IN SEARCH OF MONSTERS TO DESTROY?

American Foreign Policy, Revolution, and Regime Change, 1776-1900

Patrick J. Garrity

Published in 2012 by
National Institute Press ®
9302 Lee Highway, Suite 750
Fairfax, Virginia 22031

Copyright ©2012 by National Institute Press ®

Library of Congress Cataloging-in-Publication Data

Garrity, Patrick J.
In search of monsters to destroy? : American foreign policy, revolutions, and regime change, 1776-1900 / Patrick J. Garrity.
  p. cm.
Includes index.
1. United States--Foreign relations--1783-1865. 2. United States--Foreign relations--1865-1898. 3. Revolutions--History--18th century. 4. Revolutions--History--19th century. 5. Regime change--History--18th century. 6. Regime change--History--19th century. 7. World politics--To 1900. I. Title.
E183.7.G37 2012
327.73009'033--dc23
                2011050846

Table of Contents

Acknowledgements vii

Introduction ix

CHAPTER ONE

The American Revolution and Regime Change:
Adams, Franklin and the Indirect Approach to Promoting the Rights of Man 1

CHAPTER TWO

Jefferson, the Barbary Regencies and Regime Change:
The Attractions and Limits of Limited Liability. 75

CHAPTER THREE

She Goes Not Abroad, in Search of Monsters to Destroy:
The Dispute Between John Quincy Adams and Henry Clay Over the South American Revolutions 147

CHAPTER FOUR

"The High, Plain, Yet Dizzy Ground" of Influence:
American Views on Regime Change and the European Revolutions of 1848 253

CHAPTER FIVE

The American Regime Change Debates of the 1890s:
A Matter of Principle and Interest 339

About the Author 425

Index 427

Acknowledgements

This book has long been in contemplation and preparation – far too long. It has required the patience, as well as the assistance, of many friends and colleagues. I would like to acknowledge the Smith Richardson Foundation, which encouraged the project and funded my research. The staff of the National Institute for Public Policy and its Press provided courteous, prompt and thoroughly professional support. Let me note especially the commitment of Keith Payne and Amy Joseph to the book's publication, and the careful editorial work of Beth Payne.

The staff members at the Ashbrook Center of Public Affairs at Ashland University have generously provided their time and talents to aid me with activities related to the topic of the United States and foreign regime change. Ashbrook's Director, Peter Schramm, as always, put himself and his resources at my disposal. This included the technical support of Ben Kunkel and the research and proofreading skills of a number of students (thanks to you all). Allow me to single out Joshua Distel in this regard.

The Miller Center of Public Affairs has been a wonderful place to think and write. My colleagues with the Center's Presidential Recordings Project – David Coleman, Erin Mahan and Ken Hughes – have kindly worked around my occasional lapses in our work on Nixon and SALT while I turned my attention to this book. Mike Greco and Sheila Blackford have patiently taken care of my research and library needs. Joseph Taylor, Andrew Chauncey and Robin Kuzen ably handled my administrative needs on behalf of the Miller Center Foundation.

I remain in intellectual debt to my friends at the Claremont Institute and the *Claremont Review of Books,* particularly Chris Flannery, Charles Kesler, Brian Kennedy and John Kienker. Steven Everley, while in residence at the Institute, provided much useful research on the First Barbary War. I draw continuously on the wisdom of Professors Harry V. Jaffa and W.B. Allen and note sadly the passing of Professor Harold W. Rood, scholar and gentleman. My long-time teacher, coach, and friend in Idaho, Garry Matlock, is a constant and welcome source of encouragement.

Permission to quote from the unpublished Adams Papers was granted by the Massachusetts Historical Society. I thank the editors of *Comparative Strategy* for permission to publish Chapter Two, an earlier version of which appeared in that journal.

Finally, let me thank my ever-friendly Charlottesville walking companions, Christine and Cholita, who offered much stimulating company while putting up with my endless stories about John Quincy Adams – and tales of March Madness.

Introduction

The recent wars in Iraq and Afghanistan, coupled with subsequent U.S. efforts to promote democracy in those countries, have raised fundamental questions as old as – even older than – the Republic itself. To what extent does the character of other nations and peoples, especially their form of government, affect American national security? Under what circumstances are Americans justified in becoming involved in the domestic affairs of others? To put the issue in its sharpest relief: Should the United States intervene actively to bring about the change of a foreign regime – or take sides in a civil war among contending factions – even to the point of governing other peoples without their consent?

This book will explore five notable occasions, from the time of the Founding through the end of the 19th century, during which American public officials and citizens debated seriously the feasibility and morality of adopting a policy of foreign regime change. Regime change, in its most direct sense, involved not merely the replacement of a particular foreign leader (although some leaders are so closely identified with their regime as to make this distinction irrelevant), but a deliberate decision by the United States to bring about a complete alteration in the character of a foreign political system through the use of force, coercion or subterfuge. The United States, moreover, explored less direct efforts to alter the political system of other states, through moral suasion and through efforts to change the character of international politics and commerce in a way that favored certain types of regimes and disadvantaged others.

Americans have demonstrated consistent patterns of thought about regime change but there has also been a significant evolution of their views to accommodate new conditions in the international environment and domestic politics. The political and intellectual dynamic of the debates, as well as their particular outcomes, have had major significance for the overall direction of basic U.S. national security policy. Indeed, the debaters often went to the core of what constituted the American national interest. These controversies have been as much about the character of our own regime as that of others.

The American understanding of regime change has not necessarily been synonymous with "democratization." Americans have accepted the legitimacy of other forms of government and have acknowledged that non-democratic regimes abroad are necessary and even preferable under certain circumstances. Americans have disagreed about the theoretical and practical meaning of "democracy" and the relationship of human rights to different types of regimes. Their deliberations have not been two-sided, between interventionists and abstentionists, or between promoters of democracy and advocates of benign neglect. The policy debate has always been complex and surprisingly dynamic. Individuals and entire schools of foreign policy thought have altered or even reversed views. These debates typically involved shifting political coalitions and complicated policy perspectives. They did not move in a straight line. The political, strategic and economic difficulties associated with a policy of directly-enforced regime change have led Americans frequently to prefer compromise policies or an indirect approach – including reliance on international institutions and norms, general economic progress, or dynamic local forces. Nonetheless, compromises and the indirect approach have had their difficulties. The impersonal forces of history, globalization and international good will often have failed to meet the expectation of American moral sensibilities and interests in critical areas such as the Middle East.

The reader may well question the value of a set of case studies that ends more than a century ago. It is my contention that the patterns of American thought about regime change run very deep in U.S. history. Much can be learned from a detailed examination of a few representative debates in which some of the greatest early American statesmen developed their views on foreign regime change. Some readers may find these case studies to be too detailed or repetitive but I rely on those whose insight is greater than mine to wade through those of particular interest to them and to separate the wheat from the chaff. Each chapter can be read independently of the others. Other readers may ask why certain important situations and debates have not been included. For example, the American reaction to the French Revolution; the decision to invade Canada in 1812; the practice of filibustering along the unsettled borderlands or in other countries by American adventurers, with or without the support of the U.S. government; and the American Civil War and Reconstruction, would all merit close study. I can only plead the lack of space and detailed knowledge, and encourage others to look at these and other instances of regime change for themselves.

The American Revolution and Regime Change: Adams, Franklin and the Indirect Approach to Promoting the Rights of Man. "It is a common observation here that our cause is the cause of all mankind, and that we are fighting for their liberty by defending our own." Benjamin Franklin's statement, written from Paris in 1777, was indeed commonplace among the American Revolutionary leaders and the progressive thinkers of Europe. But what precisely did this mean? How exactly did American liberty relate to that of other peoples? Did Americans have any responsibility to do more than defend their own liberties, to work or fight actively for the liberties of others? Chapter

One considers the Founders' view of how the United States might, and might not, properly promote the cause of liberty, and especially foster changes in foreign governments. This is not a comprehensive review or assessment of the thinking of the American revolutionaries about regime change; rather, it is a selective introduction to the Founders' concepts and disagreements concerning the relationship of the new nation with other peoples and governments.

The chapter begins with an assessment of the colonial background in which American thinking about regimes first developed – especially the colonists' admiration for the British Constitution and the cutting-edge thought of the European Enlightenment. After the French and Indian War, however, a significant number of Americans interpreted London's effort to rationalize the imperial structure as an immense conspiracy against their individual and corporate liberties – an effort by the political center to force regime change on the peripheries of the empire, as well as to destroy the liberties of the home country itself. The American revolutionaries did not seek to achieve their aims through world revolution. Nor did they claim the right to alter and abolish other governments. Indeed, they sought the aid and cooperation of former enemies such as France and Spain, which the colonists once had regarded as the essence of despotism. The Americans, however, sought to limit U.S. foreign relationships to the realm of commerce in order to avoid "entangling" political-military alliances. They hoped that American entrance into the Euro-Atlantic state system would bring about a new configuration of international power and rules of behavior; this arrangement would be conducive not only to American security but also to domestic political reform in nations like France, as well as to the cause of liberty and republicanism more generally. They appealed to the national interest of the rulers but also to enlightened public opinion among the European nations.

The American revolutionaries assumed that France, which was the most powerful nation on the continent and the long-standing enemy of Britain, would be the linchpin of this strategy. The necessities of war caused American diplomats, led by Benjamin Franklin and the American Congress, to agree to a conditional political-military alliance with France and to defer increasingly to French leadership. John Adams, who represented a minority in Congress – and who was a minority of one in many respects – challenged this drift in American policy. He believed that the French had their own distinct interests in the conflict and that the United States was best served by multiplying its political-commercial contacts throughout Europe, especially with compatible regimes such as the Dutch Republic.

Adams' independent, activist approach – his so-called "militia diplomacy" – not only circumvented the French but also challenged, directly or indirectly, the rulers and entrenched interests in those nations being asked to align themselves with the United States. Adams, in order to obtain loans and to develop commercial ties with the Netherlands, developed a close relationship with the Patriot movement in that nation – a movement that opposed the pro-English House of Orange and favored major domestic political changes. Adams insisted that he was not interfering in Dutch politics or supporting regime change there; he acknowledged, however, that his public arguments and private efforts on behalf of the American cause stimulated interest in popular participation in government and in political reform throughout Europe, including a possible British Revolution.

For Franklin and his supporters in Congress, Adams' efforts represented a vast overreaching of limited American power, which threatened to undermine the essential ties with France. Adams perversely encouraged those in Britain and America who sought to restore an Anglo-American Union. Militia diplomacy would unnecessarily alarm European political and strategic conservatives, who still held the upper hand in most nations. Franklin, of course, was no reactionary (some of his closest friends in France would become leaders of the early stages of the French Revolution). He insisted that he had no intention of making the United States a French satellite or subservient to despotism. Indeed, Franklin thought that America should bide its time and wait for the natural increase of its power, rather than engage in an overly-aggressive diplomacy, to improve the prospects for enlightened rule elsewhere.

In the end, the path to liberty and enlightenment proved to be neither straight nor sure. "The Nations of Europe, appeared to me, when I was among them, from the beginning of 1778, to 1785, i.e., to the commencement of the troubles in France, to be advancing by slow and sure Steps towards an Amelioration of the condition of Man, in Religion and Government, in Liberty, Equality, Fraternity Knowledge Civilization and Humanity," Adams reflected decades later to Thomas Jefferson. Events, however, outran the ability and power of the United States to influence the evolution of a liberal international order that would be conducive to gradual reform and (relatively) peaceful regime change. In the coming decades, American statesmen like Adams and Jefferson (just like Adams and Franklin previously) could not agree upon the proper policies to conduct the indirect approach, especially after the outbreak of the French Revolution in 1789. American commerce did not change the nature of international relations but rather sucked the United States into the maelstrom of European conflicts. The idea of an indirect approach to foreign regime change was not forgotten, only deferred.

Jefferson, the Barbary Regencies, and Regime Change: The Attractions and Limits of Limited Liability. For the first few decades of its existence as an independent nation, the United States faced a threat to its commercial interests in the Mediterranean and eastern Atlantic from the Barbary "pirates" – popularly known as corsairs – who sailed under the auspices of four Islamic polities on the North African coast (Tripoli, Tunis, Algiers and Morocco). Americans debated whether their national interest in the Mediterranean was best achieved through accommodation of the Barbary rulers or through a more assertive policy designed to change the behavior of those rulers, perhaps even to overthrow them. Chapter Two examines American policy and the policy debate concerning the Barbary regencies at the turn of the 19th century.

Thomas Jefferson became the central figure in this debate. As a diplomat and Secretary of State, he favored strongly the change-of-behavior alternative through a form of international containment of the corsair threat. As president, he waged war against Tripoli and allowed military commanders on the scene to provide support to the domestic opponents of its ruler. However, because the indigenous opposition against the government in Tripoli could not bring about regime change and rule in its own name, Jefferson decided that the United States was at liberty to follow its own interests and settle the dispute on the best available terms with the existing regime.

This policy of limited liability, which seemed an attractive middle ground between the extremes of appeasement and imperialism, had its own problems and critics. By cooperating with the opponents of a hostile regime to gain tactical advantages over the current ruler, the United States created a sense of obligation from which it was difficult to disengage with honor. The United States risked developing a negative reputation for fomenting revolution with promises of political or military support that did not materialize – a reputation that was bound to undermine the limited liability approach over the long term. Opposition factions could exploit the ambiguity of such a policy and promote their own cause among individual U.S. government officials, Congress, and the American public. Finally, rulers previously threatened by the United States in this fashion would likely harbor a sense of grievance and continue to work against U.S. interests. Americans, nevertheless, came to regard the First Barbary War as a triumph of U.S. strategy and military skill and as a template for future policy toward non-European strategic contingencies.

She Goes Not Abroad, in Search of Monsters to Destroy: The Dispute Between John Quincy Adams and Henry Clay Over the South American Revolutions. On July 4, 1821, Secretary of State John Quincy Adams delivered an oration on the Declaration of Independence that contained the famous aphorism about American foreign policy: "Wherever the standard of freedom and independence has been or shall be unfurled, there will her [America's] heart, her benedictions and her prayers be. But she goes not abroad, in search of monsters to destroy." Adams' argument became the point of departure for an entire strain of thought about American foreign policy. To call his views "isolationist," however, would be too limited, as would other commonly used terms such as "realist" or "anti-interventionist." The Address clearly warned America against going abroad in search of monstrous regimes to destroy – Adams meant what he said – but neither did he assume thereby that monsters should be given an entirely free hand or that America must sit passively by, merely thinking happy thoughts.

To help make sense of Adams' argument, Chapter Three examines his July 4 Address as a whole, and the context in which it was delivered. Adams himself explained that he meant to argue, first and foremost, against European-style colonialism. Second, he meant to combat what he termed the "doctrine of Lexington" (Henry Clay's proposal for an American hemispheric alliance against the Holy Alliance of despots) and the "doctrine of Edinburgh" (the appeal of English liberals for Anglo-American cooperation on behalf of political reform and revolution in Europe). Adams thought there was a practical, yet elevated middle ground between the cold pursuit of material national interests and the hot-blooded advocacy of revolution and foreign regime change. In the immediate case at hand, that of the proper approach of the United States toward the movements for independence in South (or Spanish) America, Adams initially argued for a cautious approach. He resisted pressures to recognize the new South American regimes until he felt that the strategic and political circumstances had matured sufficiently. Once that had occurred, however, Adams shifted to a policy of more active engagement with the South Americans, in hopes of influencing at least indirectly their internal development in a republican direction. Adams offered one of the first in a long line of arguments that American foreign policy idealism and realism are not stark alternatives, but rather two sides of the same coin.

Adams believed that the laws of political gravity and the emerging spirit of the age worked in favor of the United States and the advancement of the rights of mankind. The process of working out the transcendent principles of the Declaration of Independence and the full potential of Western and Christian civilization, however, would be a very long one. Success was not assured, especially in the short term. Bad policy choices by the United States, especially those intended to hurry history and foreign cultures beyond their capacity to change progressively, could be catastrophic because human nature itself is unchangeable. This was especially true if it meant becoming entangled in European wars and revolutions. American statesmen should be patient and restrained, take care of the internal improvement of their own regime first, and then allow other peoples to work out their own destinies, all the while stoutly defending the principle of the inalienable right of peoples to do so. America could best aid the process indirectly, by promoting a civilizational agenda of peace, commerce, and the elimination of barbaric practices, rather than through "propagandism" or the use of force to overthrow foreign despotisms. The United States could pursue this agenda in cooperation with regimes of all types, including despotisms, knowing that the effect would be to advance the cause of liberalism and constitutionalism.

Adams' position was assailed by those who judged such a middle ground to be unsupportable. On the one hand, Clay argued that by distancing itself initially from South American revolutionary movements, the United States missed an historic opportunity, at relatively low cost, to move the world's political balance of forces in a progressive direction. Millions were condemned to live in oppression while the United States sat on the sidelines, cheerfully (and selfishly) assuming that history would resolve everything for the better over centuries or millennia. This lost opportunity involved not only the defeat of revolutions and national independence movements because of despotic resistance, but also the inability of victorious revolutionary regimes to sustain their commitment to republicanism and the rights of mankind. The moral force of America's example to guide others toward ordered liberty would be lost unless its good words and sympathies were matched with real, tangible assistance – which Clay insisted did not mean the use of force, but rather steps such as the prompt diplomatic recognition of the new regimes. The argument that the United States should let others work out their own destiny – that the success or failure of revolutionary movements and friendly regimes abroad did not fundamentally affect America's well-being and happiness – was a fallacy. The cause of liberty was ultimately indivisible. Far-seeing despots realized that they could not coexist with free governments. Sooner or later the forces of reaction would ally against the forces of liberty, and the United States would be far better off if it had republican allies in that world-historic contest.

Adams was hardly free from challenges by those who argued that his apparent foreign realism and caution was based on a comfortable fallacy: that the United States could credibly make a distinction between sympathy and action, and that statesmen like Adams could wave an ideologically charged document like the Declaration of Independence in front of other nations, while piously insisting that it followed a policy of neutrality and peace. What became the Monroe Doctrine was the source of much mischief, because its insistence on the ideological separation of the two hemispheres was erroneously based on the airy distinction between regime types, and not on the solid ground of American national interest. The national interest certainly did not require a comprehensive and open-ended "doctrine" that pretended that all regimes in the Western Hemisphere were or should be "republican" and that the entire hemisphere must be defended by the United States on those grounds. Furthermore, Adams' civilizational agenda, which at least notionally was regime-neutral, actually constituted interference in the domestic affairs of others. It was sure to be resented, as such. For instance, freedom of trade affected domestic economies in a way that privileged some and disadvantaged others, and created avenues for foreigners to influence internal affairs of weaker states.

Adams' generally-recognized status as the greatest American diplomatist, or at least Secretary of State, suggests that he enjoyed considerable practical success in transcending the realist-idealist divide that runs through the history of U.S. foreign policy. (He was certainly not a realist of the European style, as is sometimes supposed.) Critics of his policy approach, on both sides of the fence, have had their days and scored their points throughout American history as well. Nonetheless, Adams defined the terrain of the debate – a debate that is partly, yet not wholly, realist versus idealist – in a manner that remains with us today.

The High, Plain, Yet Dizzy Ground of Influence: Daniel Webster and American Views on the European Revolutions of 1848. Chapter Four examines how American attitudes toward the European Revolutions of 1848 renewed the national debate over whether and how to support foreign political reforms and regime change. The intellectual and political impetus for a more assertive approach to foreign policy and for the promotion of foreign regime change came largely from a new generation of Democrats, who sought to advance American interests and ideals through territorial expansion, free trade, and support for liberal movements abroad. The New Democrats sought to overcome factional and intellectual resistance to such activism from within their own party and from the opposition Whigs, who traditionally held that America's world-historic mission was one of democratic example rather than the conquest of foreign territories or the subversion of other regimes. Nevertheless, the Whig persuasion also contained a strain of activism on behalf of human rights, marked by strong rhetorical support for republican government and national self-determination. The New Democrats thus had potential allies among up-and-coming progressive Whig politicians and the Free Soil movement. This raised the prospect that a political majority might emerge across parties in favor of a more activist or even interventionist foreign policy – a national majority that might transcend differences over slavery.

Popular interest in foreign regime change reached its peak with the arrival in the United States of Hungarian revolutionary leader Lajos (Louis) Kossuth, after the Hungarian Revolution was suppressed by Russian and

Austrian intervention. Kossuth, and some of his American supporters, envisioned a second revolution, which would be enabled by an American-British-Turkish military alliance directed at Austria and Russia, or by some other type of American "intervention for non-intervention." However, most New Democrats, such as Stephen A. Douglas, and progressive Whigs, including William Seward, carefully avoided taking such provocative ground. They argued that American moral and diplomatic support alone would alter the political climate in Europe sufficiently to allow a future Hungarian revolution to succeed, if the Hungarians were truly capable of self-government. Even this modest approach was opposed by eminences such as Kentucky Senator John J. Crittenden, a Whig, who argued that it was impossible to establish a clear distinction between moral-diplomatic support for the Hungarian cause and outright military intervention. Either the United States would find itself on the slippery slope that led to war for matters that were not vital to the nation, or it would be forced to back down in humiliating fashion.

These conservative Whigs successfully aligned with the Fillmore administration and a strong majority of Southerners of both parties to create an effective opposition to the New Democrats and progressive Whigs on the Kossuth issue. As the nation slid deeper into domestic crisis over slavery during the 1850s, the prospect of a new political coalition based on an assertive foreign policy and an aggressive approach to foreign regime change, disappeared.

This foreign policy debate was in many respects the most "modern" of those which took place during the American Republic's 1st century, in that the protagonists anticipated many of the arguments and policy options that later emerged when the United States became a world power. Daniel Webster, as Senator and Secretary of State, was in many ways the central character in this mid-19th century search for ways to maximize American influence in favor of regime change without crossing the line into direct political-military intervention. Webster's soaring rhetoric about human liberty seemingly put him on the side of those who challenged the perceived tradition of American non-involvement in the political affairs of Europe. At the same time, however, Webster's official actions were cautious, taking into account the fragile state of the Union and the limits of American power.

The American Regime Change Debates of the 1890s: A Matter of Principle and Interest. The late 19th century was a time of great hope and anxiety for the United States. Several decades of extraordinary growth had transformed it into the world's leading industrial power, despite a financial panic in 1893 which plunged the nation into a major economic depression. Americans watched with concern as the major European powers scrambled for new colonies and influence in Africa, the Middle East, and Asia. These revitalized European empires threatened to exclude American business from vital overseas markets and to expand into the Western Hemisphere, thereby challenging American security. New technologies, especially steam power, the telegraph, and railroads, pointed to major changes in the conduct of warfare, and arguably lessened the traditional security provided to the United States by its distance from Europe. Yet there was considerable hope that science, commerce and civilization had reached the point where great power conflict might be prevented or at least limited by international cooperation.

Many Americans felt that their bourgeoning economic power and the moral authority of their democratic society entitled – indeed, compelled – them to exert greater influence over this brave yet frightening new world. They disagreed considerably over the means and ends of doing so, however – especially when the exertion of American power, or the claims of American example, required the United States to consider actively intervening in the affairs of other peoples and nations. Chapter Five examines two such controversies that emerged during the 1890s: (1) the 1896-1898 debate over possible American intervention in the Cuban civil war (or insurrection or revolution, depending on one's viewpoint), which focused on the desirability and feasibility of removing the Spanish imperial regime in favor of Cuban independence, or some other form of political governance over the island; and (2) the "imperial debate" of 1898-1900, in which Americans deliberated whether their national interest and moral authority required them to go beyond the removal of a European power in the Philippines and replace it with a regime, either temporarily or permanently, under American political control.

These debates were driven, in a conceptual sense at least, by those who considered themselves "large Americans"—heirs to the expansionist tradition of the pre-Civil War republic who believed that their traditions should be revived and adapted properly to conditions of the time. The unification of the nation in the years following the Civil War, and the increased threat represented by European colonialism, required the United States to become more "outward-looking." Events in East Asia, as well as in Latin America, directly affected the economic strength and security of the United States. To retain its freedom of action, America would have to increase substantially its naval forces and enhance its ability to operate away from its shores by acquiring strategically located bases. There seemed to be no good reason why America's Manifest Destiny should halt at the eastern edge of the Pacific Ocean. War was an essential, even beneficial element of national policy; the maintenance of armed forces and the most modern weapons were the best guarantees of peace and security.

The "large Americans" did not believe that the United States would have to expand territorially, save in a few strategically critical locations (e.g., Hawaii), but they wanted America to widen its methods of political control outside of the continental United States. These methods included protectorates and neo-colonial arrangements (the "large Americans" generally insisted that they did not favor establishing European-style empires). To the extent that foreigners, whether colonial powers or natives, resisted American political intervention, they would be subject to more forceful action and a change of regime. Alfred Thayer Mahan, Theodore Roosevelt, and Henry Cabot Lodge were among those promoting the "large" view, but it was supported by substantial figures from the old-line Republican Party, such as Benjamin Harrison.

The opposing intellectual camp went under various names, including "little Americanism," anti-expansionism, and anti-imperialism. As a rule, those in this camp did not regard the activities of the European powers as representing a significant threat to the security of the United States. The economic well-being of the nation was best secured through free trade, a small, non-offensive navy, and the absence of overseas bases. Any further territorial expansion (with the possible exception of Canada) was unnecessary, and would only involve the United States in foreign entanglements. Armaments were the cause of war and hence ought to be limited or abolished through international agreement or unilateral actions. The anti-imperialists emphasized morality rather than self-interest as the core of their argument: the principles of the American regime compelled policymakers to concern themselves first with the welfare of the citizens of the United States, and to avoid interference with or intervention in the affairs of other nations. The health of the American regime would be undermined if it attempted to emulate the Europeans and establish a full-blown empire in which it would rule other peoples without their consent, or deny other peoples their right to national and political self-determination. The leading anti-imperialists included individuals from various backgrounds and from both major political parties, including Carl Schurz, David Starr Jordan, and William Jennings Bryan; this outlook was particularly identified with the Democratic Party.

In the practical, political arena, as this chapter demonstrates, the division between these two foreign policy schools was not quite that clear-cut. Many of those who considered themselves anti-imperialists, such as Bryan, came to support what they regarded as humanitarian intervention in Cuba, which meant the overthrow of the Spanish colonial regime. Bryan, for tactical political reasons, also supported ratification of the Treaty of Paris and with it the acquisition of the Philippines. Some of those who might have counted themselves in the "large" American camp, such as Harrison, opposed the acquisition of the Philippines because they were "a bridge too far." Overshadowing the debate was the enigmatic William McKinley, who was considered to be aligned with the business interests of the Republican Party, which by and large opposed war. McKinley promised "no jingo nonsense" yet led the nation into conflicts in which regime change was actively promoted.

At the heart of these debates and shifting points of view, was the political goal of creating an enduring and decisive domestic political realignment based in large part on foreign policy issues, either imperialism or anti-imperialism. That political realignment never occurred, as such. The McKinley administration's policy, and that of the political middle ground, did not point toward the establishment of a formal U.S. empire. Public opinion was deeply influenced by the arguments of the anti-imperialist movement, even if the anti-imperialists did not always win out on particular policy matters. Interest, ideals and experience pointed toward solutions other than territorial expansion and a foreign policy that actively promoted regime change. Americans retained a deep attachment to the principle that peoples could be governed only with their own consent. The United States arguably could obtain access to overseas markets and military bases without establishing colonies. Perhaps domestic economic and political change could provide the answer to industrial overproduction. In terms of culture, racist assumptions cut both ways. Many supporters of an interventionist American foreign policy, as well as their opponents, did not want the country "tainted" by acquiring non-white peoples. If foreign cultures were indeed highly resistant to change, perhaps the costs and risks of "civilizing" others was simply too great. The coming 20th century would witness Americans trying to operate in the difficult, contentious middle ground between empire and non-intervention.

CHAPTER ONE

The American Revolution and Regime Change:

Adams, Franklin and the Indirect Approach to Promoting the Rights of Man

"It is a common observation here that our cause is the cause of all mankind, and that we are fighting for their liberty by defending our own." [1] Benjamin Franklin's statement, written from Paris in 1777, was indeed commonplace among the American Revolutionary leaders and among the progressive thinkers of Europe. But what precisely did this mean? How exactly did American liberty relate to that of other peoples? Did Americans have any responsibility to do more than defend their own liberties, to work or fight actively for the liberties of others?

This chapter considers the Founders' view of how the United States might, and might not, properly promote the cause of liberty, and especially foster changes in foreign governments. It begins with an assessment of the colonial background in which American thinking about regimes first developed, especially the colonists' admiration for the British Constitution and for the cutting-edge thought of the European Enlightenment. After the French and Indian War, however, a significant number of Americans interpreted London's effort to rationalize the imperial structure as an immense conspiracy against their individual and corporate liberties – an effort by the political center to force regime change on the peripheries of the empire, as well as to destroy the liberties of the home country itself. Americans debated the best means to resist the presumed corruption of the British Constitution, both on their behalf and on that of the reformist political project of the Enlightenment. The most radical elements of the American resistance concluded that fundamental regime change – independence and republican government – was necessary to

---

[1] Franklin to Samuel Cooper, 1 May 1777, Francis Wharton, ed., *The Revolutionary Diplomatic Correspondence of the United States*, 6 vols. (Washington, D.C.: U.S. Government Printing Office, 1889), 2: 312-3. Hereafter referred to as *RDC*. To deal with the varied spelling and punctuation from documents of the period, I have used the original version wherever possible from the indicated published sources.

achieve these objectives. The American revolutionaries formulated far-reaching arguments about the nature of politics and the right to alter and abolish governments. These arguments were designed to persuade those who feared that the breakup of the British Empire would be a grave setback for human liberty and a boon to the forces of despotism.

The American revolutionaries did not seek to achieve their aims through world revolution. Nor did they claim the right to alter and abolish other governments. Indeed, they sought the aid and cooperation of former enemies such as France and Spain, which the colonists had once regarded as the essence of despotism. The Americans, however, sought to limit U.S. foreign relationships to the realm of commerce, avoiding "entangling" political-military alliances. They hoped that American entrance into the Euro-Atlantic state system would bring about a new configuration of international power and rules of behavior, which would be conducive not only to American security but also to domestic political reform in nations like France and, more generally, to the cause of liberty and republicanism. They appealed to the national interest of the rulers but also to enlightened public opinion among the European nations.

The American revolutionaries assumed that France, which was the most powerful nation on the continent and the long-standing enemy of Britain, would be the linchpin of this strategy. The necessities of war caused American diplomats, led by Benjamin Franklin, and the American Congress to agree to a conditional political-military alliance with France and to defer increasingly to French leadership. John Adams, who represented a minority in Congress – and who was a minority of one in many respects – challenged this drift in American policy. He believed that the French had their own distinct interests in the conflict and that the United States was best served by multiplying its political-commercial contacts throughout Europe, especially with compatible regimes such as the Dutch Republic.

Adams' independent, activist approach – his so-called "militia diplomacy" – not only circumvented the French but also challenged, directly or indirectly, the rulers and entrenched interests in those nations being asked to align themselves with the United States. Adams, in order to obtain loans and to develop commercial ties with the Netherlands, developed a close relationship with the Patriot movement in that nation – a movement that opposed the pro-English House of Orange and that favored major domestic political changes. Adams insisted that he was not interfering in Dutch politics or supporting regime change there; he acknowledged, however, that his public arguments and private efforts on behalf of the

American cause stimulated interest in popular participation in government and in political reform or regime change throughout Europe, including a possible British revolution.

For Franklin and his supporters in Congress, Adams' efforts represented a vast overreaching of limited American power that threatened to undermine the essential ties with France and, perversely, to encourage those in Britain and America who wanted to restore an Anglo-American Union. Militia diplomacy would unnecessarily alarm European political and strategic conservatives, who still held the upper hand in most nations. Franklin, of course, was no reactionary (some of his closest friends in France would be the leaders of the early stages of the French Revolution). He insisted that he had no intention of making the United States a French satellite or subservient to despotism; America should instead bide its time and wait for the natural increase of its power, rather than engage in an overly-aggressive diplomacy, to improve the prospects for enlightened rule elsewhere.

This chapter is not a comprehensive review or assessment of the thinking of the American revolutionaries about regime change, but rather a selective introduction to the Founders' concepts, and disagreements, about their relationship to other peoples and governments. The line of argument is suggestive, designed to provoke thought and stimulate further research, and not intended to put forward a definitive analysis of this complicated topic.

The Colonial Background

By the middle of the 18th century, the British North American colonists, those who would come to think of themselves as Americans, possessed a multifaceted view of their way of life, history and place in the world. They, or their ancestors, had fled to the New World above all (so their story went) to obtain the liberties that had been suppressed in Europe by the tyranny of canon and feudal law. The leading edge of the white colonists, especially in the North, had come from the British Isles to escape religious persecution and discrimination against non-English ethnic groups (and the poverty that went along with them). Some of the early colonists had hoped to use their outpost in the New World to bring about a change of religious regime in the Mother Country; others wanted to create a New Jerusalem apart from the fallen Old World; still others simply wanted to make their own way and their own fortunes. Whatever their motive, according to John Adams, the British North Americans believed that the existence of the colonies had marked "the opening of a grand scheme and design in Providence for the illumination of the ignorant, and the emancipation of the slavish part of mankind all over the earth." [2]

As a practical matter the colonists assumed, for reasons of security and economics, that their liberties had to be achieved within the British Empire. France, Spain, and their native allies threatened the existence of British North America. The struggle for survival had an ideological as well as geopolitical dimension: the colonists saw themselves as part of an Anglo-American Protestant bulwark of liberty against the aggressive designs of continental tyranny and popery, which aimed to create a Universal Monarchy. Despite their historic differences with their governors in London, the colonists nevertheless believed that they were part of the world's freest political regime. Historian Gordon Wood notes it is impossible, "to overestimate the degree to which eighteenth century Englishmen," including those in British North America, "reveled in their worldwide reputation for freedom." The French and Indian War was seen in British North America as a great victory for the global forces of liberty, and the colonists believed they had played the decisive role in that war. They assumed that the subsequent growth of power and territory by Anglo-America would also serve to spread liberty. [3]

The colonists also reveled in the defense of their particular form of government – that of the British Constitution. As historian Bernard Bailyn notes: "No one doubted that liberty, as the colonists knew it, rested on, had in fact been created by, the stable balancing of the three essential socio-constitutional orders, the monarchy, the nobility and the people at large, each with its appropriate organ of government." The balance of contending forces needed to be so institutionalized, "that no one contestant could monopolize the power of the state and rule without effective opposition." [4] There was, to be sure, a distinction between savagery and barbarism on the one hand, and civilized society on the other. Continental monarchies like France might be highly advanced in the arts and sciences, literature, commerce and refinement, but their propensity toward luxury and inequality made them inferior to societies such as England which were based on respect for equality and political virtue. Americans would stress the *British*, not merely *English*, Constitution,

---

[2] See, for example, David Hackett Fischer, *Albion's Seed: Four British Folkways in America* (New York: Oxford University Press, 1989); and John Adams, *A Dissertation on the Canon and Feudal Law*, Charles Francis Adams, ed., *The Writings of John Adams, 10 vols.* (Boston: Little and Brown, 1851), 3: 452. Hereafter referred to as *WJA*.

[3] Eric Foner, *The Story of American Freedom* (New York: W.W. Norton, 1994), pp. 4-7 (Wood quotation, p. 7).

[4] Bernard Bailyn, *Faces of Revolution: Personalities and Themes in the Struggle for American Independence* (New York: Alfred A. Knopf, 1990), p. 70.

for its role in creating an empire of liberty that was grounded in both national interests and imperial concerns. In Benjamin Franklin's opinion, London had wisely granted autonomy to its provinces and thus solved the great imperial problem in which "great empires had crumbled first from their extremities" because the central government lacked the necessary information to reign in bad governors. [5] The French and Indian War had demonstrated graphically to men like Franklin that the imperial core actually gained strength from the periphery. The colonists saw themselves playing an increasingly elaborate and vital role in the Anglo-American regime as time went on. [6]

British North Americans also saw themselves as part of a larger Enlightenment project, with all the qualifications that term entails. In all realms of life – political, scientific, cultural – men were to be judged by merit and not birth. The Enlightenment was reformist in spirit, designed to work within existing institutional frameworks and to improve those institutions through a process of gradual and consensual change. The object was not to tear the social fabric apart but rather to achieve far-reaching effects over time as reforms accumulated and began to reinforce one another. [7] The New World had a distinctive role and path in the unfolding of the Enlightenment, as Bailyn notes:

> British North America had long been the subject of intense scrutiny by European thinkers – partly out of interest in the effect of environment on human development, but mainly out of the need for proof of what a society of Europeans would look like if the burdens of European establishments were radically reformed or eliminated: if powerful established churches, with their priesthoods and wealth and inquisitions, were eliminated; if feudal landowning, which gave great wealth, leisure, and power to the few and guaranteed poverty for the masses, were abolished; and if oppressive economies, bound down by medieval restrictions and encumbrances, were rationalized and modernized. In America the enlightened reformers believed they had found the answers, and answers that gave lie to conservatives who argued that the powerful institutions

---

[5] Franklin's Narrative of Negotiations in London, 22 March 1775, *RDC*, 2: 12.

[6] See, for example, Eliga H. Gould, *The Persistence of Empire: British Political Culture in the Age of the American Revolution* (Chapel Hill: University of North Carolina Press, 2000); and Linda Colley, *Britons: Forging the Nation, 1707-1837* (New Haven: Yale University Press, 1992).

[7] See the Introduction in Darren Staloff, *Hamilton, Adams, Jefferson: The Politics of the Enlightenment and the American Founding* (New York: Hill and Wang, 2005); and also Peter Onuf and Nicholas Onuf, *Federal Union, Modern World: The Law of Nations in the Age of Revolution, 1776-1814* (Madison, Wisconsin: Madison House, 1993).

of the *ancien regime* alone protected Europe from barbarism, that if the structure of civilization as it was known were eliminated the result would not be Elysium but savagery. America, the philosophes, especially Voltaire said, was there to prove the opposite.[8]

The leading figures of the Enlightenment regarded themselves as members of a transnational and transpolitical regime – the Republic of Letters. They sought to reinforce one another by transmitting ideas and the results of experiments, whether scientific or political, and by adopting the best practices of others. They advocated the "cause of humanity" and sought to create an enlightened public opinion among elites that would give authority and support to the reform process within particular political regimes of various types. Different individuals had different programs but as political scientist Ralph Lerner observes, this enlightened public opinion was united in pursuit of a "generic republicanism" that was "neutral, by and large, toward the office of kingship, but not toward a system of exemption and privileges based on hereditary orders. It would respect or at least make grudging allowance for national or historic differences, but focus its attention mainly on the shared qualities and aspirations of newly enlightened regimes. For such republicanism, legitimacy stems not from divine grant, not from time-honored prescription, but from the consent of citizens who have matured in their freedom. A people brought to an awareness of their interests and rights can be relied on to care for themselves and hold their trustees to account."[9]

The Enlightened were interested in improving the general lot of humanity but also increasing the power of their particular states. They debated among themselves about what type of regime best served the dual role of engine of Enlightenment and of national greatness. Some, following one line of Montesquieu's analysis, argued that regimes ought to be tailored to the national character, which was a byproduct of climate, topography, and history. The advocates of the English Constitution of King, Lords and Commons, following another line of Montesquieu, pointed to their regime's success both as a liberal regime and as a powerful and wealthy state, and to the Glorious Revolution as a model for political reform. As political scientist Harvey Mansfield notes: "It established the English Constitution as the model constitution, in Locke, Montesquieu, Burke and others. The model constitution is the best, practical

---

[8] Bailyn, *To Begin the World Anew: The Genius and Ambiguities of the American Founders* (New York: Alfred A. Knopf, 2003), pp. 67-8.

[9] Ralph Lerner, "America's Place in the Enlightenment," in William Rusher and Ken Masugi, eds., *The Ambiguous Legacy of the Enlightenment* (Lanham, MD: University Press of America, 1995), p. 88.

constitution made actual. Even if it is not a universal pattern that would work everywhere, it is a model for the best circumstances." [10]

Advocates of reform on the continent, in contrast, tended to prefer enlightened despotism on the grounds that a strong central authority, in the form of a monarch devoted to modernization, was needed to overcome the entrenched aristocratic and clerical obstacles to progress. Enlightened advisers would provide the monarch with the necessary expertise (and prestige) to recast their state and society, the role that Voltaire aimed to assume in Prussia and Russia. More radical thinkers warned, however, that the monarchs' own survival was so tied up with the *ancien regime* that they would inevitably come to oppose reform before it reached that critical threshold. Modernization therefore required political liberalization – republican government (however defined) should be the aim of the Enlightenment project. Rousseau offered an influential radical critique of the entire notion of political reform through gradual improvement of the status quo. [11]

For most of the Enlightened, however, the *process* of reform was thought to be more important than the exact type of regime in which that reform was to be conducted. Reform would be top-down, not bottom-up (that is, mass violence would not drive it). It would occur nation by nation, as Enlightened leaders on the spot judged the proper pace and scope of change according to their particular circumstances.

There was an international as well as transnational dimension to the Enlightenment, a Republic of Nations as well as a Republic of Letters. The reformist spirit aimed to moderate the intensity of state-to-state conflict and thereby support the conditions for domestic reform. Enlightened leaders were expected to apply the "improved science of politics," as well as natural science, to strengthen their respective states, but they also believed that the pursuit of national interest should take place within a structure that had rules of the road – the law of nature and nations – that would increasingly be liberalized over time. The law of nations included the principles of the equality of nations and non-interference in domestic affairs, and it made no distinction among types of regimes, only in their external behavior. There was an argument

---

[10] Harvey Mansfield, "The Unfinished Revolution," in Ralph C. Hancock and L. Gary Lambert, eds., *The Legacy of the French Revolution* (Lanham, MD: Rowman & Littlefield, 1996), pp. 28-9. See also the essay by Pierre Manent, "The French Revolution and French and English Liberalism," in this volume.

[11] For review of these ideas, see Eric J. Hobsbawm, *The Age of Revolution, 1789-1848* (New York: New American Library, 1962), pp. 20-5. On Rousseau, see Charles Kesler, "The Different Enlightenments: Theory and Practice in the Enlightenment," in Rusher and Masugi, eds., *The Ambiguous Legacy of the Enlightenment*, p. 111.

whether the balance of power was a progressive or regressive concept, but the most respected authorities of the law of nations, such as Emmerich de Vattel, conceived of Europe as a political system in which equilibrium was crucial to liberty as well as order. As political scientist Daniel George Lang notes: "As Hume would suggest, the balance of power system would help encourage the development of limited government within states because the denial of universal claims abroad would moderate absolutist claims at home." [12]

According to the main current of Enlightenment thought, commerce played an important role in reducing state-to-state violence and arbitrary domestic rule. This was the case even if one did not fully embrace the notion, attributed to Montesquieu, that commerce softened the morals and manners of men. As historians Peter and Nicholas Onuf have written:

> Diplomacy conducted in accordance with the principles of the balance of power promised to rationalize, even domesticate power. But its greatest contribution to the progress of European civilization was to promote peaceful, mutually beneficial exchanges across national boundaries. The enlightened self-interest of sovereigns converged with their subjects to serve the common good of humanity. The liberal equation of interest with prosperity, or rationality with a preference for maximal over relative gains, resolved all conflicts in an ultimate harmony of interests. Enlightened statecraft worked toward this revolution by dismantling artificial impediments to trade. [13]

To be sure, many of these Enlightenment ideals often were honored in the breach. Britain and the colonies frequently pursued their own specific interests as aggressively as any other power (as well as against each other, on occasion). But at least in this highly stylized world, the colonists saw themselves as participants in the global geopolitical struggle between the opposing political systems – one representing ordered liberty and the other, despotism – and in the corresponding intellectual and moral struggle between enlightenment and non-enlightenment.

The immediate role of British North America in this struggle was to serve as the commercial and strategic anchor of the Empire. The colonists had their differences with England but these were thought to be manageable because

---

[12] Gerald Stourzh, *Benjamin Franklin and American Foreign Policy*, 2nd ed. (Chicago: University of Chicago Press, 1969), p. 7; and Daniel Lang, *Foreign Policy in the Early Republic: The Law of Nations and the Balance of Power* (Baton Rouge: Louisiana State University Press, 1985), pp. 7-12. See also Onuf and Onuf, *Federal Union, Modern World*.

[13] Onuf and Onuf, *Federal Union, Modern World*, p. 18.

of the prestige of the mother country, the protection she offered them, and the tacit willingness of London to allow colonial self-government. As Franklin noted, this was a very different relationship, in terms of liberty and prosperity, from that between England and Ireland. Over time, however, British North Americans expected that their subordinate role would change. Franklin's famous 1751 essay, "Observations Concerning the Increase of Mankind," predicted that within a century the greatest number of Englishmen would be in North America. He foresaw a glorious future in which the seat of empire would transfer to the West, and the differences between the imperial core and periphery would adjust naturally on American terms and in an evolutionary fashion. Young, virtuous and vigorous America would strengthen the cause of liberty in aging Britain and provide the dynamic element in the continued and ordered expansion of that liberty. An ever-stronger Anglo-America meant the corresponding weakening of despotism, a power-political trend that would also open up opportunities for enlightenment and political reform among the states of Europe. [14]

The Crisis of the Imperial Regime

The breakdown of this stylized model of Anglo-American ordered liberty is a familiar story. After the French and Indian War, a majority of the colonists interpreted the policies of the British Ministry to rationalize the imperial structure as an immense conspiracy to assault their individual and corporate liberties – that is, an effort by the center to force regime change on the peripheries of the empire. Britain's hostility toward the colonies was not just the result of bad policies but also because of the corruption of the English Constitution. That regime had deteriorated to the point where Britain herself had become an agent of tyranny and a threat to the entire Enlightenment project. American resistance, then, was conceived not just in terms of an intra-imperial dispute over specific legislation but as part of the global conflict between freedom and despotism, and the eternal domestic contest between liberty and power. For instance, the colonists previously had been willing to accept the British Navigation Acts because they saw them as being in the interests of the Empire as a whole and not as an instrument of special privileges for Britain itself. The authorities in London and their delegates in the Western

---

[14] On Franklin's views, see Stourzh, *Benjamin Franklin*, pp. 100-2; Bailyn, *The Ordeal of Thomas Hutchinson* (Cambridge: Harvard University Press, 1974), p. 234; John Ferling, *A Leap in the Dark: The Struggle to Create the American Republic* (New York: Oxford University Press, 2003), p. 22; and H.W. Brands, *The First American: The Life and Times of Benjamin Franklin* (New York: Doubleday, 2000), pp. 439-41.

Hemisphere traditionally had signaled their acceptance of this understanding through lax enforcement of the Acts against American shipping, especially in the West Indies trade. Now, things had changed and colonists such as John Hancock were being brought up on charges of smuggling. When American juries and officials resisted complying with this change of policy, Britain threatened to remove the cases to an Admiralty Court outside of the colonies. A growing number of Americans came to consider British maritime policy as tyrannical and inimical to commercial freedom.[15]

The American response to the perceived threat of London-imposed regime change was resistance, ultimately in the form of violence (real or threatened), but to a first order through commercial retaliation (real or threatened) that presumably put at risk Britain's prosperity and its financial trump card over the continental despotisms. They sought to restore the de facto autonomy that the colonial governments, especially their popular assemblies, had enjoyed (sometimes as much imagined as real); to insist on their rights as Englishmen (e.g., not to be taxed without their own consent); and to have their growing role in the Empire recognized. The Americans also warned their friends in England that their own liberties were at stake in the contest. "We call for & confide in the good offices of our fellow subjects beyond the Atlantic," Thomas Jefferson wrote. "Of their friendly dispositions we do not yet cease to hope; aware, as they must be, that they have nothing more to expect from the same common enemy than the humble favor of being last devoured."[16]

The American colonial agents in London, especially Benjamin Franklin, insisted that the colonists were acting in a constitutional fashion to resist the unconstitutional acts of Parliament and, as the argument played itself out, the King-in-Parliament. Their declared objective was not separation from the Empire but the defense of the British regime, properly understood, and its restoration to former glory. "England must be saved in America," John Dickinson argued. Eventually, the mother country "will rejoice that we resisted – and thank us for having offended her." Joseph Warren expressed the hope that "Britain's liberty, as well as ours, will eventually be preserved by the virtue of America." John Adams believed that the direction of reform was clear: "The improvements to be made in the English Constitution lie entirely in the House of Commons." If there was a substantial measure of electoral reform, and if

---

[15] For a thorough overview, see Robert Middlekauff, *The Glorious Cause: The American Revolution, 1763-1789* (New York: Oxford University Press, 1982).

[16] Jefferson's Draft of the Declaration of the Causes and Necessities for Taking Up Arms, Julian P. Boyd and others, eds., *The Papers of Thomas Jefferson* (Princeton: Princeton University Press, 1950-), I: 203.

the popular arm of the legislature was thus strengthened, "it would be impossible to corrupt the people of England." It was up to those people to "take care of the balance, and especially their part of it." [17] These appeals were made not only to the people of Britain but to other parts of the Empire, including Quebec, Jamaica and Ireland.

As these political appeals went unanswered and as London responded by reasserting its authority through measures such as the Coercive Acts, American leaders, who characterized themselves as Whigs, began to fear that the British regime could not be reformed, at least from the outside, and certainly not on a time scale that would save American liberties. The British Ministers, for their part, insisted it was the colonists who were conspiring to bring about regime change in England by calling into question the constitutional settlement of 1688. Even the friends of America such as Burke, however much they might sympathize in practice with the colonists and urge conciliatory measures, disagreed with the evolving American interpretation of the nature of the imperial regime. From this lack of support for the American cause, John Adams and other American Whigs decided that the King, Parliament, the administration, and the electorate "have been now many years trained and disciplined by Corruption" in their oppressive ways. The conclusion seemed clear that "the Cancer is too deeply rooted, and too far spread to be cured by anything short of cutting it out entire." [18]

The process of resisting British policies at the political-moral as well as practical level led American Whigs to rethink the entire nature of government and not merely the British-American constitutional relationship. The cutting edge of American opinion moved beyond an appeal to rights and liberties of Englishmen to an appeal to the rights of man, which (as these Americans now saw it) had once been the animating spirit of the British Constitution. The sovereignty of the people became the new or at least newly-asserted standard by which regimes should be judged, an argument in line with the larger Enlightenment project. A people had a right to determine their own form of government. They had a right to threaten, and even carry out, revolution to secure those rights when confronted by tyrannical rule. The most radical of the Americans began to argue openly that the colonists had to free themselves from the British Empire not only for their own self-preservation and liberty

---

[17] Quotations cited by H. Trevor Colbourn, *The Lamp of Experience: Whig History and the Intellectual Origins of the American Revolution* (Chapel Hill: University of North Carolina Press, 1965), pp. 103, 114-5, 123, 187.

[18] Adams to Moses Gill, 10 June 1775, Robert J. Taylor and others, eds., *Papers of John Adams* (Cambridge: Harvard University Press, 1977-), 3: 21. Hereafter referred to as *PJA*.

but also on behalf of the larger cause of humanity, a cause that the British had abandoned. Theirs would not be a purely selfish act but one designed to preserve and advance the cause of liberty writ large. America would assume the mantle of defender of Protestant and republican liberty, through the creation of a "New Order of the Ages." The American Revolution would be fought for the rights of mankind. America would bear the torch of human liberty and take the lead in promoting an enlightened constitutionalism. If America was to reach its full potential and play its full role as the Laboratory of Enlightenment, it would have to separate itself from the British Empire and become an American Empire.[19]

The Case Against American Regime Change

That was a hard argument to swallow for many colonists who not only retained their historic attachment to the Mother Country but who held a somewhat different view of government, liberty, and regime change. For years, even the most radical colonial leaders had insisted publicly that they were loyal to the crown and that they only wanted to bring about constitutional reform, not independence. Those who became Loyalists, and not a few moderate American Whigs, had warned from the beginning that independence was the logical outcome of resistance to England. The Loyalists argued that there could be no middle ground between a regime based on the principle of Parliamentary supremacy, and the complete separation of America from Britain. Given the disastrous consequences that the Loyalists believed would result from independence, they saw no alternative but to accept the former relationship. Massachusetts Governor Thomas Hutchinson acknowledged the premise of the Enlightenment: that this was indeed an age of liberty, and that the desire for liberty throughout the world had grown markedly since the Glorious Revolution. But truly free government required a balance between power and liberty. The peoples of continental Europe had begun tentatively to seek the restoration of their former liberties against despotic rule. In these circumstances, at least in principle, the expansion of liberty could have a positive outcome. But in already free societies, the excessive pursuit of liberty would degenerate into anarchy unless checked by power.[20] Religious minorities also needed protection from overbearing local majorities. "The destruction of Old England

---

[19] Janice Potter, *The Liberty We Seek: Loyalist Ideology in Colonial New York and Massachusetts* (Cambridge: Harvard University Press, 1983), pp. 170-1.

[20] Bailyn, *The Ordeal of Thomas Hutchinson*, especially pp. 80-2.

would hurt me," lamented New York Dutch-French Huguenot John Jay. "I wish it well. It afforded my ancestors an asylum from persecution." [21]

For the Loyalists, the British government provided the essential balancing element of power for the colonies. First, British North Americans needed the protection of the mother country to defend their lengthy and exposed coastline, a vulnerable frontier on the interior, and their commerce. Second, because the individual colonies differed so widely in their interests, they needed an external force – Parliament – to impose order in their internal relationships and, through appointed governors and officers, to protect the rights of individual citizens from oppressive local majorities. According to Massachusetts loyalist Daniel Leonard, a friend and political opponent of John Adams, the colonial governments "have no principle of stability within themselves;" they would "become wholly monarchical, or wholly republican, were it not for the checks, controls, regulations, and supports of the supreme authority of the empire." There could be no divided constitutional authority: "the supreme authority of Parliament to legislate for the empire was the vital constitutional ligament in the imperial connection and the most basic symbol of the oneness of the Empire." [22]

Hutchinson argued that the only practical alternative to the existing imperial arrangement for the colonists was not a freer, independent America, but rule by another external power, "which would allow them less liberty than they are sure of always enjoying while they remain English subjects. . . . I hope it will never be our misfortune to know by experience the difference between the liberties of an English colonist and those of the Spanish, French, or Dutch." [23]

Pennsylvania's Joseph Galloway agreed. If America rejected the authority and protection of the mother country, "she must in all probability soon become the slave of an arbitrary power – of Popish bigotry and superstition." [24] According to Galloway, the imperial relationship had served the colonies well. Their commerce had flourished, they enjoyed unprecedented freedoms, they could depend on imperial protection from foreign threats and they could look forward to a happy and prosperous future that included a rapid expansion across the continent. Galloway doubted that the colonists – with no army or navy to speak of and no military infrastructure – could wage war successfully against

---

[21] Potter, *The Liberty We Seek*, p. 2.

[22] Potter, *The Liberty We Seek*, pp. 143-4.

[23] Bailyn, *The Ordeal of Thomas Hutchinson*, pp. 80-2, 209.

[24] Colbourn, *The Lamp of Experience*, p. 14.

Britain. America's only hope of victory would be to ally itself with France and Spain, Roman Catholic countries with far more absolutist traditions than the mother country. Galloway and others doubted that the continental despotisms, which possessed their own empires and which had concerns about the stability of their own domestic rule, would be eager to legitimize popular rebellion, even against their ancient enemy. That said, if America, aided by France and Spain, actually defeated Britain, it would find itself at the mercy of foreign regimes far worse than that of King George III and the British Parliament. What was more probable, however, was the likelihood that the colonies would be defeated and ruled henceforth with an iron hand by London.[25]

According to the Loyalists and the cautious Whigs, an Anglo-American civil war would also be devastating for the general cause of human freedom and the prospect for the evolution of enlightened regimes throughout Europe. America's alliance with despotic regimes like France and Spain would strengthen those particular despotisms and weaken the case for balanced constitutions and ordered liberty. The dynamic liberalizing factor and example of America would be lost, for Britain in particular and for enlightened opinion in general. "But I cannot please myself with contemplating the Ruin and destruction of Great Britain – Avert it Heaven! May she ever continue the Mistress of Nations – the grand support of *Liberty*, the Scourge of Oppression and Tyranny!" wrote one loyalist.[26]

The best choice for Americans as the Loyalists saw it was to stay in the Empire and continue to fight the good fight for liberty, for themselves and for their brethren in England, as their ancestors had done. Franklin, for a long time, was of this persuasion. Even if the King and the Ministry were engaged in a malevolent conspiracy, time, in the form of geography, demography, and economic growth, was on the side of British North America. The colonists should not force the issue, especially as they had been incapable in the past of uniting for the common defense (as the failed Albany Plan had demonstrated). When Great Britain, burdened with debt, next found itself at war, the colonies then would be in the best position to bargain and define the imperial regime properly. "Then is the time to say, redress our grievances," Franklin argued. "Cling fast to every right privilege and just claim, but avoid violence and open conflict. Keep in mind not only the inevitable growth of America and its destined domination of the English-speaking world, but the condition of Europe and England's fate in a universe of warring nations. Remember

---

[25] Ferling, *A Leap in the Dark*, pp. 116-9.

[26] Quoted in Potter, *The Liberty We Seek*, pp. 110-1.

that the Protestant country (our mother, though lately an unkind one) is worth preserving, and that her weight in the scale of Europe, and her safety in a great degree, may depend on our union with her." [27]

The more moderate Whigs were not content with the constitutional or political status quo, however. They still sought a middle ground where the principle of Parliamentary supremacy could be reconciled with a practical division between imperial and local affairs. The colonists should be granted a responsibility for matters that did not concern the Empire as a whole. The moderates considered various reforms such as an imperial parliament, in which Americans would be directly represented. They supported a policy of resistance and commercial coercion but with the object of reconciliation, rather than separation, by compelling London to integrate the colonies more fully into the Empire and thus better secure their rights and liberties. [28]

Even Loyalists like Galloway thought in terms of major constitutional reforms that would alter the internal government of the colonies as a means of adjusting the imperial relationship. Unlike the Whigs, however, he believed that republicanism was an enemy of liberty because it destroyed the necessary constitutional balance. He decried the growing "democratic" drift in American thinking about government. "An entire Democracy without the checks of Aristocracy and Monarchy would be dangerous to the State." Galloway favored lessening the power of the popular assemblies and strengthening the non-elective branches, to make those colonial governments less responsive to public pressure. He favored creating an American nobility appointed by the King, perhaps in the form of councilors. According to Galloway, the colonists should get over the notion that there was a politically influential group in England that supported the radical American Whig understanding of the proper nature of the imperial regime. "However closely we may hug ourselves in the opinion, that parliament has no right to tax or legislate for us, the people of England hold the contrary opinion as firmly." Daniel Leonard warned: "We hear, by every

---

[27] Bailyn, *The Ordeal of Thomas Hutchinson*, p. 234. Or, as Franklin wrote to a colleague from Massachusetts: "There seem to be among us some violent spirits who are for an immediate rupture. But I trust the general prudence of our countrymen will see that by our growing strength we advance fast to a situation in which our claims must be allowed; that by a premature struggle we may be crippled and kept down another age; that as between friends every affront is not worth a duel, between nations every injury is not worth a war; so between the governed and the governing every mistake in government, every encroachment on rights, is not worth a rebellion." Brands, *The First American*, p. 458.

[28] See the characterization of John Jay and others in Ron Chernow, *Alexander Hamilton* (New York: Penguin Press, 2004), p. 57.

arrival from England, that it is no longer a ministerial (if it ever was) but a national cause." [29]

Benjamin Franklin, after being humiliated in front of the Privy Council for his arguments on behalf of the colonies, concluded reluctantly that the Loyalists were correct. There was no politically viable enlightened opinion in England to which the colonists could appeal. But rather than surrender the larger issue, he and other American leaders soon decided to appeal to enlightened opinion elsewhere.[30]

The Case for American Regime Change

The would-be American revolutionaries needed to make a persuasive case for regime change that would address the criticisms of Loyalists and bring the moderates into their camp. Regime change meant not only separation from the British Empire and assertion of American nationhood but also, as it soon became clear, the adoption of a republican form of government. The revolutionary leadership had to demonstrate that such an independent America was viable internally and externally; that separation from the British Empire would advance and not damage the larger cause of human liberty, enlightenment, and political reform; and that the new nation would not be forced to align itself with despotism. Well before the Continental Congress officially declared independence, its representatives had begun sounding out foreign opinion and seeking military and economic assistance from abroad. They realized that outside aid, in some form and at some level, would be necessary to succeed in a conflict with the world's leading military and economic power. John Adams, for instance, thought that while the United States could achieve independence on its own, the costs (broadly considered) would be so excessive as to make good government impossible after the war.[31]

The nascent Congressional government had considerable confidence, contrary to Galloway's warnings, that the geopolitical imperative among continental European powers to weaken Britain – aided, in France's case, by the desire for revenge from defeat in the Seven Years' War – would override potential allies' concern about American republicanism. As for the prospects of an alliance with France after over a century of conflict with the French in North America, American leaders noted that sudden rever-

---

[29] Information and quotations from Potter, *The Liberty We Seek*, pp. 134, 154, 172-3, 175.

[30] Colbourn, *The Lamp of Experience*, p. 188.

[31] L. H. Butterfield, Leonard C. Faber, and Wendell D. Garrett, eds., *Diary and Autobiography of John Adams*, 4 vols. (Cambridge: Harvard University Press, 1961), 4: 38-9. Hereafter referred to as *D&A*. Adams to James Warren, 4 August 1778, *RDC*, 2: 676.

sals of alliance among European powers were hardly unknown. George Mason observed that the Dutch had been able to secure outside support in their revolt against Spain from Spain's traditional enemies, including those regimes that were hardly sympathetic to the religion or politics of the Dutch. "The same causes will generally produce the same effects . . . what has happened may happen again." [32] The revolutionary leaders may also have calculated that their adoption of republican institutions was actually an advantage in soliciting an alliance with a proud monarchy like France. If anything, the French royalists "believed that the republican form of government was destined to keep the US so weak and powerless that Europe would not have to be afraid of it." [33]

Nevertheless, the American revolutionaries were not prepared merely to rely on old-style European diplomacy or the calculations of despots. They appreciated the need to appeal to the politically influential enlightened classes of Europe – the lawyers, merchants, writers, and sympathetic government officials who constituted the Republic of Letters and who considered themselves the defenders of the rights of mankind. These appeals would have to be made in terms other than crass individual or national self-interest. The Americans expected to draw upon, shape, and strengthen the cause of Enlightenment – call it liberalism or generic republicanism – throughout Europe. The Enlightened, in turn, would appreciate that the success of the American Revolution would improve the prospects for domestic reform and, in the long term, for regime change in Europe. In 1775, Franklin, on behalf of Congress' Secret Committee of Correspondence, wrote to ask C.W.F. Dumas, a Swiss-born authority on international law living at The Hague, whether there were "any disinterested powers acting on behalf of humanity." Dumas responded: "When I remarked, in my last letter to you, 'that all Europe wishes you the most happy issue in your defense of your liberty,' I meant the unprejudiced, equitable, humane European public; in a word, the citizens of universal society, men in general." [34] The French playwright Pierre Beaumarchais, who had friends in the French Court and among the literati of Paris, was a fitting example of the audience that the Americans were trying to target. Beaumarchais was an Enlightenment enthusiast who founded a commercial enterprise, secretly supported by the

---

[32] Colbourn, *The Lamp of Experience*, p. 151.

[33] Henry Blumenthal, *A Reappraisal of Franco-American Relations, 1830-1871* (Chapel Hill: University of North Carolina Press, 1959), p. 3.

[34] Franklin quotation, Stourzh, *Benjamin Franklin*, pp.121-4; Dumas to Franklin, 30 April 1776, *RDC*, 2: 86.

French government, which supplied the Americans with weapons, clothes and provisions. Indeed, Americans held out some hope for a time that individuals like Beaumarchais, with the tacit approval of their governments, would for reasons of glory (and profit) provide enough private aid that formal government-to-government alliances would not be necessary.

The American revolutionaries issued a number of documents, official and unofficial, designed to shape the domestic and international battlefield of ideas in their favor. Thomas Paine's *Common Sense* was a milestone in shifting American public opinion in favor of independence and republican government (although Adams groused that it contained nothing that had not been bandied about behind closed doors in the Continental Congress). The Declaration of Independence established what turned out to be the canonical arguments for opposing oppressive rule and justifying regime change. The Model Treaty set out the desired place of the United States in the Euro-Atlantic state system and the means by which the United States could influence that system – and the regimes that constituted the Republic of Nations – for the better. American representatives, publicists and sympathizers abroad saw that these arguments were circulated throughout Europe, suitably tailored to the appropriate audiences.

The Declaration of Independence and the Model Treaty

The Declaration of Independence would have a privileged place in articulating the role of the United States in the world. Scholars have long debated the precise purpose and target audience of the Declaration, as well as the short-term impact of the document itself. Historians such as Pauline Maier argue that the Declaration was not remarkably original or important at the time, especially in contrast to the significance that later generations would assign to it as the foundational document of the American Republic.[35] But it is fair to say that the Declaration was, as Jefferson put it, "an expression of the American mind" at the time of the Revolution, and that the Declaration offered a template of advanced liberal thinking about the nature of regimes and regime change. The Declaration was also part of the new nation's diplomatic campaign to attract the support of foreign allies. That campaign had to walk a fine line: one of influencing enlightened public opinion abroad without alienating the non-enlightened rulers and ministers

---

[35] Pauline Maier, *American Scripture: Making the Declaration of Independence* (New York: Vintage Books, 1997).

who as a rule controlled the guns, loans and troops on which the success of the Revolution would ultimately depend.[36]

A New Standard for Regime Change

The Declaration of Independence was famously addressed "to a candid world," by which the American revolutionaries meant especially the enlightened (or those who thought themselves enlightened). It sought to demonstrate that the American cause was much more than mere rebellion; that this particular revolution, and revolution rightly understood, was a legitimate means of affecting regime change. The Declaration invoked the rights of mankind and the sovereignty of the people as the ultimate standards of political justice and pushed the boundaries of legitimate regime change beyond that established by the Glorious Revolution. But at the same time, the Declaration was carefully qualified by terms, explicit or implicit, that did not threaten established rulers everywhere. The *right* that a sovereign people had to alter or abolish their government was not the same as a *categorical imperative* to do so.

First, any people contemplating regime change must suffer demonstrably from an oppression that went well beyond the ordinary difficulties between rulers and the ruled. Governments should not be overturned for "light and transient causes" – there must be a "long train of abuses" that clearly demonstrated a design to establish an absolute despotism. (At the same time, a sovereign people was entitled to draw the logical conclusion that a long train of abuses portends such a design – they are not condemned to wait to resist until an absolute despotism is established, because a successful revolution may then be impractical.) Second, the revolutionaries must demonstrate that they have exhausted all other avenues short of revolution to seek redress for their grievances. Third, the revolution must be practical. ("When a people find themselves cruelly oppressed by the parent state, they have an undoubted right to throw off the yoke, and to assert their liberty, if they find good reason to judge that they have sufficient power and strength to maintain their ground," as the Boston cleric Samuel West argued.[37]) Fourth, the revolution of any particular people must cause more good than harm for humanity as a whole, and not merely be for the immediate benefit of those people.

---

[36] Gerald Stourzh, *Alexander Hamilton and the Idea of Republican Government* (Stanford: Stanford University Press, 1970), p. 23.

[37] Samuel West, "On the Right to Rebel Against Governors," Election Day Sermon, 1776, at http://oll.libertyfund.org/?option=com_staticxt&staticfile=show.php%3Ftitle=2066&chapter=188670&layout=html&Itemid=27.

Those generic standards established a rather high threshold for legitimate regime change. The Declaration – unlike *Common Sense* – did not condemn monarchy in general but rather the actions of a particular monarch. Indeed, the Declaration demonstrated an inherent respect for the decision of other peoples about their form of government, including their willingness to live under despotism.[38] The American revolutionaries did not call for world revolution or demand the independence of all colonies from their mother countries. The Declaration set the American Revolution and the claim of national independence in the context of the existing international system – "to assume among the powers of the earth, the separate and equal station to which the Laws of Nature and of Nature's God entitle them" (a point which would be emphasized in other policy documents and decisions, such as the Model Treaty). This followed the authority of Vattel – that all nations, like all men, were created equal and had equal rights. As historian David Armitage writes of the Declaration: "Its primary intention was to turn a civil war among Britons, and within the British Empire, into a legitimate war between states under the law of nations." Paine, in the first edition of *Common Sense*, argued that the "custom of nations" demanded a declaration of American independence. Without a declaration, Paine concluded, "[t]he custom of all courts is against us, and will be so, until, by an independence, we take rank with other nations."[39]

The Declaration's generalized appeal to foreign audiences and potential allies raised the question whether, under the law of nature and nations, it was legitimate for those seeking independence or regime change to ask for the assistance of outside powers and whether, in light of the general doctrine of non-interference in the domestic affairs of others, it was legitimate for those outside powers to offer assistance. The American answer, of course, was yes, at least in terms of aiding a people establishing their independence from a repressive (and distant) government. The revolutionary regime, for its part, had to be sufficiently powerful to accept that assistance on equal terms rather than as a supplicant. Independence or regime change could not be justified if it resulted merely in exchanging one tyrant for another. Those outsiders who were considering whether to support independence or regime change, like the revolutionaries themselves, must take into account the probability of success and the effect of their actions on third parties. France and Spain, for instance, would be entitled to consider the impact of the American Revolution on their

---

[38] Nathan Tarcov, "Principle and Prudence in Foreign Policy," *Public Interest* 76 (Summer 1984): 47-50.

[39] See quotes and analysis in David Armitage, *The Declaration of Independence: A Global History* (Cambridge: Harvard University Press, 2007), pp. 36-40.

own colonies, and to insist upon reassurance from the United States that it did not intend to promote revolution in those colonies.

The New Standard for Regimes

The American revolutionaries laid claim to the Enlightenment standard of the best modern regime – one previously asserted for the British Constitution – and a new model of regime change based on reflection and choice, not force and accident.[40] The American regime would be a New Order of the Ages. It would demonstrate to the world the feasibility of a wholly popular government (non-monarchical and non-aristocratic) on a continental scale. The United States would also be a (con)federal republic. The American revolutionaries believed that it was possible to arrange their federation so that no outside agent, like the British Parliament, would be required to impose unity and order among the constituent members. Although the American Revolution was not formally anti-monarchical, its success would clearly point the way to identifying self-government with republican government, understood to be government without Kings and Lords.[41]

There was, to be sure, great deliberation among American leaders about the precise form of government that best suited this new federal republic, both within the new states and for the central (confederation) government. They also debated the proper relationship between and among the states and the central authorities. Paine argued for a simple form of government based on a unicameral legislature; the Pennsylvania Constitution of 1776 incorporated these ideas. Adams insisted that complexity, in terms of a constitutional balance among branches of government representing distinct socio-economic (but not hereditary) orders, was essential to maintain ordered liberty; he was the principal author of the Massachusetts Constitution of 1780. The American political debate, of course, would carry on into the 1780s, the Constitutional Convention and ratification, and beyond. But in any case, the United States was a breathtaking and dynamic experiment in self-government, the lessons of which could be applied by wise leaders elsewhere to reform their own particular regimes according to their own particular circumstances.

At the heart of the justification for the American Revolution was the belief that this was an experiment in self-government that would favorably impact all mankind and the prospects for reform and regime change elsewhere.

---

[40] Mansfield, "The Unfinished Revolution," pp. 28-9.

[41] For the argument that the Declaration of Independence did offer authoritative guidance about the preferred type of regime, see Harry V. Jaffa, *How to Think About the American Revolution* (Durham: Carolina Academic Press, 1978), pp. 49-140.

American leaders assumed that the mere fact of their Revolution would have good effects. Adams argued that any rebellion for freedom – as the English did against King John, the Dutch against the Spanish, the Swiss against the Austrians, and the Romans against the Tarquins – tended to promote the general cause of liberty in unexpected ways. [42] The revolutionaries speculated that at the very least America would become an asylum for the oppressed of mankind, especially if the European regimes could not be reformed. The existence of this asylum by itself would increase the prospects for reform by bolstering the courage of the enlightened who could now run greater risks, knowing that they had assurances of safety if things went badly. Despots would have to consider the losses to their own national power if their populations (especially the best and brightest) fled to the New World because of domestic repression. [43]

A New International System and Standard for International Behavior

Finally, the Declaration of Independence put the United States forward as a sovereign and equal member of the existing international system. The American revolutionaries proposed, however, to join that system on their own terms rather than those set by the European great powers. They believed they could reform that system and fundamentally reconfigure international politics in a way that would promote the opportunities for enlightened domestic reform and, if a sovereign people so chose, for regime change. As Peter S. Onuf writes: "Visionary republican revolutionaries wanted to change the world: by extending the boundaries of the European system, by enhancing the system's capacity for progressive improvement through the practice of enlightened diplomacy, by perfecting a legal regime among their own state-republics that would eliminate the causes and pretexts of war." [44]

The Archimedean lever that would allow the United States to move the Euro-Atlantic world so fundamentally was commerce. The American revolutionary leaders assumed that the lure of their commerce, once liberated from the British Empire, was so powerful that it would overcome the reluctance that the nations of Europe might have toward aiding the cause of independence. As noted above, there were other reasons to believe that the Europeans would

---

[42] Colbourn, *The Lamp of Experience*, p. 95, from Adams' *Novanglus* essays.

[43] See Bailyn, *Faces of Revolution*, chapter on "1776." The American revolutionaries' promotion of emigration was qualified in important respects, however. For example, both Franklin and Jefferson were cautious about letting in aristocrats or peasants because their characters had been tainted, in different ways, by living under a monarchy. Brands, *The First American*, pp. 633-4.

[44] Peter S. Onuf, *Jefferson's Empire: The Language of American Nationhood* (Charlottesville: University of Virginia Press, 2001), p. 60.

be friendly; the Americans assumed, however, that the commercial imperative would convince all but the most regressive European regimes that they could not afford to be left out of the economic bonanza. Put in these terms, the American cause would appeal to those among the enlightened who advocated greater commercial freedom but who did not necessarily identify the cause of political freedom with that of republican government. The United States would offer its commerce on the open market, without preference to regime type, ideally on a reciprocal basis. Under these conditions, "all nations would join in protecting the common mart" and resist Britain's efforts to reestablish her monopoly over this trade.[45] As Peter and Nicholas Onuf write: "By challenging Britain's mercantilist regime, the Americans appeared not only to serve their own interests, but also those of prospective trading partners and of the trading world generally."[46]

At the outset of the Revolution, Americans assumed that they were in such a strong position that they would not have to enter into any binding political arrangements ("entangling alliances") with the European powers, either during the Revolutionary War or thereafter. The political and geographical separation between the Old and New Worlds would protect American republicanism as well as American interests. The United States would deal with all nations strictly on a commercial basis and would promote a correspondingly enlightened understanding of the law of nations – especially the maritime law of nations, where England had long been at odds with the continental powers. American representatives promoted the law of nations as interpreted by authorities such as Vattel, who held that the natural state of nations was peace, not war, which further justified the American policy preference of avoiding the wars and entanglements of European diplomacy.[47] In *Common Sense*, Paine had famously written: "Any submission to, or dependence on, Great Britain tends directly to involve this Continent in European wars and quarrels, and set us at variance with nations who would otherwise seek our friendship, and against whom we have neither anger nor complaint." Paine did so in part to refute the argument that American security required that the colonies remain under the protection of Britain. But in a larger sense, Paine believed that continued ties with England made unnatural enemies of those nations and peoples who would otherwise be

---

[45] James H. Hutson, *John Adams and the Diplomacy of the American Revolution* (Lexington: University Press of Kentucky, 1980), p. 16.

[46] Onuf and Onuf, *Federal Union, Modern World*, p. 19.

[47] Jesse S. Reeves, "The Influence of the Law of Nature Upon International Law in the United States," *American Journal of International Law* 3 (July 1909): 554, 559.

friends – and that such friendship was the natural state of affairs in a commercially-focused international system, one not driven by classic military/naval/imperial considerations.[48]

Toward the end of the war, Paine would argue that the progressive aim of the American Revolution was not to spread republican government but to foster the growth in international harmony between nations of different political systems and principles – the creation of world community based on compacts or treaties of commerce and peace between sovereign countries. The 18th century had demonstrated that wars were not profitable. The only barrier to political compacts of nations was the prejudice nations had developed toward each other during previous periods of history. "Forms of government have nothing to do with treaties," Paine wrote. "The former are the internal policy of the countries severally; the latter their external policy jointly; and so long as each performs its part, we have no more right or business to know how the one or the other conducts its domestic affairs, than we have to inquire into the private affairs of a family."[49]

The Americans would also follow the authority of Vattel that all nations, like all men, were created equal and had equal rights; that among these (with some important and well-defined exceptions) was the right of non-interference in their domestic affairs. Of course, nations, like men, varied in their size, character, wealth, and circumstances; and great powers claimed their prerogatives. But the law of nations, interpreted in an enlightened fashion, would check excessive claims by the great powers – including their right to interfere in the domestic affairs of others – and support the right of peoples to choose their own form of government. To be sure, the balance of power still existed as a motive force in relations among the European powers and the United States could not ignore the balance in its prudential calculations. "That it never could be our Interest to unite with France, in the destruction of England, or in any measures to break her Spirit or reduce her to a situation in which she could not support her Independence," John Adams concluded. "On the other hand it could never be our Duty to unite with Britain in too great a humiliation of France."[50] The trick was to ensure that the balance of power operated in a progressive rather than regressive

---

[48] Thomas Paine, *Common Sense,* Michael Foot and Isaac Kramnick, eds., *The Thomas Paine Reader* (New York: Penguin Classics, 1987), p. 83. For an overview, see David M. Fitzsimons, "Tom Paine's New World Order: Idealistic Internationalism in the Ideology of Early American Foreign Relations," *Diplomatic History* 19 (Fall 1995): 569-82.

[49] For Paine's full analysis, see his Letter to the Abbé Raynal, *The Thomas Paine Reader,* pp. 147-66.

[50] Adams, Autobiography, *WJA,* 2: 505.

manner. An independent, non-aligned, and commercially powerful United States best promoted such a progressive balance.

The Continental Congress approved what became known as the Plan of 1776, or the Model Treaty, which codified the preferred American approach to foreign policy and international relations.[51] The American approach to international commerce and the law of nations did not formally discriminate among regime types or promote domestic regime change; the geo-economic revolution caused by American independence and by general access to American trade would, however, effectively preference certain types of political rule over time. Commerce and liberty were twins, as Alexander Hamilton would later explain: "As commerce enlarged wealth and civilization increased," slowly illuminating the darkness of mediaeval times, "the people began to feel their own weight and consequence . . . they grew tired of their oppressions" and, joining forces with their monarchs, "threw off the yoke of aristocracy." "Commerce did more than contribute to the strength of the nation: it ensured its liberties," as political scientist Darren Staloff observes. "A steady stream of revenues from taxes on trade meant government no longer need plunder its people or threaten private property. Indeed, one of the central themes of Scottish social theory from Smith and Ferguson to Hume and William Robertson had been the role of commerce in producing modern liberty. It was the rise of commerce that had destroyed the baronial despotism of the feudal epoch, redistributing property from the landed aristocracy to the urban tradesman and people at large."[52] Hume and Adam Smith argued in turn that the enhanced prosperity of one nation did not necessarily mean the ruin of another. Smith spoke of a great mercantile republic uniting all the merchants of all nations.[53] Even if the merchant class did not constitute "men of *no* nation," they would represent a powerful constituency within non-republican regimes to which the American cause would appeal.

The American republicans believed that by promoting law-governed international commerce, they would promote moderate relations among nations and strengthen the forces and interests of liberalism within regimes

---

[51] See the detailed discussion of the Model Treaty in Gregg L. Lint, "The Law of Nations and the American Revolution," Lawrence S. Kaplan, ed., *The American Revolution and a Candid World* (Kent, OH: Kent State University Press, 1977).

[52] Hamilton quote and discussion in Staloff, *Hamilton, Adams, Jefferson*, p. 80.

[53] Stourzh, *Benjamin Franklin*, pp. 108-9.

of all types.[54] The old warlike international system, by contrast, retarded the progress of mankind because it strengthened those interests and elements most inimical to liberty and reform. It led to the accumulation of power by the government at the expense of the people. Liberalized regimes, based on a fundamental respect for the rights of their citizens, were more likely to be respectful of the rights of others and, hence, less likely to threaten each other.[55] American independence would not lead to a full and instant reformation of the international system but it would initiate this virtuous circle and create space for enlightened leaders to foster further improvement in their domestic regimes. "The progress of the law of nations, under the influence of science and humanity, is mitigating the evils of war, and diminishing the motives to it, by favoring the rights of those remaining at peace, rather than of those who enter into war," James Madison would later argue. "Not only are the laws of war tempered between the parties at war, but much also in relation to those at peace."[56]

Standing in the way of the creation of this virtuous circle of commerce, peace and domestic reform was a particular despotism: the maritime tyranny of Britain. Americans might debate among themselves whether monarchies or mixed regimes like that of Britain were inherently tyrannical or merely subject to corruption; they hoped, however, that the continental European governments could be brought to agree that London's naval practices threatened to undermine the security and prosperity of all nations, irrespective of regime type. "The one fighting to oppress and enslave a free people," Robert R. Livingston of New York characterized the conflict, "The other to establish their rights, the one attempting to Tiranize over the Ocean, and fetter the Commerce of the World, the other resisting that Tyranny, and rendering Trade as free as nature made it."[57] The enlightened of Europe could take this argument one step

---

[54] As Pierre Manent observes, Americans were not uncritical supporters of commerce. In the commercial system, members of society behave less passionately and more rationally, not because they become intrinsically wiser but because they are more aware of their own interests and that the system is conceived precisely for the satisfaction of their interests. They were also concerned with the threat to virtue caused by the luxury associated with certain types of commerce. Manent, *A World beyond Politics? A Defense of the Nation-State,* trans. Marc A. Lepain (Princeton: Princeton University Press, 2006), p. 88.

[55] On this general reformist tendency, see John C. Rainbolt, "Americans' Initial View of Their Revolution's Significance for Other Peoples, 1776-1788," *Historian* 35 (May 1973): 418-33.

[56] James Madison, *Examination of the British Doctrine, Which Subjects to Capture a Neutral Trade, Not Open in Time of Peace* (Washington, D.C., 1806), available at http://oll.libertyfund.org/?option=com_staticxt&staticfile=show.php%3Ftitle=1938&chapter=119003&layout=html&Itemid=27.

[57] Robert R. Livingston to Adams, 9 January 1782, *PJA,* 12: 176.

further: the British maritime tyranny fostered a zero-sum international environment that retarded domestic political reform. Franklin argued that Britain had followed the wrong path to commercial prosperity. She had displayed, "a fondness for conquest as a warlike nation, her lust for ambition was an ambitious one, and her thirst for a gainful monopoly was a commercial one . . . the true and sure means of extending and securing commerce is the goodness and cheapness of commodities; and . . . the profit of no trade can ever be equal to the expenses of compelling it and holding it by fleets and armies."[58] An independent America not only would demonstrate a better path to national prosperity, it would promote the best domestic political practices among all nations and regime types.

The American leaders, then, did not rely upon a global war of peoples against kings, or revolutionary changes of regime elsewhere, to help bring about their own change of regime. They instead relied on appeals to the geopolitical and economic interests of existing European governments, and the common goals of the enlightened classes, to gain necessary assistance in their war for independence. But they also hoped that the American Revolution would be the catalyst for the emergence of a more moderate international system in which states, republican and non-republican, respected each other's sovereignty. The cumulative effect, by strengthening liberal interests within nations and by removing the repressive pressures created by threats to national security, would improve the conditions of mankind and create openings for domestic political reform – and, if particular sovereign peoples so desired, for regime change. The successful American experiment in republican government would provide further incentive and guidance for reform and peaceful revolution throughout the civilized world.

Strategy and Diplomacy of the War

These concepts about regime change were all well and good to contemplate within the theoretical confines of the Republic of Letters, but the principles of the American Revolution had to be made operational to meet the needs of wartime strategy and diplomacy. Under the pressure of events Americans would come to disagree about the degree to which the letter and spirit of the "new diplomacy" – with its implications for foreign regime change – ought to guide their actions.

The American representatives abroad had the immediate task of announcing the formal existence of the new nation. They cited various

---

[58] Franklin to Lord Howe, 20 July 1776, *RDC*, 2: 103-4.

actions and pronouncements of the Continental Congress and other American governmental bodies as evidence of American seriousness. Above all, they sought to reassure governmental officials and influential Europeans that the colonies would not reconcile with England. "Our Articles of Confederation being by our means translated and published here, have given an appearance of consistence and firmness to the American States and Government that begins to make them considerable," Franklin wrote shortly after he arrived in France in late 1776 with a diplomatic commission from Congress. "The separate constitutions of the several States are also translating and publishing here, which afford abundance of speculation to the politicians of Europe . . ."[59]

Congress certainly did not to try to hide from foreign rulers the Declaration of Independence, despite its potentially revolutionary appeal. Quite the contrary. "The reasons of this act of independence are so strongly adduced in the declaration itself that further argument is unnecessary," the President of Congress, John Hancock, informed William Lee, the representative-designate to the courts of Berlin and Vienna.[60] The Committee of Secret Correspondence instructed Silas Deane, its first informal representative to France: "With this you will receive the Declaration of the Congress for a final separation from Great Britain. It was the universal demand of the people, justly exasperated by the obstinate perseverance of the Crown in its tyrannical and destructive measures, and the Congress were very unanimous in complying with that demand. You will immediately communicate the piece to the Court of France, and send copies of it to the other Courts of Europe. It may be well also to procure a good translation of it into French, and get it published in the gazettes."[61] Deane later complained to Congress about the tardy arrival of the document. "I presented the Declaration of Independence to this court, after it had, indeed, become an old story in every part of Europe," he reported in December 1776. He was happy to report, "it was well received . . ."[62]

Franklin agreed with Deane's assessment: "The good will of all Europe to our cause as being the cause of liberty, which is the cause of mankind, still continues, as does the universal wish to see the English

---

[59] Franklin and Deane to Committee of Secret Correspondence, 12 March 1777, *RDC*, 2: 287-8.

[60] Hancock to William Lee, 1 July 1777, *RDC*, 2: 359.

[61] Committee of Secret Correspondence to Silas Deane, 8 July 1776, Paul H. Smith, ed., *Letters of Delegates to Congress, 1774-1789* (Washington, D.C.: Library of Congress, 1976-), 4: 405.

[62] Deane to John Jay, 3 December 1776, *RDC*, 2: 213-14.

pride humiliated and their power curtailed." [63] Franklin did not foresee any immediate loosening of grip of despotism in Europe but he verified the earlier speculation that the American Revolution would have a positive effect on the cause of human liberty. "Tyranny is so generally established in the rest of the world, that the prospect of an asylum in America for those who love liberty, gives general joy, and our cause is esteemed the cause of all mankind. Slaves naturally become base, as well as wretched. We are fighting for the dignity and happiness of human nature." [64]

> All Europe is on our side of the question, as far as applause and good wishes can carry them. Those who live under arbitrary power do nevertheless approve of liberty, and wish for it; they almost despair of recovering it in Europe; they read the translations of our separate colony constitutions with rapture, and there are such numbers everywhere who talk of removing to America with their families and fortunes as soon as peace and independence shall be established, that it is generally believed that we shall have a prodigious addition of strength, wealth, and arts, from the emigration of Europe; and it is thought that to less or prevent such emigrations the tyrannies established there must relax and allow more liberty to their people. Hence it is a common observation here that our cause is the cause of all mankind, and that we are fighting for their liberty by defending our own. [65]

Over time, American diplomats found the European view of republican America to be a bit more complicated. "The Courts of Europe ... dread the Forms of Government in America," Adams observed after spending several years on the continent. "They dread that high Sense and Spirit of Liberty, and those popular Principles, with which America is full. They are afraid of their Spreading in Europe and propagating like a Contagion, So as to produce Revolutions. But the People of Europe, and the Men of Letters ought for the opposite Reasons, to cherish America as their only remaining Barrier against Despotism. For if the Spirit of Liberty is Subdued in America there is now an end of it in the World." [66] To help finesse the revolutionary implications of

---

[63] Franklin to Cooper, 27 October 1779, *RDC*, 3: 396.

[64] Franklin and Deane to Committee of Secret Correspondence, 12 March 1777, *RDC*, 2: 287-8.

[65] Franklin to Samuel Cooper, 1 May 1777, *RDC*, 2: 312-3; Stourzh, *Benjamin Franklin*, p. 234.

[66] Adams to Edmund Jenings, 27 February 1781, *PJA*, 11: 164-6.

their mission for the *ancien regime*, American diplomats offered reassurances that the United States would respect the colonial possessions of the European powers. Adams used this line of argument:

> Those Powers, which have as large Possessions as any beyond Seas, have already declared against England, apprehending no such Consequences. Indeed there is no Probability of any other Power of Europe following the Example of England, in attempting to change the whole System of the Government of Colonies, and reducing them by Oppression to the Necessity of governing themselves. And without such manifest Injustice and Cruelty on the Part of the Metropolis, there is no danger of Colonies attempting Innovations. Established Governments are founded deeply in the Hearts, the Passions, the Imaginations and Understandings of the People, and without some violent Change from without to alter the Temper and Character of the whole People, it is not in human Nature to exchange Safety for Danger, and certain Happiness for very precarious Benefits. [67]

Adams was well aware that the Spanish were particularly sensitive on this point. "But when they are led to consider the Difference between their Colonies and the English, that there is no Probability or Possibility of their ever undertaking as the English did, to subvert the fundamentals of an Established Government—and the Nature of their Governments which can suppress in an instant the first Symptom of discontent, they easily give it up." [68] Spain, France and the other European colonial powers should realize that the real threat to their overseas possessions was not American-inspired revolt but the threat posed by a British Empire that had re-conquered its American colonies: "Put America again in dependance on England, and it would be in their joint Power in twenty years, to conquer all the Possessions of the Spaniards French Dutch and Portuguese in the East and West Indies in Spight of all that the rest of Mankind could do to prevent it." [69]

American representatives also relied heavily on appeals to honor. "His most Christian majesty in rendering himself a protector of the rights of mankind became entitled to the assistance from the friends of man," Samuel Huntington, then serving as President of Congress, wrote to the French Minister

---

[67] "A Memorial to their High Mightinesses, the States General of the United Provinces of the Low Countries," 19 April 1781, *PJA*, 11: 280.

[68] Adams to Elbridge Gerry, 11 December 1779, *PJA*, 8: 295.

[69] Adams to Jean de Neufville and Fils, 24 March 1781, *PJA*, 11: 227.

to the United States. "This title could not but be recognized by a monarch whose diadem is adorned with equity and truth."[70] Arthur Lee appealed to "the magnanimity of a great and opulent prince," his Most Catholic Majesty, King of Spain: "Nor can anything give more lasting satisfaction to the royal mind than the reflection of having employed those means which God has put into his hands in assisting an oppressed people to vindicate those rights and liberties which have been violated by twice six years of incessant injuries and insulted supplications; those rights which God and nature, together with the convention of their ancestors and the constitution of their country, gave to the people of the States."[71]

The War, the Regime Question, and Regime Change

American revolutionary leaders viewed war and its accoutrement, such as debts and standing armies, as engines of despotism, an inherent threat to liberty and to republican government. As Franklin famously said, "I have been apt to think that there has never been, nor will ever be, any such thing as a *good* war, or a *bad* peace."[72] By fighting for their independence, American republicans were aware that they might paradoxically be planting the seeds for their own future destruction. They believed, however, that specific wars fought out of necessity, if waged properly and for the right ends, could actually strengthen the forces of liberalism and reform among the Republic of Nations and within particular regimes. If Americans properly waged the present war of necessity, they would strengthen their union and self-government and create, or at least facilitate, a favorable international configuration of power that would preserve American independence over the long run, as well as promote the general cause of human liberty.

To this end, Americans sought to internationalize the war and orient it toward the common goal of truncating or destroying the maritime tyranny of Britain. "It is a connection with America, which must in future decide the Balance of maritime Power, in Europe," Adams insisted.[73] If Britain retained control over America's expanding population and commerce, the European balance of power would be destroyed and "there would be an end of the liberty of all other nations upon the seas. All commerce and navigation of the world would be swallowed up in one frightful despotism." France's existence as a

---

[70] President of Congress (Samuel Huntington) to Luzerne, 17 November 1779, *RDC*, 3: 410.

[71] Arthur Lee to Florida Blanca, 17 March 1777, *RDC*, 2: 291.

[72] Franklin to Jonathan Shipley, 10 June 1782, cited in Brands, *The First American*, p. 620.

[73] Adams to Patrick Henry, 9 July 1778, *D&A*, 4: 153-4.

maritime and commercial power would be destroyed as would Spain and the Netherlands. Britain would realize the ancient dream of despots by becoming a universal monarchy.[74]

To deal with this common threat of British maritime tyranny in the context of winning the current war, American strategists pressed their European allies or potential associates (specifically, France) to dispatch a strong naval force to American waters to combine with the armies of the United States. "We must have a superiour naval Force in the West Indies and on the Coast of this [American] Continent," Adams insisted. "England will never be brought to her senses untill this Plan is adopted. Get Convoys to Trade, and a superiour naval Power in the American seas, and all will be easy, I think."[75] The American Commissioners in France (Franklin, Adams and Lee) appealed to the French Foreign Minister, comte de Vergennes:

> It is obvious to all Europe that nothing less is at stake than the dominion of the sea, at least the superiority of naval power, and we can not expect Great Britain will ever give it up, without some decisive effort on the part of France. With such an exertion as that of sending a superior fleet to America we see nothing in the course of human affairs that can possibly prevent France from obtaining such a naval superiority without delay. Without it the war may languish for years, to the infinite distress of our country, to the exhausting both of France and England, and the question left to be decided by another war....[76]

At the outset of the conflict, American leaders did not expect that independence would be achieved by militarily conquering or forcing regime change on Britain. Having abandoned their claims of common citizenship and rights under the British Constitution, the American revolutionaries did not assume the moral authority they once possessed as fellow citizens to become involved in Britain's domestic affairs. The British people were now like any other people: enemies in war, friends in peace. Rebellion might well occur in the British Isles but this would be the by-product rather than the aim of war. George Washington, for one, believed that the British would muddle through their governmental problems, as they had always done, and

---

[74] Hutson, *John Adams and the Diplomacy of the American Revolution*, p. 10.

[75] Adams to Henry Marchant, 25 October 1779, *PJA*, 8: 228.

[76] Franklin, Lee and Adams to Vergennes, 1 January 1779, *RDC*, 3: 5-6.

that Americans could not count on such a simple solution as the fall of the Monarchy to absolve them of the need to fight and win a hard war.[77]

The newly-constituted United States did not entirely neglect this dimension of the conflict, however. American forces invaded Canada even before independence was formally declared and had invited the accession of the Canadians to the North American Union. Franklin argued for raids by allied naval forces against the English coast (one of which was executed by John Paul Jones) for the purpose of retaliation and strategic leverage rather than the overthrow of King George. "It is scarcely conceivable how great a panic, the success in any one of these projects, would occasion in England," Jones argued. "It would convince the world that their coasts are vulnerable, and would, consequently, hurt their public credit." [78] The French and Spanish planned an invasion of Britain but this plan had limited resources and goals and was soon aborted. William Lee suggested to Adams that it would be "good Policy in France to have a good stock of muskets and other Military Stores lodged at Dunkirk and other sea Ports ready to throw into England at a short warning if circumstances there should ever require such a measure." [79] Paine suggested to Congress that he be smuggled into England and spread revolutionary propaganda but, like Lee's proposal, nothing came of this idea. [80]

Loyalist émigrés like Joseph Galloway took the threat of subversion seriously. They argued that a transatlantic cabal based in England, in collusion with Franklin and other American rebels, had created the revolution. Their tactics, according to Galloway, were domestic sedition in England and "conflagration of massacres" in America. The aim of the cabal was to create such discord as to bring about the collapse of the Ministry, the destruction of the monarchy, and the republicanization of British society and institutions. Franklin, from Paris, did stay in touch with such intellectual liberals in Britain as Richard Price, Joseph Priestly, David Hartley, Benjamin Vaughan, and William Hodgson. He did so not

---

[77] R. R. Palmer, *The Age of the Democratic Revolution: The Challenge* (Princeton: Princeton University Press, 1959), p. 184.

[78] Jones to the Commissioners, 4-5 July 1778, *PJA*, 6: 262.

[79] William Lee to Adams, 9 April 1780, *PJA*, 8: 119-20.

[80] Craig Nelson, *Thomas Paine: Enlightenment, Revolution, and the Birth of Modern Nations* (New York: Viking, 2006), p. 150.

to encourage sedition, however, but rather to nurture moves toward peace talks and British acceptance of American independence.[81]

For most American leaders, Bourbon France, despite the differences in regime type, was the natural linchpin of their wartime strategy and the key to a new postwar configuration of international power conducive to American security and human liberty. Next to Britain it was the most powerful state in Europe; its leaders burned to avenge the humiliating defeat in the Seven Years' War; and it could call on the family compact with Spain. To make the relationship work, both sides had to overcome long-standing prejudices. Franklin was an inspired choice to mediate between the two peoples, as he shrewdly played upon his image as a savant of the Enlightenment and a "natural American," while flattering the French character. Adams also offered reassurances to his countrymen that the religion-based regime differences were no longer to be feared.

> The spirit of crusading for religion is not in France. . . . The rage for making proselytes, which has existed in former centuries, is no more. There is a spirit more liberal here in this respect than I expected to find. Where has been the danger to the religion of the Protestant cantons of Switzerland from an alliance with France, which has subsisted with entire harmony for one hundred and fifty years, or thereabouts? But this subject is fitter for ridicule than serious argument, as nothing can be clearer than that, in this enlightened tolerant age, at this vast distance, without a claim or color of authority, with an express acknowledgment and warranty of sovereignty, this, I had almost said tolerant nation, can never endanger our religion.[82]

Monarchical and Catholic France, to be sure, was hardly an exemplar of a progressive regime or crusader on behalf of the rights of mankind. Nevertheless, France's acceptance in February 1778 of a liberal commercial relationship with the United States through a Treaty of Amity and Commerce, based on the Model Treaty, was a landmark event. As John Quincy Adams would reflect decades later:

> The commercial treaties negotiated by other nations were almost always combinations for exclusive privileges or concessions of

---

[81] Esmond Wright, *Franklin of Philadelphia* (Cambridge: Harvard University Press, 1986), p. 322; John Ferling, *The Loyalist Mind: Joseph Galloway and the American Revolution* (University Park: Pennsylvania State University Press, 1977), p. 105.

[82] Adams to Warren, 4 August 1778, *RDC*, 2: 676.

monopoly. But the spirit of the American revolution was emphatically the spirit of liberty and of equal rights. It was manifested not only in their internal institutions, but in the influence which they exercised from the first moment of their admission into the community of nations. It was proclaimed to the world, in a manner appropriate to its own excellence and to their dignity, in the first treaty that they concluded with a European power that of 6th February, 1778, with France. . . . It may be a subject at once of honest exultation and of serious admonition to Americans of this day, that while their declaration of independence contained the first solemn recognition by a nation at the moment of its bursting into birth of the great and sacred principles of civil society, upon which alone rightful government can be founded, their first national compact, though concluded with an absolute monarchy, proclaimed in like manner the only just and magnanimous principles which ought to govern the intercourse of nations with each other.[83]

The Foreign Policy Debate Emerges

The reality of the situation did not quite match the goals of idealized American diplomatic and military strategy, however, as Adams – father and son – well knew. Nations did not automatically flock to cultivate and protect American commerce. Franklin and his colleagues were unable to secure a commerce-only relationship with France. In order to entice the French openly into the war, the American Commissioners agreed to a second treaty that brought the United States into a conditional political-military alliance with France. Although Spain eventually joined the fighting, the Spanish Court refused American applications for loans or diplomatic recognition. The war dragged on. The Continental Congress became essentially bankrupt. Elements of the Continental Army mutinied. Non-belligerent European powers, including Russia, proposed a mediation that might have sacrificed American interests and even its independence.

In 1779, in the midst of this emerging crisis, Congress engaged in the first major debate over foreign policy since the decision for independence. The debate was initially triggered by a request from Conrad Alexander Gerard, the French Minister to the United States, to determine its terms for peace and to appoint a minister plenipotentiary to conduct the negotiations. The ensuing

---

[83] John Quincy Adams to George Washington Campbell, 28 June 1818, Worthington C. Ford, ed., *The Writings of John Quincy Adams*, 7 vols. (New York: Macmillan, 1913-1917), VI: 367-8.

Congressional deliberations revealed major sectional and factional disagreements about the way forward. To complicate matters Gerard schemed behind the scenes to ensure that Congress adopted limited war aims – terms acceptable to France and likely to lead to an early resolution of the war. He also pressed Congress to select a pliable diplomat.

Gerard was disappointed with the selection of personnel. New Englander John Adams, who had already rubbed Vergennes the wrong way before returning to the United States on his own accord in 1779, was named as the U.S. Peace Commissioner. (As part of the compromise agreement over policy and personnel, John Jay of New York, then regarded as pro-French, was selected over Francophobe Arthur Lee of Virginia for the post in Madrid.) Gerard was much more successful in determining the content of Adams' instructions. Congress' initial terms fell short of the full American wish list; for instance, Adams was not required to obtain access to the fisheries of Newfoundland or to acquire all of Canada and Florida. By 1781, Congress, under the influence of a new French Minister, the Chevalier de la Luzerne, was even more accommodating to Versailles. Adams was subsumed into a five-member Peace Commission which now included presumed Francophiles Jay, Franklin and Thomas Jefferson. They were instructed to subordinate themselves in the peace negotiations to the French government: "You are . . . to undertake nothing . . . without their knowledge and concurrence; and ultimately to govern yourselves by their advice and opinion." [84]

The underlying factional differences in Congress were extraordinarily complicated and cannot be divided simply into pro- and anti-French parties. For our purposes, what appears to be extraordinary subservience to France can be explained by growing Congressional fears that the Revolution was about to founder militarily and politically without a rapid settlement, and particularly by the belief that substantial elements of American society secretly aimed to reintegrate the United States into the British Empire. Only the closest possible ties with France could keep America from falling back into the English orbit. Those opposing this position argued that independence made on French terms would leave the United States as an enfeebled satellite of France, having merely exchanged one European master for another (precisely as Galloway had predicted). [85] Some of those in the so-called

---

[84] Continental Congress, Instructions to American Peace Commissioners, 15 June 1781, Mary A. Guinta and J. Dane Hartgrove, eds., *Documents of the Emerging Nation: U.S. Foreign Relations, 1775-1789* (Washington, D.C.: National Historical Publication and Records Commission, 1998), pp. 78-9.

[85] Ferling, *A Leap in the Dark*, pp. 210-3; Bradford Perkins, *The Creation of a Republican Empire, 1776-1865* (New York: Cambridge University Press, 1993), pp. 32-6.

anti-French camp might indeed be described as pro-English but, for the most part, their experience in the war had reinforced their views on the need for an independent American foreign policy and on the unique relationship of the United States to other regimes, including that of Britain. The most influential, if idiosyncratic, member of this camp was John Adams.

Adams, American Strategy and the French Alliance

Adams' diplomatic experience in Europe had persuaded him that the American Revolution – particularly the liberation of American commerce, but also its republicanism – had wide-ranging effects beyond those appreciated by Congressional members preoccupied with the short-term problems of fighting the war.

> Although my Mind has been full twenty Years preparing to expect great Scenes, yet I confess the Wonders of this Revelation exceed all that I ever foresaw or imagined. That our Country so young as it is, so humble as it is, thinking but lately, so meanly of itself should thus Interest the Passions, as well as employ the Reason of all Mankind in its favour, and effect in so short a Space of Time, not only thirteen Revolutions of Government at home, but so compleatly accomplish a Revolution in the system of Europe, and in the Sentiments of every Nation in it, is what no human Wisdom perhaps could foresee." [86] America, Adams insisted, "is certainly the great Wheel in the political Machine of the World at present. [87]

Adams believed that the United States should exploit this opportunity to bring about significant changes in the emerging Euro-Atlantic state system (and, *inter alia*, encourage major reforms of Europe's domestic institutions). It was imperative, as a matter of national interest as well as the betterment of mankind, for the United States, and particularly its foreign representatives, to guide the process as far as possible through activist diplomacy. Adams assumed that this could be accomplished without violating the stricture against binding political connections with any of the European powers. The war, to be sure, had to be fought and won, and peace negotiated, on its own terms. But Adams did not see a contradiction between the near-term demands of the conflict and America's longer term aims of bringing about a liberal trading

---

[86] Adams to the President of Congress, 28 April 1780, *PJA*, 9: 243-4.

[87] Adams to Edmund Jenings, 20 January 1781, *PJA*, 11: 62.

order, supporting the rights of mankind, and strengthening enlightened and popular elements in foreign regimes.

Adams acknowledged that American wartime strategy, as a practical matter, rested on the French alliance. Although the conditional treaty of alliance with France violated Adams' warning against political connections with Europe, he recorded no immediate objection to Franklin's decision to make such an agreement. As noted above, Adams' first experience in Paris confirmed his pre-war judgment that the political, cultural and religious differences between the American Republic and Monarchical Catholic France were not an obstacle to cooperation. "The longer I live in Europe and the more I consider our Affairs the more important our Alliance with France appears to me," Adams wrote in August 1778. "It is a Rock upon which we may safely build, narrow and illiberal prejudices peculiar to John Bull with which I might perhaps have been in some degree infected when I was John Bull, have now no Influence with me." [88] Because Britain was certain to be America's long-term enemy, France would remain America's natural ally. "As long as Great Britain shall have Canada Nova Scotia, and the Floridas, or any of them So long will Great Britain be the Enemy of the United States, let her disguise it as much as she will. It is not much to the Honour of human Nature, but the Fact is certain that neighbouring Nations are never Friends in Reality. . . . France and England as Neighbours and Rivals never have been and never will be Friends. The Hatred and Jealousy between the Nations is eternal and ineradicable." Because France had no possessions on the North American continent, "We therefore, as on the one Hand we have the surest Ground to expect the Jealousy and Hatred of Great Britain, so on the other We have the Strongest Reasons to depend upon the Friendship and Alliance of France." The connection with France, furthermore, "will forever secure a Respect for our states in Spain Portugal and Holland too, who will always chose to be upon friendly terms with Powers who have numerous Cruisers at sea, and indeed in all the rest of Europe." [89]

But as time went on, Adams came to believe that American and French interests – at least those pursued by Vergennes and much of the French Court – were substantially at odds. (Adams always retained a high opinion of Louis XVI.) His testy conversations and correspondence with Vergennes and other senior French officials, coupled with reports of the French-influenced shift in Congressional attitudes, persuaded Adams that France wanted to truncate

---

[88] Adams to James Warren, 4 August 1778, *PJA*, 6: 346-9. Adams added: "I never was however much of John Bull. I was John Yankee and such I shall live and die."

[89] Adams to Samuel Adams, 28 July 1778, *PJA*, 6: 325-7.

America's growth by limiting its territory, controlling its diplomacy, and particularly by influencing its domestic politics. "There is Danger to the Simplicity of our Manners and to the Principles of our Constitution, and there may be dangers that too much will be demanded of Us. . . . There is Danger, that French Councils and Emmissaries and Correspondents, may have too much Influence in our Deliberations," he warned Roger Sherman, a Congressman from Connecticut.[90]

Adams rejected the argument that the wartime emergency, coupled with the threat of British subversive influence and the divisions among American states and regions, required Congress to accede to French diplomatic leadership and to limit American wartime aims. Adams believed that the American Revolution naturally created the leverage that wise statesmen could use to chart a truly independent course and to set a liberal tone for international relations. But for America to use that leverage for its own advantage and for the cause of mankind, it had to establish itself and be recognized as a great power – a major planet – in the Euro-Atlantic state system, and not as a client state (satellite) of France.

> N. America is a new primary Planet, which taking its Course in its own orbit, must have an Effect upon the orbit of every other, and shift the common Center of Gravity of the whole system of the European World. She is de facto, an independant Power, and must be so, de Jure. . . . She is mistress of her own fortune, knows that she is so, and will manage that Power which she feels herself possessd of, to establish her own System and change that of Europe.

For its own sake, Adams argued, the United States must occupy a unique position in the international "solar system" – that is, by being politically detached and able to exercise its "gravity" through commerce rather than through the traditional devices of war and the manipulation of political alliances. The existence of such a new planet – geographically distant, non-aligned, republican, pacific and commercial – would also benefit the Europeans as well, if they understood (or could be made to understand) their interests properly. "The natural Effects of the Seperation of them, and of the Independance of America, upon the commercial and political state of Europe . . . may by Wisdom and Benevolence, [be] wrought into the greatest Blessing of Peace, Liberty and Happiness, which the World hath yet seen. . . . America, will then become the arbitress of the commercial . . . and perhaps . . . the mediatrix of peace, and of the political business of the World." This

---

[90] Adams to Roger Sherman, 6 December 1778, *PJA*, 7: 254-5.

"political business" would include altering the domestic affairs of nations, at least indirectly.

> If the Sovereigns of Europe, should find in the Example of England, that the System of Colonies in distant regions for the Purpose of Monopolies, is at an end, and turn their Attention, to give Exertion to their own internal powers like the police of China, cultivate their waste lands, improve Agriculture, encourage manufactures, abolish Corporations: as all the remnants of Barbarism, shall be removed, the powers of the Community will create those surpluses which will become the Source, and open the channells of commerce. . . . they should see with pleasure, that the manners of mankind, softening by degrees have become more humanized; their Police more civilized: and altho many of the old oppressive Institutions of Government, as they respect Husbandmen, Manufacturers, Merchants, Marketts and Commerce, have not yet been formally abolished; yet that Practice, by various Accommodations, have abrogated their most mischeivious operations. That the Activity of Man finds every day, a freer Course: that there are a thousand Ways, which altho pride will not open, prudence will connive at, through which the intercourse of Marketts finds every year, a freer vent: and that the active Spirit of commerce is like the Spirit of Life, diffusing itself through the whole Mass of Europe. [91]

In declaring the United States to be a new and independent primary planet, Adams, in his own mind, did not propose to turn against France. He proposed instead to develop American leverage over this unfolding revolution in the Euro-Atlantic state system by stirring up British public opinion against the war and forcing Britain to the negotiating table; by multiplying diplomatic contacts and influential relationships elsewhere in Europe; and, by persuading the established powers to recognize American independence and to accord it proper diplomatic status. Commerce was to be the wedge that opened the door. The American market and American goods would be available to all on equal footing but Adams pointed out that those European merchants, bankers and nations that entered into a formal commercial relationship with the United States first would have a natural advantage over late-comers.

Adams wanted to complement economic self-interest by appealing to the currents of enlightenment among some segments of European society as a means of pressuring non-republican governments to recognize the United

---

[91] Adams to the President of Congress, 19 April 1780, *PJA*, 9: 176-7, 179-80, 188-9.

States. Public opinion, even among the enlightened, always tended to lag behind events and needed to be shaped actively. The enlightened classes already appreciated the generic value of commerce, but it was the task of the American diplomat to demonstrate forcefully that the entry of the United States into the European state system represented a remarkable shift in the balance of power and that it served as the catalyst for commercial and political liberalization. In doing so American representatives should not take no for an answer or defer to established opinion about proper etiquette. "Your Veterans in Diplomaticks and in Affairs of State consider Us as a kind of Militia, and hold Us perhaps, as is natural, in some degree of Contempt," Adams told Livingston, who had been appointed by Congress as Secretary of Foreign Affairs, "but wise Men know that Militia sometimes gain Victories over regular Troops, even by departing from the Rules." [92]

Franklin Objects

Franklin and his political allies, including Livingston, to the extent they understood Adams' position, opposed it as a vast and presumptuous over-reaching on the part of the United States. Militia diplomacy would unnecessarily alarm European political and strategic conservatives, who still held the upper hand in most nations. "A virgin state should preserve the virgin character, and not go about suitoring for alliances, but wait with decent dignity for the application of others," Franklin had observed shortly after arriving in Europe. [93] Livingston was of the view that Adams embarrassed the United States by insisting on his public character, which only revealed the weakness of the American diplomatic position absent French support. [94] Adams' bull-in-the-China-shop approach threatened America's essential connection with France and undermined Vergennes' carefully calibrated diplomacy. "It is our firm connection with France that gives us weight with England, and respect throughout Europe," Franklin maintained. "If we were to break our faith with this nation, on whatever pretence, England would again trample upon us, and every other nation despise us." [95] Franklin insisted that he had no intention of making the United States a French satellite; rather, America should for now occupy a close, parallel orbit, in which French "gravity" would shield the United States from the

---

[92] Adams to Livingston, 21 February 1782, *PJA*, 12: 253-6.

[93] Franklin to Arthur Lee, 21 March 1777, *RDC*, 2: 298.

[94] Livingston to Adams, 20 November 1781, *PJA*, 12: 72-6.

[95] Franklin to Samuel Cooper, 26 December 1782, in Brands, *The First American*, p. 600.

dangerous "debris" of European interstate relations that would otherwise cross the "orbit" of the new Republic.

Franklin believed that Adams fundamentally misunderstood France's motivation in supporting American independence. Frenchmen, whether of enlightened or traditional views, thought of themselves as magnanimous. As a people they were susceptible to emotional appeals made by the apparently weak and oppressed, but not to threats or to material inducements. American gratitude, not American commerce, would be the essential binding agent of the relationship for the immediate future. For the cold-eyed realists like Vergennes who actually implemented French policy, such gratitude also demonstrated America's appreciation of the proper power-political relationship between France and the United States – Franklin knew his place, and that of his nation, whereas Adams did not.

> He [Adams] thinks, as he tells me himself, that America has been too free in expressions of gratitude to France, for that she is more obliged to us than we to her, and that we should show spirit in our applications. I apprehend that he mistakes his ground, and that this court is to be treated with decency and delicacy. The king, a young and virtuous prince, has, I am persuaded, a pleasure in reflecting on the generous benevolence of the action in assisting an oppressed people, and proposes it as a part of the glory of his reign. I think it right to increase this pleasure by our thankful acknowledgments, and that such an expression of gratitude is not only our duty, but our interest. A different conduct seems to me what is not only improper and unbecoming, but what may be hurtful to us.[96]

Time revealed that Franklin, no less than Adams, was a devoted advocate of American interests. Franklin believed that American's strength would manifest itself naturally over time.[97] For Adams, however, the time was now. He believed that Franklin favored an attitude of gratitude and deference to France as an end in itself, rather than as a means to an end. As Adams wrote to Francis Dana, a friend and diplomatic colleague:

> Although I am convinced by every thing I see, and read and hear, that all the Powers of Europe, except perhaps the House of Austria, and I am not very clear in that Exception, rejoice in the American Revolution, and consider the Independence of America as for their

---

[96] Franklin to President of Congress, 9 August 1780, *RDC*, 4: 22-3.

[97] For an explanation and defense of Franklin's position, see Bailyn, *To Begin the World Anew*, pp. 66-7.

Interest and Happiness, in many Points of View, both respecting Commerce and the Ballance of Europe, yet I have many Reasons to think that not one of them, not even Spain nor France, wishes to see America rise very fast to Power. We ought therefore to be cautious how we magnify our Ideas and exaggerate our Expressions of the Generosity and Magnanimity of any of these Powers. Let us treat them with Gratitude, but with Dignity. Let us remember what is due to ourselves and our Posterity, as well as to them. Let us above all things, avoid as much as possible, entangling ourselves with their Wars or Politicks. Our Business with them and theirs with Us, is Commerce, not Politicks, much less War. America has been the Sport of European Wars and Politicks long enough.

Adams was determined to carve out as much diplomatic room for maneuver as possible, certainly while the war was still in progress. "America, my dear Sir has been too long Silent in Europe. Her Cause is that of all Nations and all Men: and it needs nothing but to be explained to be approved," Adams insisted. "At least these are my Sentiments. . . . The Effects of it may not appear in Sudden and brillant Success: but the Time was exactly chosen and the happy fruits of it will appear in their Course." [98] Adams wanted the United States to seek foreign loans without the assistance of France by propagandizing and by seeking diplomatic recognition where the American presence was not (yet) welcome.

Franklin objected. "Our Credit and Weight in Europe depend more on what we do than on what we say: And I have long been humiliated with the Idea of our running about from Court to Court begging for Money and Friendship, which are the more withheld the more eagerly they are solicited, and would perhaps have been offer'd if they had not been asked," he warned Adams. "The supposed Necessity is our only Excuse. The Proverb says *God helps them that helps themselves*, and the World too in this Sense is very Godly." [99] In August 1780, Franklin reported to Congress with considerable alarm about Adams' aggressive, independent diplomacy.

> M. de Vergennes, who appears much offended, told me yesterday that he would enter into no further discussions with Mr. Adams, nor answer any more of his letters. He is gone to Holland to try, as he told me, whether something might not be done to render us less dependent on France. He says the ideas of this court and those of

---

[98] Adams to Dana, 18 April 1781, *PJA*, 11: 267 70.

[99] Franklin to Adams, 2 October 1780, *PJA*, 10: 194-5.

the people of America are so totally different, that it is impossible for any minister to please both. He ought to know America better than I do, having been there lately, and he may choose to do what he thinks will best please the people of America. But when I consider the expressions of Congress in many of their public acts, and particularly in their letter to the Chevalier de la Luzerne, of the 24th of May last, I can not but imagine that he mistakes the sentiments of a few for a general opinion.

"It is my intention, while I stay here, to procure what advantages I can for our country by endeavoring to please this court," Franklin added, "and I wish I could prevent anything being said by any of our countrymen here that may have a contrary effect and increase an opinion lately showing itself in Paris, that we seek a difference, and with a view of reconciling ourselves to England. Some of them have of late been very indiscreet in their conversations." [100]

Adams' arguments and actions unquestionably contributed to the French (and Congressional) concern that some Americans secretly planned to resume political ties with the British regime and to terminate the alliance with France. Such accusations did not deter him from pressing on with an aggressive diplomatic campaign, however. He did not regard that campaign as begging but as demanding that the new American regime be given its due.

A British Revolution?

Adams thought that Britain, above all nations, would be impacted by the change in the Euro-Atlantic state system that was occurring because of the American Revolution. As he refined his diplomatic strategy, Adams revisited the question of whether American independence and the destruction of Britain's maritime tyranny might require a change in the British regime.

Adams thought that Britain, or at least England, would survive the war: "the Annihilation of a Nation never takes place." The more important question was "whether she shall sink down into the Rank of the middling powers of Europe or whether she shall maintain the second place in the Scale." [101] Adams believed that Britain could maintain second place only if it reestablished its commercial relationship with the former colonies and if it abandoned the exclusionism of the Navigation Acts. Adams argued that the first step in achieving these ends was to notify the British government officially of his powers to negotiate peace and establish a treaty of commerce.

---

[100] Franklin to the President of Congress, 9 August 1780, *RDC*, 4: 22-3.

[101] Adams to James Warren, 4 August 1778, *PJA*, 6: 346-9.

By doing so, "he would force the British government to clarify its position on negotiations, encourage those in Great Britain who wanted peace, dispel rumors that France enjoyed exclusive privileges under the Franco-American Treaty of Amity and Commerce, and take advantage of the forces that were tearing at the fabric of British society." [102]

Vergennes, with Franklin's support, angrily warned the American envoy against making his credentials public. By raising prematurely the prospect of peace negotiations, Adams, in Vergennes' opinion, would sabotage France's efforts to bring Spain fully into the war and to coordinate the diplomatic machinery necessary to bring about American independence. Adams, frustrated by the opposition of Vergennes and Franklin, sought less formal channels to make his case to the British. He reworked and published in French and English the arguments made in a pamphlet by Thomas Pownall, the former governor of Massachusetts. Pownall argued for the importance of American commerce to Britain and for adopting free trade principles suitable to promoting trade with the former colonies. Adams also prepared a response to a publication, *Cool Thoughts*, written by exiled loyalist Joseph Galloway, which had called on England to prosecute the war with more vigor. Adams sought to convince British leaders and opinion-makers that formal acknowledgement of American independence was the necessary first step toward peace, mutually profitable commerce, and the preservation of Britain's great power status (even if that status would necessarily be reduced). [103] He wrote letters to those Englishmen whom he believed to be sympathetic to the American cause, both in the British Isles and on the continent. He hoped they would promote these arguments, and his anonymous writings, with their peers.

Adams hoped that the logic of his case would persuade rational Englishmen, particularly those in opposition to the North Ministry who might come to power in a change of government. But he also considered the possibility that the prospects for peace and the long-term development of a beneficial Anglo-American commercial relationship might be improved by full-scale regime change in Britain and not merely by a change in public or elite opinion over immediate policy issues. Adams believed that a British Revolution was certainly possible as a consequence of the war. He thought that the King and his ministers might relinquish their pretensions to rule in

---

[102] Editorial Note, *PJA*, 9: 517.

[103] Adams first sent a redacted version of the Pownall pamphlet to the President of Congress on 19 April 1780; the published versions appeared in Amsterdam (in French) later that year, and in London in 1781. Adams' response to *Cool Thoughts* was not published until 1782.

America only when they stood on the precipice of national bankruptcy and civil war, or had already plunged off those cliffs. "What their Pride will end in, God only knows," he wrote Franklin. "For my own Part, I cannot See, a Probability, that they will ever make Peace, untill their Finances are ruined and such Distresses brought upon them as will work up their Parties into a civil War." [104] As he put it to an English correspondent: "So far from expecting any serious, sensible proposals for Peace, I think the Parties in England will go to War with each other, and they must fight their Battle out, before we shall know, which has the national Power in its Hands to make peace with Us. They have a point to settle first, whether we shall make Peace with a British King or a British Congress." [105] If events came to such a climax, Adams concluded, "a Revolution in her Government may possibly take place, but whether in Favor of Despotism or Republicanism is the Question." [106]

Adams had little doubt that the British Empire was doomed if London continued to prosecute the war, a fact which, at least in the early years of the war, inclined him to think that a British Revolution would lead to tyranny in the home islands. "The few Men in the Nation who think seriously of this Business See clearly in the long Train of Consequences of American Independance, the Loss of their West India Islands, a great Part, of their East India Trade, the total Loss of Canada, Nova Scotia, the Floridas, all the American Fisheries, a Diminution of their Naval Power, as well as national Bankruptcy and a Revolution in their Government in Favour of Arbitrary Power," he wrote in 1778. [107]

Two years later, however, it seemed to Adams as if republicanism rather than despotism was the more likely course. Adams was intrigued by the development of county associations in England and the volunteer and non-importation movements in Ireland, which he likened to their earlier American counterparts. "You will see by the public Papers, that your Committee of Correspondence is making greater progress in the World, and doing greater things in the political World than the Electrical Rod ever did in the Physical," he wrote to Samuel Adams. "Ireland and England have adopted it, but mean Plagiaries as they are, they do not acknowledge who was the Inventor of it." In the short term such movements could aid the American cause. Adams noted

---

[104] Adams to Franklin, 13 June 1782, *PJA*, 13: 116-8.

[105] Adams to Edmund Jenings, 26 April 1780, *PJA*, 9: 235-7.

[106] Adams to James Warren, 4 August 1778, *PJA*, 6: 346-9.

[107] Adams to the President of Congress, 8 December 1778, *PJA*, 7: 268-9.

that, "the Speakers of these Meetings go great Lengths, some of them openly justifying and applauding the Americans, and others even applauding France and Spain for stepping in to our Assistance." [108]

Looking beyond the war itself, Adams believed that America had demonstrated to the Enlightened of Europe the existence of popular mechanisms to bring about regime change. "Its Invention will make an Epocha in the History of the Progress of Society, and of the human Understanding," Adams wrote to an English correspondent. [109] He told his old friend Elbridge Gerry:

> The Boston Committee of Correspondence, and the Military Associations which grew out of it, are likely to prove the greatest Engines for pulling down Tyranny, that were ever invented. The Electrical Rod, which deprives the Clouds of their Thunder, does it not so effectually, as these Committees wrest the Iron Rod out of the Hands of a Tyrant. Ireland has already obtained, purely by the Use of this Machine, great Advantages, and as She has not yet laid it down, She will obtain more, or give England further Trouble. [110]

Adams also hoped that America's regime-building activities would become a positive model to guide a similar process in England (and elsewhere) – to demonstrate that reflection and choice could build up as well as tear down institutions of government. He had in mind the recently-ratified Constitution of the Commonwealth of Massachusetts, of which he was the principal author. "The Massachusetts are exhibiting a Phenominon in the political World, that is new and Singular. It is the first People, who have taken So much Time to deliberate upon Government—that have allowed such Universal Liberty to all the People to reflect upon the subject, and propose their objections and Amendments—and that have reserved to themselves at large, the right of finally accepting or rejecting the form. It forms a Kind of Epocha, in the History of the Progress of Society." [111] He hoped that the report of the Massachusetts Constitution Convention (of which he too was principal author) would be circulated widely: "I wish this was printed in England. I think it would much assist their Committees and Associations. The Principles, of it, must be the Principles on which, those Committees

---

[108] Adams to Samuel Adams, 23 February 1780, *PJA*, 8: 353-4.

[109] Adams to Edmund Jenings, 27 February 1780, *PJA*, 8: 369-71.

[110] Adams to Elbridge Gerry, 23 February 1780, *PJA*, 8: 357.

[111] Adams to William Gordon, 26 May 1780, *PJA*, 9: 342-4.

must proceed or they will fail." [112] "No Government was ever made so perfectly upon the Principle of the Peoples Right and Equality," Adams argued. "It is Locke, Sydney and Rousseau and Mably reduced to Practice in the first Instance. I wish every step of their Progress printed and preserved. These Principles ought to be Spread in England at this time as much as possible." [113]

Adams clearly hoped that his correspondents and others would effectively propagandize the British in this manner; he did not, however, propose to interject the United States directly into the process of fomenting regime change or major political reform in Britain. (He did note that John Paul Jones' raids along the Irish coast had led to the formation of militia bodies for defense purposes, and that those bodies might later constitute a threat to British rule.) Adams was skeptical that reform in Britain that stopped short of revolution, including liberalization which might improve the lot of the British people, would actually benefit the United States. Adams feared that clever British leaders would channel the pressures away from political reform into economic reform, as a way to wage the war more effectively. "Will they be of any Use to Us, if the Persons who take the lead in these Correspondences Associations and Congress, should prevail and get into Power, will not their Aeconomical Projects rather injure than serve our Cause, by enabling them to command more Money, and make greater Exertions?" Adams wondered. [114] He doubted that political reform of the existing system was even possible at this late date –

> all Endeavours in parliament to reform, will be ineffectual. Reformation must be made in a Congress if any Way. Corruption has too many hereditary, and legal Supporters in Parliament. Whether it has or not out of parliament [sic] is the question. Whether there is enough of Unanimity and Firmness among the people, to struggle against this formidable phalanx? But one thing seems clear, that either the remaining Virtue in the Nation must overcome the Corruption, or the Corruption will wholly exterminate the remaining Virtue. I see but one Alternative and no middle Way. Either Absolute Monarchy, or a Republic and Congress. [115]

Adams was even skeptical that a British Revolution, ending in a British (or English) Republic and Congress, would necessarily solve the problems between the two nations. English culture, high and low, was too deeply

---

[112] Adams to Edmund Jenings, 7 June 1780, *PJA*, 9: 388-9.

[113] Adams to Edmund Jenings, 20 June 1780, *PJA*, 9: 446-7.

[114] Adams to Thomas Digges, 14 March 1780, *PJA*, 9: 45-6.

[115] Adams to Edmund Jenings, 29 April 1780, *PJA*, 9: 250-2.

ingrained with a spirit of jealousy against rising America. "The permanent and lasting Friendship of the Dutch, may be easily obtained by the United States; that of England never," Adams wrote to Franklin. "It is gone with the days before the Flood. If we ever enjoy the Smallest degree of Sincere Friendship again from England I am totally incapable of Seeing the Character of a Nation or the Connections of Things, which however may be the Case, for what I know." [116]

> There never was given by any Nation, more dreadful proofs of deadly Hate, than have been constantly given these five Years by the English to Americans. Lord Mansfield's Words have been adopted in all their Actions. Kill them, kill them, right or wrong, by fas and nefas, kill them or they will kill you. Do You know the deep political Motive for ringing the everlasting Knell of Rebel and Rebellion. Have you not considered that the Nation have habitually settled it in their minds and Hearts, that Rebels have no Rights, that every thing is lawful against them. They are Insects, they are Reptiles, they are Serpents, they are wild Boars and Tygers, they are Devils in the English Imagination. Have not Parliament, Gazettes, Pamphlets, Common Prayers, Sermons, and every thing for these six years, shot this Word down deep into the minds of the People of England and produced its Effect. The Government, the Church, the Nation itself means to establish an ineradicable Hatred and Animosity against us. [117]

As a result of this propagandizing, the common people in England (unlike those throughout the rest of Europe), as well as the hereditary orders, were hostile to America and to its cause. Adams believed that mobs would threaten any regime in Britain, monarchical or republican, that sought peace and reconciliation with the United States.

> The Nation will stand by the King and Ministry through every loss, while they persevere: whereas both would sink into total Contempt and Ridicule, if they were to make Peace. While they persevere, they are Masters of the Purses and the Commerce too of the whole Nation: make Peace, and they lose a great part of this Influence. National Pride when it has become an habitual Passion by long Indulgence, is the most obstinate thing in the World; and this War

---

[116] Adams to Franklin, 13 June 1782, *PJA*, 13: 116-8.

[117] Adams to Edmund Jenings, 11 June 1780, *PJA*, 9: 407-9.

has been made so completely though so artfully the national Act, as well as that of King and Ministers, that the Pride of the Nation was never committed more entirely to the support of any thing. It is not to be supposed that the present Ministry will Treat with America; and if there should be a Change, and the Leaders of Opposition should come in, They will not treat with America in any Character, that She can with Honor or Safety assume. [118]

Adams came to realize that neither political reform nor revolution was in the cards for Britain. The Gordon Riots in June 1781, the course of which Adams followed closely, were suppressed with massive military force. Parliamentary reform was essentially at an end. Some government prints, to taint all such activities as traitorous, alleged that the riots were the result of American or French agitators. [119] The fall of the North Ministry in March 1782 in the aftermath of the defeat at Yorktown did not instantly lead to peace either, because the new coalition government held out the seductive idea of an Anglo-American federal regime which would wage war against the old despotic enemies, France and Spain. Neither Adams nor Franklin would stand for this. The best that could be hoped for was a cold peace with England, based on mutual geopolitical and commercial interests. There could be neither political nor cultural reconciliation, much less a far-reaching alliance based on an understanding between two regimes, one republican, the other liberalizing.

The New International System

Rather than depending on regime change in Britain to win the war and to create a favorable post-war international environment, Adams looked increasingly to develop non-binding ties with other nations and peoples, besides France, which shared similar interests, irrespective of the form of their regime. He felt that he could exploit the popular sentiment in favor of America, which Franklin and others had commented upon. "Indeed Sir, you would be flattered with the Attention that is shown to our States, and with the high Eulogiums, that are every where bestowed, by learned and ingenious Men, upon our Constitutions, our Laws, our Wisdom, Valour and Universal Virtue," he wrote to Patrick Henry. "Partial as I am to my Country, and dearly as I love it, I cannot but say that I think they do Us, rather more honour than We

---

[118] Adams to the President of Congress, 15 October 1781, *PJA*, 11: 16-20.

[119] The Gordon Riots are described in PJA, 9: 398-9. See also Richard B. Morris, *The Peacemakers: The Great Powers and American Independence* (New York: Harper and Row, 1965), pp. 67–87.

deserve. But We are Combattants for Liberty, and it is a fashionable Saying in this Country, that every Man who combats for Liberty is adorable. There is more Liberality of Sentiment in every part of Europe, except England . . . than former Ages have known, and it will increase every day." [120] Adams believed it imperative to demonstrate that "in general Usages, and in the Liberality of Sentiments in those momentous Points, the Freedom of Inquiry, the Right of private Judgment and the Liberty of Conscience, of so much Importance to be supported in the World, and imparted to all Mankind . . . at this Hour are in more danger from Great Britain, and that intolerant Spirit which is secretly fermenting there, than from any other Quarter. . ." [121]

Adams, harkening back to the logic of the Model Treaty, believed that the specific "liberty" on which all regime types and peoples, except the British, could unite was the liberty of the seas. When it came to commercial transactions, any similarity of laws, language and religion were important but not decisive – the goodness and cheapness of goods was the overriding factor. "The two greatest Objects of the Negotiations and Wars of the present Age," Adams claimed, were "American Independance and the rights of neutral Vessells." [122] The League of Armed Neutrality, promoted by Catherine the Great as a means of resisting British wartime naval practices against neutral shipping, was for Adams "one of the most brilliant Events, which has yet been produced by the American Revolution." [123] Adams hoped to associate the United States with the principles of the League as a backdoor means of gaining diplomatic recognition during the Revolution – a plan which did not succeed – but he celebrated nevertheless the American-led shift toward a more liberal international system. The old balance of power system, promoted particularly by the British, had been aimed at preventing any nation from dominating the European continent. Adams argued, however, that "universal monarchy on land is chimera – impractical – but universal monarchy at sea" – that is, the British Empire – "is well nigh established." The new international system, one necessarily including the United States, should be built to a first order on resisting naval tyranny, whether that of Britain (currently) or prospectively by a nation like France: "America herself will never suffer any power of Europe again that decided superiority over all commercial nations, which we have vainly boasted of, and which the

---

[120] Adams to Patrick Henry, 9 July 1778, *D&A*, 4: 153-4.

[121] "A Memorial To their High Mightinesses, the States General of the United Provinces of the Low Countries," 19 April 1781, *PJA*, 11: 277.

[122] Adams to Jean de Neufville & Fils, 21 March 1781, *PJA*, 11: 222.

[123] Adams to the President of Congress, 1 February 1781, *RDC*, 4: 244-8.

past tameness of mankind has permitted. And America, little as she is thought of, will, for ever have it in her power, by joining with a majority of maritime powers, to preserve their Freedom." [124]

To promote these ideas, and to develop loans, commercial ties and non-binding relationships with states other than France, Congress, in Adams' opinion, should

> send Ministers to every great Court in Europe, especially the Maritime Courts, to propose an Acknowledgment of the Independence of America, and Treaties of Amity and of Commerce is no more than becomes Us, and in my Opinion is our Duty to do: it is perfectly consistent with the genuine System of American Policy, and a piece of Respect due from new Nations to old ones. . . . It is necessary for America to have Agents in different parts of Europe, to give some Information concerning our affairs, and to refute the abominable Lies that the hired Emissaries of Great Britain circulate in every Corner of Europe, by which they keep up their own Credit and ruin ours. [125]

The Dutch Option

The Republic of the Seven United Netherlands, popularly known as the Dutch Republic or the United Provinces, had long been of particular interest to Adams as a potential partner of the United States outside of the orbit of France. "The Similitude of Manners, of Religion and in Some Respects of Constitution; the Analogy, between the Means, by which the two Republicks arrived at Independancy, but above all the Attractions of commercial Interests, will infallibly draw them together," Adams pointed out to Congress in 1779, after he returned from his first assignment in Europe. He predicted, however, that "This Connection will not probably shew itself, in a public Manner before a Peace, or a near Prospect of Peace. Too many Motives of Fear or Interest place the Hollanders in a Dependance on England, to suffer her to connect herself openly, with Us, at present." [126] During his second mission to Europe, Adams' falling out with Vergennes – and the deteriorating economic position of the United States – led him to consider a more assertive approach toward the Dutch Republic.

---

[124] Adams, Letters from a Distinguished American, No. 3, ca. 14-22 July 1782, *PJA*, 9: 552.

[125] Adams to Franklin, 14 October 1780, *PJA*, 10: 267-8.

[126] Adams to President of Congress, 4 August 1779, *PJA*, 8: 112.

In July 1780, Adams finally obtained permission from Vergennes to travel northward and explore the possibility of obtaining loans from the Bankers of Amsterdam, even though he had no direct authority from the United States to execute such an assignment. He figured that a little informal spade-work could not hurt. "I cannot but lament however, that there is no Representation of Congress in this Republick, vested with Powers to borrow Money," he wrote to the President of Congress shortly after arriving in the Netherlands. "This would be a double Advantage. We should avail ourselves of a Loan, and at the same Time lessen the Loan of England. A Loan once begun here, would rapidly increase so as to deprive the English of this Resource. This is the Method, in which Commerce may be extended between the two Republicks, and the political Sentiments and System of Holland changed." [127]

Congress did appoint Henry Laurens of South Carolina as its envoy to the Netherlands but his ship had been seized by a British frigate and Laurens taken to the Tower of London. Congress then placed Dutch affairs temporarily in Adams' care and, in the winter of 1780-81, named him Commissioner of the United States to the United Provinces. Dutch officials, fearful of British reprisals, refused to meet with him. Anglo-Dutch relations had already deteriorated as Dutch shippers, claiming neutral rights (or simply acting as smugglers), traded with the French and the Americans. The States-General, the sovereign governing body, sought protection for its commerce under Catherine's proposed League of Armed Neutrality. The city of Amsterdam was particularly active in this campaign. In retaliation, the British declared war in December 1780. Britain cited as one pretext its discovery in Laurens' papers of a 1778 treaty of commerce secretly negotiated by the Amsterdam banker Jean de Neufville and William Lee, with the support of high-ranking Amsterdam officials. The treaty had no authority and no effect but it tainted the future prospects of a Dutch-American relationship. The collective Dutch heart was hardly in the war effort against its century-old ally, and the States-General had no intention of complicating matters by reprising the Neufville-Lee fiasco and engaging in talks with another American agent.

All this worked against Adams' plans. Adams initially hoped to obtain loans through private channels but, after one attempt failed miserably, he concluded that the political groundwork must be first laid. Bankers would not pay out money unless they had political cover. "The true Cause of the Obstruction of our Credit here is Fear, which can never be removed but by the States General acknowledging our Independence," Adams explained to Congress.

---

[127] Adams to the President of Congress, No. 3, 23 August 1780, *PJA*, 10: 85-7.

> This Country is indeed in a melancholy Situation – sunk in Ease – devoted to the Pursuits of Gain – overshadowed on all sides by more powerful Neighbours – unanimated by a Love of military Glory, or any aspiring Spirit; feeling little Enthusiasm for the Public; terrified at the loss of an old Friend, and equally terrified at the prospect of being obliged to form Connections with a new one: encumbered with a complicated and perplexed Constitution, divided among themselves in Interest and Sentiment, they seem afraid of every thing. Success on the Part of France, Spain and especially of America raises their Spirits, and advances the good Cause somewhat: but Reverses seem to sink them much more. The War has occasioned such a Stagnation of Business, and thrown such Numbers of People out of Employment, that I think it is impossible things should remain long in the present insipid State. One System or another will be pursued: one Party or another will prevail – much will depend on the Events of the War. [128]

Adams meant to wean the Dutch away from their long-standing pro-English sentiments and fears by reviving the independent "Batavian spirit" of liberty and commercial enterprise that had been in decline over the previous century. To do so, Adams naturally gravitated to those individuals – known as the Patriots, or Republicans – who wanted to change, in some fashion, the government of the United Provinces.

The Dutch Republic was a complicated political regime. It was a confederation of seven provinces, the wealthiest and most important of which was Holland. The provinces had their own governing bodies (estates) and retained considerable independence from the federal government. The provinces, in turn, were controlled by towns and cities that were governed by councils typically dominated by well-established families and/or by leading merchants. Certain cities had particular privileges and weight in their respective provinces. Amsterdam, the commercial and banking center of Holland, practically conducted its own foreign policy. The federal government consisted of the States-General, in which the provincial estates were represented. There was a semi-royal executive, traditionally the Prince of Orange, who was appointed as the "stadtholder" in each of the provinces and also served as captain-general of the Union. The House of Orange had very close ties with the English monarchy: William II, William III, and William IV had all married daughters of English kings. The present Stadtholder, William V (who had married a

---

[128] Adams to the President of Congress, 16 May 1781, *PJA*, 11: 317-20.

Prussian princess) was regarded by his Dutch Patriot critics as genial but indecisive, a puppet of the English who would resist vigorous prosecution of the current Anglo-Dutch war.[129]

The Patriot movement had many facets. There was a democratic, or popular, element, strongly influenced by the European Enlightenment and enthused by the American cause. Other Patriots partook of a traditional centuries-long resistance by the city and town oligarchs against the House of Orange and its dependency on British maritime and naval power. The practical political goal of the Patriots was to weaken or eliminate the office of the Stadtholder. They did not, in the end, agree on what sort of regime ought to emerge from this process but, for the time being, were able to cooperate against William V. The English and the Stadtholder's (Orange) party, by contrast, wanted to use the crisis to strengthen his position, and to undermine or eliminate traditional opponents among the entrenched elites, particularly the regents of cities like Amsterdam. As Adams judged the situation:

> The ancient and intimate Connection between the Houses of orange, and Brunswick, the Family Alliances, and the vast Advantages which the Princes of orange have derived from them in creating, establishing and at last perpetuating the Stadhouderat against the Inclination of the Republican Party, and the Relyance which this Family Still has upon the Same Connection to support it, have attached the Executive Power of this Government in such a manner to England, that nothing but Necessity could cause a seperation. On the Contrary, the Republican Party, which has heretofore been conducted, by Barnevelt, Grotius, De Wit and other immortal Patriots, have ever leaned towards an Alliance with France, because she has ever favoured the Republican Form of Government in this Nation. . . . All Parties too, See, that it would be dangerous to the Commerce and even Independance of the united Provinces, to have America again under the Dominion of England: and the Republicans See, or think they see that a change in this Government and the Loss of their Liberties would be the Consequence of it too.

"Those Persons who are both able and willing to lend Us Money, are the Patriots, who are willing to risk British and Stadthouderian Resentment for the Sake of extending the Commerce, Strengthening the political Interests, and preserving the Liberties of their Country," Adams concluded. "They

---

[129] For an overview of Dutch government and politics, see Palmer, *The Age of the Democratic Revolution*, pp. 323-40.

think that lending Us Money, without forming a political Connection with Us will not answer these Ends. That Cause, Stands very insecurely which Stands upon the shoulders of Patriotism in any Part of Europe. And in such Case if Patriotism is left in a state of doubt whether they ought to sustain it, the Cause must fall to the Ground." [130]

Adams recognized that those calling themselves Patriots or Republicans were not united among themselves on the proper constitutional reforms. For the most part they were not advocates of purely popular rule. Many of them wanted to preserve or enhance the position of the aristocracy, or the ancient liberties of the provinces and cities, against what they regarded as the aggrandizing tendencies of the Orange Party and William V. [131]

> The opposite, which is called the Republican Party, is suspected of Desires and Designs of introducing Innovations. Some are supposed to aim at the Demolition of the Stadtholdership—others of introducing the People to the Right of choosing the Regencies: but I think these are very few in Number, and very inconsiderable in Power, though some of them may have Wit and Genius. There is another Party, at the Head of which is Amsterdam, who thinks the Stadtholdership necessary, but wish to have some further Restraint or Check upon it. Hence the Proposition for a Committee to assist his Highness. But there is no appearance that the Project will succeed. All the Divisions of the Republican Party are thought to think well of America, and to wish a Connection with her and France. [132]

Adams believed that the Patriots of whatever stripe were the natural political allies of the United States – and, at least indirectly, the allies of

---

[130] Adams to the President of Congress, 25 September 1780, *PJA*, 10: 176-9.

[131] As Adams later recalled the Dutch political situation: "The sovereignty, by the constitution, is a pure aristocracy, residing in the regencies, which consist of about four thousand persons. The common sense, or rather the common feelings, of human nature, had instituted, or rather forced up by violence, an hereditary stadtholder, to protect the common people, or democracy, against the regencies, or aristocracy. But as the stadtholdership was always odious to the aristocracy, there had been frequent disputes between them, which must have terminated in the expulsion of the house of Orange, and the abolition of the stadtholdership, if it had not been for the interposition of the commons, the common people. These having no house of commons, no house of representatives to protect them, or even to petition, had no mode of interposing but by mobs and insurrections. This kind of democracy has always been dreadful, in all ages and countries. Accordingly Barneveldt had been sacrificed at one time, the De Witts at another, and in 1748, more sacrifices would have been made, if the aristocracy had not learned some wisdom by tragical experience, and given way in some degree to the popular enthusiasm." Adams to the President of Congress, 25 December 1780, *PJA*, 10: 438, footnote 3.

[132] Adams to Livingston, 19 February 1782, *PJA*, 12: 242.

enlightened republicanism – and that Americans and Dutch Patriots had a common defensive interest in preventing regime change that effectively made the Stadtholder a pro-English despot. The connection between the Patriots and the American cause was not self-evident, however. Adams needed to cultivate the Patriots if they were to act successfully as a pressure group that favored American independence and commerce. He discovered that the Patriots had little knowledge of the United States and generally considered it to be the project of rebels. "Even in the City of Amsterdam, which is the most Attentive to our Affairs, and the best inclined towards Us there are few, who do not consider the American Resistance, as a desultory Rage of a few Enthusiasts, without order, Discipline, Law or Government." [133]

Adams therefore set about to educate the Patriots about the American cause and to stress the natural ties between them. For instance, he took the opportunity to reply to inquiries about the American Revolution made by Hendrik Calkoen, an Amsterdam lawyer and Patriot. Adams' twenty-six letters, addressed to Calkoen but intended to be circulated informally to a much wider audience, compared the Revolution with the Dutch drive for liberty and against despotism in the 17th century. He sought to assure the Dutch that the Americans would not succumb to factionalism but were committed to the fight and were certain to prevail. [134]

As Adams set about this process of cultivating Dutch opinion and arguing behind the scenes for formal recognition of the United States, he ran afoul of French foreign policy interests. Despite the protests of the French Ambassador to The Hague, Duke De La Vauguyon, Adams finally decided to go public with his case in an effort to get around the opposition of the States-General, as then composed, and of the Stadtholder's party and its pro-English supporters. In his *Memorial To their High Mightinesses, the States General of the United Provinces of the Low Countries*, dated 19 April 1781, the anniversary of the battles of Lexington and Concord, Adams formally announced his presence as a diplomatic representative of the United States. He made the case for the stability of the American government, the surety of victory over the British, and the advantages which American commerce would provide to the Dutch Republic. He cited the close ties of culture and "a Similitude of Religion, although it is not deemed so essential in this as it has been in former Ages to the Alliance of Nations, is still, as it ever will be thought a desirable Circumstance." He explained in some detail the advantages of Dutch-American commerce. As

---

[133] Adams to the President of Congress, 25 September 1780, *PJA*, 10: 176.

[134] Replies to Hendrik Calkoen, 4-27 October 1780, *PJA*, 10: 200-52.

to the regime question, Adams argued that "a natural Alliance may be formed between the two Republicks, if ever one existed among Nations."

> A Similarity in the Forms of Government is usually considered as another Circumstance, which renders Alliances natural: and although the Constitutions of the two Republicks are not perfectly alike, there is yet Analogy enough between them to make a Connection easy in this respect. In general Usages, and in the Liberality of Sentiments in those momentous Points, the Freedom of Inquiry, the Right of private Judgment and the Liberty of Conscience, of so much Importance to be supported in the World, and imparted to all Mankind, and which at this Hour are in more danger from Great Britain, and that intolerant Spirit which is secretly fermenting there, than from any other Quarter, the two Nations resemble each other more than any others. The Originals of the two Republicks are so much alike, that the History of one seems but a Transcript from that of the other: so that every Dutchman, instructed in the Subject, must pronounce the American Revolution just and necessary, or pass a Censure upon the greatest Actions of his immortal Ancestors; Actions which have been approved and applauded by Mankind, and justified by the Decision of Heaven.

Adams concluded his *Memorial* with an appeal to the enlightened instincts of the Dutch people and their leaders by reporting that Congress was "impressed with an high Sense of the Wisdom and Magnanimity of your High Mightinesses, and of your inviolable Attachment to the Rights and Liberties of Mankind, and . . . desirous of cultivating the Friendship of a Nation, eminent for its Wisdom, Justice and Moderation . . ."[135]

Adams was well aware that the States-General, as then constituted, would not accept the *Memorial*, much less act favorably upon it. But he hoped that it would influence opinion over time in the various provincial governments, which could then instruct their representatives at The Hague to support recognition of American independence. (It was in this specific context that Adams made reference to "militia diplomacy.") Adams and his Dutch Patriot allies saw that the *Memorial* received wide circulation by printing it in English, French and Dutch versions, and by publishing it in various prominent European, British and American newspapers. Through Adams' *Memorial*,

---

[135] "A Memorial to Their High Mightinesses, the States General of the United Provinces of the Low Countries," 19 April 1781, *PJA*, 11: 272-81.

many sympathetic individuals throughout Europe received their first serious exposure to the ideas behind the American Revolution. [136]

Adams did not expect or obtain an immediate result from his *Memorial*: "The public Voice has not that Influence upon Government in any part of Europe, that it has in every part of America, and therefore I cannot expect that any immediate effect will be produced upon the States General," he explained to Congress. That change would require further developments in diplomacy. "They will probably wait, until they can sound the disposition of the Northern Powers, Russia particularly, and if they should not join in the War, their High Mightinesses will probably be willing to be admitted to accede to the Treaty of Alliance between France and America." [137] Adams did not believe that the United States should remain passive in this area of European politics. In another example of militia diplomacy, Adams dispatched Dana to Russia to seek diplomatic recognition from Catherine and the accession of the United States to the principles of the League of Armed Neutrality. Adams did not propose, however, to apply his highly public approach in the Netherlands to all circumstances. "The Nature of the Government in an absolute Monarchy" like Spain or Russia "would render it improper to make any application or Memorial public. The Nature of this Government rendered it indispensibly necessary." [138]

The Amsterdam regents escalated the Dutch political crisis in June 1781, when they pressed for constitutional reforms, including the creation of a federal privy council, and for the removal of the Duke of Brunswick, the Stadtholder's chief adviser. This challenge went to the heart of the Dutch political system. Adams believed that his *Memorial* had been the catalyst for this boldness: "Intelligence came to Amsterdam from all the Provinces and cities, that the memorial, so far from exciting resentment against Amsterdam or America, was generally approved, and the popular cry was 'Health to Myn Heer Adams, and success to the brave Americans.' A discovery that greatly raised the spirits of the people of Amsterdam, and consequently emboldened the regency." [139]

Adams also kept up the pressure on the Dutch in the form of a second Memorial to the States-General, dated 9 January 1782, which categorically demanded a formal reply to his earlier missive for diplomatic recognition.

---

[136] See the Introduction to JQA, 11: xv-xvi ; Adams to the Secretary for Foreign Affairs, 21 February 1782, *RDC*, 5: 192-9.

[137] Adams to the President of Congress, 16 May 1781, *PJA*, 11: 316-7.

[138] Adams to Livingston, 19 February 1782, *PJA*, 12: 245.

[139] Adams to the President of Congress, 26 June 1781, *PJA*, 11: 395, with references to Adams' subsequent correspondence in the Boston *Patriot*.

Adams' implicit threat was that the Dutch would lose out on American trade if they did not act soon. Vauguyon, presumably acting under Vergennes' orders, strongly recommended a less confrontational approach. Adams, according to his later account, was initially agreeable to the French plan, but

> I thought [it] however rather too tame and timid. I was therefore determined to consult my own privy council of Dutch patriots, who had never deceived me; who had never concealed from me any danger or difficulty, but who had always communicated to me every information, without exaggeration, which could afford me encouragement or hope. These were unanimously in favor of my memorial and against the Comte De Vergennes's project. I asked them whether I ought not to strike out the epithet 'categorical.' Oh! no. By no means; that is the best word in the whole memorial. Our nation likes such hints: They think them manly. That word will excite more attention than all the rest, and you are sure now of the current in your favor. But if it should do no good, it will certainly do you no harm. We think you have hit the taste of our people. – I took this advice and proceeded . . . [140]

The *Memorial* and its follow-on (at least as Adams saw things) reverberated throughout Dutch politics and served to energize the Patriots as well as the cause of American independence and commerce. "If it had not been presented and printed, I am very sure I could not long have resided in the Republick, and what would have been the Consequence to the Friends of Liberty here I know not," Adams later reflected. "They were so disheartened and intimidated, and the Anglomanes were so insolent, that no Man can say, that a sudden Phrenzy might not have been excited among the Soldiery and the People to demand a Junction with England, as there was in the Year 1748. Such a Revolution would have injured America and her Allies, have prolonged the War and have been the total Loss and Ruin of the [Dutch] Republick." [141]

Several months after Adams published the *Memorial*, a Dutch Patriot, Joan Derk van der Capellen tot den Pol, sent Adams a pamphlet that he had just published, *Aan het Volk van Nederland*. As the editors of the Adams Papers have noted:

> The anonymously printed pamphlet was unique in Dutch political literature to that time because it appealed to the people of the

---

[140] Duc de La Vauguyon to Adams, 30 December 1781, *PJA*, 12: 168. Adams published this letter, translated into English, in the Boston *Patriot* of 19 September 1810.

[141] Adams to Livingston, 21 February 1782, *PJA*, 12: 253.

Netherlands rather than to a province, city, or class. The pamphlet, which was clandestinely distributed across the Netherlands on the morning of 26 Sept. through the efforts of François Adriaan Van der Kemp, was an impassioned attack on the Orangist party and called for the Dutch people to rise in rebellion. It was immediately banned, copies were burned, and a reward offered for information regarding the identities of the pamphlet's author and those involved in its printing and distribution. Nevertheless, it was soon translated into English, French, and German.[142]

Van der Capellen and Van der Kemp were more radical members of the circle of Dutch Patriots into whom John Adams had been drawn. "It is a shame that your Excellency does not understand Dutch," van der Capellen wrote to Adams, linking his own argument with the political controversies surrounding the American envoy. "It is a thunderclap, and I would not want to guarantee the author's head if he is found out. . . . No one has ever written in this manner." In the pamphlet, van der Capellen argued that the States-General's refusal to recognize Adams as a representative from the United States was made in the same spirit as that body's refusal to recognize Walter Strickland as ambassador from the English Commonwealth in 1650. In both cases the Orange Party rejected the natural alliance of fellow republicans.[143]

When the Dutch authorities attempted to suppress van der Capellen's pamphlet, Adams predicted: "They will have, however, a contrary effect, and will make a pamphlet which otherwise perhaps would have been known in a small circle familiar to all Europe. The press can not be restrained; all attempts of that kind in France and Holland are every day found to be ineffectual." Adams believed that the flap over van der Capellen's pamphlet and the recent disturbances in Geneva against the ruling oligarchy were an indication that the tide of public opinion throughout the continent was becoming sympathetic to "democratical principles."

> When I say democratical principles, I do not mean that the world is about adopting simple democracies, for these are impracticable; but multitudes are convinced that the people should have a voice, a share, and be made an integral part; and that the government should be such a mixture, and such a combination of the powers of one,

---

[142] Joan Derk van der Capellen tot den Pol to Adams, 6 October 1781, *PJA*, 12: 7.

[143] Joan Derk van der Capellen tot den Pol to Adams, 6 October 1781, *PJA*, 12: 5-7. See also Simon Schama, *Patriots and Liberators: Revolution in the Netherlands, 1780-1813* (New York: Knopf, 1977), pp. 64-7; I. Leonard Leeb, *The Ideological Origins of the Batavian Revolution: History and Politics in the Dutch Republic 1747-1800* (The Hague: Nijhoff, 1973), pp. 136-7, 155-60.

the few, and the many, as is best calculated to check and control each other, and oblige all to co-operate in this one democratical principle, that the end of all government is the happiness of the people; and in this other, that the greatest happiness of the greatest number is the point to be obtained. These principles are now so widely spread that despotisms, monarchies, and aristocracies must conform to them in some degree in practice, or hazard a total revolution in religion and government throughout all Europe. [144]

"Who and what has given rise to the assuming pride of the people, as it is called in Europe?" Adams' answer: "The American Revolution. The precepts, the reasonings, and example of the United States of America, disseminated by the press through every part of the world, have convinced the understanding and have touched the heart." As to the matter of international relations, too, "the American Revolution is working its necessary Effects in Europe," Adams reflected with satisfaction. "It has operated So among the nations, it has set so many Wheels in Motion, that it has now forced the Dutch into a War. . . . it was necessary that the Affections should be alienated between the English and Dutch, in order to bring about the more certainly and compleatly, a great Change in the Affairs of Mankind." [145]

Adams believed that active American diplomacy – primarily his own – had been necessary to bring about these changes in the affairs of mankind. Further: "The longer the American war lasts, the more the spirit of American government will spread in Europe, because the attention of the world will be fixed there while the war lasts. I have often wondered that the sovereigns of Europe have not seen the danger to their authority which arises from a continuance of this war. It is their interest to get it finished, that their subjects may no longer be employed in speculating about the principles of government." [146]

Adams' intervention in Dutch politics, although not directly aimed at regime change, pointed to a specific method by which American diplomacy could help crystallize foreign public opinion in a liberal direction. "The Constitution of this Country [the Netherlands] is such, that it is difficult to discover the general Sense," Adams explained to Congress. "There have been all along Circumstances in which it might be discerned; but these were so feeble, and so susceptible of Contradiction and Disguise, that some

---

[144] Adams to President of Congress, 25 October 1781, *PJA*, 12: 48. On the circumstances of Geneva, see Palmer, *The Age of the Democratic Revolution*, pp. 127-9, 358-60.

[145] Adams to Edmund Jenings, 3 January 1781, *PJA*, 11: 10-2.

[146] Adams to President of Congress, 25 October 1781, *PJA*, 12: 48.

extraordinary Exertions were necessary to strike out unquestionable proofs of the Temper and Opinion of the Nation."

In these critical Circumstances, something uncommon was necessary to arouse the Nation, and bring forth the public Voice. The first Step of this kind was the Proposition of the United States of America to their high Mightinesses, which being taken ad referendum became a subject of deliberation in every City of the Republick, and the publication of the Memorial of the nineteenth of April 1781, which made the American Cause the primary Object and main spring of the War, the Topick of Conversation in every private Circle, as well as in every public Assembly. This Memorial gave all Parties an Opportunity to know with Certainty the public opinion: and accordingly such a general and decided approbation was discovered every where, that the few who detested it in their hearts never dared to open their Mouths.

"When the public Councils of a Country have taken a wrong bias, the public Voice, pronounced with Energy, will sometimes correct the Error, without any violent Remedies," Adams concluded. "Thus altho' the Enemies of England in this Republick do not appear to have carried any particular point against the opposite Party, yet it appears that they have forced into Execution their System, by means of the national Voice, and against all the Measures of the Anglomanes. The national Spirit is now very high: so high that it will be dangerous to resist it. In time all things must give way to it." [147]

"If I ever did any good since I was born," Adams told Franklin, "it was in stirring up the pure Minds of the Dutchmen, and setting the old Batavian Spirit in motion, after having slept so long." [148]

Having contributed to putting this process of reviving the Dutch spirit into motion, Adams was anxious that it not get out of control, however. America must be seen as the spirit of enlightened reform, not rebellion, especially at this crucial moment in the war and the negotiations for peace. Although he remained friendly with van der Capellen, he did not embrace his call for a popular revolution. Adams told a friend that "he might with the greatest ease in the World have thrown the whole [Dutch] States into commotion so great was their desire for the American Independence and their dislike to the Stateholder and Duke of Brunswick." [149]

---

[147] Adams to the President of Congress, 22 August 1781, *PJA*, 11: 461-4.

[148] Adams to Benjamin Franklin, 25 August 1781, *PJA*, 11: 469.

[149] *Matthew Ridley Journal*, 20 May 1781, *PJA*, 13: 67.

Adams, in fact, did not believe that most of Europe was then (if ever) ready for wholly popular governments. He thought that a good monarch, properly balanced by the other elements of society, would probably be necessary for peoples who were not far removed from feudalism and religious despotism. When Lafayette, after returning to France from America, assured Adams that "the Court Air Has not So Much Altered My Republican Principles as to Make me Believe the Opinion of a King is Every thing," [150] Adams replied with a warning:

> Have a Care, however, how you profess Friendship for me: there may be more danger in it, than you are aware of. I have the Honour, and the Consolation to be a Republican on Principle. That is to Say, I esteem that Form of Government, the best, of which human Nature is capable. Almost every Thing that is estimable in civil Life, has originated under Such Governments. Two Republican Towns, Athens and Rome, have done more honour to our Species, than all the rest of it. A new Country, can be planted only by Such a Government. America would at this moment have been an howling Wilderness in habited only by Bears and Savages, without Such forms of Government. And it would again become a Wilderness under any other. I am not however an enthusiast, who wishes to overturn Empires and Monarchies, for the Sake of introducing Republican Forms of Government. And therefore I am no King Killer, King Hater or King Despizer. There are Three Monarcks in Europe for whom I have as much Veneration as it is lawfull for one Man to have for another. The King of France, the Emperor of Germany and the King of Prussia, are constant objects of my Admiration, for Reasons of Humanity Wisdom and Beneficence which need not be enlarged on. [151]

With respect to the existing quasi-republican polity of the Netherlands, Adams believed that although sensible political reform could not be achieved without being driven by "the assuming pride of the people . . . the people of the seven United Provinces appear to me of such a character that they would make wild steerage at the first admission to any share in government; and whether any intimation of a desire of change at this time will not divide and weaken the nation is a problem. I believe rather it will have a good effect, by convincing

---

[150] Lafayette to Adams, 7 May 1782, *PJA*, 13: 12-3.

[151] Adams to Lafayette, 21 May 1782, *PJA*, 13: 65-6.

the government that they must exert themselves for the good of the people to prevent them from exerting themselves in innovations." [152]

Adams also feared that excessive enthusiasm for popular rule in the Netherlands (and throughout Europe generally) would create a backlash among moderate elements concerned about their property and safety, and thereby provide an opening for entrenched conservative and foreign influences to reassert their influence by fomenting class warfare. He believed that this very nearly happened in the Netherlands when Sir Joseph Yorke, the British Ambassador, with the support of the Stadtholder's party, had threatened retaliation against those Patriots who supported the American cause by stirring up violence among those "lower class" elements of the population that had traditionally been pro-Orange and that were suspicious of the aristocracy and the merchant classes. Adams reflected:

> This Plan was so daringly supported by Writers of the first Fame on the side of the Court, that Multitudes of Writings appeared attempting to shew that what Temmink and Van Berkel [men sympathetic to the Patriots] had done was high Treason. All this had such an Effect, that all the best Men seemed to shudder with Fear. ... You can have no Idea, Sir. No Man who was not upon the Spot, can have any Idea of the Gloom and Terror that was spread by this Event [the British capture of the Dutch West Indies island of St. Eustasia]. The Creatures of the Court openly rejoiced in this, and threatened some of them in the most impudent Terms. I had certain Information that some of them talked high of their Expectations of popular Insurrections against the Burgomasters of Amsterdam and Mr. Van Berkel, and did Mr. Adams the honor to mention him as one, that was to be hanged by the Mob in such Company. [153]

Adams believed that the ultimate aim of mob action provoked by the Orangists, and the Orangist opposition to the war with England and to recognition of America, was the destruction of the Patriot cause and that of popular reform. "There are strong suspicions, that this whole Contest and War is excited, purposely to alter the Constitution of this Country," in favor of the Stadtholder, Adams observed. [154] This recalled the events of 1748, when "the Populace arose in Amsterdam to demand, that the City should be for joining England and making an hereditary Stadholder." Adams, citing his Patriot sources,

---

[152] Adams to President of Congress, 25 October 1781, *PJA*, 12: 48.

[153] Adams to Livingston, 21 February 1782, *PJA*, 12. 253-6.

[154] Adams to Edmund Jenings, 3 January 1781, *PJA*, 11: 10-2.

suspected that "the Plan was concerted between the two Courts of London and the Hague." Once again he claimed that his own actions, particularly the *Memorial*, had been important for the cause of the Patriots as well as the United States: "A Gentleman, of excellent Character, and profound Discretion as well as Learning told me, within this Week, 'We were Saved by Miracle. If Sir Joseph had advised his Master to have declared War against Amsterdam alone, We should have been undone, past all Remedy. Your Memorial, contributed somewhat to our Salvation. It was a good Antedote to Yorks Poison.'" [155]

In April 1782, Adams claimed victory. Some of the Dutch provinces, and finally the States-General, accorded diplomatic recognition to the United States. Adams soon finalized a loan with a consortium of Amsterdam Bankers. In October 1782, he completed a Treaty of Amity and Commerce with the Netherlands, which Congress ratified the following year. According to Adams, America achieved these successes without resorting to the bullying tactics of England or the backstairs machinations of France – "availing itself only of the still small Voice of Reason, urging general Motives and national Interests, without Money, without Intrigue, without imposing Pomp, or more imposing Fame, it has prevailed against the utmost Efforts of Intrigue and Corruption, against the almost universal Inclination of Persons in Government, against a formidable Band of Capitalists, and the most powerful mercantile Houses in the Republick, interested in English Funds and too deeply leagued in English Affairs." [156] Adams asked of Samuel Adams:

> What Say you, to the alliance of the first Commercial Power in Europe, next to England a Republican and a Protestant Power? Is it an Event of any Importance or no? There are who dispute it. The two Houses of orange and Brunswick have heretofore acted Sublime Parts in favour of the Cause of Liberty. They have lately acted too much in Concert against it. That of orange must now return to its old System and Principles. I confess I felt a great Pleasure to be introduced to that Court, where William the first and William the third, accomplished Such great Things, in favour of the Protestant Religion and the Rights of Mankind, and to their hereditary successors. [157]

Adams' critics would point out that Dutch recognition of the United States came about only after the combined American-French force at Yorktown

---

[155] Adams to James Lovell, 25 February 1782, *PJA*, 12: 269.

[156] Adams to Livingston, 16 May 1782, *PJA*, 13: 48-9.

[157] Adams to Samuel Adams, 15 June 1782, *PJA*, 13: 125.

had forced Cornwallis' surrender. They argued that facts on the ground, not profound political arguments, had brought about the change of Dutch policy (just as the American victory in the Battle of Saratoga had influenced the French decision to recognize the United States and join the war). The regime question in the Netherlands, according to Adams' critics, was peripheral to the overriding geopolitical realities.

Livingston Takes Exception

Adams' aggressive diplomatic approach in the Dutch Republic was opposed by Franklin, as noted above, and it earned him several rebukes from Livingston after he assumed the position as Congress' Secretary of Foreign Affairs in late 1781. "We find from your letters as well as from other accounts of the United Provinces that they are divided into powerful parties, for and against the War, and we are sorry to see some of the most distinguished names among what are called the *Anglomanes*," Livingston wrote. He complained that Adams had not provided Congress with a detailed analysis of the "views and principles of each party." But that aside: "It is so important to the due execution of your mission, to penetrate the views of all parties, *without seeming to be connected with either*, that I have no doubt you have insinuated yourself into the good graces and confidence of the leaders, and that you can furnish the information we require[.] [Y]ou may be persuaded, no ill use will be made of any you give, and it is expected from You." [158]

> Your first Object then, if I may Venture my Opinion, is to be well with the Government, your Second, to appear to be so, and to take no measures which may bring upon you a publick Affront; You will naturally treat the friends we have, with the politeness and attention that they justly merit, and even with that Cordiality, which your heart must feel for those who wish your Country well, but your prudence will suggest to you to avoid giving Offence to Government, by the appearance of intrigue.

In Livingston's opinion, Adams had lost sight of his mission and failed singularly in these basic tasks. By becoming embroiled in Dutch politics and by stirring up popular unrest, Adams had actually strengthened the pro-English faction and its effort to bring about an early and separate peace between Britain and the Netherlands – a peace that would be detrimental both to the Dutch and the American causes.

---

[158] Livingston to Adams, 20 November 1781, *PJA*, 12: 74-6. Emphasis added.

> ... the State you are in, divided by powerful Parties, and the bias that Every Man has to his own Country, naturally gives him a predilection for that which most favors its Interests. But this, tho' the Child of Virtue, is often the greatest Obstacle to successful Negociations, it creates distrust and Jealousies, it Excites prejudices, which unfits us for conciliating the affections of those whose Assistance we require, and induces too fond a reliance upon the information of those who wish to serve us. Aristocratic Govermts. are of all others the most Jealous of popular Commotions, the rich and the powerful are Equally engaged to resist them, and nothing will, in my Opinion, So soon contribute to a peace between Great Britain and the United provinces, as the commotions which now clog the Government of the latter.[159]

Livingston clearly did not think that Adams had avoided the appearance, much less the reality, of political intrigue. As to Adams' decision "to declare your public character, before the States were disposed to acknowledge it," Livingston complained about "the humiliating light in which it places us."

> I may form improper ideas of the government, interests and policy of the United Provinces, but I frankly confess that I have no hope that they will recognize us as an independent state and embarrass themselves in making their wished for peace with our affairs. What inducements can we hold out to them? They know that our own interest will lead us to trade with them, and we do not propose to purchase their alliance by giving them any exclusive advantage in commerce. Your business, then, I should think lies in a narrow compass. It is to "conciliate the affections of the people, to place our cause in the most advantageous light, to remove the prejudices that Great Britain may endeavour to excite, to discover the views of the different Parties, to watch every motion that leads to peace between England and the United provinces, and to get the secret aid of government in procuring a loan, which is almost the only thing wanting to render our affairs respectable at home and abroad."

"As our objects in Holland must be very similar to those of France," Livingston concluded pointedly, "I should suppose it would be prudent for

---

[159] Livingston to Adams, 23 October 1781, *PJA*, 12: 40-4.

you to keep up the closest Connexion with her minister to advise with him on great leading objects, and to counteract his opinion only upon the most mature deliberation." [160]

Adams was stung by Livingston's accusation that he had meddled in Dutch politics. He insisted that he had not favored any particular Patriot faction or supported any particular form of regime change. He had merely aided, indirectly, the arguments of those who had prevented a pro-English revolution in Dutch politics and foreign policy. Adams thought that he had redefined the grounds of those politics in a way that ultimately would stand the United States in good stead with all native parties in the Netherlands. Adams, for instance, believed that the various political factions in the Netherlands (except for a few highly influential individuals who represented an extreme pro-English viewpoint) all agreed upon the need for peace with Britain. Adams believed he could persuade Dutch opinion across the political spectrum that such a peace could not be achieved without American independence. "It is the United States of America, which must save this Republick from Ruin. It is the only Power that is externally respected by all Parties, altho' no Party dares as yet declare openly for her. One half the Republick nearly declares every day very indecently against France— the other against England: but neither one nor the other declares against America, which is more beloved and esteemed than any other Nation of the World." Adams insisted that he had not taken sides among domestic factions: "I have endeavoured to have the good Graces of the Leaders, and I have no Reason to suspect that I do not enjoy their Esteem, and I have received from the Prince [the Stadtholder] repeatedly and in strong Terms by his Secretary the Baron de Lerray Assurances of his personal Esteem." [161]

> In the parties which divide the Nation I have never taken any Share. I have treated all Men of all Parties whom I saw alike, and have been used quite as well by the Court Party as their Antagonists. Both Parties have been in bodily Fear of popular Commotions, and the Politicks of both appear to me to be too much influenced by the alternate Fears and I must add Hopes of Popular Commotions. . . . Your Advice to be well with the Government and to take no Measures which may bring upon me a public affront, is perfectly just. All appearance of Intrigue, and all the Refinements of

---

[160] Livingston to Adams, 20 November 1781, *PJA*, 12: 74-6. The editors of the *Papers of John Adams* note that the source of Livingston's quotation is not known.

[161] Adams to Livingston, 19 February 1782, *PJA*, 12: 240-5.

Politicks have been as distant from my Conduct, as You know them to be from my natural and habitual Character. [162]

As Adams put it to one of his Congressional allies:

> My Memorial, contrived as it was, and coming out as it did, compelled all Parties to Speak in its Praise. The Courtiers themselves were obliged to say, it is cunningly drawn up, it is sensible it is eloquent, it is fine, it is elaborate &c &c. The opposite Party cryed it is admirable, it is excellent, it is noble, it is the best Thing that ever was writ. I am well informed that the common People, read it, with the Utmost Greediness and often with Tears in their Eyes. I dont believe that any Letters which have gone from hence, have Spoke much in its Praise. The reason is the Friends of Liberty dare not. Letters from the opposite Party may have condemned it in America, although they dared not to disapprove it here... [163]

Adams contended that his "militia diplomacy" in general and the *Memorial* in particular were justified not only in terms of their positive effect on Dutch foreign policy and on the future of the Dutch regime, but also on the views of enlightened statesmen throughout Europe. He told his Congressional ally James Lovell that he had worded parts of *Memorial* carefully, to persuade the Hapsburg Emperor, Joseph II, that Austria was taking a considerable risk if it ignored the future value of American commerce. "When I wrote in that Memorial, those Words, 'a System, (that of making equitable Treaties with all the Commercial Powers, without being goverd or monopolized by any) from which the Congress never will depart unless compelled by Some Powers declaring against them, which is not expected,' had the Emperor and him alone in View." Adams told Lovell that he could easily imagine the Emperor's response:

> When he [Joseph II] saw that Memorial, was it not natural for him to Say, "the manner in which my Mother [Maria Theresa] recd the American Minister Mr Lee, and the continual Puffs of the English, have made the Americans Suspect me. Whom else, except Portugal can they Suspect? All the other Powers have declard themselves in their favour or neutral. I'le remove this Jealousy. Il even See this memorialist. I'l join the armed Neutrality. Il visit my maritime Towns make Regulations to favour their Commerce, with America.

---

[162] Adams to Livingston, 14 February 1782, *PJA*, 12: 233-4.

[163] Adams to James Lovell, 25 February 1782, *PJA*, 12: 269.

Nay more, I will do America a greater Honour, than even France has done. I'l adopt their Sublime Systems of Reason, Philosophy and Civility, in adopting their Code of religious Liberty, by which I shall favour my Commerce with them as much, as I shall do them honour. I will do this memorialist the Honour to show him and all the World that I am of his opinion that it is of vast Importance that the Freedom of Inquiry, the Right of private Judgment and the Liberty of Conscience should be imparted to all Mankind." [164]

Adams was convinced that Joseph II's recent grants of religious toleration to Protestants throughout the empire, including the "Edict of Toleration" issued by the governors general of the Austrian Netherlands (Belgium), was the direct result of the American Revolution's effect on the calculations of foreign rulers. [165] But the logic of the American Revolution was not completely self-evident; it required demonstration through activist American diplomacy. Adams catalogued these positive and widespread effects for the benefit of Secretary Livingston:

The Memorial, as a Composition, has very little Merit, yet almost every Gazette in Europe has inserted it, and most of them with a Compliment, none with any Criticism. When I was in Paris and Versailles afterwards, no Man ever expressed to me the smallest disapprobation of it, or the least apprehension that it could do any harm. On the contrary, several Gentlemen of Letters expressed higher Compliments upon it than it deserved. The King of Sweden has done it a most illustrious honor, by quoting one of the most material Sentiments in it, in a public Answer to the King of Great Britain; and the Emperor of Germany has since done the Author of it the honor to desire in the Character of Count Falkenstein to see him, and what is more remarkable has adopted the sentiment of it concerning religious Liberty into a Code of Laws for his Dominions, the greatest Effort in favor of Humanity, next to the American Revolution, which has been produced in the eighteenth Century.

"By comparing Facts and Events and Dates, it is impossible not to believe, that the Memorial had some Influence in producing some of them," Adams insisted. "When Courts and Princes and Nations have been long contemplat-

---

[164] Adams to James Lovell, 25 February 1782, *PJA*, 12: 268-9.

[165] Walter W. Davis, *Joseph II: An Imperial Reformer for the Austrian Netherlands* (The Hague: Nijhoff, 1974), pp. 189–219.

ing a great system of affairs, and their Judgments begin to ripen, and they begin to see how things ought to go and are agoing, a small Publication, holding up these objects in a clear point of View, sometimes sets a vast Machine in motion at once like the springing of a mine. What a Dust We raise, said the Fly upon the Chariot Wheel?" [166]

Adams was convinced that Livingston's criticism of his behavior in the Netherlands was prompted by the French legation in America, which was acting under the instructions of Vergennes (and the views of Franklin). Adams never moved off his ground. Nearly three decades later, to defend his actions as a Revolutionary War diplomat, Adams published his response to Livingston along with documents relating to his controversial diplomatic mission. "There is not an effect of that memorial, suggested in this letter as possibly or probably flowing from it, that I do not now in 1810, after near thirty years of examination and reflection, believe to have been produced by it." [167]

Conclusion

The notion that John Adams' *Memorial* to the States-General of the Netherlands had not only advanced the cause of liberty in the Dutch Republic but also persuaded political leaders throughout Europe to adopt enlightened policies surely struck Benjamin Franklin as fantastic. "He means well for his country, is always an honest man, often a wise one, but sometimes and in some things, absolutely out of his senses," was Franklin's famous and enduring judgment of his Revolutionary War colleague. [168]

Franklin, however, was hardly indifferent to the global fate of liberty and enlightenment or the role that America, and Americans, could play in fostering political reform. While in France he became a member and later grand master of the Masonic Lodge of the Grand Sisters; many future leaders of the French Revolution were members of the same lodge. For these Masons, according to Franklin's biographer Carl Van Doren, "the American constitutions were looked upon as a grammar of liberty. This was a lodge of constitutionalists, hoping that France might put constitutional limits to its monarchy." Whatever Franklin said or did with this group remained behind closed doors. When the news of the French Revolution reached America in the winter of 1789-90 just before his death, Franklin reflected:

---

[166] Adams to Livingston, 21 February 1782, *PJA*, 12: 253-6.

[167] Adams to Livingston, 21 February 1782, *PJA*, 12: 256.

[168] Carl Van Doren, *Benjamin Franklin* (New York: Viking Press, 1938), p. 694.

> The convulsions in France are attended with some disagreeable circumstances; but if by the struggle she obtains and secures for the nation its future liberty, and a good constitution, a few years enjoyment of those blessings will amply repair all the damages their acquisition may have occasioned. God grant that not only the love of liberty, but a thorough knowledge of the rights of man, may pervade all the nations of the earth, so that a philosopher may set his foot anywhere on its surface, and say, 'this is my country!' [169]

Historian Robert R. Palmer, whose study of the "age of democratic revolution" remains the most thorough analysis of the topic, offered this conclusion:

> The effects of the American Revolution, as a Revolution, were imponderable but very great. It inspired the sense of a new era. It added a new content to the conception of progress. It gave a whole new dimension to ideas of liberty and equality made familiar by the Enlightenment. It got people in the habit of thinking more concretely about political questions. It made them more readily critical of their own governments and society. It dethroned England, and set up America, as a model for those seeking a better world. It brought written constitutions, declarations of rights, and constituent assemblies into the realm of the possible. The apparition on the other side of the Atlantic of certain ideas already familiar in Europe made such ideas seem more truly universal, and confirmed the habit of thinking in terms of humanity at large. . . . America made Europe seem unsatisfactory to many people of the middle and lower classes, and to those of the upper classes who wished them well. It made a good many Europeans feel sorry for themselves, and induced a kind of spiritual fight from the Old Regime. [170]

This chapter focused on the "indirect approach" that typically marked the Founders' line to foreign regime change. First, the American Revolution and an independent United States would demonstrate the viability of republican government and a commercially-oriented foreign policy. The result, second, would be a new configuration of power in the Euro-Atlantic state system, and more liberal rules of international behavior, which would be conducive not only to American security but also to the cause of political reform and

---

[169] Ibid., pp. 656-7, 773 (quote).

[170] Palmer, *The Age of the Democratic Revolution*, p. 282.

popular sovereignty, rightly understood. Third, American statesmen would take the national interests of various states into account while encouraging this transformation, while appealing in parallel to enlightened public opinion throughout Europe. They believed that this opinion, over time, would be in an ever stronger position to guide those national interests in a moderate direction and to undertake liberal domestic political reform, while necessarily taking into account the particular circumstances of each foreign regime.

The path to liberty and enlightenment proved to be neither straight nor sure. "The Nations of Europe, appeared to me, when I was among them, from the beginning of 1778, to 1785 i.e. to the commencement of the troubles in France, to be advancing by slow and sure Steps towards an Amelioration of the condition of Man, in Religion and Government, in Liberty, Equality, Fraternity Knowledge Civilization and Humanity," Adams reflected decades later to Thomas Jefferson. [171] But events outran the ability and power of the United States to influence the evolution of a liberal international order that would be conducive to gradual reform and (relatively) peaceful regime change. American statesmen like Adams and Jefferson (just like Adams and Franklin) could not agree upon the proper policies to conduct the indirect approach, especially after the outbreak of the French Revolution in 1789. American commerce did not change the nature of international relations but rather sucked the United States into the maelstrom of European conflicts. However, the idea of an indirect approach to foreign regime change was not forgotten, only deferred.

---

[171] Adams to Jefferson, 15 July 1813, Lester J. Cappon, ed., *The Adams-Jefferson Letters* (Chapel Hill: University of North Carolina Press, 1959), p. 357.

CHAPTER TWO

Jefferson, the Barbary Regencies and Regime Change:
The Attractions and Limits of Limited Liability

For the first few decades of its existence as an independent nation, the United States faced a threat to its commercial interests in the Mediterranean and eastern Atlantic from the Barbary "pirates" – popularly known as corsairs – who sailed under the auspices of four Islamic polities on the North African coast (Tripoli, Tunis, Algiers and Morocco). For centuries the corsairs had seized merchant vessels whose nation of origin had not purchased protection from the Barbary rulers. They enslaved their crews until ransomed. From 1801-1805 the United States waged a political-military campaign to compel Tripoli to cease its depredations against American ships while simultaneously dissuading the other polities from joining the conflict. [1]

This chapter will examine American policy toward the Barbary states at the turn of the 19th century. To a first order, Americans debated whether their national interest in the Mediterranean was best achieved either through a policy of accommodation of the Barbary rulers – based on an economic cost-benefit calculation and a sense of relative strategic priorities – or through a more assertive policy designed to change the behavior of those rulers by the application of an appropriate mix of threats and incentives. To the extent that the United States sought an enduring and fundamental change in the use of corsairs, it also threatened (or promised, depending on one's point of view) to alter the entire way of life on the Barbary coast. At the extreme, the United States had the option of attempting to enforce a change of behavior by overthrowing the existing rulers and replacing them with friendly or compliant individuals or regimes.

Thomas Jefferson became the central figure in this debate. As a diplomat, he favored strongly the change-of-behavior alternative through a form of international containment of the corsair threat that would lead to a more pacific existence for the Barbary peoples. As president, he came to embrace a policy toward Barbary (Tripoli in particular) in which, in the midst of war, the United States provided enough support to the domestic opponents

---

[1] An earlier version of this chapter was published in the October-December 2007 edition of the journal *Comparative Strategy*.

of a hostile ruler to make them self-sustaining and to create leverage for the United States over that ruler. Because that opposition faction proved unable to bring about regime change and rule in its own name, the United States was at liberty to follow its own interests and settle the dispute on the best available terms, even if it left the original ruler in place. The United States was obligated only to do its best to leave its former allies in a position no worse than when they began to cooperate.

This policy of limited liability, which seemed an attractive middle ground between the extremes of appeasement and imperialism, had its own problems and critics. By cooperating with the opponents of a hostile foreign regime to gain tactical advantages over the current ruler, the United States created a sense of obligation from which it was difficult to disengage with honor. Senior American officials were tempted to rely on "plausible deniability" – that is, privately encouraging or turning a blind eye to local U.S. representatives who pushed beyond a policy of limited liability – while leaving Washington the option of disclaiming national responsibility later if things went badly. The United States thereby risked developing a negative reputation for fomenting revolution with promises of political or military support that did not materialize – a reputation that was bound to undermine the limited liability approach. Opposition factions could exploit the ambiguity of such a policy and promote their own popularity among individual U.S. government officials, Congress, and the American public, to their own particular advantage. Finally, rulers once threatened by the United States in this fashion would likely foster a sense of grievance and avoid a long-term cooperative relationship.

Several points should be made about the selection of this particular case study. These North African Islamic regimes – usually referred to as regencies – fall somewhere between what we generally characterize today as "states" and "non-state actors." Islamic notions of sovereignty and statehood and the relationship between religion and politics were different from those that had emerged in Europe under the Christian natural law tradition and the subsequent influence of the Enlightenment. The Islamic world did not have the equivalent of the Peace of Westphalia to define and legitimize regimes based upon the nation-state, or the American or French Revolution to set the standards for political self-determination. In a more practical sense, the Barbary rulers exercised various and often limited degrees of control over the territories they claimed to control, especially the Berber (Moorish) and Arab peoples of the interior. One authority described Tripoli as "a loose polity held together, mainly by the personal authority of the Pasha."[2] With the exception of Morocco, an independent kingdom,[3] the regencies were still nominally part of the Ottoman Empire and the Sultan still had important influence in them.[4] Turkish mercenary forces often became involved in their domestic affairs. Corsair captains or regional governors sometimes decided to undertake cruises against merchant ships without authority of the ruler – or at least without his explicit permission. The closest analogy to the regencies for Americans might have been Native American tribes or nations with which the United States had diplomatic relations of sorts but which the U.S. government did consider as fully independent "states."

The Barbary Threat

Some contemporary scholars and commentators have challenged the traditional American depiction of the Barbary threat and the U.S. claim of victory in the counter-piracy campaign. They point out that Christian nations for centuries had also enslaved Muslims captured during wartime, but without hope of ransom or release. They contend that what the United States and the Europeans condemned as "piracy" was actually not dissimilar to privateering, a form of warfare sanctioned by the existing law of nations. During the French Revolution and the Napoleonic Wars, the regular navies and privateers of Britain and France seized hundreds of American merchant vessels, worth tens of millions of dollars. Britain impressed thousands of sailors from American ships. These losses vastly exceeded the rather paltry level of American commercial assets that the Barbary regencies seized over several decades (a dozen small vessels and a few hundred men). Further, European courts routinely made demands for presents and bribes from foreign diplomats, as Americans should have

---

[2] Kola Folayan, *Tripoli During the Reign of Yusuf Quaramanli* (Ile Ife, Nigeria: University of Ife Press, 1979), p. 43.

[3] To simplify matters, this text generally includes Morocco in the discussion of the "regencies." American officials did not treat its sovereign status differently from that of Tripoli, Tunis and Algiers.

[4] The precise relationship between the Porte and the various regencies is very much a matter of scholarly dispute. For a discussion about the importance of the relationship in the case of Algiers, and recent review of the literature, see Tal Shuval, "The Ottoman Algerian Elite and Its Ideology," *International Journal of Middle East Studies* 32 (2000): 323-44.

realized from the XYZ controversy with France that immediately preceded the outbreak of the Tripolitan War. [5]

Even granting these points, the conflict between the United States and the Barbary regencies, in the eyes of the participants, was qualitatively different from the conflicts between America and various European powers. Americans of the time thought that the Barbary regimes were based on a way of life fundamentally at odds with the United States and the rest of the civilized world, of which the overtly Islamic nature of the Barbary states was only the most obvious difference. For U.S. officials like Thomas Jefferson, the law of nations, at best, only partly covered the regencies. John Adams considered them merely "nests of banditti." [6]

The Barbary corsairs had menaced European shipping and terrorized coastal communities for centuries. In the course of the 17th and 18th centuries, after the regencies obtained autonomous status from the Ottoman Empire, they entered into treaties with European nations, wherein individual Christian powers paid agreed-upon levels of tribute and presents in exchange for the safety of their merchant shipping. From time to time, one or more of the regencies would find pretext to declare war on a European power, capture its merchant vessels, and hold their crews for ransom. To protect its shipping the European state might convoy its ships or blockade or bombard the corsairs' ports. At some point the belligerents would arrange for ransom and agree to a new treaty, the regencies would find a new victim, and the process would start over.

Americans like Benjamin Franklin wondered why the European nations, especially the British and French, put up with this game. The simple answer – attributed variously to Louis XIV and various British merchants – was that, "if Algiers did not exist, we would have to build it." That is, the great European naval powers were more than happy to have the Barbary regencies keep in check their commercial rivals in the Mediterranean. Britain and France could easily afford to subsidize the regencies and stir them up against third parties – or to chastise them if they became too dangerous. The regencies, whose relative power in

---

[5] For contrasting discussions of the Barbary "pirates," compare Ray W. Irwin, *The Diplomatic Relations of the United States With the Barbary Powers, 1776-1816* (New York: Russell and Russell, 1910), pp. 1-19; and Gardner W. Allen, *Our Navy and the Barbary Corsairs* (Boston: Houghton, Mifflin and Company, 1905), pp. 1-2; with Syed Z. Abedin, *In Defense of Freedom: America's First Foreign War, A New Look at U.S.-Barbary Relations, 1776-1816*, Ph.D. Dissertation, University of Pennsylvania, 1974, pp. xxxiv-xxxviii, pp. 14-45; and Daniel Panzac, *Barbary Corsairs: The End of a Legend, 1800-1820* (Leiden and Boston: Brill, 2005), pp. 1-43.

[6] John Adams to Thomas Jefferson, 31 July 1786, Lester D. Cappon, ed., *The Adams-Jefferson Letters* (Chapel Hill: University of North Carolina Press, 1959), p. 146.

relation to the West, like that of the Islamic world as a whole, had been declining, existed in this tenuous niche. The regencies discovered that the tribute and presents, together with their own privately conducted commerce, was considerably more lucrative than the booty and slaves their corsairs might bring home. As a result, the regencies had strong incentives for peace as well as war. The regents walked a fine line. They had to threaten European commerce enough to keep the tribute coming but not so much as to trigger overwhelming military reprisals. The rulers of the regencies also relied on corsair operations to maintain domestic stability and preserve their own rule. One American diplomat was told by the Dey of Algiers: "If I were to make peace with everybody, what should I do with my corsairs? What should I do with my soldiers? They would take off my head for want of other prizes, not being able to live upon their miserable allowances." [7]

The regencies' justification for the corsair activities was also tied to their sense of identity as Islamic polities. As one authority described the rationale for the campaigns:

> It had an effective part of the economic activity of the region, involving, directly or indirectly, a considerable segment of the population; it had a strong influence on the diplomatic orientation of the leaders, and provided a justification for the very existence of these states; the corsairs were the heroes of Dar el-Islam (land of Islam), and fought its enemies in the Dar el-Harb (land of war, land of infidels). Those involved in the corsair activities participated in this double role: on the one hand, they exercised an essential socio-economic activity, and on the other, they carried out an important religious mission. [8]

The Barbary regencies were distinct entities with different histories, ethnic elites, and economic profiles. Although they tended to associate with each other when it came to dealing with the Christian powers, they were otherwise often at odds with each other. For instance, Tunis and Algiers, the most powerful of the four entities, were long-time rivals. During this period, the Bey of Tunis provided support or safe haven for Tripolitan opposition leaders, including (at different times) the two warring Karamanli brothers.

---

[7] Cited by Allen, *Our Navy and the Barbary Corsairs*, pp. 51 2.

[8] Panzac, *Barbary Corsairs: The End of a Legend*, pp. 56-7.

The U.S. Experience, 1775-1801

Prior to the outbreak of the American Revolution, colonial merchant shipping enjoyed the protection against Mediterranean piracy afforded by the British flag. The newly-constituted United States, however, found its commerce exposed to attacks by the corsairs. The American Congress initially attempted to persuade other European powers, notably its new ally, France, to extend their protection. France did agree to employ its good offices to assist the United States with the Barbary regencies but Foreign Minister Vergennes informed American diplomats that Versailles would not force the corsairs to respect U.S. shipping. The Netherlands took the same attitude in its commercial treaty with the United States. British hostility to any post-war rapprochement with America reinforced London's long-standing attitude about the strategic value of the regencies. Lord Sheffield, in his highly influential 1783 pamphlet, wrote: "It is not probable that the American States will have a very free trade in the Mediterranean; it will not be the interest of any of the great maritime powers to protect them from the Barbary States. If they knew their interests, they will not encourage the Americans to be carriers – that the Barbary States are advantageous to the maritime powers is obvious." [9]

The actual and potential value of the American trade held at risk by the Barbary regencies was always a matter of debate. Jefferson calculated that a reasonable baseline was the amount of trade between the colonies and Mediterranean ports before the American Declaration of Independence (subsequent trade was interrupted or distorted by the Revolution, the lack of treaty arrangements, and later the Quasi-War with France). Jefferson believed this figure to be "about one Sixth of the Wheat and Flour exported from the United States, and about One Fourth in Value of their dried and picked Fish, and some Rice . . . that the Commerce loaded outwards from Eighty to one hundred Ships, annually, of Twenty thousand Tons, navigated by about Twelve Hundred Seamen." More than that, for Jefferson and other American officials, the Mediterranean trade offered a major alternative outlet for commerce, as they sought to wean American merchants, financiers and shippers away from English-oriented trade. In that sense, the Mediterranean represented an object for Americans something like the (supposedly) untapped China market of the 19th and 20th centuries, the future center of commerce. [10]

---

[9] Cited by Allen, *Our Navy and the Barbary Corsairs*, p. 26. See also Irwin, *The Diplomatic Relations of the United States With the Barbary Powers*, p. 106.

[10] Thomas Jefferson, *Report on American Trade in the Mediterranean*, 28 December 1790, Julian P. Boyd, ed., *The Papers of Thomas Jefferson* (Princeton: Princeton University Press, 1950-), 18: 423; and preceding Editorial Note. Hereafter referred to as *PTJ*.

In 1784-1785, the U.S. Confederation Congress sought to supplement its appeals to European states for their intervention against the corsairs with a plan to negotiate treaties directly with the regencies. Congress authorized $80,000 for that purpose.[11] To help them set specific negotiating objectives, the principal American diplomats in Europe, Thomas Jefferson and John Adams, studied agreements in place between the Barbary regencies and various European powers. The Americans approached the French government for assistance in dealing with Morocco, which had seized but then released an American vessel as a means of prompting negotiations with the new republic. The French Minister of Marine offered the opinion that a treaty would likely be very expensive – certainly much more than authorized by Congress – but that without such contributions the United States could not expect to maintain peace. He thought, however, that if the United States could settle its affairs with Morocco and Algiers, the other two regencies, Tunis and Tripoli, "would easily follow their example, and certainly at less expense." This was apparently the beginning of the view, long held by American officials, that a U.S. treaty relationship with one of the Barbary regencies would provide leverage to deal with others. An American agent, Thomas Barclay, reached a surprisingly liberal agreement with the Moroccan Emperor in June 1786. It included no stipulation for presents or tribute and an agreement that, in case of war, neither country would enslave their captives but would exchange them within one year of capture. The Emperor also agreed to send letters to Constantinople, Tunis and Algiers, encouraging those entities to conclude treaties with the United States.[12]

The initial round of American negotiations with the three Barbary regencies was not nearly as successful. The resources allotted by Congress were wholly inadequate to establish treaties. Algiers, the most powerful of the regencies, became the major problem when it attacked American shipping in the mid-1780s and its corsairs captured and held for ransom 21 Americans. When approached by American agents about a settlement, the Dey of Algiers refused to negotiate a general treaty of peace and set a price of approximately $60,000 for the captives, which was well above what the U.S. Congress was willing to pay (roughly $4,200). The United States explored the possibility of securing a treaty with Algiers by forming a prior arrangement with

---

[11] Payments in Western treaties with the Barbary States were typically denominated in Spanish dollars, but Congressional and U.S. government documents usually do not make clear to which sort of "dollars" they are referring. To avoid confusion I have used the figure given by U.S. officials. They do indicate the order of magnitude of the transaction.

[12] See text and citations, Irwin, *The Diplomatic Relations of the United States With the Barbary Powers*, pp. 26-9.

the Ottoman Porte – the nominal sovereign of the Algiers – but French and Spanish officials discouraged the United States from exploring this path. Vergennes told Jefferson that any attempt to purchase Constantinople's support would require far greater funds than the United States possessed. In any event the Turks did not have sufficient leverage over Algiers. "The only two agents at Algiers are money and fear," Vergennes insisted. Jefferson and Adams also found Tripoli's asking price for a treaty to be far too high. [13]

The financial and political weakness of the American confederation during the 1780s meant that few diplomatic resources were available to Adams and Jefferson. There was no money and no navy. In light of this discouraging situation, the two diplomats debated the proper course for the United States: tribute or force. Their debate is of considerable interest because it bounded the set of policy options available to the United States; further, it set Jefferson's mind in the particular direction that he would later pursue as President.

Adams, although a staunch nationalist and advocate of U.S. naval power, favored paying tribute, at least while the United States remained in a weakened condition. "If it [peace] is not done, this war will cost us more millions of sterling money in a short time, besides the miserable depression of the reputation of the United States, the cruel embarrassment of all our commerce, and the intolerable burden of insurance, added to the crisis of our countrymen in captivity." The increase on maritime insurance rates alone, Adams argued, would be larger than payments to the regencies. It was not good economy to sacrifice "a million annually to save one gift of two hundred thousand pounds." The United States, Adams argued, did not have the means to coerce the regencies because of a basic asymmetry. Those powers had no substantial commerce that the United States could hold at risk even if it had a navy; moreover, America could not easily protect its substantial merchant shipping. Since the major maritime powers of Europe tolerated or even encouraged piracy in the Mediterranean, the United States would always be the odd-power out if it tried to oppose the regencies. [14]

> As long as France, England, Holland, the Emperor, etc., will submit to be tributaries to these robbers, and even encourage them, to what purpose will we make war upon them? The resolution might be

---

[13] Vergennes cited by Irwin, *The Diplomatic Relations of the United States With the Barbary Powers*, p. 44. This paragraph based on ibid., Chapter 3.

[14] Adams to John Jay, 17 February 1786, 20 February 1786, 22 February 1786, Charles Francis Adams, ed., *Works of John Adams* (Boston: Little, Brown, 1853), 8: 372, 373, 379; Adams to Jefferson, 3 July 1786, *The Adams-Jefferson Letters*, p. 129; Allen, *Our Navy and the Barbary Corsairs*, p. 33.

heroic, but would not be wise. The contest would be equal, but we cannot hurt them in the smallest degree.... Unless it was possible, then, to persuade the great maritime powers of Europe to unite in suppression of those piracies, it would be very imprudent for us to entertain any thoughts of contending with them, and will only lay a foundation, by irritating their passions and increasing their insolence and their demands, for long and severe repentance.[15]

Adams' bottom line to Jefferson: "We ought not to fight them at all, unless we determine to fight them forever. The thought is, I fear, too rugged for our people to bear."[16]

Jefferson disagreed. He insisted to his colleague that paying tribute to the regencies was dishonorable, whereas successful American military action would increase the standing of the United States with European powers. Jefferson studied successful French military actions in the Mediterranean and concluded that a small naval force and maritime blockade would rapidly bring the regencies to heel. Several decades earlier, for instance, France had brought Algiers to terms within three months, employing only "one large and two small frigates." Jefferson thought that a league of second-tier naval powers, such as Portugal, Naples, Venice, Malta, Sweden and Denmark, joined by the United States, could easily constitute a blockading force of that size. Although it might not be cost-effective for any one such power to oppose the regencies, such a combination would bring the expenses for each to a manageable level. The league would also address the odd-power out problem because, confronted by a collective security arrangement among the Christian states, the regencies would be left with no easy victims to attack. "There is no barbarian power, thus confined, which would not sue for peace," Jefferson argued. Jefferson believed that the regencies resorted to piracy not because of their Islamic character or their warrior culture but because they calculated that corsair operations provided a somewhat higher rate of return than peaceful commerce. He thought that cooperative military countermeasures by Western naval powers would easily tip that balance of self-interest in the other direction.

Jefferson did not favor the other principal tactic of the larger naval powers, that of bombarding the main ports of the regencies in order to coerce good behavior. "Bombardments are but transitory. It is, if I may so express myself, like breaking glass windows with guineas. None have produced the desired effect against the barbarians." Nor was the blockade to be an end in

---

[15] Adams to John Jay, 15 December 1784, *Works of John Adams*, 8: 218.

[16] Adams to Jefferson, 31 July 1786, *The Adams-Jefferson Letters*, p. 146.

itself. Jefferson envisioned coercing the regencies into a more normal, state-to-state relationship with the Christian nations – in essence, to alter their way of life and, indirectly, the character of their political regime. Once the regencies were cut off from the sea and denied easy prey by the anti-piracy league, Jefferson believed that they would "change their habits and characters from a predatory to an agricultural people." To ensure deterrence, the cooperating powers would maintain a small force along the coast of North Africa under the direction of a multinational committee. Jefferson thought the United States, even with its limited resources, should be able to provide one frigate. He envisioned a campaign that would be directed first against Algiers and then extended, if necessary, to the other regencies. [17]

Jefferson's plan went nowhere. Spain, having just concluded an expensive treaty with Algiers ($3,000,000), showed no interest. The evident coolness of Britain and France toward the enterprise discouraged the smaller naval powers. The Confederation Congress failed to authorize American participation. [18] The United States during the 1780s had neither the resources nor the will to engage in successful diplomacy or military operations at such a distance and against such established practices.

The U.S.-Barbary Treaty Structure Emerges

The creation of a more powerful central government under the new U.S. Constitution offered new possibilities for dealing with the piratical threat to American commerce. The Washington administration decided initially to take the traditional route of negotiating with the regencies for peace and to defer the establishment of a regular American navy that could resist piracy.

Jefferson, however, had not given up entirely on the idea of resorting to military force. As Washington's Secretary of State, Jefferson submitted several reports to Congress in which he reintroduced the idea of an international blockade of Algiers. In 1792, John Paul Jones was appointed to negotiate with Algiers, in the hope that the American revolutionary war hero's reputation as an aggressive naval commander would translate into diplomatic respect by the regencies. Jefferson instructed Jones to reject any payment of ransom that did not include a general treaty of peace. He was authorized to pay no more than $25,000 annually in tribute or more than $27,000 in ransom. The latter figure was held deliberately low so as

---

[17] For the above two paragraphs, with citations, see the Editorial Note, *PTJ*, 10: 560-6.

[18] Irwin, *The Diplomatic Relations of the United States With the Barbary Powers*, pp. 48-9.

not to encourage future hostage taking. Algiers was to receive payments in cash rather than maritime stores (this condition was later changed to permit one-time only provision of naval supplies). "We have also understood that peace might be bought cheaper with naval stores than with money," Jefferson wrote, "but we will not furnish them with naval stores, because we think it not right to furnish them with the means which we know they will employ to do wrong." [19]

Jones died before reaching Algiers and, in any case, the Dey refused to negotiate with any American agent. The outbreak of war between Britain and France in 1793 triggered a new wave of piracy, particularly after Britain brokered a truce between its ally Portugal and Algiers, which had the effect of allowing Algerine corsairs to enter into the Atlantic. Americans assumed that Britain arranged this truce – contrary to Lisbon's own wishes – in order to encourage the corsairs to prey on neutral U.S. commerce destined for France or French-controlled territory. The Algerines soon captured eleven American ships and approximately one hundred new captives. Maritime insurance rates rose from ten to thirty percent. [20]

President Washington now recommended the creation of a regular U.S. naval force specifically designed to deal with the Barbary threat. It was to consist of six frigates and ten smaller vessels, to be reduced when peace with Algiers was achieved. The establishment of the navy, however, provoked serious political opposition. Congressional critics of the President's plan warned that the British could subsidize the Algerines far more cheaply than the United States could build and support a navy suitable for service in the Mediterranean. U.S. naval patrols in the Mediterranean would likely provoke wars with the other regencies and create international complications with European nations. The Algerines would retaliate against the captured Americans if the United States showed a disposition to fight. [21]

Given this domestic opposition, the complications of an ongoing European war that threatened to embroil the United States, and the length of time it would take to build an effective naval force, the Washington

---

[19] Jefferson to Jones, 1 June 1792, *PTJ*, 24: 3-10; Irwin, *The Diplomatic Relations of the United States With the Barbary Powers*, pp. 56-7; Allen, *Our Navy and the Barbary Corsairs*, pp. 45-6.

[20] Irwin, *The Diplomatic Relations of the United States With the Barbary Powers*, pp. 59-60.

[21] Congressman James Madison, an ally of Jefferson, introduced a resolution to subsidize the Portuguese in their contest with the Algerines. Irwin, *The Diplomatic Relations of the United States With the Barbary Powers*, pp. 63-5.

administration decided not to neglect the diplomatic track. In July 1794, the administration authorized up to $800,000 for peace and ransom – an order-of-magnitude increase over previous proposals – and abandoned much of the tough line that Jefferson had wanted to pursue (Jefferson had resigned office in December 1793). The Dey of Algiers responded with a counter-demand of nearly $2.5 million. In 1795, American diplomats David Humphreys and Joel Barlow finally reached a treaty arrangement with Algiers. The settlement committed the United States to pay $642,000 in cash and an annual tribute of $21,600 in naval stores along with informal promises to provide Algiers with a frigate and large consular presents. This was an extraordinary concession: the size of the entire federal budget was $2.3 million in 1802 (a peacetime year). The settlement reflected a clear American strategy of giving priority to its relations with the Dey of Algiers – presumed to be the strongest of the Barbary rulers – and encouraging the Dey to lend his good offices to settle affairs with the other two regencies. The frigate, named the *Crescent* and built in Portsmouth, New Hampshire, arrived in January 1798 bearing Richard O'Brien, the new consul to Algiers and Consul-General to all of Barbary, another clear indication of the relative importance that the United States accorded to Algiers.[22]

The generous American settlement with Algiers – which amounted in total to nearly $1,000,000 – alarmed the smaller European powers. "Denmark and Sweden complain heavily that we have . . . materially disturbed the economy with which they have immemorially managed their affairs with those regencies," Rufus King, the American Minister to Britain, warned. The United States soon called on the Dey to carry out his part of the bargain in dealing with the other regencies. When the negotiations between Tunis and the United States stalled, the Dey threatened to compel Tunis to make peace. Through the agency of the French consul, Joseph Famin, the United States finally reached a treaty with Tunis for peace and ransom – but no annual tribute – with an estimated value of $107,000. The French consul warned, however, that the involvement of the Dey of Algiers in the process had created considerable resentment in Tunis. American diplomats in the region suspected that the Dey had his own motives for these threats and they doubted that his intervention was particularly useful. Nevertheless, in June 1797, Washington's successor, John Adams, told Congress that he considered the United States "to be under peculiar obligations" to the Dey, and agreed

---

[22] Irwin, *The Diplomatic Relations of the United States With the Barbary Powers*, pp. 80-1.

to his request that two cruisers be built and equipped for him in the United States, at Algiers' expense.[23]

At the insistence of the U.S. Senate, the treaty was later revised to eliminate two provisions. One provision would have allowed Tunis to commandeer (with compensation) the use of American merchantmen. The second provision would have required the United States to provide a barrel of gunpowder each time Tunis' guns saluted arriving American vessels (a clause which, *inter alia*, would have discouraged visits by U.S. Navy). William Eaton, the new U.S. consul to Tunis, was disgusted by the situation. "Can any man believe that this elevated brute has seven kings of Europe, two republics, and a continent tributary to him, when his whole naval force is not equal to two line-of-battle ships? It is so!"[24]

The Dey also sent a letter to the Pasha of Tripoli, Yusuf Karamanli, demanding that he make peace with the United States for $40,000. Yusuf turned down the initial American offer but later agreed to that amount after O'Brien, serving under the orders of then-Consul General Joel Barlow, promised informally to provide a vessel in addition to consular presents of $12,000 cash and some naval stores. The total value of the treaty with Tripoli was estimated at nearly $57,000. The agreement formalized a role for the Dey of Algiers as the treaty's guarantor and facilitator of adjustments of any disputes that might emerge between the United States and Tripoli.[25] It also included an unprecedented clause:

> As the Government of the United States is not, in any sense, founded on the Christian religion; as it has in itself no character of enmity against the laws, religion, or tranquility, of Mussulmen; and, as the said States never entered into any war, or act of hostility against any Mohomentan nation, it is declared by the parties, that no pretext arising from religious opinions, shall

---

[23] King to Eaton, 28 December 1800, Charles R. King, ed., *The Life and Correspondence of Rufus King* (New York: G.P. Putnam, 1894), 3: 355. Hereafter cited as LCRK. Irwin, *The Diplomatic Relations of the United States With the Barbary Powers*, ibid., with the quote from Adams. Eaton suspected Famin of undercutting American interests and pursuing his own financial interests, to the point where the two men came to blows. Joseph Wheelan, *Jefferson's War: America's First War on Terror, 1801-1805* (New York: Carroll & Graf, 2003), pp. 89-92. The treaty complicated rather than simplified American efforts to settle affairs elsewhere. A new Emperor in Morocco demanded new presents and tribute, since the United States had agreed to an annuity for Algiers. American diplomats refused tribute.

[24] Irwin, *The Diplomatic Relations of the United States With the Barbary Powers*, pp. 86-90; Eaton cited in Allen, *Our Navy and the Barbary Corsairs*, p. 64; Irwin, *The Diplomatic Relations of the United States With the Barbary Powers*, ibid.

[25] Irwin, *The Diplomatic Relations of the United States With the Barbary Powers*, pp. 83-4.

ever produce an interruption of the harmony existing between the two countries. [26]

Some contemporary writers have pointed to this clause as a definitive statement of the Founders' position on domestic church-state relations. The American negotiators on the spot, however, undoubtedly considered it a means to remove the religious issue from U.S.-Barbary relations as much as possible.

The Treaty Structure Begins to Collapse

By 1797, then, the United States had a series of treaties in place with the Barbary regencies designed to provide for the security of American commerce in the Mediterranean. The treaty structure immediately showed signs of strain. One critical problem, not then fully appreciated, was the gross asymmetry between size and terms of the American settlement with Algiers and those with the other polities. This disparity created considerable resentment – and sense of future entitlement – on the part of the smaller regencies. The constant demands for presents and outright bribes from the rulers and subordinate officials frustrated U.S. officials; in the end these demands amounted to little more than disguised tribute. The regencies, for their part, complained with considerable justice about non-performance on the part of the Americans. U.S. shipments of presents and tribute arrived months and years late, if at all. The regencies often found the stores that did arrive to be unsatisfactory and incomplete – something that the U.S. consuls privately acknowledged was the case. [27] On top of everything else Eaton believed that France and England were instigating trouble for the United States. [28]

Matters reached a point of crisis when the U.S. frigate *George Washington* arrived in Algiers in September 1800 with a delayed payment of tribute. The Dey demanded that the American warship be sent under Algerine flag to Constantinople in order to deliver an ambassador and presents to the Sultan. The Dey was anxious to placate the Turks because he had previously signed a treaty with France even though Napoleon had

---

[26] The full treaty text is available at http://avalon.law.yale.edu/18th_century/bar1796t.asp, accessed 7 October 2009.

[27] The regencies could also find fault with a perfectly good shipment if they were searching for a pretext for war or for additional presents. American slowness in official payments was not limited to the Barbary Coast. The U.S. government often struggled to maintain its accounts with its official bankers in Amsterdam, despite the importance of maintaining American credit in Europe.

[28] Wheelan, *Jefferson's War*, p. 93.

invaded Ottoman territories in Egypt and Syria. The Dey feared that the local Turkish troops would overthrow him or that the Ottoman fleet would punish him. O'Brien and the ship's commander, William Bainbridge, initially refused the request but, as the frigate had already anchored under the city's batteries, Bainbridge decided to comply. Algiers also threatened an immediate declaration of war. The Dey told Bainbridge: "You pay me tribute, by which you become my slaves. I have, therefore, a right to order you where I think proper." "There was no alternative but war with the Regency," Bainbridge explained to Rufus King. O'Brien estimated that the cost of diverting the *George Washington*, about $40,000, was much less than the price of war. Bainbridge, as it turned out, was well received in Constantinople and obtained from the Sultan a firman (official edict) which guaranteed him protection in Turkish ports. Bainbridge used the firman to resist a new set of demands from the Dey, including another attempt to impress the *George Washington*. However, America's problems continued: "At Algiers we are 2½ years behind in arrears of annuities [and] we are threatened with war if the stores do not arrive shortly," O'Brien warned the new Secretary of State, James Madison, in May 1801.[29]

Meanwhile, Tunis and Tripoli continued to make clear their dissatisfaction with the relative inferiority of their treaties with the United States. The Bey of Tunis, hearing of the affair of the *George Washington*, wanted an American ship to carry goods to Marseilles. Eaton reminded him that, according to the Treaty of 1796, he had no right to demand that service. To avoid a potential conflict, however, Eaton arranged for the use of the ship for $4,000. The Bey also complained to Eaton about the failure of the United States to provide naval supplies (Eaton had tried to substitute cash). He demanded as compensation presents of jewels and a cruiser. He threatened to make war on the United States beginning in January 1800 unless the U.S. met his demands. When some of the promised American supplies finally arrived, he complained of their quality. During 1800, the Bey gained significant concessions from Spain, Denmark, Sicily and Sweden, which pointed to a new corsair campaign against someone else. "I consider it sufficient to state that the United States are the only nation which have, at this

---

[29] Allen, *Our Navy and the Barbary Corsairs*, pp. 77-84. The Sultan, or Grand Seignior, sent back a message to Algiers demanding that it declare war on France and send him a million piasters within sixty days. The Dey complied by declaring war. Bainbridge to King, 28 November 1800, *LCRK*, 3: 381; Irwin, *The Diplomatic Relations of the United States With the Barbary Powers*, pp. 92-5; Wheelan, *Jefferson's War*, p. 96; O'Brien to SecState, 12 May 1801, *Papers of James Madison, Secretary of State Series* (Charlottesville: University of Virginia Press, 1986-), I: 167. Hereafter cited as *PJM-SS*.

moment, a rich and unguarded commerce in the Mediterranean, and that the Barbary regencies are pirates," Eaton warned the U.S. government.[30]

Tripoli increasingly represented the most serious threat to American shipping. The current Pasha, Yusuf, was a member of the local Karamanli dynasty that had ruled Tripoli since 1711. He had come to power through a coup against his brother, Hamet (Ahmad), several years after he murdered the presumptive heir, his eldest brother Hassan. In addition to struggles within the family, Yusuf had to overcome an Algerine adventurer, Ali Borghul, who ruled Tripoli for eighteen months with the support of Turkish mercenaries. Yusuf was well aware that for some years Constantinople had contemplated resuming direct control over Tripoli because of fears that this regency might otherwise fall victim to Britain or France. Years of misrule by the Karamanli family had left their lands economically backward, divided by civil war and unrest, with insecure control of the lands outside the port. Tripoli had almost no naval force and thus lacked the prestige and access to tribute and revenue provided by privateering.[31]

Yusuf was determined to change things. Westerners who dealt with the Pasha described him as violent, uncontrollable, highly intelligent and inordinately ambitious for himself and his regime. He sought to make Tripoli a first-class Mediterranean power by building a strong navy and using it to gain international recognition of his independence and status from the Christian powers, the Porte and his Barbary neighbors. By 1797, the Ottoman Sultan sent the Pasha several warships, confirmed Yusuf in power, and elevated Tripoli to equal status with his other nominal provinces, Algiers and Tunis. By 1800, the Tripolitan fleet had expanded from three to nineteen corsair ships of various sizes, plus additional skiffs and gunboats. Yusuf expected the various European powers to reestablish proper treaty relationships (many of which had been allowed to lapse over the years) by forwarding the consular presents traditionally accorded a new ruler. Spain, Venice, and France complied. Those powers that did not immediately do so, including

---

[30] Wheelan, *Jefferson's War*, p. 99; Irwin, *The Diplomatic Relations of the United States With the Barbary Powers*, pp. 98-100; Eaton to SecState, 8 December 1800, *American State Papers: Foreign Relations* (Washington, D.C.: Gales and Seaton, 1832), II: 355. Hereafter referred to as ASPFR. The arrival of one U.S. shipment caused the Bey to divert his cruisers, which had been awaiting orders to sail against the Americans, to attack the Danes instead. Eight Danish vessels soon were captured. Allen, *Our Navy and the Barbary Corsairs*, p. 71.

[31] For a discussion of Yusuf and *Tripoli, see especially* Folayan, *Tripoli During the Reign of Yusuf Quaramanli*, Chapters 1-2; Wheelan, *Jefferson's War*, pp. 102-3. See also the Editorial Note, PJM-SS, I: 197-9, which observes that the Americans misinterpreted the link between the regencies of Algiers and Tripoli. The changes that Tripoli was undergoing – the growing navy, and political and economic independence in the area – rapidly altered the subordinate position that Tripoli had held to Algiers and Tunis throughout the 18th century.

Sweden, Denmark, Holland, Austria and Naples, soon found their ships at risk. During 1797-1798, Sweden and Denmark decided to pay $100,000 for restoration and ransom and agreed to an annual subsidy of $5,000. The following year Denmark paid $13,000 in penalties for allowing the unlawful use of its passports. Ragusa ($30,000) and Sardinia ($40,000) paid for their failure to promptly renew their treaties. In 1800, Russia contributed another $100,000. Yusuf was also able to persuade many of these powers to increase the level of their annual tributes.[32]

Soon it was the turn of the United States which, according to its treaty, paid no annual tribute. Yusuf refused at first to receive the new American consul, James Leander Cathcart, and complained that the United States failed to deliver a frigate and various articles promised by O'Brien. He made clear that he was especially resentful of any American suggestion that Tripoli was a dependency of Algiers. He insisted that he stood better with the Grand Seignior than did the Dey. Cathcart, once Yusuf had received him, agreed to furnish the Pasha with $18,000 in cash in lieu of naval stores, and a consular present of $4,000. Yusuf wrote directly to President Adams to accept these terms, on the condition that the United States would henceforth treat Tripoli on par with the other regencies. He continued to urge Cathcart to provide him with a cruiser or brig as had been provided to the Dey of Algiers. He was also angry to hear reports that the Bey of Tunis had received "splendid presents" from the United States. Additionally, he resented Cathcart's repeated efforts to invoke the good offices of Algiers to settle their differences, per the terms of the Treaty.[33]

Yusuf finally showed all of his cards. He demanded some substantial proof of American goodwill and declared to Cathcart that if he did not receive satisfaction and a new treaty – $250,000 up front, an annual tribute of $20,000, and no reference to Algiers or any other nation – he would declare war. (Sweden had just concluded a preliminary peace with those precise monetary terms.) To demonstrate the seriousness of the Pasha's intent, a Tripolitan corsair captured an American brig from New York, but released it several months later. Cathcart, for $20,000, purchased a promise that the Pasha would delay any decision until he could secure a reply from

---

[32] Wheelan, *Jefferson's War*, pp. 102-3; Folayan, *Tripoli During the Reign of Yusuf Quaramanli*, p 7.

[33] Cathcart to SecState, 18 April 1800, *ASPFR*, II: 350; Cathcart to SecState, 4 January 1801, *ASPFR*, II: 354. Cathcart had been told that Yusuf had written to the Dey about the situation; in his opinion, "If the Dashaw of Algiers peremptorily orders him to accept my offer; I think not withstanding all his bravado, that he will acquiesce." Cathcart to SecState, 13 March 1801, *PJM-SS*, I: 14-15.

the U.S. government; in February 1801, however, the American consul warned Washington and American merchants in the region that hostilities were now likely.[34]

The Consular Plan to Overturn the Treaty Structure

In light of these ongoing difficulties, the American consuls in the region warned that the United States could not sustain its current approach toward the regencies. They informed Washington that if the United States wanted to maintain the current treaty structure that it must, at a minimum, follow the best practices of the European states: first, remove the sources of grievances by paying promptly the required annuities and presents; and second, deter the regents from illegitimate demands by maintaining and displaying a significant naval force.[35] When the United States provided the jewels demanded by the Bey of Tunis, for instance, Cathcart recommended that an American ship of war deliver the presents. "This would work upon the Bey like electricity," Cathcart assured the Secretary of State. He added: "I, therefore, can see no alternative but to station some of our frigates in the Mediterranean; otherwise, we shall be continually subject to the same insults which the Imperials, Danes, Swedes and Ragusans have already suffered, and will continue to suffer." The United States must also do more than just show the flag, especially given the loss of prestige which the United States suffered from the affair of the *George Washington*. "History shall tell," Eaton wrote sourly, "that the United States first volunteered a ship of war, equipt, a carrier for a pirate ... Nothing but blood can blot the impression out." No permanent peace could be established, Eaton contended, without "gold or cannon balls." War alone, he insisted, could make the United States respected at Algiers. "There is but one language which can be held to those people, and that is terror." In its relationship with the regencies, the U.S. government has "very much mistaken the character" of the regencies, "whose rulers regard

---

[34] Irwin, *The Diplomatic Relations of the United States With the Barbary Powers*, pp. 96-8; Folayan, *Tripoli During the Reign of Yusuf Quaramanli*, p. 35; Cathcart to SecState, 18 October 1800 [misdated 1801], *ASPFR*, II: 352.

[35] It should be noted that the American consuls were themselves often bitterly at odds over personal issues and private commercial matters, conflicts that would later spill over into their relations with U.S. naval commanders. The tension between Eaton and O'Brien, for instance, was based on Eaton's belief that O'Brien had improper ties with Jewish merchants in Algiers. As merchants, Cathcart and O'Brien had been captured by Algiers earlier in the 1790s and developed a dislike for each other during captivity.

courtesy as cowardice, moderation as diffidence, and civility as submission" – "temporizing with these people will not do." [36]

The most immediate threat remained a preemptive attack on American merchant shipping by Tripoli. The American consuls insisted that the United States must resist the demands of Yusuf Pasha, as the U.S. diplomats commonly referred to him. If the United States capitulated, Eaton warned, it would have to pay double that amount to Tunis and even more to Algiers, given their sense of the proper ranking among the regencies. Tripoli again would soon be dissatisfied and the demands would spiral out of control. "So long as they hold their own terms, no estimate can be made of the expense of maintaining a peace," Eaton insisted. "They are under no restraints of honor or honesty. There is not a scoundrel among them, from prince to the muleteer, who will not beg and steal." [37]

U.S. diplomats in Europe, who were concerned about the general reputation of the United States, reinforced this recommendation. "To chastise that haughty but contemptible Power which now dares first to insult us by its aggression would certainly serve, not only as a salutary example to other piratical states, but it would produce an almost incalculable effect in elevating our national character in the estimation of all Europe," Humphreys argued from his post in Lisbon. [38] John Quincy Adams, the American Minister to Prussia, advocated following up a proposal by Sweden for cooperative naval activities to protect merchant shipping in the Mediterranean. Adams rejected the argument that such cooperation was contrary to America's treaty engagements with the regencies.

> The United States have since then experienced themselves how little reliance can be placed upon the faith of those Treaties, even when purchased at prices unusually burdensome. The expense of an armament like that proposed by the king of Sweden would probably not be heavier than that of the tribute we presume to pay. It would be a more efficacious protection to our navigation in the Mediterranean; and I presume, an expense infinitely more reconcilable to the feeling of every American. [39]

---

[36] Irwin, *The Diplomatic Relations of the United States With the Barbary Powers*, pp. 95, 101-2; Cathcart to SecState, 27 May 1800, *ASPFR*, II: 352; Allen, *Our Navy and the Barbary Corsairs*, pp. 68-9; Eaton to SecState, 10 September 1801, *PJM-SS*, II: 98.

[37] Eaton to SecState, 10 April 1801, *PJM-SS*, I: 79; Allen, *Our Navy and the Barbary Corsairs*, loc. cit.

[38] Humphreys to SecState, 14 April 1801, *PJM-SS*, I. 92.

[39] John Quincy Adams to SecState, 25 June 1801, *PJM-SS*, I: 348-9.

John Quincy Adams, of course, was the son of John Adams, the man who had once argued for the cost-effectiveness of accepting a tributary relationship with the regencies. Implicit in John Quincy's argument was the rejection of the entire treaty relationship with the Barbary rulers, not merely resistance to the latest demands of Tripoli.

The American consuls in the region made this argument explicitly. They saw the crisis with Tripoli as an opportunity to revise the U.S. relationship with the regencies across the board, to eliminate any payment of tribute and the threat of enslavement (hostage-taking). Their general recommendations included the following points:

- Although America's concessionary relationship with Algiers was the ultimate source of the problem, the United States should begin by focusing on changing its relationship with Tripoli which the consuls regarded as the least capable, if most immediately threatening, regency. "Prudence seems however to dictate the Necessity of adjusting our acct. with Tripoli first, which I hope will be the means of obtaining respect at Tunis," Cathcart wrote to the Secretary of State, reflecting his views and those of Eaton. To take on the entire problem at once was beyond America's immediate capabilities. "Should we break with the whole of the Barbary States at once we must have a considerably greater force in this river of Thieves. I purpose [sic] chastising them one at a time . . ."[40]

- To lay the groundwork for this comprehensive approach, the United States must establish a reputation throughout the Mediterranean for being willing to use force. "We must harass them until they become sensible of their inferiority, we must establish a National Character in this River of Thieves, as yet we are an infant Nation but little known & our flag has suffer'd & will continue to receive insults until we resolve to maintain our dignity among the Nations of the Earth by the rigorous laws of retaliation."[41] A successful campaign against Tripoli would establish American credibility and, over the longer term, reduce the eventual amount of military power that would be required to coerce the other regencies.

- The United States should opportunistically seek the support of others to achieve its short- and long-term goals. First, America should explore

---

[40] Cathcart to SecState, 2 July 1801, *PJM-SS*, I: 370-2.

[41] Cathcart to SecState, 2 July 1801, *PJM-SS*, I: 370-1.

tactical and operational cooperation with willing European powers, while recognizing that such powers could not be depended upon to stay the course if they saw advantages in treating separately with Tripoli and the other regencies. Second, the United States, without sacrifice of its primary interests, should encourage Algeria to pressure Tripoli, according to the terms of the existing treaties with both regencies. In Cathcart's opinion, "if the Bashaw of Algiers peremptorily orders him [Yusuf] to accept my offer; I think not withstanding all his bravado, that he will acquiesce." The United States should implicitly threaten Algiers with adverse consequences if it failed to carry out its obligations. "If the Dey does not use his mediation in our favor in the present instance it can answer no purpose whatever to continue the [U.S.-Algiers] treaty in its present form." [42]

- Perhaps most importantly, America should seek a treaty and relationship with the Ottoman Sultan that would encourage him to exercise his legitimate sovereignty over the regencies – a backdoor form of regime change brought about by a strengthening of rule by the Ottoman Empire. "His influence is almost absolute over the Barbary States," William Willis, an American consul in the region, argued. The American republic, oddly enough, had a certain status beyond its commerce that would appeal to the Sultan (Grand Seignior). "It would be much easier of the United States to support a preference with him than for any of the powers of Europe, as they each of them [is] almost undistinguished among the crowd of powers of Europe. But as America stands alone, his vanity would be much gratified in having his friendship sought from so great a distance, as he is proud of having his friendly influence extend over a great part of the globe." [43] Cathcart believed that Washington and Constantinople had a fundamental common interest. "You will observe the many

---

[42] Cathcart to SecState, 13 March 1801, *PJM-SS*, I: 14-15. "Upon the whole our Peace being guaranteed by Algiers has been a service to our interests here, & I should recommend to government to continue the treaty in its present form was it not for the consideration that should we have a rupture with Algiers that Tripoli will immediately take the opportunity to break with us . . ."

[43] William Willis to SecState, 22 April 1801, *PJM-SS*, I: 110-11. Robert R. Livingston, American Minister to France, wrote jokingly to the new Secretary of State, James Madison: "Novelty, & superstition may perhaps allure their statesmen. By showing them a few federal election papers I can convince them that the presidents Christianity will not stand in the way of his proselytism to the doctrine of Mahomet, & tho I would not go so far as to stipulate for his circumcision, or even for that of his grand Vizer [Madison], I shall not scruple at building a mosque at Washington provided they destroy the prisons at Algiers." Livingston to SecState, 1 July 1801, *PJM-SS*, I: 368.

causes the Grand Seignior has had to complain of the arrogance of Yusuf Pasha, and no doubt will join with me in opinion that the war in which he was engaged [with France] was the only reason which prevented him from chastising him as he deserved; and that he only waits for a proper opportunity I believe is evident," Cathcart wrote to the Secretary of State. ". . . no act could ensure the Grand Seignior a revenge so prompt and efficacious, and attended with so little expense of both blood and treasure; . . . as well as set a precedent to the other states of Barbary, whose incorrigible insolence has become insupportable at the Sublime Porte, and render an example not only expedient, but absolutely necessary." [44]

The American consuls had recent evidence that the use of force against the Barbary regencies would have its effect. Cathcart reported to Washington that in May 1799, a Portuguese ship of 64 guns had destroyed a Tripolitan cruiser and captured a senior naval commander, after which Lisbon concluded a highly favorable treaty with Yusuf Pasha. Secretary of State Pickering found this report "encouraging" and "a happy demonstration of a mode of treatment of the Barbary Powers which all maritime Christian nations might successfully adopt." On the other hand, Sweden had reached a provisional settlement with Tripoli for $250,000 for peace and ransom and $20,000 in annual tribute – precisely the amount that Yusuf demanded from the United States. The Pasha, in Cathcart's opinion, was clearly looking for a new enemy, and America perfectly fit the bill. [45]

The United States and the regencies were at a crossroads in 1800-1801. None of the parties was satisfied with the existing relationship. The regencies were dissatisfied with the failure of the United States to meet its treaty obligations, as they understood those obligations, and they still regarded America as a potential source of new revenue. Tripoli went even further and demanded a fundamental revision to its relationship with the United States, as part of a more ambitious program to achieve equality with Algiers and establish itself as a major player throughout the Mediterranean. American officials on the scene argued for a highly confrontational strategy – at a minimum to deter the regencies from challenging the treaty structure, and maximally to coerce those regencies into a more normal, "civilized" relationship with the United States. (Behind this lay an even more fundamental

---

[44] Cathcart to SecState, 25 August 1802, *ASPFR*, II: 700.

[45] Cited by Irwin, *The Diplomatic Relations of the United States With the Barbary Powers, 1776-1816*, p. 102; Wheelan, *Jefferson's War*, p. 100.

ambition, in the words of David Humphreys, "that the United States would be the Authors of the System for exterminating the piracies.") [46] Neither side accurately understood the extent of the other's objectives, motivations or capabilities. Americans did not fully appreciate how their coercive program, aimed at changing the regencies' behavior, threatened to bring about regime change. In addition, although the American consuls had laid out a rationale for the use or threatened use of force against the regencies, they had not defined precisely how that force should be applied.

The Conflict With Tripoli, First Phase: Failure of Limited Measures

These consular warnings about the breakdown of the treaty structure and the imminence of war, together with news of the treatment of the *George Washington*, reached the United States just as the Jefferson administration was entering office in the spring of 1801. "The sending to Constantinople [of] the national ship of war the *George Washington*, by force, under the Algerine flag, and for such a purpose, has deeply affected the sensibility, not only of the President, but of the people of the United States," the new Secretary of State, James Madison, wrote to O'Brien. It demanded "a vindication of national honor." The *George Washington* was then about to sail back to the Mediterranean to deliver the latest annuity to Algiers. Madison ordered O'Brien to refuse any impressments of American ships in the future, and to reserve the right to claim reparations from Algiers for the original incident. [47]

Madison's instructions reflected the administration's general reconsideration of American policy toward the Barbary regencies. Jefferson, as noted above, had long advocated a more assertive policy in dealing with the threat of Mediterranean piracy. The circumstances of 1801 permitted him greater latitude than his predecessors had enjoyed. The Quasi-War with France recently had been resolved. American naval forces were now free for duty elsewhere. With the end of that war, and with the anticipation of a general European peace, American merchant traffic flooded across the Atlantic; those ships would be vulnerable in the event of hostility with one or more of the regencies. Jefferson had the desire of every new president to distinguish his policies from those of his predecessor and his party would enjoy a decided Congressional majority when the new Congress convened in December 1801.

---

[46] Humphreys to SecState, 10 September 1801, *PJM-SS*, II: 96.

[47] Wheelan, *Jefferson's War*, p. 98; SecState to O'Brien, 17 July 1801, *PJM-SS*, I: 424-5.

After consultation with the members of the Cabinet in May 1801, Jefferson dispatched to the Mediterranean a squadron of three frigates and a schooner, totaling 124 guns, as a "fleet of observation." [48] The squadron commander, Richard Dale, was instructed to deter any or all of the Barbary regencies from breaking out of the existing treaty structure or, if war had been declared, to "protect our commerce and chastise their insolence – by sinking, burning or destroying their ships and vessels wherever you find them." In case of war with Tripoli, Dale was specifically authorized to blockade the port. The Navy Department deemed this force "fully adequate to the Destruction of the Naval Power of Tripoli & to meet the Navies of Algiers and Tripoli united." The two 44-gun frigates were judged fully competent to blockade Tripoli because the forces of Tripoli were "contemptible." "The Bashaw has but one ship Carrying 18 guns the other few Vessels that he possesses are of 12 Guns and under." Given the uncertainties of the situation, Dale was not authorized to negotiate peace or a new treaty, although Cathcart was provided with $10,000 to encourage Yusuf Pasha to remain at peace. Dale's squadron was to have an important deterrent purpose. "Tis thought probable, that a small squadron of well appointed frigates, appearing before their Ports, will have a tendency to prevent their breaking the Peace which has been made & which has subsisted for some years, between them & the United States. It is also thought that such a squadron . . . will give confidence to our Merchants, & tend greatly to increase the commerce of our country within those Seas." Jefferson sent messages to Morocco, Algiers and Tunis, offering assurances that he did not intend in any way for the American squadron to threaten them. He also took steps to ensure prompt payment of overdue annuities and stores, particularly to Algiers. Madison urged O'Brien to call upon the Dey of Algiers to exercise his influence over Tripoli to prevent or halt piratical actions. [49]

Taken at face value, Jefferson's new policy toward the regencies was much more limited than the aggressive revisionist course advocated by the American consuls. The President signaled that he did not intend to challenge the tributary system generally. He continued the American policy of

---

[48] The Peace Reduction Act of 1801, passed by the outgoing Congress, required that six frigates be maintained in active service. The new President decided to retain two 12-gun schooners, *Enterprise and Experiment*. The latter was soon sold.

[49] Acting SecNav to Dale, 20 May 1801, Dudley Knox, ed., *Naval Documents Related to the United States Wars With the Barbary Powers, 1785-1807* (Washington, D.C.: U.S. Government Printing Office, 1939-1944), I: 465-7. Hereinafter referred to as *Naval Documents*. Acting SecNav to Tom Fitzsimons, 4 June 1801, *Naval Documents*, I: 486; Jefferson to Hamouda Bashaw, 19 September 1801, *ASPFR*, I: 356; SecState to O'Brien, 21 May 1801, *PJM-SS*, I: 213.

giving pride of place to Algiers. The United States would prevent an outbreak of piracy through a combination of incentives (meeting formal treaty commitments, coupled with spontaneously rewarding good behavior) and deterrence (the implicit threat of punishment from the squadron). Jefferson also intended this combination of policies to discourage the regencies from making new demands for presents or tribute. If one of the regencies, most likely Tripoli, had already begun cruising for American merchant ships, the U.S. squadron was to act in an appropriate manner to coerce that regency to restore the existing treaty arrangement, while deterring the others from taking advantage of the situation. The policy gave the squadron commander considerable discretionary authority to determine exactly how coercion was to be applied, but the administration's clear preference was for the imposition of a naval blockade. The traditional choices of the European powers – either convoying merchant ships to deny the corsairs easy access to their prizes, or bombarding the main ports in order to signal determination and frighten the leaders of the regencies into peace – were decidedly less preferable to the Jefferson administration. Convoys gave little incentive for the regency to return to the original treaty arrangement, while Jefferson always believed that one-time bombardments were likely to fail. Direct attacks against the port of Tripoli proper would require larger forces and expenditures than Jefferson was willing to accept in light of his plans to reduce dramatically the federal budget, including the U.S. Navy.[50]

Jefferson, however, clearly did not believe Dale's cruise would be a one-time exercise that would solve the piracy threat or that the existing treaty structure was either legitimate or self-sustaining. "We have taken these steps towards supplying the deficiencies of our predecessors merely in obedience to the law; being convinced it is money thrown away, and there is no end to the demand of these powers, nor security in their promises," Jefferson wrote to one of his Congressional allies, referring to the overdue payments to Algiers. "The real alternative before us is whether to abandon the Mediterranean or to keep up a cruise in it, perhaps in rotation with other powers who would join us as soon as there is peace. But this is for Congress to decide." He told Madison, "I am an enemy to all these douceurs, tributes & humiliations. What the laws impose on us let us execute faithfully; but nothing more. . . . I know that nothing will stop the eternal increase of demand from these pirates but the presence of an armed force, and it will be more economical & more

---

[50] For a good account of this strategy, see Christopher McKee, *Edward Preble: A Naval Biography* (Annapolis, MD: Naval Institute Press, 1972), pp. 87-94.

honorable to use the same means at once for suppressing their insolences." [51] Jefferson still held to the opinion that the United States could successfully coerce the regencies if it shifted their cost/benefit analysis in the direction of peaceful commerce which meant, at least over the long term, some form of regime change for the regencies. Jefferson was also prepared to act alone if other nations were not prepared to cooperate. In that case, the United States would behave like a major naval power in its dealings with the regencies and claim the same level of respect.

The Initial American Naval Deployment

When Commodore Dale's squadron reached Gibraltar, he discovered that Tripoli had already declared war on the United States and that its corsairs were out hunting for American merchant ships. The first appearance of an American naval force in the Mediterranean caught the Tripolitans off guard. Dale blocked two Tripolitan cruisers, which he caught anchored at Gibraltar, including the *Meshuda* commanded by Tripoli's grand admiral Murad Reis, the former Scotsman Peter Lisle. Dale presumed that these cruisers would have been deployed in the Atlantic, where they could have done extensive damage to American traders. John Gavino, the U.S. consul at Gibraltar, estimated that the Tripolitans might have captured as many as twenty American merchant vessels if Dale's forces had arrived only a fortnight later. This coup seriously would have damaged the American negotiating position. "One single merchantman's crew in chains at Tripoli would be of incalculable prejudice to the affairs of the United States with that regency," Eaton warned Madison. [52]

The Americans soon scored a major victory of their own when the schooner *Enterprise* defeated a Tripolitan polacca, the *Tripoli*. The Americans disabled the ship and allowed her to make her way back to port, where Yusuf Pasha punished and publicly humiliated her captain. For some time thereafter, very few Tripolitan cruisers ventured from the port. Murad Reis and his crews abandoned their ships at Gibraltar and set out for home by various means, an act which the Americans again attributed to demoralization caused by the victory of the *Enterprise*. The American squadron began to convoy American merchant ships in the western Mediterranean, operating in cooperation with Sweden, itself again at war with Tripoli after Stockholm rejected the preliminary settlement with Yusuf Pasha. Dale duly made appearances at Algiers and

---

[51] Jefferson to Nicholas, 11 June 1801, cited in Wheelan, *Jefferson's War*, pp. 110-1; Jefferson to SecState, 28 August 1801, *PJM-SS*, II: 71.

[52] Gavino to SecState, 24 July 1801, *PJM-SS*, I: 530; McKee, *Edward Preble*, p. 91; Eaton to SecState, 3 February 1802, *PJM-SS*, II: 438-9.

Tunis, carrying cash and asking their rulers for patience with overdue naval stores. O'Brien informed Dale that he had been warned by the Dey of Algiers "that the U.S. had not made its annual payments and had gone so far as to say he would not put up with it much longer." After a few days at Algiers, Dale reported to the Secretary of the Navy: "He [O'Brien] was now confident . . . that the Dey would not speak so big, and had no doubt that the arrival of the *President* [one of the 44-gun frigates] at Algiers had much more weight with the Dey than if the *Washington* had arrived with stores. . . . From Mr. Eaton's information . . . the appearance of our ships will have the same effect on the great and mighty Bey of Tunis." [53]

The squadron also appeared off Tripoli and briefly instituted a blockade of the port. Through the Danish consul, Nicholas Nissen, Dale requested a statement of the Pasha's grievances with the United States, offered Yusuf a truce and a $10,000 present from President Jefferson, and reminded the Pasha that the treaty required Algiers to mediate the disputes. Yusuf replied by demanding direct negotiations with the United States for a new treaty of peace. American insistence on interjecting the Dey of Algiers into Tripoli's affairs, Yusuf said, was the problem, not the solution. Dale refused the demands, citing his lack of negotiating authority. [54] Rough winter weather soon intervened and the American squadron returned to the United States, per the original orders.

U.S. Strategic Options: The View From the Mediterranean

On the face of things, the initial naval deployment of the United States to the Barbary Coast was a success, given the fact that Tripoli had already initiated hostilities. The U.S. government had followed the advice of the American consuls and demonstrated a willingness to use force to secure its interests in the region. The American naval squadron apparently provided enough cash and visible military presence to deter Algiers and Tunis from taking advantage of the situation and attacking U.S. shipping. The U.S. Navy had demonstrated its credibility by defeating a Tripolitan ship of war. Tripoli had seized no American merchant vessels and no U.S. citizen was a captive. [55]

---

[53] Allen, *Our Navy and the Barbary Corsairs*, pp. 95-8; Dale to SecNav, 19 July 1801, *ASPFR*, II: 360.

[54] Charles O. Paullin, *Diplomatic Negotiations of American Naval Officers, 1778-1883* (Baltimore: Johns Hopkins Press, 1912), pp. 63-5. The precise sequence of Dale's activities is not clear. Wheelan, *Jefferson's War*, p. 114; Dale to Bashaw of Tripoli, 25 and 28 July 1801, *Naval Documents*, I: 531-3.

[55] Cathcart to SecState, 10 August 1801, *PJM-SS*, II: 33.

Despite these tactical successes, the American consuls believed that the United States had missed a major strategic opportunity to coerce Tripoli. The sudden American deployment to the Mediterranean caught Yusuf Pasha off guard. His military buildup was in its early stages and food was scarce that season. Tripoli held no American citizens as negotiating leverage. The consuls calculated that if the United States had been able to maintain a close blockade of the coast, they might have brought Yusuf around to acceptable terms within a reasonable period. Unfortunately Dale's squadron had been too small and wrongly configured. His instructions did not allow him to undertake offensive operations, such as a direct attack on Tripoli – or at least Dale so interpreted his orders.[56]

Commodore Dale and the U.S. consuls put forward to Washington their own ideas about how to proceed. The consuls now agreed that the option of using Algiers as a mediator or intermediary was not viable, despite the fact that the Dey had supposedly written letters of warning to Yusuf Pasha. "They [Algiers] might in some respect check the plundering ideas of Tripoli but to arrange and secure this business, it will be requisite on the part of the US to give an extraordinary present and to show a respectable force in this sea," O'Brien informed Madison. Cathcart told the Secretary of State that the Dey of Algiers would never intercede on behalf of the United States but rather would come down in favor of "his brother pirate of Tripoli." O'Brien noted that the Dey had already received letters from Tripoli that requested help with food shortages and in obtaining the release of the ships blockaded at Gibraltar. Tunis and Tripoli both appealed to Algiers to reject the American right of blockade on the grounds that it could become a custom "very prejudicial" to them. When push came to shove, the consuls noted, the regencies would likely make a common front against the infidels. Nor were the long-term prospects for U.S. strategic cooperation with the smaller European powers encouraging. Cathcart informed Madison that the Danes had recently adjusted their terms of tribute with Tripoli rather than take advantage of the current opportunity to eliminate payments. The Danish commodore predicted to him that Jefferson's planned general reductions in the U.S. Navy would result in America's acceptance of every demand of the Barbary States, no matter how unjust. The Swedes were friendly but Cathcart thought they

---

[56] Allen, *Our Navy and the Barbary Corsairs*, p. 98. "I have no orders to make any attack on shore." Dale to Rufus King, 7 February 1802, *Naval Documents*, II: 54. See the Cabinet discussion of war power in *PJM-SS*, I: 198-9.

were unlikely to maintain a common cause with the United States and would seek an early peace treaty. [57]

That left the unilateral military route. Dale thought that the United States had two basic choices. First, the U.S. Navy could engage in a passive blockade of the port of Tripoli with two frigates and two sloops of war, along with a small gunboat that could direct occasional harassing fire into the city. Second, the President could approve a combined arms attack on Tripoli and shipping in the harbor. For this purpose, the U.S. Navy needed four frigates and three bomb ketches to operate against the port. The naval operations would be aided by a ground force landed on the coast to threaten the city from inland, where the defenses were much less formidable. A detachment of gunboats would also be necessary to protect the frigates when they moved closer to shore from attack by Tripolitan gunboats. Dale himself favored the more aggressive course, especially if he could add Sweden's four frigates to the attacking force: "I would be answerable for Tripoli's being taken in two days after the force arrived off there." At the very least the shipping in the harbor could be destroyed without major risk to the attackers. Eaton agreed with the recommendation. "To avoid the expense of prolonging the war, Tripoli should be bombarded. This is a very practicable measure." [58]

For the ground component of the campaign, Eaton thought that two thousand troops would be adequate to the task. He undoubtedly suspected that the American government was not likely to approve sending an army of this size to the Mediterranean; he and the other consuls had already arrived at another means to threaten Yusuf Pasha. They had begun to appreciate Yusuf's larger regional ambitions and concluded that the United States must do more than compel him to back down from his immediate demands. "For so long as Yusuf Bashaw lives, our commerce will not be secure, allowing that we conclude a peace upon our own terms; the first time our frigates are off our guard or employed upon other service his cruisers will capture the Americans in retaliation for having imposed upon him terms which he may consider humiliation." [59]

---

[57] O'Brien to SecState, 24 June 1801, *PJM-SS*, I: 346; O'Brien to SecState, 22 July 1801, *PJM-SS*, I: 457; Cathcart to SecState, 10 August 1801, *PJM-SS*, II: 33; O'Brien to SecState, 26 September 1801, *PJM-SS*, II: 138; Cathcart to SecState, 27 September 1801, *PJM-SS*, II: 141.

[58] Cited by McKee, *Edward Preble*, p. 93; Allen, *Our Navy and the Barbary Corsairs*, pp. 100-1.

[59] Eaton to Cathcart, 29 June 1801, *Naval Documents*, I: 494.

The consuls therefore advocated creating a "second front" that would threaten regime change in Tripoli, by supporting the claims of Yusuf's deposed brother. Hamet Pasha had signaled a willingness to deal more favorably with the United States. He would either form an army from his supporters or simply appear in a U.S. ship off the coast, provoking a revolt against Yusuf. The consuls believed conditions for such a change in leadership were in place. "The subjects in general of the reigning Bashaw are very discontented and ripe for revolt; they want nothing but confidence in the prospect of success: this confidence may be inspired by assurances of our determination to chastise the Bashaw for his outrage against U.S.," Eaton asserted. "The Bey of Tunis, though prudence will keep him behind the curtain, I have strong reasons to believe, will cheerfully prompt the scene: He is in favor of the elder brother [Hamet]." The other Barbary regents, insecure in their own realms, would undoubtedly take note of America's willingness to strike directly at Yusuf Pasha. "The idea of dethroning our enemy and placing a rightful sovereign in his seat makes a deeper impression on account of the lasting peace it will produce with that regency, and the lesson of caution it will teach the other Barbary States." [60]

The Administration Plans for a Second Deployment

The Jefferson administration considered these naval and consular recommendations as it prepared to deploy an expanded relief force to the Mediterranean in the spring of 1802, under the command of Richard Morris. The administration interpreted the Tripolitan diplomatic overtures to Commodore Dale as a sign that the initial American military actions had had a substantial effect on the Pasha and that he was eager for peace. The President obtained from Congress a Use of Force Resolution – "an Act for the protection of the commerce and seamen of the United States against the Tripolitan cruisers." The executive was given full discretion in the employment of the navy and authorized to commission privateers. [61]

The Secretary of the Navy instructed Morris to take a more visibly aggressive posture against Tripoli. "Holding out the olive Branch in one hand & displaying in the other the means of offensive operations, may produce a peaceful disposition towards us in the mind of the Bashaw,

---

[60] Eaton to SecState, 5 September 1801, *PJM-SS*, I: 569-70.

[61] McKee, *Edward Preble*, p. 94.

and essentially contribute to our obtaining an advantageous treaty with him.... You will proceed with the whole squadron under your command and lay off Tripoli, taking every care to make the handsomest and most military display of your force, and so conduct your maneuvers as to excite an impression that, in the event of negotiations failing, you intend a close and rigorous blockade." Although the administration granted Morris wide discretion to meet unexpected circumstances, it clearly indicated its strategic preference for blockade. "Convoy must be given to our vessels as far as it can be done consistently with the plan of blockading." The American General Consul, Cathcart, was authorized to negotiate with Tripoli, with the expectation of making peace without purchase – essentially, a return to the *status quo ante* of the 1797 Treaty. Madison instructed Cathcart to let Yusuf make the first overture so that "awe inspired by a display of our force" could have its effect. Don't buy a peace, Madison warned. "To buy a peace with Tripoli, is to bid for War with Tunis . . ."[62]

The administration, as it calculated the difficult strategic and diplomatic geometry of deterring the other regencies while coercing Tripoli back into the treaty structure, believed that the expanded American naval deployment was adequate to the task. "Although I have directed you to lay your whole force before Tripoli," the Secretary of the Navy instructed Morris, "you will yet consider yourself authorized, should you deem it necessary, to leave one vessel to watch the motions of the Emperor of Morocco, and to prevent the escape of the Tripolitan vessel at Gibraltar."[63]

The Jefferson administration also considered the consuls' proposal to support Hamet Pasha.[64] Although the regencies did not qualify as "states" or "governments," Madison was clearly squeamish about the broader implications of becoming involved in the domestic affairs of Tripoli and becoming an instrument of regime change. Nevertheless, Madison told Cathcart, "It cannot be unfair, in the prosecution of a just war or the accomplishment of a reasonable peace, to turn to . . . advantage the enmity and pretensions of others against a common foe." Madison attempted to draw a distinction between American strategic objectives and those of Hamet, a distinction that Madison knew would be difficult to maintain in practice. "How far success

---

[62] McKee, *Edward Preble*, pp. 94-5; SecNav to Morris, 20 April 1802, *Naval Documents*, II: 130; Wheelan, *Jefferson's War*, pp. 127-8; Madison to Cathcart, 22 August 1802, *PJM-SS*, III: 504-5.

[63] SecNav to Morris, 20 April 1802, *Naval Documents*, II: 130; Allen, *Our Navy and the Barbary Corsairs*, p. 114.

[64] On the firman, see Folayan, *Tripoli During the Reign of Yusuf Quaramanli*, p. 37.

in the plan ought to be relied on, cannot be decided at this distance and with so imperfect a knowledge of many circumstances. . . . Should the rival brother [Hamet] be disappointed in his object, it will be due to the honor the United States to treat his misfortunes with the utmost tenderness, and to restore him as nearly as it may to the situation from which he was drawn, unless some other proper arrangements should be more acceptable to him." The Secretary of the Navy offered somewhat clearer instructions to Morris. "In adjusting the terms of peace with the Dey [Pasha] of Tripoli, whatever regard may be had to the situation of his brother, it is not to be considered by you, of sufficient magnitude to prevent, or even to retard a final settlement with the Dey." The American government considered Hamet's cause of regime change, if not Hamet himself, to be expendable.[65]

Tripoli Gains the Upper Hand, 1802-1803

Despite the buildup of the U.S. squadron and plans for a more aggressive military and diplomatic posture, the American strategic position in the Mediterranean, apparently so promising in 1801, deteriorated considerably over the next two years. The Tripolitans captured an American merchant ship, the *Franklin* – the first and, as it turned out, the only prize of the war. Two corsairs ran the American and Swedish blockade and, with the *Franklin* as prize, slipped back into Tripoli. The event considerably boosted Tripolitan morale and the Pasha's leverage. The United States eventually ransomed her captain and small crew for $6500 through the agency of Algiers, which confirmed to all the regencies that, despite their bluster, the Americans would pay for captives. The Swedes soon decided to make their peace for $150,000 and an annual tribute of $8,000. France provided the Pasha with $40,000 in gifts and an 18-gun cruiser. The Danish consul, Nissen, told the Americans that "Tripoli this year is well provided with provision by a rich harvest. [T]here are plenty of European goods by the arrival of several ships, & the Bashaw having Swedish money has wherewith to maintain his people & defray his expenses. . . . Under such circumstances it seems Sir that a *simple* blockade is as expensive as useless & that your navigation is not secure as seen last year." The Pasha continued to build up his navy and especially improve Tripoli's fortifications and coastal batter-

---

[65] Madison to Cathcart, 22 August 1802, *PJM-SS*, II: 505-7; SecNav to Morris, 28 August 1802, ASPFR, II: 45; Folayan, *Tripoli During the Reign of Yusuf Quaramanli*, loc. cit.; Irwin, *The Diplomatic Relations of the United States With the Barbary Powers*, p. 144.

ies, the latter of which had been judged negligible in 1801 – "barely enough to fire a salute" – but which consisted of 115 cannons two years later.[66]

The Hamet Pasha option also seemed to be closed. Hamet had taken up refuge in Tunis and Yusuf held his immediate family hostage in Tripoli. Yusuf, who was well aware of the American contacts with Hamet, offered his older brother the governorship of Derne, an important port town, as well as security for his family. Hamet accepted the post but continued to plot against Yusuf. When a revolt in Derne failed in early 1804 Hamet was forced to flee, eventually making his way to Egypt.[67]

Commodore Morris, despite his orders, did not maintain a continuous blockade of Tripoli but focused instead on convoy duties. In May-June 1803, Morris at last brought the bulk of the squadron off Tripoli. He launched an attack against a number of gunboats and succeeded in destroying one large cruiser. A senior Tripolitan official, Sidi Mohammad Dghies, proposed a settlement based on U.S. payment of $200,000, plus the expense of the war. He hinted that this offer was merely an opening gambit and that the Pasha was prepared to reduce the amount. Morris countered with an ultimatum: either $5,000 as a consular present and a second gift of $10,000, to be paid after five years assuming there had been no violations of the treaty, or a 12-month truce while the Pasha stated his terms directly to the President. Morris' preemptory tone angered Dghies, who was generally regarded as well disposed to the Americans. The negotiations were broken off – Morris himself nearly became a captive when he came ashore – and the Commodore soon raised the blockade. With the withdrawal of the American squadron the official price of peace from Tripoli rose, to a payment of $500,000 and annual tribute of $20,000.[68]

The American consuls were appalled by Morris' lack of activity and by what they regarded as his presumption in assuming the lead role in the negotiations. They were taunted by the other regencies. "Our operations of the last and present year produce nothing in effect but additional enemies and national contempt . . . . The Minister [of Tunis] puffs a whistle in my face, and says, 'We find it all a puff! We see how you carry on the war with Tripoli,'" Eaton informed Madison. Distant or paper blockades and the use of convoys would not coerce Tripoli or deter other regencies from piracy over the long term.

---

[66] Wheelan, *Jefferson's War*, pp. 130-2, 183; Eaton to Morris, 16 October 1802, *Naval Documents*, II: 297; Nissen to Cathcart, 4 June 1803, *Naval Documents*, II: 440.

[67] Folayan, *Tripoli During the Reign of Yusuf Quaramanli*, pp. 38-9.

[68] Wheelan, *Jefferson's War*, pp. 153-4; Allen, *Our Navy and the Barbary Corsairs*, pp. 153-6, Irwin, The *Diplomatic Relations of the United States With the Barbary Powers*, p. 135. Wheelan, *Jefferson's War*, p. 153, reverses the order of the Pasha's offer as indicated by Allen and Irwin.

Eaton insisted that it was "absolutely necessary that the United States should once, and at once, show themselves on the *Barbary,* and not the European coast; and in a manner to make themselves known." [69]

Morris countered by arguing that the American squadron under his command had been too small and improperly configured to meet the full range of missions that the Jefferson administration set out. He insisted that a system of convoys offered the most cost-effective protection of American merchant shipping. He could not blockade Tripoli without a larger and much more diverse naval force. Small merchant ships and shallow-draft Tripolitan corsairs could hug the waters along the coast where the larger American frigates could not safely operate. "It is impossible to block Tripoli with large ships so as to prevent these row-boats from stealing out; it is equally impossible for large ships to catch them when out: they may have a rendezvous in every port on the Barbary coast, where they may sell their prizes and take in provisions," Eaton acknowledged. Morris added: "It is impossible a frigate can have any chance of capturing those cruisers in moderate weather: they generally cruise close in with the land, and make use of oars to get into shoal water, or some port." The harbor at Tripoli likewise did not allow safe access to the frigates, thus precluding a direct attack against shipping there. Nor was the U.S. Navy large enough to cover the entire coast. Nissen reported that vital military stores, including gunpowder, were being conveyed to Tripoli overland from Tunis or from smaller ports elsewhere along the coast. [70]

Morris, with considerable justice, pointed out that he needed to keep the squadron available to deter or meet other outbreaks of piracy. The naval campaign against Tripoli naturally caused incidents with the shipping of the other regencies, which refused to recognize the principle of blockade. The regencies wanted to use the cover of their flags in order to provide Tripoli with arms and ammunition as well as provisions, whether out of economic opportunism or solidarity with their fellow Islamic ruler. The Moroccan Emperor, for instance, claimed that he had obtained title to the Tripolitan cruiser *Meshuda* and demanded an American passport to sail that ship and another vessel, full of grain, to Tripoli. This would not only violate the

---

[69] Wheelan, *Jefferson's War*, pp. 138-9; McKee, *Edward Preble*, p. 113. A naval court of inquiry convened in the United States agreed with the consuls: Morris was censured for failing to display "the diligence or activity necessary to execute the important duties of his station." Irwin, *The Diplomatic Relations of the United States With the Barbary Powers*, p. 129; Findings of the Court, *Naval Documents*, II: 528-9.

[70] Eaton to Summert and Brown, 9 July 1802, *Naval Documents*, II: 196; Morris to SecNav, 15 October 1802, *Naval Documents*, II: 296ff.

American blockade of Tripoli but the American agents assumed that the Emperor would then turn the ship back over to Yusuf Pasha. When the American consul in Tangier, James Simpson, refused the passport, the Moroccan Emperor declared war on the United States. When Commodore Morris appeared off the coast with part of the American squadron, Simpson soon negotiated a return to peace, but his arguments with the Emperor continued.[71]

There were other trouble signs. Algiers and Tunis lodged the usual complaints that the United States had failed to provide agreed-upon annuities and consular presents. The Bey of Tunis demanded a 36-gun frigate as a present from the United States. Morris was concerned with information (incorrect, as it turned out) that Tunisian corsairs appeared to be cruising together in preparation for attacks on American shipping. Morris hoped to coerce Tunis and Algiers into attitudes that were more reasonable by appearing off the ports with most of his squadron. The Bey claimed to be unimpressed, declared that he would continue to send ships to Tripoli, and threatened reprisals against American commerce if the U.S. Navy interfered with that trade. While Morris was ashore at Tunis, the Bey briefly detained him for non-payment of an American debt incurred to support Hamet Pasha. The Commodore agreed to pay $22,000 in claims for Tunisian property seized by the U.S. Navy.[72]

Morris's argument reflected the position of some senior officers in the Navy, who believed that the Jefferson administration's strategic objective – to coerce Tripoli to return to the terms of the 1797 Treaty, while deterring other regencies from breaking their own treaty commitments – greatly exceeded the present capabilities of the Navy and ignored the essential facts on the ground. "They are not a commercial people; therefore, we can make no impression on them," Captain Alexander Murray, who had deployed with Morris, reported when he returned to the United States. The blockade of one of the regencies, he argued, would simply cause unnecessary trouble with the others and defeat the purpose of the administration's strategy of deterrence and conciliation. It was laudable to try to do away with tribute but unless the other European

---

[71] Morris to Cathcart, 5 April 1803, cited in Irwin, *The Diplomatic Relations of the United States With the Barbary Powers*, pp. 126-7; Allen, *Our Navy and the Barbary Corsairs*, p. 113; Wheelan, *Jefferson's War, pp. 127-8*.

[72] McKee, *Edward Preble*, p. 111; Paullin, *Diplomatic Negotiations of American Naval Officers*, pp. 65-7. Morris also had to sail to Algiers and attempt to deal with the Dey of Algiers, who objected to a consignment of $30,000 cash in place of the annual shipment of timber and other maritime stores.

powers cooperated with the United States more generally, it would be more prudent to submit and pay.[73]

The Jefferson Administration Reevaluates the Situation: 1802-1803

During the fall of 1802 and the spring of 1803, President Jefferson and his Cabinet reconsidered their policy toward Tripoli in light of these discouraging reports and in the context of an emergent strategic danger closer to home. After years of rumors, it was now clear that France had finally obtained title to the Louisiana Territory from Spain. The administration scrambled to prevent Napoleon from establishing a French strategic empire in the Caribbean and the American West. The peace between Britain and France was also on the verge of collapse. Once the two great European powers and their allies resumed war on the seas, as they did in May 1803, navies with far greater reach and capacity than the Barbary corsairs would again put American neutral shipping at risk.

Secretary of the Treasury Albert Gallatin was strongly influenced by Murray's reports on the deteriorating U.S. position and by the administration's overriding domestic goal of fiscal retrenchment. Gallatin argued for a quick resolution to the war in the Mediterranean. "Our object must clearly be to put a speedy end to a contest which unavailingly wastes our resources, and which we cannot, for any considerable period of time, pursue with vigor without relinquishing the accomplishment of the great and beneficial objects we have in view," he wrote to Jefferson in August 1802.

> ... I sincerely wish you could reconcile it to yourself to empower our negotiators to give, if necessary for peace, an annuity to Tripoli. I consider it no greater disgrace to pay them than Algiers. And indeed we share the dishonor of paying those barbarians with so many nations as powerful and interested as ourselves, that, in our present situation, I consider it a mere calculation whether the purchase of peace is not cheaper than the expense of a war which shall not even give us the free use of the Mediterranean trade. . . . Eight years hence we shall, I trust, be able to assume a different tone; but our exertions at present consume the seeds of our greatness and retard to an indefinite time the epoch of our strength.[74]

---

[73] Cited by McKee, *Edward Preble*, pp. 108-9.

[74] Cited by McKee, *Edward Preble*, pp. 102-3.

Secretary of the Navy Robert Smith, to the contrary, argued for a substantial increase in the American deployment to the Mediterranean to meet the collective threat posed by the regencies. "So far from considering that Tripoli is to be our only enemy, I am rather inclined to believe that nothing but a formidable squadron will prevent all the Barbary Powers waging war against us," he told Jefferson. "A superior force in the Mediterranean will insure us an early peace and will enable us to dictate the terms that will be the most honorable and beneficial to us. A feeble force, on the contrary, will subject us to the necessity of purchasing a peace upon the same terms that have from time to time been imposed upon the small powers of Europe." The United States ought to compel the regencies to recognize the United States to be in a class with the great European naval powers, a position Smith knew Jefferson was determined to obtain. "A formidable force displayed at this time will make a favorable impression, will repress every disposition hostile to us, and thus will save us a great trouble and much expense. It will acquire to us a character that will hereafter protect us against all such aggression." Smith believed that an expansion of the American Mediterranean squadron would force Tripoli to conclude peace within a year. "With less force the war may continue for years, which would be playing a hazardous game." One of the senior American naval officers in the squadron, Captain John Rodgers, supported this position – with "5 frigates, two brigs or schooners, and one mortar-ship we would be able to force a peace on any terms we care to dictate within two weeks after their arrival before the port of Tripoli."[75]

Jefferson sought a compromise between the two positions. The Cabinet agreed to explore a negotiated peace with Tripoli that included a major concession – annual tribute. Madison explained to Cathcart, in the spring of 1803,

> Considering that the Bashaw is no longer under the domestic distresses which at one time humbled his pretensions, that all the other nations at war with him have yielded to the customary terms of peace, and that the new terms which the concurrent policy of all civilized nations ought to force on those barbarians would now be pursued by the United States at a very great expense, not only without the cooperation of a single other power, but in opposition to the example of all, and at a period in different respects critical to their affairs, it is thought best that you should not be tied down to a refusal of the presents, whether

---

[75] Quotations from McKee, *Edward Preble*, pp. 103, 118.

to be included in the peace, or to be made from time to time during its continuance, especially as in the later case the title to the presents will be a motive to its continuance.

The Secretary of State authorized Cathcart to offer Tripoli an initial payment of $20,000 for peace, and an annuity of $8-10,000 in cash, but not naval stores. Madison encouraged Cathcart to keep such a commitment out of a formal treaty, if possible. Madison acknowledged that if Tripoli received presents and tribute from the United States, Tunis would demand the same. Cathcart was therefore authorized to offer annuities (tribute) to Tunis up to $10,000 prior to beginning negotiations with Tripoli.[76]

At the same time, to encourage a quick settlement from Tripoli, the administration decided to push its naval commanders toward a more aggressive posture. Jefferson had previously resisted an expansion of American naval deployments on the grounds that Congress had authorized the executive to employ no more force than was necessary. He eventually agreed to a new squadron with more ships (although about the same number of guns) under the command of Edward Preble, which would arrive in the Mediterranean in the summer of 1803. The administration also took steps to reconfigure the American force to meet the special needs of blockading Tripoli and other Barbary ports. Congress voted funds to construct as many as fifteen gunboats and other smaller craft. The Secretary of the Navy authorized Preble to explore the loan or purchase of gunboats, bomb ketches and other shallow-bottom craft in Europe, which could aid in the campaign against the port.[77]

Smith's instructions to Preble were similar to those issued to Morris. He was to blockade the enemy and otherwise exert appropriate coercive pressure on Yusuf Pasha, while cooperating with the senior American diplomat in the region (now Tobias Lear, replacing Cathcart) to achieve a negotiated solution. Smith reminded Preble that the American squadron had multiple tasks – "for it is not only to overawe Tripoli, that the equipping of the squadron was incurred, but upon a calculation of its salutary effect upon the other Regencies and especially Tunis, whose unfriendly conduct might require its presence." Smith made the point that the administration expected Preble to be more aggressive

---

[76] Madison to Cathcart, 9 April 1803, *PJM-SS*, 4: 494-5; McKee, *Edward Preble*, p. 129; Irwin, *The Diplomatic Relations of the United States With the Barbary Powers*, p. 128. Fortunately for the United States, the Bey of Tunis rejected the terms – and Cathcart as consul. The Bey also repeated demands for a frigate. Allen, *Our Navy and the Barbary Corsairs*, p. 133.

[77] Wheelan, *Jefferson's War*, p. 136. A further defect of the frigates was that they were not equipped for bombarding enemy land fortifications, as only the largest (44-gun ships) carried long guns heavier than 18 pounders; their carronades, although of large caliber, were not suited to that purpose. Allen, *Our Navy and the Barbary Corsairs*, p. 137.

than his predecessor: "The conduct for sometime past pursued by our squadron in the Mediterranean has, unhappily, not been calculated to accomplish the object of the government nor to make a just impression upon the enemy of our national character." [78]

Second Phase: The Americans Take the Offensive

In the fall of 1803, Commodore Preble arrived in the Mediterranean determined to follow Smith's injunction to adopt a more aggressive strategy toward Tripoli, rather than to continue the passive approach of convoying merchant vessels and maintaining a distant blockade. Preble decided that the key to coercing Yusuf Pasha was to prevent Tripoli from carrying on its coastal trade and from deploying its corsairs, by denying those ships safe haven.[79] "If Tripoli does not make peace, I shall hazard much to destroy their vessels in port if I cannot meet them at sea. I shall endeavor to convince them their ports are not sufficient protection for them," he informed the Secretary of the Navy. Preble envisioned "distressing the coast" – that is, destroying the smaller ports through which Tripoli received many of its military supplies and from which Yusuf received much of his personal revenue. This campaign would drive most of the population of the smaller coastal towns into Tripoli, where they would strain the resources of the capital. Preble then planned to carry out the reduction of Tripoli by direct naval action.[80]

Or, even better, Preble hoped to use Hamet Pasha to capture rather than destroy those towns and roll up Tripoli from the land. "[Hamet] is now at Alexandria and has Arabs and mamelukes and wishes to march to the siege of Tripoli but is destitute of money, powder and field artillery," Preble informed Secretary Smith. "This he thinks with our assistance by sea would put him in possession of Tripoli; and I am certain that it would in less than two months. He promises perpetual peace & will give us hostages and allow us to hold the

---

[78] Madison to Lear, 6 June 1804, *PJM-SS*, 7: 287-8; Irwin, *The Diplomatic Relations of the United States With the Barbary Powers*, p. 142; Smith's orders in Wheelan, *Jefferson's War*, p. 209.

[79] Morris, at least for the record, had considered a similar approach. He said that he had planned to deploy the squadron off Tripoli in January 1803 and then attempt to burn the shipping in the harbor, but that the weather had prevented the operation. He claimed that he would have destroyed most, if not all, of the Tripolitan cruisers that spring had he been supplied rather than ordered home. At the very least, he said, the destruction of the cruisers would have prevented the molestation of American commerce for some time. Allen, *Our Navy and the Barbary Corsairs*, pp. 119-121; McKee, *Edward Preble*, p. 110; Murray Journal, 29 January 1803, *Naval Documents*, II: 350.

[80] Preble to Henry Dearborn, 9 August 1803, cited in McKee, *Edward Preble*, pp. 138-9; Preble to SecNav, 9 August 1803, *Naval Documents*, II: 508; Preble to Smith, 16 July 1803, cited in McKee, *Edward Preble*, pp. 130-1.

principal fort at the entrance of the harbor, plus release of all Christian prisoners. I wish earlier notice had been taken of this man and his views." Preble was "astonished the first and second squadron didn't compel peace" – he calculated that he faced ten times the Tripolitan force as had Dale and Morris. Even so, "if you will allow me one hundred thousand dollars in such additional naval force as I think proper, I will take Tripoli or perish in the attempt. I am confident it may easily be destroyed or taken in the summer with Gun & Mortar boats protected by our cruisers." Preble thought that word of the new American deployment, and the U.S. support of Hamet Pasha, might lead to a quick settlement of the war without further military action.[81]

In the event, Preble's campaign against Tripoli was delayed for the rest of the season when he was forced to deal with an emerging crisis in October 1803, just as he reached the western Mediterranean. He found that Moroccan corsairs were at sea with orders from the Governor of Tangier to open hostilities against the United States, even though the Emperor himself had not formally declared war. Several American merchant ships had been captured and the American consul, James Simpson, was in detention. Simpson informed Preble that the Moroccan goal was to replace the Treaty of 1786 with one that required the United States to pay tribute.

The unexpected presence of Preble's squadron preempted that plan. Preble insisted upon the release of the captured American merchantmen, the punishment of any Moroccan officials or sailors who had acted without the Emperor's permission, and the formal reaffirmation of the treaty of 1786 for the duration of the Emperor's reign. Preble lectured Moroccan officials on the value of American trade and argued that commercial advantages far outweighed anything they could hope to gain from war. If Morocco chose war, however, he made it clear that he was prepared "not only to destroy all their vessels, which would not require much of our force to do, but we should send ships and batter down every seaport town in the Empire." Preble was able to assemble a particularly impressive force – six warships of 168 guns – which included two frigates under the command of John Rodgers that were just about to rotate back to the United States. "The activity of the Squadron was equal to its unexpected appearance – Every Sea port in the Empire, from Mogador to Tituan, had or more [sic] cruisers off, to prevent the entrance or departure of any Vessels. . . . Our Frigates were drawn up to destroy his town, if he should determine on hostilities. The impression

---

[81] Paullin, *Diplomatic Negotiations of American Naval Officers*, pp. 72-3; Preble to SecNav, 17 January 1804, *Naval Documents*, III: 339; Preble to SecNav, 11 March 1804, *Naval Documents*, III: 485.

was strong," Tobias Lear noted from Tangier. American naval forces also seized several Moroccan ships, including the ubiquitous *Meshuda*, which they had caught trying to run the blockade of Tripoli. The Emperor now insisted that he knew nothing of the orders to capture American merchant ships. After Simpson supplied presents to senior officials to expedite the negotiations, the Emperor agreed to recognize the American blockade of Tripoli, to ratify the treaty of 1786, to release an American brig, and to punish the Governor. [82]

While Preble dealt with Morocco, any hopes for a cheap and quick settlement with Tripoli were dashed in October 1803 when the U.S. frigate *Philadelphia*, under the command of William Bainbridge, ran aground outside the port while attempting to chase down a blockade-runner. The crew failed to destroy the ship prior to its capture, and the Tripolitans soon managed to recover it intact. The stake of the war with Tripoli escalated dramatically. The Pasha now demanded $3,000,000 for peace and ransom of the *Philadelphia*'s complement, about 300 men in total. "Would to God, that the Officers and crew of the Philadelphia had, one and all, determined to prefer death to slavery; it is possible that such a determination might save them from either," Preble complained to the Secretary of the Navy. "If it had not been for the Capture of the *Philadelphia*, I have no doubt, but we should have had peace with Tripoli in the Spring; but now I have no hopes of such an event." [83]

Preble was particularly concerned that Algiers or Tunis would take advantage of the weakened psychological as well as military position of the United States. Reports circulated that Yusuf Pasha planned to sell the *Philadelphia* to one of those regencies. If the Americans tried to prevent the transfer, they would likely find themselves at war with yet another Barbary power and be labeled as the aggressor. The addition of an advanced American warship to one of the regencies threatened to tip an already uncertain naval balance against the United States. "The Barbary Powers are daily increasing their naval force," Preble reported to the Secretary of the Navy, "and will soon become powerful, if not seasonably checked." The Bey of Tunis, meanwhile, once again demanded indemnification for property confiscated by Americans during the blockade, under the threat of an immediate declara-

---

[82] Cited in McKee, *Edward Preble*, p. 152; Lear to Davis, 12 December 1803, *Naval Documents*, III: 265; Irwin, *The Diplomatic Relations of the United States With the Barbary Powers*, pp. 132-3; McKee, *Edward Preble*, pp. 139-59. The Governor of Tangier was eventually able to buy his way out of punishment by the Emperor. McKee, *Edward Preble*, p. 171.

[83] Preble to SecNav, 10 December 1803, *Naval Documents*, III: 256-7.

tion of war. A Tunisian minister told the U.S. consul that "the Americans are now like the ground."[84]

Preble was not in a position to undertake any comprehensive military campaign for some months, given the winter weather and the need to assemble the smaller craft for direct action against Tripoli. He did, however, take action to deal with the problem at hand. In January 1804, an American assault force, carried by a disguised merchant ship, burned the *Philadelphia* in Tripoli harbor. The American consul in Tunis, George Davis, reported that "the success of this enterprise added much to the reputation of the Navy, both at home and abroad." British Admiral Nelson called it "the most bold and daring act of the age." But in the short term, positions hardened on both sides. Before the destruction of the *Philadelphia*, the Tripolitan agent at Malta had suggested that the Pasha would agree to a ransom of $120,000 (after the Americans repatriated the 60-odd Tripolitan prisoners they held) and to an exchange of a schooner for the *Philadelphia*. Lear thought these terms better than the Jefferson administration had expected and advised their acceptance. Now, however, the Pasha refused to negotiate at all, reflecting his anger over the destruction of the *Philadelphia* and reports that the Americans had massacred some of the Tripolitan crew aboard the ship, an accusation that Preble indignantly denied. Lear authorized Preble to pay a ransom of $600 per man – on the order of $150,000-$180,000 – in addition to whatever costs might be associated with the formation of a new treaty.[85]

Preble consistently took a harder line on treaty terms than did Lear, who remained at his post in Algiers during most of this period. In June 1804, with campaign season approaching, Preble, with the assistance of former consul Richard O'Brien, offered a total settlement of $60,000: $40,000 in ransom, $10,000 to various public figures, and the equivalent of $10,000 in consular presents to be paid every ten years. Preble believed that Tripoli would likely have accepted Lear's more generous proposal but Preble thought that the United States would be mistaken offering those terms. They would merely stimulate the other Barbary regencies to

---

[84] Preble to SecNav, 11 March 1804, *Naval Documents*, III: 485; Irwin, *The Diplomatic Relations of the United States With the Barbary Powers*, p. 140; Davis to SecState, 28 December 1803, *PJM-SS*, 6: 238-9.

[85] Allen, *Our Navy and the Barbary Corsairs*, p. 173; Paullin, *Diplomatic Negotiations of American Naval Officers*, pp. 74-5; Wheelan, *Jefferson's War*, p. 198; Preble to Bainbridge, 12 March 1804, *Naval Documents*, III: 489; Irwin, *The Diplomatic Relations of the United States With the Barbary Powers*, p. 136. These secondary accounts differ somewhat in detail and the timing of proposals.

demand an upward revision of their arrangements with the United States. In any case, Yusuf Pasha rejected Preble's terms. The Pasha had recently concluded peace agreements with Holland and Denmark for $80,000 and $40,000, respectively, even though he held no citizens of those countries. Preble's offer was also well below that made by Commodore Morris before the Tripolitans captured the *Philadelphia*'s crew. Preble argued to his superiors that the presence of a reinforced American squadron changed matters greatly. The United States, he said, should insist now on concessionary terms from Tripoli or press the matter home militarily. Preble was particularly insistent that the United States should never pay tribute; it would only stimulate the avarice of the other regencies and probably lead to a new outbreak of piracy.[86]

The possibility of international cooperation was renewed when Robert R. Livingston, the outgoing American Minister in Paris, sought Napoleon's good offices to mediate affairs with Tripoli. (The U.S. representative in Russia, Levitt Harris, made the same request of the Tsar.) Talleyrand, the French Foreign Minister, told Livingston that he had instructed the French consul at Tripoli, Beaussier, to aid the American prisoners and, if possible, secure their freedom. When Beaussier quoted a higher price for ransom and peace than Preble had received from other sources – first, $250,000, then $500,000 – Preble decided that the consul was working against American interests and decided to hold the negotiations strictly in American hands, insofar as possible. Preble also heard that the Spanish consul arranged for Spanish carpenters to build gunboats for the Pasha. He concluded that all the foreign representatives, except the Danish consul, Nissen, were working against the United States because they feared that settlement with America would cause the Pasha to unleash his corsairs on their commerce.[87]

The Jefferson administration was irritated when it received word of these diplomatic initiatives. Madison, in his instructions to the new Minister to France, John Armstrong, stated firmly that "it was certainly better in all cases that our own objects be effected by our own means, than that resort should be

---

[86] Paullin, *Diplomatic Negotiations of American Naval Officers*, pp. 72, 78-80; Irwin, *The Diplomatic Relations of the United States With the Barbary Powers*, p. 137; Preble to SecNav, 17 January 1804, *Naval Documents*, III: 339.

[87] Irwin, *The Diplomatic Relations of the United States With the Barbary Powers*, pp. 136-8; Allen, *Our Navy and the Barbary Corsairs*, p. 180. Preble did not rule out any foreign assistance: "Would it not do for the Interest of our Country to have a Minister Plenipotentiary or Ambassador at the Ottoman Porte? Such a character might influence the Grand Seignior to guarantee our treaties with the Barbary Powers, and they would then never dare to infringe them." Preble to SecNav, 11 March 1804, *Naval Documents*, III: 485.

had to the favor of other powers, and happily there is reason to expect that the means now provided for the existing case will be sufficient." [88]

Preble's Campaign

With the diplomatic track stalled, Preble prepared for an active campaign against Tripoli. He obtained from the King of the Two Sicilies, six gun boats and two bomb-vessels – partially crewed with Neapolitan sailors and gunners – and he mounted longer-range guns aboard the *Constitution*. He also took steps to see that the other regencies remained quiet so that he could turn his full attention to Tripoli. The American consuls had reported a direct correlation between the length of time between port visits by U.S. warships and the size and frequency of demands by their rulers. Preble made a point of bringing part of the squadron periodically before Tunis, the regency most likely to engage in an opportunistic corsair campaign against American shipping. He and Davis concluded that they could deter the Tunisians successfully because of the substantial American presence in the Mediterranean, a shortage of grain, and the fact that the Bey was occupied with war against Naples. Davis also reported that Tunis was waiting to see the outcome of the impending attack on Tripoli. He thought it imperative that these operations be successful in order to establish America's reputation – "It must be dreadful to Barbary." Tobias Lear sent a message to William Bainbridge, still captive in Tripoli, which Lear obviously intended to be passed on to Tripolitan officials. "We are a Nation different from all others, we are now powerful, if we choose to exert our strength; and we are rising rapidly to a great pitch of importance, while most other nations, which are now here, are at their full growth, or on the decline." [89]

Preble opened his campaign on August 3, 1804 with a bombardment of the town and attack on the Tripolitan gunboats. He followed this strike with another daylight strike and three night attacks over the next three weeks. The pauses were caused by bad weather and the need to reassemble the ships, assess the damage, and plan the next attack. Preble's operational objective seems to have been to negate the harbor's defenses – the gunboats, fortifications and defensive batteries – so that he could operate his own forces with impunity and destroy, or at least hold at risk, the merchant shipping and

---

[88] Madison to Armstrong, 15 July 1804, *PJM-SS*, 7: 453-4; Irwin, *The Diplomatic Relations of the United States With the Barbary Powers*, p. 138.

[89] Allen, *Our Navy and the Barbary Corsairs*, pp. 182, 219; Irwin, *The Diplomatic Relations of the United States With the Barbary Powers*, p. 142; Wheelan, *Jefferson's War*, p. 202; Lear to Bainbridge, 28 August 1804, *Naval Documents*, IV: 471.

corsair vessels in the port. Preble may also have hoped that the shock of the attack alone would persuade the Pasha to settle, or perhaps trigger a revolt against his rule. Preble tried several different methods of attack on the port itself. He did not have the time or resources to destroy the smaller port cities first, as he had initially planned. Nor had he been able to arrange to engage Hamet Pasha in the campaign.

The Americans enjoyed some clear successes, including the capture or destruction of three Tripolitan gunboats in hand-to-hand fighting. This was regarded as a signal success for America's fighting reputation, as Christian navies were regarded as having superior seamen and gunners, while the corsairs supposedly held the edge in personal combat. "Some Turks died like men," one officer reported, "but most behaved like women." An American gunboat was destroyed with considerable loss of life, however; a final attempt to damage or destroy the port by sailing a fire ship into the harbor failed when the American vessel blew up prematurely, taking most of its crew with it. Preble was never able to force the Tripolitan gunboats to engage outside the protection of the port's batteries. American counter-fire put some of those cannons out of commission but the defensive fortifications remained largely intact. Most of the shells from the mortar boats, at least early in the campaign, did not explode, apparently because of their poor quality. In mid-September 1804, Preble broke off the campaign. Deteriorating weather and low ammunition meant that he could no longer use the gunboats and mortar ketches. His own ships were operating at the limits of their crews and provisions.[90]

During the operational pauses, Preble continued to negotiate by various indirect means with Yusuf Pasha. After the first attack, which he hoped had demonstrated the seriousness of America's intent, Preble renewed his previous offer – a $60,000 package, including ransom but no tribute. He warned that four new American frigates were expected to join the squadron momentarily. Preble claimed that he would then agree to no payment whatsoever and would dispatch a frigate to Alexandria to bring Hamet Pasha to the scene. "I am convinced by what I have already seen, that we can reduce Tripoli to a heap of Ruins: the destruction of Derne & Benghazi will follow, and the blockade will be constantly continued, unless the present terms are accepted," Preble informed Beaussier, the French consul in Tripoli. Yusuf Pasha did not reply.[91]

---

[90] This account based on Allen, *Our Navy and the Barbary Corsairs*, pp. 192-7.

[91] Paullin, *Diplomatic Negotiations of American Naval Officers*, p. 81; Preble to Beaussier, 11 August 1804, *Naval Documents*, IV: 397-8.

Commodore Preble – perhaps influenced by the news that Captain James Barron would soon replace him as squadron commander – later increased his offer to $90,000 and then to $120,000, including ransom and presents. The Pasha reduced his demands to $150,000. Preble refused to go that high. Although the difference seemed relatively insignificant, Preble consistently held to the view that $150,000 exceeded the threshold at which the other regencies would demand changes to their treaties. (Had Tobias Lear been on the scene, he likely would have recommended or even ordered Preble to settle on those terms.) The Pasha, apparently growing in confidence that he could withstand the assault, eventually raised his demands to $400,000. The French consul reported that Yusuf had sworn "to encounter all your forces in Order that Europe & Africa may conceive a favorable opinion of his strength & courage." [92]

During the attacks, Preble received mixed reports on the damage the Americans had inflicted on Tripoli and its defenses. The captain of a Spanish merchant ship who had been in the town during the bombardment reported that the second attack had wreaked "great havoc and destruction" and killed "a vast number." Beaussier, on the other hand, reported that the American bombardments had little effect. More importantly, this was the view of Nissen, the Danish consul, whom the Americans regarded as a friendly and reliable source. "On the whole bombardment & cannonade, have not had an effect sufficient to force the Bashaw, who, don't care much about his Town or his Subject's life." The foreign consuls all agreed that Preble had made a serious error in making settlement offers in between attacks. "The Bashaw takes it as a necessity for peace & grows more obstinate," Nissen concluded. "After every attack, there has been the next day a flag of truce – this is no good policy towards an Enemy as Tripoli." Preble would have been better off, Nissen argued, had he continued the attacks without pause and forced Yusuf Pasha to make the first offer. (Preble, given his limited ability to assess battle damage and his uncertainty about the Pasha's mindset, may have adopted this fight-and-talk course as the only way of gaining intelligence about what types of attacks were having the most effect on Yusuf.) [93]

Bainbridge, who was able to communicate surreptitiously with the American squadron from his prison in Tripoli, was another important source

---

[92] Irwin, *The Diplomatic Relations of the United States With the Barbary Powers*, pp. 138-9; Allen, *Our Navy and the Barbary Corsairs*, pp. 181-97, 217; Wheelan, *Jefferson's War*, pp. 222-4.

[93] Wheelan, *Jefferson's War*, p. 221; Nissen to Davis, 1 September 1804, *Naval Documents*, IV: 495.

of intelligence. He had long been skeptical of Preble's plan to coerce Tripoli solely with naval force. The city itself, he argued, was too well fortified to be forced to submit by bombardment alone (by chance, Bainbridge himself was nearly killed when an American shell struck near his living quarters). Bainbridge argued that the city was vulnerable only to attack by land, and that the deployment of three or four thousand U.S. troops would be necessary to force the Pasha to capitulate. Bainbridge did favor continuing to bombard Tripoli at night. Such harassing fire might drive the inhabitants into the country and encourage the Pasha to accept more moderate terms, even if not all those that the United States had sought.[94]

The Final Phase: The Regime Change Option

In early autumn 1804, Commodore Barron officially relieved Preble. He commanded an expanded naval force and received orders to prosecute the counter-piracy campaign with still greater vigor. The Jefferson administration made the decision for further military escalation after receiving news of the capture of the Philadelphia, and well before Preble engaged in the first direct attacks against Tripoli.

> . . . the President immediately determined to put in commission and send to the Mediterranean a force which would be able, beyond the possibility of a doubt, to coerce the enemy to a peace on terms compatible with our honor and our interest. A due regard to our situation with Tripoli, and precautionary considerations in relation to the other Barbary powers, demanded that our forces in that quarter should be so augmented as to leave no doubt of our compelling the existing enemy to submit to our own terms, and of effectually checking any hostile dispositions that might be entertained towards us by any of the other Barbary powers.[95]

The Secretary of the Navy acknowledged to Barron that the forces under Preble's command had not been adequate to these multiple tasks, but "with this force it is conceived that no doubt whatever can exist of your coercing Tripoli to a Treaty upon our own Terms and of your preventing the effects of hostile dispositions which may be entertained towards us on the part of any other of the Barbary Powers." The following summer, when the entire force was assembled, Barron would have available at least thirty-one

---

[94] Allen, *Our Navy and the Barbary Corsairs*, p. 170; Wheelan, *Jefferson's War*, p. 202.

[95] SecNav to Preble, 22 May 1804, cited in Allen, *Our Navy and the Barbary Corsairs*, pp. 198-9.

ships: six frigates, four brigs, two schooners, one sloop, two bomb-vessels, and sixteen gunboats.[96]

Madison also toughened Lear's negotiating instructions by returning to the original U.S. position of no tribute. In view of the strong force under Barron's command, the Jefferson administration now believed that it should effect peace "without any price or pecuniary compensation whatever." Lear was authorized to make a one-time purchase of peace and the payment of ransom only in case of adverse events, such as an accident to the squadron or hostilities on the part of other Barbary powers. The administration, once it received reports of the American naval campaign against Tripoli of August-September 1804, concluded that the American bargaining position had been further strengthened. "The possibility of any considerable sacrifices being necessary should be considered as diminished by the spirited attack made on the enemy of Commodore Preble, and the comparison which will naturally be made of their effect, with what may be expected from a repetition of them when the season opens, with equal animation on a larger scale."[97]

The Jefferson administration was also more open to the option of supporting Hamet Pasha, at least as an adjunct to the American strategy of coercing Yusuf into abandoning the war. William Eaton returned to the region with Barron's squadron as the newly-designated Navy Agent to the Barbary regencies, with authority to deal with Hamet. Eaton had consistently maintained that a ground campaign would be necessary to deal with Tripoli. If the United States was not prepared to conduct a substantial amphibious attack itself, it must use Hamet to recruit local troops for that purpose. But was the United States prepared to go so far as to support Hamet's efforts to overthrow Yusuf? Secretary Smith's instructions to Barron were predictably vague: "With respect to the ex-Bashaw of Tripoli, we have no objection to your availing yourself of his co-operation with you against Tripoli, if you shall, upon a full view of the subject, consider his co-operation expedient. The subject is committed entirely to your discretion." At the same time, Barron was informed that Lear was "invested by the President with full power and authority to negotiate a treaty of peace with the Bashaw of Tripoli" – which indicated the administration had limited objectives that stopped short of the overthrow of Yusuf. Madison authorized Lear to spend up to $20,000 on the Hamet Pasha

---

[96] SecNav to Barron, 6 June 1804, *Naval Documents,* IV: 152-3; Irwin, *The Diplomatic Relations of the United States With the Barbary Powers,* p. 157.

[97] Madison to Lear, 6 June 1804, cited in Allen, *Our Navy and the Barbary Corsairs,* p. 254; Madison to Lear, 20 April 1805, *ASPFR,* II: 702.

project, but he added that the primary instrument of pressure was to be the U.S. naval force, which should be "sufficient for any exercise of coercion which the obstinacy of the Bashaw may demand." [98]

Barron found that it was too late to do more than blockade Tripoli briefly in 1804 before he took up winter quarters. He deployed two or three ships to maintain a distant blockade of the port. The frigate USS *Essex* was stationed at Gibraltar to monitor events in Morocco because the Emperor continued to make noises that the Americans interpreted as part of a design by the regencies to divert American warships away from Tripoli. Barron began his initial planning for a resumption of naval attacks on Tripoli during the coming summer. [99]

Eaton, meanwhile, actively pursued the second-front, regime-change option. He persuaded Barron to support a ground campaign conducted under the auspices of Hamet Pasha. "Bringing Hamet forward with all his influence," Eaton explained to the Secretary of the Navy, would aid Barron's efforts by "intercept[ing] the supplies of the Enemy and to cut[ing] off his escape in the rear." Eaton traveled to Egypt to meet Hamet, who was engaged in fighting with the Mamelukes then in rebellion against Turkish authorities. Eaton reported that Yusuf Pasha's agents encouraged the Turks to prevent Hamet from being allowed to return. "The subjects of Tripoli were getting weary of the war with these new infidels," Eaton quoted the agents as saying. "They could not learn from their movement their intentions, and were attacked unaware: the Bashaw [Yusuf] believed he could resist them with his batteries; but if they made a descent with his brother, his people would all leave him." [100]

Eaton's original idea had been to convoy Hamet by ship directly to Tripoli. He decided instead to conduct an overland march with Hamet's forces across the desert to Bomba, where the troops would be supplied by the U.S. Navy, and move on to take Derne, the town where Hamet had once been governor. Hamet assured Eaton that he continued to have much local support there. In exchange for American participation in his campaign against Yusuf, Hamet agreed to a Convention extraordinarily favorable to the United States. Hamet promised upon resuming his station in Tripoli

---

[98] SecNav to Barron, 6 June 1804, *ASPFR*, II: 702; see also Madison to Lear, 6 June 1804, cited in Allen, *Our Navy and the Barbary Corsairs*, pp. 254, 259; Madison to Lear, 20 April 1805, *ASPFR*, II: 702, says those instructions still hold.

[99] Allen, *Our Navy and the Barbary Corsairs*, p. 219; Paullin, *Diplomatic Negotiations of American Naval Officers*, pp. 82-3.

[100] Eaton to SecNav, 9 August 1805, *Naval Documents*, IV: 213-8.

to indemnify the United States for the war, release all American prisoners without ransom, and conclude a permanent treaty with the United States that involved no tribute. A secret article committed Hamet to hand over Yusuf and Murad Reis to the Americans. Eaton was given title of general and commander in chief of the invasion force. [101]

Eaton's march across the desert with a motley collection of Moors, Arabs, adventurers of other ethnicities, and a few U.S. Marines soon became part of American folklore. Eaton overcame repeated threats of mutiny and desertion (some of which came from Hamet himself), and shortages of food, water and military supplies to reach Derne in late April 1805. It was a trek worthy of Lawrence of Arabia. Several U.S. warships supported the attack against that town, which fell on April 27. The expeditionary force fought off several counterattacks from forces dispatched from Tripoli by Yusuf Pasha. Eaton thought that the expedition was on the verge of success. He wanted Barron to resupply Hamet's forces so that they could press immediately on to seize Benghazi, 100 miles away. Once that attack succeeded, U.S. warships could carry the army the last 400 miles to Tripoli itself. [102]

Commodore Barron, remote from the scene at Malta and suffering from a serious illness, was not nearly as sanguine. That winter he had been persuaded by Eaton's enthusiasm to support the overland campaign but he had become alarmed at reports from his officers about the difficulties that accompanied the dealings with Hamet. Yusuf, meanwhile, sent signals of his serious intention to negotiate. Through the agency of Nissen, Sidi Mohammad Dghies, who had been opposed to the war from the beginning, said that peace could probably be bought at $120,000, the figure which Preble had earlier proposed. Dghies said he was strongly in favor of peace, partly because his private fortune had suffered from the war – an indication that the commercial interests in Tripoli might now be willing to pressure Yusuf for a settlement. Bainbridge also predicted that Yusuf could be brought down to $120,000. According to Bainbridge's sources, the Pasha did fear that the United States would mount an even more serious naval attack against Tripoli in 1805. But if the attack did not meet those

---

[101] Wheelan, *Jefferson's War*, p. 251. Hamet pledged to use the tribute of Denmark, Sweden and the Batavian Republic to compensate the United States.

[102] Wheelan, *Jefferson's War*, p. 245. American officials typically used the term "Moors" and "Arabs" at various times to describe various ethnic groups, with little attempt to make precise distinctions.

expectations, Bainbridge warned, the price of peace would undoubtedly be ratcheted back up. [103]

Barron and Lear interpreted these signals from Yusuf as reflecting recognition of his growing weakness, especially given Tripoli's economic difficulties (grain was known to be scarce) and Yusuf's concern with internal threats other than Hamet. Yusuf was reported to have detained relatives of the senior officers who had been dispatched to the relief of Derne, to ensure their loyalty while away from the town. But the prospect of Hamet's campaign was also a mixed blessing to the American cause. It increased pressure on Yusuf but it also ran the risk of hardening his terms and provoking a serious retaliation. "The Bashaw is now very attentive upon your transactions with his brother . . ." Nissen informed the Americans. "Give me leave to tell you that I have found your plan with the Bashaw's brother very vast, and that you sacrifice your prisoners' lives here in case of success." Bainbridge concurred. Yusuf told Bainbridge directly that if the Americans continued to support his brother, he would strike the United States "in the most tender part." When news of the fall of Derne reached Tripoli, Yusuf convened his council, the Divan, announcing to them that he wished to execute the American prisoners. [104]

The Americans on the scene thus faced a critical choice. Barron decided that the Convention that Eaton signed with Hamet was inconsistent with his instructions because it seemed to preclude a negotiated settlement with Yusuf Pasha. "You must be sensible, Sir, that in giving their sanction to a cooperation with the exiled Bashaw, [the] Government did not contemplate the measure as leading necessarily and absolutely to a reinstatement of that Prince in his rights on the regency of Tripoli," Barron chided Eaton. Once the peace was signed, he insisted, "our support to Hamet Bashaw must necessarily be withdrawn." Barron thought that the overland expedition had already reached the point of diminishing returns. Eaton's request for resources to carry on went far beyond the approved level of $20,000. If Hamet's pretensions to rule – and his claims of popular support – were to be taken seriously, he should be able to sustain himself with nothing more than limited U.S. naval support. "They [the

---

[103] Allen, *Our Navy and the Barbary Corsairs*, p. 248; Bainbridge to Davis, 27 January 1805, *ASPFR, II: 703*.

[104] Lear to Madison, 5 July 1805, cited in Irwin, *The Diplomatic Relations of the United States With the Barbary Powers*, pp. 150-1; Bainbridge to Davis, 27 January 1805, *ASPFR*, II: 703; Wheelan, *Jefferson's War*, pp. 246, 267, 289.

U.S. government] appear to have viewed the cooperation in question as a means, which, provided there existed energy and enterprise in the Exile, and attachment to his person on the part of his former subjects, [he] might be employed to the common furtherance and advantage of his claims and of our cause, but without meaning to fetter themselves by any specific or definite attainment *as an end,* as the tenor of my instructions . . . and the limited sum appropriated for that special purpose, clearly demonstrate." The point of no return, Barron told Eaton, was Derne. Hamet, according to reports reaching Barron, was barely able to maintain control of that town, much less recruit and supply his own army. [105]

Eaton argued vehemently that Barron was applying the wrong standards in judging Hamet. Poor harvests, the American blockade of Tripoli, and years of heavy taxation by Yusuf had left few resources for either brother to call upon. Absent American support, Hamet could only raise money by adopting draconian measures that were sure to alienate the population, just as Yusuf had done. The United States could tip the balance decisively – and gain considerable future influence over the new ruler of Tripoli – if it provided ready cash and military supplies at this critical moment. The Arab troops especially were at the disposal of the highest bidder – "poor, avaricious, accustomed to despotism, [they] are therefore generally indifferent about the name or person of their despot, provided he imposes no new burdens." Eaton believed he could easily raise an army of 20-30,000 Arabs and Moors. If this force successfully marched on Tripoli and installed Hamet, this example of American-sponsored regime change would reverberate throughout the region and "would very probably be a death blow to the Barbary system." America's reputation as well as its interest was now at stake. If the United States betrayed Hamet, it would dishonor itself in a culture that valued honor (at least in principle), and would weaken its long-term position in the region by eliminating or alienating those forces of opposition that might in the future become assets for the United States with the other regencies. [106]

---

[105] Wheelan, *Jefferson's War,* pp. 290ff; Barron to Eaton, 22 March 1805, cited in Allen, *Our Navy and the Barbary Corsairs,* p. 260. See also John Quincy Adams' record of conversation with Barron the following year in Washington: "Barron says Eaton had no authority; when he learned of the commitment he decided to support him until he got to Derne with full warning that after that he must maintain himself at his own risk and on his own strength. But when he got there he was as impotent as before – utterly unable to maintain himself a moment or to be of the smallest use to us." Charles Francis Adams, ed., *Memoirs of John Quincy Adams* (Philadelphia: J.B. Lippincott, 1874), 2: 429-30. Diary entry for 6 April 1806.

[106] Eaton to SecNav, 13 February 1805, *ASPFR,* II: 704; Wheelan, *Jefferson's War,* pp. 292, 312; Allen, *Our Navy and the Barbary Corsairs,* pp. 232, 242.

The deciding voice in the matter was the American consul general, Tobias Lear. Lear had long been an opponent of any sort of cooperation with Hamet; he thought that the man had little ability or influence. If the Americans did succeed in installing Hamet in Tripoli by the force of arms, they would find themselves allied with an unpopular and incapable ruler, the worst possible combination. A deal with Yusuf, on the other hand, was much more likely to stick. "I should place much more confidence in the continuation of peace with the present bashaw, if he is well beaten into it, than I should with the other, if he should be placed on the throne by our means," Lear argued. In fact, Lear doubted that Hamet himself really posed a threat to Yusuf – it was the presence of the small American contingent with Hamet and the supplies that the United States could provide the rebels, which had truly alarmed Yusuf. "I found that the heroic bravery of our few countrymen at Derne, and the idea that we had a large force and immense supplies at that place, had made a deep impression on the Bashaw." But whatever the case, Barron (just before he relinquished command of the American squadron due to his illness) and Lear agreed that the time was ripe to open direct negotiations with Tripoli. Barron refused to provide Eaton with any further military supplies for a campaign beyond Derne and offered him only limited naval support. [107]

Lear proceeded to Tripoli in late May and, through the agency of Nissen, began discussions on a settlement. The U.S. assault squadron remained over the horizon to provide coercive leverage in the negotiations. According to Nissen, the Pasha acknowledged that he was defeated and that the American squadron in the Mediterranean was sufficient to reduce Tripoli. [108] Yusuf, however, threatened to abandon the town along with his American prisoners and retire to the interior, where he would continue resistance. The Pasha gave up his demand for a payment for peace and reduced his ransom requirements to $130,000. Lear countered with what amounted to an ultimatum: a ransom payment of $60,000 and the delivery of 81 Tripolitan prisoners held by the United States, in exchange for the crew of the *Philadelphia*. The United States would offer no tribute although it was understood that America would observe the custom of giving a present (not exceeding $6,000) upon the appearance of a new consul. In the event of a future war between the United States and Tripoli,

---

[107] Wheelan, *Jefferson's War*, p. 273; Lear to Eaton, 6 June 1805, *ASPFR*, II: 715.

[108] It is certainly possible that Nissen phrased Yusuf Pasha's views on the war in a way he felt most likely to promote a settlement.

prisoners would not be enslaved and would be exchanged without ransom at the conclusion of peace or with payment based on a fixed exchange rate if one side held more prisoners than the other. [109]

The new treaty made no reference to a special role for Algiers. The Pasha also insisted on an article to the effect that American troops would be withdrawn from Derne and U.S. pressure would be placed on Hamet to withdraw his pretensions. Lear asked in return that Yusuf commit formally to restore Hamet's family to him – but Lear also agreed to a secret clause that gave the Pasha four years to do so. Lear did not convey this qualification to Washington (at least not officially), which later caused considerable embarrassment when it became public in the United States. [110] The Treaty also contained an article, following on that of the Treaty of 1797, which attempted to remove the religious dimension from the relationship between the regimes (at least from the standpoint of the United States):

> Article 14 (in English translation). As the Government of the United States of America, has in itself no character of enmity against the Laws, Religion or Tranquility of Musselmen, and as the said States never have entered into any voluntary war or act of hostility against any Mahometan Nation, except in the defence of their just rights to freely navigate the High Seas: It is declared by the contracting parties that no pretext arising from Religious

---

[109] Treaty of Peace and Amity between the United States of America and the Bashaw, Bey and Subjects of Tripoli in Barbary, Article 16 (in English translation; text of the treaty at http://avalon.law.yale.edu/19th_century/bar1805t.asp): "If in the fluctuation of Human Events, a War should break out between the two Nations; The Prisoners captured by either party shall not be made Slaves; but shall be exchanged Rank for Rank; and if there should be a deficiency on either side, it shall be made up by the payment of Five Hundred Spanish Dollars for each Captain, Three Hundred Dollars for each Mate and Supercargo and One hundred Spanish Dollars for each Seaman so wanting. And it is agreed that Prisoners shall be exchanged in twelve months from the time of their capture, and that this Exchange may be effected by any private Individual legally authorized by either of the parties."

[110] Article 3, in English translation: "All the forces of the United States which have been, or may be in hostility against the Bashaw of Tripoli, in the Province of Derne, or elsewhere within the Dominions of the said Bashaw shall be withdrawn therefrom, and no supplies shall be given by or in behalf of the said United States, during the continuance of this peace, to any of the Subjects of the said Bashaw, who may be in hostility against him in any part of his Dominions; And the Americans will use all means in their power to persuade the Brother of the said Bashaw, who has co-operated with them at Derne &c, to withdraw from the Territory of the said Bashaw of Tripoli; but they will not use any force or improper means to effect that object; and in case he should withdraw himself as aforesaid, the Bashaw engages to deliver up to him, his Wife and Children now in his powers." American consul George Davis succeeded in bringing about a reunion of Hamet with his family in 1807. Irwin, *The Diplomatic Relations of the United States With the Barbary Powers*, p. 159. In 1806, apparently unaware of the secret understanding, Jefferson's Cabinet had considered restoring the blockade to force the release of Hamet's family. Wheelan, *Jefferson's War*, p. 326.

Opinions, shall ever produce an interruption of the Harmony existing between the two Nations; And the Consuls and Agents of both Nations respectively, shall have liberty to exercise his Religion in his own house; all slaves of the same Religion shall not be Impeded in going to said Consuls house at hours of Prayer. The Consuls shall have liberty and personal security given them to travel within the Territories of each other, both by land and sea, and shall not be prevented from going on board any Vessel that they may think proper to visit; they shall have likewise the liberty to appoint their own Dragomen and Brokers.

The new commander of the U.S. squadron, John Rodgers, informed Eaton that a peace had been signed and ordered him to remove himself and the small American contingent from Derne. Eaton reluctantly complied. The Americans and Hamet were evacuated by the U.S. Navy, leaving Hamet's furious Arab tribal allies and the citizens of Derne to make the best of the situation.

Addendum: Maintaining Deterrence in the Absence of Regime Change

The settlement with Tripoli was an essential but not decisive point in the American campaign to establish a stable and favorable treaty structure with the Barbary regencies without pursuing a strategy of regime change. The United States still had to deal with outstanding problems with the other regencies, especially Tunis. For the moment, at least, the United States had a surplus of military capabilities in the region to apply to the problem. Commodore Rodgers was determined to take advantage of that situation before the inevitable drawdown of U.S. forces took place when the administration and Congress became aware of the peace with Tripoli.

The Bey of Tunis had never recognized the American blockade of Tripoli and, in the spring of 1805, threatened to declare war over the disposition of three Tunisian-flagged ships that had been captured by the blockading forces. Rodgers deployed the main American squadron off Tunis in August 1805. He was accompanied by Lear, despite the Bey's previous insistence that he would not make a treaty with any American consul general. The Bey initially took a hard line; he complained that the appearance of the squadron was provocative and demanded its withdrawal. The Bey insisted that he would not be treated as Tripoli had been. "Europe shall never say that half a dozen frigates have overawed a prince who has kept in subjection such superior powers," he told the American consul, George Davis. If he submitted to a second-rate power like the Americans, how could he expect to be treated by more powerful states? He insisted that "never while I have a soldier to fire a gun will I accord peace." Davis told Rodgers and Lear that he was uncertain about the Bey's intentions. On the one hand, his pride might push him to extreme measures now that he had been confronted directly by the Americans. On the other hand, the general famine along the Barbary Coast, and the associated prospect of civil disorder in his realm, might incline him to peace. The Bey acknowledged to Davis that these latter factors had hitherto restrained him from sending out his cruisers against the United States.[111]

Rodgers felt he was in a strong position to compel Tunis to affirm its pacific relationship with the United States. He demanded a written promise to abide by the terms of the Treaty of 1796. If the Bey did not comply, Rodgers threatened to place the regency under immediate blockade. Rodgers later wrote that he believed the American force "was sufficient, in ten days, to have made him call for mercy on his bended knees." Rodgers made this threat even though he did not have positive instructions from his superiors to coerce Tunis. He told Lear that he understood that he ran the risk of being disavowed by Washington. When the Bey tested American resolve by attempting to sail a merchant vessel out of the harbor, the U.S. squadron turned it back with gunfire. The Bey then agreed to enter into negotiations with Lear. He disavowed all threats against the United States, granted most favored nation trading status, and offered to send his own envoy to the United States to negotiate the disposition of the captured Tunisian ships. He also dropped his long-standing demand that the United States provide him with a frigate and assured Lear that he would keep the peace with the United States until the return of his ambassador.[112]

Rodgers took considerable satisfaction in the outcome. "I think I can almost with certainty say that he never will again attempt to behave in a similar manner, as I feel satisfied this lesson has not only changed his opinion of our Maritime strength, but has caused him to discover more distinctly his weakness in every sense," he wrote to the Secretary of the Navy. "If the government decides to chastise him, provided that intention is made known to me by March 1 [1806], before the ensuing September I will not only obtain an honorable peace but make him pay the expenses of

---

[111] Lear to Madison, *ASPFR*, II: 718; various other quotes in Allen, *Our Navy and the Barbary Corsairs*, p. 268; Paullin, *Diplomatic Negotiations of American Naval Officers*, pp. 92-3; Irwin, *The Diplomatic Relations of the United States With the Barbary Powers*, pp. 161-2.

[112] Cited by Paullin, *Diplomatic Negotiations of American Naval Officers*, p. 95; Allen, *Our Navy and the Barbary Corsairs*, p. 269.

the war, and this too with no more force than what remains this winter in the Mediterranean." [113]

The Debate Over the Settlement With Tripoli

The Jefferson administration had no interest in fighting another war in the Mediterranean. It quickly embraced the settlement with Tripoli obtained by Lear and welcomed negotiations with the Tunisian envoy. The United States, by the President's calculations, had now successfully protected American commerce and resisted the demands of an ambitious, predatory entity in a way that discouraged future compensatory claims by the other regencies. Yusuf Pasha had obtained nothing like his maximum demands. He committed himself to a relationship that was much closer to the Western ideal of proper state-to-state relations: no tribute, no future ransom, and most favored nation trading ties. The United States, having established a credible deterrent relationship with the other regencies during the war with Tripoli, and having recently reinforced its position with Tunis, had laid the groundwork for a more defensible and stable treaty structure.

Lear's settlement with Tripoli, however, immediately became the source of considerable controversy in the United States. Jefferson's political opponents claimed that the United States had squandered the decisive political-military advantages which it obtained over Yusuf. America, they said, far from paying ransom, should have obtained an indemnity for war expenses and other concessions from Tripoli. The United States had acted dishonorably in its treatment of Hamet Pasha by failing to follow through on its promised support for regime change. America should have pressed its advantages much further with the other regencies, particularly Algiers, to eliminate that tributary relationship. These criticisms harkened back to the 1800-1801 maximalist proposals of the American Barbary consuls. Prominent Federalists such as Fisher Ames of Massachusetts argued that Jefferson's willingness to compromise with Yusuf, rather than to fight on to victory, signaled unmistakable weakness to Napoleon, whom the Federalists regarded as the greatest threat to U.S. security and Western civilization:

> Would Buonaparte calculate on the vigor of our government, as an insuperable obstacle to his military attempt on the United States? Would the congress majority, like a Roman senate, create means and employ them, with a spirit that would prefer death to servitude or tribute? The French Hannibal, surely, with our fifteen millions

---

[113] Cited by Allen, *Our Navy and the Barbary Corsairs*, pp. 269-70.

of tribute money already in his treasury, would have no discouraging fear of this sort. When he reads our treaty with Tripoli, by which it appears, that we chose tribute, when victory was within our reach; when he sees that the bey of Tunis presumes to say, by his minister at Washington, pay or fight, what can Buonaparte conclude, but that honor is a name, and in America an empty one; and that our national spirit can never be roused to a higher pitch, than to make a calculation. With us honor is a coin, whose very baseness confines it at home for a currency. Such a people, he will say, are degraded, before they are subdued. They are too abject to be classed or employed among my martial slaves. Let them toil to feed their masters, and to replenish my treasury with tribute. [114]

William Eaton, not surprisingly, was first and foremost among the post-war critics of Jefferson. After he returned to the United States, Eaton publicly challenged Lear's disparagement of the strategic leverage provided by Hamet Pasha and his threat of regime change, as well as Lear's willingness to settle at the expense of American honor. "What rendered the moment highly favorable to peace?" Eaton asked. It was not the American naval squadron under Commodore Barron, which had exhibited no visible preparations to engage Tripoli. "Nor was it 100 Christians on a coast left totally destitute of supplies. ... No it was the dread of revolution moved by Hamet Bashaw being brought to his capital through our assistance that made the impression on the enemy." As to Lear's observation that the United States should make peace with the man best able to keep it: "If parricide, fatracide, [sic] treason, perfidy to treaty, already experienced and systematic piracy are characteristic guarantees of good faith Mr. Lear has chosen the fittest of the two brothers [Yusuf] for his confidence: Their ability to keep the peace is less essential than our ability to keep it, undoubtedly nothing but terror would bind either of them nor any other Barbary chief to a faith[ful] observance of treaty stipulation."

Lear, in Eaton's opinion, had completely missed one critical point. "Our negotiation ought however to have considered that Hamet Bashaw's was the popular cause and that this is fast gaining ground in Barbary – It was the cause of Liberty and freedom." At the very least Lear should have waited for favorable naval weather and for further orders from the United States before he cut short the regime change option. As to the Pasha's threat to execute the American prisoners, Yusuf had issued the same warning before Preble

---

[114] Fisher Ames, "Dangerous Power of France," *Repertory*, May 1806, in William B. Allen, ed., *Works of Fisher Ames, as Published by Seth Ames* (Indianapolis, IN: Liberty Classics, 1983), I: 337.

attacked Tripoli but never carried out that threat. "On the contrary when ever that determined officer approached his walls after the first attack the terrible bashaw's first care was to provide for his own safety and he uniformly took refuge in his gardens or in his Bomb-proof and all experience has taught us that the more roughly he was handled and the nearer danger approached him the more tractable he has been rendered . . . " Eaton excoriated Lear and, by extension, the Jefferson administration for dishonorably cutting its ties with Hamet and abandoning the expeditionary forces at Derne.[115]

In Lear's defense, he seems to have gauged accurately the essential objectives of his superiors in Washington, as well as the limited resources they were prepared to commit to achieve them. Jefferson had never embraced the maximal object of using the war with Tripoli to overthrow Yusuf or overturn the tributary system, which would have meant confronting Algiers and the other regencies. In the midst of multiple international crises with the major European powers, and still committed to a policy of fiscal conservatism, the President was not in a position to insist on a more ambitious outcome. The war with Tripoli alone was costing $2 million per year. The original deployment of four warships had expanded to twelve (plus the vessels obtained locally), manned by two thousand sailors. In early 1805, before news of the settlement with Tripoli reached America, Jefferson had already determined to reduce the American profile in the region back to the model he had always preferred. "If in the course of the summer they cannot produce peace, we shall recall our force, except one frigate and two small vessels, which will keep up a perpetual blockade," he wrote to a Virginia friend. "Such a blockade will cost us no more than a state of peace, and will save us from increased tributes and the disgrace attached to them." He added optimistically that, "the example we have set begins already to work in the disposition of the powers of Europe to emancipate themselves from the degrading yoke. Should we produce such a revolution there, we shall be amply rewarded for what we have done."[116]

Given Jefferson's views, and the likelihood that America's expanded military posture in the Mediterranean would not be sustained beyond the present campaign, Lear understandably sought a settlement on less than maximum terms – one that included important substantive concessions and face-saving elements for Tripoli. Most importantly, Lear agreed to provide Tripoli with relief from the implied subservience to Algiers that marked the first treaty, which Yusuf regarded as one of the chief irritants in his relationship with the

---

[115] This and the preceding paragraph taken from Eaton to SecNav, 9 August 1805, *Naval Documents*, VI: 213-8. I have inserted punctuation to make Eaton's meaning clearer.

[116] Cited by Allen, *Our Navy and the Barbary Corsairs*, p. 222.

United States. (This was a point of far greater importance to the Pasha than to the United States; the American consuls had long since concluded that Algiers was either unwilling or unable to exercise its influence in a way favorable to the United States.) Yusuf also succeeded in separating the United States from Hamet Pasha, thus strengthening his own rule while discrediting his older brother as the feckless tool of a foreign power. Yusuf received ransom – albeit below "market value" – for the release of the crew of the *Philadelphia*. Some scholars argue that these provisions, taken in the context of Yusuf's situation and ambitions, actually represented a considerable victory for Tripoli. This is something of an overstatement but Lear undoubtedly felt that tougher peace terms – e.g., no ransom, Tripolitan indemnities for the cost of the war, the U.S. right to hold fortifications that controlled the harbor at Tripoli – would likely spur Yusuf to seek revenge as soon as the main American naval forces departed the Mediterranean.

What if the United States had sought, instead, to obtain these maximum terms by restoring Hamet Pasha's rule over Tripoli and by placing American-regency relations on the basis of the Eaton-Hamet Pasha Convention? Lear, based on his assessment of Hamet's character – one that history seems to have borne out – simply did not believe that the man was up to the task of governing Tripoli and implementing a treaty opposed by significant elements of his own population. Lear reasoned that if Hamet had been left to his own devices, he probably would have been overthrown by Yusuf or some other rebel ill-disposed to the United States. Hamet conceivably might have preserved his rule with military support by the United States, but Lear had no reason to believe that President Jefferson was prepared to sponsor a problematic client state on the North African coast.

The Jefferson administration did not rule out U.S. support for a change of foreign leadership under the right circumstances, as long as it did not become an end in itself. The President, in a message to the Congress that addressed Eaton's criticisms of U.S. policy, accepted the criteria for the support of regime change set out by Commodore Barron.

> [C]oncerted operations against a common enemy are entirely justifiable, and might produce effects favorable to both, without binding either to guarantee the objects of the other. But given the distance and difficulties and uncertainty of intelligence, it [support of Hamet] was committed to our agents as one option which might be resorted to, if it promised to promote our success. . . . In the event it was found, that, after placing the ex-Bashaw in possession of Derne, one of the most important cities and provinces of the country, where he

had resided himself as Governor, he was totally unable to command any resources, or to bear any part in cooperation with us. This hope was then at an end, and we certainly have never contemplated, nor were we prepared to land an army of our own, or to raise, pay, or subsist an Army of Arabs, to march from Derne to Tripoli, and to carry on a land war at such a distance from our resources. Our means and our authority were merely naval . . . [117]

The Jefferson-Madison policy came down to this. In this war of limited objectives, the United States was justified in supporting a foreign opposition faction for American purposes – up to the point where that faction should reasonably be expected to become self-sustaining. If that faction could not demonstrate the ability to rule in its own name, the United States was at liberty to follow its own interest and settle its dispute with the present leaders. The United States was obligated only to do its best to leave its former allies in a position no worse than when they began to cooperate. As far as Jefferson was concerned, if Eaton made any commitment to the contrary, he exceeded the letter and spirit of his instructions. Any dishonor rested personally with him, not with the United States government. [118]

Congressional critics of the President's approach to foreign policy and the Barbary regencies had opportunities to register their disapproval during the Senate's debate over the ratification of the Treaty with Tripoli. They also pressed to obtain official compensation to Eaton and Hamet as a way of rebuking the Jefferson administration. When the treaty was submitted to the Senate in December 1805, it was referred to a three-member committee that reported a resolution of consent to ratification. A few days later Connecticut Federalist Uriah Tracy, the minority member of the committee, submitted a resolution that reflected his own and his colleagues' general dissatisfaction with the affair – a dissatisfaction shared by many Republicans. Tracy's resolution was adopted with slight alterations. The fate of Hamet's family weighed particularly heavily on the Senate deliberations, both for reasons of honor and

---

[117] Jefferson to the Senate and House of Representatives of the United States, 13 January 1806, James D. Richardson, ed., *A Compilation of the Messages and Papers of the Presidents,* Volume I, Part 3, available at Project Gutenberg, http://www.gutenberg.org/dirs/1/0/8/9/10893/10893.txt, accessed 12 January 2007.

[118] In Eaton's defense, the Jefferson administration and its successors demonstrated a disquieting tendency to rely on "plausible deniability" – to encourage its representatives privately to push beyond the limits of official policy and later to deny official responsibility if things went bad. As a result, the United States acquired something of a reputation for encouraging foreign opposition groups – including Kurds, Hungarians and Iraqi Shiites – with at least implicit promises of political or military support, which did not materialize in the end.

because the retention of the family by Yusuf would complicate, if not prevent, a renewed strategy of regime change if Yusuf resumed his predations. [119]

> *Resolved,* That the President of the United States be, and he is hereby, requested to cause to be laid before the Senate, the instructions which were given to Mr. Lear, the Consul General at Algiers, respecting the negotiations for the treaty with the Bey and Regency of Tripoli; which treaty is now before the Senate for their consideration; and, also, the correspondence of the naval commanders, Barron and Rodgers, and of Mr. Eaton, late Consul at Tunis, respecting the progress of the war with Tripoli, antecedent to the treaty, and respecting the negotiations for the same; and whether the wife and children of the brother of the reigning Bashaw of Tripoli, have been delivered up, pursuant to the stipulation in said treaty; and what steps have been taken to carry the said stipulation into effect; and also, to lay before the Senate any other correspondence and information, which, in the President's opinion, may be useful to the Senate, in their deliberations upon said treaty. [120]

Jefferson responded to the general demand for information in two messages on the subject. One was addressed to both Houses of Congress (cited above) and offered an explanation of the cooperation between the United States and Hamet. It also contained an application for assistance from Hamet. The other message was addressed to the Senate in its executive capacity, claiming that all relevant documentation had been provided. The President's messages were referred to a select committee of five members, of which Tracy was the only Federalist. Even so, the Republican-controlled committee was clearly concerned that the President was not being forthcoming. The committee proposed and the Senate approved another resolution that requested Jefferson to transmit copies of eight particular documents, which they described in great detail. The administration subsequently provided these documents or extracts from them.

In the full Senate, one of the select committee members, Vermont Republican Senator Stephen R. Bradley, proposed to ask the President to ascertain whether the wife and children of Hamet had been released. On behalf of the select committee, Bradley also presented a report and a bill favorable

---

[119] This account of the Senate deliberations and debate, unless otherwise indicated, is taken from Ralston Hayden, *The Senate and Treaties, 1789-1817* (London: Macmillan & Co., 1920), pp. 156-78.

[120] Cited by Hayden, *The Senate and Treaties,* p. 159.

to Hamet's application for relief. Bradley laid out the case that the Jefferson administration, from the beginning, had given its officials on the ground necessary flexibility to support a policy of regime change; moreover, those officials had made binding commitments to that effect to Hamet.

> This unfortunate prince, by the treason and perfidy of his brother, the reigning Bashaw, was driven from his throne, an exile, to the Regency of Tunis, where the agency of the United States, in the Mediterranean, found him; and as early as August, eighteen hundred and one, entered into a convention to co-operate with him, the object of which was to obtain a permanent peace with Tripoli, to place the ex-Bashaw on his throne, and procure indemnification for all expense in accomplishing the same. This agreement was renewed in November following, with encouragement that the United States would persevere, until they had effected the object; and in eighteen hundred and two, when the reigning Bashaw had made overtures to the ex-Bashaw to settle on him the two provinces of Derne and Bengazi, and when the ex-Bashaw was on the point of leaving Tunis, under an escort furnished him by the reigning Bashaw, the agents of the United States prevailed on him to abandon the offer, with assurance that the United States would effectually co-operate, and place him on the throne of Tripoli.
>
> The same engagements were renewed in eighteen hundred and three, and the plan of co-operation so arranged, that the ex-Bashaw, by his own exertions and force, took possession of the province of Derne; but the American squadron, at that time under the command of Commodore Morris, instead of improving that favorable moment to co-operate with the ex- Bashaw, and to put an end to the war, unfortunately abandoned the Barbary coast, and left the ex-Bashaw to contend solely with all the force of the reigning Bashaw, and who in consequence was obliged, in the fore part of the year eighteen hundred and four, to give up his conquest of Derne, and fly from the fury of the usurper into Egypt. [121]

According to Bradley's report, then, the Jefferson administration's policy of regime change and its commitment to Hamet as the agent of that change was well in place before the fateful events of 1805. "After encountering many difficulties and dangers, the ex-Bashaw [Hamet] was found in Upper Egypt

---

[121] This and subsequent references to Bradley's report are taken from the *Annals of Congress*, 9th Congress, 1st session, pp. 185-8.

with the Mamelukes, and commanding the Arabs; the same assurances were again made to him, and a convention was reduced to writing, the stipulations of which had the same objects in view; the United States to obtain a permanent peace and their prisoners, the ex-Bashaw to obtain his throne." Hamet was on the verge of success:

> in several battles afterwards, one of which he fought without the aid of the Americans, (they having been restrained by orders, not warranted by any policy, issued as appears by Mr. Lear, the American Consul), defeated the army of the usurper with great slaughter, maintained his conquest, and, without the hazard of a repulse, would have marched to the throne of Tripoli, had he been supported by the co-operation of the American squadron, which in honor and good faith he had a right to expect.

Unfortunately, according to Bradley's report, Tobias Lear stepped in and snatched defeat from the jaws of victory and thus prevented a change of regime in Tripoli, which would have solved America's strategic and commercial predicament in the Mediterranean:

> . . . the committee [will not] condescend to enter into a consideration of pretended reasons, assigned by Mr. Lear to palliate his management of the affairs of the negotiation; such as, the danger of the American prisoners in Tripoli, the unfitness of the ships for service, and the want of means to prosecute the war; they appear to the committee to have no foundation in fact, and are used rather as a veil to cover an inglorious deed, than solid reasons to justify the negotiator's conduct. The committee are free to say, that, in their opinion, it was in the power of the United States, with the force then employed, and a small portion of the sixty thousand dollars, thus improperly expended, to have placed Hamet Caramalli, the rightful sovereign of Tripoli, on his throne; to have obtained their prisoners in perfect safety, without the payment of a cent, with assurance, and probable certainty, of eventual remuneration for all expenses; and to have established a peace with the Barbary Powers, that would have been secure and permanent, and which would have dignified the name and character of the American people.

Massachusetts Senator John Quincy Adams, then in the process of shifting from the Federalist to the Republican Party, was the principal opponent of the bill for the relief of Hamet. Adams, who earlier had advocated an assertive policy toward the Barbary regencies, did not record in detail his views on the morality or practicality of a policy of regime change against Tripoli. (In an editorial note that accompanied his published edition of Adams' journal, his son, Charles Francis Adams, opined: "the whole proceeding ... appears at this day singularly in contravention of the established policy of the country, not to give aid or support in any internal struggles of foreign nations, however insignificant." [122]) Adams objected less to the monetary relief of Hamet than to the argument in Bradley's report that it was owed as a matter of right and justice.

Adams argued that the Bradley report had wrongly construed the policy and commitments of the Jefferson administration, which the President's Message (in Adams' view) had accurately described as one of limited liability toward the cause of Hamet and regime change. "[T]he committee represent Hamet Bashaw as having been inveigled, deceived, amused with promises to place him on his throne, and finally betrayed and sacrificed. They appear to think the United States were bound, at all events, and, by their exclusive exertions, to restore him to his dignity, and that the mere act of withdrawing their aid, without accomplishing that object, was a treacherous violation of their faith plighted to him." But as Adams saw it:

> ... the discretionary power of Commodore Barron, to avail himself of Hamet's co-operation, was not unlimited – neither by the intention of the Executive, nor in his own understanding. It was limited both as to the nature of the engagement he was to contract, and as to the sum appropriated for the purpose; cooperation is a term of reciprocal import – it certainly means that there should be some operation on both sides. The operation in this case by sea, was to be conducted entirely and exclusively by the squadron of the United States. Hamet Bashaw could contribute, and was expected to contribute, nothing to that. His operation was to be by land; and, upon principles of ordinary reciprocity, it might have been required that this also should be exclusively at his expense. The Government, however, were willing to furnish him some aid even there. And the sum of twenty thousand dollars had been appropriated for that purpose. This was going as far as prudence would warrant, or as good faith could require. Hamet himself could have entertained no other expectation, since, in his letter to Mr. Eaton, of 8d January, he says: "Your operations should be carried on by sea; mine by land." And even after the peace was made, in his letter to

---

[122] 1 April 1806, *Memoirs of John Quincy Adams*, I: 425.

Mr. Eaton, of 20th June, he acknowledges, as clearly as language can express it, that the failure of co-operation was not on our part, but his own; that his means had not been found to answer our reasonable expectations; and that he was "satisfied with all our nation has done concerning him."

. . . If Hamet, after the capture of Derne, was totally unable to command any resources, or bear any part in co-operation with us, how can it be said that he would, without the hazard of a repulse, have marched to the throne of Tripoli, had he been supported by the co-operation of our squadron? But, further, I ask what were the means, what were the resources, of this sovereign prince, from the hour when Mr. Eaton received his orders to withdraw from him? The event, sir, is worth a thousand arguments. He could not support himself a day. He was compelled to take instantaneous refuge on board our vessels, and was saved from destruction only by being brought away. Does this look like marching to the throne of Tripoli? [123]

Adams reviewed sympathetically Lear's claim that the American prisoners would have been in serious jeopardy if he had not come to an agreement that paid some ransom and that effectively abandoned the regime change option. Adams was inclined to think that they were not actually at risk – "I do not believe that in any event the Bashaw [Yusuf] would have sacrificed the lives of the prisoners. I believe he would have followed the course most useful to himself, and that, at the last extremity, he would have turned them to such account as he could, and given them up for peace rather than put them to death." But reasonable and well-informed men on the spot held other opinions; moreover, Lear and Barron did not have all the information indicating otherwise at their disposal. "Yet, sir, when I consider the extreme solicitude manifested through this whole country for the fate of these our unfortunate fellow citizens, and how anxious we all were for their redemption, I can excuse that error which consisted in too tender a regard for their situations, though I cannot justify it altogether; I certainly can never brand as treachery, what, at worst, was virtue carried too far, on the borders of weakness."

As to the assertion of the Bradley report that Hamet's family had not been delivered up and that Yusuf did not intend to do so, Adams argued that

---

[123] Adams' statement to the Senate here and below is taken from the *Annals of Congress*, 9th Congress, 1st session, pp. 211-24.

the United States could not press for their release until it had ratified the Treaty. Adams flatly rejected the accusation that Lear had secretly agreed with Yusuf not to demand their restitution. (Adams was wrong, at least in part; Lear, in fact, had stipulated that they could remain in Yusuf's custody for four years.) Such a secret agreement or article would have been communicated to the Senate. "Had he [Lear] incurred the guilt and folly of assenting to such a bargain, it could not take from us the right of insisting, as I hope we shall effectually do, upon the real and formal stipulation of the treaty. Such an intention must have defeated itself."

Bradley's bill for the compensation of Hamet was recommitted (by a 15-14 vote) to an expanded special committee, of which Adams was named a member. The committee sessions were marked by contentious debate. Adams was not averse to settling with Hamet on the proper grounds, that of "liberality and magnanimity," rather than of national obligation. Adams privately approached Secretary of State Madison for his ideas about how to handle the matter; Madison suggested that some temporary provision for Hamet would suffice, which course Adams began to pursue. Bradley and his supporters now favored putting the matter off until the next session, in December 1806, when they might be able to bring additional political pressure to bear. While Adams was out of the Senate on other business, Bradley hurried through a resolution of postponement.

Bradley also argued for postponing consideration of the Treaty itself – at least partially (so Adams believed) to leave in place a duty surcharge that Congress had levied specifically to support the war in the Mediterranean, but whose revenue the Republicans found generally useful and wished to retain. Bradley's resolution, supported by the opponents of the Treaty, was defeated 20-10. The Treaty's opponents also failed (20-9) to make the Senate's advice and consent contingent upon prior delivery of Hamet's family. On April 12, 1806, the Senate approved the Treaty by a vote of 21-8. After the ratification of the treaty, Adams brought in a bill for the temporary relief of Hamet that passed before the end of the session.[124]

Conclusion

This leads us to consider the critical question: By what means did the United States coerce Tripoli into a favorable, if not optimal, settlement? Perhaps better put, what was the calculation of incentives, disincentives, and independent variables that caused Yusuf largely to agree to peace on

---

[124] Hayden, *The Senate and Treaties*, pp. 166-7.

American terms? In addition, what role did the threat of regime change play? Any answers must be provisional, given the lack of records and authoritative information about the deliberations and policies of the regencies during this period. There are, however, several plausible conclusions.

First, the United States – as much by accident as design – was able to put at *comprehensive* risk Yusuf's longer-term, revisionist ambition to raise his own standing, and that of Tripoli, to the first rank among the rulers and regencies of Barbary. This ambition, as much as his own survival imperative, formed the basis of Yusuf's calculations when he dealt with the Americans.

- Neither the protection of American merchant shipping by convoy, nor the periodic blockade of Tripoli, proved sufficient to bring Yusuf to accept reasonable terms. Such defensive measures, nevertheless, did limit an important source of revenue and leverage for Tripoli, and they raised the cost of the conflict, especially when the United States cooperated with European powers.
- The U.S. Navy, by its assault on Tripoli harbor, threatened to destroy in place the source of Tripoli's military power in the Mediterranean – its corsair fleet and the defenses that protected the harbor. Although Preble did not succeed in that task in 1804, Yusuf was undoubtedly concerned that subsequent attacks would prove more effective, especially if they included a land component. (That calculation would have changed had Yusuf been aware of Jefferson's determination to return to the blockade system after the campaign of 1805.) Perhaps equally important, the United States thereby made Tripoli a much less attractive destination for other regencies, neutrals, and freelancers, as the port was no longer a safe haven for shipping.
- Some sort of direct threat to Tripoli on the ground was probably necessary for the United States to achieve anything like its preferred outcome. American support for Hamet Pasha had the added advantage of threatening Yusuf's rule while obviating the need for a major American ground force. Yusuf, to be sure, had demonstrated complete ruthlessness when it came to getting and maintaining power. His threat to continue the war from the countryside even if the Americans reduced Tripoli and reinstalled Hamet was hardly an idle threat – he had done it before. However, the costs and delays of a civil war, even if Yusuf eventually

returned to power, would have retarded and probably destroyed his ambitions for future Tripolitan greatness under his rule.

Any one of these coercive elements – including the threat of regime change – probably would not have been enough for the United States to obtain a favorable peace in 1805, especially given the negotiating leverage that Yusuf possessed by holding the captives of the *Philadelphia*. Taken together with the ability of the United States to deter the other regencies from joining the conflict, however, this comprehensive threat to Yusuf's desire for regional status and prestige provided the necessary foundation for a relatively successful policy outcome. In the years after 1805, Yusuf emphasized a policy of strengthening Tripoli by consolidating his rule and developing his inland resources, rather than by expanding his naval capabilities and conducting corsair operations. This decision may already have been part of Yusuf's long-term plans, but the American campaign against Tripoli might well have influenced him to turn inward. [125]

Second, the United States allowed Yusuf to save face by conceding certain points that were not essential to U.S. interests, particularly by excluding Algiers from an intermediate role in their relationship and by ceasing its support for Hamet's pretensions. The United States thereby signaled its limited objectives toward Tripoli and the other regencies. In doing so, the United States ran the risk of offending Algiers, the most capable of the regencies, and perhaps provoking its Dey to seek a revision of his treaty with the United States under the threat of war. In the short term, this risk was manageable through a policy of deterrence and coercion. The United States had temporarily deployed a surplus of naval power in the Mediterranean and had recently demonstrated its willingness to use that power. But the long-term problem of Algiers remained unresolved. The underlying logic of the Jefferson administration's policies was indeed revisionist – it pointed to the rejection of all tributary relationships with the Barbary regencies – but the United States would not be in a position to act on that point with Algiers for over a decade, until after the War of 1812.

Third, the long-term success of the American strategy of developing a stable treaty structure with the Barbary powers depended on the U.S. ability to deter the other regencies from directly or indirectly supporting Tripoli's cause. The expansion of U.S. naval forces operating in the Mediterranean beyond the level required immediately to deal with Tripoli provided the

---

[125] Folayan, *Tripoli During the Reign of Yusuf Quaramanli*, Chapters 2 and 3; and Panzac, *Barbary Corsairs: The End of a Legend, 1800-1820*, pp. 102-32, discuss Yusuf's change of strategy after 1805.

necessary means to support a policy of deterrence. Some degree of conciliation also entered into the equation. The Jefferson administration worked to improve America's performance in meeting its treaty obligations with the regencies; further, U.S. consuls proved to be quite creative in satisfying unexpected demands for presents. The deterrent threshold seems to have been rather low. Periodic visits by even a single American warship generally calmed the diplomatic waters with Tunis, Algiers and Morocco. These regencies appear to have been waiting upon the outcome of the U.S. campaign against Tripoli before coming to a final judgment on American capability and seriousness. Further, by 1805, Algiers and the other regencies may have pressed Yusuf to settle with the Americans because they found the ever-increasing activities of the U.S. squadron in the region to be detrimental to their particular interests.

Fourth, the United States gained from selective international cooperation. However, such cooperation did not itself provide essential leverage to coerce Tripoli or deter the other regencies. The most promising avenue – a form of indirect regime change by encouraging the Ottoman Sultan to exercise his sovereign authority over the regencies – never materialized. The United States lacked the political and economic leverage to engage the Porte, unlike some of the European powers, such as Austria, which did successfully call on Constantinople to take action against the regencies. Jefferson's anti-piracy league of small naval powers never materialized due to the opposition of Britain and France and to the general polarization of international politics after 1793. The United States did take advantage of temporary tactical opportunities, such as the naval cooperation with Sweden in 1801-1802, while recognizing that such cooperation was likely to be transitory. Friendly individual relationships with foreign nationals also aided the American cause. The Danish consul in Tripoli, Nissen, was a reliable source of intelligence and diplomacy. British officials in ports like Gibraltar and Malta, for reasons not perfectly clear, also allowed the U.S. Navy considerable privileges.

Fifth, various independent factors may have worked in America's favor, at least in the context of its disputes with the Barbary regencies. The maritime war between Britain and France, and the competing efforts of those nations to control American and European neutral commerce, seem to have created lucrative new peaceful trading opportunities for the regencies, at least in North Africa and the Levant. Commerce became for a time considerably more attractive to the regencies than the spoils of piracy/privateering. A marked decline in corsair activity began in 1806, after the United

States reached a settlement with Tripoli, so this calculation was not likely a direct cause of Yusuf's decision to agree to peace. It is likely that the lure of commerce contributed to the maintenance of the U.S. treaty structure with the regencies despite the drawdown and eventual withdrawal of the U.S. Navy from the Mediterranean. When the economic calculus of the regencies changed after the end of the Napoleonic Wars and vigorous corsair activity resumed, the United States and various European powers decided independently to end the regency threat once and for all. [126]

---

[126] Panzac, *Barbary Corsairs: The End of a Legend, 1800-1820*, pp. 259-92.

CHAPTER THREE

She Goes Not Abroad, in Search of Monsters to Destroy:
The Dispute Between John Quincy Adams and Henry Clay Over the South American Revolutions

On July 4, 1821, Secretary of State John Quincy Adams stood before an audience in the chamber of the U.S. House of Representatives to deliver an oration on the Declaration of Independence. Adams originally had been asked merely to read the Declaration, the original of which he possessed in his official capacity, and which he held up before the assembly. But when the sponsors of the event failed to find "an orator equal to the theme of the day," they invited him "to accompany the reading with an appropriate address." His initial reaction – besides annoyance that he had not made the first cut among those thought competent to address the subject – had been to decline. First, "I was tongue-tied by my place." Any honest discussion of context and content of the Declaration of Independence from an American Secretary of State was bound to sit poorly with the diplomatic representatives of other nations, and with one nation in particular. Second, his domestic political enemies would seize on any misstep – "this address, if it attracted more notice than a common fourth of July oration, would rouse the crest of every snake or Medusa's head against itself and against its author." *Nullum numen adest ne sit prudentia,* he told himself.[1]

Adams, however, typically chose the bolder course. "I brooded over the idea, till I made up my mind to risk it and take the consequences." The balance was tipped in his mind when he saw that an English writer, George Robert Gleig, had argued that England should pursue terroristic tactics, such as the burning of cities, in a future war with the United States. Gleig, according to

---

[1] John Quincy Adams [hereafter JQA] to Walsh, 10 July 1821, and JQA to Ingersoll, 23 July 1821, in William Chauncey Ford, ed., *Writings of John Quincy Adams,* 7 vols. (New York: The Macmillan Company, 1917), 7: 113-4 and 119-23, respectively. Hereafter referred to as *WJQA*. For background on the Address and its setting, see Samuel Flagg Bemis, *John Quincy Adams and the Foundations of American Foreign Policy* (New York: Alfred A. Knopf, 1950), pp. 355-9; and Lynn Hudson Parsons, *John Quincy Adams* (Madison, WI: Madison House, 1998), p. 149. The Latin expression is quoted as transcribed in *WJQA,* 7: 122. It is typically rendered, *nullum numen abest si sit prudentia.*

Adams, insisted that such tactics were justified in conflicts with republics, although not in wars between monarchs. "I had just seen the extract from the work containing this sample of British humanity published in twenty of our newspapers, without a single word of comment upon it," Adams fumed. "And I thought it high time that we should be asking ourselves, where we were in our relations with that country." From Adams' perspective, Gleig's argument was only the latest in a long line of British attacks and slights against the United States, her principles, and her special place in the world. This anti-American attitude was shared, in different forms, by the continental European despots and their apologists.[2]

Adams decided to use the opportunity to defend his country by reminding his listeners of "our peculiar and imperishable principles," which constituted the glory of America. He dismissed prudence, this "sly insinuating lass," "by asking her to step into the next door, while I should be holding a talk with my countrymen." As to the foreign diplomats, they were already used to plain speaking from him, behind closed doors. He had no intention "to waft incense to any member of the *corps diplomatique* among us," even though he insisted stiffly that none of them had the right officially to take exception to his views. Neither the British Minister, Stratford Canning, nor his Russian counterpart, the Chevalier Pierre de Poletica, attended the event, although both sent back accounts of the speech to their governments. The latter was especially scathing, asking rhetorically about the justice of America's treatment of blacks, Indians, and weak nations such as that of Spain.[3]

As a concession to form, Adams delivered his remarks while wearing an academic robe – befitting a former Professor of Rhetoric and Oratory at Harvard University – to signal that his remarks were to be understood as those of a private citizen. He did not consult in advance on the content with President Monroe or any of his colleagues in the Cabinet.[4]

The oration would be long remembered for these words:

> Wherever the standard of freedom and independence has been or shall be unfurled, there will her [America's] heart, her benedictions and her prayers be. But she goes not abroad, in search of monsters to destroy. She is the well-wisher to the freedom and independence of all. She is the champion and vindicator only of her own. She will

---

[2] JQA to Ingersoll, 23 July 1821, *WJQA*, 7: 120, 123; JQA to Walsh, 10 July 1821, WJQA, 7: 115. Adams was referring to Gleig, *The Campaigns of the British Army at Washington and New Orleans in the Years 1814-1815* (London, 1821).

[3] JQA to Ingersoll, 23 July 1821, *WJQA*, 7: 120; Bemis, *John Quincy Adams*, p. 357.

[4] JQA to Walsh, 10 July 1821, *WJQA*, 7: 114.

recommend the general cause, by the countenance of her voice, and the benignant sympathy of her example. She well knows that by once enlisting under other banners than her own, were they even the banners of foreign independence, she would involve herself, beyond the power of extrication, in all the wars of interest and intrigue, of individual avarice, envy, and ambition, which assume the colors and usurp the standard of freedom. The fundamental maxims of her policy would insensibly change from liberty to force. The frontlet upon her brows would no longer beam with the ineffable splendor of freedom and independence; but in its stead would soon be substituted an imperial diadem, flashing in false and tarnished lustre the murky radiance of dominion and power. She might become the dictatress of the world: she would be no longer the ruler of her own spirit.[5]

Adams' aphorism – "she goes not abroad, in search of monsters to destroy" – became the epigrammatic departure for an entire strain of thought about American foreign policy. To call that strain "isolationist" would be too limited, as would other commonly used terms such as "realist" or "anti-interventionist." Adams' assertion on this point actually came at the end of the Address. At first glance, it seemed almost an afterthought, an idea dropped abruptly into a speech that his critics called an ungracious and inelegant diatribe against the British polity. Canning, Poletica, and other European diplomats were struck by Adams' moralistic and aggressive tone, not his diplomatic realism.

To make sense of Adams' argument, we need to examine the Address as a whole, and the context in which it was delivered. Adams himself explained that he meant to argue, first and foremost, against European-style colonialism. Second, he meant to combat what he termed the "doctrine of Lexington" (calling for an American Hemispheric alliance against the Holy Alliance of despots) and the "doctrine of Edinburgh" (calling for Anglo-American cooperation on behalf of political reform and revolution in Europe).[6] More broadly, the Address can be seen as an index to Adams' entire political thought, including the U.S. role (if any) in promoting foreign regime change and democratization (or, in Adams' way of thinking, republicanization). The Address clearly

---

[5] John Quincy Adams, *An Address Delivered at the Request of a Commission of Citizens of Washington; on the Occasion of Reading the Declaration of Independence, on the Fourth of July, 1821* (Washington, D.C.: Davis and Force, 1821), p. 29. Hereafter referred to as JQA, *July 4, 1821 Address*.

[6] JQA to Walsh, 10 July 1821, *WJQA*, 7: 117.

warned America against going abroad in search of monstrous regimes to destroy – Adams meant what he said – but as we will see, Adams also did not assume that monsters should be given an entirely free hand or that America must sit passively by, merely thinking happy thoughts.

In this chapter, we review briefly the strategic and political context in which Adams made his argument. Next, we examine the Address in greater detail and use it as a means to discover more about Adams' thinking about regime change and foreign revolution – and about the alternatives to his position. We note contemporary reactions to the Address and to Adams himself. We conclude with an assessment of Adams' views and policies in the months and years after his Address, as reflected in the Monroe Doctrine and in his policy toward the Panama Congress.[7]

The Context for the Address

The United States in the summer of 1821 was far from a settled place. The nation had just concluded a war with the world's greatest military and economic power. Its territory had been invaded, its capital had been burned, and a significant portion of the Union had seemed on the verge of separation. The peace that ended the War of 1812 – negotiated by a delegation that included John Quincy Adams, then U.S. Minister to Russia – turned out surprisingly well, in a return to the *status quo ante bellum*, but this agreement left a variety of critical issues unsettled. Most Americans, to be sure, celebrated the war as a great success, a second War for Independence, which confirmed that a confederated republic was capable of holding its own against monarchy. In 1819, however, the United States experienced a major financial panic. That same year, the crisis over the admission of Missouri as a state brought to the surface the latent problem of slavery and sectionalism. For a time it seemed nearly certain that the Union would break apart. The compromises that settled the crisis were fresh and of uncertain duration. The political wounds opened by the debate still festered.

---

[7] The Monroe Doctrine, which was outlined in President Monroe's Annual Message of December 1823 and in associated diplomatic documents, was not commonly referred to as such for some years thereafter. For convenience sake, however, we will refer to it in that manner here. Otherwise, for the sake of consistency, we use the terms most commonly applied by American officials and writers at the time, such as the American Hemisphere (rather than Western Hemisphere or New World); South America, which typically included, in a political sense, Mexico and Central America (rather than Spanish America or Latin America); and the Emperor Alexander (rather than Czar or Tsar). To avoid confusion between the Quadruple Alliance, the Quintuple Alliance, and the Holy Alliance – distinctions that Americans often did not make or understand – we generally use the generic terms, continental allies or European monarchs.

Adams, for his part, had been startled by the frank pro-slavery arguments made privately to him by the Cabinet member to whom he had felt the closest, Secretary of War John C. Calhoun. Calhoun had added another disquieting note: "He said he did not think it would produce a dissolution of the Union, but, if it should, the South would be from necessity compelled to form an alliance, offensive and defensive, with Great Britain. I said that would be returning to the colonial state. He said, yes, pretty much, but it would be forced upon them."[8]

Adams, as Secretary of State, had carefully avoided intruding on these hot-button political topics. His official attention was focused on strengthening the strategic position of the United States in a trans-Atlantic world still reeling from two decades of global war. (Adams was also not unmindful of the political advantages that this detachment provided him in the upcoming race for presidential succession.) Europe had settled into an uneasy strategic equilibrium maintained by a concert of the victorious powers, supported by the restored monarchy in France. A grouping of these powers on the continent, under the nominal rubric of the so-called Holy Alliance, had proclaimed the determination to bring about a new era of peace and justice. The father of the Holy Alliance, Emperor Alexander of Russia – with whom Adams was well acquainted from his diplomatic service in St. Petersburg – portrayed himself as the great enlightened monarch who would bring top-down political and social reform and national self-determination to Europe. Skeptics saw this as masking Russia's bid for continental hegemony. In any case, Alexander's liberal instincts increasingly had succumbed to the reactionary view that political change of any sort in Europe must be suppressed.

Adams believed that the major continental states were sincerely anxious to preserve a period of interstate peace but he could not be sure how long that period might last – particularly in light of the enormous social strains that threatened the European monarchies. Adams, as we will see, did not believe that the United States had an immediate or vital interest in the social or political struggles of Europe. He assumed, however, that England would become embroiled in any new European-wide war and that, as always, it would use its sea power ruthlessly for military and commercial advantage. As a consequence, all the familiar Anglo-American conflicts over the rights of neutrals and impressment would again emerge. Adams, first as Minister to Britain and then as Secretary of State, had been working to put British-American relations

---

[8] Journal entry for 24 February 1820, in Charles Francis Adams, ed., *Memoirs of John Quincy Adams, Comprising Portions of his Diary from 1795 to 1848*, 12 vols. (Philadelphia: J.B. Lippincott & Co., 1877), 4: 530-1. Hereafter referred to as *MJQA*.

on better footing, partly in anticipation of heading off future crises. He wanted to buy time to strengthen American finances, naval power, and geographic security, so as to deter Britain from provoking war with the United States, and eventually to negotiate their outstanding differences from a position of American strength.

As part of this grand strategy, Adams had been working to resolve several outstanding issues with Spain, whose unstable colonial borderlands abutted the United States. Adams sought to acquire Spain's possessions in Florida and to secure favorable boundaries in the south and west. The negotiations with Spain had been tricky for domestic and international reasons. Spanish control of its colonies throughout the New World had been in disarray for some time. Several of the colonies had declared their independence and had sought aid and diplomatic recognition from the United States. Ordinary Americans were naturally sympathetic to the independence movements and some of them offered their services to the insurgents, for glory or for gain.[9]

The tide of battle between various governments in Spain and the colonial insurgents had ebbed and flowed for years but the general trend was in favor of the movements for independence. In September 1815, President Madison issued a proclamation of neutrality that warned U.S. citizens to refrain from enlisting in any military expeditions in the Spanish dominions. However, the United States treated the conflict as a civil war which meant, for instance, that vessels flying insurgent flags were admitted into American ports. In 1817 and 1818, following the wishes of the Monroe administration, Congress passed legislation further aimed at prohibiting American sympathizers from committing unneutral acts against Spain. Agents representing or claiming to represent the insurgent regimes flocked to the United States to seek arms and funds. The entire city of Baltimore, Adams observed, seemed to have gone over entirely to the South American cause, in violation of U.S. law.[10] The South American insurgents continued to press the Monroe administration for formal diplomatic recognition. Prominent Americans, including Speaker of the House Henry Clay, pressured the U.S. government to do so.

The Monroe administration held back, however, despite the President's own sympathy for the South American cause (in the 1790s, he had been one of the most adamant American supporters of the French Revolution). Under Adams' guidance, the U.S. government clearly placed priority on settling matters with Spain. South American representatives and their U.S. supporters

---

[9] For an overview, see John Lynch, *The Spanish American Revolutions, 1809-1826*, 2nd ed. (New York: W.W. Norton, 1986).

[10] 29 March 1819, *MJQA*, 4: 315-6.

resented Adams' apparent coolness toward the cause. The Secretary of State, as we shall see, believed that South American independence was inevitable and that American recognition of the new regimes should and would occur in due course. Year after year, however, the President's Annual Message held out only words of sympathy to the South Americans, with no promise of material support and no acknowledgement of their independent status.

Behind the scenes, as detailed below, the United States encouraged the major European powers, particularly Britain, to persuade Spain that its cause in most of the American Hemisphere was lost and that it should cut its losses (and thereby preserve its most valuable possession, Cuba). Adams was concerned that the United States might be drawn into war if one or more of the major European powers chose to back Spain in any crisis or conflict with the United States. Adams refused to undermine his carefully crafted diplomatic approach to ease Spain out of North America by moving precipitously on the matter of South American recognition. As of July 1821, none of the European players had yet signed on to the U.S. approach of persuading Spain to give up the game in its rebellious colonies. In the opinion of impatient Americans like Clay, Adams had supinely ceded control of U.S. foreign policy on South American liberty to the reactionary Holy Alliance.

The Spanish government, for its part, protested vigorously that the United States was negligent in its duties under the law of nations by adopting, but not enforcing, a formal position of neutrality. The conflict in South America was illegal rebellion against legitimate rule. Spanish officials suggested an obvious *quid pro quo* to Adams. Spain would agree to a settlement, presumably one favorable to the United States, in the negotiations over Florida and territorial boundaries, in exchange for an agreement or understanding that Washington would not recognize the South American insurgents. Adams had successfully resisted any formal connection between the two issues and – taking advantage of the military pressure exerted by Major General Andrew Jackson against Florida – he had reached an agreement in February 1819 with the Spanish representative, Don Luis de Onís, in what became known as the Transcontinental (or Adams-Onís) Treaty. That the United States did not rush to recognize the South American nations after the treaty was signed, however, strongly suggested that there was indeed a tacit understanding linking the two issues.

As it turned out, the Spanish government procrastinated in ratifying the Adam-Onís agreement, and it sent a special envoy (General Francisco Vives) to seek clarification and further concessions by the United States. The Spanish terms included an explicit American commitment not to recognize any of the rebellious provinces. (To make matters worse, there was a disagreement over the status of certain Spanish land grants in Florida.) Adams took the position that the treaty, under the law of nations, was binding on Spain because Onís had been given full authority by his sovereign to negotiate. The United States therefore was entitled to enforce the terms of the agreement unilaterally, for example, by occupying Florida, if it so chose. That action might have led to war with Spain, and perhaps with Spain's European allies, something that the country (with the exception of a few War Hawks) did not want, especially in light of the financial panic and the crisis over Missouri.

To complicate the situation further, a revolt at Cadiz of Spanish troops en route to South America sparked a widespread domestic insurrection against the monarchy. To retain his throne, Ferdinand VII agreed to restore the liberal Constitution of 1812, but the King regarded this as only a temporizing measure. Spanish politics continued in near chaos, while South America drifted further away. The other European monarchs, particularly the restored Bourbon regime in France, signaled their unhappiness at this turn of events and made noises about military intervention in Spain on behalf of the legitimate ruler. Adams spent the better part of two years untangling the diplomatic knots in the context of this unstable political situation. When pressed by Vives, Adams did not disagree with the impression that Vives said had been left with Onís – that the United States "probably" would not "precipitately" recognize the South American revolutionary regimes. Ratifications of the Transcontinental Treaty were finally exchanged in the spring of 1821.[11]

When Adams stood to deliver his July 4 Address, three months later, he felt that he still did not yet have complete diplomatic freedom of action. The treaty was yet to be implemented and he could be accused of bad faith by the Spanish if the United States rushed to recognize the new South American nations. That accusation might resonate in European capitals hostile to the United States. The situation on the ground in South America was also in flux. Several of the revolutionary regimes recently had suffered military setbacks and civil disturbances. Some privateers operating under the flag of those regimes preyed indiscriminately on foreign commerce and the South American insurgents seemed unable or unwilling to bring them under control. It was not out of the question that Britain or another European power, in order to preserve commercial interests, would take military action against the "pirates" and the regimes that protected them.

---

[11] This at least is how Bemis, *John Quincy Adams*, p. 352, interprets their conversation. See journal entries for 1 and 4 May 1820, *MJQA*, 5: 86, 94-5, 104.

Under those circumstances, Adams feared that U.S. recognition of the South American regimes might provoke the European monarchs to side with Madrid in any dispute with the United States, especially because those monarchs were under growing pressures at home. Popular insurrections in Lisbon and Oporto in August 1820 had resulted in the establishment of a liberal constitution in Portugal, modeled after that of Spain. The Kings of Naples and Piedmont also succumbed to popular movements and likewise granted liberal charters (the latter abdicated in favor of his brother). Just a few months before Adams delivered his Address, several Danubian principalities of the Ottoman Empire had revolted against Turkish rule and Alexander Ypsilantis, a Greek then serving as a general in the Russian army, had issued a proclamation calling on all Greeks and Christians to rise up against the Ottomans.

Many Americans were naturally thrilled at the apparent revival of constitutional liberalism in Europe – and they were equally horrified when the absolutist regimes intervened to repress the movements for constitutions and national self-determination. In October 1820, the Conference at Troppau authorized an Austrian army, backed if necessary by Russian troops, to move into Naples to suppress the constitution and restore absolutist rule. The conference members also issued a protocol that claimed the general right to undertake such interventions on behalf of legitimacy. Austria also successfully acted against the liberal regime in Piedmont. Britain, the bastion of freedom and advocate of non-interference in the affairs of others, distanced itself from the affair, despite the calls of some prominent liberals to support the popular movement in Europe. In Britain proper, the activities of those agitating for parliamentary reform or more radical measures had been restricted by new laws. At a large public meeting for reform in Manchester in August 1819, a dozen participants were killed and hundreds injured when cavalry units were ordered by the authorities to disperse the group.[12]

As Secretary of State, with extensive personal experience and contacts in Europe, Adams had naturally followed these revolutionary developments closely. As he prepared for his July 4 Address, he was well aware that two lines of argument – which contrasted sharply with ideas of U.S. neutrality and well-wishing – demanded much more assertive American policy in support of revolution and foreign regime change on both sides of the Atlantic.

---

[12] The critical European developments for this period are detailed in Frederick B. Artz, *Reaction and Revolution, 1814 1832* (New York: Harper Brothers, 1934), especially pp. 110-83. For their impact on the United States, see W.P. Cresson, *The Holy Alliance: The European Background of the Monroe Doctrine* (New York: Oxford University Press, 1922).

The Lexington Doctrine

In May 1821, Henry Clay was feted at a public dinner in his honor in Lexington, Kentucky. After steering the Missouri Compromise legislation through Congress, Clay had announced his retirement from politics to return to his law practice and recover his financial fortune (no one doubted that this was a temporary measure and that Clay would actively seek the presidency in 1824). In his brief remarks acknowledging the evening's toasts, Clay urged the United States "to countenance, by all means short of actual war," the great cause of South American independence, in large part because Americans' support of their southern brethren "would give additional tone, and hope, and confidence to the friends of Liberty throughout the world" at a time of great crisis for the cause of the rights of mankind.

In light of recent developments in Europe, Clay elaborated, the friends of liberty needed hope. The European despots had assembled in meetings over the years in the name of legitimacy – "a softer and covered name for despotism" – "to decide, without ceremony, upon the destiny and affairs of Foreign Independent States." Clay pointed out that the European despots had recently authorized Austrian intervention against the new constitutional government in Naples, which had been reformed "peaceably, without bloodshed, and with the unanimous and enthusiastic concurrence of the whole nation, prince and people. This is the crime of Naples; and for this crime, three individuals [the emperors and king of Austria, Russia, and Prussia], who if they have reached the height of human power, are displaying what is too often its attendant, the height of human presumption, are threatening to pour their countless hordes into her bosom and to devastate her land." Clay reminded his listeners that the United States was "the greatest offender of all against the principle of legitimacy," and that its survival as a republic to date had been due to its distance from Europe and the bravery of its citizens. But would not the "giddiness and intoxication of power" created by the success of the Holy Alliance tempt the despots to test these barriers?

> It had seemed to him that a sort of counterpoise to the Holy Alliance should be formed in the two Americas, in favor of National Independence and Liberty, to operate by the force of example and by moral influence; that here a rallying point and an assylum [sic] should exist for freemen and for freedom.[13]

---

[13] "Toast and Response at Public Dinner," 19 May 1821, Lexington, Kentucky, in James F. Hopkins and others, eds., *The Papers of Henry Clay*, 11 vols. (Lexington: University of Kentucky Press, 1959-1992), 3: 80-1. Hereafter referred to as PHC.

Clay's "Lexington Doctrine," as Adams termed it, was not a sudden or ill-considered concept. Clay's listeners – and those who would soon read his speech throughout the nation – were well aware of his long-standing advocacy of a more assertive U.S posture toward South America. As early as 1813, he had expressed his enthusiasm for their cause. In 1817, he had opposed President Madison's efforts to strengthen U.S. neutrality laws so as to prohibit insurgents from arming and outfitting ships in American ports and waters. "We have a right to take part with them, that it is in our interest to take part with them, and that our interposition in their favor would be effectual." He considered that the separation "of any part of America from the dominions of the old world" would "add to the general security of the new."[14]

When Monroe succeeded Madison in 1817, he did not choose Clay as his Secretary of State, an office that Clay deeply desired and that he was widely expected to receive. Clay believed that his leadership in Congress in the run-up to the War of 1812, and his role in the Ghent peace negotiations, entitled him to become the Republican Party's principal leader on foreign affairs. (The individual holding that Cabinet office was also generally regarded as having the inside track to the presidency.) The post went instead to Clay's colleague and rival on the Ghent peace commission, John Quincy Adams, whom many Republicans still regarded as a turncoat Federalist and crypto-monarchist. Clay now made it clear that, as Speaker of the House, he would not cede control of American foreign policy to the executive, especially when it came to promoting South American independence. He developed close relations with some of the prominent representatives of the South American revolutionary movements. When Monroe's first Annual Message, in December 1817, indicated that the new administration would continue the American policy of "impartial neutrality" (albeit with expressions of friendship to the insurgents), Clay responded by calling on Congress to "interpose its authority." By this Clay meant instructing the House Committee on Foreign Affairs to consider new legislation that would ensure that the United States was practicing "a just observance" of neutrality in relation to the struggle in the Spanish colonies in the Americas.[15]

In March 1818, Clay urged Congress to go further down the road of interposition. He moved for an appropriation of $18,000 to outfit an American

---

[14] Speech of 29 January 1817, *PHC*, 2: 155. For Clay's legislative activities on behalf of the South American revolutionaries, see Halford L. Hoskins, "The Hispanic American Policy of Henry Clay, 1816-1828," *Hispanic American Historical Review* 7 (November 1927): 460-78; and Robert Remini, *Henry Clay: Statesman for the Union* (New York: W.W. Norton & Company, 1991), pp. 155-61.

[15] Remini, *Henry Clay*, pp. 155-6.

Minister to the independent provinces of the River Platte (generally referred to as Buenos Aires) whenever the President deemed it expedient to do so. Such an appropriation by Congress would force the President's hand: he must either veto the legislation and publicly desert the popular cause of South American liberty or acquiesce and formally recognize Buenos Aires. Monroe and Adams rallied the friends of the administration in the House and Clay's proposal was defeated 115-45. Despite the lopsided legislative loss, Clay continued to press the matter. In April 1820, he sponsored a resolution in the House that declared such appropriations as expedient, and that called on the President (with the consent of the Senate) to appoint ministers to any of the South American regimes that had established their independence. This resolution, to the disquiet of Monroe and Adams, passed the House by a small majority. Clay tried and narrowly failed in February 1821 to authorize the appropriation directly but he did secure a large majority in favor of a resolution authorizing the President "whenever he may deem it expedient to recognize the sovereignty and independence of any of the said provinces."[16]

Clay justified his position on South America in several major Congressional speeches and public comments, which culminated in his remarks in Lexington. He insisted that he was not advocating revolution in other countries or going to war on behalf of those seeking political independence or a change of regime. Clay insisted that "he was no propagandist. He would not seek to force upon other nations our principles and our liberty, if they did not want them. He would not disturb the repose even of a detestable despotism. But if an abused and oppressed people willed their freedom; if they sought to establish it; if, in truth, they had established it, we had a right, as a sovereign power, to notice the fact, and to act as our circumstances and our interest required." Clay rejected the notion that the only alternative to war was to do nothing, to sit passively behind the façade of "impartial neutrality."[17]

Clay sought to persuade Americans of the moral, strategic, and material stakes they had in the success of the South American independence movements. He condemned the selfish and misguided reluctance to embrace the South American cause by those who argued that these were rebellions, not legitimate revolutions, which were bound either to fail or to end up in despotic rule. He identified Secretary of State Adams as the principal figure behind the administration's recalcitrant views on the subject. Clay was especially irritated by arguments that the South Americans were incapable of independence

---

[16] Hoskins, "Hispanic American Policy of Henry Clay," p. 468.
[17] Motion and Speech of 24-25 March 1818, *PHC*, 2: 517.

and liberty because their character had been deformed by centuries of Spanish misrule. Clay argued instead that the South Americans had actually demonstrated many favorable traits. He cited cutting-edge scholarship by Alexander von Humboldt and others that "the people of Spanish America [exhibit] great quickness, genius, and particular aptitude for the acquisition of the exact sciences, and others which they have been allowed to cultivate." In 1820, during the Missouri crisis, he added provocatively: "On the point which had been so much discussed on this floor during the present session, they were greatly in advance of us. Grenada, Venezuela, and Buenos Ayres had all emancipated their slaves. He did not say that we ought to do so, or that they ought to have done so, under different circumstances; but he rejoiced that the circumstances were such as to permit them to do it."[18]

But even acknowledging for the sake of argument the effects of Spanish misrule, how was the South American character supposed to improve if the people were not freed from bad government? "If Spain succeeded in riveting their chains upon them would not that ignorance and suspicion be perpetuated? ... For his part, Mr. C said, he wished their independence. It was the first step towards improving their condition. Let them have free government, if they are capable of enjoying it; but let them have, at all events, independence." To say that men were not capable of governing themselves under anything but ideal circumstances was the doctrine of thrones – and a denial of the principles of the American Revolution. Clay insisted that the two revolutions were fundamentally the same; indeed, the South American cause, on the merits, was actually much stronger than that of the British North American colonists of 1776, who had suffered comparatively little. To those who argued that the South American independence movements were stained by excessive violence and "execrable outrages," Clay rejoined that retaliation begets retaliation. The South Americans faced a despotic adversary that was much worse than that faced by the Americans in their revolution. Retribution was sometimes necessary in dealing with extreme circumstances.[19]

Clay emphasized the beneficial effects that revolutionary experience itself would have on the political character of South Americans, especially because the revolutionaries had naturally sought to emulate their elder (republican) brothers in the north. Clay challenged the contention that the South Americans were doomed to despotism because of their religion. Clay denied that Roman Catholicism as such was a barrier to good government; it was the

---

[18] Ibid., *PHC*, 2: 520-1; Speech of 10 May 1820, *PHC*, 2: 858.

[19] Speech of 24 January 1817, *PHC*, 2: 291; Speech and Motion of 24-25 March 1818, *PHC*, 2: 517; Speech of 28 March 1818, *PHC*, 2: 551.

union of church and state – *any* church – that corrupted politics and religion. The United States had amply demonstrated this point and the South Americans were bound to follow and disestablish the Church.[20]

Clay famously posited the existence, or at least the great potential, of a hemispheric "American System," of which the United States would be the leader, both politically and economically. Once the South Americans were released from Spanish despotism, Clay was convinced that the new regimes would "be animated by an American feeling, and guided by an American policy. They would obey the laws of the system of the New World, of which they would compose a part, in contradistinction to that of Europe." Those "laws" included the overriding self-interest to avoid being sucked into the "European vortex" – that is, of remaining apart from the wars and quarrels of the Old World and of embracing and enforcing a liberal system of neutrality. The American Hemisphere constituted a self-sufficient economic system that could dictate the terms of international commerce, especially during the frequent European wars. Clay challenged the argument that the United States and the South Americans were commercial rivals because they produced many of the same things, largely agricultural products. Americans should take the longer view: Maritime commerce was increasingly global and dynamic and the economic connection between North and South America would evolve accordingly.

> And he would ask again, as he had on another occasion, ask gentlemen to elevate themselves to the actual importance and greatness of our republic; to reflect like true American statesmen, that we were not legislating for the present day only; and to contemplate this country in its march to true greatness, when millions and millions will be added to our population and when the increased productive industry will furnish an infinite variety of fabrics for foreign consumption in order to supply our wants. The distribution of precious metals has hitherto been principally made through the circuitous channel of Cadiz. No one can foresee all the effects which will result from the direct distribution of them from the mines which produce them. One of the effects will probably be to give us the entire command of the India trade. The advantage we have on the map over Europe, in that respect, is prodigious.[21]

---

[20] Speech and Motion of 24-25 March 1818, *PHC*, 2: 520-2.

[21] Speech of 10 May 1820, *PHC*, 2: 856-69; Speech and Motion of 24-25 March 1818, *PHC*, 2: 520-5.

Finally, "American laws" were those of free men and free government. Although the South Americans had the right to choose their own regime type, Clay was "strongly inclined" to believe that they would choose governments similar to that of the United States: "We were their great examples."[22]

Clay argued that, in concrete policy terms, the available choice was not between U.S. military intervention and complete indifference to the cause of South American independence. That was a false dichotomy emanating from the monarchical (and Federalist) position that force was the only arbiter of affairs among men. There was a new factor in the Enlightened Age – that of "moral power" – with force representing only an auxiliary element. There was a "vast stream of public opinion, which, sooner or later must regulate the physical action upon the great interests of the civilized world." At a time when American policy should have brought its moral power to bear on behalf of the revolutionary movements, it had done exactly the opposite. "The brilliant costumes of the Ministers of the royal government are seen glittering in the circles of our drawing rooms, and their splendid equipages rolling through the avenues of the Metropolis, but the unaccredited Minister of the republic [Buenos Aires], if he visit our President or Secretary of State at all, must do it *incog.* lest the eye of Don Onís should be offended by so unseemly a sight!"[23]

There were a number of practical measures short of war that the United States could take to bring its moral force to bear, especially by adopting a "just" neutrality rather than an "impartial" position. Justice demanded that, should the United States err in applying its laws, the error be on the side of liberty and happiness. Americans should not confuse piracy with the actions of those patriots legitimately defending their own country by acting as privateers. Moreover, the most important policy change would be to recognize the new regimes, thus leveling the playing field with the Spanish government. Governments must be recognized if they have control of the territory that they claim to rule and if they are stable, just as the Washington administration had recognized the French Republic in 1793 even though no other nation had done so. Clay believed that there was a critical point at which enduring impressions of friendship (or hostility) are made on men and nations. Prompt American recognition of the new regimes would have a positive effect on South American opinion of the United States and of republican government. But if the United States lagged and conferred recognition grudgingly – and especially if it did so after the European monarchies – the impact on South American attitudes could be devastating. Clay thought that the critical moment had arrived in

---

[22] Speech and Motion of 24-25 March 1818, *PHC*, 2: 520.

[23] Speech of 28 March 1818, *PHC*, 2: 552-3; Speech of 23 January 1824, *PHC*, 3: 605.

1818, when the future of the revolutionary regimes seemed problematic and therefore U.S. influence would be at its highest. That was why he had tried to force the executive's hand.[24]

> Did any man doubt the feelings of the south towards us? In spite of our coldness towards them, of the rigor of our laws, and the conduct of our officers, their hearts still turned towards us, as to their brethren; and he had no earthly doubt, if our government would take the lead and recognise them, they would become yet more anxious to imitate our institutions, and to secure to themselves and to their posterity the same freedom which we enjoy.[25]

The United States also diluted its influence by trying to concert its recognition policy with that of the European monarchs. That policy cost the United States its influence in South America and also around the world. "The opinions of the friends of Freedom in Europe is, that our policy has been cold, heartless, and indifferent, towards the greatest cause which could possibly engage our affections and enlist our feelings in its behalf."[26]

Would not a more assertive policy embroil the United States in war? Not with Spain, Clay insisted. She would have no just cause for complaint if U.S. recognition was not accompanied by aid. In practical terms, Spain, with its huge debt and internal problems, was incapable of waging war against the United States. And if Spain nevertheless foolishly did do, this would ensure the success of the revolutionaries, even in those parts of South America where they still had some prospect of maintaining her dominions – and certainly in Florida, Mexico and Cuba. Such a war would be terminated favorably in two years, if no other power interposed.[27]

But would the European monarchs interpose on behalf of Spain in a war with the United States and the South American revolutionaries? Once again, Clay insisted, no. They had commercial interests that would be benefited by South American independence. Would they act against their material interests in order to suppress the spirit of revolt and liberty? No. Nations, like peoples, seldom act upon remote dangers. The spirit of allied monarchical cohesion had been annihilated by Waterloo. European despots no longer had the threat of Napoleon and the French universal empire to unite them; even when France was a revolutionary power, they could not unite against her. The continental

---

[24] Speech and Motion of 24-25 March 1818, *PHC*, 2: 525-7.

[25] Speech of 10 May 1820, *PHC*, 2: 857.

[26] Ibid., *PHC*, 2: 859.

[27] Speech and Motion of 24-25 March 1818, *PHC*, 2: 530-2.

powers realized they could not wage war successfully against England, and England had powerful reasons to support independence. Clay concluded that "our Government, I believe, sincerely wishes success to their cause, but it indulges apprehensions, with regard to the power of Europe, which I think groundless, and which I fear may restrain it from doing even the little which I think we ought to do, and which in my opinion would not compromise our peace or neutrality."[28]

Clay rejected the argument that the U.S. government's delay in recognizing South American independence had been necessary to ensure the success of the negotiations with Spain over Florida and the western boundaries. Whereas Monroe and Adams had attempted to appeal to the "justice and affections" of Spain with respect to encouraging the independence of South America, Clay thought that the United States should also have appealed to Spain's fears, "by a recognition of the independent governments of South America, and [by] leaving her in a state of uncertainty as to further steps we might take in respect to those governments." Clay believed that Adams had been unduly frightened by a single comment made by British Foreign Secretary, Lord Castlereagh, while Adams was Minister in London: "Don't aggrandize yourself at the expense of your neighbors to the South." From this simple remark Adams had conjured up all sorts of exaggerated fears of British and European intervention.[29]

Over time, Clay increasingly linked the cause of South American independence with the cause of "the friends of freedom in Europe," both of which were under direct assault by the despots of the Old World. He spoke up on behalf of the Spanish people, whose efforts to reestablish the liberal constitution of 1812 was threatened by the spectre of invasion by the Holy Alliance, as well as by the Greek independence movement. "If Spain succeeded in establishing her freedom, the [South American] colonies must also be free," Clay deduced. "The first desire of a government itself free, must be to give liberty to its dependencies." The European despots had no cause to force regime change on Spain even by their own standards of order because the constitutionalist government there did not threaten other states, as the revolutionary French republicans had once done. Constitutional Spain had not propagated revolution abroad, threatened to invade France, or executed its monarch; it only sought to reform its domestic institution. "Her revolution has been characterized by no excesses, sullied by no atrocities, stained

---

[28] Ibid., *PHC*, 2: 532; Clay to William D. Lewis, 25 January 1818, cited by Remini, *Henry Clay*, p. 155.

[29] Clay to Jonathan Russell, 24 March 1820, *PHC*, 2: 797-8; Speech of 3 April 1820, *PHC*, 2: 803.

by no blood, except that which has been shed at the instigation or with the countenance of foreign powers."[30]

As to practical policy, Clay insisted that "he would not intermeddle in the affairs of Europe. We wisely kept aloof from their broils." But neither did he believe that the Founders' dictum of the separation of the Old and New World prevented the United States from expressing its sympathies irrespective of the location of the struggle for freedom: "Whatever may be the issue, we shall, at least, have the consolation of cherishing our own principles, and of giving all, that is consistent with our posture and our institutions to communicate – our fervent prayers and our best wishes for every people, wherever situated, whether in the old or new world, who are struggling to establish and preserve their liberties." That included appointing agents or commissioners to evaluate the conditions in Europe. If they reported that circumstances warranted, the United States should extend diplomatic recognition to new regimes, such as an independent Greece.[31]

Such expressions, whether by Congress or the executive, Clay admitted, might have limited effect across the Atlantic, where (for the moment) "all Europe may be encircled in the thick and dark mantle of inexorable despotism."[32] Even so, they were necessary to help prepare the American people for the day when European despots decided to try to suppress the source of the popular infection – the American Republic. For that reason, the Lexington Doctrine should become the corollary to the Washington Doctrine, as laid out in the first President's Farewell Address. In defending his proposal to send American agents to Greece, Clay argued:

> It has been admitted by all, that there is impending over this country a threatening storm, which is likely to call into action all our vigor, courage and resources. Is it a wise way of preparing for this awful event, to talk to this nation of its incompetency to resist European aggression, to lower its spirit, to weaken its moral force, and do what we can to prepare it for base submission and easy conquest? ... But, sir, it is not first and chiefly for Greece, that I desire to see this measure adopted. It will give them but little aid, and that aid purely of a moral kind. It is, indeed, soothing and solacing in distress, to hear the accents of a friendly voice,

---

[30] Speech of 20 May 1820, *PHC*, 2: 858; Toasts and Speech at a Public Dinner, 29 March 1823, *PHC*, 3: 404.

[31] Speech of May 1818, *PHC*, 2: 530; Toasts and Speech at a Public Dinner, 29 March 1823, *PHC*, 3: 405; Speech of 23 January 1824, *PHC*, 3: 607.

[32] Toasts and Speech at a Public Dinner, 29 March 1823, *PHC*, 3: 405.

(we know this as a people). But, sir, it is principally and mainly for America herself, for the credit and character of our common country, that I hope to see this resolution pass: it is for our own unsullied name that I feel.[33]

Although Clay seldom made the connection, it is evident that he thought a more assertive and pro-liberal American foreign policy – even if war was the result – would help unite the country and heal the political wounds caused by the recent debate over Missouri and slavery. American international activism would direct the impulse for liberty outside the country, where it could be safely exercised (or exorcised).[34]

The Edinburgh Doctrine

Adams was also confronted by those who argued specifically that the United States should abandon its long-standing determination not to become involved in purely European interests and quarrels, because "it is the duty of America to take an *active* part in the future political reformation of Europe."[35] That idea, which went beyond that of Clay's call for moral support for European liberal movements, had been broached in a May 1820 essay in the *Edinburgh Review*. The *Review*, one of Britain's most prestigious political literary journals, represented reformist Whig (opposition) opinion. One of the *Review*'s founders and principal contributors, Henry Brougham, was a leading Whig in the House of Commons. Although there was no definitive Whig foreign policy *per se* – the group was more of a persuasion than an organized party – Whig opinion was generally anti-slavery, pro free-trade, sympathetic to liberal movements on the continent, and opposed to what they regarded as the reactionary settlement at the Congress of Vienna.

This particular *Review* essay had caught the eye of Adams because it examined a book by Robert Walsh, an American editor and polemicist. Walsh had criticized the *Review* and other British writers and publications, including *The Quarterly Review*, the Tory rival of the *Edinburgh Review*, for their hostility toward America. Walsh had objected especially to their incessant argument that the United States lacked literary accomplishments, scientific and intellectual achievements, and cultural refinement. This degradation of American culture by Europeans in general, and by the British in

---

[33] Speech of 23 January 1824, *PHC*, 3: 607, 609-10.

[34] This is at least implicitly suggested in his Toasts and Speech at a Public Dinner, 29 March 1823, *PHC*, 3: 405, although he does not specifically mention the Missouri crisis.

[35] JQA to Walsh, 10 July 1821, *WJQA*, 7: 117. Emphasis in original.

particular, had long been a sore point for Adams and many of his fellow citizens. Walsh noted, for example, that the *Review* had reflected poorly on John Marshall's *Life of Washington* and on a travelogue (*Letters on Silesia*) that had been authored two decades earlier by the then-U.S. Minister to Prussia, John Quincy Adams. Walsh's book also detailed various social and political shortcomings and outright failures in Britain.[36]

The *Review*'s essayist responded that, quite to the contrary, his journal, and Whig opinion generally, had been almost universally friendly toward the United States, especially because of its liberal principles and representative institutions. The essayist decried polemics like those of Walsh, which were designed to stir up anti-English sentiment in America; by creating a vicious circle, American Anglophones would stir up anti-American sentiment in England. The essayist noted that the *Review*'s evaluation of John Marshall's book – that it was rather dull – had not been intended in any way to slight the great Washington himself (in fact, Marshall's book had been rather poorly received in the United States as well).[37] As to the review of Adams' travelogue, the essayist insisted that his *Letters* had been treated with sufficient courtesy and respect for a book that was "easy, and pleasant, and entertaining." The *Review* had no obligation to offer extravagant compliments just because its author happened to be the son of a President of the United States. To be sure, individual writers in the *Review* had noticed the obvious faults of American politics and society, just as they commented on those of England and other nations. These faults of the United States included, above all, Negro slavery. Walsh, however, had willfully confounded the distinctly anti-American and anti-republican views of the Tories with the more liberal attitudes of the Whigs. In fact, the popular majority in Britain was strongly disposed toward Anglo-American cooperation.[38]

In the midst of defending British and Whig opinion against Walsh's accusations, the *Review* essayist argued that the two English-speaking nations now had a priceless opportunity to strengthen their natural bonds of affinity.

---

[36] Robert Walsh, *An Appeal from the Judgments of Great Britain respecting the United States of America, Part First, Containing an Historical Outline of their Merits and Wrongs as Colonies, and Strictures on the Calumnies of British Writers* (Philadelphia and London, 1819).

[37] Although the Review's essayists could not know it, John Adams' private opinion of Marshall's biography of Washington was similar: "a Mausoleum, 100 feet square at the base and 200 feet high." Joseph Ellis, *Passionate Sage: The Character and Legacy of John Adams* (New York: W.W. Norton, 1993), p. 67.

[38] *Edinburgh Review* 33 (May 1820), pp. 409, 412-4, 430-1. Full text available, with registration, at http://pao.chadwyck.com/journals/displayItemFromId.do?QueryType=journals&ItemID =4091#listItem431.

Europe was in the midst of "a greater and more momentous contest impending, than ever before agitated human society." The essayist continued:

> In Germany – in Spain – in France – in Italy, the principles of Reform and Liberty are visibly arraying themselves for a final struggle with the principles of Established Abuse, – Legitimacy, or Tyranny – or whatever else it is called, by its friends or enemies. Even in England, the more modified elements of the same principles are stirring and heaving, around, above and beneath us, with unprecedented force, activity, and terror; and everything betokens an approaching crisis in the great European commonwealth, by the result of which the future character of its governments, and the structure and condition of its society, will in all probability be determined. The ultimate result, or the course of events that are to lead to it, we have not the presumption to predict. The struggle may be long or transitory – sanguinary or bloodless; and it may end in a great and signal amelioration of all existing institutions, or in the establishment of one vast federation of military despots, domineering as usual in the midst of sensuality, barbarian [sic], and gloom.[39]

The *Review* essayist expressed confidence that "the cause of Liberty will be ultimately triumphant." But how long would this process take, and at what cost? "In this, as in every other respect, we conceive that much will depend on the part that is taken by America; and on the dispositions which she may have cultivated towards the different parties concerned." He reflected on the position of the United States:

> Her great and growing wealth and population – her universal commercial relations – her own impregnable security – and her remoteness from the scene of dissension – must give her prodigious power and influence in such a crisis, either as a mediator or umpire, or, if she take a part, as an auxiliary and ally. That she must wish well to the cause of Freedom, it would be indecent, and indeed impious, to doubt – and that she should take an active part against it, is a thing not even to be imagined: – But she may stand aloof, a cold and disdainful spectator; and, counterfeiting a prudent indifference to scenes that neither can nor ought to be indifferent to her, may see, unmoved, the prolongation of a lamentable contest, which her interference might either have prevented, or brought to a speedy and happy termination. And this course she will most probably

---

[39] Ibid., p. 403.

follow, if she allows herself to conceive antipathies to nations for the faults of a few calumnious individuals: And especially if, upon grounds so trivial, she should nourish such an animosity towards England, as to feel a repugnance to make common cause with her, even in behalf of their common inheritance of freedom.[40]

The *Review* essayist acknowledged that Americans might reasonably be suspicious of the current Tory Ministry in England, but "there is yet no other country in Europe where the principles of liberty, and the rights and duties of nations, are so well understood as with us." The English government, "has partaken, or at least has been controlled by the general spirit of freedom; and we have no hesitation in saying, that the Free Constitution of England has been a blessing and protection to the remotest nations of Europe for the last two hundred years. Had England not been free, the worst despotism in Europe would have been far worse than it is, at this moment." Whatever the faults of the Tories, "the effects of her Parliamentary Opposition – the artillery of her Free Press – the voice, in short, of her People" worked on behalf of liberty in Europe. "We still venture to hope that the dread of the British Public is felt as far as Petersburgh and Vienna; and would fain indulge ourselves with the belief, that it may yet scare some Imperial spoiler from a part of his prey, and lighten, if not break, the chains of many distant captives."[41]

For Britain to exercise its "generous, though perhaps decaying influence," it needed "an associate or successor in the noble office of patronising and protecting General Liberty . . . we now call upon America to throw from her the memory of all petty differences and nice offences, and to unite herself cordially with the liberal and enlightened part of the English nation, at a season when their joint efforts may be all little enough to crown the good cause with success, and when their disunion will give dreadful advantages to the enemies of improvement and reform." The mere *example* of America, to be sure, "has done much for that cause; and the very existence of such a country, under such a government, is a tower of strength, and a standard of encouragement, for all who may hereafter have to struggle for the restoration or the extension of their rights. It shows within what wide limits popular institutions are safe and practicable; and that a large infusion of democracy is consistent with the authority of government, and the good order of society." But mere example was not enough – "her *influence*, as well as her example, will be wanted in the crisis which seems to be approaching: – and that influence must be paralysed

---

[40] Ibid., p. 404.

[41] Ibid., pp. 404-5.

and inoperative, if she shall think it a duty to divide herself from England; to look with jealousy upon her proceedings, and to judge unfavourably of all the parties she contains."[42]

Adams bristled when he read these words. Some Americans, as Adams well knew, were sympathetic to the argument that mere example was not enough with respect to promoting liberty in Europe. Clay's argument for an American System to oppose the principles of the Holy Alliance in the New World could certainly be extended to take the battle for liberty preemptively to the Old World. American intervention of some sort in Europe was arguably a matter of prudence and self-interest. Massachusetts Congressman Daniel Webster, for instance, would soon challenge the views of those Americans who argued that "the thunder . . . rolls at a distance," and that "the wide Atlantic is between us and danger; and however others may suffer, we shall remain safe."

> The near approach or the remote distance of danger may affect policy, but cannot change the principle. The same reason that would authorize us to protest against unwarrantable combinations to interfere between Spain and her former colonies, would authorize us equally to protest, if the same combinations were directed against the smallest state in Europe, although our duty to ourselves, our policy, and wisdom, might indicate very different courses as fit to be pursued by us in the two cases. We shall not, I trust, act upon the notion of dividing the world with the Holy Alliance, and complain of nothing done by them in their hemisphere if they will not interfere with ours.[43]

Adams also knew that activist views in the United States toward the European revolutions were not confined to Congress or the political press. In late May 1821, a little over a month before Adams delivered the July 4 Address, President Monroe expressed regret to his Secretary of State that the United States had not sent a minister or agent to Naples while that kingdom had been under constitutional rule.

> Had we taken that step it would have voiced our sentiments in strong term of the doctrines issued from Troppau and elsewhere by the allied powers, which in principle strike at our government almost as directly as at that of Naples, and are perhaps more

---

[42] Ibid., p. 405. Emphasis in original.

[43] Daniel Webster, "Independence of Greece," 19 January 1824, in Charles M. Wiltse and Harold D. Moser, eds., *The Papers of Daniel Webster: Speeches and Formal Writings* (Hanover, NH: University Press of New England, for Dartmouth College, 1974-), 1: 97-8.

directly applicable to it. Will it not be proper that a paper should be presented on the part of this government to those powers, to be addressed to their ministers here, or by our ministers with them, in obedience to instructions, examining calmly the extent of those doctrines, asking their scope, if any doubt should remain respecting it, and protesting against them, if there be none, in the view taken of them? I am aware that this is a most delicate topic, and which ought not to be touched without the most thorough conviction of its policy. It may make us a party, in a certain sense, when it may be the object of all to leave us out of the great movement on foot. It may avert a danger which, tho now latent, may assume a visible form hereafter, since it may animate the friends of human rights everywhere, and thereby check the progress which is making, or intended to be made, in favor of universal despotism.[44]

Monroe, to be sure, had not advocated direct intervention in Europe, just as Clay had insisted that he did not propose to use military force to resist the despotic principles of the Holy Alliance in the American Hemisphere. However, as he stood before his audience on July 4, 1821, Adams feared that the drift toward dangerous political shoals of foreign interventionism and the promotion of revolution and regime change was all too likely.

The Formal Argument of the Address

We can now turn to Adams' argument in the July 4 Address itself. In light of the later attention paid to Adams' epigram – "she goes not abroad, in search of monsters to destroy" – what strikes the reader of the Address is that Adams was focused on the defense of *American* independence and its republican regime. The major rhetorical thrust of the Address was to answer the question, "what has the United States done for mankind?" – a question that had been phrased in the form of a taunt by America's English critics, including those writing for the *Edinburgh Review*. The short answer, Adams said, was that America had proclaimed to mankind the inextinguishable rights of human nature, which was the only lawful foundation of government. America's glory was not that of dominion but of liberty. (p. 31)[45]

The longer answer involved Adams' review of how the American Founders had come to undertake such a glorious and world-historic task.

---

[44] Monroe to Adams, 28 May 1821, *WJQA*, 7: 110-1.

[45] Page numbers in parentheses are taken from the original 1821 publication printed by the sponsors of the event, which can be accessed at http://ia700302.us.archive.org/12/items/address-delivered00adamiala/addressdelivered00adamiala.pdf.

Adams reminded his listeners that Western Christendom for centuries had been in the thrall of a "portentous system of despotism and of superstition." That had been a time in which the rights of man had been overwhelmed by the claims to power of "the Crown and the Mitre." But "the baleful effects of ecclesiastical imposture and political oppression" could not permanently extinguish "the light of reason in the human mind." The inventions of modern science and technology, such as the mariner's compass, the printing press and gunpowder, had led to the age of exploration and a revolution in the art and science of war and of peacetime pursuits. But more decisive still were the improvements in the science of the mind initiated by the leaders of the Reformation. Although the reformers took aim immediately at the corruptions and usurpations of the Church, "at the foundation of all their exertions, there was a single, plain, and almost self-evident principle – that man has a right to the exercise of his own reason." From that conclusion, the transition of that almost self-evident principle to the political and civil realm "was natural and unavoidable." (pp. 6-8)[46]

It was also natural that the political as well as religious reformers were met by the weapons of reactionary temporal power. The double contest of human reason against Crown and Mitre was "too appalling for the vigor, or too comprehensive for the faculties of the reformers of the European Continent." In Britain alone was this contest attempted. Adams did not elaborate on the precise reasons that the British nation (as he called it) distinguished itself in this respect, other than to remark upon the particular intelligence and spirit of its people. In any case, through a series of prolonged and violent civil wars waged between "the oppressions of power and the claims of right," the British people succeeded in emerging from "the impenetrable gloom of this intellectual darkness, and the deep degradation of this servitude." Britons, Adams did not have to remind his audience, gloried in their hard-won liberties and held them up to the world. (pp. 7-8)

Adams said, however, that the British had succeeded only up to a point. They were governed "by a race of kings, whose title to sovereignty had originally been founded in *conquest*." (p. 1)

Over time the British people had "extorted from their tyrants, not *acknowledgments*, but *grants*, of right. With this concession, they had been content to stop in the progress of human improvement." (pp. 5-6) This was "a faltering assertion of freedom." There were those in Britain who had

---

[46] Adams' arguments follow and tailor those of his father, John Adams, particularly in the latter's *Dissertation on the Canon and Feudal Law* (1765) and the *Novanglus* essays (1775), which were then at the cutting edge of the American Whig's rethinking of the proper relationship between the colonies and the mother country.

understood the matter properly – "spirits capable of tracing civil government to its foundation in the moral and physical nature of man" (p. 9) – but, Adams implied, they recognized that British society and culture were capable of taking things to their logical conclusion:

> It was then, that, released from the fetters of ecclesiastical domination, the minds of men began to investigate the foundations of civil government. But the mass of the nation surveyed the fabric of their Institutions as it existed in fact. It had been founded in conquest; it had been cemented in servitude; and so broken and moulded had been the minds of this brave and intelligent people to their actual condition, that instead of solving [sic] civil society into its first elements in search of their rights, they looked back only to conquest as the origin of their liberties, and claimed their rights but as donations from their kings. . . . conquest and servitude were so mingled up in every particle of the social existence of the nation, that they had become vitally necessary to them, as a portion of the fluid, itself destructive of life, is indispensably blended with the atmosphere in which we live. (pp. 8-9)

Adams was not necessarily critical of this considered choice of the British nation. The British went about as far as they could in the direction of ordered liberty.

It was here that the British North American colonies entered the picture. In the midst of the contest between right and power in Britain and throughout Europe, "our forefathers sought refuge from its fury, in the then wilderness of this Western World." They were "exiles of liberty and conscience, dearer to them even than their country." But, even so, they did not want to abandon that country. They came with Charters from the British kings and hoped, "by the corresponding links of allegiance and protection to preserve" the ties of their connection. Soon, however, their experience diverged from that of the mother country. That experience, most notably of the Plymouth colony, was one of a true social compact, a voluntary charter, "formed upon the elementary principles of civil society, in which conquest and servitude had no part," and "which no royal charter could provide." The colonists had always been treated by the parent state "with neglect, harshness and injustice." And, just as the American colonists were attaining their political maturity by the "natural vigor of their constitution," Parliament, in violation of the fundamental principle on which British freedom had been cemented, undertook to tax them without their consent. (pp. 9-10)

For Adams, the Declaration of Independence was the Rosetta Stone that made this and subsequent events perfectly clear. In a narrow sense, the Declaration was merely state paper, announcing and justifying the separation of one people from another, based on time-honored claims of resistance to tyranny. "The names of Pharaoh and Moses, of Tarquin and Junius Brutus, of Geisler and Tell, of Christiern and Gustavus Vasa, of Philip of Austria and William of Orange, stand in the long array through the vista of Time, like the Spirit of Evil and the Spirit of Good, in embattled opposition to each other . . . For the Independence of North America, there were ample and sufficient causes in the law of moral and physical nature."[47] (pp. 11-2)

American resistance to British rule had a particular place in the history of man's natural resistance to tyranny. The next step in Adams' argument was to make the specific case against European-style colonialism. Justice – "the greatest moral purpose of civil government . . . the constant and perpetual will of securing to everyone his right" – cannot be dispensed to a people by a government that is thousands of miles away and separated by an ocean. Justice, one might argue, is the same in London as in Boston or Kingstown (or in Madrid and as in Buenos Aires). Adams believed, moreover, that because "time and space cannot be annihilated," in a practical sense the dispensation of justice, and the administration of the wants of man, require "sympathy." Sympathy begins with the affections of domestic life, which "spread through the social and moral propinquities of the neighbor and friend, to the broad and more complicated relations of countryman and fellow citizen." These ties extend to all humanity, but they weaken as the circle of acquaintance is enlarged. "The tie which binds us to our country, is not more holy in the sight of God, but it is more deeply seated in our nature, more tender and endearing, than the looser link which merely connects us with our fellow mortal man." (pp. 12-4)

> It is a common government that constitutes our country. But in THAT association, all the sympathies of domestic life and kindred blood, all the moral ligatures of friendship and of neighbourhood, are combined with that instinctive and mysterious connection between man and physical nature, which binds the first perceptions

---

[47] The Declaration of Independence was the rhetorical foundation of Adams' approach to American politics and international relations. The Fourth of July was thus the occasion for some of his most significant public statements: about the Declaration and the wars of the French Revolution and American foreign policy (1793); the Constitution and the doctrine of nullification (1831); and slavery and the rights of man (1837). For an assessment of Adams, the Founders, and the Declaration, see Gary V. Wood, *Heir to the Fathers: John Quincy Adams and the Spirit of Constitutional Government* (Lanham, MD: Lexington Books, 2004).

of childhood in a chain of sympathy with the last gasp of expiring age, to the spot of our nativity, and the natural objects by which it is surrounded. These sympathies belong and are indispensable to the relations ordained by nature between the individual and his country. They dwell in the memory and are indelible in the hearts of the first settlers of a distant colony. . . . But these sympathies can never exist for a country, which we have never seen. They are transferred in the hearts of succeeding generations, from the country of human institution, to the country of their birth; from the land of which they have only heard, to the land where their eyes first opened to the day. The ties of neighbourhood are broken up, those of friendship can never be formed, with an intervening ocean; and the natural ties of domestic life, the all-subduing sympathies of love, the indissoluble bonds of marriage, the heart-riveted kindliness of consanguinity, gradually wither and perish in the lapse of a few generations. All the elements, which form the basis of that sympathy between the individual and his country, are dissolved. (p. 14)

Long before the Declaration, "the great mass of the People of America and the People of England, had become total strangers to each other." Even Edmund Burke, who sympathized most with the distresses of America, admitted that he considered its peoples to be strangers. Colonial establishments, in Adams' view, were justifiable only when the subordinate peoples could otherwise not protect themselves, and by the 1770s that was no longer the case for the American colonies. "The connexion was unnatural; and it was in the moral order, no less than in the positive decrees of Providence, that it should be dissolved." (pp. 14-5)

For Adams, however, neither the claim of resistance to a particular tyranny, nor the rejection of this "unnatural connexion" because of the lack of sympathy, was the principal justification the Declaration assigned to America her independence.[48] At an even higher level, it was a revolution based "upon the adamantine rock of human rights," undertaken only as a "last stand" after a long train of abuses. It was not a rebellion "driven by the restive and ungovernable spirit of ambition bursting from the bonds of colonial subjection." (p. 16) Even after some forty-five years, Americans, and a candid world, remained interested in the Declaration not because of the specific wrongs that it enu-

---

[48] Adams later stated that the argument based on "sympathy" for American independence in particular, and for self-determination in general, "is merely incidental to the demonstration from the moral and physical nature of man that *colonial establishments cannot fulfil the great objects of government in the just purpose of civil society.*" He thought some readers had missed the point. JQA to Edward Everett, 31 January 1822, *WJQA*, 7: 200.

merated – or even because it proclaimed the independence of America – but because "it was the first solemn declaration by a nation of the only legitimate foundation of civil government."

> It was the corner stone of a new fabric, destined to cover the surface of the globe. It demolished at a stroke the lawfulness of all governments founded upon conquest. It swept away all the rubbish of accumulated centuries of servitude. It announced in practical form to the world the transcendent truth of the unalienable sovereignty of the people. It proved that the social compact was no figment of the imagination; but a real, solid, and sacred bond of the social union. . . . It stands, and must forever stand alone, a beacon on the summit of the mountain, to which all the inhabitants of the earth may turn their eyes for a genial and saving light, till time shall be lost in eternity, and this globe itself dissolve, nor leave a wreck behind. It stands forever, a light of admonition to the rulers of men; a light of salvation and redemption to the oppressed. So long as this planet shall be inhabited by human beings, so long as man shall be of social nature, so long as government shall be necessary to the great moral purposes of society, and so long as it shall be abused to the purposes of oppression, so long shall this declaration hold out to the sovereign and to the subject the extent and the boundaries of their respective rights and duties; founded in the laws of nature and of nature's God. (pp. 21-2)

Adams referred pointedly to "the genuine Holy Alliance" of the Declaration's principles and called upon his fellow citizens "to recognize them as eternal truths, and to pledge ourselves, and bind our posterity, to a faithful and undeviating adherence to them." (pp. 22-3)

The story did not end there, even with a successful war for independence. The United States of America was of right free and independent, but "the people of this Union collective and individual [were] without government." Contrary to the expectations of the "profoundest of British statesmen," however, they were not in a state of anarchy. Adams listed the near-ideal conditions – the natural connections – that helped lead to the profoundly favorable outcome of the Revolution.

> From the day of the Declaration, the people of the North American Union and of its constituent States, were associated bodies of civilized men and Christians, in a state of nature, but not of Anarchy. They were bound by the laws of God, which they

all, and by the laws of the gospel, which they nearly all, acknowledged as the rules of their conduct. They were bound by the principles which they themselves had proclaimed in the declaration. They were bound by all those tender and endearing sympathies, the absence of which, in the British government and nation, towards them, was the primary cause of the distressing conflict in which they had been precipitated by the headlong rashness and unfeeling insolence of their oppressors. They were bound by all the beneficent laws and institutions, which their forefathers had brought with them from their mother country, not as servitudes but as rights. They were bound by habits of hardy industry, by frugal and hospitable manners, by the general sentiments of social equality, by pure and virtuous morals; and lastly they were bound by the grappling-hooks of common suffering under the scourge of oppression. Where then, among such a people, were the materials for anarchy! Had there been among them no other law, they would have been a law unto themselves. (pp. 26-7)

The American Founders wisely did not assume that such favorable conditions translated themselves automatically into utopia, however. They had a positive agenda for their Revolution, which involved three great objects: "the first, to cement and prepare for perpetuity their common union and that of their posterity; the second, to erect and organize civil and municipal governments in their respective states: and the third, to form connexions of friendship and of commerce with foreign nations." The states were organized in republican forms, on the principles of the Declaration. The Articles of Confederation were adopted unanimously and when they proved "not adequate to the purposes of the country, the people of the United States, without tumult, without violence, by their delegates all chosen upon principles of equal right, formed a more perfect union, by the establishment of the federal constitution." Since that time, "in all the changes of men and parties through which it has passed, it has been administered on the same fundamental principles. . . . In the progress of forty years since the acknowledgement of our Independence, we have gone through many modifications of internal government, and through all the vicissitudes of peace and war, with other powerful nations. But never, never for a moment have the great principles, consecrated by the Declaration of this day, been abandoned or renounced." (pp. 27-8)

As to the third great object – that of foreign relations – the United States had offered to all nations treaties of commerce "in which, for the first time, the same just and magnanimous principles, consigned in the Declaration of Independence, were, so far as they could be applicable to the intercourse between nation and nation, solemnly recognized." (p. 27) These principles were a template for how a nation founded on the rights of mankind should conduct itself abroad. They had been realized during the Revolution in treaties with (monarchical) France and the (republican) Netherlands.

> America, in the assembly of nations, since her admission among them, has invariably, though often fruitlessly, held forth to them the hand of honest friendship, of equal freedom, of generous reciprocity. She has uniformly spoken among them, though often to heedless and often to disdainful ears, the language of equal liberty, equal justice, and equal rights. She has, in the lapse of nearly half a century, without a single exception, respected the independence of other nations, while asserting and maintaining her own. She has abstained from interference in the concerns of others, even when the conflict has been for principles to which she clings, as to the last vital drop that visits the heart. (pp. 28-9)

Adams foresaw centuries-long contests in "that Aceldama the European world" between "inveterate power and emerging right." It is at this point in the Address that he famously explained to his fellow countrymen the proper spirit and policy that they should adopt in those contests:

> Wherever the standard of freedom and independence has been or shall be unfurled, there will her [America's] heart, her benedictions and her prayers be. But she goes not abroad, in search of monsters to destroy. She is the well-wisher to the freedom and independence of all. She is the champion and vindicator only of her own. She will recommend the general cause, by the countenance of her voice, and the benignant sympathy of her example. She well knows that by once enlisting under other banners than her own, were they even the banners of foreign independence, she would involve herself, beyond the power of extrication, in all the wars of interest and intrigue, of individual avarice, envy, and ambition, which assume the colors and usurp the standard of freedom. The fundamental maxims of her policy would insensibly change from liberty to force. The frontlet upon her brows would no longer beam with the ineffable splendor of freedom and independence; but in its stead would soon be substituted an imperial diadem, flashing in false and tarnished lustre the murky radiance of dominion and power. She

> might become the dictatress of the world: she would be no longer the ruler of her own spirit. (p. 29)

Adams now threw back the taunts of British critics of America: "Stand forth, ye champions of Britannia, ruler of the waves! Stand forth, ye chivalrous knights of chartered liberties and the rotten borough! Enter the lists, ye boasters of inventive genius! Ye mighty masters of the palette and the brush! Ye improvers upon the sculpture of the Elgin marbles! Ye spawners of fustian romance and lascivious lyrics! Come and enquire what has America done for the benefit of mankind! In the half century which has elapsed since the Declaration of American Independence, what have you done for the benefit of mankind?" That is, besides inventing the Congreve rocket, the shrapnel shell, and the torpedo. Adams said he might, but would not contrast these British instruments of destruction to useful American inventions such as the steamboat and the cotton gin, because these would be dismissed by the British as a "provincial barbarism." Instead, he was content to rest the American case on the Declaration of Independence. (pp. 29-31)

> Her glory is not dominion, but liberty. Her march is the march of mind. She has a spear and a shield: but the motto upon her shield is, Freedom, Independence, Peace. This has been her Declaration: this has been, as far as her necessary intercourse with the rest of mankind would permit, her practice.
>
> My Countrymen, Fellow-Citizens, and Friends, could that spirit which dictated the Declaration we have this day read; that spirit, which "prefers before all temples the upright heart and pure," at this moment descend from his habitation in the skies, and within this Hall, in language audible to mortal ears, address each one of us here assembled, our beloved Country, Britannia ruler of the waves, and every individual among the sceptred lords of human kind; his words would be
>
> GO THOU, AND DO LIKEWISE. (p. 31)

Elaboration of the Address

Adams was pleased with the immediate reaction of his audience: "Its effect upon the crowded auditory who heard me was as great and as favorable as I could have desired – the effect of unremitting rivetted attention, with more than one occasional burst of applause." The reaction in the wider public, when the Address was reprinted in newspapers around the country, was less positive. "Criticism fastened at once upon the writer and upon the work. Opinions became various. The address was *read* by friend and foe, and it was judged more by the spirit of feeling than by that of scrutiny, more by what was thought of the author than by what was found in the discourse." [49] For the most part, the critics focused on what they judged to be the literary and rhetorical demerits of the Address – an assessment that wounded deeply the feelings of the former Professor of Rhetoric and Oratory. As to substance, Adams was chided for his strident anti-British tone, which seemed in particularly bad taste given his criticism of the mentally ill and recently-deceased George III.

Adams wrote to his young friend from Massachusetts, Edward Everett – who was developing something of a reputation for oratory himself – that he was frustrated by the fact that "neither friend nor foe, so far as I have observed, discovered what was really in the address and what I had thought the most noticeable thing in it." Adams blamed the misapprehension, and any inelegance of expression, on the fact that he had "indulged myself" in an "experimental mood," writing "more for effect than was perhaps always wise," together with the fact that "it was a hasty composition, prepared in the midst of a multitude of other avocations, and I had no time for the labor of the file."[50]

Adams could not defend himself in public but he attempted privately to explain the purpose and argument of the Address to personal friends or political allies like Everett and Walsh, so that they could support Adams' case in their own names. In fact, Adams had a number of different arguments and purposes in mind. He was always sorely provoked by accusations of American inferiority, especially coming from the British, and he could not help answering such slights. He denied that he set out to provoke or offend England.

> Yet in commenting upon the Declaration of Independence, it was impossible to point out that which distinguishes it from any other public document ever penned by man, and that which alone can justify its annual public reperusal, forty years after the close of the conflict of which it was the manifesto, without touching upon topics of peculiar delicacy at this time, and without coming into collision with principles which the British government itself disclaim, but which Emperors and Kings yet maintain at the point of all their bayonets and at the mouths of all their cannon. Far from thinking that this was an occasion for flinching from the assertion of our peculiar and imperishable principles, I am free to confess that one

---

[49] JQA to Edward Everett, 31 January 1822, *WJQA*, 7: 199. Emphasis in original.
[50] Ibid.

of my reasons for assenting to the request that I would deliver an address was to avail myself of the opportunity of asserting them.[51]

The "most notable thing" in the Address, Adams explained to Edward Everett, was "the demonstration from the moral and physical nature of man that *colonial establishments cannot fulfil the great objects of government in the just purpose of civil society*." (Adams underlined the point for emphasis.) This demonstration, in Adams' opinion, was something entirely new, and "complete and unanswerable." He listed the main points of the Address, as they related to "the past, present and future history of mankind, upon the system of political morality, and upon the future improvement of the human character."

1. It places on a new and solid ground the *right* of our struggle for independence, considering the intolerable oppression which provoked our fathers to the revolt only as its proximate causes, themselves proof of the viciousness of the system from which they resulted.

2. It settles the justice of the present struggle of South America for independence, and prepares for an acknowledgment upon the principle of public law of that independence, whenever it shall be sufficiently established by the fact.

3. It looks forward prospectively to the downfall of the British Empire in India as an event which must necessarily ensue at no very distant period of time.

4. It anticipates a great question in the national policy of this Union which may be nearer at hand than most of our countrymen are aware of: Whether we too shall annex to our federative government a great system of colonial establishments.

5. It points to a principle proving that such establishments are incompatible with the essential character of our political institutions.

6. It leads to the conclusion that great colonial establishments are but mighty engines of *wrong*, and that in the progress of social improvement it will be the duty of the human family to abolish them, as they are now endeavoring to abolish the slave trade.[52]

---

[51] JQA to Walsh, 10 July 1821, *WJQA*, 7: 113-4.

[52] JQA to Edward Everett, 31 January 1822, *WJQA*, 7: 200-1. Emphasis in original.

What precisely was the "duty" of the United States, as a member of the "human family," with respect to the abolition of the great colonial establishments? For Adams, the beginning of practical wisdom for American policymakers was the realization that the breakdown of the colonial systems would occur naturally, in the course of human events. All colonial empires, whether established by absolutist regimes like Spain or more liberal states like Britain, were "an outrage upon the first principles of civil society." The natural rebellion against such injustice, which first occurred in North America and later in the South, "together with the progress of the human mind towards emancipation, which no efforts of existing power can suppress, must within a period not very remote demolish all the remnants of that absurd and iniquitous system."[53] The same was also true of the interventionism of the Holy Alliance to defend despotism in the Old World. "It is tasking severely the patience of the human race to hear Louis the 18th of France proclaim in the face of the world, that he who had not legs to stand upon will send a hundred thousand Frenchmen into Spain to ravage the land with fire and sword, to teach them to receive their liberties from the grant of Ferdinand the 7th," Adams later remarked. "This doctrine cannot be much longer maintained in Europe. It grows too absurd."[54]

In part because of this generally progressive direction of human affairs, Adams concluded that the United States need not and should not indulge in a crusading spirit or take part directly in the "conflicts between power and right." Americans had learned by experience the full costs and risks of foreign crusades, especially when the protagonists did not share the American understanding of ordered liberty as set out in the Declaration and the Constitution. The interventionist doctrines of Lexington and Edinburgh had "already twice in the course of our history brought the peace and the permanent welfare of the Union into jeopardy: under Washington's administration at the early stage of the French Revolution; under the present administration in the efforts to entangle us in the South American conflict."[55]

For Adams, reflection on the principles of the Declaration and experience with the Constitution pointed to a different approach. The federal government should support the development of a great federal, republican North American Union, secure from foreign threats, steadily improving the physical and moral condition of its citizens, and contributing to the common benefit of human (Christian) civilization through the fruits of its science, the arts, and literature. What we might call Adams' "civilizational agenda" did have a specific foreign

---

[53] JQA to Alexander H. Everett, 10 August 1818, *WJQA*, 6: 423.

[54] JQA to Daniel Cony, 28 April 1823, *WJQA*, 7: 368.

[55] JQA to Edward Everett, 31 January 1822, *WJQA*, 7: 201.

policy dimension – the promotion of peace and commerce, moral opposition to colonial establishments, and the elimination of certain barbarous practices.[56]

Adams insisted that such goals were not utopian. He believed that these great civilizational objectives could be achieved prudently, in stages. For the most part, they would not involve the use of force.[57] Each nation could decide for itself how it would contribute to these ends but Adams expected that the United States would play a leading international role. For instance, by advocating strongly freedom of commerce in peacetime and the rights of neutrals in wartime – and by making that advocacy credible by its own economic and naval strength – the United States would make war a much less attractive option for all concerned. Similarly, by achieving international agreements to outlaw privateering, the United States would close off a specific avenue that made war profitable and that provided a cover for piracy, one of those barbarous practices that a civilized world should not tolerate.[58]

In 1823, Adams proposed to offer Britain and other maritime powers of Europe a comprehensive convention to regulate neutral and belligerent rights in time of war. "My plan involves nothing less than a revolution in the laws of war – a great amelioration in the condition of man. Is it the dream of a visionary, or is it the great and practicable conception of a benefactor of mankind? I believe it the latter; and I believe this to be precisely the time for proposing it to the world. Should it even fail, it will be honorable to have proposed it." The cool and realistic diplomatist known to history admitted to his diary: "When I think, if it possibly could succeed, what a real and solid blessing it would be to the human race, I can scarcely guard myself from a spirit of enthusiasm, which it becomes me to distrust."[59]

Adams believed in a hierarchy of societies and in the superiority of western, Christian civilization. In the inevitable clashes between civilizations,

---

[56] For an exploration of the broader dimensions of Adams' approach to foreign policy, see Greg Russell, *John Quincy Adams and the Public Virtues of Diplomacy* (Columbia: University of Missouri Press, 1995).

[57] Adams, however, recognized that the end of slavery in the United States might well be accomplished only through or during a period of violence. For a considered discussion of Adams' views, see William Lee Miller, *Arguing about Slavery: John Quincy Adams and the Great Battle in the United States Congress* (New York: Vintage, 1998).

[58] As part of his civilizational agenda, Adams favored strong measures to bring about the abolition of the transatlantic slave trade – but unfortunately, to his mind, the British stubbornly tied their cooperation to their unfettered right of search on the high seas, and thus to their claimed right of impressment, which Adams regarded as a violation of human rights even greater than that of the slave trade itself (a point which the African slaves might have contested). 29 April 1819, *MJQA*, 4: 353-5.

[59] 28 July 1823, *MJQA*, 6: 164-5; Day, July 1823, *MJQA*, 6: 166-7. For the text of JQA's *Project of a Convention for Regulating the Principles of Commercial and Maritime Neutrality*, see Bemis, *John Quincy Adams*, pp. 579-85.

he naturally favored what he considered to be the more advanced stages of mankind, even if they were not perfect. (Justice, to be sure, was always to be done to the inferior party). Adams was a strident critic of Islam and was sympathetic with Russia in its battles with the Turks (although he did not propose American interference in that conflict). He would later argue in support of Britain's unwillingness to accept China's economic restrictions and the refusal of its envoys to kowtow to the Chinese Emperor.[60]

In the process of dealing with barbarous behavior by purportedly inferior civilizations, Adams believed that there were occasions when the United States itself might contemplate going abroad in search of monsters to destroy – at least to prevent barbarities, if not to destroy the monsters themselves. Adams, like most Americans, regarded the Islamic polities on the Barbary Coast as monsters, particularly because of their piratical attacks on merchant vessels and the enslavement and ransoming of their crews. In the First Barbary War (1801-1805) against Tripoli, Adams, while a U.S. Senator, had favored strong American measures (although he stopped short of advocating American diplomatic and military action to overthrow the current ruler and replace him with his presumably more pliant brother).[61] While U.S. Minister to England, he followed closely the actions of the U.S. Navy's Mediterranean Squadron led by Commodore Stephen Decatur against Algiers in 1815-1816, but regretted that more had not been done.

> Pacific as I am, I hope we shall never again, after beating Algiers, truckle to her in substance, and then swagger as if we had obtained a triumph. A real and a glorious triumph awaits us there, if we will but undertake to win it. But we must have fighting as gallant and skilful as heretofore, and no trifling negotiations, no gratuitous restitutions, no consular presents, no bullying articles against tribute, and tacit ticklings of the pirates palm. This war, if we have it, will be quite as much as we can manage well, and will not necessarily, nor even probably, lead us into any other. Its tendency would on the contrary be to cement our peace with the rest of the world, by increasing at once our moral strength in the respect of mankind,

---

[60] On the general hierarchy of societies, from the hunter to the inhabitants of cities, see JQA, "Society and Civilization," *American Whig Review* 2 (July 1845): 80-9. On Russia and Islam, see JQA, Chapters X and XI, *The American Annual Register for the Years 1827-8-9* (New York: William Jackson and E. & B.W. Blunt, 1835), pp. 267-316. On Britain and China, see "John Quincy Adams: The Opium War and the Sanctity of Commercial Reciprocity," *Proceedings of the Massachusetts Historical Society* 43 (February 1910): 303-26.

[61] See Patrick J. Garrity, *Jefferson, the Barbary Regencies, and Regime Change: The Attractions and Limits of Limited Liability*, Working Paper Series on American Foreign Policy and Regime Change (Ashland, OH: Ashbrook Center, October 2009), pp. 50-2.

and our physical power of defense in the naval bulwark. War! say I, with Algiers, and peace with the universe beside.[62]

Here are Adams' criteria for seeking out monsters, or at least monstrous (uncivilized) behavior, to destroy. According to Adams, the successful use of force must be well within the means of the United States; the action must not result in a wider war (and especially not entangle the United States in purely European struggles); it should contribute to the general peace of mankind; it should enhance America's moral standing; and, it should result in an improvement in America's defensive military capacity, which Adams understood principally to mean the U.S. Navy. In the context of America's position in the world in 1821, these were high standards indeed.

This brings us back to what Adams regarded as the central line of argument of his July 4 Address: "that colonial establishments cannot fulfil the great objects of government in the just purpose of civil society," and that, "in the progress of social improvement it will be the duty of the human family to abolish them, as they are now endeavoring to abolish the slave-trade." The South American cause of independence was indeed a civilizational cause – but it did not meet Adams' criteria for the American use of force. The United States would, at a minimum, have provoked a wider war that would have exceeded its means to wage effectively. Adams also believed that American public opinion was opposed to such a war – and (as we will see) he assumed that the political stability of an independent, republican South America was problematic.

In Adams' opinion, the Lexington Doctrine took the United States down the slippery slope of political entanglement and military intervention. He did not propose, however, that the United States should be entirely passive toward the South American cause. He believed that there was a middle ground between disinterest and the use of force – that is, a diplomatic and moral tilt toward the South Americans that would offset the diplomatic and moral tilt of the European monarchs against colonial independence, and that it would allow progressive political and historical forces to work themselves out favorably on behalf of the South Americans. The revolutionaries, meanwhile, had to prove they were capable of winning their independence. The critical policy card that the United States had to play was the timing and nature of its recognition of the independence of the new South American states. At the margins, but only

---

[62] JQA to Erving, 10 June 1816, *WJQA*, 6: 46. When an Anglo-Dutch fleet under the command of Lord Exmouth bombarded Algiers, compelled the release of more than a thousand Christian prisoners, and obtained a treaty that formally outlawed the slavery of Europeans – "a deed of real glory" – Adams was disappointed that the United States had not won the palm of honor. 16 September 1816, *MJQA*, 3: 442-3; JQA to Secretary of State, 18 September 1816, *WJQA*, 6: 87-8.

at the margins, Adams believed that this non-interventionist, middle-ground course could influence the formation of the South American regimes in a republican and constitutional direction that was respectful of human liberty and the rights of mankind. This diplomatic tilt, in turn, required the United States to reinforce publicly its rejection of the Edinburgh Doctrine and avoid any hint of interference in the social and political struggles of Europe proper.

South American Independence: Diplomatic Recognition and Regime Change

To a first order, the outbreak of movements for South American independence fit perfectly into Adams' expectation of the progressive evolution of civilization. These movements would eventually break down the great European colonial establishments, in which a distant homeland governed a people from afar and maintained exclusivity of trade. Spain had been the worst example of the lot.

> Resting for the right upon the most degraded superstition; pursuing for its means brutal force alone, Spain had taken a grant of half the world from the Bishop of Rome, to teach to its inhabitants the most benevolent of all religions. And after ravaging under these pretences those extensive regions with fire and sword; after subduing their people by force and treachery, and extirpating them by millions, had taken possession of nearly the whole continent of South America, and of a great portion of the north, and locking them up from all other human intercourse but with herself, claimed, and for three hundred years maintained, exclusive property of the inhabitants and of the soil, excluding all foreigners from setting foot on their shores upon the penalty of death.[63]

Adams thought that the breakup of the Spanish Empire in the Americas was inevitable, whenever the time was ripe, without any outside military support by the United States. "It was impossible that such a system as Spain had established over her colonies should stand before the progressive improvement of the understanding in this age, or that the light shed upon the whole earth by the results of our revolution should leave in utter darkness the regions immediately adjoining upon ourselves."[64] Because of his confidence that the

---

[63] JQA to Anderson, 27 May 1823, *WJQA*, 7: 441-2. These words were deleted on reflection, probably because they were too inflammatory to communicate in a diplomatic instruction, but they did reflect Adams' views.

[64] Ibid., 7: 442. This text was also deleted in the final version of the instructions to Anderson.

South American cause would succeed on its own when the time was right – and not before – Adams rejected for the United States the path of Bourbon France during the American Revolution. That strategy would have been one of surreptitious support for the revolutionaries, followed by diplomatic recognition, treaties of commerce and alliance, military aid, and then the direct use of troops and ships against the colonial power. Adams believed that the U.S. government had instead correctly adopted and enforced a policy of neutrality toward the belligerents and that it had wisely resisted the pressure of Clay and others for early recognition of the South American states.[65]

Adams agreed with Clay that diplomatic recognition was the most powerful diplomatic, legal, and political tool for the United States to support independence and to influence regime change in South America. But he believed that tool should be applied much later in the process, not at the beginning – and then only when certain favorable conditions within the new states and in the international environment had been demonstrated amply.

In Adams' view, the argument by Clay and the lobbyists for the South American revolutionaries – that early diplomatic recognition could be granted without risk to the United States – was disingenuous or naïve. Spain was bound to claim that diplomatic recognition was a hostile act, incompatible with proclaimed American neutrality, which Madrid already insisted was a sham. The United States would find itself on the slippery slope to war. The revolutionaries and their U.S. supporters would not be satisfied merely with recognition. Adams believed, for instance, that they would demand the revision or non-enforcement of laws that barred U.S. citizens from active military or logistical support for the revolutionaries. Formal U.S. military involvement was the next logical step in this escalatory process, even if Spain did not declare war against the United States.[66]

Adams was concerned that many Americans regarded the Spanish with contempt as a military opponent, in part because they did not realize the virtual certainty that war with Spain would draw in other European powers. Clay

---

[65] To be sure, American neutrality between the belligerents in the midst of a civil war involving a mother country and colony did not mean equal treatment of the parties. One party, after all, was a recognized nation-state, and the other was not. "We consider it, however, as among the obligations of neutrality to obviate this inequality as far as may be practicable without taking a side, as if the question of the war was decided." This led to complaints by both Spain and the South Americans that they were being treated unfairly by the United States – and to Clay's arguments that the United States should practice a "just" rather than "impartial" neutrality. For a detailed discussion of Adams' views on this point, see JQA to Rush, 1 January 1819, *WJQA*, 6: 520-6.

[66] William Earl Weeks, *John Quincy Adams and the American Global Empire* (Lexington, KY: University Press of Kentucky, 1992), Chapter 4, reviews Adams' approach to the South American question. Weeks emphasizes the primacy of the negotiations with Spain for Adams, with the South American revolutions treated as a distinctly secondary concern (pp. 133-4).

later professed to Adams that he was unconcerned by that prospect, although he did not think it likely – "he believed even a war for it against all Europe, including even England, would be advantageous to us." Such a war, if successful, would strengthen the Union, Clay insisted. Adams strongly disagreed; this smacked of American overconfidence leading up to the War of 1812. "I told him I believed a war for South American independence might be inevitable, and, under certain circumstances, might be expedient, but that I viewed war in a very different light from him – as necessarily placing high interests of different portions of the Union in conflict with each other, and thereby endangering the Union itself."[67] The War of 1812 had been a damned near-run thing in this respect. New England had almost separated from the Union. The Missouri crisis reminded Adams of how internal divisions, especially over slavery, had not been fully resolved.

Adams, to repeat, believed that South American independence was natural, legitimate and inevitable, and that U.S. diplomatic recognition of the new regimes would and should follow in due course. But the timing and context was critical. Premature diplomatic recognition would derail a policy that Adams thought was best for the United States, the South Americans, and the cause of the rights of man. Adams summarized that policy to Clay: "That the final issue of their present struggle would be their entire independence of Spain I had never doubted. That it was our true policy and duty to take no part in the contest I was equally clear. The principle of neutrality to *all* foreign wars was, in my opinion, fundamental to the continuance of our liberties and of our Union."[68]

Adams believed that the principled and self-interested bedrock of U.S. foreign policy toward all foreign wars was that of neutrality. American statesmen had supported the concept, rightly understood, as an operative principle of the law of nations even during their own revolution. The Washington administration had embraced neutrality during the wars of the French Revolution and Washington himself had enshrined it in his immortal Farewell Address. As a young attorney, Adams had written a prominent series of newspaper essays that defended a policy of strict neutrality.[69] By insisting on and enforcing this historic policy in the case of the South American revolutions, the United States put itself in the best diplomatic position to encourage other powers to

---

[67] JQA to George W. Erving, 28 March 1816, *WJQA*, 5: 547. Clay acknowledged that "a successful war, to be sure, created a military influence and power, which he considered as the greatest danger of war." 2 December 1823, *MJQA*, 6: 223-4.

[68] 9 March 1821, *MJQA*, 5: 323-4.

[69] Bemis, *John Quincy Adams*, pp. 37-8; the Columbus essays are printed in *WJQA*, 1: 148ff.

stay out of the fight as well. And in a fair, straight-up fight, Adams believed that the South Americans were bound to win. Spain, by itself, was incapable of maintaining or recovering its rule in most of its American possessions. The only game-changing card that Spain had left to play was to enlist the other European monarchs actively on its behalf. At the Congress of Aix-la-Chapelle in 1818, however, the continental allies and Britain, as Adams saw it, effectively agreed that they would not offer military assistance to Spain.

Adams seized on this European restraint as something that American policy should encourage. He argued that overt U.S. involvement on behalf of the revolutionaries would cause the European allies to reconsider their position. This would turn a limited war between a single, weak mother country and her colonies into a transatlantic war between republicans and monarchs. England would be hard-pressed to stay out of such a war. If London chose to fight on the side of Spain and the monarchs in South America, America would find itself in a desperate position with little ability to influence the outcome. But if England took the side of revolutionaries, she would do so for selfish commercial reasons, which would work against the United States even though the two English-speaking peoples would nominally be on the same side. This was the terrain that the United States would face in 1823, under somewhat different circumstances, when it responded with what became known as the Monroe Doctrine.

Adams did not propose to adopt a purely passive policy toward South America, however. Neutrality still left room for diplomacy. The United States sought to persuade the various governments in Madrid that "every effort of Spain to recover the South American continent must thenceforward be a desperate waste of her own resources, and that the truest friendship of other nations to her would consist in making her sensible that her own interest would be best consulted by the acknowledgment of that independence which she could no longer effectually dispute." Adams wanted, if possible, to internationalize the process of recognition. The Monroe administration had informal contacts along these lines with the French, Russian and British governments in 1817. In August 1818, "a formal proposal was made to the British government, for a concerted and cotemporary [sic] recognition of the independence of Buenos Ayres, then the only one of the South American states which, having declared independence, had no *Spanish* force contending against it, within its borders, and where it therefore most unequivocally existed *in fact*."[70]

Adams knew that such appeals to the continental allies and to the British had to rest ultimately on the pursuit of their perceived national interests rather

---

[70] JQA to Anderson, 27 May 1823, *WJQA*, 7: 444-6. Emphasis in original.

than their sense of abstract justice. Until the South American states were recognized as full members of the community of nations, Adams pointed out, they could not be required "to observe on their part the ordinary rules of the laws of nations in their intercourse with the civilized world. We particularly believe that the only effectual means of repressing the excessive irregularities and piratical depredations of armed vessels under their flags, and bearing their commissions, will be to require of them the observance of the principles sanctioned by the practice of maritime nations. It is not to be expected that they will feel themselves bound by the ordinary duties of sovereign states while they are denied the enjoyment of all their rights." The U.S. made it known that it would refuse any invitation to a European conference on South America unless its purpose was to ratify independence. [71]

Britain was the key to American diplomatic strategy because she had the most to gain, or lose, from the opening (or closing) of the markets of South America, as well as protection from attacks against her merchant shipping. The British alone had the naval and economic power to make their policy preference stick. To prompt London, Adams instructed U.S. Minister Richard Rush to inform the British in early 1819 that President Monroe intended to recognize Buenos Aires "before long." The proposed British-American action would not be one "of formal compact, but of common good understanding." Castlereagh's decision to decline the American initiative confirmed to Adams the view that premature unilateral U.S. recognition could be disastrous because it would put the two English-speaking nations directly at odds. Britain's preferred outcome, as Adams understood it, was to develop trade with the dissolving Spanish Empire but delay recognition, in hopes that King Ferdinand could salvage some sort of sovereignty over a reformed colonial system that would be open to British trade. Britain's second choice, as Adams suspected, was for a constellation of South American monarchies under British tutelage. Neither of these was an acceptable outcome for the United States. Moreover, it was still not out of the question that London, to maintain a balance of power in Europe, would eventually come around to supporting intervention against the independence movements.[72]

In light of Britain's policy, despite what Rush was instructed to tell Castlereagh, U.S. recognition of any of the new South American states was deemed too risky in the years before Adams' July 4, 1821 Address. As Adams saw it, the United States still needed to buy time for things to mature favorably

---

[71] JQA to Rush, 1 January 1819, *WJQA*, 6: 525.

[72] 7 December 1818, *MJQA*, 4: 186-7; 2 January 1819, *MJQA*, 4: 203-8; Bemis, *John Quincy Adams*, p. 343.

on the ground in South America, while he resolved the United States' bilateral negotiations with Spain. Although the British government had declined the proposal to cooperatively recognize Buenos Aires, it had not taken exception to the idea, and Adams believed that the approach had moved Britain closer to the American position. In Adams' opinion, the quiet American diplomatic campaign for cooperative action on behalf of South American independence had influenced favorably the deliberations of the European powers at the crucial Congress at Aix-la-Chapelle in 1818.

> There is reason to believe that it disconcerted projects which were there entertained of engaging the European alliance in active operations against the South Americans, as it is well known that a plan for their joint *mediation* between Spain and her colonies, for restoring them to her authority, was actually matured and finally failed at that place only by the refusal of Great Britain to accede to the condition of employing *force* eventually against the South Americans for its accomplishment.[73]

According to Adams' analysis, the United States had run some risk on behalf of South American independence through its initiative to encourage Britain and other European states to recognize Buenos Aires. However, it had mitigated that risk by assuring Britain and the continental allies that its preference – under the present circumstances at least – was to avoid getting out ahead of Europe on the matter.

> Anxious, however, to fulfil every obligation of good neighborhood to Spain, notwithstanding our numerous and aggravated causes of complaint against her, and especially desirous to preserve the friendship and good-will of all the allied European powers, we have forborne under circumstances of strong provocation to take any decisive step which might interfere with the course of their policy in relation to South America. We have waited patiently to see the effect of their mediation, without an attempt to disconcert or defeat any measures upon which they might agree for assuring its success.[74]

Adams believed that such quiet diplomacy offered the best way to aid the cause of the South Americans. He disagreed with Clay about the value of public diplomacy or grandiose pronouncements in favor of national indepen-

---

[73] JQA to Anderson, 27 May 1823, *WJQA*, 7: 447. Emphasis in original.

[74] JQA to Rush, 1 January 1819, *WJQA*, 6: 524.

dence movements – unless (as we shall see) there was severe provocation in which the rhetorical defense of republicanism was clearly justified. Otherwise, in Adams' opinion, these pronouncements merely angered the Europeans while idiomatically complicating America's essential interests closer to home. Each year, Monroe insisted on inserting a paragraph or two in his Annual Message, which commented on the situation in South America and offered a favorable prognosis for the independence movements. Adams did his best to tone down these words. "I have always thought these paragraphs exotics [sic] to the proper region of the message; which might just as well descant upon the wars of the English in India, or more suitably upon the treaties and Congresses of the European allies. . . . My objection to it is, that, our system being professedly neutrality, any avowal of partiality for the South Americans was inconsistent with it, and liable to raise doubts of our sincerity."

The President, Adams realized, probably thought it necessary politically to use such language to counteract Clay's insinuation that the administration was hostile to the South American cause. However, they resulted in unfortunate repercussions in the diplomatic realm: "I believe that these paragraphs of the message have been the principal real cause of the delay of Spain to ratify the Florida Treaty."[75]

Adams' Criteria for Recognition and Regime Change

Adams recognized that the South American situation was dynamic and that, at some point, the United States would have to consider going beyond its policy of encouraging European governments to recognize the new regimes coincidentally with the United States. That meant unilaterally offering recognition to some or all of the South American states. Adams developed a political-strategic matrix to determine the point at which such a shift in policy would be justified. He explained to Monroe, in 1818, that "there is a stage in such contests when the party struggling for independence have, as I conceive, a right to demand its acknowledgment by neutral parties, and when the acknowledgment may be granted without departure from the obligations of neutrality. It is the stage when the independence is established as a matter of fact, so as to leave the chance of the opposite party to recover their dominion utterly desperate."[76] This was in contrast to the view taken by European reactionaries, in which "the rebels against legitimate authority" were entitled to recognition by third parties only after the colonial state had done so.

---

[75] 12 November 1820, *MJQA*, 5: 199-201.

[76] JQA to Monroe, 24 August 1818, *WJQA*, 6: 441-3.

First, Adams believed that each new regime claiming independence must demonstrate that it exercised effective physical control over a specific territory. It could only demand recognition of territory that it actually possessed and not of areas still undeniably controlled by the colonial power – or of territory claimed by other revolutionary actors. In the case of Buenos Aires, its claims of territorial sovereignty had been so excessive as to undermine a persuasive case for recognition of the lands it did unmistakably control.

Second, true sovereignty meant the ability and willingness to abide by and enforce the law of nations. The new regimes, for example, must offer credible assurances that they would not allow privateers to use their territory or the cover of their flags to attack neutral commerce.

Third, the revolutionary regime must agree to put the United States economically on the footing of most favored nation, a status to which other nations were also entitled as a precondition for recognition. The new regime could not reserve special favors to the former colonial power, in this case, Spain, as compensation for its abandonment of claims of sovereignty. Nor could it grant special commercial favors to other nations (Adams had Britain in mind). Any such special economic arrangements would put the new regimes back in a state of colonial subservience. To be sure, the United States, as a practical matter, might acknowledge the "imperfect" existence of such subservient states by sending and receiving consuls and other agents. That, however, was not the same as recognizing "entire" independence.[77]

Fourth, the new nation must demonstrate its *political* independence. According to the principles of the Declaration, peoples were entitled to establish whatever form of government they believed to be conducive to their safety and happiness. The South American states, in theory, did not need to be republics in order to be accorded recognition by the United States, although the leading revolutionaries typically proclaimed themselves to be republican. Adams, however, was alarmed by reports that the leaders of Buenos Aires and other would-be South American nations were willing to offer thrones to members of European royal families in exchange for diplomatic recognition. He was not prepared to support diplomatic recognition under those circumstances – and he fully intended to use the threat of U.S. non-recognition to persuade the South Americans not to go down the path of dependent monarchies.[78]

Adams' policy matrix did not stop with his assessment of the internal makeup of the new states. The right of a revolutionary regime to demand

---

[77] JQA to Monroe, 24 August 1818, *WJQA*, 6: 441-3; JQA to de Forrest, 31 December 1818, *WJQA*, 6: 514-9.

[78] JQA to Rodney, 17 May 1823, *WJQA*, 7: 426.

acknowledgement of its independence when it had met those necessary domestic conditions did not *require* the United States (or any other neutral power) to grant recognition.

> The neutral nation must, of course, judge for itself when this period [of de facto independence] has arrived, and as the belligerent nation has the same right to judge for itself, it is very likely to judge differently from the neutral and to make it a cause or a pretext for war, as Great Britain did expressly against France in our Revolution, and substantially against Holland. If war thus results in point of fact from the measure of recognizing a contested independence, the moral right or wrong of the war depends upon the justice, and sincerity, and prudence with which the recognizing nation took the step. I am satisfied that the cause of the South Americans, so far as it consists in the assertion of independence against Spain is just. But the justice of a cause, however it may enlist individual feelings in its favor, is not sufficient to justify third parties in siding with it. The fact and the right combined can alone authorize a neutral to acknowledge a new and disputed sovereignty. The neutral may indeed infer the right from the fact, but not the fact from the right.[79]

Among the facts to be taken into account by the U.S. government was the likelihood that American recognition might draw in other powers on the opposite side, thereby creating a wider war in which the security of the United States might be placed at risk – and in which the world as a whole would be worse off. Misplaced words or diplomatic acts, as well as the direct use of force, could result in a destructive conflict that would overwhelm the immediate justice of the case at hand. The U.S. decision to delay recognition, in Adams' view, went beyond the self-interested need to avoid antagonizing Spain at a critical point in the bilateral negotiations for what became the Transcontinental Treaty. The United States must not be responsible for the outbreak of a global war over South America that could otherwise have been avoided through American restraint.[80]

---

[79] JQA to Monroe, 24 August 1818, *WJQA*, 6: 441-3.

[80] Adams asserted that when the United States finally decided to offer recognition to a new regime, it would not become an active party to the conflict if the former colonial power persisted in trying to reestablish its rule. The United States would still remain neutral according to its understanding of the law of nations, with the necessary adjustments to account for the fact that the war had now legally become a conflict between two or more nations, rather than a civil war.

The Republican Cause in North and South America: Deconstructing the Lexington Doctrine

Clay, as we have seen, disagreed with Adams' general approach toward South America, as well as his particular calculations about the strategic situation. Clay felt that the risks of a wider war, and of Spain's breaking off the talks with the United States, were much lower than Adams estimated. Clay also believed that the United States, by standing aloof from its southern brethren, was missing a golden opportunity to shape the independence movements in a republican and pro-American direction (American in the broader sense, as well as pro-United States). If the sympathies of the United States were not actively made manifest to the South Americans, Clay insisted, they would naturally look to other powers for support and for models of government.

Adams, at the time of his July 4, 1821 Address, was doubtful that the United States could do much directly to influence the formation of the South American states. In his opinion, American policymakers should examine closely the cause professed by these "republics" or "republican" revolutionaries, and not assume automatically that their cause was the same as that of the United States. There were ample historical grounds for such caution. During the 1790s, Adams had argued strenuously that the causes and objects of the French Revolution should not automatically be conflated with those of the American Revolution. The United States, he believed, had wisely remained neutral in the wars of the French Revolution not only because of its obligation under the law of nations and its national self-interest but because what passed for republicanism in France was wrong-headed and likely to end in a military dictatorship. He had held this view well before Napoleon arrived prominently on the scene. The French Republic's supposed crusade to free the peoples of Europe merely masked traditional French expansionist aims. At the same time, Adams believed that the French people were entitled to whatever form of government they felt best suited their safety and happiness, and that the opposing alliance had no right to intervene to change that government, be it republican or Napoleonic.[81]

Adams applied the same scrutiny to the cause of the South Americans. He had no doubt that their liberation from Spain and their soon-to-be-consummated entry into the family of nations was "among the most important events in modern history." In that sense it followed "the development of

---

[81] See, for example, JQA to Nathaniel Freeman, Jr., 3 August 1797, *Microfilms of the Adams Papers* (Boston: Massachusetts Historical Society, 1954-), Reel 130. Hereafter referred to as *MAP*. JQA to John Adams, 10 August 1797, *MAP*, Reel 385.

principles first brought into action by the separation of these states from Great Britain, and by the practical illustration given in the formation and establishment of our Union to the doctrine that voluntary agreement is the only legitimate source of authority among men, and that all just government is a compact."[82] But in the larger sense, "the independence of the Spanish colonies, however, has proceeded from other causes, and has been achieved upon principles, in many respects different from ours. In our revolution the principle of the social compact was, from the beginning, in immediate issue. It originated in a question of *right* between the government in Europe and the subject in America. Our *independence* was declared in defence of our *liberties*, and the attempt to make the yoke a yoke of oppression was the cause and justification for casting it off.

> The revolution of the Spanish colonies was not caused by the oppression under which they had been held, however great it had been. Accustomed to the combined weight of military and ecclesiastical despotism, secluded from all intercourse with the rest of the world, subdued in mind and body, with a people heterogeneously composed of European adventurers, of Creole natives of the country but of Spanish descent, of aboriginal Indians, and of African slaves, all under the actual government of the small number of Spaniards composing the first class, there was no spirit of freedom pervading any portion of this population, no common principle of reason to form an union of mind; no means of combining force for exertions of resistance to power. The independence of the Spanish colonies was first forced upon them by the temporary subjugation of Spain herself to a foreign power [Napoleonic France]. They were by that event cast upon themselves and compelled to establish governments of their own.[83]

Such a defective political culture meant that true republican government in South America was unlikely to emerge. As a boy, Adams had traveled through northern Spain with his father, who was en route to Paris to take up his diplomatic post for the U.S. Congress during the Revolutionary War. Here he had experienced the results of Catholic absolutism: fat priests and lean peasants, widespread poverty, ignorance and superstition. His exposure to various scholarly writings, conversations with merchants and mariners, and diplomatic

---

[82] JQA to Richard C. Anderson, 27 May 1823, *WJQA*, 7: 441.

[83] Ibid., 7: 442-3. The first two sentences in this block quote were deleted from the final instructions, but they do reflect Adams' considered view.

contacts and reports, led Adams to later conclude that the same cultural deformities existed throughout South America, albeit intensified by centuries of colonial exploitation.[84] As Adams told Clay in a private conversation just a few months before he delivered the July 4 Address:

> I had seen and yet see no prospect that they would establish free or liberal institutions of government. They are not likely to promote the spirit either of freedom or order by their example. They have not the first elements of good or free government. Arbitrary power, military and ecclesiastical, was stamped upon their education, upon their habits, and upon all their institutions. Civil dissension was infused into all their seminal principles. War and mutual destruction was in every member of their organization, moral, political, and physical. I had little expectation of any beneficial result to this country from any future connection with them, political or commercial. We should derive no improvement to our own institutions by any communion with theirs. Nor was there any appearance of a disposition in them to take any political lesson from us. –As to the commercial connection, I agreed with him that little weight should be allowed to arguments of mere pecuniary interest; but there was no basis for much traffic between us. They want none of our productions, and we could afford to purchase very few of theirs. Of these opinions, both his and mine, *time* must be the test; but, I would candidly acknowledge, nothing had hitherto occurred to weaken in my mind the view which I had taken of this subject from the first.[85]

"They will be independent, no doubt, but will they be free?" Adams asked his father in 1818. "General ignorance can never be free, and the Roman religion is incompatible with free government. South America, then, independent of Spain, will be governed by a dozen Royalists independent of each other, and each seeking alliances in Europe, and in the United States. Suppose a Confederation of these little sovereigns, will it not be a perpetual struggle which shall be first?"[86]

Adams, it should be stressed, did not make this sort of comment publicly or incorporate it in official policy documents. He said nothing of the sort in

---

[84] Parsons, *John Quincy Adams*, p. 19. Adams' views were confirmed by the findings of a Commission that Monroe sent to South America to survey developments there (although the Commissioners disagreed about the policy implications). Bemis, *John Quincy Adams*, p. 347.

[85] 9 March 1821, *MJQA*, 5: 324-5.

[86] JQA to John Adams, 5 January 1818, cited in Bemis, *John Quincy Adams*, pp. 342-3.

his July 4 Address. Yet it is unlikely that Clay was the only one to whom he expressed such doubts about the political future of South America. The South American representatives clearly understood that Adams was the principal barrier in the Cabinet to their pleas for recognition and a more accommodating U.S. approach.

Adams did not agree with Clay that U.S. caution had weakened its ability to influence the South Americans in their internal deliberations about their form of government. As far as Adams was concerned, the revolutionary leaders simply did not want to listen to the United States – "although we have done more than any other nation for the South Americans, they are discontented because we have not espoused their cause in arms, and, with empty professions of friendship, they have no real sympathy with us." He continued: "There is something disheartening in all our correspondence and transactions relating to South America. We have done everything possible in their favor, and have received from them little less than injury in return. No satisfaction has been obtained from them upon any complaint, and they have been constantly endeavoring to entangle us with them and their cause."[87]

Adams did not want to confound the great political experiment that was the United States, with the dubious prospects of South America. Adams had long believed that geography, economics, and a republican and Christian (Protestant) political culture pointed to the creation of "a nation, coextensive with the North American continent, destined by God and nature to be the most populous and powerful people ever combined under one social compact." His great fear had been that the project of Union would fail and that North America would fall into "an endless multitude of little insignificant clans and tribes at eternal war with one another for a rock, or a fish pond, the sport and fable of European oppressors."[88] Adams did not want to distract his countrymen from the essential task at hand by engaging in foolhardy projects like Clay's proposal for an American System – an idea echoed in some fashion by certain South American leaders, such as Simon Bolivar – that would encompass the entire American Hemisphere and that, *inter alia*, putatively would give the United States the means to influence the process of republican regime formation in South America (a prospect welcomed by Clay, if not Bolivar). "As to an American system, we have it; we constitute the whole of it; there is no community of interests or of principles between North and South America," Adams insisted. "Mr. Torres and Bolivar and

---

[87] 6 January 1820, *MJQA*, 4: 498; 8 July 1820, *MJQA*, 5: 164.

[88] JQA to Abigail Adams, 30 June 1811, *WJQA*, 4: 128.

O'Higgins talk about an American system as much as the Abbé Correa, but there is no basis for any such system."[89]

There were strong strategic as well as political reasons to separate the causes of North and South America. Adams did not want to create an alarm in Europe that the United States was forming a Hemispheric Alliance to take the republican struggle to the Old World – in other words, that Washington was planning to combine the Lexington Doctrine with the Edinburgh Doctrine. Adams' famous observation – that it was necessary that "the world shall be familiarized with the idea of considering our proper dominion to be the continent of North America" – was intended as a statement of America's *limits* as well as its ambitions. Adams believed in a political law of gravity that would eventually bring Spanish and British colonial territories in North America into the Union: "It was impossible that centuries should elapse without finding them annexed to the United States; not that any spirit of encroachment or ambition on our part renders it necessary, but because it is a physical, moral, and political absurdity that such fragments of territory, with sovereigns at fifteen hundred miles beyond the sea, worthless and burdensome to their owners, should exist permanently contiguous to a great, powerful, enterprising, and rapidly-growing nation."[90]

The Adams-Onís treaty was a benchmark and model for this peaceful, consensual process because it legitimized peacefully the United States' transcontinental position in North America. The same principle guided Adams' efforts to negotiate northern boundary settlements with Britain and Russia – "in all our negotiations upon this subject our interest was to gain time; for in the natural course of events we must outgrow all the obstacles which European powers are so desirous of opposing to us." Adams insisted that American expansion of this sort was not colonialism. Regime change, or regime formation, for the new states of the North American Union would be achieved peacefully and voluntarily, based on the principles of the Declaration of Independence, and not through force and military occupation, which were the means of rule by regimes based on divine right or chartered liberties. "The people of other nations, inhabitants of regions acquired not by conquest, but by compact, have been united with us in the participation of our rights and duties, of our burdens and blessings." He had no doubt that

---

[89] 19 September 1820, *MJQA*, 5: 176. José Correia da Serra, who was associated with the European Enlightenment, was the Portuguese Minister to the United States. He was commonly referred to as the Abbé Correa. The others were South American revolutionary leaders.

[90] 16 November 1819, *MJQA*, 4: 438-9.

"a Government by federation would be found practicable on a territory as extensive as this continent."[91]

Adams had no master plan to consummate the greater Union completion or delineate its precise final boundaries. For the near to intermediate term, he clearly envisioned incorporating the "unoccupied" areas of the trans-Mississippi region and the Pacific Northwest, those to which the United States could claim as part of the Transcontinental Treaty. Eventually, perhaps over "centuries," he believed that it was a "law of nature" that the United States would acquire British possessions to the north and perhaps (he was not clear on this point, especially once Mexico and Central America obtained their independence) all of Spain's former colonies in North America.[92] In his letter to Edward Everett, in which Adams outlined the principal arguments of the July 4 Address, he had mentioned India as the British colony most at risk for revolution, not Canada.[93]

Whatever the case, Adams insisted that the Union must have definite boundaries, in time and in space. The law of political gravity – physical and moral – placed natural limits on the expansion of the republic, to the North American continent and to certain critical offshore features that were integral to the continent, such as the island of Cuba. It was just as important to the health of the regime, and to its standing in the community of nations, to observe those limits as to realize the full potential of the Union. For Adams, this mandated a certain detachment from South America and a reassurance to

---

[91] 26 December 1824, *MJQA*, 6: 454-5; John Quincy Adams, Inaugural Message, 4 March 1825, accessed at http://millercenter.org/scripps/archive/speeches/detail/3513; 9 March 1824, *MJQA*, 6: 251.

[92] 16 November 1819, *MJQA*, 4: 438-9. As to the change of regime for the Native American tribes who lived in those territories over which the United States claimed sovereignty, Adams argued that, by the law of nature, the tribes had forfeited claims to the land by their failure to develop and improve it. They should be treated justly, according to American law and legitimately negotiated treaties, and individuals who accepted American citizenship should be accorded full rights. Over time their cultures would simply wither away. See Lynn Hudson Parson, "'A Perpetual Harrow upon My Feelings:' John Quincy Adams and the American Indian," *New England Quarterly* 46 (September 1973): 339-79. Slavery was a more difficult problem and Adams did not embrace a single solution to it. At times, he seemed to think that the reconstitution of the Union would eventually be necessary, perhaps in the aftermath of a servile revolt and civil war. But Adams' preferred solution at this time seemed to be that slavery, like the retrograde Indian culture, would simply wither away in the context of the progressive Union he had in mind.

[93] The quotation above suggested that Adams considered both Canada and the former Spanish possessions in North America to be in play. But Adams, in a subsequent confrontation with British Minister Stratford Canning over the boundaries of the Oregon Territory, denied that America's claims included the "northern provinces on this continent." "No," said I, "there the boundary is marked, and we have no disposition to encroach upon it. Keep what is yours, but leave the rest of this continent to us." Of course, this did not rule out later accommodations, perhaps over "centuries," which would lead to the independence of the British North American provinces and their subsequent incorporation into the Union. 27 January 1820, *MJQA*, 5: 252.

the Europeans that the United States was not about to create a Hemispheric Alliance that would engage in a crusade for European revolution.

This brings us to Adams' warning in the July 4 Address, that by going abroad "in search of monsters to destroy" and by "enlisting under other banners than her own," America risked a situation in which "the fundamental maxims of her policy would insensibly change from liberty to force." Americans would thereby sacrifice the "ineffable splendor of freedom and independence" in exchange for "an imperial diadem," which offered "the murky radiance of dominion and power." This warning reflected, in part, Adams' agreement with the Anglo-American Whig view that war, with its concomitant standing armies (or at least large armies) and massive debts, was the engine of despotism. But Adams disagreed with the stereotypical Whig opposition between liberty and power – "liberty is power," he would famously and controversially state in his First Annual Message – if power was applied properly to the betterment of the citizens of the United States and to mankind in general. For Adams, that meant carefully working out his plan for a peaceful and prosperous North American confederation, in which republican government based on the equality of mankind (the Declaration of Independence) would once and for all give lie to the claims of despots that only monarchies and aristocracies were capable of reaching higher social states of civilization.[94]

Adams believed that this great ambition would be thwarted if the United States abandoned its commitment to "internal improvement" (understood more broadly than the building of physical infrastructure) and to the carefully calibrated advancement of certain civilizational tasks abroad. The alternative for the United States was an imperial agenda that abandoned the moral cause of self-government and the geographical limits imposed by the laws of nature. Adams had been deeply troubled by the way in which the Jefferson administration had executed the Louisiana Purchase. Unlike some Federalists, Adams believed that federal republican government was possible on a continental scale, and that the purchase itself was constitutional. The federal government had the power to acquire *territory* from a foreign state; the federal government, however, had neither the constitutional power nor the moral right to acquire and govern a foreign *people* without their consent. That was a violation of

---

[94] For Adams' larger political purposes, see the reflections in Daniel Walker Howe, *The Political Culture of the American Whigs* (Chicago: University of Chicago Press, 1979) and *What Hath God Wrought: The Transformation of America, 1815-1848* (New York: Oxford University Press, 2009); the section on John Quincy Adams in Richard Samuelson, "The Adams Family and the American Experiment," Ph.D. dissertation, University of Virginia, 2000; and David Tucker, "John Quincy Adams on Principle and Practice," in Bryan-Paul Frost and Jeffrey Sikkenga, eds., *History of American Political Thought* (Lanham, MD: Lexington Books, 2003), pp. 271-86.

the principles of the Declaration of Independence. Adams acknowledged that necessity sometimes overrode a strict adherence to principle and that under the conditions at hand in 1803 there was no practical way to obtain the consent of the peoples of Louisiana prior to the purchase. Nevertheless, Adams insisted that the United States should have obtained that consent after the fact and it should not have governed the territory despotically prior to its subsequent incorporation into the Union in the form of States.[95]

In the end, Adams believed that the de facto acquiescence of the peoples of the original Union and of Louisiana to the arrangement settled the matter.[96] The precedent, nonetheless, was deeply troubling. The dissolution of the Spanish Empire in the American Hemisphere created the opportunity for the ordered, limited and constitutional expansion of the Union – but it also led to the imperial temptation to overreach geographically and morally, and to establish colonial-type systems, under the guise of liberating other peoples, who would then have to be ruled for their own good. Clay's Lexington Doctrine, whatever its high-sounding words and intentions, offered a poisoned pill to the principle of the Declaration. If the South American regimes turned out to be as disorderly and weak as Adams feared they would be, U.S. policymakers would have to be especially vigilant against the siren song of militant and imperial expansionism into these unruly lands.

In the years after the July 4, 1821 Address, Adams saw this dynamic at work in the efforts to annex Texas, which had achieved its independence from a weak and unstable Mexican regime that still claimed sovereignty over its former province. The advocates of Manifest Destiny, such as the journalist John O'Sullivan, claimed that the United States had a mission to spread freedom through the acquisition of Texas, even if war with Mexico was the necessary result, because Mexico too would benefit. Adams decried that argument:

> The annexation of Texas to this Union is the first step to the conquest of all Mexico, of the West India Islands, of a maritime, colonizing, slave-tainted monarchy, and of extinguished freedom. ... This Texas annexation we deem the turning-point of a revolution which transforms the North American Confederation into a conquering and warlike nation. Aggrandizement will be its passion and its policy. A military government, a large army, a costly navy,

---

[95] For Adams' position on Louisiana, see his Notes on Speech of Motion, January 1804, *WJQA*, 3: 26–30.

[96] JQA to John Adams, 31 August 1811, *WJQA*, 4: 204-10.

distant colonies, and associate islands in every sea, will follow of course in rapid succession.[97]

The imperial temptation could be "smuggled in" through a variety of forms, well short of outright invasion and conquest. Slaveholders and their northern allies would be especially prone to these schemes. In 1819, Adams had objected to proposals that the United States government purchase territory on the coast of Africa, which would become an American colony "where all the free blacks and people of color of the United States may be sent and settled." The initial group of inhabitants would consist of slaves seized under the terms of the Slave-Trade Act of 1819, which authorized "armed vessels of the United States, to be employed to cruise on any of the coasts of the United States . . . or the coast of Africa" to interdict slave traders. This project was promoted by the American Colonization Society, a group and cause that (in various guises) had the support of such notables as Monroe, Jefferson, Madison, Clay and, in later years, Abraham Lincoln. Adams, for his part, thought this idea was dangerous stuff and nonsense.

> There are men of all sorts and descriptions concerned in this Colonization Society: some exceedingly humane, weak-minded men, who have really no other than the professed objects in view, and who honestly believe them both useful and attainable; some, speculators in official profits and honors, which a colonial establishment would of course produce; some, speculators in political popularity, who think to please the abolitionists by their zeal for emancipation, and the slaveholders by the flattering hope of ridding them of the free colored people at the public expense; lastly, some cunning slaveholders, who see that the plan may be carried far enough to produce the effect of raising the market price of their slaves.

Adams noted the irony that many of those most anxious to limit the power of the federal government were also among the foremost proponents of "engrafting of a colonial establishment upon the Constitution of the United States, and thereby an accession of power to the National Government transcending all its other powers." Adams denied that the Louisiana Purchase, or the U.S. government's support for an American settlement at the mouth of

---

[97] 10 and 16 June 1844, *MJQA*, 12: 49, 57. Adams' critics pointed out that, while serving as President, he had attempted to purchase Texas from Mexico; Adams himself noted that during the negotiations with Onís in 1818-1819, he had advocated a boundary line that would have included much of Texas. The difference, Adams insisted, was that he sought peacefully to acquire territory that at the time was free of slavery and thus was perfectly consistent with his vision of a great, free North American Union.

the Columbia River, constituted precedent for acquiring territory for colonial purposes. "The acquisition of Louisiana, and the establishment at the mouth of Columbia River, being in territory contiguous to and continuous with our own, could by no means warrant the purchase of countries beyond the seas, or the establishment of a colonial system of government subordinate to and dependent upon that of the United States."[98]

Non-interventionism in Europe: Deconstructing the Edinburgh Doctrine

The risks of exchanging liberty for power increased exponentially if the United States followed anything like the Edinburgh Doctrine and ventured outside of the American Hemisphere to promote liberty and national independence. Adams believed that the United States had no reason to abandon its Foundational determination to remain out of purely European interests and quarrels – to avoid becoming, as his father had said, a makeweight in the European balance of power. "The political system of the United States is also essentially extra-European. To stand in firm and cautious independence of all entanglement in the European system, has been a cardinal point of their policy under every administration of their government from the peace of 1783 to this day," Adams concluded. "If at the original adoption of their system there could have been any doubt of its justice or its wisdom, there can be none at this time. Every year's experience rivets it more deeply in the principles and opinions of the nation."[99]

Adams recognized that the need for such restraint was not self-evident to all Americans, however, and he feared that a Clay-like policy toward South America would habituate the United States to unrestrained foreign interventionism, especially as power of the expanding North American Union was likely to increase exponentially. "In proportion as the importance of the United States as one of the members of the general society of civilized nations increases in the eyes of the others, the difficulties of maintaining this system, and the temptations to depart from it" – both domestically and internationally – "increase and multiply with it." Temptations for intervention in the

---

[98] 12 March 1819, *MJQA*, 4: 292-4. Adams' own view at the time, which later underwent modification (although he consistently opposed colonization schemes), was that "the mass of colored people who may be removed to Africa by the Colonization Society will suffer more and enjoy less than they would if they should remain in their actual condition in the United States; that their removal will do more harm than good to this country, by depriving it of the mass of their industry, and thus that the result of the whole, to both parties, will be evil and not good." 30 April 1819, *MJQA*, 4: 356.

[99] JQA to Middleton, 5 July 1820, *WJQA*, 7: 49.

Old World had increased further because, since 1783, the locus of conflicts in Europe had changed: "The warlike passions and propensities of the present age find their principal ailment, not in the enmities between nation and nation, but in the internal dissensions between the component parts of all. The war is between nations and their rulers." This was a "controversy between ancient establishments and modern opinions, between prejudice and innovation, . . . At the present moment the struggle of Europe is to return to the politics and the religion of the 15th century." Adams had no doubt that the United States was the inspirational source of liberal resistance to the restoration of divine right monarchy and priestly superstition in Europe – a fact of which the monarchs and priests were well aware: "The influence of our example has unsettled all the ancient governments of Europe. It will overthrow them all without a single exception. I hold this revolution to be as infallible as that the earth will perform a revolution around the sun in a year" – just as it was inevitable that the South Americans and their brethren in places like India would emancipate themselves from their colonial masters.[100]

Although Adams took the success of the European revolutions for granted, he did not think regime change on the continent would come about easily or quickly or that it would follow the American path to constitutional self-government.

> Our great superiority is in political science, government and political morality. The European and South American nations which have received and are acting under the impulse given by us seem destined only to illustrate that superiority. They have all caught from us the infection of making constitutions, and not one of them has yet been able to make a constitution which will work to secure the enjoyment of liberty, property and peace. Their constitutions result in nothing but civil war. In forty years we have not had one execution for treason, with a population multiplied from three to ten millions. The Europeans improve upon our theories till they become impracticable. In 1793 France set herself and the world on fire for a legislature in a single assembly. In 1823 Spain is doing the same thing. They are unable to form the conception of a legislature in two branches without privileged orders. We have reduced it universally to practice. . . . whether Europe will ever establish governments capable of securing to individuals all the benefits of good

---

[100] JQA to Middleton, 5 July 1820, *WJQA*, 7: 48-9; JQA to Kirkland, 30 November 1815, *WJQA*, 5: 530; JQA to Ingersoll, *WJQA*, 19 June 1823, 7: 488.

government, almost without use of force, and altogether without violence, is doubtful. If ever, certainly not within half a century.[101]

Adams did not believe that the United States could actively influence the slow process of establishing good government by taking the side of European peoples against their rulers. Time had demonstrated that the United States had few, if any, natural allies among the enlightened classes of Europe – or among the potentially revolutionary peoples, for that matter. Moreover, it had many natural enemies among the unenlightened, who still wielded the force of arms and who were in a position to threaten American commerce and security. "There is already in all the governments of Europe a strong prejudice against us as Republicans, and as the primary causes of the propagation of those political principles, which still make the throne of every European monarch rock under him as with the throes of an earthquake."[102]

> The conduct and issue of the late war [War of 1812] has undoubtedly raised our national character in the consideration of the world; but we ought also to be aware that it has multiplied and embittered our enemies. . . . All the restored governments of Europe are deeply hostile to us. The Royalists everywhere detest and despise us as Republicans. All the victims and final vanquishers of the French Revolution abhor us as aiders and abettors of the French during their career of triumph. Wherever British influence extends it is busy to blacken us in every possible manner. In Spain the popular feeling is almost as keen against us as in England. Emperors, kings, princes, priests, all the privileged orders, all the establishments, all the votaries of legitimacy, eye us with the most rancorous hatred. Among the crowned heads the only friend we had was the Emperor Alexander, and his friendship has, I am afraid, been more than cooled.[103]

By this calculation (made in 1816), all of Europe seemed to be united against America. This was a dangerous position for the United States to be in, especially because Adams believed that England was spoiling for another fight with America. And, even if Britain did not provoke a third Anglo-American war, intra-European quarrels were likely to result in another global conflict that would inevitably involve America and England in a dispute over maritime rights.

---

[101] JQA to Ingersoll, *WJQA*, 19 June 1823, 7: 488.
[102] JQA to Plumer, 17 January 1817, *WJQA*, 6: 142.
[103] JQA to John Adams, 1 August 1816, *WJQA*, 6: 58-9.

Fortunately, within a few years the risk of a general European war had declined. Adams soon concluded that the continental monarchs, under Russian leadership, were united on the overriding principle of "preserving peace *in our time*."[104] That provided the United States with the necessary diplomatic breathing space to push forward with its ambition to create a continental republic and to offer benevolent neutrality to the South American revolutionary regimes. Still, the threat of some sort of reactionary Europe united against America and republicanism could not be ruled out. Adams, to be sure, was not inclined to appease the reactionary regimes, especially when he thought he stood on favorable political ground (as will be seen). But in his own mind, he drew the line at actively fomenting revolution – "propagandism" in the expression of the times – as a means of preempting the potential threats by undermining the rule of despots at home, in Europe. Instead, he used the differences between the two basic regime types to reinforce the political barriers between the Old and New World.

The matter came up in 1820, when the Russian Minister in Washington, Chevalier de Poletica, approached Adams about formal American adherence to the Holy Alliance, "as a pledge of mere principles," whose "professed purpose was merely the general preservation of peace." As inducement, Poletica had "intimated that if any question should arise between the United States and other governments of Europe" – by which Adams understood primarily to mean England – "the Emperor Alexander, desirous of using his influence in their favor, would have a substantial motive and justification for interposing, if he could regard them as *his allies,* which as parties to the Holy Alliance he would be." For domestic political reasons, as well as his views on the separation of America and Europe, Adams had no interest in following up this initiative. He was careful not to insult the Russian Emperor with an outright refusal (a point with which President Monroe agreed), but Adams took the occasion to make one important counterpoint to Alexander, through his instructions to the new American Minister to Russia, Henry Middleton:

> But independent of the prejudices which have been excited against this instrument [the Holy Alliance] in the public opinion, which time and an experience of its good effects will gradually wear away, it may be observed that for the repose of Europe as well as of America, the European and American political systems should be kept as separate and distinct from each other as possible. If the United States as members of the Holy Alliance could acquire

---

[104] JQA to Ingersoll, 19 June 1823, *WJQA,* 7: 488. Emphasis in original.

a right to ask the influence of its most powerful members in their controversies with other states, the other members must be entitled in return to ask the influence of the United States for themselves or against their opponents. In the deliberations of the league they would be entitled to a voice, and in exercising their right must occasionally appeal to principles, which might not harmonize with those of any European member of the bond.[105]

Adams thus issued an implicit warning – American involvement in the European equilibrium would be destabilizing for Europe and its monarchs because of the differences in regimes as well as the growing strength of the United States. The United States would, in the interests of domestic and international peace, stick to its political-strategic hemispheric isolation, and Adams hoped that the Emperor would continue to appreciate that American restraint was in the interest of all concerned.[106] If the Europeans, however, ever forced an ideological confrontation with the United States in the American Hemisphere, the United States had at its disposal a potent ideological counter, that of adopting the Edinburgh Doctrine. Adams had no intention of playing that card but it was nevertheless on the table.

Britain was the wild card (so to speak) in this high-stakes diplomatic game. By 1818, Britain had begun to distance itself from the continental allies. There was widespread sympathy in England for the liberal cause and national independence movements in Europe. The *Edinburgh Review* essayist had put forward the idea that the two liberal, Anglo-Saxon powers might decisively throw their combined weight onto the scale of European revolution. In such a scheme, the United States would rely on the Royal Navy and the Atlantic Ocean to protect it from reprisal by the Holy Alliance and, effectively, to guarantee the success of South American independence movements. Adams was well aware that this was not Castlereagh's policy, or that of the Tory government, but he feared that the intoxicating notion itself could disorient Americans by obscuring the true nature of British policy, which Adams believed was still fundamentally hostile to republicanism and the United States.

To begin with, Adams smelled a rat in the proposal. The *Edinburgh Review* essayist, "foreseeing times of future turbulence in his own country, and panting for a revolution with English and Scottish Whigs at its head, descanted largely upon the importance of a good understanding between the Americans

---

[105] JQA to Middleton, 5 July 1820, *WJQA*, 7: 49-51.

[106] The United States, of course, would not be completely isolated from the Old World; it would continue to trade with Europe and to promote its civilizational agenda, ideally in concert with European regimes of whatever type.

and that party."[107]   Adams suspected that the proposed Anglo-American crusade for liberty in Europe was a cover for the cause of political revolution in Britain proper. He knew that a radical faction of Whigs went so far as to advocate the overthrow of the English Constitution and its replacement with a wholly republican (democratic) regime.

Adams had no desire for the United States to become a pawn in the game of British domestic politics. In addition to principled objections to any sort of intervention in the domestic affairs of another nation, Adams did not favor the radical Whig agenda on its merits. He believed that the English Constitution, rightly understood, was the best possible for Britain, given the state of society in the British Isles. It contained the essential element of balance without which there had never been political stability in any regime where civil and religious liberty was valued. Adams did not favor the English Constitution for the United States (as his critics, and the critics of his father, alleged). The English Constitution was properly applied to one state of society, the U.S. Constitution to another. Adams believed that the English Constitution would be destroyed, not by any inherent defect, but by debt – the same cause that destroyed the French monarchy. He concluded that proper political reform in Britain would elevate the democratic element in the Constitution, but that such reform should not dominate or destroy other elements of society. He thought, moreover, that the future of the British policy – whether status quo, reform or revolution – was for the British people to decide. America could not really influence the process, even if it wanted to – it had few natural allies in British society and its name would simply become a tool in factional disputes.[108]

The overriding point for Adams was the deep-seated British hostility to America that cut across the political spectrum and class. No change in the Constitution would affect this attitude. In Adams' experience, the Whigs and Tories no longer differed fundamentally in their respective attitudes toward the United States, whatever the *Edinburgh Review* might argue for its own partisan purposes. "The opposition party and its leaders before the war were much more liberally disposed towards America than the ministerialists; but after the war commenced they joined the ministers in full pack, and since the peace their party tactics have constantly been to cavil against any liberality or concession of the ministers to America." The British had never forgiven the Americans for their Revolution and those feelings had not mellowed with

---

[107] JQA to Edward Everett, 31 January 1822, *WJQA*, 7: 201.

[108] See, for example, JQA to Alexander Hill Everett, 28 September 1817, *WJQA*, 6: 200-4; and JQA to Alexander Hill Everett, 15 October 1817, *WJQA*, 6: 221-5. In the United States, the democratic (popular) element was naturally and properly preponderant; that element had to be balanced by other means, with a strong executive and an independent judiciary.

time. "The animosity which we have now to encounter from Britain is purely national. It is rather discountenanced than stimulated by the government, and is inspired by the two deepest and most malignant passions of the human heart – revenge and envy – revenge for the national humiliation of two successive wars, envy at the unparalleled growth and prosperity which associate with all their thoughts of America the torturing terror of a rival growing every day more formidable to them."[109]

Adams, therefore, reacted vehemently against the suggestion of Anglo-American cooperation on behalf of liberal revolution, even though such a proposal was hardly likely to come from the conservative government of Liverpool and Castlereagh, which was hardly sympathetic either to American or to European revolutions. Adams believed, however, that perfidious Albion, under the right circumstances and/or a future Whig government, was perfectly capable of manufacturing such a scheme in order to ensnare American power on behalf of narrow British interests – and, *inter alia* – to clip America's wings. The British offered a competing model to American republicanism, a faux liberalism – one of chartered liberty, economic exclusivity, and British domination of the high seas. The British may have gloried in their defense of national liberties in the war with Napoleon but, in Adams opinion, this war merely masked the furtherance of British economic interests and London's desire to establish global maritime hegemony.

Adams concluded that the British were the only nation to have figured out the means to profit economically from war; in doing so, however, they had amassed an enormous debt that could be managed only with financial legerdemain and the dominance of trade enforced by the Royal Navy. The British economy languished in times of peace; this created popular unrest and pressures to go to war to relieve economic depression. In the long run, the reliance of a war-based economy was a losing strategy. It had become a narcotic of which stronger and stronger doses were constantly required. Britain, in the opinion of Adams, would not collapse in a moment of revolutionary upheaval, as some Americans had been predicting for years. Adams was convinced, moreover, that Britain was in a state of long-term decline. In the meantime, the United States was at risk of being drawn into Britain's latest war, either as an antagonist – which would be immensely popular in England – or (as the *Edinburgh Review* essayist proposed) as an ally in a putative crusade on behalf of liberty in Europe. Adams believed that the proper course for the United States was to avoid the trap of war against England, increase American strength, and wait for Britain's gradual decline to take effect. British cal-

---

[109] JQA to Plumer, 17 January 1817, *WJQA*, 6: 142; JQA to Walsh, 10 July 1821, *WJQA*, 7: 115.

culations of interest would change as American power naturally increased. Certain benchmarks would signal a fundamental change of British policy – especially London's acceptance of the liberalization of trade, its diplomatic recognition of South America without special privileges, and its abandonment of the right of impressment. Even then, cooperation with Britain, not alliance, was the proper model. Under no circumstances, however, should the United States try to short-cut the process by throwing its lot in with Britain by embracing the Edinburgh Doctrine.[110]

Adams also believed that any foreign intervention on behalf of European revolutionaries, especially if it required military occupation to support the new liberal regime, would generate indigenous opposition. "Government, whether founded upon the will of the people, or upon the will of God, never yet had a durable foundation upon the basis of a foreign and hostile soldiery." He had seen that process at work in the 1790s, when the French revolutionary armies soon wore out their welcome in places like the Netherlands and Italy – even among the local leaders who favored republican government, and certainly among the ordinary population, which was generally indifferent to politics or attached to the old way of life.[111] .

Adams' concern with Britain's not-so-hidden agenda to trap the United States would return in full force two years later, in 1823, when it seemed (to some at least) that South American liberty was in jeopardy by a full-scale European counterattack. Adams' own policy toward the new governments in South America, in the meantime, had evolved to take a more active role.

Influencing Regime Change in a Republican Direction

By the winter of 1821-1822, President Monroe, Adams, and the rest of the Cabinet finally agreed that the fundamental conditions for diplomatic recognition by the major claimants to power in South America had now been established. Adams pointed to recent decisive military successes by the revolutionary armies; to the concession by local Spanish officials of the virtual independence of the new regimes, notably in Mexico; to the organization of governments and constitutions on popular principles; and, to initiatives by South American representatives for the negotiation of treaties of commerce and navigation "founded upon the bases of reciprocal utility and perfect equality."

---

[110] See, for example, JQA to John Adams, 29 February 1816, *WJQA*, 5: 520-2; 18 April 1817, *MJQA*, 3: 504-6.

[111] JQA to Murray, 23 March 1799, *MAP*, Reel 133; JQA to John Adams, 16 December 1815, *WJQA*, 5: 447.

The U.S. House of Representatives, even though Clay was no longer in the Chair, had pressed the matter. In January 1822, the House voted to request the executive to provide it with diplomatic communications and information on the state of war between Spain and the revolutionary regimes. On March 8, 1822, Monroe sent a message to Congress, which announced his intention to acknowledge the independence claimed by Spain's American provinces. In May, by near-unanimous votes in each House, Congress approved appropriations for funding diplomatic missions to "the independent nations on the American continent as the President should deem proper." Within a few years the President deemed those regimes to be Buenos Aires (the United Provinces of the Rio de la Plata), Colombia, Chile, Mexico, Peru and Central America. Monroe received the first accredited diplomat from South America, Manuel Torres, as the Columbian *chargé d'affaires* in June 1822.[112]

By recognizing the independent nations of South America at this time, Adams did not believe that the United States had gone abroad in search of monsters to destroy, because America's duty and interest had finally become aligned. To be sure, the choice was still not without risks. The Monroe administration did not consult with or inform any of the European powers – including Britain – about its change of policy, even though the continental monarchs, who were in the process of suppressing revolutionary movements in Europe, might conceivably have taken offense. The Spanish Minister in Washington immediately protested against the American action and Spain continued to assert its right to rule over its American possessions. Adams, however, believed that circumstance and policy had combined to minimize the larger risks – including the danger that Spain might try to renege on the Transcontinental Treaty (although he favored informing Congress that Spain might take offense and that the United States should be prepared for that eventuality). Adams feared that to delay recognition further would have ceded the political initiative to Clay's supporters in Congress, who almost certainly would now have won a vote to authorize funding missions to South America even without executive approval. As Adams saw things, Clay, despite being out of office, would effectively have seized control of American foreign policy and would have been in a position to promote American activism toward the revolutions in Europe. And, not coincidentally, Clay would

---

[112] The chronology of events in these two paragraphs is set out in JQA to Anderson, 27 May 1823, *WJQA*, 7: 441-86. See also JQA to Don Joaquin de Anduaga, 6 April 1822, *WJQA*, 7: 216-9.

have strengthened his own presidential prospects in 1824, at the expense of those of Adams.[113]

Adams' policy calculations at this point, and going forward, are a matter of considerable interest because he now clearly adopted a more assertive and positive attitude toward the new regimes in South America. Historians have seen a growing coincidence of the views of the head (Adams) and the heart (Clay) of American foreign policy, which culminated in their approach to the Panama Congress of 1826, when they were President and Secretary of State, respectively. Contemporary critics of Adams accused him of a politically opportunistic shift in which he abandoned the solid ground of U.S. detachment and paved the way to dangerous entanglements with the affairs of South America. When confronted with such criticism, Adams commented: "I do not recollect any change of policy, but there has been a great change of circumstances."[114]

One can say with some confidence that Adams' negative views of South American history and culture did not change and that he must have retained strong doubts about the long-term stability and republican character of the new regimes. He believed, however, that the United States did have some influence at the margins that it could and should exercise to encourage a relatively positive outcome in terms of regime development and inter-American relations. By taking an optimistic public tone and keeping his doubts private, Adams undoubtedly hoped to dispel the anti-South American bias of which he was accused and also to make his highly positive, even breathless rhetoric about South America become the father of reality. Adams also believed that the South Americans might be enlisted on behalf of his civilizational agenda, for which he was becoming, despite his cautious nature, an "enthusiast."

Adams certainly concluded that if the United States held back, it ran the risk of alienating the leaders of the new South American states, many of whom were already suspicious of the United States. These leaders might look to Europe for diplomatic support and models for their internal organization. Adams, therefore, urged the President to recognize at once all the viable regimes, including Mexico, which seemed to have the most tenuous existence (and whose territories, especially the province of Texas, some Americans

---

[113] Dexter Perkins, *The Monroe Doctrine, 1823-1826* (Cambridge: Harvard University Press, 1932), pp. 49-51; 26 February 1822, unpublished JQA Diary, Massachusetts Historical Society, accessed at http://www.masshist.org/jqadiaries/doc.cfm?id=jqad33_25. One prominent American historian, Ernest R. May, argued that one could explain the foreign policy positions of Clay, Adams and other prominent politicians during this period largely or solely on the basis of their campaign needs for the presidency in 1824. *The Making of the Monroe Doctrine* (Cambridge, Mass.: Belknap Press of Harvard University Press, 1975).

[114] 8 December 1825, *MJQA*, 7: 75.

coveted). Adams favored this course even though reports indicated that Mexican revolutionary politics leaned toward monarchy (in May 1822, a native-born General, Agustín de Iturbide, was proclaimed Constitutional Emperor of the Mexican Empire). "My main reason for acting now, and including all, being to take the lead with recognition," Adams noted in his journal.[115]

Adams wanted to use the process of recognition, and of establishing diplomatic relations, to influence the South Americans in a liberal and republican direction. "Of this mighty movement in human affairs, mightier far than that of the downfall of the Roman Empire, the United States may continue to be, as they have been hitherto, the tranquil but deeply attentive spectators. They *may* also, in the various vicissitudes by which it must be followed, be called to assume a more active and leading part in its progress." (Adams underlined "may.") The South Americans were entitled by fact and right to their independence, but the form of government they chose was still in play, and Adams believed that, marginally at least, the United States might influence positively the evolution of their governments. The regime question was not fixed in concrete at the moment of independence, but it was an evolutionary process that might take years or decades to play out. After all, the U.S. Continental Congress had adopted the Articles of Confederation in 1776, although these had not been ratified by all the states until 1781. When the Articles proved to be inadequate, the American people, acting through extraordinary conventions, had composed and ratified the Constitution. Such success certainly was not guaranteed, as France had demonstrated after 1789; neither was a stable and republican outcome impossible, even with an imperfect start.[116]

Based on his experience with representatives of the independence movements, Adams could not be sure that leaders of the new regimes would be amenable to American example or persuasion; nonetheless, the stakes were too high not to try. In his instructions to American envoys to the new regimes, Adams stressed that U.S. diplomats should establish or reestablish American credibility as the true friend of South American independence, rightly understood; further, they should warn against the blandishments of the European governments, which would attempt to gain special privileges and tamper with internal politics.

In these instructions, Adams picked up on the themes of his July 4 Address. The South Americans should be informed or reminded by American diplomats that "the European alliance of emperors and kings have assumed

---

[115] 7 March 1822, unpublished JQA Diary, Massachusetts Historical Society, accessed at http://www.masshist.org/jqadiaries/doc.cfm?id=jqad33_28.

[116] JQA to Anderson, 23 May 1823, *WJQA*, 7: 471.

as the foundation of human society the doctrine of unalienable *allegiance*. Our doctrine is founded upon the principle of unalienable *right*. The European allies, therefore, have viewed the *cause* of the South Americans as rebellion against their lawful sovereign. We have considered it as the assertion of natural right. *They* have invariably shown their disapprobation of the revolution, and their wishes for the restoration of the Spanish power. We have as constantly – favored the standard of independence and of America."

> In contrasting the principles and the motives of the European powers, as manifested in their policy towards South America, with those of the United States, it has not been my intention to boast of our superior purity, or to lay a claim of merit to any extraordinary favor from South America in return. Disinterestedness must be its own reward; but in the establishment of our future political and commercial intercourse with the new republics it will be necessary to recur often to the principles in which it originated; they will serve to mark the boundaries of the rights which we may justly claim in our future relations with them, and to counteract the efforts which, it cannot be doubted, European negotiators will continue to make in the furtherance of their monarchical and monopolizing contemplations.[117]

Adams sought to discourage the South Americans from "hankering after monarchy," which Buenos Aires and Mexico in particular had seemed inclined to do. Leaders in these proto states had previously floated the idea of inviting a European royal family member to assume the throne, as a means of encouraging European recognition. The United States, to be sure, acknowledged the right of the peoples of South America to choose whatever form of government they judged to be most compatible with their own safety and happiness. However, this right held only if the new regimes were truly independent and not mere appendages of the divine-right European monarchical system.[118]

This raised the question of whether the United States would recognize an indigenous South American monarch, or a member of a European royal family who claimed to be the unfettered choice of the people of that state. Adams argued that "monarchical projects" of any sort were contrary "to the general feeling of all the native Americans and to the liberal institutions congenial to the spirit of freedom," as well as to "the true policy" of the new states. Adams did not believe that monarchy was a viable solution to the defects of the politi-

---

[117] Ibid., 7: 452-3. Emphasis in original.
[118] JQA to Rodney, 17 May 1823, *WJQA*, 7: 426-7.

cal culture of South America. Nor was it a regime type that its peoples would embrace without compulsion. Referring to a border dispute between Buenos Aires and Brazil, Adams ventured the opinion that "the republican hemisphere will endure neither emperor nor king upon its shores."[119]

The former Portuguese colony of Brazil was something of a special case. In 1808, the Portuguese royal family fled from Napoleon's invading force and took up residence at Rio de Janeiro, as capital of the entire Portuguese Empire. The United States soon dispatched consular agents to Brazil. In 1821, King Dom Joao (John) VI returned to Portugal. His son declared Brazil's independence in September 1822, and became emperor with the title of Dom Pedro I. In 1824, a Brazilian agent, Silvestre Rebello, arrived in Washington and asked to be received as *chargé d'affaires* of the independent Empire of Brazil. In deliberations with the Cabinet, Attorney General William Wirt raised the question whether it was proper to recognize the new government because it was a monarchy and because "it would be represented as favoring the views of the Holy Alliance and a partiality for monarchies."

Calhoun disagreed with this line of argument. "The established policy of this country in relation to South America had been to look only to the question of independence, and invariably to recognize the Governments 'de facto;' . . . to decline the recognition of the Empire of Brazil because it was monarchical, would be a departure from the policy hitherto observed, and would introduce a new principle of interference in the internal government of foreign nations." Calhoun argued that there were material interests involved as well – "the acknowledgment of the independence of Brazil was highly important, our trade thither being already very considerable, and promising to be more valuable than with all the rest of South America." The United States, Calhoun pointed out, had recognized the Imperial Government in Mexico during its brief period of existence, and had received its Minister. The President, meanwhile, "observed that the recognition of Brazil as an empire would lessen the offensiveness to the Holy Alliance of the acknowledgments, as it would show that we did not make a difference with regard to the forms of government."

Adams agreed in principle with Calhoun: "there were reasons for the recognition of Brazil yet stronger than those which had operated in the case of South America, inasmuch as the King of Portugal himself, while he resided in Brazil, had proclaimed it an independent kingdom and abolished the colonial system of government altogether." [120] The facts on the ground, however, had yet to be established officially. In Adams' mind, there was some doubt

---

[119] Ibid., 7: 426; JQA to Anderson, 23 May 1823, *WJQA*, 7: 471.
[120] 6 April 1824, *MJQA*, 6: 281-3.

whether Brazil actually controlled its territory, particularly its coastline, and also whether there was in fact a secret conspiracy between royal father and son, and with the French government, to return Brazil to the colonial fold. As soon as these matters were resolved to Adams' satisfaction, he recommended to the President that Rebello be received and an American *chargé* be appointed to serve at Rio.[121]

The fundamental question of recognition for Adams, then, was not one of regime type but whether Brazil had indeed authoritatively established independence from its former mother country and from other European states. Because there was no risk of war with Portugal or entanglement at stake, the United States could judge the matter strictly on its merits. Moreover, Adams could take a relaxed view because he believed that time and progress would soon eliminate the anomaly of an American monarchy. He assumed that the Brazilian Empire would "probably [be] as ephemeral as that of Mexico" – Iturbide's imperial regime, after all, had lasted less than a year. Rebello reinforced that impression: Empire "was a mere word," he told Adams. "It implied an extensive territory, which could not be applicable to Portugal, but was eminently so to Brazil. Its meaning, however, was only that Brazil was an independent nation, and its Government was in principle republican – the Emperor himself being more inclined to republicanism than the people of the country."[122]

Adams wanted to encourage the South American governments of whatever internal makeup to embrace foreign and commercial policies that reflected "the broad and liberal principles of *independence, equal favors,* and *reciprocity*." For Adams, this was republicanism, rightly understood, as applied to international affairs. "The foundation of our municipal institutions is equal rights. The basis of all our intercourse with foreign powers is reciprocity."[123] The February 1778 Treaty of Amity and Commerce with France, and not the Franco-American Treaty of Alliance, signed at the same time, was coeval with the Declaration of Independence as an authoritative statement of America's place in the world.

---

[121] 29 April 1824, *MJQA*, 6: 310-1; 1 May 1824, *MJQA*, 6: 314; 22 May 1824, *MJQA*, 6: 348.

[122] JQA to Rodney, 17 May 1823, *WJQA*, 7: 430; 7 April 1824, *MJQA*, 6: 283-4. Adams also likely agreed with Henry Clay when the latter, as Adams' Secretary of State, privately expressed the opinion that, although the Brazilian monarchy was out of place in the American Hemisphere, its likely difficulties and failure would serve to show the superiority of the republican model. See Clay's instructions to Anderson and Sergeant, 8 May 1826, *PHC*, 5: 344. This point was deleted in the final text of these instructions, presumably for diplomatic reasons, but they likely reflected Clay's views.

[123] JQA to Anderson, 23 May 1823, *WJQA*, 7: 460; JQA to Rodney, 17 May 1823, *WJQA*, 7: 432. Emphasis in original.

The preamble is believed to be the first instance on the diplomatic record of nations, upon which the true principles of all fair commercial negotiation between independent states were laid down and proclaimed to the world. That preamble was to the foundation of our commercial intercourse with the rest of mankind, what the declaration of independence was to that of our internal government. The two instruments were parts of one and the same system, matured by long and anxious deliberation of the founders of this Union in the ever memorable Congress of 1776; and as the declaration of independence was the foundation of all our municipal institutions, the preamble to the treaty with France laid the corner stone for all our subsequent transactions of intercourse with foreign nations. Its principles should be therefore deeply impressed upon the mind of every statesman and negotiator of this Union, and the first four articles of the treaty with France contain the practical exposition of these principles, which may serve as models for insertion in the projected treaty, or in any other that we may hereafter negotiate with any of the rising republics of the south.[124]

Adams did not believe that it was necessary to negotiate formal commercial treaties of this sort, as long as the South Americans followed the rule of reciprocity; to the extent that the South Americans desired such treaties, however, they opened an avenue to encourage the independence and republicanism of the new regimes. Commercial treaties, for instance, provided the United States with a means to introduce clauses recognizing the liberty of conscience and religious worship for the citizens of one state residing in or engaged in commerce with another state, and to drive home the point about the interrelatedness of the various true forms of liberty.

Civil, political, commercial and *religious* liberty, are but various modifications of one great principle founded in the unalienable rights of human nature, and before the universal application of which, the colonial domination of Europe over the American hemisphere has fallen, and is crumbling into dust. Civil liberty *can* be established on no foundation of human reason which will not at

---

[124] JQA to Richard C. Anderson, 23 May 1823, *WJQA*, 7: 460. Adams added: "There is indeed a principle of still more expansive liberality, which may be assumed as the basis of commercial intercourse between nation and nation. It is that of placing the *foreigner*, in regard to all objects of navigation and commerce, upon a footing of equal favor with the *native* citizen; and to that end of abolishing all discriminating duties and charges whatsoever. This principle is altogether congenial to the spirit of our institutions, and the main obstacle to its adoption consists in this: that the fairness of its operation depends upon its being admitted universally." (p. 461)

the same time demonstrate the *right* to religious freedom; and the control of a Bishop of Rome and a conclave of cardinals on the banks of the Tiber over *the freedom of action of* American nations on the shores of the Orinoco, or the Magdalena, is as incompatible with their independence, as the arbitrary mandate of a Spanish monarch and a Council of the Indies at Madrid. The tendency of the spirit of the age is so strong towards religious liberty, that we cannot doubt it will soon banish from the constitutions of the southern republics of this hemisphere all those intolerant religious establishments with which they have hitherto been trammelled. Religious and military coercion will be alike discarded from all the institutions framed for the protection of human rights in civil society of independent nations; and the freedom of opinion and of faith will be guaranteed by the same sanctions as the rights to personal liberty and security. To promote this event by all the moral influence which we can exercise by our example, is among the duties which devolve upon us in the formation of our future relations with our southern neighbors; . . .

Freedom of religion and conscience was thus only one of the standards that the United States, by its own example, its indirect influence, and its direct encouragement, could recommend to its new southern neighbors in the ongoing battle between "the principles of civil liberty" and "the prejudices of inveterate ignorance, despotism, and superstition." The principles of civil liberty included "the subordination of the military to the civil power," which was necessary to avoid the rise of Bonapartism as an alternative to divine right monarchy and republicanism. Adams was already seeing worrisome indications that the South Americans would fail to adopt this essential element of popular and constitutional government.[125]

Adams did not propose to urge a certain form of republican order on the South Americans. When he heard reports that Colombia, which then claimed territory much larger than that of the United States, planned to establish a unitary rather than a federal government, he was skeptical of its success. "Whether this attempt will be found practicable in execution, may be susceptible to doubt; but in the new organizations of society upon this hemisphere, even unsuccessful experiments lead to results by which the science of government is advanced and the happiness of man is promoted." As long as the

---

[125] Ibid., 23 May 1823, *WJQA*, 7: 454-5, 466-7. The language about the argument between principles and prejudices was deleted from the text of the final instructions, undoubtedly for reasons of political and cultural sensitivity. Emphasis in original.

government was "entirely republican," with "articles declaratory of the natural rights of the citizen to personal security, property and reputation, and of the inviolable liberty of the press," there were no grounds for criticism.

> With such a constitution, in such a country, the modifications which experience may prove to be necessary for rendering the political institutions most effectually competent to the ends of civil government, will make their own way by peaceable and gradual conquests of public opinion. If a single government should be found inadequate to secure and protect the rights of the people living under it, a federation of republics may without difficulty be substituted in its place. Practical effect having once been given to the principle that lawful government is a compact and not a grant, the pretences for resorting to force for effecting political revolutions disappear.[126]

There were, however, limits on the degree of experimentation with regime type with which Adams was prepared to countenance – at least in principle. A unitary republic was one thing. Empire through conquest, as the Colombian government reportedly contemplated with respect to the island of Cuba, was quite another.

> If the natural advantages bestowed upon the Colombian territory were to be improved by its inhabitants only for purposes of empire, that which nature has bestowed as a blessing upon them would in its consequences prove a curse inflicted upon the rest of mankind. . . . Let her look to *commerce* and *navigation*, and not to empire as her means of communication with the rest of the human family. These are the principles upon which *our* confederated republic is founded, and they are those upon which we hope our sisters of the southern continent will ultimately perceive it to be for their own welfare, no less than for that of the world, that they should found themselves.[127]

Adams believed, as we have seen, that the laws of political gravitation would eventually lead the Union to expand and become coterminous with North America. Was there an equivalent critical mass that could, or would, eventually constitute a *South* American Union? Should the United States accept or encourage this development on the grounds that political union there would be, as in the North, the best vehicle for the preservation of republican

---

[126] Ibid., 7. 454-5.
[127] Ibid., 7: 468-9.

government and peaceful relations among its constituent members? What if this process of unification was carried out by force rather than persuasion? Would a unified South America, of whatever regime type, constitute a strategic threat to the North? Or would a formal North-South partnership be the next evolutionary step in regime development?[128]

Adams was well aware of various ideas that were in circulation for some sort of political alliance, confederation or unification of all or part of the Americas. Clay's Lexington Doctrine – an American System (vaguely defined) – was only one of the notions in play. "Floating, undigested purposes of this great American confederation have been for some time fermenting in the imaginations of many speculative statesmen." Adams did not think that such ideas should "be disdainfully rejected, because its magnitude may appal [sic] the understanding of politicians accustomed to the more minute but more complicated machinery of a contracted political standard." Nonetheless, they had to pass the close scrutiny of the principles of the Declaration of Independence, as set out in Adams' July 4 Address, and of historical experience.

Adams easily dismissed proposals being floated by the government in Lisbon for "a general confederacy of all America, North and South, together with the constitutional governments of *Portugal* and *Spain,* as a counterprise to the European *Holy Alliance*." That violated the United States' traditional insistence on the political-strategic separation of the hemispheres as well as the stricture against entangling alliances. Adams approached somewhat cautiously the concept of a South American confederation or offense-defense alliance based on "an union in support of a representative system throughout, and of preventing partial associations with any one of the powers of Europe." In its most prominently advocated form, this South American confederation would establish a common foreign policy while its constituent republican members retained control of their domestic affairs. "So far as its purposes may be to concert a general system of popular representation for the government of the several independent states which are floating from the wreck of the Spanish power in America, the United States will still cheer it with their approbation, and speed with their good wishes its success." As to whether the United States might be willing to preside or attend a meeting, or congress, "intended to assimilate the politics of the south with those of the north," Adams advised his diplomatic agents in the spring of 1823 that "a more particular and definite view of the end proposed by this design and

---

[128] These issues are explored in detail in James E. Lewis, Jr., *John Quincy Adams: Policymaker for the Union* (Wilmington, DE: SR Books, 2001), especially pp. 85-9, 112.

of the means by which it is to be effected, will be necessary to enable us to determine upon our concurrence with it."[129]

Toward the Monroe Doctrine

A few months after Adams issued these optimistic instructions to American diplomats assigned to South America, the political and strategic situation seemed to change dramatically for the worse. For the small group of American statesmen who were in the know, the future of republicanism seemed to be at a tipping point. Over the spring and summer of 1823, France, with the political support of continental allies, had invaded Spain to restore the unchallenged rule of Ferdinand VII. Rumors circulated that a French fleet was preparing to embark with Spanish troops for South America to suppress the new regimes there – whether by restoring Spanish rule, coercing the South Americans to establish kingdoms ruled by members of the Bourbon family, or paving the way for the partition of South America among various European powers. In October 1823, the new Russian Minister in Washington, Baron de Tuyll, informed Adams that Emperor Alexander would not receive ministers or agents from any of the new regimes in South America. This was a policy undertaken by the Emperor as being "faithful to the political principles which he follows in concert with his Allies." Tuyll also offered what could have been construed as a warning to the United States to remain neutral during an intervention by the continental allies on behalf of Spain. Russia, meanwhile, continued to assert claims of exclusive commercial rights far down the northwest coast of North America, which possibly presaged the Empire's expansive territorial ambitions.[130]

To add spice to the mix, in London, the new British Foreign Secretary, George Canning, proposed to Minister Rush that the United States and Britain issue a joint declaration of principles that would, in essence, express Anglo-American opposition to any continental project to suppress South American independence.

This leads us to the familiar story of the Monroe Doctrine, the details of which need not detain us here. It is worth exploring briefly, however, how

---

[129] Material from these two paragraphs taken from JQA to Anderson, 27 May 1823, *WJQA*, 7: 471-2.

[130] Bradford Perkins, *The Cambridge History of American Foreign Relations*, Volume 1: *The Creation of a Republican Empire* (New York: Cambridge University Press, 1993), pp. 161-5; Worthington C. Ford, "John Quincy Adams and the Monroe Doctrine, Part I," *American Historical Review* 7 (July 1902): 685-6. For a review of U.S.-Russian relations during the period, see Hiroo Nakajima, "The Monroe Doctrine and Russia: American Views of Czar Alexander I and Their Influence upon Early Russian-American Relations," *Diplomatic History* 31 (June 2007): 439-63.

Adams attempted to apply the framework of his July 4 Address to the apparent crisis of late 1823. Adams continued to reject the Lexington and Edinburgh Doctrines as a way out of the problem. If his own account is to be believed, he single-handedly prevented serious exploration of an Anglo-American alliance or entente based on the defense of the liberty and independence of South America. Adams instead saw the situation as an opportunity to reinforce and systematize unilateral American efforts to strengthen political, commercial and religious liberty in the American Hemisphere – all the while keeping the U.S. out of Europe and Europe out of the American Hemisphere. Adams had to deal with the arguments of the President and his Cabinet colleagues who, in some instances, favored a bolder policy than he did, but in other cases advocated a more cautious approach.

Adams' first inclination evidently was to ignore publicly the apparent new European threat to South America and to focus instead on reinforcing the non-colonization principle, which he believed to be the key point of his July 4 Address. Adams still believed that it was highly unlikely that the continental powers would ever be able to agree to joint military action in South America, especially in light of Britain's stated opposition. Even if they did, he told the Cabinet, "I did not deny that they might make a temporary impression for three, four, or five years, but I no more believe that the Holy Allies will restore the Spanish dominion upon the American continent than that the Chimborazo will sink beneath the ocean. But, I added, if the South Americans were really in a state to be so easily subdued, it would be but a more forcible motive for us to beware of involving ourselves in their fate."[131]

As a statesman, however, Adams had to account for the fact that his assessment could be wrong – or, better put, that circumstances could change. He had to be prepared to deal with various plausible contingencies. He also had to account for the fears of President Monroe and his colleagues and for Congressional reaction if the diplomatic and strategic situation deteriorated. Monroe and some in the Cabinet, especially Calhoun, seemed to Adams to be on the verge of panic, crediting the European allies not only with bad intentions but with the military capacity to make good their threats unless the United States and Britain formally and effectively cooperated. Monroe and Calhoun were clearly intrigued by Canning's proposal. Monroe had already decided to consult privately by letter with his predecessors, Thomas Jefferson and James Madison. "Has

---

[131] Perkins, *The Monroe Doctrine*, pp. 74-5; 15 November 1823, *MJQA*, 6: 186. Adams felt that "they [the continental allies] must take time, and we can act coolly." 12 November 1823, unpublished JQA Diary, Massachusetts Historical Society, accessed at http://www.masshist.org/jqadiaries/doc.cfm?id=jqad34_155.

not the epoch arrived when G. Britain must take her stand, either on the side of the monarchs of Europe, or of the U States, & in consequence, either in favor of Despotism or of liberty . . . My own impression is that we ought to meet the proposal of the British gov't. . ."[132]

Both Jefferson and Madison agreed that the President should explore this avenue. Jefferson was opposed to abandoning "our first and fundamental maxim . . . never to entangle ourselves in the broils of Europe." But he thought that in this case, Britain could be enlisted usefully in the cause of liberty: "By acceding to her proposition, we detach her from the bands, bring her mighty weight into the scale of free government, and emancipate a continent at one stroke, which might otherwise linger long in doubt and difficulty."[133]

Madison concurred. He had no illusions that Britain had suddenly become enlightened about the principles of human liberty or republican government. Nevertheless, in the case at hand mutual self-interest pointed in the same direction. Indeed, Madison believed that Anglo-American cooperation in the matter of South America might alter Britain's calculations of her self-interest and cause her to be less warlike and to adopt more liberal views toward commerce and neutral rights. The fourth president thought it possible to go even further with the British in the promotion of human liberty:

> Will it not be honorable to our Country, & possibly not altogether in vain to invite the British Govt. to extend the 'avowed disapprobation' of the project agst. the Spanish Colonies, to the enterprise of France agst. Spain herself, and even to join in some declaratory Act in behalf of the Greeks. On the supposition that no form could be given to the Act clearing it of a pledge to follow it up by war, we ought to compare the good to be done with the little injury to be apprehended to the U. S., shielded as their interests would be by the power and the fleets of G. Britain united with their own.

Madison wrote privately to Jefferson: "With the British power & navy combined with our own we have nothing to fear from the rest of the World;

---

[132] Monroe to Jefferson, 17 October 1823, in Stanislaus Murray Hamilton, ed., *The Writings of James Monroe*, 7 vols. (New York: G.P. Putnam's Sons, 1898-1903), 6: 324. Adams was away in Massachusetts at the time. Monroe did not immediately inform him of this correspondence, nor did he do so when Adams first returned to Washington.

[133] Jefferson to Monroe, 24 October 1823, Merrill D. Peterson, ed., *The Portable Thomas Jefferson* (New York: Penguin Books, 1977), pp. 574-6.

and in the great struggle of the Epoch between liberty and despotism, we owe it to ourselves to sustain the former in this hemisphere at least."[134]

Adams disagreed strongly. Because Britain was acting only in its self-interest, not from the elevated desire to promote human liberty, the United States would be held hostage to a reversal of British policy if circumstances changed or if the continental monarchs could offer her sufficient incentives to switch sides or to remain neutral. Cuba was the obvious prize to tempt London to acquiesce to French-Russian intervention in South America. Adams doubted that Spain or the continental monarchs were prepared to go that far but he believed that did not matter. Canning's real game was to protect Britain's commercial interests and to entice the United States to make a binding pledge not to acquire Cuba or any other Spanish possessions. Adams discounted the argument that the United States could co-opt the British into supporting independent and republican governments in the American Hemisphere. It was more likely that Britain would use the connection to drag the United States into Europe, perhaps via the Edinburgh Doctrine. Adams was prepared to take matters with the British further only if Canning agreed in advance to follow the American lead and to offer diplomatic recognition to the new South American regimes. And even then, Adams argued that Washington and London should act in concert, not jointly, a view which he expressed pithily: "It would be more candid as well as more dignified, to avow our principles explicitly to Russia and France than to come as a cock-boat in the wake of a British man-of-war." His basic argument carried the day in the Cabinet.[135]

Adams was not surprised when Canning declined to recognize the South American governments and instead reached a bilateral understanding with the French (the Polignac Memorandum). Dispatches from Rush would later confirm Adams' judgment about Britain's motivations in the matter, which had nothing to do with advancing the rights of mankind. Rush described British policy succinctly: "It is France that must not be aggrandized, not South America that must be made free."

---

[134] Madison to Monroe, 30 October 1823, accessed at http://oll.libertyfund.org/?option=com_staticxt&staticfile=show.php%3Ftitle=1940&chapter=119281&layout=html&Itemid=27; and Madison to Jefferson, 1 November 1823, cited in Robert Kagan, *Dangerous Nation: America's Place in the World from its Earliest Days to the Dawn of the Twentieth Century* (New York: Alfred A. Knopf, 2006), p. 168.

[135] 7 November 1823, *MJQA*, 6: 177-81. See also the entries for 15 and 17 November 1823. Adams obtained consent from the President to send instructions to Rush to this effect. He successfully persuaded Monroe to resist the pressure of his colleagues, particularly Calhoun, to provide Rush with the discretion to make a deal in an emergency. Monroe directed, however, that Rush should not make South American recognition a sine qua non in an emergency.

> This nation in its collective, corporate capacity has no more sympathy with popular rights and freedom now, than it had on the plains of Lexington in America; than it showed during the whole progress of the French Revolution in Europe; than it exhibited lately at Naples in proclaiming a neutrality in all other events, save that of the safety of the royal family there; or still more recently, when it stood aloof whilst France and the Holy Alliance avowed their intention of crushing them too upon pretexts so wholly unjustifiable . . . With a king in the hands of his ministers, with an aristocracy of unbounded opulence and pride, with what is called a House of Commons constituted essentially by the aristocracy and always moved by its influence, England can, in reality, never look with complacency upon popular and equal rights, whether abroad or at home. She therefore moves in her natural orbit when she wars, positively or negatively, against them. For their own sakes alone, she will never war in their favor.[136]

The opportunity that Adams saw was not that of an Anglo-American alliance in which the United States would be a junior partner beholden to London. It was rather an occasion to reinforce, in the minds of his countrymen as well as foreign powers, the moral distinction between liberty and despotism, between the rights of man and divine right; and between self-government and imperialism (governing other peoples without their consent). This was the doctrine of the Declaration of Independence and his July 4 Address, rightly understood, a doctrine that Adams believed Britain had never accepted.

Despite his earlier concern to cool overheated official rhetoric, Adams believed that the time had come for the U.S. government to make clear America's position – that of his July 4 Address – and to do so publicly, if necessary. Adams was provoked to do so in mid-November 1823, in the midst of the intense Cabinet debate over South America. He had received from Tuyll an extract from a circular dispatch issued by the Russian Foreign Minister, Count Nesselrode. The dispatch contained (in Adams' words)

> an exposition of principles relating to the affairs of Spain and Portugal, in a tone of passionate exultation at the counter-revolution in Portugal and the impending success of the French army in Spain; an 'Io Triumphe' over the fallen cause of revolution, with sturdy promises of determination to keep it down; disclaimers

---
[136] Ford, "Adams and the Monroe Doctrine, Part I," pp. 687-9.

of all intention of making conquests; bitter complaints of being calumniated, and one paragraph of compunctions, acknowledging that an apology is yet due to mankind for the invasion of Spain, which it is in the power only of Ferdinand to furnish, by making his people happy.

The Russian Emperor and his European allies, according to the circular, would never treat with revolutionaries. Forcible intervention in the affairs of others was designed only "to guarantee the tranquility of all the states of which the civilized world is composed." In these Russian demarches there was no open threat of intervention to restore the "tranquility" in the American Hemisphere. But it was certainly unusual, and perhaps ominous, for a Russian Minister to the United States to call attention to his government's policy toward purely European matters.[137]

The provocative Russian dispatch was one factor that led Adams to support a broader statement of American foreign policy toward South America than that of the principle of non-colonization. Monroe's Annual Message, submitted to Congress on December 2, 1823, in which Adams had a substantial hand, explained why the United States had a vital interest in the American Hemisphere that it did not have in Europe.

> The citizens of the United States cherish sentiments the most friendly in favor of the liberty and happiness of their fellow men on that side of the Atlantic. In the wars of the European powers in matters relating to themselves we have never taken any part, nor does it comport with our policy so to do. It is only when our rights are invaded or seriously menaced that we resent injuries or make preparation for our defense. With the movements in this hemisphere we are of necessity more immediately connected, and by causes which must be obvious to all enlightened and impartial observers.

At this point in the Message, Monroe seemed to be making a strategic case for the priority of U.S. interests in the American Hemisphere, including South America – in essence, arguing for a U.S. sphere of influence, at least with respect to European penetration. Yet given the relative disparity between

---

[137] 17 November 1823, *MJQA*, 6: 190. The text of Nesselrode's Circular, in French, dated 30 August 1823, is in Worthington C. Ford, "John Quincy Adams and the Monroe Doctrine, Part II," *American Historical Review* 8 (October 1902): 30-3. The translation is from Dexter Perkins, *The Monroe Doctrine*, p. 71. Bemis, *John Quincy Adams,* p. 386, reports that Tuyll verbally told Adams that this applied to South America as well as to Europe, but that does not seem to be what Adams recorded in his diary.

the combined military power of Europe and that of America – and the substantial commercial interests of the British, Spanish and other European powers in the American Hemisphere – any *material* claim to a special geopolitical interest by the United States was arguably a vast strategic overreach. Material interests did not exhaust the U.S. claims, however, which ultimately had to do with disparate forms of government.

> The political system of the allied powers is essentially different in this respect from that of America. This difference proceeds from that which exists in their respective Governments; and to the defense of our own, which has been achieved by the loss of so much blood and treasure, and matured by the wisdom of their most enlightened citizens, and under which we have enjoyed unexampled felicity, this whole nation is devoted. . . . . It is impossible that the allied powers should extend their political system to any portion of either continent without endangering our peace and happiness; nor can anyone believe that our southern brethren, if left to themselves, would adopt it of their own accord. It is equally impossible, therefore, that we should behold such interposition in any form with indifference.[138]

Even so stated, Monroe's assertion of the differences between American and European regime types was qualified. He offered it as a fact, on which objective observers presumably could agree, but he did not offer any defense of republicanism as such, or claim its universal superiority over other forms of government.

One might reasonably infer a claim of republican superiority from the Annual Message but Adams felt the need for a stronger assertion, at least for the record. During the Cabinet deliberations over the text of the Message, Adams argued that although the United States should not take the ideological *offensive*, America was not only justified, it was required, to *defend* the principles of republican government when those were openly challenged. Adams originally wanted to do so in a written reply to Tuyll's October observations about Alexander's attitude toward South American ministers. At the time, Monroe and the Cabinet watered down Adams' communication to avoid offense. The Secretary of State now insisted, moreover, that Nesselrode's circular in defense of absolutism, and its right and duty to intervene in the affairs of others, could not go unanswered.

---

[138] Quotes from Monroe's Seventh Annual Message are taken from http://millercenter.org/scripps/archive/speeches/detail/3604.

> My purpose would be in a moderate and conciliatory manner, but with a firm and determined spirit, to declare our dissent from the principles avowed in those communications; to assert those upon which our own Government is founded, and, while disclaiming all intention of attempting to propagate them by force, and all interference with the political affairs of Europe, to declare our expectation and hope that the European powers will equally abstain from the attempt to spread their principles in the American hemisphere, or to subjugate by force any part of these continents to their will.[139]

Adams wanted to make it clear to Tuyll that, although the United States would not contest the rule of the monarchs where it existed, it would resent and resist the spread of monarchical principles where its own vital interests were at stake.

> It was meant also to be eventually an exposition of the principles of this Government, and a brief development of its political system as henceforth to be maintained: essentially republican – maintaining its own independence, and respecting that of others; essentially pacific – studiously avoiding all involvement in the combinations of European politics, cultivating peace and friendship with the most absolute monarchies, highly appreciating and anxiously desirous of retaining that of the Emperor Alexander, but declaring that, having recognized the independence of the South American States, we could not see with indifference any attempt by European powers by forcible interposition either to restore the Spanish dominion on the American Continents or to introduce monarchical principles into those countries, or to transfer any portion of the ancient or present American possessions of Spain to any other European power.[140]

Adams' draft of his "Observations on the Communications recently received from the Minister of Russia," which he intended to submit to Tuyll, began with the observation that "the Government of the United States is Republican," and that "the principles of this form of polity are:

> 1. that the Institution of Government, to be lawful, must be pacific, that is founded upon the consent, and by the agreement of those who are to be governed; and 2. that each Nation is exclusively the judge of the Government best suited to itself, and that no other Nation, can

---

[139] 21 November 1823, *MJQA*, 6: 194.
[140] 25 November 1823, *MJQA*, 6: 199-200.

justly interfere by force to impose a different Government upon it. The first of these principles may be designated, as the principle of *Liberty* – the second as the principle of National *Independence* – They are both Principles of *Peace* and Good Will to Men.[141]

Following the principle of national independence, "the United States recognize in other Nations the right which they claim and exercised for themselves, of establishing and modifying their own Governments, according to their own judgments, and views of their interests, not encroaching upon the rights of others." Although "the Monarchical principle of Government, is different from the United States," the American government had never sought conflict with that principle, "for interests not their own," but rather it "desired Peace, Commerce, and Honest Friendship with all other Nations, and entangling alliances with none."[142]

> From all the combinations of European Politics relative to the distribution of Power, or the Administration of Government the United States have kept themselves studiously aloof. They have not sought, by the propagation of their principles to disturb the Peace, or to intermeddle with the policy of any part of Europe. In the Independence of Nations, they have respected the organization of their Governments, however different from their own, and [Republicans to the last drop of blood in their veins], they have thought it no sacrifice of their principles to cultivate with sincerity and assiduity Peace and Friendship even with the most absolute Monarchies and their Sovereigns.

Adams then recapitulated American policy toward the revolutions and regime change, including George Washington's policy of neutrality and his decision to recognize the independence of a new regime once it had been established physically beyond all reasonable doubt. (He did not refer to all of the qualifications that guided his approach toward South American independence.) Adams also affirmed that U.S. neutrality depended on the European monarchs also being willing to remain neutral toward the Spanish-South American conflict.

Then to Adams' fundamental *quid pro quo*: As to the assertion of the Russian government that the Allies were prepared to intervene against

---

[141] The following quotes are taken from Ford, "Adams and the Monroe Doctrine, Part II," pp. 41-3. Emphasis in original.

[142] Here Adams cited Jefferson's familiar formulation about entangling alliances, from his First Inaugural Address, rather than that of Washington in the Farewell Address.

revolutionary regimes and movements to ensure the "tranquility" of the civilized world, the President "wishes to perceive the sentiments, the application of which is limited, and intended in their result to be limited to the Affairs of Europe."

> That the sphere of their operations was not intended to embrace the United States of America, nor any portion of the Western Hemisphere. . . . That the United States of America, and their Government, could not see with indifference, the forcible interposition of any European Power, other than Spain, either to restore the dominion of Spain over her emancipated Colonies in America, or to establish Monarchical Governments in those Countries, or to transfer any of the possessions heretofore or yet subject to Spain in the Western Hemisphere, or to any other European power.

Adams' Cabinet colleagues were alarmed at the tone of the draft. Perhaps, they said, it was unwise to make such a bold declaration, even if it did not become public. (Adams actually suggested to Tuyll that the two publish all their correspondence on the matter.) The Russians would surely share Adams' note with other powers, including Britain. Wirt objected to the first part of it as being "a hornet of a paragraph, and, he thought, would be exceedingly offensive." Monroe worried that this would be taken as "a direct attack" on the Holy Alliance. The President also believed that the British were torn between liberal and illiberal impulses. By making such ideological pronouncements, the United States would actually weaken the forces of reform in Britain:

> The President seemed to entertain some apprehension that the republicanism of my paper might indispose the British Government to a cordial concert of operations with us. He said they were in a dilemma between their anti-Jacobin policy, the dread of their internal reformers, which made them sympathize with the Holy Allies, and the necessities of their commerce and revenue, with the pressure of their debts and taxes, which compelled them to side with South American independence for the sake of South American trade. He believed they must ultimately take this side, but if we should shock and alarm them upon the political side of the question, and the Holy Allies could hold out to them anything to appease the craving of their commercial and fiscal interest, they might go back to the allies – as Portugal has gone back – insignificant and despised, but leaving us in the lurch, with all Europe against us.

Calhoun, "with many professions of diffidence and doubt, but only to prompt discussion," asked whether it was appropriate to communicate such sentiments directly to the Russian government through its Minister. "The paper contained rather an ostentatious display of republican principles; it was making up an issue, perhaps too soon, with the Holy Alliance. It would perhaps be offensive to the Emperor of Russia, and perhaps even to the British Government, which would by no means relish so much republicanism." Calhoun suggested that it might be less offensive merely to provide Tuyll with a copy of the relevant portions of Monroe's Annual Message, which did not identify any particular nation as the source of concern, and let him draw his own conclusions. In Calhoun's judgment, the form of the Annual Message, which was directed toward a domestic rather than international audience, would be less provocative to Russia and the European monarchs, than a diplomatic communication.

Adams insisted that it was essential to respond to ideological challenges that "beard[ed] us to our faces upon the monarchical principles of the Holy Alliance.

> It was time to tender them an issue. In the last resort, this was a cause to be pleaded before the world of mankind. Our country, and the world, would require that our ground should be distinctly taken, as well as resolutely maintained. Now, in my belief, was the time for taking it; and as I thought the Holy Alliance would not ultimately invade South America, and firmly believed that the Emperor Alexander did not mean to include us, or any consideration of us, in his invectives against revolution, I wished to give him an opportunity of disclaiming any such intention.[143]

Adams insisted that there was a justifiable distinction between defending republicanism and promoting it aggressively. "We avowed republicanism, but disclaimed propagandism." U.S. diplomatic strategy should aim to put despotism in the wrong, when it needed to be put in the wrong – "if the Holy Alliance were determined to make up an issue with us, it was our policy to meet, and not to make it. We should retreat to the wall before taking to arms, and be sure at every step to put them as much as possible in the wrong." Adams was sure that his language would not be offensive to the Emperor, "unless he had determined to invade South America; and if he had, this paper, which was to be our protest against it, could not too distinctly set forth the *principles* of our opposition to his design." The U.S. government should establish strategic

---

[143] This discussion is taken from 25 November 1823, *MJQA*, 6: 199-204.

and political red lines, based on principle, which made sense to the American people and which coincided with America's interest and power.[144]

This line of argument raised the question of whether the United States should use military force if the continental allies intervened to depose the regimes in the former Spanish colonies. Did the language of the President's Annual Message mean to warn that European military action in South American was a *casus belli* for the United States? Adams believed that, on the merits, the United States would be fully justified in using force, although he still regarded intervention as a low-probability event. If the United States simply stood by, the end result would not be the restoration of weak Spanish rule but a new set of European colonies – Russia, for instance, would take California, Peru and Chile, and France would govern Mexico and Buenos Aires, probably under a Bourbon Prince. Britain, is this scenario, would be bought off with Cuba. "The danger therefore was brought to our doors, and I thought we could not too soon take our stand to repel it." Calhoun, who thought that Allied intervention was both likely and imminent, agreed emphatically: "The next step the allies would then take would be against ourselves – to put down what has been called the first example of successful diplomatic rebellion." The United States could not hesitate to resist European intervention in South America or it would be compelled to fight on its own soil for its independence and form of government.[145]

To be sure, it was far more likely that should this occur, Britain would oppose the European allies' action. Adams assumed that, given Britain's naval superiority, she would undoubtedly preserve the independence of South America even without American support. The problem for the United States, if it remained neutral, was that the new regimes would likely then become protectorates, if not outright colonies of Britain, and lose their republican form. Britain was known to have favored the establishment of monarchical regimes in the event that some sort of Spanish sovereignty was not preserved. By contrast, American participation in the war to defend the South Americans would give Washington some means and moral authority to resist Britain's political domination of South America and to support the republican cause. Adams noted that the Executive could not formally commit the United States to go to war – that power resided with Congress – but the way in which the President framed his policy in his Annual Messages and in diplomatic communications would surely prejudice the Congressional deliberations in one way

---

[144] 22 November 1823, *MJQA*, 6: 197; 25 November 1823, *MJQA*, 6: 204; 27 November 1823, *MJQA*, 6: 211. Emphasis in original.

[145] 26 November 1823, *MJQA*, 6: 207-8.

or another. The firmer the statements that the President made, the stronger would be the implicit commitment and the political pressure to use force. Adams still believed that these contingencies were a very low probability but he opposed bluffing to try to deter or avoid conflict. As it was, the Annual Message avoided any unequivocal threat to use force in the event of European intervention in South America.[146]

In making such pronouncements, whether public or private, Adams believed that the proper assessment of the intended foreign and domestic audience for the U.S. warnings was critical. His official instructions to the new American Minister to France, for instance, avoided the use of charged language even though France was the most assertive of the European powers in supporting Spain's right to recover its colonies.[147] In contrast, Adams believed that the Russian Emperor would not be offended and that he therefore could be lectured safely in a way that would send a message to other, less friendly states. Adams thought he had divined the key to the riddle of Alexander's apparently schizophrenic approach to the world. "I believed the Emperor Alexander was honestly wedded to his system; that he was profoundly penetrated with the conviction that he was laboring for the good of his people and for the welfare of mankind." Based on his personal experience with Alexander, as well as on a close study of his policies, Adams concluded that "there was no man living more sensitive to public opinion." The Emperor relished the image of being a peacemaker and the friend of mankind. "My object in this paper [Adams' response to Tuyll] was to appeal much to the personal feelings of the Emperor Alexander: to his love of peace; to his religious impressions; to his sensibility to public opinion; to his old friendly offices and good will towards the United States. I would search all these sources of action, and bring him either to a formal disavowal of any dispositions unfriendly to the United States, or to an express declaration of what his intentions are."[148]

In order to avoid giving unnecessary and dangerous offense to the European monarchs, Adams insisted that the United States must credibly

---

[146] 26 November 1823, *MJQA*, 6: 206-7; Bemis, *John Quincy Adams*, p. 390. Calhoun concurred with Adams' general line of argument about the use of force; Calhoun concluded, however, that Britain could not successfully resist the Allies if the United States remained neutral, and therefore that London would go along with European intervention unless Washington agreed to support the British and South Americans.

[147] Perkins, *The Monroe Doctrine*, p. 90.

[148] 25 November 1825, *MJQA*, 6: 201-2. Albert Gallatin, who had just returned from Paris after the conclusion of his appointment as Minister to France, argued that Adams' view of Alexander's liberal sensibilities had been overtaken by events and that the Emperor would be offended by Adams' proposed language on the distinction between republicanism and monarchy. 27 November 1823, *MJQA*, 6: 215-6.

reinforce the distinction that it had made consistently between the Old World and the American Hemisphere. Emperor Alexander, in their first conversation in St. Petersburg in 1809, had expressed to Adams his understanding and appreciation of America's policy of avoiding entanglement in the affairs of Europe. From this Adams concluded that "the avowal of principles connected with the disclaimer of interference in European affairs, of proselytism, and of hostile purposes, could not offend him. I thought it most essential." The United States must do nothing, in word or deed, to suggest that it did not respect its no-exceptions disclaimer of interference in purely European affairs.[149]

The possibility of American support for the revolutionary and liberal movements in Europe was not purely hypothetical. The *Edinburgh Review*, after all, had proposed Anglo-American cooperation to this end. Monroe, as we have seen, regretted the lack of opportunity to weigh in on the revolutionary movement in Naples in 1821. In the summer of 1823, Monroe wrote to ask Jefferson: "Can we, in any form, take a bolder attitude in regard to it, in favor of liberty, than we did" during the time of the French Revolution? "Can we afford greater aid to that cause, by assuming such an attitude, than we do now, by the form of our example?" Practical opportunities seemed to be open. Greek agents in London had approached Rush for American assistance to their independence movement. No less a personage than Albert Gallatin, who was retiring as U.S. Minister to France, proposed that the United States send warships to the Mediterranean on behalf of the Greeks. Madison had speculated in his letter to Monroe about the possibility of some American action with respect to Greece and Spain.[150]

Monroe, in his Annual Message, originally had drafted language that (in Adams' words) "alluded to the recent events in Spain and Portugal, speaking in terms of the most pointed reprobation of the late invasion of Spain by France, and of the principles upon which it was undertaken by the open avowal of the King of France." Monroe's draft also "contained a broad acknowledgment of the Greeks as an independent nation, and a recommendation to Congress to make an appropriation for sending a Minister to them." As to the propriety of the United States inserting itself verbally and diplomatically into European wars and revolutions, Monroe and Calhoun argued to the Cabinet that circumstances had changed since the unhappy days of the French Revolution. "This last invasion of Spain

---

[149] 26 November 1823, *MJQA*, 6: 209. For JQA's first meeting with Alexander, see 5 November 1809, *MJQA*, 3: 50-4.

[150] Monroe to Jefferson, 2 June 1823, cited in Dexter Perkins, *The Monroe Doctrine*, p. 60.

by France ... was a more direct attack upon the popular principle; and that although no former message ever censured those overthrows and conquests before, yet it might be very proper to censure this now."[151] A few weeks later, Webster introduced a resolution in the House to recommend defraying the expense of an agent or commissioner to Greece, whenever the president might deem such an appointment expedient – which clearly followed Clay's strategy with respect to South American independence. It was designed to encourage, or force, the administration to recognize and even aid the Greek revolutionaries. Clay supported the proposal.[152]

Adams was frustrated that Monroe had completely missed the point of his argument about how best to support human liberty and the rights of mankind – and American national interests – without engaging in an ideological crusade. He warned the President that the proposed language "would be a summons to arms – to arms against all Europe, and for objects of policy exclusively European – Greece and Spain.

> It would be as new, too, in our policy as it would be surprising. For more than thirty years Europe had been in convulsions; every nation almost of which it is composed alternately invading and invaded. Empires, kingdoms, principalities, had been overthrown, revolutionized, and counter-revolutionized, and we had looked on safe in our distance beyond an intervening ocean, and avowing a total forbearance to interfere in any of the combinations of European politics. This message would at once buckle on the harness and throw down the gauntlet. It would have the air of open defiance to all Europe, and I should not be surprised if the first answer to it from Spain and France, and even Russia, should be to break off their diplomatic intercourse with us. I did not expect that the quiet which we had enjoyed for six or seven years would last much longer. The aspect of things was portentous; but if we must come to an issue with Europe, let us keep it off as long as possible. Let us use all possible means to carry the opinion of the nation with us, and the opinion of the world.[153]

In offering his analysis to Monroe, Adams certainly recognized the basic power gradient that governed international relations. The United States

---

[151] 21 November 1823, *MJQA*, 6: 194, 196.

[152] David S. Heidler and Jeanne T. Heidler, *Henry Clay: The Essential American* (New York: Random House, 2010), p. 165. Adams may have wanted to avoid any Congressional endorsement for the Monroe Doctrine to be sure that it did not become entangled with such matters.

[153] 21 November 1823, *MJQA*, 6: 195.

simply lacked the means to make any real military difference in great power conflicts across the Atlantic or to intervene effectively on behalf of European movements for independence or constitutional government. Notwithstanding that fact, Adams never wavered in his view that the cause of "the banners of freedom" in Europe was probably hopeless in its own right for the foreseeable future – because that cause was at best imperfectly understood by its advocates and because it was not self-sustaining, in the way that the South American cause (however imperfect) had proven to be. Adams, to be sure, did not believe that military occupation by the European despots could suppress the desire for independence or reform in Europe, but neither would that resistance necessarily be successful or sustainable for the foreseeable future. American, or Anglo-American, intervention on behalf of the republican cause, even if it was militarily feasible, would not succeed in light of national assertiveness and reactionary resistance. Only when the peoples of Europe were ready and able to sustain themselves – and only when the international environment was much more favorable – would a republican government, or a truly constitutional monarchy, become possible.

Adams opposed breaching the line between Europe and the American Hemisphere even where the case for U.S. intervention was strong, such as with the Greek independence movement. The Greeks were seeking independence from an Empire that Adams believed to be far more regressive than that of Catholic Spain. Most Greek revolutionaries espoused republican (democratic) principles, yet they enjoyed high-level support among Russian elites (due to Orthodox and ethnic connections) and strong popular support in England. With the U.S. Navy's Mediterranean squadron and its substantial commerce in the region, the United States arguably had the material means to support the Greeks. Adams, nevertheless, strongly resisted this line of argument. In fact, one of the reasons he may have become more friendly toward the new South American regimes was because it helped focus his nation's political attention on the American Hemisphere and thereby forestall a disastrous foray into Europe.

> The ground that I wish to take is that of earnest remonstrance against the interference of the European powers by force with South America, but to disclaim all interference on our part with Europe; to make an American cause, and adhere inflexibly to that. The President said he had spoken of the Greeks and of the Spaniards in his last year's message. I said I should not object to paragraphs of a like description, in general terms and pledging nothing, but I would

be specially careful to avoid anything which may be construed as hostility to the allies.[154]

"I have not much esteem for the enthusiasm that evaporates in words," Adams observed, "and I told the President I thought not quite so lightly of a war with Turkey." In 1824, Adams was asked to make a personal contribution for humanitarian aid to the Greeks. He declined and recommended that the President do so as well. "We had objects of distress to relieve at home more than sufficient to absorb all my capacities of contribution; and a subscription for the Greeks would, in my view of things, be a breach of neutrality, and therefore improper."[155]

At the end of the day, both sides compromised. The purportedly offensive ideological language in the response to Tuyll – what Adams referred to as "the cream of my paper," especially the "hornet of a paragraph" dealing with the principles of a republican polity – was removed. Monroe later authorized Adams to restore the text, at least when reading the paper to Tuyll, if Adams thought it that important – but the Secretary decided not to go against the clear wishes of his superior, and did not do so. Monroe, meanwhile, agreed to remove his proposed language about Greece and Spain from the Annual Message and to include the strongly worded statement about the separation of America from Europe.[156]

A Word on the Panama Congress

Monroe's foreign policy pronouncements in the Annual Message were well received generally by American opinion leaders and by the public, neither of which was aware of the apparent crisis created by the threat of European intervention in South America. Nonetheless, a few dissenting voices were heard, whose themes would echo down the years. The New York *Advertiser*, a vehicle of the remnants of the Federalist Party, found the language to be "too broad and comprehensive for the occasion." An essay in the Boston *Advertiser* asked: "Is there anything in the Constitution which makes our Government the Guarantors of the Liberties of the World? of the Wahabees? the Peruvians? the Chilese? the Mexicans or Colombians?" Clay, now back in Congress, told Adams that he thought the section on foreign policy was "the best part" of the Annual Message, but Clay was unable to generate any enthusiasm for a resolu-

---

[154] 15 August 1823, *MJQA*, 6: 172-3; 22 November 1823, *MJQA*, 6: 197-8; 24 November 1823, *MJQA*, 6: 198-9.

[155] 15 November 1823, *MJQA*, 6: 173; 10 May 1824, *MJQA*, 6: 324-5. At this time, Adams was also quietly exploring the possibility of a commercial agreement with Turkey.

[156] 27 November 1823, *MJQA*, 6: 211-3.

tion that would support the President's warning against forcible intervention in South America. John Randolph, the quixotic but influential representative from Virginia, declared that if the new regimes were not capable of maintaining their own independence, then the United States should not commit itself to defend their cause.[157]

One vital precinct was also considered, but only very late in the game. Adams did not discuss the situation with Jose Maria Salazar, the new Minister from Colombia and the only accredited South American diplomat in Washington, until November 29, three weeks after the Cabinet had begun urgent deliberations on the presumed threat to South America. By then, Monroe and the Cabinet had already made the basic policy decisions that were to be reflected in the Annual Message. Adams had been authorized earlier to brief Salazar but he had not done so until the end of the month. The delay presumably resulted from the press of events but also, most likely, from the low priority that Adams placed on South American views. Adams, according to his diary, informed Salazar "of the negotiation between Mr. Rush and Mr. Canning, recently commenced, and of the manifestations of the disposition of the Emperor of Russia regarding South America. And I told him he would see by the President's message to Congress the deep interest we were taking in the maintenance of their independence; and Mr. Ravenga [the Colombian agent in London] would inform his Government how earnestly we were pressing the acknowledgment of it by Great Britain." The Secretary of State apparently gave Salazar no opportunity to comment on a draft of the Message or otherwise to explore cooperation with the United States.[158]

Nor did Adams provide American diplomats with information about the situation, or about U.S. policy, to pass on to the governments in South America. In the coming months, the United States would continue to deflect South American efforts to turn the unilateral U.S. policy approach – what history would later come to know as the Monroe Doctrine – into a binding bilateral or multilateral security guarantee. Adams, in fact, made it clear that in a real emergency, the United States would first have to reach a prior understanding "with those European powers, whose interests and principles would secure from them an active and efficient cooperation in the cause" – in other words, Britain – before it would consider negotiating any sort of alliance or security relationship with a South American power.[159]

---

[157] Quotations and citations taken from Dexter Perkins, *The Monroe Doctrine*, pp. 146-7.

[158] 29 November 1823, *MJQA*, 6: 220-1.

[159] Dexter Perkins, *The Monroe Doctrine*, pp. 149-61, 185-93.

In December 1824, the representatives in Washington from Colombia, Mexico and Central America transmitted an invitation for the United States to attend a Pan-American Congress in Panama to discuss means of ensuring greater hemispheric cooperation. This Congress was the brainchild of Simon Bolivar, although Bolivar originally planned to exclude the United States. He favored British participation, however, and regarded London as a much more natural partner and ally of the South American cause than the United States. The responsibility whether to respond to the invitation, as it turned out, fell to the new administration of President John Quincy Adams and his successor at the Department of State, Henry Clay.

Adams chose Clay for the post despite their longstanding rivalry. Clay's support had been essential for Adams to win enough votes in the House of Representatives to obtain the presidency, when none of the candidates achieved a majority in the Electoral College. The two men denied that there had been any "corrupt bargain," by which Clay obtained the senior position in the Cabinet, and other concessions, in exchange for his support for Adams. The new president sincerely believed that Clay was politically the best choice for the post. He gave the West a senior representative in the Cabinet. Adams and Clay supported a domestic "American System" of internal improvements and modest protective tariffs. As to foreign policy, however, there were reasons to doubt that the two men could work well together. Clay and Adams had often been at loggerheads during their service on the U.S. Commission at Ghent in 1814, and more recently had disagreed over the proper policy toward South American independence movements.

Clay favored accepting the invitation to the Panama Congress as a means to help restore U.S. ability to promote republican government in South America. Clay feared that Washington's moral authority had been lost because of the impression that the U.S. government in general – and Adams in particular – had acted out of narrow self-interest in its dealing with the South Americans. Clay, in his communications with South American representatives, therefore portrayed the unilateralist Monroe Doctrine in the best possible light.[160]

Adams agreed with Clay that the United States should attend the Congress. He may well have hesitated initially because of his lingering doubts about the stability of the South American republics. Adams also believed that Cabinet officers should be granted considerable authority within their respective areas of responsibility, as long as the president did not fundamentally disagree with their approach; the Cabinet member, in turn, owed loyalty to his chief. The president certainly should not micromanage his team, even in

---

[160] Ibid., pp. 198-200.

an area where the president had considerable or even unprecedented expertise, as Adams did in the diplomatic realm. For Adams to try to run the State Department over Clay's shoulder would have been disastrous. Adams knew how important good South American relations were to Clay; on its own merits, the Panama Congress provided Adams with the opportunity to promote his civilizational agenda – especially the Freedom of the Seas – and to reinforce the message to the South Americans that true independence depended on rejecting burdensome trading conditions and exclusive commercial privileges.

Adams, of course, also wanted to defend and advance America's particular interests. He wanted to send a clear message of U.S. opposition to any South American invasion of Cuba and to counteract any extra-American influence (Britain was to be represented at Panama by an observer). American participation would be limited, however. The United States would maintain its position of neutrality in the ongoing war between the South Americans and Spain and would not engage in any discussions among the participants about their military operations. Further, as Adams assured Congress, the U.S. government would not regard the meeting as anything like a Constitutional Convention or predecessor to a hemispheric federal government or regime.[161] As Clay wrote in his instructions to the American delegation:

> All notion is rejected of an Amphyctionic [sic] Council, invested with power finally to decide controversies between the American states, or to regulate, in any respect, their conduct. Such a Council might have been well enough adapted to a number of small, contracted States, whose united territory would fall short of the extent of that of the smallest of the American Powers. The complicated and various interests which appertain to the Nations of this vast Continent, cannot be safely confided to the superintendence of one Legislative authority. We should almost as soon expect to see an Amphyctionic Council to regulate the affairs of the whole globe. But even if it were desirable to establish such a tribunal, it is beyond the competency of the Government of the United States, voluntarily to assent to it, without a previous change of their actual Constitution.[162]

The American decision to accept the invitation did not represent Adams' conversion to the Lexington Doctrine. The United States, as Clay's instruc-

---

[161] Adams, Special Message to Congress, 26 December 1825. John T. Woolley and Gerhard Peters, *The American Presidency Project* [online]. Santa Barbara, CA. Available from World Wide Web: http://www.presidency.ucsb.edu/ws/?pid=66660.

[162] Clay to Anderson and Sergeant, 8 May 1826, *PHC*, 5: 314.

tions made clear, no longer saw any threat of intervention in South America by the Holy Alliance, and therefore saw no need to consider an offense-defense alliance. The United States was not prepared to multilateralize the tenets of the Monroe Doctrine, as some of the South American governments had hoped, or otherwise give the South Americans any substantial voice in the U.S. foreign policy decision-making process. The Adams administration did not portray the Panama Congress as a meeting of republican regimes but rather as a gathering of independent, sovereign states. There was no mention of ideological solidarity with the revolutionaries in Europe.

Adams did, however, hope to strengthen the cause of republicanism in South America, at least indirectly. He stressed the importance of persuading the South Americans to acknowledge the principle of non-colonization that he had originally regarded as the centerpiece of his July 4 Address. This was to be done through a general statement (not a treaty) that each nation would "guard by its own means against the establishment of any future European colony within its borders." In terms of human rights (the rights of mankind) that flowed from popular sovereignty, Adams singled out "the advancement of religious freedom" as an area where the United States could exercise its moral influence at the Congress.

> Some of the southern nations are even yet so far under the dominion of prejudice that they have incorporated with their political constitutions an exclusive church, without toleration of any other than the dominant sect. The abandonment of this last badge of religious bigotry and oppression may be pressed more effectually by the united exertions of those who concur in the principles of freedom of conscience upon those who are yet to be convinced of their justice and wisdom than by the solitary efforts of a minister to any one of the separate Governments.[163]

In his instructions to the U.S. Commissioners, Clay elaborated on the argument that they were to make.

> It would be deemed rash to assert that civil liberty, and an established church cannot exist together in the same State; but it may be safely affirmed that history affords no example of their union where the religion of the State has not only been established, but exclusive. If any of the American Powers think proper to introduce into their systems an established religion, although we should

---

[163] Adams, Special Message to Congress, 26 December 1825.

regret such a determination, we should have no right to make a formal complaint unless it should be exclusive.

The ground for the complaint was that such exclusivity would deny American citizens, on their lawful occasion in those countries, the right to worship as they saw fit. The U. S. commissioners were authorized to propose a joint declaration that there would be free toleration of religious worship. "And you will also, in any Treaty or Treaties that you may conclude, endeavor to have inserted an article stipulating the liberty of religious worship in the territories of the respective parties.... And this new guarantee will serve to give strength to the favorable dispositions of enlightened men in the various American States, against the influence of bigotry and superstition."[164]

In his public messages to Congress, Adams was circumspect about any advice – or direct means – that the United States might use to promote republican government in South America. Clay left this matter to the end of his official instructions, where he observed that Americans, as a rule, cautiously avoided touching "on a subject so delicate." "The United States never have been, and are not now animated by any spirit of propagandism. They prefer, to all other forms of government, and are perfectly contented with, their own confederacy. Allowing no foreign interference, either in the formation or in the conduct of their government, they are equally scrupulous in refraining from all interference in the original structure or subsequent interior movement of the governments of other independent nations." Americans were not indifferent to the form of government that the various South American nations might choose "because they cannot be indifferent to the happiness of any nation. But the interest which they are accustomed to cherish in the wisdom or folly which may mark the course of other powers, in the adoption and execution of their political systems, is rather a feeling of sympathy than a principle of action."

Clay instructed the Commissioners to go beyond their natural restraint on one point, however. "There is reason to believe that one European Power, if not more, has been active in both Colombia and Mexico, if not elsewhere, with a view to subvert, if possible, the existing forms of free Government there established, to substitute the monarchical in place of them, and to plant, on the newly erected thrones, European Princes." The information available to Clay indicated that such projects had been repulsed, but "the spirit which dictated it never slumbers, and it may be renewed." For the record, Clay asserted his belief that the American Commissioners would be preaching to the republican choir on this point. "You will, however, take advantage of every fit opportu-

---

[164] Clay to Anderson and Sergeant, 8 May 1826, *PHC*, 5: 338.

nity to strengthen their political faith, and to inculcate the solemn duty of every Nation to reject foreign dictation in its domestic concerns. You will also, at all proper times, manifest a readiness to satisfy inquiries as to the theory and practical operation of our Federal and State constitutions of Government, and to illustrate and explain the manifold blessings which the people of the United States have enjoyed, and are continuing to enjoy under them."[165]

Adams reported that he had accepted the invitation to the Panama Congress, pending Congressional approval of his nominations for the U.S. Commission, in his highly controversial First Annual Message of December 1825. In that Message, Adams laid out an ambitious national agenda of internal improvements – promoting moral, intellectual and scientific achievements, as well as great projects like roads and harbors. Liberty, Adams insisted provocatively, is power. Such an assertion raised the hackles of various Republican factions who saw this as the dangerous rebirth of High Federalism, and of slaveholders who feared that the federal government would assert the right to interfere with the peculiar institution. Adams' discussion of the Panama Congress was only briefly noted in the Message, but his opponents viewed his request for a U.S. Commission to Panama as being animated by the same dangerous principle of expanding the powers of the federal government.

American participation in the Panama Congress quickly became the target of opportunity around which Adams' opponents could rally. His critics in the Senate attempted to defeat the nominations for the Commission and, when that failed, the anti-Adams elements in the House attempted to deny appropriations for the mission. Observers at the time, and historians since, have pointed out that the opposition to the Panama mission was a partisan political device. New York Senator Martin Van Buren played a critical role in formulating the coalition that became the Democrat Party. The opposition was driven particularly by southern concerns (and those of their northern allies) that the Panama Congress would support measures that would affect slavery in the United States.[166]

The Opposition to American Participation

The opposition's foreign policy position was expressed most fully in a report issued by the majority of the Senate Committee on Foreign Relations (SCFR), chaired by Nathaniel Macon of North Carolina. The report, to be

---

[165] Ibid., 5: 339-40.

[166] The critical debate and vote in the House actually occurred over a resolution reported by the Committee on Foreign Relations in favor of President Adams' policy, rather than over the appropriations bill itself. Dexter Perkins, *The Monroe Doctrine*, p. 210.

sure, reflected the agenda of American domestic slavery, for example, in its expression of concern that the Panama Congress would become a vehicle to recognize an independent black regime (Haiti). Additionally, the report reflected an important and enduring critique of an activist, cooperative U.S. foreign policy.[167] Adams' critics regarded his approach to South America, and to U.S. participation in the Panama Congress, as a violation of the sacred tenets of Washington's Farewell Address (as embraced by Jefferson in his First Inaugural Message) – that of non-entanglement and non-interference in the domestic affairs of others.

> The first question which suggested itself to the Committee, at the very threshold of their investigation, was, what cogent reasons now existed, for adopting this new and untried measure, so much in conflict with the whole course of policy, uniformly and happily pursued by the United States, from almost the very creation of this government to the present hour? By the principles of this policy, inculcated by our wisest statesmen in former days, and approved by the experience of all subsequent time, the true interest of the United States was supposed to be promoted, by avoiding all entangling connexions with any other nation whatsoever. Steadily pursuing this course, while they have been desirous to manifest the most cordial good will to all nations, and to maintain with each relations of perfect amity, and of commerce, regulated and adjusted by rules of the most fair, equal, and just reciprocity, the United States have hitherto sedulously abstained from associating themselves in any other way, even with those nations for whose welfare the most lively sensibility has been at all times felt and otherwise manifested.[168]

The SCFR report took many of Adams' earlier critiques of Clay and applied them to his own policies. For instance, the report pointed to the profound differences between Anglo-American and Spanish cultures, thereby questioning the capacity of the South Americans to maintain republican

---

[167] For a review of the debate of the Panama Congress in the U.S. Congress, in which the criticisms of Adams' policy track those of the SCFR report, see Jeffrey J. Malanson, "The Congressional Debate over U.S. Participation in the Congress of Panama, 1825-1826: Washington's Farewell Address, the Monroe Doctrine, and the Fundamentals of U.S. Foreign Policy," *Diplomatic History* 30 (November 2006): 813-38.

[168] Senate Committee on Foreign Relations, *Report on Nominations of Richard C. Anderson and John Sergeant to be Envoys Extraordinary and Ministers Plenipotentiary to the Assembly of the American Nations at Panama, 16 January 1826, in Compilation of Reports of Committee on Foreign Relations, United States Senate, 1789-1901* (Washington, D.C.: U.S. Government Printing Office, 1901), Volume 4, p. 14.

government. Just as Adams had once warned that premature diplomatic recognition of the South American regimes would place the United States on the slippery slope toward entanglement and war, Adams' critics in the Senate insisted that the negotiations in Panama would create their own momentum and sweep the United States into commitments it would later regret.

Specifically, the SCFR report contended that the objective of the South Americans at Panama was to bring about a concert of the participants in the war against Spain. If the United States refused to go along, the American delegates would create discord and might find themselves in conflict with the South American representatives. However, if the American delegation went along to get along, the Senate's power to refuse its consent to treaties was an insufficient safeguard, because "long experience must have informed the Senate that it is generally exceedingly difficult, and sometimes even impossible, to escape from the embarrassments produced by the mere act of entering into a negotiation; and that it is much better to abstain from doing so until its objects are distinctly known and approved than to confide in the power of the Senate, in the last resort, to refuse their assent to the ratification of an agreement after it is adjusted by means of such negotiation."[169]

Adams' critics warned that the Panama Congress would likely end in a duplication of the form of the European Congress system, which was animated by the spirit of the Holy Alliance. That is, it would result in something like the American System called for in Clay's Lexington Doctrine. This system would surely be regarded as hostile and provocative by the old European order. To the extent the United States wanted to aid the new regimes, it would be better served by remaining independent, in order to retain its influence with Europe. The United States could then credibly assure the Europeans that it could help restrain the South American republicans from propagandizing the Old World and thereby discourage retaliatory attacks against the American Hemisphere. The SCFR report preferred bilateral discussions and negotiations on particular issues with particular South American states rather than an attempt to deal with outstanding issues through a multilateral arrangement.[170]

The SCFR report criticized Adams' civilizational agenda of gaining South American assent to principles of liberal trade, the rights of neutrals, cooperation on the abolition of the slave trade, and the like. Adams believed that such mutual assent would, at least indirectly, strengthen republican tendencies among the South American regimes. The SCFR report argued that this constituted unwarranted interference in their domestic affairs; the

---

[169] Ibid., pp. 16, 20.

[170] Ibid., pp. 19-20, 24.

United States, for instance, should not lecture the South Americans on liberal principles of trade.

> In considering these reasons, it can not escape the observation of any that in manifesting dispositions to establish such commercial relations the Southern American nations must have been actuated by the only motive that ever operates either upon nations or individuals in regard to their mere commercial intercourse – a desire fairly to advance their own interests, and a belief that they could by such means properly accomplish this end. If in this belief these nations are right, then the United States can scarcely be viewed as acting toward them in that spirit of generous kindness and fraternal friendship they have professed when they would strive to induce them to establish as liberal principles such as would be injurious to the interests of these southern nations themselves. . . . The interests of commerce are necessarily peculiar; they grow out of numerous circumstances produced by locality, climate, population, manners, customs, and other causes, no one of which exists alike in any two nations on the globe. Few general principles, therefore, can ever apply with equal truth to so many peculiarities, and such as do so apply need not the sanction of solemn compact to give them effect. They may be very safely confided to the natural disposition of man promptly to discover and eagerly to advance his own best interests.[171]

As to the slave trade, the SCFR report piously insisted that the United States was doing all it could to bring about its abolition – there was no need to dictate to others how they should view this civilizational mission. "The United States, however, have not certainly the right, and ought never to feel the inclination, to dictate to others who may differ with them upon this subject; nor do the committee see the expediency of insulting other States with whom we are maintaining relations of perfect amity, by ascending the moral chair and proclaiming from thence mere abstract principles of the rectitude of which each nation enjoys the perfect right of deciding for itself."[172]

Adams' Senate critics objected particularly to his emphasis on obtaining a general commitment to the principle of non-colonization – with its explosive relationship to the natural rights of mankind, although the Committee report did not explicitly point this out. The SCFR report chose

---

[171] Ibid., p. 21.
[172] Ibid., pp. 18-9.

to critique Adams' argument at the practical level. There was no such threat to the South Americans except that posed by Spain, a conflict in which the United States must not become entangled, as the South Americans clearly hoped the U.S. would do.[173]

The SCFR report challenged Adams' assertion that the United States was justified in promoting religious liberty in South America, through its diplomatic argument that established churches – if the South Americans choose to create such establishments – should not prohibit individuals from practicing other faiths. Any argument about religion, according to Adams' critics, would become a source of controversy, not unity.

> And if there be any such subject more sacred and delicate than another, as to which the United States ought never to intermeddle, even by obtrusive advice, it is that which concerns religious liberty. The most cruel and devastating wars have been produced by such interferences; the blood of man has been poured out in torrents, and, from the days of the crusades to the present hour, no benefit has resulted to the human family from discussions carried on by nations upon such subjects. Among the variety even of Christian nations which now inhabit the earth rare indeed are the examples to be found of States who have not established an exclusive church, and to far the greater number of these toleration is yet unknown. In none of the communications which have taken place is the most distant allusion made to this delicate subject by any of the ministers who have given this invitation, and the committee feel very confident in the opinion, that if ever an intimation shall be made to the sovereignties they represent, that it is the purpose of the United States to discuss at the proposed congress their plans of internal civil polity, or anything touching the supposed interests of their religious establishments, the invitation given would soon be withdrawn.[174]

Adams' Rejoinder

In a Special Message that responded to the House's request for further information on the appropriation for a delegation to the Panama Congress, Adams addressed the criticisms of the Senate report. He insisted that "my first and greatest inducement was to meet in the spirit of kindness and

---

[173] Ibid., pp. 17-8.
[174] Ibid., p. 23.

friendship an overture made in that spirit by three sister Republics of this hemisphere. . . . From them the proposition to us appeared respectful and friendly; from us to them it could scarcely have been made without exposing ourselves to suspicions of purposes of ambition, if not of domination, more suited to rouse resistance and excite distrust than to conciliate favor and friendship." The United States did not want to forfeit the moral capital that it had built up through its sympathy and recognition: "In the intercourse between nations temper is a missionary perhaps more powerful than talent. Nothing was ever lost by kind treatment. Nothing can be gained by sullen repulses and aspiring pretensions."[175]

Adams argued again that his civilizational agenda of "the improvement of the condition of mankind on earth," through liberalized trade in peacetime, and Freedom of the Seas in wartime, could be advanced powerfully through American participation in the Congress. "It may be that in the lapse of many centuries no other opportunity so favorable will be presented to the Government of the United States to subserve the benevolent purposes of Divine Providence; to dispense the promised blessings of the Redeemer of Mankind; to promote the prevalence in future ages of peace on earth and good will to man, as will now be placed in their power by participating in the deliberations of this congress." Adams pointed out that the United States had attempted to do this with various European nations, and the Barbary regencies, through a commercial commission, shortly after it achieved its independence. The delegation consisted of Jefferson, Franklin and Adams' own father.

> At that time in the infancy of their political existence, under the influence of those principles of liberty and of right so congenial to the cause in which they had just fought and triumphed, they were able but to obtain the sanction of one great and philosophical, though absolute, sovereign in Europe [Frederick the Great of Prussia] to their liberal and enlightened principles. They could obtain no more. Since then a political hurricane has gone over three-fourths of the civilized portions of the earth, the desolation of which it may with confidence be expected is passing away, leaving at least the American atmosphere purified and refreshed. And now at this propitious moment the new-born nations of this hemisphere, assembling by their representatives at the isthmus between its two continents to settle the principles of their future international inter-

---

[175] This and the following references, from Adams' Special Message to Congress of 15 March 1826, is taken from Woolley and Peters, *The American Presidency Project* [online]. Available from World Wide Web: http://www.presidency.ucsb.edu/ws/?pid=66632.

course with other nations and with us, ask in this great exigency for our advice upon those very fundamental maxims which we from our cradle at first proclaimed and partially succeeded to introduce into the code of national law.

In his Special Message, Adams chose to downplay the one issue where he had proposed to "intervene" – the promotion of religious freedom. He stressed only that the U.S. would try to gain the right of worship for its citizens.

Adams attempted to address what he took to be the principal criticism of his approach to South America and the Panama Congress – "whether the measure might not have a tendency to change the policy, hitherto invariably pursued by the United States, of avoiding all entangling alliances and all unnecessary foreign connections." George Washington's famous guidance on this point, Adams contended, was contingent upon a particular set of circumstances. Those circumstances had not changed with respect to America's "distant and detached situation" vis-à-vis the Old World. "Europe has still her set of primary interests, with which we have little or a remote relation." But the United States had grown much stronger over the past thirty years, in terms of population, wealth, territory and power. And the American Hemisphere as a whole had been transformed from a time when,

> we were surrounded by European colonies, with the greater part of which we had no more intercourse than with the inhabitants of another planet. Those colonies have now been transformed into eight independent nations, extending to our very borders, seven of them Republics like ourselves, with whom we have an immensely growing commercial, and must have and have already important political, connections; with reference to whom our situation is neither distant nor detached; whose political principles and systems of government, congenial with our own, must and will have an action and counteraction upon us and ours to which we can not be indifferent if we would.

> Reasoning upon this state of things from the sound and judicious principles of Washington, must we not say that the period which he predicted as then not far off has arrived; that *America* has a set of primary interests which have none or a remote relation to Europe; that the interference of Europe, therefore, in those concerns should be spontaneously withheld by her upon the same principles that we have never interfered with hers, and that if she should interfere, as she may, by measures which may have a great and dangerous recoil

upon ourselves, we might be called in defense of our own altars and firesides to take an attitude which would cause our neutrality to be respected, and choose peace or war, as our interest, guided by justice, should counsel. The acceptance of this invitation, therefore, far from conflicting with the counsel or the policy of Washington, is directly deducible from and conformable to it. Nor is it less conformable to the views of my immediate predecessor as declared in his annual message to Congress of the 2d December, 1823.

That is, the Monroe Doctrine. Adams was taking the position that with expanded American power, the United States would increasingly be able to consult its rights and duties, and not be restrained by its fears.

Conclusion

We have seen that John Quincy Adams' classic aphorism for American foreign policy – "she goes not abroad, in search of monsters to destroy" – reflected a deep line of principle and policy, not merely a disposition against interventionism on behalf of liberal ideals and national independence. Adams thought there was a practical, yet elevated middle ground between the cold pursuit of material national interests and the hot-blooded advocacy of revolution and foreign regime change. It was one of the first in a long line of arguments that American foreign policy idealism and realism are not stark alternatives, but rather two sides of the same coin.

To simplify things greatly, Adams believed that the laws of political gravity and the emerging spirit of the age worked in favor of the United States and the advancement of the rights of mankind. The process of working out the transcendent principles of the Declaration of Independence and the full potential of Western and Christian civilization, however, would be a very long one. Success was not assured, especially in the short term. Bad policy choices by the United States, particularly those that tried to hurry history and culture beyond their capacity to change progressively, could be catastrophic, because human nature itself was unchangeable. American statesmen should be patient and restrained, take care of the internal improvement of their own regime first, and allow other peoples to work out their own destinies, all the while stoutly defending the principle that it was the inalienable right of peoples everywhere to do so. America could best aid the process indirectly, by promoting a civilizational agenda of peace, commerce, and the elimination of barbaric practices, rather than through "propagandism" or the use of force to overthrow foreign despotisms. The United States could pursue this agenda in cooperation with regimes of all types, including despotisms, knowing that the ultimate effect would be to advance the cause of liberalism and constitutionalism.

Adams' position was assailed by those who argued that such a middle ground was unsupportable. Opponents like Henry Clay argued that the United States, by distancing itself from revolutionary movements, missed a near-term opportunity, at relatively low cost, to move the world's political balance of forces in a progressive direction. Millions would be condemned to live in oppression while the United States sat on the sidelines, cheerfully (and selfishly) assuming that history would resolve everything for the better over centuries or millennia. This lost opportunity involved not only the defeat of revolutions and national independence movements because of despotic resistance, but also the inability of victorious revolutionary regimes to sustain their commitment to republicanism and the rights of mankind. The moral force of America's example to guide others toward ordered liberty would be lost unless its good words and sympathies were matched with real, tangible assistance (which did not necessarily involve the use of force.) Arguments that the United States should let others work out their own destiny, and that the success or failure of revolutionary movements and friendly regimes abroad did not fundamentally affect America's well-being and happiness, were dangerous fallacies. The cause of liberty was ultimately indivisible. Far-seeing despots realized that they could not coexist with free governments. Sooner or later the forces of reaction would ally themselves against the forces of liberty, and the United States was far better off if it had republican allies in that world-historic contest.

Adams was hardly free from challenges by those who argued that his apparent foreign realism and caution were based on a comfortable fallacy: that the United States could credibly make a distinction between sympathy and action, and that statesmen like Adams could wave an ideologically charged document like the Declaration of Independence in front of other nations, yet piously insist that they followed a policy of neutrality and peace. The Monroe Doctrine became a source of such mischief because its insistence on the separation of the two hemispheres was erroneously based on the airy distinction between regime types, and not on the solid ground of American national interest. The national interest certainly did not require a comprehensive and open-ended "doctrine" that pretended that all regimes in the Western Hemisphere were or should be "republican" (which was not true) and that the entire hemisphere must be defended by the United States on those grounds. A rhetorically charged foreign policy of this sort could not be restrained in practice. Adams himself understood this at times and tried to tone down the language of President Monroe, but he often was unable to follow his own rule, an inevitable constraint for any foreign policy based on ideological distinctions among regime types.

Furthermore, Adams' civilizational agenda, which at least notionally was regime-neutral, actually constituted interference in the domestic affairs of others. It was sure to be resented, as such. For instance, freedom of trade affected domestic economies in a way that privileged some interests and disadvantaged others, while it created avenues for foreigners to influence internal affairs of weaker states. In the case of the Barbary regencies, the Western-enforced abolition of Christian slavery and of the system of privateering and ransoming on which it was based, arguably brought about regime change and led to the conquest and colonization of North Africa by the European powers.

Adams' generally-recognized status as the greatest American diplomatist, or at least Secretary of State, suggests that he enjoyed considerable practical success in transcending the realist-idealist divide that runs through the history of U.S. foreign policy. (He was certainly not a power-political realist of the European style, as is sometimes supposed.) Critics of his policy approach, on both sides of the fence, have had their days and scored their points throughout American history. Adams, nonetheless, defined the terrain of the debate – a debate that is partly, yet not wholly, realist versus idealist – in a manner that remains with us today.

CHAPTER FOUR

"The High, Plain, Yet Dizzy Ground" of Influence:
American Views on Regime Change and the European Revolutions of 1848

This chapter examines American attitudes toward the European Revolutions of 1848 and the national debate over whether and how to support foreign political reforms and regime change. This foreign policy debate was, in many respects, the most "modern" of those which took place during the American Republic's first century, in that the protagonists anticipated many of the arguments and policy options that later emerged when the United States became a world power. Most of the proposals for an active U.S. response to the Revolutions of 1848 (but not all) stopped short of military intervention and focused on the ability of the United States to shape world public opinion in a way that would facilitate the cause of human rights and liberalized regimes. Rufus Choate, a leading Massachusetts politician and orator, aptly captured this perspective when he described the approach of his friend, Senator and later Secretary of State Daniel Webster:

> ... to occupy the high, plain, yet dizzy ground which separates influence from intervention, to avow and promulgate warm good-will to humanity, wherever striving to be free, to inquire authentically into the history of its struggles, to take official and avowed pains to ascertain the moment when its success may be recognized, consistently, ever, with the great code that keeps the peace of the world, abstaining from everything which shall give any nation a right under the law of nations to utter one word of complaint, still less to retaliate by war.[1]

Webster was, in many ways, the central character in this mid-19th century search for ways to maximize American *influence* in favor of regime change without crossing the line into direct political-military *intervention*. Webster's

---

[1] Samuel Gilman Brown, ed., *The Works of Rufus Choate, with a Memoir of his Life*, 2 vols. (Boston: Little, Brown and Company, 1862), 1: 520.

soaring *rhetoric* about human liberty seemingly put him on the side of those who challenged the perceived tradition of American non-involvement in the political affairs of Europe. But at the same time, Webster's official *actions* were cautious, taking into account the fragile state of the Union and the limits of American power.

This chapter begins with a brief examination of the historical background of the U.S. approach to regime change as news of the Revolutions of 1848 first reached the American shore. The intellectual and political impetus for a more assertive approach to foreign policy and for the promotion of foreign regime change came largely from a new generation of Democrats, who sought to advance American interests and ideals through territorial expansion, free trade, and support for liberal movements abroad. The New Democrats sought to overcome factional and intellectual resistance to such activism from within their own party and from the opposition Whigs, who traditionally held that America's world-historic mission was one of democratic example rather than the conquest of foreign territories or the subversion of other regimes. The Whig persuasion, moreover, contained a strain of activism on behalf of human rights, especially strong rhetorical support for republican government and national self-determination. The New Democrats thus had potential allies among up-and-coming progressive Whig politicians and advocates of the Free Soil movement. This raised the prospect that a political majority might emerge across parties in favor of a more activist or even interventionist foreign policy – a national majority that might transcend differences over slavery.

The possibility of such a domestic political coalition first emerged when the unpopular July Monarchy of Louis-Philippe was overthrown by yet another French Revolution in February 1848. The U.S. Minister in Paris, Richard Rush, almost immediately recognized the new republic, an action which was ratified by the Polk Administration on the grounds that early and favorable U.S. action toward republican government in Europe could encourage and strengthen the stable development of such regimes. The U.S. Congress – then in the midst of controversy over ratification of peace with Mexico – debated the wisdom of a policy of active encouragement of republican governments in France and elsewhere in Europe. These deliberations revealed substantial opposition among Southern Democrats and conservative Whigs even to rhetorical support for the latest experiment in French republicanism. One of the most prominent spokesmen for caution was South Carolina Democrat John C. Calhoun. Calhoun's arguments generated the first major defense of an activist foreign policy by leading Democratic Senators such as Michigan's Lewis Cass and Illinois' Stephen A. Douglas. The debate, especially in the House, soon became diverted by those who wanted to use the French Revolution as a means to highlight their opposition to slavery and American territorial expansion.[2]

As the revolutions spread across the continent, the American government and public had to grapple with the policy issues raised by other forms of regime change, including the unification of Germany – presumably but not necessarily on republican and confederal lines – and the autonomy or independence of Hungary from the Hapsburg Empire. This chapter reviews the approaches of the Polk (Democrat) and Taylor-Fillmore (Whig) administrations toward these developments. Both administrations adopted or embraced diplomatic policies that were sympathetic toward the prospective new regimes but that stopped short of outright intervention. Congressional members again debated whether and how the United States should proceed, especially after the Hungarian Revolution was suppressed by Austria with the aid of Russian troops. Cass and Whig grandee Henry Clay argued about the former's proposal to withdraw U.S. diplomatic recognition of Austria to protest the intervention and to signal American support for a future Hungarian independence movement. Whig Secretary of State John Clayton and his successor, Daniel Webster, engaged in an acrimonious public controversy with the Austrian diplomat, Baron Hülsemann, about his allegations of improper American interference in Austro-Hungarian affairs. The Hülsemann dispute provided additional grist for Congressional advocates and critics of an activist American foreign policy.

This chapter also examines the most important of these public debates over the proper American approach toward regime change, which was triggered by the appearance of the Hungarian revolutionary leader Lajos (Louis) Kossuth. The Taylor administration successfully urged Kossuth's release from confinement in Turkey and, with Congressional approval, dispatched a U.S. frigate to convey him to the United States, where presumably he would live out his life in quiet exile. Kossuth and many of his American supporters, however, saw his release merely as the next step in a second Hungarian Revolution, which would be enabled (according to his most aggressive U.S. supporters) by an American-British-Turkish military alliance directed at Austria and Russia, or by some other type of "intervention for non-intervention." But most New Democrats, such as Douglas, and progressive Whigs, including New York Senator William Seward, carefully avoided taking such provocative ground. They argued that active American moral and diplomatic support would alter

---

[2] For a more detailed account of U.S. reactions to developments in France in 1848, see an expanded version of this essay, Patrick J. Garrity, *American Views on Regime Change and the European Revolutions of 1848* (Ashland, OH: Ashbrook Center of Public Affairs, November 2009), pp. 17-47.

the political climate in Europe sufficiently to allow a future Hungarian revolution to succeed on its own terms, if the Hungarians were truly capable of self-government. The critics of such an approach, such as Kentucky Senator John J. Crittenden, argued that it was impossible to establish a clear line between moral-diplomatic support for the Hungarian cause, and outright military intervention. The United States would either find itself on the slippery slope that led to war for matters that were not vital to the nation, or it would be forced to back down in humiliating fashion.

In the end, the conservative Whigs, aligned with the Fillmore administration, and a strong majority of Southerners of both parties, constituted an effective opposition to the New Democrats and progressive Whigs on the Kossuth issue. As the nation slid deeper into domestic crisis over slavery during the 1850s, the prospect of a new political coalition based on an assertive foreign policy and an aggressive approach to foreign regime change disappeared.

This chapter does not attempt to provide a comprehensive or definitive account of the American response to the Revolutions of 1848, but rather seeks to highlight the substantive arguments that emerged during the public debate. Three limitations must be noted in particular. First, the controversy over the future of slavery increasingly dominated American domestic politics and affected the debate over the proper response to the European revolutions. The chapter identifies the points at which the foreign policy debate was directly affected by arguments about the peculiar institution. The entire subtext, however, cannot be disentangled entirely in a limited monograph; for instance, one of the main options for promoting regime change in the Western Hemisphere was filibustering expeditions – a tactic which became increasingly identified with the promotion of slavery – yet it is not covered in any depth. Second, some of the political alignments during the foreign policy debates of the late 1840s and early 1850s were dictated by factional and personal differences within the parties rather than by high-minded substantive considerations. Third, Americans were not always fully aware of the differences between their own concept of republican self-government and those espoused by various European revolutionaries, who often sought dramatic social change that would have been unacceptable in the American context.

Background

Most historians of American foreign relations now recognize that it is inaccurate, or better put, incomplete, to describe the U.S. approach to the world (or Europe) during the 19th century as "isolationist." The rapid growth and importance of American international commerce alone generated important financial, diplomatic and strategic interests outside of North America and the Western Hemisphere. Since the days of their own Revolution, Americans naturally sympathized with liberal reforms and independence movements abroad, notably the French Revolution of the 1790s, the Spanish-American revolts after the War of 1812, and the Greek independence movement of the 1820s. These sympathies generated political pressures which influenced U.S. foreign policy to a greater or lesser degree, especially when the sense of national interest coincided with aims of foreign revolutionaries (as with the Republican Party and the original French Revolution). Americans saw themselves as the wave of the political future and at the cutting edge of the Enlightenment project for promoting the rights of mankind and self-government, as so memorably set out in the Declaration of Independence.[3]

That said, the default position of the United States when it came directly to supporting foreign regime change was represented by the Washington-Adams policy of neutrality, enshrined in Washington's Farewell Address: that of non-entanglement in the European system of alliances (and thus non-involvement in European wars), and of non-interference in the domestic affairs of others. John Quincy Adams famously articulated this position in his July 4, 1821 Address:

> America, with the same voice which spoke herself into existence as a nation, proclaimed to mankind the inextinguishable rights of human nature, and the only lawful foundations of government. America, in the assembly of nations, since her admission among them, has invariably, though often fruitlessly, held forth to them the hand of honest friendship, of equal freedom, of generous reciprocity. She has uniformly spoken among them, though often to heedless and often to disdainful ears, the language of equal liberty, of equal justice, and of equal rights. She has, in the lapse of nearly half a century, without a single exception, respected the independence of other nations while asserting and maintaining her own. She has abstained from interference in the concerns of others, even when conflict has been for principles to which she clings, as to the last vital drop that visits the heart. She has seen that probably for centuries to come, all the contests of that Aceldama the European world, will be contests of inveterate power, and emerging right.

---

[3] This important strand of American foreign policy is highlighted by Robert Kagan, *Dangerous Nation: America's Foreign Policy from Its Earliest Days to the Dawn of the Twentieth Century* (New York: Alfred A. Knopf, 2006).

Wherever the standard of freedom and Independence has been or shall be unfurled, there will her heart, her benedictions and her prayers be. But she goes not abroad, in search of monsters to destroy. She is the well-wisher to the freedom and independence of all. She is the champion and vindicator only of her own. She will commend the general cause by the countenance of her voice, and the benignant sympathy of her example. She well knows that by once enlisting under other banners than her own, were they even the banners of foreign independence, she would involve herself beyond the power of extrication, in all the wars of interest and intrigue, of individual avarice, envy, and ambition, which assume the colors and usurp the standard of freedom. The fundamental maxims of her policy would insensibly change from liberty to force. . . . [4]

Historian David Hendrickson summarized the traditional American view: "that every people had a right of revolution that could not be denied; outsiders were obliged to recognize that new status when it was achieved but should neither foment revolution nor come to the aid of despotic governments against internal enemies. To do either would be illegitimate intervention and equivalent to aggression. Self-government . . . meant above all freedom from external rule." [5]

The practical problem for those Americans who hoped for a better world and liberal regime changes abroad was the apparent strength of foreign despotisms. These regimes typically united to preempt or suppress any experiments in liberalism or popular revolution within themselves and among their neighbors. Republican government or national self-determination, proceeding naturally in individual countries as the people better understood and exercised their rights, seemed impossible. Historian Sean Wilentz characterized the depressing circumstances facing democrats around the world in the early 1840s:

That situation was terrible. In Britain, the Reform Bill of 1832 had left the vast majority of urban and rural workingmen disenfranchised. Radicals from William Cobbett (who wrote an admiring brief biography of [Andrew] Jackson) to the Chartists were struggling through one setback after another, on the road to Chartism's

---

[4] John Quincy Adams, *Address before the U.S. House of Representatives*, July 4, 1821, at http://millercenter.org/scripps/archive/speeches/detail/3484.

[5] David Hendrickson, *Union, Nation, or Empire: The American Debate over International Relations, 1789-1941* (Lawrence: University Press of Kansas, 2009), p. 322.

collapse in 1848. In France, the hopeful revolution of 1830 had produced a stockjobber monarchy that hesitated not at all to repress popular republican stirrings in blood . . . In Ireland, Daniel O'Connell's nonviolent mass movement for repeal of the union with Britain was stirring great crowds, but getting nowhere fast against the obdurate ministry of Sir Robert Peel. Across the face of Europe, nationalist as well as democratic aspirations remained stifled by Metternichian reaction.[6]

Under these circumstances, to a growing number of Americans forbearance in the political affairs of others simply conceded the game to the forces of reaction, because despotism observed no such niceties. The growth of American economic power, and the nation's latent military potential, apparently provided the United States with options that preceding generations had lacked to exercise influence abroad. Paradoxically, as the American Republic grew stronger, it also became a greater ideological threat to European despotisms, which might soon decide to unite and extirpate the republican contagion in the New as well as the Old World. The default position of non-entanglement and non-intervention remained strong, especially given the national divisions over slavery and concern with the prospect of popular revolt *within* the Union (Dorr's rebellion in Rhode Island). But two distinct groups of party leaders and publicists searched for a way out of the narrow constraints of principled and pragmatic non-intervention.

The New Democrats

The intellectual and political impetus for a more assertive approach to foreign policy and the promotion of foreign regime change came largely from a new generation of Democrats, who sought to advance American interests and ideals through territorial expansion, free trade, and support for liberal movements abroad.[7] They included such politicians as Douglas of Illinois, Robert Walker of Mississippi, and James Buchanan of Pennsylvania, and journalist-activists like John L. O'Sullivan and George Sanders. Veteran Democrats such as Louis Cass of Michigan, although sometimes lumped in with other conservative "Old Fogies," sympathized with the aims of the New

---

[6] Sean Wilentz, *The Rise of American Democracy: Jefferson to Lincoln* (New York: W.W. Norton, 2005), pp. 562-3.

[7] In this section, I use the term "New Democrats" to cover a spectrum of similar opinion in the Democratic Party, from the Young Democrat faction of the mid-1840s to Young America in the early 1850s – while acknowledging the difficulties that any such generalization about policy views can create.

Democrats. Louisiana's Pierre Soulé succinctly captured their goal by characterizing "the mission of America" as casting the deciding weight in the scales of republicanism throughout the world.[8] The dominant policy questions for these New Democrats concerned how precisely to "expand the area of freedom" – how much weight could the United States effectively wield to promote liberalization and regime change? On which scale of power and influence – political, economic, diplomatic and military – should it seek to make the difference?

The New Democrat agenda in the Western Hemisphere was famously captured by O'Sullivan's invocation of Manifest Destiny. "And that claim is by the right of our manifest destiny to overspread and to possess the whole of the continent which Providence has given us for the development of the great experiment of liberty and federated self-government entrusted to us." Under Manifest Destiny, regime change would occur through a natural and peaceful process of "Americanization." American emigrants would fill up adjoining territories, assume positions of leadership alongside local allies, regenerate the common population (to the extent possible given cultural and/or racial limitations), develop republican self-government, and naturally gravitate into the Union. The process of regime change and self-determination within the borderlands might have a violent local revolutionary phase if it became necessary for the enlightened to overthrow despotic rule, but the final outcome would be the peaceful and voluntary accession as equal partners in the Union. The local rights and customs of the new states would be respected under the federal principle. "Communities grow up mostly by immigration from the United States. Such communities therefore invariably establish the same form of government which they left behind and *demand* admittance into the Union. The government does not *demand* of them that they come into the Union." The process of Manifest Destiny would eventually encompass North America and the Caribbean and possibly the entire Western Hemisphere.[9]

For the New Democrats, Texas was supposed to be the prime example of cultural assimilation, political regime change, and incorporation into the greater American Union. As historian Daniel Walker Howe observed, "The Texian [sic] revolution broke out over economic and constitutional issues

---

[8] Siert F. Riepma, "'Young America': A Study in American Nationalism Before the Civil War," Ph.D. dissertation, Western Reserve University, 1939, p. 292; Amos Aschbach Ettinger, *The Mission to Spain of Pierre Soulé, 1853-1855: A Study in the Cuban Diplomacy of the United States* (New Haven: Yale University Press, 1932), pp. 174-7 (mission).

[9] Robert D. Sampson, *John L. O'Sullivan and his Times* (Kent, Ohio: Kent State University Press, 2003), p. 199 (demand).

not very different from those that provoked the American Revolution." American settlers, many with their slaves, had settled in northern Mexico with the encouragement or at least the benign neglect of the central government. When that government attempted to restore an earlier, more centralized constitution, one that abolished slavery, the Anglo-Texans (including some Hispanics) first sought to create a separate state within a federal Mexico and later declared independence with a manifesto carefully modeled on the American version of 1776. They drafted a constitution similar to that of 1787 (and which also sanctioned slavery). Volunteers like former Tennessee Congressman Davy Crockett crossed the border to aid the revolt. President Jackson professed official neutrality but did little to restrain the filibusters or prevent the Texans from obtaining money and supplies from the United States. (This approach was in contrast with much stricter American efforts to restrain filibustering against British Canada.) Jackson also dispatched the U.S. Army to the Sabine River, which the Mexican government took as a threat to intervene if the revolution seemed on the verge of collapse. When the independence of the new Texas Republic was acknowledged by Santa Anna after his defeat at San Jacinto, the United States government quickly recognized the new regime (despite the protests of the Mexican government, which refused to accept Santa Anna's action) and began negotiations for Texas' accession into the Union. [10]

Outside the Western Hemisphere, the New Democrats did not completely rule out the possibility that "the wisdom of democratic convictions would become so self-evident, that populations world-wide would desire U.S. protection." Levi Woodbury of New Hampshire wanted "to extend the blessings of our government as widely as practicable. . . . States might be admitted, not only contiguous, but . . . even Europe." The more common theme, however, was that of helping European republicans achieve enlightened regime change and, where appropriate, national independence. The New Democrats' advocacy of aggressive commercial diplomacy was part of this campaign. As historian Siert Riepma noted, the New Democrats believed that the "friendly intercourse" of free trade, with the stimulating powers of "press-steam-commerce-cotton-electricity" would quietly bring

---

[10] Daniel Walker Howe, *What Hath God Wrought: The Transformation of America, 1815-1848* (New York: Oxford University Press, 2007), pp. 661-2, 669-70; George Herring, *From Colony to Superpower: U.S. Foreign Relations Since 1776* (New York: Oxford University Press, 2008), p. 194 ; Hendrickson, *Union, Nation, or Empire*, p. 165. To avoid complicating the election campaign of his chosen successor, Martin Van Buren, Jackson waited until his last day of office to recognize the Texas Republic. Jackson was at best ambivalent about Texas' independence, which he thought might complicate American efforts to annex the region.

about "triumphs over horary despotism and barbarisms." Revolutions against monarchs anywhere would abolish old feudal barriers to commerce and open up ports and markets for American shippers and for U.S. suppliers of grains, cotton, and raw materials.[11]

Beyond that, O'Sullivan had written that Manifest Destiny included a mission to spread four freedoms around the world: conscience, person, trade, and the "universality of freedom and equality." Regime change, from despotism to democracy, was the logical outcome of the four freedoms. "Why should not England be republican?" the *Democratic Review* asked. The New Democrats also were intrigued with the idea that republican movements in Europe might at the very least deter monarchs from intervening forcefully in the Western Hemisphere. A new American diplomatic style marked, for instance, by wearing plain republican clothes rather than elaborate ceremonial uniforms, would be one means of peacefully influencing European thinking and encouraging liberal opinion.[12]

The New Democrat paradigm of peaceful regime change through Manifest Destiny and the New Diplomacy did not always meet the requirements of the real world. History sometimes needed a little help to overcome those who forcibly resisted change. Despotism would not always quietly go into the dark good night of extinction. In the Western Hemisphere, the New Democrats accused Britain and France of attempting to encircle and contain the United States, and of waging ideological war against republicanism by supporting monarchical ideas and factions in Central and South America. Britain – the oppressor of the Irish and the alleged center of the moneyed interests that sought to dominate the U.S. government and economy – was the particular *bête noire* of the Democrats, New and Old. Slaveholders warned against an international abolitionist conspiracy, centered in London, whose philanthropic pretensions covered Britain's plan of world domination through the destruction of the U.S. economy and the fomenting of slave rebellions. The monarchies were said to oppose the progress of Manifest Destiny and democracy by retaining and expanding their territorial possessions in the New World; supporting existing native

---

[11] Yonatan Eyal, *The Young America Movement and the Transformation of the Democratic Party, 1828-61* (New York: Cambridge University Press, 2007), p. 130; Hendrickson, *Union, Nation, or Empire*, p. 180; Levi Woodbury, *Writings of Levi Woodbury, LL.D. Political, Judicial and Literary*, 3 vols. (Boston: Little, Brown and Company, 1852), 1: 357; Riepma, "Young America," pp. 40-1, 73.

[12] Wilentz, *The Rise of American Democracy*, pp. 562-3 (four freedoms); Henry Blumenthal, *A Reappraisal of Franco-American Relations, 1830-1871* (Chapel Hill: University of North Carolina Press, 1959), p. 4; Eyal, *The Young America Movement*, p. 104.

regimes (e.g., Mexico) and emerging regimes (e.g., Texas); and enforcing restrictions on free trade. [13]

The external resistance to the New Democrat agenda in the Western Hemisphere was complicated by the corresponding domestic opposition to territorial expansion. From the early days of the republic, there had always been a strong political viewpoint that opposed territorial over-extension on classical political grounds. These critics argued that further expansion would lead to war, or the danger of war, and thus would require a dangerously large and expensive military force.

To New Democrats, the fate of Texas after 1836 demonstrated the risk that the natural process of republican regime change and peaceful assimilation would be frustrated by these countervailing internal and external forces. The annexation of Texas had been blocked for nearly a decade by the Whigs and some anti-slavery northern Democrats. During that period, some Texas leaders promoted the idea of a permanently independent Texas Republic (or at least they kept that option open to provide them with diplomatic leverage). An independent Texas, aligned with Britain, was a nightmare for the New Democrats; the Lone Star Republic would have a secure market for its cotton and the support of a major European ally in what would be a multi-polar Western Hemisphere security system. Texas might well expand to the Pacific and become a major power in its own right, competing with the United States for territory and influence. New Democrats and slaveholders of both parties feared that the British alliance might become so necessary and attractive to the Texans that the new regime would be persuaded or compelled to abolish slavery if it was spurned by the United States. [14]

The New Democrats thus confronted the possibility that Manifest Destiny would be truncated and result in the encirclement of the United States by a number of new and unfriendly regimes, including Texas, California, Oregon, Cuba and Canada. Lord Ashburn, for instance, spoke of a new "Pacific republic" governed neither by Britain nor America. These nations might be republics (slaveholding or abolitionist), clients of Britain or France, or even monarchies. The French historian and statesman François

---

[13] Blumenthal, *A Reappraisal of Franco-American Relations*, pp. viii-ix; Eyal, *The Young America Movement*, p. 118; Donald S. Spencer, *Louis Kossuth and Young America: A Study of Sectionalism and Foreign Policy 1848-1852* (Columbia: University of Missouri Press, 1977), pp. 18-22; Herring, *From Colony to Superpower*, p. 183.

[14] Donelson to Calhoun, 8 January 1848, *Papers of John C. Calhoun* (Columbia: University of South Carolina Press, 1959-), vol. 25: 105 (hereafter referred to as PJCC); H.W. Brands, *Andrew Jackson, His Life and Times* (New York: Doubleday, 2005), pp. 545-6; Howe, *What Hath God Wrought*, pp. 671-7.

Guizot proposed: "What was not good for Europe under the form of a universal monarchy would not be good for America under the form of universal republicanism." Thomas Jefferson had been relaxed about the idea of "sister republics" populated by Anglo-Saxons emerging on the far side of the continent but under the circumstances of the mid-19th century; the New Democrats were not. Even loyal American emigrants would be tempted by the lure of power and driven by necessity to support independent and even non-republican regimes if they were excluded from the Union upon declaring their independence. [15]

The New Democrats conceived of a variety of policy tools to deal with the "unnatural" resistance to the spread of republican government. They believed it was sometimes essential actively, even forcefully, to defend and accelerate the process of republicanization and Americanization. The most controversial option was filibustering, in which American citizens and sympathetic native exiles would infiltrate or invade an "oppressed" territory and overthrow the existing regime, after which the new government would petition to join the Union. The most famous filibusterer of the 1840s was Narciso Lopez, a Venezuelan, who engaged in several campaigns against Spanish rule in Cuba with the aid of American volunteers and financial support. Filibustering was justified not only as a means of relieving the oppressed by bringing them republican government but also as a defensive instrument to prevent regime changes detrimental to American interests and security. For example, filibustering against Canada was designed not only to trigger a revolt against British rule but also to preempt local advocates of independence like William Lyon McKenzie, who declared his aversion to "American democracy as it presented itself in the form of political corruption, crass materialism and human slavery." Many Southerners, and some northern commercial interests, supported or were sympathetic to Lopez because of fears that Spain might transfer the island to Britain or France or, worse, abolish slavery there. Even more worrisome was the prospect of a slave revolt on the island that would turn Cuba into a second Haiti. [16]

Few prominent Democrats, New or Old, were willing publicly to support the flouting of domestic and international laws that prohibited organizing filibustering expeditions on American soil. Slaveholders and businessmen under-

---

[15] Eyal, *The Young America Movement*, pp. 122-23 (Ashburn); Hendrickson, *Union, Nation, or Empire*, p. 179 (Guizot).

[16] Elbert B. Smith, *The Presidencies of Zachary Taylor & Millard Fillmore* (Lawrence: University Press of Kansas, 1988), p. 74 (McKenzie); Thomas Chaffin, "'Sons of Washington': Narciso Lopez, Filibustering, and U.S. Nationalism, 1848-1851," *Journal of the Early Republic* 15 (Spring 1995): 94.

stood the importance of the rule of law when it applied to their own interests. New Democrat Douglas argued that filibustering was actually counterproductive. According to Douglas, history demonstrated that such campaigns, at least without the active support of the U.S. government, were almost certain to fail and thus weaken the forces of native resistance. However, Douglas and other New Democrats drew the line against the active suppression of filibusters outside the territory and waters of the United States, which they claimed was not sanctioned by American law. Some were prepared to argue for amending U.S. neutrality legislation to give the benefit of legal doubt to filibusters. The same argument would later be made for those who wanted to find private means of supporting European revolutionaries. [17]

That left coercive diplomacy as the preferred instrument of the New Democrats in the Western Hemisphere when the passive options failed. Coercive diplomacy required credible military options and a willingness to resort to war. President James Polk, who shared many of the predispositions (if not the romanticism) of the New Democrats, was unwilling to wait for time and goodwill to resolve the outstanding issues of the day: the status of the Oregon territory (which status, after a period of bluster, he decided to compromise with Britain, despite the opposition of some New Democrats and anti-slavery Whig nationalists like John Quincy Adams); the security of Texas, whose existence and boundaries remained in dispute with Mexico; and America's future ambitions on the west coast and the Pacific Ocean, which Mexico, Britain and France wished to truncate. In his Inaugural Address, he stated what became known as the Polk Corollary to the Monroe Doctrine: "We must ever maintain the principle that the people of this continent alone have the right to decide their own destiny. Should any portion of them, constituting an independent state, propose to unite themselves with our Confederacy, this will be a question for them and us to determine without any foreign imposition." [18]

The crisis with Mexico brought several important strands of New Democrat policy together. The Polk administration and its New Democrat allies hoped not only to fast-forward the process of extending the area of hemispheric freedom; they also strove to overcome domestic limits against expansion by taking advantage of a new wave of patriotism to create a new and more favorable party alignment. Although Polk's Whig critics accused him

---

[17] Chaffin, "Sons of Washington," pp. 92-9.

[18] Howe, *What Hath God Wrought*, p. 809; James K. Polk, Inaugural Address, 4 March 1845, at http://millercenter.org/scripps/archive/speeches/detail/3550.

of a pro-southern, pro-slavery agenda, he viewed his policies as aiming to bring about national unity. [19]

When coercive diplomacy with Mexico failed, Polk used the opportunity of a Mexican attack on U.S. troops in disputed territory to ask Congress for a declaration that a state of war existed. For the New Democrats, the territory to be acquired as a result of the war – as an "indemnity" from Mexico – would be freed from Mexican misrule and would extend the area of human liberty and happiness. According to the activist *Democratic Review*, there was a great danger in conquering only to enslave, but "a free nation, which shows equal toleration and protection to all religions, and conquers only to bestow freedom, has no such danger to fear." O'Sullivan generally opposed the use of force on behalf of Manifest Destiny; he felt, however, that war was justified in this case in part because it would destroy Mexico's "mock republic," with its temptation to be "the cat's paw of European monarchies to assail the progress of republican institutions." Some New Democrats believed that the shock of the war might regenerate Mexico's failing republican institutions; Commodore Robert Stockton argued that the war should be fought "for the express purpose of redeeming Mexico from misrule and civil strife." Others of the "All-Mexico" movement argued that this regeneration could take place only by incorporating all Mexican territory into the Union after a probationary period during which the business community and other agents of liberalization would reform her institutions. [20]

New Democrats perceived an even broader purpose in pursuing Manifest Destiny actively in the Western Hemisphere. As the New York *Herald* wrote about the Mexican War, American assertiveness on behalf of human freedom in the New World would "lay the foundation of a new age, a new destiny, affecting both this continent and the old continent of Europe." By successfully attacking European monarchical interests and possessions in the Western Hemisphere, the United States would undermine the power and legitimacy of those monarchies at home and create new opportunities for liberal reform and revolution in those regimes. The outbreak of revolution in

---

[19] Wilentz, *The Rise of American Democracy*, pp. 584-6.

[20] Albert K. Weinberg, *Manifest Destiny; a Study of Nationalist Expansionism in American History* (Baltimore: Johns Hopkins University Press, 1935), p. 178 *(Democratic Review)*; Sampson, *John L. O'Sullivan*, p. 203 (Sullivan); Hendrickson, *Union, Nation, or Empire*, p. 180 (Stockton); Eyal, *The Young America Movement*, pp. 131-2. A few anti-slavery advocates fell into the All-Mexico camp as well, on the assumption that some or all of Mexico's nineteen states could apply for admission to the Union as free states and thus tilt decisively the constitutional balance against the slaveholding interests. Wilentz, *The Rise of American Democracy*, p. 611.

France, which occurred just as the United States had completed its military triumph over Mexico, struck the New Democrats as something more than mere coincidence. Their next challenge was to take advantage of the favorable momentum created by the success against Mexico – to develop tools and policies that would assist the European revolutionaries and to create an enduring domestic political majority that would embrace the vision of expanding the area of freedom.[21]

Progressive Whigs and Free Soilers

The New Democrats movement, it should be stressed, was not monolithic; nor did it represent a majority even within the Democratic Party. The democracy was divided by factional and personal rivalries – most notably within the key state of New York – and by growing sectional differences over whether the expansion of American sovereignty also meant the expansion of slavery. These divisions made it difficult to promote an activist American foreign policy. On the other side of the political fence, the Whig Party also represented a substantial barrier to the development of a national majority supportive of an assertive American foreign policy.

The objectives of the New Democrats ran counter to the opposition Whig Party's long-standing "persuasion" that internal improvement, rather than external expansion, represented the proper path of republicanism. According to the Whigs, America's world-historic mission was one of democratic example rather than the conquest of foreign territories or the subversion of other regimes. That mission had been badly tarnished by the war of aggression against Mexico. Whigs did not reject entirely the long-term possibility of territorial expansion if it came about through "masterly inactivity," in the words of New York's William Seward; and if it reflected the organic development of the conditions of freedom that would make voluntary accessions to the Union genuinely possible. American expansion in the present circumstances, however, inevitably brought up the divisive question of slavery in the new territories and the existence of the Union itself. The Whigs were much more interested in *commercial* expansion, especially in the Pacific and Asia. Seward argued that American-led globalization (to use a modern term) would extend the "civilization of the world westward . . . across the continent of America," across the Pacific to Asia, on through Europe until it reached "the other side, the shores of the Atlantic Ocean."

---

[21] Wilentz, *The Rise of American Democracy*, p. 582 (Herald); Eyal, *The Young America Movement*, pp. 120, 131-2; Chaffin, "Sons of Washington," p. 84.

The United States would "furnish a political alembic which, receiving the exhausted civilization of Asia and the ripening civilization of Western Europe, and commingling them together . . . would disclose the secret of the ultimate regeneration and reunion of human society throughout the world." The progressive Whig approach to the world was "based on the equality of nations of races of men. . . . One nation, race or individual, may not oppress or injure another, because the safety and welfare of each is essential to the common safety and welfare of all. If all are not equal and free, then who is entitled to be free, and what evidence of his superiority can he bring from nature or revelation?" [22]

The Whigs regarded Britain more as a rival in the competition for markets than as a strategic and ideological enemy, as did the New Democrats. Whig administrations were prepared to cut deals with London (e.g., the Webster-Ashburton Treaty) and to seek access to British capital for the development of the American economy, especially after the Panic of 1837. Some Whigs admired British culture and the stability of British political institutions. Daniel Webster, who served as Secretary of State in two Whig administrations, had once implicitly classified Britain along with the United States on the side of free institutions.

> It cannot be denied that the great political question of this age is that between absolute and regulated governments. The substance of the controversy is whether society shall have any part in its own government. Whether the form of government shall be that of limited monarchy, with more or less mixture of hereditary power, or wholly elective or representative, may perhaps be considered as subordinate. The main controversy is between that absolute rule, which, while it promises to govern well, means, nevertheless, to govern without control, and that constitution system which restrains sovereign discretion, and asserts that society may claim as a matter of right some effective power in the establishment of the laws which are to regulate it. The spirit of the times sets with a most powerful current in favor of these last mentioned opinions.

---

[22] George E. Baker, ed., *The Works of William H. Seward*, 5 vols. (Boston and New York: Houghton, Mifflin and Company, 1887), 1: 91, 247-9; 3: 13, 113; 4: 124, 128; *Congressional Globe*, 36th Congress, 2nd session, p. 251 (hereafter referred to as *Congressional Globe*. See also Ernest N. Paolino, *The Foundations of the American Empire; William Henry Seward and U.S. Foreign Policy* (New York: Cornell University Press, 1973); Hendrickson, *Union, Nation, or Empire*, p. 289; Charles Vevier, "American Continentalism: An Idea of Expansion, 1845-1910, *American Historical Review* 65 (January 1890): 323-35.

It is opposed, however, whenever and wherever it shows itself, by certain of the great potentates of Europe.[23]

Whig foreign policy was, of logic and necessity, open to the possibility that independent "regulated" regimes would develop on the periphery of the United States, and that cooperation, rather than competition, could mark America's relationship with those regimes. As Whig elder statesman Henry Clay, an opponent of Texas annexation, wrote in 1844:

> ... it is probable that there will be a voluntarily or forcible separation of the British North American possessions from the parent country. I am strongly inclined to think that it will be best for the happiness of all parties that, in the event, they should be erected into a separate and independent republic. With the Canadian republic on one side, that of Texas on the other, and the United States, the friend of both, between them, each could advance its own happiness by such constitutions, laws, and measures, as were best adapted to its peculiar condition. They would be natural allies, ready, by cooperation, to repel any European or foreign attack upon either. Each would afford a secure refuge to the persecuted and oppressed driven into exile by either of the others. They would emulate each other in improvements, in free institutions, and in the science of self-government.[24]

Hawaii was another case where the Whigs were prepared to accept the existence of an independent regime – and a monarchy at that – rather than to seek or compel its annexation, which was the preferred Democratic policy. The native Hawaiian regime, to be sure, had been influenced deeply by American missionaries and economic interests, so much so that by the 1840s the islands appeared to some visitors like a transplanted New England. The indigenous population had suffered greatly from Western diseases. To deter European powers (particularly France) from attempting to conquer Hawaii, the Whig Tyler administration announced a *de facto* American protectorate over the islands. To some contemporary scholars, this was a classic example of American commercial and cultural imperialism, regime change in substance if not in form. From the Whig perspective, however, enlightened missionar-

---

[23] Daniel Webster, "Independence of Greece," 19 January 1824, *The Papers of Daniel Webster* (Hanover, NH: University Press of New England, 1974-), Speeches and Formal Writings, 1: 89-104.

[24] Hendrickson, *Union, Nation, or Empire*, p. 179; Congressional Speech, 17 April 1844, *The Papers of Henry Clay,* 11 vols. (Lexington: University of Kentucky Press, 1959-1992), 10: 45.

ies and economic activity had assisted Hawaii's rulers in adapting Western ideas and forms of "regulated" government to their own circumstances while protecting essential native sovereignty.[25]

The Whig persuasion did include within it a tradition of activism on behalf of human rights, especially strong rhetorical support for republican government and national liberation movements. Henry Clay had been a notable defender of the Spanish American independence movements after the War of 1812. He had gone so far as to push the Monroe administration to revise the neutrality laws to favor the revolutionaries, to recognize their governments, and to promote the idea of a republican alliance in the Western Hemisphere to counteract the despotic Holy Alliance. Clay and Webster also spoke out strongly in favor of American moral support for Greek freedom from the Ottoman Empire. The Whigs' humanitarian sympathizers considered themselves natural allies of the middle-class reformers of Europe.[26]

Young progressive Whig politicians such as Seward and Ohio's Joshua Giddings, and journalists such as Horace Greeley, saw the opportunity to revive this Whig tradition of support for republican government and human rights abroad. In part, they perceived the need to counter New Democrats in the contest for immigrant voters who had fled European poverty and oppression. However, they also believed it possible to link the politically-attractive appeal for human rights abroad with a campaign for human rights at home. They imagined a domestic political coalition united by its opposition to the expansion of slavery, which would include northern Democrats who had become disgusted with what they regarded as the domination of their party by southern slaveholders, and those who were drifting away from both parties in support of the Free Soil movement. According to historians Daniel Walker Howe and Timothy Roberts, the Free Soilers "saw themselves as challenging the political status-quo in the United States and welcomed the revolutions in Europe as heralding a world-wide change in public opinion, one that might sweep away all established tyrannies, including American racial slavery." The United States could serve as a beacon to the world only if it restricted the spread of slavery as a step toward its ultimate abolition. The progressive Whig-Free Soil position tended to emphasize the defensive, not aggressive, role of the United States in the process of the spread of liberty

---

[25] Howe, *What Hath God Wrought*, pp.706-7; Herring, *From Colony to Superpower*, pp. 208-12.

[26] Timothy M. Roberts and Daniel Walker Howe, "The United States and the Revolutions of 1848," in R.J.W. Evans and Hartmut Pogge von Strandmann, eds., *The Revolutions in Europe, 1848-1849: From Reform to Reaction* (New York: Oxford University Press, 2002), p. 169.

abroad. America would help protect liberty where it had been previously established, but not force liberty on other peoples.[27]

This progressive Whigs argument linking global liberty, republican government, and legitimate regime change self-consciously opposed the position of the New Democrats, whom the progressive Whigs associated with slavery and its expansion. For instance, after word of the European disturbances of 1848 reached the United States, Greeley's New York *Tribune* offered this comparison: "The 'revolutions in Europe' which the *Tribune* has favored all look to the Enfranchisement and Elevation of the Laboring Class – the Cultivators of the Soil – as their chief end. The 'revolution in Cuba' proposes to leave the cultivators of *her* soil in the position of beasts and chattels, subject to be flogged or starved, sold or tortured as the caprice or fancied interest of the landlord caste shall dictate."[28] The possibility existed, however, that on particular issues involving foreign regime change, such as Hungarian independence, progressive Whigs, Free Soilers, and New Democrats might find enough common ground to move American foreign policy in a new and more assertive direction.

Revolutions in Central Europe and the Hülsemann Affair

The outbreak of revolutionary politics and violence in 1848 against the established European orders was hardly unexpected to serious observers on both sides of the Atlantic; the speed, scope and sweep of events, however, proved astonishing. What began immediately as a popular revolt against despotism in the Kingdom of the Two Sicilies spread to the rest of the Italian peninsula. In France, the unpopular July Monarchy of Louis-Philippe gave way to another French Revolution and a Republic was established. In the Austrian Empire, the notorious reactionary Prince Metternich was deposed and the various constituent nationalities in central Europe (especially the Hungarians) and in Italy sought autonomy or independence. Rioting encouraged by republican or socialist leaders occurred throughout the German lands, including Prussia. Monarchs wavered, abdicated or promised to accept written constitutions. An assembly in Frankfurt began the process of creating a united, liberal and constitutional German state. The Chartists planned a massive demonstration in London.

Many American foreign policy activists were greatly encouraged by the revolutionary developments in central Europe. From his post in Berlin,

---

[27] Roberts and Howe, "The United States and the Revolutions of 1848," p. 168.

[28] Chaffin, "Sons of Washington," p. 91 *(Tribune)*.

Minister Andrew Donelson initially warned American citizens against participation in political upheavals in Prussia and elsewhere; he soon became an enthusiast for the efforts of the Frankfurt Assembly to establish a united and liberal Germany. He noted that the American Declaration of Independence and the U.S. and state constitutions were being circulated and studied by reformers in Berlin and Frankfurt. Donelson urged the U.S. government to send a naval detachment to the Baltic to be "ready for eventualities." The arrival of the frigate USS *St. Lawrence* and the appearance of American naval officers in Berlin were taken by the Germans as signs of fraternal republican sympathies. The Frankfurt Assembly, facing war with Demark over Schleswig-Holstein, inquired about the prospects for purchasing warships from the United States and requested that an American naval officer serve as admiral of the navy of a united Germany. The German representatives also asked that American junior officers be assigned to help crew the ships.[29]

Donelson was aware of, and approved, Minister Richard Rush's initiative in Paris to recognize the Provisional Government there. He believed likewise that prompt American recognition of a united German government could promote U.S. commercial interests and, of greater importance, affect the liberal evolution of the development of the new German regime. Donelson requested authority from the President, "without taking any part in the struggle of the German states," to follow his own discretion about whether to recognize the new regime. After receiving no immediate response from Washington, he decided to travel to Frankfurt and act as he saw fit.[30]

The Polk administration and many leading American opinion makers were very much of the same mind as Donelson to anticipate events in Germany. The President disavowed a private citizen who claimed to be acting as a U.S. envoy to the Frankfurt Assembly; in July 1848, Secretary of State Buchanan ordered Donelson to proceed to Frankfurt as the accredited American representative to that body (he was later nominated and received Senate confirmation as Minister Plenipotentiary and Envoy Extraordinary to the Federal Republic of Germany). He was instructed to recognize the new government if he deemed it to be operating successfully and to promote American commercial interests (e.g., through reciprocal tariff reductions). The President assumed that the Berlin mission would be closed once the United States had been notified that the federal government had assumed

---

[29] Arthur James May, *Contemporary American Opinion of the Mid-Century Revolutions* (Philadelphia: University of Pennsylvania Press, 1927), pp. 8-11; James A. Field, Jr., *America and the Mediterranean World, 1776-1882* (Princeton: Princeton University Press, 1969), p. 226.

[30] May, *Contemporary American Opinion of the Mid-Century Revolutions*, pp. 14-5.

responsibility for German foreign relations. In his Annual Message to Congress in December 1848, Polk reaffirmed "the great and fundamental principle of our foreign policy of noninterference in the domestic concerns of other nations," and the right of peoples to determine their own form of government. Polk also hailed:

> the efforts in progress to unite the States of Germany in a confederation similar in many respects to our own Federal Union. If the great and enlightened German States, occupying, as they do, a central and commanding position in Europe, shall succeed in establishing such a confederated government, securing at the same time to the citizens of each State local governments adapted to the peculiar condition of each, with unrestricted trade and intercourse with each other, it will be an important era in the history of human events. Whilst it will consolidate and strengthen the power of Germany, it must essentially promote the cause of peace, commerce, civilization, and constitutional liberty throughout the world.

The Polk administration responded cautiously but affirmatively to the German request for naval assistance, authorizing two officers to provide advice and permitting a German warship to be outfitted in the Brooklyn Navy Yard.[31]

As noted above, Calhoun was one of those enthusiastic about the possibility of regime change in Germany. He was presented with an unexpected opportunity to influence that process in May 1848 when Baron Friedrich von Gerolt, Prussia's Minister Resident, solicited Calhoun's suggestions for the constitution of a united Germany. Calhoun acknowledged the limits of any outside advice. "Every constitution, to succeed, must be adapted to the community for which it is made, in all respects; and hence no one, in forming a constitution for itself, can derive much aid from that of others." He lacked "that full, accurate knowledge of the existing institutions in Germany . . . or of the character, feelings, and opinions of the German people, or the different interests of the communities of which they are composed, that is indispensable to form a constitution which would suit them, or to pronounce with any certainty, whether the proposed plan, or any other, would."

---

[31] May, *Contemporary American Opinion of the Mid-Century Revolutions*, pp. 26-8; Roberts and Howe, "The United States and the Revolutions of 1848," pp. 164-5; Polk, Annual Message to Congress, 5 December 1848, at http://www.presidency.ucsb.edu/ws/index.php?pid=29489; Field, *America and the Mediterranean World*, pp. 226-7. By October 1848, however, the Navy ordered its officers to observe strict neutrality among the contending parties and avoid any indication that it recognized revolutionary regimes. Field, *America and the Mediterranean World*, p. 224.

That said, Calhoun felt confident in warning that "it seems to me that the project errs in proposing to base the Constitution on *national unity* and to vest the union, or Empire, as it is called, with so vast an extent of power, as it does. It strikes me, that it would be impossible to induce the several communities of which Germany is composed" – above all, the great monarchies of Prussia and Austria – "to agree to it."

> But even if it could be adopted, it strikes me, that it would not be advisable. A constitution based on national unity, and with such extreme powers, would, it seems to me, form too intimate and close a union, for a people divided into communities, with political institutions so very different and interests so very conflicting. . . . experience has shown, that the tendency to concentrate all powers in the federal government is far stronger than that towards dissolution, contrary to the anticipation of many of the most experienced and wise of our statesmen, when the Government went into operation. Judged, then, by our experience, the constitution proposed for Germany, would end either in absorbing all the powers belonging to the Governments of the several communities and concentrate the whole in the Empire; or what is more probable, a conflict would occur between it and them, resulting from the Union being closer, than what the interest and the sympathy of the parts would permit, which would end in the dissolution of the former.

Calhoun was therefore "inclined to think, that the existing confederation should be preserved, but improved and strengthened." The Diet might be invested with powers related to foreign affairs and military defense, and to preserving the harmony among its member communities, "but with no more [power], than may be indispensable for either purpose. . . . It would be safer, at first, to give too little rather than too much power. It would be easier to add, whatever experience might show to be necessary, than to divest the Diet of such as may be found mischievous." Calhoun took no position on the character (republican, monarchical, or mixed) of the German federal regime or its constituent members.[32]

When Donelson received positive instructions from Secretary of State Buchanan in July 1848, he presented himself to the Frankfurt Assembly's temporary executive, the Hapsburg Archduke John, as the duly accredited

---

[32] Calhoun to Baron von Gerolt, 28 May 1848, printed with commentary in Merle E. Curti, "John C. Calhoun and the Unification of Germany," *American Historical Review* 40 (April 1935): 476-8. For a discussion of the divisions among the Germans, see Mike Rapport, *1848: Year of Revolution* (New York: Basic Books, 2008), pp. 117-25.

American representative. He told the Archduke that American opinion strongly favored efforts to unite Germany. In November, he informed the Prussian King, Frederick William IV, who was one of the possible contenders for the crown of Germany, that "the United States, though attached to the scheme of federal unity does not obtrude its example or experience on other sovereigns." American recognition of the Frankfurt Assembly was not intended to make the United States a party for or against "any scheme of reform which was of doubtful bearing on the prospects of the German states whether viewed as a Federal whole or as sovereigns." [33]

Donelson, however, had distinct personal views about how regime change in the German lands might lead eventually to a republican federation. In a letter to Calhoun, Donelson speculated that:

> the attempt at Frankfurt will have the good effect of enlightening the public mind, and preparing monarchs to abdicate positions which the changes of society make no longer necessary. Some of them I believe would now do so if they could be sure of the quiet possession of their personal estates. . . . No people will consent to be taxed to keep up two sets of Kings [for the central government and the states]: and if they submit to the one created at Frankfurt it may be expected that after he shall have assisted them in dethroning the local monarchies, these last will unite in depriving him in his turning this privilege: and then there will remain nothing but republics united as ours by a limited constitution, but possessing more centralizing powers. [34]

The Prussian monarch had something different in mind. He cracked down on reformers in his own lands and prorogued the Prussian assembly. Donelson and other American diplomats began sending back to Washington a chain of reports indicating the failure both of German unification and of the liberal revolutions.

This negative turn of events coincided with the inauguration of the Taylor administration, which took a generally more cautious view of an active American role in European affairs and of expansion in the Western Hemisphere. The new Secretary of State, John M. Clayton, had been an opponent of the Mexican War while in the Senate, but he also had the reputation of not being "averse to introducing a little 'eagle-screaming' into his

---

[33] May, *Contemporary American Opinion of the Mid-Century Revolutions*, pp. 15-17 (attached).

[34] Donelson to Calhoun, 8 July 1848, *PJCC*, 25: 573-4.

diplomatic intercourse, for the purpose of rousing popular enthusiasm for the Government." Clayton instructed Donelson to assure the Archduke John of America's sympathies and willingness to "cheer" new governments "in every progressive movement that has for its aim the countless and priceless blessing of freedom." Donelson, however, was told to adopt a lower diplomatic profile and if no progress was made toward German unification, his mission in Frankfurt would be abolished. Clayton added that "we should not renew the experiment of sending a minister to another Government before it should be organized and capable of treating with us." Donelson was recalled in September 1849 and the mission "for the present" was suspended. The Taylor administration also withdrew American support for the creation of a new German Navy.[35]

Austria and Hungary: The Views and Activities of William H. Stiles

When the revolution broke out in the Hapsburg lands in the spring of 1848, the American *charge* in Vienna, William H. Stiles, expressed optimism that the Austrian monarchy might be substantially liberalized as a result. He believed, however, that a republican government was beyond the capabilities of the mass of the peoples of the empire and the leadership of those in the radical movement.

Stiles, along with the other American diplomats in Europe, had to walk a fine line between his sympathies and official duties. He dispelled the claims of a delegation which purported to bear official American promises of financial and military aid to the Viennese revolutionaries. In December 1848, a friend of Louis Kossuth, the leader of the Hungarian (Magyar) cause for autonomy and later independence from Austria, approached Stiles and asked him to intervene diplomatically "for the settlement of the differences now existing between the imperial government and the Kingdom of Hungary." Stiles demurred: "I frankly stated, on that occasion, the difficulties which such a step suggested to my mind, arising from the fact that it was a domestic quarrel between the government of the Austrian empire and one of its dependencies, and with which no foreign power could properly have any concern." Stiles (as he reported to Secretary of State Buchanan) told the Hungarian intermediary, "that it was a subject which the United States had ever regarded with peculiar

---

[35] Mary Wilhelmine Williams, "John Middleton Clayton," in Samuel Flagg Bemis, ed., *The American Secretaries of State and Their Diplomacy*, 10 vols. (New York: Alfred A. Knopf, 1928), 6: 9-11 (eagle screaming); May, *Contemporary American Opinion of the Mid-Century Revolutions*, pp. 25-9; Field, *America and the Mediterranean World*, p. 227. The Taylor administration also recalled Richard Rush and replaced him with a new minister regarded as being friendly to Louis Napoleon, William C. Rives. Roberts and Howe, "The United States and the Revolutions of 1848," p. 171.

jealousy, and that I could not, therefore, reconcile it to myself to be in any manner instrumental in committing her; that, besides, so extensive, as I understood, had been the preparations made by the imperial government for the subjugation of Hungary, that it was scarcely to be expected that it would, at this eleventh hour, listen to any proposals of settlement short of the unconditional submission to imperial authority." [36]

Stiles' interlocutor responded that Kossuth and the Hungarian government had been unable to communicate its desire for a settlement and reconciliation to the imperial authorities in Vienna. He pleaded for the United States to serve as a conduit of such a communication to avoid the immense bloodshed that would result if the conflict escalated.

> I then inquired whether the object for which the interposition was sought was the separation of Hungary from Austria; or, if not, whether it was to gain time in order to make a more successful resistance; that if either of these objects were in contemplation, I could not listen for one moment to the application. On being solemnly assured to the contrary, and that no other end was in view but an amicable adjustment of the impending difficulties, I stated that the only ground upon which I could consent to interfere was that of humanity, and to save the useless effusion of blood; that such an appeal I should not consider myself justified in resisting; but that even in that event, my interference, if approved by the imperial government, would simply go to the extent of opening the door of reconciliation between the opposing parties, and by which the unhappy differences which distract the two countries might be, between themselves and through the instrumentality of their respective authorities, peaceably and satisfactorily arranged.

Stiles immediately contacted Prince Schwartzenberg, the Austrian Minister of Foreign Affairs, stressing that "I had no disposition to interfere between the Austrian government and one of its provinces, and that I would only take such action or pursue such a course in the matter as might be agreeable to the imperial government." Schwartzenberg responded that, "matters had progressed too far – that they could enter into no negotiation with rebels, and that nothing short of unconditional surrender could now be submitted to by the government."

---

[36] The following account is taken from Stiles to Buchanan, 12 December 1848, William H. Stiles, *Austria in 1848-9: Being a History of the Late Political Movements in Vienna, Milan, Venice, and Prague . . . [and] a Full Account of the Revolution in Hungary*, 2 vols. (London: Sampson Low, 1852), 2: 401-4.

A week later, Stiles received an official written plea from Kossuth himself, asking the United States to initiate a negotiation with the imperial government for a military armistice during the winter. Stiles decided again to approach the Austrian authorities, including Field Marshal Windischgrätz, while warning Kossuth:

> . . . in the mean time, as the matter is attended with great difficulties arising from the facts, first, that the controversy is a domestic one, and Austria may, consequently, be unwilling to permit of any foreign interference; and, second, that as the preparations for the attack of Hungary on the part of the imperial government are said to be very extensive, and any delay in their operations they may conceive detrimental to their interests, I can hold out to you but little hopes of success in obtaining the desired armistice. For the cause of humanity, however, and to prevent the useless effusion of blood, the only ground upon which I can consent to take any step toward opening the door of reconciliation between Austria and Hungary, and by which the difficulties which now unhappily distract the two countries may be adjusted between themselves, you may rest assured that no exertion on my part shall be spared which may be calculated to effect so desirable an object.

Windischgrätz, as Stiles predicted, would have none of it. "I can do nothing in the matter." "I must obey the orders of the emperor." "Hungary must submit." "I will occupy Pesth with my troops, and then the emperor will decide what is to be done." "I have received orders to occupy Hungary, and I hope to accomplish this end – I cannot, therefore, enter into any negotiations." "I can not consent to treat with those who are in a state of rebellion."

Stiles, like his colleagues Rush and Donelson, naturally was concerned that his diplomatic activism, however limited, might meet with the disapproval of his superiors in the Polk administration. "Before closing this communication, I have only to add, sir, that as in this (to me) entirely novel situation, I have endeavored to act with all the circumspection which the delicate nature of the subject so imperiously required; as I have studiously avoided the least step which I thought could in any manner compromise my country," he wrote to the Secretary of State, "and as, if any error has been committed, it has been done for the sake and in the cause of humanity, I trust that the course which, without time for special instruction, I have thought proper to pursue in this matter, will not meet the disapprobation of my government."

Secretary of State Buchanan subsequently approved Stiles' actions but offered no encouragement for taking any more ambitious steps in the future:

... I am gratified that your prudence and ability were equal to the occasion. In our foreign policy, we must ever be governed by the wise maxim not to interfere with the domestic concerns of foreign nations; and from this you have not departed. You have done no more, in your own language, than to attempt to open the door of reconciliation between the opposing parties, leaving them to adjust their differences without your intervention. Considering there was reason to believe that the previous offers of the Hungarian government for a reconciliation had never reached the imperial government, and that no other practicable mode of communicating these offers existed, except through your agency, you acted wisely in becoming an intermediary for this purpose alone. Had you refused thus to act upon the request of Mr. Kossuth, you might have been charged with a want of humanity, and been held, in some degree, responsible for the blood which has since been so profusely shed in the war. The president entirely approves your conduct.[37]

Stiles reflected on the larger implications of the Hungarian Revolution for European reform and liberal regime change. "[I]f Hungary is subdued (which will most certainly be the case, from the superior strength and discipline of the imperial army), such a result will only aggravate the feelings of hostility which now exist; and as a country determined to be free cannot, in these days, be held in subjection for any length of time by mere military force, this very conclusion may lead eventually to the liberation of Hungary and in total separation from the Austrian empire," he wrote in December. In the spring of 1849, after the Hungarians issued a Declaration of Independence and Russian troops came to the aid of Austria and non-Magyar ethnic groups, Stiles concluded that this had now become a struggle between "peoples and thrones" and warned that if Russian intervention succeeded in suppressing the rebellion, all of Europe was at risk of Russian despotism. He contended that the Hungarians had a sound legal basis for claiming independence. Stiles, Donelson and Rush all predicted the likelihood that Russian intervention would provoke a European-wide war.[38]

---

[37] Buchanan to Stiles, 9 February 1849, *Austria in 1848-9*, pp. 405-6.

[38] Stiles, *Austria in 1848-9*, p. 403 (subdued); Merle E. Curti, *Austria and the United States, 1848-1852. A Study in Diplomatic Relations* (Northampton, Mass: Smith College, 1926), pp. 150-2; May, *Contemporary American Opinion of the Mid-Century Revolutions*, pp. 33-40; Rapport, *1848: Year of Revolution*, p. 312.

Stiles' dispatches influenced the attitude of the otherwise cautious Whig administration of Zachary Taylor. Although conservative members of the party warned about getting too far ahead of events, the cause of Hungary drew the particular support of the Progressive Whigs as well as New Democrats. Secretary of State Clayton had received numerous petitions and requests from Hungarian immigrants and visitors to dispatch a diplomatic envoy to their homeland. Public meetings, including one in Philadelphia chaired by former Vice President George M. Dallas, implored the United States to recognize Hungarian independence. In Illinois, Whig Congressman Abraham Lincoln served on a citizens committee that drafted resolutions offering sympathy with the Hungarian people; calling on the United States to acknowledge Hungarian independence "at the very earliest moment consistent with our amicable relations" with Austria; and opining that the immediate acknowledgement of that independence was "due from American freemen, to their struggling brethren, to the general cause of Republican liberty, and not a violation of the just rights of any people." Other public meetings, such as in Philadelphia, went even further – the United States should recognize Hungary "not with reference to the success or defeat of the revolutionary progress there but because our republican brethren are fighting for liberty." [39]

Senator John J. Crittenden, a close friend of the new Secretary of State, urged Clayton to find some means to voice American sympathy for the Hungarian people and to denounce the interference of despotism in the struggle for freedom. If he were president, Crittenden reflected, he would "speak aloud the great doctrines of liberty and free government." Clayton responded:

> You never wrote a more sensible letter in your life than that in which you gave me your lessons in diplomacy. I agree with you in everything, and you will see *by-and-by* that I have sent an agent to recognize the independence of Hungary on the first favorable indication. . . . The same policy (sympathy with the advance of republican principles) will characterize all my course, if the President will allow me. On this subject do you write to me to give me a loose rein. Some of my colleagues *(who are noble*

---

[39] Spencer, *Louis Kossuth and Young America,* p. 24; Roy P. Basler, ed., *The Collected Works of Abraham Lincoln,* 8 vols. (New Brunswick, NJ: Rutgers University Press, 1953-55), 2: 62; May, *Contemporary American Opinion of the Mid-Century Revolutions,* pp. 48-9 (brethren).

fellows) are somewhat young and tender-footed. We must keep up with the spirit of the age.[40]

Clayton's agent to Hungary was A. Dudley Mann, an American diplomat based in Paris, whom Clayton instructed to proceed "towards" Hungary and to gather accurate information about the situation in Central Europe. Without departing from the "established policy of non-interference in the domestic concerns of other nations," if Mann determined that Hungary was "able to maintain the independence she had declared," the United States wished "to be the very first to congratulate her, and to hail with a hearty welcome her entrance into the family of nations." Mann was authorized in that instance to recognize Hungarian independence and conclude a commercial treaty with the new regime. President Taylor left no doubts about his sympathies in the matter, according to Clayton. Kossuth's efforts at reform and the amelioration of his countrymen's conditions had been opposed by a policy of "immobility, backed by the bayonet." The "best wishes" of the United States attended Hungary, whose cause offered "the interesting spectacle of a great people rising superior to the enormous oppression" that had "so long weighed her down." Senator Crittenden, when apprised of Clayton's orders, approved wholeheartedly. "It is glorious and will please our people to see the majesty of our Republic exhibiting itself on all proper occasions, with dignity and fearless front, in the eyes and to the teeth of kings and despots." Clayton asked Crittenden to reinforce this line of argument whenever he met with President Taylor.[41]

The United States was again pressing the boundaries of accepted diplomatic practice and the law of nations, in this case with the hope that prompt American recognition of Hungarian independence might influence world public opinion and deter or limit outside intervention. According to John Bassett Moore, one of the 19th century's leading authorities on international law, Mann's instructions conferred such powers as "had never before and have not since been confided to any representative of the United States." Some American activists thought the United States should have been even more aggressive and not waited for Mann's fact-finding expedi-

---

[40] May, *Contemporary American Opinion of the Mid-Century Revolutions*, p, 51 (speak); Clayton to Crittenden, 11 July 1849, Ann M.B. Coleman, ed., *The Life of John J. Crittenden*, 2 vols. (Philadelphia: J.B. Lippincott, 1862), 1: 344-5. Emphasis in original.

[41] Clayton to Mann, 18 June 1849, in John Bassett Moore, "Kossuth: Sketch of a Revolutionist, Part II," *Political Science Quarterly* 10 (June 1895): 262-3; Spencer, *Louis Kossuth and Young America*, pp. 25-6; Curti, *Austria and the United States, 1848-1852*, pp. 151-3 (glorious); May, *Contemporary American Opinion of the Mid-Century Revolutions*, p. 53.

tion. A leading progressive Whig journalist wrote after the fact: "We have no doubt that the timely interposition of the United States and Great Britain in the recognition of the Government of . . . Hungary . . . would have caused the Czar to hesitate before enslaving Hungary." Former President John Tyler thought that the United States should have registered strong protests in Vienna and, if they were not taken into account, the United States should have withdrawn Stiles from Austria and expelled the Austrian representative from the United States. Mann's friend, George Sumner, actively promoted the Hungarian cause in the English press and met that summer with Foreign Secretary Palmerston to encourage official recognition by London. Mann may have shown Sumner his instructions with the idea that they would be passed on to such key British officials and opinion-makers. [42]

Mann himself was of the view that "the question whether continental Europe shall be under Cossack or republican rule hereafter will, in all probability, be definitively decided on the plains and in the passes of Hungary." By the time he reached Vienna, however, it was too late to proceed further. The massive Russian intervention decided matters. In late August 1849, Kossuth fled to Turkey. The Hungarian armies soon surrendered. For some conservative journals such as the Richmond *Whig*, this was a reminder that "every nation had the degree of liberty which it deserved." Had the Hungarian people been capable and deserving of freedom, no force on earth could have conquered them. But Horace Greeley and other Progressive Whigs and New Democrats argued that the United States should not give up the fight. He recommended widely disseminating pamphlets in Europe that would stir up the minds of the oppressed peoples. President Taylor's critics took to the newspapers to attack him for not recognizing the independent Hungarian government before it was defeated. [43]

Despite the failure of his mission, Mann believed that much had been accomplished. Newspapers in England and the United States printed the gist of his instructions from Clayton, which had met with "unqualified praise of all Europeans, animated by humane and generous sentiments. To crowned heads and monarchists it cannot be otherwise than exceedingly unpalatable." Despite speculation that the European autocracies might sever diplomatic relations with the United States on this account, Mann told Clayton that they

---

[42] Moore, "Kossuth, Part II," p. 264; Gamaliel Bailey, *The National Era*, cited in Spencer, *Louis Kossuth and Young America*, pp. 24, 31; Curti, *Austria and the United States, 1848-1852*, p. 154.

[43] Spencer, *Louis Kossuth and Young America*, pp. 26-7 (Cossack); May, *Contemporary American Opinion of the Mid-Century Revolutions*, p. 50 (deserved); Smith, *The Presidencies of Zachary Taylor & Millard Fillmore*, p. 85.

were aware "that their strength would be greatly impaired by such a suspension of intercourse." Mann had not lost his enthusiasm: "It is in our power to save continental Europe from the yoke of cruel oppression prepared for its neck. What a mission! What a glory will not accrue to the administration of Gen. Taylor if it performs a noble duty." [44]

American diplomatic activism toward Hungary did not go unnoticed by Austrian authorities. The Austrian *charge* in Washington, Baron Hülsemann, had reported regularly to Vienna during the previous decade about the expansionist tendencies in the United States. He urged his superiors to avoid any breach of neutrality during the Mexican War because it might encourage American intervention in the European revolutionary movements. He also recommended that Vienna try to influence Spain to sell Cuba to the United States before American filibustering expeditions against the island succeeded. But the events of 1848 indicated to Hülsemann and his superiors that the United States was edging toward a provocative role in Europe. The Austrians followed closely the movements of the American Mediterranean squadron, which the U.S. was rumored to be planning to use to intervene on behalf of central European revolutionaries. They also followed efforts by the United States to obtain basing rights for its ships in the region. As reports of alleged Austrian and Russian atrocities in Hungary began to circulate in America, "public opinion is so enraged against Austria," Hülsemann reported, "that scarcely an editor admits anything favorable to her." [45]

The Austrian government, meanwhile, had somehow obtained a full copy of Mann's official instructions (the United States could always disavow accounts of those that had been published in the newspapers). Hülsemann's diplomatic colleagues in Washington agreed with him that the Mann mission constituted interference in Austrian affairs, according to the non-intervention standards established by the Americans themselves. Hülsemann discussed the matter with Secretary Clayton in hopes that President Taylor's Annual Message in December 1849 would address the matter satisfactorily or at least not make matters worse. Hülsemann did not succeed. Clayton insisted that the United States had not interfered in Austrian affairs because Mann was authorized to recognize Hungary only if it had in fact established its

---

[44] Curti, *Austria and the United States, 1848-1852*, pp. 167-70 (unpalatable). See Mann's cautionary views detailed in Spencer, *Louis Kossuth and Young America*, p. 27.

[45] Curti, *Austria and the United States, 1848-1852*, pp. 144-45; Spencer, *Louis Kossuth and Young America*, p. 30 (enraged).

independence. The President's Annual Message expressed sympathy for the Hungarians and officially approved the Mann mission. [46]

The De-Recognition Debate: Cass versus Clay

Americans found it particularly difficult to accept the suppression of the movement for Hungarian independence. The failure of republican regime change in France could be ascribed to domestic reasons peculiar to France. The French were certainly at liberty to reject American advice about constitutionalizing their revolution. The egregious external intervention by Russia in Hungary, however, doomed what seemed to be a promising attempt at liberal nationalism. It was as if Louis XVI had taken the British side in the American Revolution and sent French troops to America to fight against George Washington. American activists sought some effective way to protest against Russia's action and to dissuade despots from similar interventions in the future.

In the Senate, Lewis Cass introduced a resolution that would instruct the Senate Foreign Relations Committee "to inquire into the expediency of suspending diplomatic relations with Austria." Cass thereby introduced a new American tool to support the right of regime change and to marshal world public opinion on behalf of the cause of human liberty. In addition to the rapid, even preemptive *recognition* of revolutionary regimes, the United States could *withdraw* recognition from states that interfered in the internal affairs of other states, especially to suppress regime changes. Cass argued that the increased interrelationship among "the nations of Christendom" caused by the general progress of the age – scientific, commercial and the like – had "broken down the barriers of space which separated nations, [and] have opened each to the knowledge and business of all." The members of this political family thus could not be indifferent to the "internal agitations or external dangers" that

---

[46] "I have scrupulously avoided any interference in the wars and contentions which have recently distracted Europe. During the late conflict between Austria and Hungary there seemed to be a prospect that the latter might become an independent nation. However faint that prospect at the time appeared, I thought it my duty, in accordance with the general sentiment of the American people, who deeply sympathized with the Magyar patriots, to stand prepared, upon the contingency of the establishment by her of a permanent government, to be the first to welcome independent Hungary into the family of nations. For this purpose I invested an agent then in Europe with power to declare our willingness promptly to recognize her independence in the event of her ability to sustain it. The powerful intervention of Russia in the contest extinguished the hopes of the struggling Magyars. The United States did not at any time interfere in the contest, but the feelings of the nation were strongly enlisted in the cause, and by the sufferings of a brave people, who had made a gallant, though unsuccessful, effort to be free." Zachary Taylor, Annual Message to the Congress, 4 December 1849, at http://www.presidency.ucsb.edu/ws/index.php?pid=29490.

might threaten each of them. Nor could they be indifferent to a globalized public opinion that passed judgment on their actions.

> The age is an inquiring and an observing one; and the facility and rapidity of communication, among the proudest triumphs of human knowledge, come powerfully in aid of this disposition to judge and approve or censure passing events, as their character and circumstances may justify. This public opinion, imbodied by the press in the daily journals it pours forth, is borne through the civilized world, pronouncing the judgment of the present day, and anticipating that of posterity. There are none so high as to be beyond its censure – none so low as not to be encouraged by its approbation. The frontiers of a country may be armed at its approach. But it will pass them. It may be checked, but it cannot be stopped. It is stronger than the bayonet – more vigilant than the suspicions of despotism.[47]

The United States should make "this first effort to rebuke, by public opinion, expressed through an established government, in the name of a great republic, atrocious acts of despotism, by which human liberty and life have been sacrificed, under circumstances of audacious contempt for the rights of mankind and the sentiments of the civilized world, without parallel even in the age of warfare between the oppressors and the oppressed."

> ... I do not recollect that any formal act has been adopted, rendering the censure more signal and enduring. If we take the first step in this noble cause, where physical force, with its flagitious abuse, if not conquered, may be ultimately restrained by moral considerations, we shall add to the value of the lesson of 1776, already so important to the world, and destined to become far more so, by furnishing one guarantee the more for the preservation of human rights where they exist, and for their recovery where they are lost.
> ... Now, sir, I say it without reservation, that a Power thus setting at defiance the opinion of the world, and violating the best feelings of our nature, in the very wantonness of successful cruelty, has no bond of union with the American people. The sooner the diplomatic intercourse is dissolved – and dissolved with marks of indignant approbation – the sooner we shall perform an act of public duty, which, at home and abroad, will meet with feelings of

---

[47] This and the following taken from *Congressional Globe*, 31:1, Appendix, pp. 54-8.

kindred sympathy from all, wherever they may be, who are not fit subjects for the tender mercies of Austrian power.

Cass acknowledged that American suspension of diplomatic relations with Vienna would not itself restrain the immediate march of Austrian despotism – that must wait "till she is stayed by one of those upheavings of people, which is as sure to come as that man longs for freedom, and longs to strike the blow which shall make it his." Despotic pride and power was tenacious, but "many old things are passing away; and Austrian despotism will pass away in its turn." Liberalized global opinion, led by the United States, would accelerate this process of revolution. The bulwarks of despotism "will be shaken by the rushing of the mighty winds – by the voice of the world, wherever its indignant expression is not restrained by the kindred sympathies of arbitrary power." The American Republic was not alone. Expressions of support for liberalism were possible not only in republics but in constitutional monarchies, "some of the most enlightened nations of the earth," where "practical freedom" could be enjoyed. Cass pointed to a recent petition signed by over eighty members of the British Houses of Commons and Lords which expressed concern about the suppression of the Hungarian revolt on the grounds of "internal liberty, national independence, [and] European peace."

Cass insisted that the American people "do not undertake to judge what forms of government are best adapted to the conditions of the other nations of the earth, and, least of all, to attempt the establishment elsewhere of their own." But because there was an overwhelming difference between constitutional monarchy and despotism, by implication at least, the United States was at liberty to align itself with enlightened public opinion in those non-republican regimes in moral support of revolutionary "upheavings" that transformed despotisms into constitutional monarchies, if not immediately into republics.

That said, Cass argued that the United States should be sparing in its expressions of "interest and sympathy." Moreover, "The value of this kind of moral interposition would be diminished by its too frequent recurrence. It should be reserved for great events – events marked by great crimes and oppressions on the one side, and great exertions and misfortunes on the other, and under circumstances which carry with them the sympathies of the world, like the partition of Poland and the subjugation of Hungary." "We are in an age of progress," Cass insisted. Those who still had the "*spirit of standing still –* conservatism," must give way to evidence that "both in the moral and physical world . . . change is one of the great laws of nature." Conservatism "little becomes a country like ours, which is advancing in the career of improvement with an accelerated pace unknown in the history of the world."

Senator John P. Hale, the Free Soiler, immediately muddied the waters – or clarified the issue, depending on one's point of view – by asking why Russia, and not Austria, was the object of the resolution of de-recognition. Hale pointed out that Cass had admitted on other occasions that Austria had a legitimate claim under the law of nations for resisting Hungarian independence, whereas Russia did not. Hale touched on a sore point for the New Democrats, for whom Britain was the main foreign enemy and for whom Russia was therefore a natural ally. As before, however, the Senators elected not to debate Hale's line of argument, which led naturally to a condemnation of domestic slavery.[48]

The debate instead took another direction. During the course of his speech, Cass said he had anticipated "with confidence the cordial support of the distinguished Senator from Kentucky" – Henry Clay – based on Clay's strong support for the independence of Spanish America and Greece in decades past. (Whether Cass really expected that support or was merely trying to score political points against his Whig rival is unclear – Cass also tweaked Clay for being a "more zealous disciple of the *stand still* school than he was some years since.") Clay, in fact, opposed Cass's resolution, which he regarded as a direct proposition to suspend diplomatic relations with Austria, rather than a genuine call for an inquiry by the Foreign Relations Committee. Clay portrayed himself as a sincere friend of the "noble cause of the Hungarians," one who had sincerely hoped that the Hungarians would have been able to maintain their independence from Austria. In that case, Clay remarked, the United States would have been fully justified in recognizing Hungary, just as it had done with the Spanish American republics (something that had been tardily done by the Monroe administration, in Clay's opinion). Hungary's inability to do so, in Clay's view, stemmed partly from internal weakness – specifically, from the failure of its revolutionary leadership – but primarily from the intervention of Russia.

Facts were facts for Clay, however, and the suspension of diplomatic relations with Austria would do precious little good under the existing circumstances. The United States, under the form of punishing Austria, would only punish its own citizens and merchants by denying them the services that an American minister in Vienna could provide. Clay concurred with Hale that Russia, not Austria, had been the primary instrument of Hungary's demise, but this did not justify the U.S. withdrawal of recognition from Russia either. "What principle does it involve? It involves the principle of

---

[48] *Congressional Globe*, 31:1, pp. 113, 117, 293. Emphasis in original.

assuming on the part of this Government a right to pass judgment upon the conduct of foreign Powers . . . and to follow it up by some direct action, such as suspending intercourse."

> But where is to be the limit? You begin with war. You may extend the same principle of action to politics or religion – to society or to social principles and habits. . . . there is no limit or restriction as to the extent to which we may go in our investigations of the conduct of foreign nations, and as to the extent we may go in pronouncing our judgment upon that conduct. We may say, in reference to Turkey, your religion tolerates polygamy; unless you change your religion, and your habits of social life, we will cease all intercourse with you.

More worrisome, in Clay's opinion, was the tendency of Cass's resolution to assume "the right of interference in the internal affairs of other nations." There was an existing political relationship between Hungary and Austria: "The House of Hapsburg were the lawful sovereign, the more especially as they were originally elected by Hungary." However justified the Hungarians might have been in seeking their independence, the United States, in the midst of an ongoing European civil war, had no right or duty to recognize their existence as a nation. There was now certainly no such independent nation to recognize or support (which, presumably, would be the indirect intent of suspending diplomatic relations with Austria). Interference in the internal affairs of other nations was "in direct contradiction to the whole policy of this Government, first laid down by Washington and pursued by every successor he has had down to the present day." Clay doubted that it would be possible to adhere to Cass's rule of acting only in the most important and egregious circumstances. "And if we were to permit ourselves to interfere in cases of this kind, where, again, I ask, are we to stop? Why should we not interfere in behalf of suffering Ireland? Why not interfere in behalf of suffering humanity wherever we may find it?"

Clay challenged Cass's notion of progress. This was not the progress that Clay had advocated throughout his career, that of the American System of internal improvement, but rather the false "progress" of manifest destiny. "I am afraid it is progress in foreign wars. I am afraid it is progress in foreign conquest – in territorial aggrandizement. I am afraid that it is progress as the disturbers of the possessions of our neighbors throughout this continent, and throughout the islands adjacent to it." Cass's resolution to de-recognize Austria was offered in that same spirit – it will "open up a new field of collision, terminating perhaps in war, and exposing ourselves to the reaction of foreign Powers, who, when they see us assuming to judge of their conduct, will undertake in their turn to judge of our conduct." The threat to suspend diplomatic relations was, in effect, a threat to "denationalize nation after nation, according as their conduct may be found to correspond to our own notion of what is right and proper in the administration of human affairs." The idea that foreign powers, typically governed by non-republican regimes, would tolerate that behavior without some sort of retaliation was naïve and dangerous.[49]

Senator Joseph R. Underwood, a Kentucky Whig and a consistent opponent of an activist foreign policy, proposed a substitute resolution that would express the sympathy of the American people for "popular movements to reform political institutions inconsistent with the enlightened opinions of the age," while adding, "they disclaim the right to meddle with the domestic policy of other nations." Alabama Senator Henry S. Foote (Democrat) offered a substitute version favoring an activist policy. The Senate never took action on any of these resolutions, and further deliberation was truncated by the all-consuming debate over what became the Compromise of 1850. But Cass and his allies did not let the matter drop completely. Democratic newspapers praised Cass's resolution as an expression of American opinion; they attacked the Whig administration for a pusillanimous policy that favored the divine right of kings and that was hostile to the cause of liberty in Europe.[50]

In March and April 1850, Cass and his Congressional allies proposed to increase American leverage over the prospects for future regime change in central Europe – and to force the Taylor administration's hand – by removing all funding for the American legations in Vienna and Berlin. They also proposed adding appropriations for "a diplomatic agent to the Central power of Germany at Frankfurt," although – as Senator William R. King of Alabama pointed out – that Assembly was defunct and there was no evidence that an effective German central government now existed. Cass, however, wanted to make a point of protesting the Taylor administration's "arbitrary and unwarrantable" decision to "suppress" Donelson's mission to Frankfurt. In Cass's view, the withdrawal of America's recognition of a united and liberal Germany had come precisely "at a time when that mission was likely to

---

[49] *Congressional Globe*, 31:1, pp. 115-6.

[50] May, *Contemporary American Opinion of the Mid-Century Revolutions*, pp. 61-3; *Congressional Globe*, 31:1, pp. 103-6, 113-4, 244, 293; *Congressional Globe*, 31; 1, Appendix, pp. 43-7, 84-91. New Democrats derided the Whigs as "the Austrian Party." Smith, *The Presidencies of Zachary Taylor & Millard Fillmore*, p. 86.

prove highly advantageous to the cause of freedom." "There is the fountain of liberal principles," Cass insisted, referring to Frankfurt. "It is that point to which every German wishing his country to be free – wishing for the progress of liberal principles – turns his attention. Let us sympathize with this feeling, and do what little we can towards its encouragement. If there is to be a regeneration in Germany, it must depend on the central authority." In Cass's view, American diplomacy must anticipate and encourage opportunities to bring about regime change through actions such as recognition and de-recognition, and not merely ratify changes – especially counterrevolutions – after the fact. [51]

Daniel Webster and the Search for the Middle Ground

With the Congressional controversy over America's policy toward central Europe as a backdrop, the Austrian diplomat Hülsemann and Secretary of State Clayton continued to spar privately about allegations of American interference in Austrian affairs. Hülsemann suggested that Austria might retaliate by suspending the Treaty of Commerce, which would damage American cotton trade to Venice and Trieste. The Austrian government also sent Hülsemann accounts of Hungarian atrocities, to be inserted in American publications, countering reports of Austrian and Russian brutality. But Hülsemann and the Austrian government decided not to press the United States for an official disavowal of the Mann mission, in part because of the sensitive question of how exactly they obtained a copy of his instructions. [52]

In April 1850, the Taylor administration, in response to a resolution originally introduced by Senator Douglas, reignited the controversy by sending the Senate documents related to Mann's mission, including his instructions (deleting only a reference to Austria's "iron rule" within its empire). The packet of documents included a statement by the President that reiterated the fact that the United States had not accredited any agent to Hungary and had received no official communication from the *de facto* Hungarian government; it noted that, had Hungary successfully achieved independence, "we should have been the first to welcome her into the family of nations." [53]

---

[51] *Congressional Globe*, 31:1, pp. 583, 745-6. The defunding measure was defeated 28-17.

[52] Curti, *Austria and the United States, 1848-1852*, pp. 156-61.

[53] Spencer, *Louis Kossuth and Young America*, p. 39; Zachary Taylor, Message to Congress, 28 March 1850, James D. Richardson, ed., *A Compilation of the Messages and Papers of the Presidents, 1789-1897*, 10 Vols. (Washington, D.C.: U.S. Government Printing Office, 1896-1899), 5: 41.

The Austrian government, with Russian diplomatic support, now ordered Hülsemann to register a written protest to Washington (the text of which he was allowed to soften somewhat). Because of the death of President Taylor, Hülsemann waited until late July 1850 to deliver an informal note to the new Secretary of State, Daniel Webster. After several months of discussion between the two men, Hülsemann delivered a formal statement of the Austrian position on September 30. The Mann mission, Hülsemann insisted, could not be construed as innocent fact-finding; rather it betrayed the fact that the United States was "impatient for the downfall of the Austrian Monarchy, and even sought to accelerate that event by the utterance of their wishes to that effect[.]" The wording of Mann's instructions left no doubt about America's lack of neutrality and its intent to interfere – "it designates the Austrian Government as an iron rule [the phrase deleted from the text sent to the Senate], and represents the rebel chief, Kossuth, as an illustrious man; while improper instructions are introduced in regard to Russia, the intimate and faithful ally of Austria." Austria would have been justified in treating Mann not as a diplomat but as a spy and thus (Hülsemann did not add, but the implication was clear) subject to execution.

Hülsemann lectured the United States on the criteria it should have applied if it sincerely wished to maintain its professed policy of non-intervention. The American government should have realized that "a contest of a few months' duration could neither have exhausted the energies of that Power [Austria], nor turned aside its purpose to put down the insurrection. Austria has struggled against the French revolution for twenty-five years; the courage and perseverance which she exhibited in that memorable contest have been appreciated by the whole world." Furthermore:

> All countries are obliged, at some period or other, to struggle against internal difficulties; all forms of government are exposed to such disagreeable episodes; the United States have had some experience in this very recently. Civil war is a possible occurrence everywhere, and the encouragement which is given to the spirit of insurrection and of disorder most frequently falls back upon those who seek to aid it in its developments, in spite of justice and wise policy.

Hülsemann added that the Austrian government would not have protested formally if President Taylor had not provoked them by publishing Mann's instructions; and that Vienna was still "disposed to cultivate relations of friendship and good understanding with the United States." He fired a shot across the American bow, however, by warning that relations could not be seriously disturbed again "without placing the cardinal interests of the two countries in jeopardy," code words for war (or at least overt Austrian opposition, in conjunction with its European allies, to American commercial interests and territorial expansion). If the United States continued to "take an indirect part in the political movements of Europe, American policy would be exposed to acts of retaliation, and to certain inconveniences, which could not fail to affect the commerce and industry of the two hemispheres."[54]

Webster had joined the Cabinet after the death of Taylor in large part to support the successful implementation of the Compromise of 1850, which he had been instrumental in bringing about while still in the Senate. In doing so, Webster suffered much political damage in the eyes of Progressive Whigs, who hated especially the strengthened Fugitive Slave legislation that was part of the compromise. Webster decided to go public with his diplomatic clash with Hülsemann as a means of reinforcing unionist sentiment as well as recovering his own political position. Webster, as previously noted, was an opponent of Manifest Destiny and of aggressive American expansionism and interventionism. But Webster, like Cass, believed in the power of American rhetoric to "shape the battlefield" of public opinion, at home and abroad, on behalf of human liberty. Webster prided himself on his own particular abilities to marshal the rhetoric of human freedom and progressive regime change, and he was not prepared to cede this ground to the New Democrats or to Cass. He believed there was a solid and defensible middle policy of wielding influence, between the extremes of indifference and outright intervention. Webster pointed to the case of the American Revolution, in which "the majestic eloquence of Chatham, the profound reasoning of Burke, the burning satire and irony of Colonel Barré" influenced American fortunes.

> . . . there was not a reading man who did not feel stronger, bolder, and more determined in the assertion of his rights when these exhilarating accounts from the two Houses of Parliament reached him from beyond the seas. He felt that those who held and controlled public opinion elsewhere were with us; that their words of eloquence might produce an effect in the region where they were uttered; and, above all, they assured him that, in the judgment of the just, and the wise, and the impartial, his cause

---

[54] Hülsemann to Webster, 30 September 1851, *The Works of Daniel Webster*, 20th ed., 6 vols. (Boston: Little, Brown and Company, 1890), 6: 488-90.

was just, and he was right; and, therefore, he said, "We will fight it out to the last." [55]

Webster's famous Congressional speeches on behalf of Greek independence in 1824 and the American mission to the Panama Conference in 1826 were among the pillars of his claim to reputation as a great orator, an American Pitt or Burke. Those speeches had introduced many of these themes that would guide Webster's subsequent policies. The United States could not avoid being drawn into the "great political question of this age ... that between absolute and regulated government." Webster insisted that "it would be impossible for us, if we were so disposed, to prevent our principles, our sentiments, and our example from producing some effect upon the opinions and hopes of society throughout the civilized world. It rests probably with ourselves to determine whether the influence of these shall be salutary or pernicious." [56]

The United States could exercise that salutary influence primarily by demonstrating the viability of free institutions through its own growth and prosperity, and by recommending their adoption, in whole or part, to other nations. Moreover, according to Webster, America also had an active role in defending the underlying basis of free government – that is, "to resist the establishment of doctrines which deny the legality of its foundations." Those doctrines, which the European despots proposed to introduce "as part of the law of the civilized world; ... enforced by a million and a half bayonets," were (1) the divine right of kings – "that all popular or constitutional rights were held as grants from the crown"; and (2) the right of forcible interference in the affairs of other states, "to control nations in their desire to change their own government, whatever it may be conjectured, or pretended, that such a change might furnish an example to the subjects of other states." Webster trusted that "every enlightened man throughout the world will oppose" the claim of forcible interference, which was "in open violation of the public law of the world." It was especially important that "those who, like ourselves, are fortunately out of the reach of the bayonets that enforce it, will proclaim their detestation of it, in a tone both loud and decisive." Enlightened Americans must realize that there were no limits to the claims of despotism: "Why are we not as fair objects for the operation of the new principle, as any other of those who may attempt a reform of government on the other side of the Atlantic?"

---

[55] Speech at the Kossuth Banquet, *The Papers of Daniel Webster,* Diplomatic Papers, 2: 98.

[56] The following summary is taken from Webster's speeches to the House of Representatives: Independence of Greece, 19 January 1824, *The Papers of Daniel Webster,* Speeches and Formal Writings, 1: 89-104; and the Panama Mission, 14 April 1826, ibid., 1: 201-35.

In making this argument, Webster was compelled to address two obvious criticisms. First, that the "thunder . . . rolls at a distance. The wide Atlantic is between us and danger; however others may suffer, we shall remain safe." Second, that American opposition to forcible interference must either be limited to feckless rhetoric or else lead to war.

As to the claim that American geographic isolation was sufficient protection for its own free institutions, Webster rejoined:

> I think it is a sufficient answer to this to say, that we are one of the nations of the earth; that we have an interest, therefore, in the preservation of that system of national law and national intercourse which has heretofore subsisted, so beneficially for all. Our system of government, it should also be remembered, is, throughout, founded on principles entirely hostile to the new code; and if we remain undisturbed by its operation, we shall owe our security either to our situation or to our spirit. The enterprising character of the age, our own active, commercial spirit, the great increase which has taken place in the intercourse among civilized and commercial states, has necessarily connected us with other nations, and has given us a high concern in the preservation of those salutary principles upon which that intercourse is founded. We have as clear an interest in international law, as individuals have in the law of society.

Webster insisted that Americans had a duty to those threatened by despotic interventionism, one that included but went beyond narrow American interest: "What do we not owe to the cause of civil and religious liberty? To the principle of lawful resistance? To the principle that society has a right to take part in its own government? As the leading republic in the world, living and breathing in these principles, and advanced, by their operation, with unequalled rapidity in our career, shall we give our consent to bring them into disrepute and disgrace?" As to whether an expression of sympathy did struggling peoples any good, Webster responded: "I hope it may. It may give them courage and spirit, it may assure them of the public regard, teach them that they are not wholly forgotten by the civilized world, and inspire them with constancy in the pursuit of their great end."

The young Webster had insisted that American opposition to despotic transgressions of the law of nations did not mean war or forcible intervention in any European cause.

> Sir, this reasoning mistakes the age. The time has been, indeed, when fleets, armies, and subsidies, were the principal reliances

even in the best causes. But, happily for mankind, a great change has taken place in this respect. Moral causes come into consideration, in proportion as the progress of knowledge is advanced; and the public opinion of the civilized world is rapidly gaining an ascendancy over mere brutal force. It is already able to oppose the most formidable obstruction to the progress of injustice and oppression; and as it grows more intelligent and more intense, it will be more and more formidable. It may be silenced by military power but it cannot be conquered. It is elastic, irrepressible, and invulnerable to the weapons of ordinary warfare.

The United States, according to Webster, could give substance to this "moral cause" and "public opinion" by means other than expressions of sympathy – that is, by promoting and defending its own rights and the law of nations, properly understood. "We stand as an equal among nations, claiming the full benefit of the established international law; and it is our duty to oppose, from the earliest to the latest moment, any innovations upon that code which shall bring into doubt or question our own equal and independent rights" – or the equal and independent rights of other nations. The United States, for instance, defended and advanced the law of nations through its traditional stance of neutrality in foreign wars and by the Monroe Doctrine, both of which stood in opposition to the despotic doctrine of intervention.

As to the particular means which the United States might employ to defend its rights and the law of nations – including the use of force, which could not be ruled out – that was a matter of prudent adjustment to the existing circumstances. Webster, however, disagreed with those who argued that "we should wait till the event comes, without any previous declaration of sentiments upon subjects important to our own rights and interests." Explicit declarations "are often the appropriate means of preventing that which, if unprevented, it might be difficult to redress. A great object in holding diplomatic intercourse is frankly to expose the views and objects of nations, and to prevent, by candid explanation, collision and war." Illiberal declarations, such as those made by the Holy Alliance, could legitimately be countered by liberal declarations.

Those were Webster's views over two decades before the Revolutions of 1848. He believed that they applied with full force to current circumstances. Webster, as noted above, had been a private skeptic about the prospects for success for republican France, but he had held out higher hopes for Hungary until the "despotic power from abroad had intervened." Russia's suppression of Hungarian independence spurred him to revive publicly his arguments about defending the law of nations. In a speech in Boston in November 1849, while still a Senator, Webster had protested against the Czar's demands to Turkey to surrender Kossuth and his associates, a demand "made in derision of the established law of nations." Americans had "wept" at the failure of Hungary's efforts to establish a free government, but the Czar's demands made Webster even "more indignant." The Czar was the supreme lawgiver (and executor) within Russia, "but thanks be to God, he is not the supreme lawgiver or executor of [inter]national law, and every offense against that is an offense against the rights of the civilized world. If he breaks that law in the case of Turkey, or in any other case, the whole civilized world has a right to call him out, and demand his punishment." The whole world, Webster claimed, "will be the tribunal to try him, and he must appear before it, and hold up his hand, and plead, and abide by its judgment."

How were such protests to be effectual? Would not "mere force" exercised by despots like the Czar subdue "the general sentiment of mankind?" To the contrary, Webster argued, the use of force in violation of the law of nations would "diffuse . . . that sentiment, and destroy the power which he most desires to establish and secure." The blood of Kossuth, like that of Abel, "will mingle with the earth, it will mix with the waters of the ocean, the whole civilized world will snuff it in the air, and it will return with awful retribution on the heads of the violations of national law and universal justice." Webster professed not to be able to see the precise time or means in which such retribution would be exacted, "but depend upon it, that, if such an act take place, then thrones, and principalities, and powers, must look out for the consequences." Those consequences would be the violent overthrow of despotism. Webster argued that the "great republic of the world" had been given the providential mission and destiny to rally world public opinion in such cases, "with a voice not to be disregarded" – as long as Americans "take care of their own conduct . . . with hands void of offense." [57]

Webster and the Hülsemann Letter

Hülsemann's written protest about the Mann mission now provided Webster with an opportunity to develop these principles of American foreign policy publicly and authoritatively, as well as to promote the cause of Union and to defend his own political flank. Webster's reply to Hülsemann is remembered by history primarily for its nationalistic bombast but it was hardly an unconsidered or reflexive rebuttal. Webster took three months to formulate

---

[57] Speech to the Festival of the Sons of New Hampshire, 7 November 1849, *The Writings and Speeches of Daniel Webster: National Edition,* 18 vols. (Boston: Little, Brown and Company, 1903), 4: 211-3.

a response. He asked William Hunter, a senior clerk in the Department, and Edward Everett, an experienced diplomat and noted orator in his own right, to prepare initial drafts. Webster consulted those drafts when formulating the final text.[58] "If you say that my Hülsemann letter is boastful and rough, I shall own the soft impeachment," he wrote to his friend, George Ticknor. "My excuse is twofold: 1. I thought it well enough to speak out, and tell the people of Europe who and what we are, and awaken them to a just sense of the unparalleled growth of the country. 2. I wished to write a paper which should touch the national pride, and make a man feel *sheepish* and *silly* who should speak of disunion." Webster's ranking is not unimportant. As historian Donald Spencer notes: "Webster's response to Hülsemann primarily sought to impress upon Europe the reality of the United States' emerging power, and to voice official support for liberal revolutionaries who were struggling against old world monarchs."[59]

In his reply to Hülsemann, Webster dismissed allegations that Mann's mission constituted interference in the domestic affairs of Austria or was disrespectful toward that power. Webster insisted that the Mann mission and the approach of the United States toward the revolutions in central Europe were consistent with the "neutral policy, which has invariably guided the Government of the United States in its foreign relations, as well as with the established and well settled principles of national intercourse, and the doctrines of public law." The U.S. government was surely entitled to inquire into the circumstances of Hungary's claim to independence. Beyond that, Mann had not entered Hungary or tried to communicate with any of its leaders. He had not recognized Hungarian independence precisely because he was unable to find a stable and firm government there. Webster insisted that the President's Message to the Senate, which published Mann's instructions, was not a public manifesto, but was purely a matter internal to the government of the United States. Any foreign protest based on that Message therefore constituted Austrian interference in *American* domestic affairs.[60]

---

[58] Moore, "Kossuth, Part II," loc. cit. Among other political considerations, Webster was considered to be a serious candidate for the 1852 Whig Party presidential nomination.

[59] Webster to Ticknor, 16 January 1851, George Ticknor Curtis, *The Life of Daniel Webster*, 2 vols. (New York: D. Appleton and Company, 1870), 2: 537. Spencer, in *Louis Kossuth and Young America*, p. 42, however, goes too far in saying that "it was, therefore, representative of the Young America movement and of Webster's commitment to its principles." Webster consistently distinguished himself from the Young America/New Democrats agenda.

[60] Webster to Hülsemann, 21 December 1851, *The Papers of Daniel Webster*, Diplomatic Papers, 2: 49-61.

Webster extolled the virtues of the American system of government and compared "the power of this Republic, at the present moment . . . spread over a region, one of the richest and most fertile on the Globe," with "the possessions of the House of Hapsburg, [which] are but as a patch on the earth's surface." As to Hülsemann's threats of economic retaliation, Webster responded that "the Government and people of the United States are quite willing to take their chances, and abide by their destiny." If Mann had been treated as a spy, "the Cabinet of Vienna may be assured, that if it had carried, or attempted to carry, any such lawless purpose into effect, in the case of an authorized Agent of this Government, the Spirit of the People of this Country, would have demanded immediate hostilities, to be waged by the utmost exertion of the Power of the Republic, military and naval."

Webster argued that the American people and their representatives would naturally express their sympathy for such extraordinary events that "appeared to have their origin in those great ideas of responsible and popular governments, on which the American Constitutions themselves are wholly founded." Nor could they suppress "either the thoughts, or the hopes, which arise in men's minds, in other countries, from contemplating their successful example of Free Government." Webster acknowledged, "that the prevalence on the other continent, of sentiments favorable to Republican Liberty, is the result of the re-action of America upon Europe; and the source and centre of this re-action has doubtless been, and now is, in these United States. The position thus belonging to the United States is a fact as inseparable from their History, their Constitutional organization, and their character." He reminded Hülsemann, however, that there was another side to the story, represented by "the powers composing the European Alliance," whose contrary views about politics stem from "the History and Constitutional organization of the Governments of those powers. The Sovereigns, who form that alliance, have . . . in their Manifestoes and Declarations, denounced the popular ideas of the age, in terms so comprehensive as of necessity to include the United States, and their forms of Government. It is well known that one of the leading principles, announced by the allied Sovereigns after the restoration of the Bourbons, is, that all popular, or constitutional rights, are holden no otherwise than as granted and indulgences from crowned heads."

Thus, according to Webster, America would and could not be deterred from expressing its opinions and sympathies. That was its right under the law of nations and a legitimate means of shaping world public opinion. The United States refused to be "gagged" while the successors of the Holy Alliance promoted their doctrines of despotism. Webster insisted that American expressions did not constitute interference in the affairs of other peoples or hostility toward existing regimes. Russia and the United States, for instance, had always maintained relations "of the most friendly kind," which "have never been deemed by either party to require any compromise of the peculiar views upon subjects of domestic or foreign policy, or the true origins of Governments." The United States was prepared to give as well as get in this debate, confident that the tide of progress and enlightened opinion was on its side – "the government of the United States heard these denunciations of its fundamental principles without remonstrance, or the disturbance of its equanimity." But it did draw the line when the European alliance "felt it their right to interfere with the political movements of foreign states," and it rejected absolutely the notion that "neutral powers should await the recognition of the new Government by the parent state" before themselves recognizing governments "brought by successful revolutions into the family of Nations." Despots were on notice, further, that Americans would cheer even louder when the cause of liberty abroad was endangered by outside intervention.

Hungary, Webster argued to Hülsemann, met any objective standards for national independence. "The Hungarian People are three or four times as numerous as the inhabitants of these United States were when the American Revolution broke out. They possess in a distinct language, and in other respects, important elements of a separate nationality, which the Anglo Saxon race in this Country did not possess." Webster later elaborated on the criteria for national self-determination as they applied to Hungary and prospectively to all nations seeking independence and popular sovereignty:

> Thus it is evident that, in point of power, so far as power depends upon population, Hungary possesses as much power as England proper or even the Kingdom of Prussia. Well, then, there is population enough, there are people enough. Who, then, are they? They are distinct from the nations that surround them. They are distinct from the Austrians on the west, and the Turks on the east; and I will say, in the next place, that they are an <u>enlightened</u> nation. They have their own history, they have their traditions, they are attached to their own institutions – institutions which have existed for more than a thousand years.... She has shown through her whole history, for many hundreds of years, an attachment to the principles of civil liberty, and of law and of order, and of obedience to the Constitution which the will of the great majority has established.... It ought to be known that Hungary stands out from it above her [Eastern European and Asian] neighbors in

all that respects free institutions, constitutional government, and a hereditary love of liberty.[61]

As political scientist David Hendrickson observes: "External self-determination (freedom from foreign rule) was a necessary condition of internal self-determination and was itself fundamental to the 'liberty and independence' these nineteenth-century Americans prized."[62]

If Webster's reply to Hülsemann was to have its intended effect of shaping foreign and domestic opinion, it would have to be made public. The Senate, prompted no doubt by Webster, within a few days passed a resolution asking the President for the relevant correspondence between the United States and Austria. The administration did so, and included the Webster letter. The Senate debated whether to print and thereby publicize these documents, which were certain to have an inflammatory effect on public opinion. Cass told his colleagues that if these documents, and especially Webster's argument, had been available at the time he offered his resolution about withdrawing diplomatic recognition from Austria, the resolution very likely would have been adopted.

A number of Senators, however, including Jefferson Davis of Mississippi, objected to a resolution to print ten thousand copies, claiming that it was too expensive to circulate a document that contained nothing new about American foreign policy doctrines. Henry Clay warned that publicizing the Webster-Hülsemann exchange would only exacerbate relations with Austria long after Hungarian independence had been lost. He noted that Americans would be displeased if Vienna had sent an agent with authority to investigate the revolt of an American state. The resolution failed by three votes, 21-18. Upon a motion to reconsider by Douglas, the Senate subsequently agreed to print five thousand copies. Clay was the only member to vote against the final motion to print.[63]

Webster's letter, as he intended, produced an immediate sensation in America. According to American diplomats, it also had an effect abroad. The American Minister to Great Britain, Abbott Lawrence, told Webster that the principles of the Hülsemann letter would elevate the position of the United States at home and abroad and that it would strengthen those who were promoting civil rights. Lawrence provided Lord Palmerston a copy of the letter.

---

[61] Speech at the Kossuth Banquet, *The Papers of Daniel Webster*, Diplomatic Papers, 2: 101.

[62] Hendrickson, *Union, Nation, or Empire*, p. 21.

[63] Curti, *Austria and the United States, 1848-1852*, pp. 166-7, 168-9; Spencer, *Louis Kossuth and Young America*, p. 35.

The American envoy at The Hague and in Vienna reported that the friends of liberty and free government praised the letter and its author. The Washington *Union* predicted that the reply would circulate throughout Europe and inspire new confidence in republican institutions. [64]

The Austrian government was not among those disposed so favorably. Webster's reply to Hülsemann could have triggered a decision by Vienna to break diplomatic relations with the United States. The Austrian government, however, decided to take the high road and express its hope for the reestablishment of the long-standing friendly relations between the two nations. (Webster probably calculated that he could offer such insulting language without provoking a real crisis and that even if he had, Austria itself did not pose a strategic or military threat.) Hülsemann was instructed, however, to repeat his insistence that the Mann mission – along with Stiles' earlier offer of mediation, and President Taylor's expression of sympathy for the Hungarians in his Message to the Senate – constituted unwarranted interference in Austrian affairs. The Austrian government noted that Russia had recalled its ambassador from Paris because of expressions of sympathy for the Polish people that had been made in the French Chamber of Deputies. Even so, Hülsemann told Webster, the Austrians would not take official cognizance of his note.

> For what would it serve to contest the glory which Mr. Webster invokes for his country, having assured Europe of the preponderant influence of republican ideas, an influence for which it is doubtful that Europe is grateful to America? To what end would it serve to recall to Mr. Webster in reply to the pompous description which he has made of the growing prosperity of the United States, that this confederation contains the germs of disunion which the central government has up to this time tried in vain to extinguish? The question whether North America owes its prosperity exclusively to its liberal institutions, or to fortunate circumstances independent of man's will, would equally furnish material for endless discussion. But we do consider the mission of Mr. Mann as an interference in our domestic affairs and we maintain our protest.

The Austrian diplomat took the edge off his note by expressing satisfaction with President Fillmore's recently-published Annual Message, which contained an assurance of America's intention to abstain from all interference in the affairs of foreign powers. [65]

---

[64] May, *Contemporary American Opinion of the Mid-Century Revolutions*, pp. 58-59.

[65] Curti, *Austria and the United States, 1848-1852*, pp. 164-7 (Hülsemann reply).

The Kossuth Affair

Despite the close of the Webster-Hülsemann correspondence, the issue of Hungary did not go away. Over the previous year Congress and American public opinion had become increasingly interested in the fate of the exiles from the Hungarian Revolution, in particular, Louis Kossuth. After Kossuth fled to the Ottoman Empire in late 1849, the Czar and the Austrian Emperor had demanded his extradition. The British government had urged the Porte to resist these demands and to assure the safety of Hungarian refugees. At one point it appeared that the Sultan would demand Kossuth's conversion to Islam as a condition for his continued protection. A number of Polish exiles had already converted to protect their status.[66]

During his confinement, Kossuth addressed a public appeal to Americans. He asked for armed assistance and claimed that "a shot fired by an English or American vessel from the Adriatic would be like the trumpet at the city of Jericho." State legislatures and private groups in the United States passed resolutions and formulated petitions urging the federal government to seek Kossuth's release. Senator Pierre Soulé of Louisiana offered a resolution in Congress requesting the President to intercede on behalf of the Hungarian exiles. George Sanders, Samuel F. Colt and other Americans in Paris urged the U.S. legation in Constantinople to express concern for Kossuth's safety and to defend his right of sanctuary. They proposed that, if necessary, the U.S. Navy should provide shelter to the Hungarian refugees and offer its services in defense of the Sultan if he was attacked by Russia or Austria. The United States government was not willing to go this far but in January 1850, then-Secretary of State Clayton had instructed the newly-dispatched American Minister to Turkey, George P. Marsh, to seek Kossuth's release; he promised to transport him to the United States in a public vessel, with the reservation that the United States did not intend "to interfere, by entangling ourselves in any serious controversy with Russia or Austria." Marsh provided Turkish officials with extracts from Presidential statements and Congressional speeches to buttress his plea.[67]

In February 1851, Senator Henry S. Foote introduced a new resolution calling upon the Executive to intervene on Kossuth's behalf. The resolution was adopted by both Houses and signed by the President on March

---

[66] Moore, "Kossuth: Part, II," pp. 258-9.

[67] Spencer, *Louis Kossuth and Young America*, p. 43 (Jericho); John H. Komlos, *Louis Kossuth in America 1851-1852* (Buffalo: East European Institute, 1973), pp. 36, 38; Field, *America and the Mediterranean World*, p. 229 (entangling).

3. (The Senate approved the resolution without a roll call; the House vote was 126 to 42.) Secretary of State Webster, who had called for American intervention on Kossuth's behalf while a private citizen and who was now basking in the glow of support for his letter to Hülsemann, instructed Marsh to renew his efforts. Webster also reaffirmed that the United States had "no desire or intention to interfere in any manner with questions of public policy or international or municipal relations of other governments." The Turkish government welcomed the opportunity to resolve its own dilemma and, despite formal Austrian protests, agreed to the arrangement. On September 10, 1851, Kossuth and approximately sixty other refugees boarded the USS *Mississippi*.[68]

Kossuth's Congressional sponsors assumed, or professed to assume, that he and his followers would take up permanent residence in the United States and live out their lives in "retirement," along with thousands of other refugees from the failed European revolutions. Webster wrote to Marsh, confirming that this was the expectation of the U.S. government. America would play its traditional role in offering asylum – a role which was consistent with the law of nations – as a humanitarian measure, and (although Webster did not say so) as a means of offering indirect encouragement to future revolutionaries, who would feel able to run greater personal risks knowing that they had a permanent refuge if their efforts at regime change failed. Over the summer, however, Hülsemann provided Webster with documentary evidence that Kossuth retained his revolutionary ambitions. The Austrian diplomat had inserted items in American newspapers which reported Kossuth's inflammatory conduct while aboard the *Mississippi*. (Kossuth, for example, was said to have declared that he did not seek asylum in the United States but would be "an avenger . . . against the oppressors of a holy cause.") Webster and Fillmore again offered Hülsemann assurances that the United States would treat Kossuth as a private individual and would not encourage his projects against foreign governments. The United States, for instance, would not offer Kossuth a cannon salute when he arrived in the United States.[69]

---

[68] John W. Oliver, "Kossuth's Appeal to the Middle West, 1852," *Mississippi Valley Historical Review* 14 (March 1928): 483; *Congressional Globe*, 31:2, pp. 580, 777; Field, *America and the Mediterranean World*, pp. 230-1; May, *Contemporary American Opinion of the Mid-Century Revolutions*, pp. 72-74.

[69] Komlos, *Louis Kossuth in America 1851-1852*, p. 47; May, *Contemporary American Opinion of the Mid-Century Revolutions*, p. 74 (avenger); Curti, *Austria and the United States, 1848-1852*, pp. 172-7.

Kossuth, meanwhile, diverted the *Mississippi* to stops in the Mediterranean and in France, where he proclaimed the imminence of another European revolution. His presence provoked widespread demonstrations and occasional outbreaks of violence. This caused considerable difficulties for the ship's captain, John Long, who had been ordered to preserve strict American neutrality during the voyage. Kossuth eventually left the American frigate at Gibraltar and made his way to England, where he was generously welcomed by liberal Englishmen, such as Richard Cobden, and sympathetic Americans, including Robert J. Walker, former Secretary of the Treasury. Walker publicly criticized Russian intervention in Hungary and anticipated an impending conflict between liberty and despotism in which England would be supported by "millions" of Americans who would flock to Europe to fight for the cause of liberty. "England and America combined, need not fear the despotisms of the world in arms." The radical press in England called for an "Anglo-American Republic" that would lead the democratic movement, with an American force "raising the standard of universal democracy" in Europe. Given Walker's status as a former U.S. government official and prominent Democrat, Kossuth may well have taken his views as representative of American opinion, or at least that of the Democratic Party. This impression was reinforced when Kossuth received a wildly enthusiastic reception when he reached New York City in December 1851 aboard a private vessel, the *Humboldt*. His arrival included a cannon salute by the order of the commandant of forts, which Kossuth interpreted as recognition of his "official character" by the U.S. government.[70]

During his seven-month stay in the United States, Kossuth sought to raise private funds in support of renewed revolutionary activity, but he also advocated more direct and official American support of Hungarian independence – what became known as a policy of "intervention for non-intervention." In a series of speeches – one estimate is that he delivered over five hundred talks – Kossuth proposed an explicit replacement for the doctrine of neutrality and non-interference in European affairs set out in Washington's Farewell Address, and for the geographic division between the Old and New Worlds established by the Monroe Doctrine. He argued that Russian expansionism into central Europe represented the leading edge of a threat to the prospects for national independence and liberty around the world. The Czar realized that

---

[70] Komlos, *Louis Kossuth in America 1851-1852*, pp. 53, 66-7 (combined); May, *Contemporary American Opinion of the Mid-Century Revolutions*, p. 79; Riepma, "Young America," pp. 110-11 (raising); Curti, *Austria and the United States, 1848-1852*, p. 182.

his despotic rule was insecure so long as free governments existed anywhere; after conquering the continent, Russia would turn against the United States, playing upon its sectional differences.

To address this threat, Kossuth insisted that Americans must go beyond vague expressions of sympathy and support for the law of nations. The Monroe Doctrine should be extended to the gates of St. Petersburg; further, the United States should commit itself to a foreign policy that actively promoted democracy, liberty and resistance to Russian tyranny. Tangible aid, not appeals to world public opinion, would be required to win Hungarian freedom and the liberty of other nations. Specifically, the U.S. government should be prepared to recognize Hungarian independence and warn Russia that it considered intervention in Hungarian affairs to be a violation of the law of nations, a violation to which America could not be indifferent. To give credibility to that policy, the United States should form an alliance with England and send an American fleet to the eastern Mediterranean to protect key trade routes and to bolster Turkey, Russia's regional enemy, whose army was capable of defeating Russia if supported by the U.S. Navy. (A few years later, Kossuth would advocate American participation in the Crimean War coalition against Russia.) The U.S. government should offer assistance to the Hungarian cause in the form of a gift or a loan, as well as reinterpret or amend its neutrality laws to allow private citizens and businesses the maximum leeway to aid the Hungarian cause.

Kossuth, as a rule, insisted that he did not intend to embroil the United States in a European war. He argued that a forward American policy of this sort would deter the Russians, in part (one might infer) by posing the prospect of an English-Turkish alliance aided by American naval and logistical support. He argued that just as the Monroe Doctrine had prevented war in the New World, the extension of that doctrine to Europe on the principle of "intervention for non-intervention," would have a similar effect on the continent. Occasionally, however, Kossuth acknowledged that ". . . should Russia not respect the declaration of your country, then you are obliged – literally obliged – to go to war . . . But you are powerful enough to defy any power on earth . . . give to humanity the glorious example of a great people going to war, not for egotistical interest, but for justice, for the law of nations . . . It will be the last war, because it will make nations contented – contented, because free." Kossuth's supporters warned him that such overtly warlike rhetoric would defeat his cause, and he more typically argued that "a war on this account by your country is utterly impossible. . . . such a declaration of just principles would ensure to the nations of Europe 'fair play' in their struggle for freedom and independence, because the declaration ... will be respected." [71]

During his subsequent travels around the United States, Kossuth tailored his message to regional sensibilities. In the West, where there were large numbers of new European immigrants, he spoke about national liberation and warned of the Russian threat. In New England, he emphasized the need for Americans to extend the blessings of liberty. In the South, he warned that Russia might close off the European cotton market once it came to dominate the continent. He also noted that Hungary and the South both favored states' rights and were opposed to centralization and foreign interference. At the end of his stay in America, he called for a union of the Hungarian, Italian and German exile communities in the United States. A free Germany would provide a bulwark against European despotism and a rallying point for republicans elsewhere (the Germans, as the largest refugee community, would also provide votes and influence to the proper, forward-looking elements in American politics). Kossuth, however, studiously maintained a position of neutrality with regard to slavery in the United States. As he told an anti-slavery group in New York: "that as I have avowed it in Europe and everywhere, that I claim for my sovereign nation the independent right to dispose of its own domestic affairs, and that I, therefore, feel it to be my duty to respect this principle in every nation, as I wish to see it respected in my own." Kossuth explained this as a matter of consistency – for instance, when in England, he had not aligned himself with the Chartist movement and avoided an invitation to attend a working men's reception. He also evaded questions about his stance on the Irish question. [72]

Over the ensuing months, various important and would-be important figures put forward proposals for actualizing Kossuth's ideas about American intervention on behalf of non-intervention. A Tammany Hall delegation of Democrats, led by Daniel Sickles, told Kossuth that it was confident that the United States would take part in the future war for freedom. One hundred thousand men would join that war and millions more would contribute money and energy, overriding the hesitancy of the moneyed interest. Horace Greeley, from the progressive Whig perspective, argued:

---

[71] May, *Contemporary American Opinion of the Mid-Century Revolutions*, pp. 90-1; Komlos, *Louis Kossuth in America 1851-1852*, p. 85; Kossuth, Speech to the Bar of New York, in P.C. Headley, ed., *The Life of Louis Kossuth* (Auburn, NY: Derby and Miller, 1852), p. 441; Kossuth, Address at the Congressional Banquet in Washington, 7 January 1852, in Mayo W. Hazeltine and others, eds., *Masterpieces of Eloquence*, 25 vols. (New York: Collier & Son, 1905), 14: 5806.

[72] Komlos, *Louis Kossuth in America 1851-1852*, pp. 140, 144, 147-8 (avowed); Riepma, "Young America," pp. 238-9.

Yes, KOSSUTH has visited our shores – even as I write, his presence hallows and ennobles this chief city of the western world. He is here, though unconsciously, to rebuke the degeneracy and factiousness of our partisan squabbles, the hollowness of our boasted love of liberty, if we turn a deaf ear to the cry of the oppressed in either hemisphere, the sordidness of our common life and the meanness of its aims. He is here to arouse us to a consciousness of the majesty of our national position and the responsibilities it involves; to show us that we cannot safely sleep while despots are forging chains for the yet unfettered nations, as well as to bind more securely their present victims; that, even if we have no regard for others' rights, we must assume an attitude of resistance to the expanding dominion of the Autocrat if only to secure our own. That "God hath made of one blood all the nations that dwell on the face of the earth," – that we should "do to others as we would have them do to us," – that we have no right to repel solicitude as to the fate of tyranny's victims, by the callous question, "Am I my brother's keeper?" – that the free nations of earth cannot afford, even were they base enough to wish, to leave each other to be assailed in succession by the banded might of despotism, and so overwhelmed and crushed – these are solemn truths which Governor Kossuth is among us to proclaim and enforce with the earnestness of a martyr's conviction and an exiled patriot's zeal.[73]

Massachusetts Governor James Boutwell declared that the United States should assert the right "to interfere in favor of any republican or constitutional regime, whenever and wherever it might be threatened by a European monarch." The Massachusetts state legislature concurred, declaring that it was the "duty of duly constitutionally governed nations to cultivate intimate relations so that if an emergency should arise they might easily combine against despots." The governor of Pennsylvania declared himself in favor of military intervention against Russia and a prominent group of citizens in the capital endorsed the "Harrisonburg Resolutions," which embraced Kossuth's program. The Pennsylvania legislature endorsed the principle of intervention for nonintervention. At a public meeting in Pittsburgh, former Congressman Moses Hampton urged the U.S. government, if Russian interference in Hungarian affairs persisted, to "remonstrate with Emperor Nicholas, use all diplomatic

---

[73] Greeley, introduction to Headley, ed., *The Life of Louis Kossuth*, p. x.

means. But if they fail, write your commands at the point of the sword, and seal them with the cannon's mouth."

The Ohio State legislature resolved that "an attack in any form upon them [the Hungarians] is a most dangerous weakening of our own influence and power; and that all such combinations of kings against people should be regarded by us now as they were in 1776, and so far as circumstances will admit the parallel, should and will be so treated." The Ohio Senate offered the Hungarians a form of lend-lease, to loan "all the public arms and ammunitions of war belonging to the state, which remains undistributed, to be returned in good order upon the achievement of Hungarian Liberty." The Democratic Party of Ohio's state convention warned that "rather than witness the utter extinction of republicanism as a fact, and a principle in Europe," the United States should be prepared to "encounter the shock of arms in the field of battle." [74]

George Sanders, an ardent New Democrat, who had returned to the United States as editor of the *Democratic Review*, argued that "we must transfer the field of war to the soil of Europe, and change the issue from a contest, whether the monarchs will beard us here, to a contest whether they and their impious practices shall for an hour longer be tolerated there." Sanders insisted that the neutrality laws which prohibited the exportation of weapons were unconstitutional. He told Kossuth that he and his friends were prepared to crew and arm a steamer and put it at the Hungarians' disposal, with more ships to follow. The Detroit *Free Press*, from the home state of Lewis Cass, argued that "an American force in the battlefield of Europe, raising the standard of universal democracy, would call forth every people of the continent." The display of the American flag alone "would strike terror and despair to the hearts of old Despotism, conscious of its doom. Its very coming would mean victory." An officer in the Army Corps of Engineers, speaking at a Jackson Day banquet hosted by the Democrats, argued that leading military men had studied the problem and concluded that "in any contest with the United States, Russia could not float an inch board [sic] anywhere below the low water mark, except by sufferance." If

---

[74] The secondary sources cited do not always distinguish clearly between direct quotes and paraphrases of these documents. Spencer, *Louis Kossuth and Young America*, pp. 109 (Boutwell), 123; May, *Contemporary American Opinion of the Mid-Century Revolutions*, pp. 94, 113 (Massachusetts legislature); Komlos, Louis Kossuth in America 1851-1852, pp. 97, 119 (weakening; undistributed); Oliver, "Kossuth's Appeal to the Middle West, 1852," p. 486 (remonstrate); Riepma, "Young America," p. 154 (extinction).

the United States decided to intervene, "we could knock at the gates of St. Petersburg" before the Czar could recall his forces from Hungary.[75]

The Opposition to Kossuth Emerges

While Kossuth was beginning his tour of the United States, Whigs and Democrats were scrambling to position themselves for the election of 1852. For a time it appeared that "Kossuth mania" might prove to be a winning issue for whichever presidential candidate could best associate with the Hungarian cause. But Kossuth's unwillingness to remain in quiet exile, and his insistence on direct U.S. support, soon generated a public backlash in a nation increasingly divided about its role in the world and the nature of its regime at home.

Many – not all – abolitionists and strong anti-slavery activists turned against Kossuth because of his unwillingness to condemn slavery along with Russian and Austrian despotism. William Lloyd Garrison wrote a one hundred page "Letter to Louis Kossuth concerning Freedom and Slavery in the U.S.," which castigated Kossuth as a hypocrite. Many – not all – southerners opposed Kossuth because his rhetoric of human rights and national liberation held disquieting implications for slaveholders, especially when linked to calls for intervention by the national (federal) government on behalf of liberty. Southerners like Calhoun criticized such calls for intervention as a dangerous innovation in traditional American foreign policy, one that had been surreptitiously introduced by the radical northern anti-slavery movement. The New Orleans *Bulletin* noted that Kossuth's supporters included noted anti-slavery politicians like Seward, Hale and Giddings. "If we sanction interference we will be the first who will be interfered with; if we become a consenting party to the project of overthrowing European forms of government our own institutions will be the first to be crushed beneath the juggernautic wheels of unlicensed, unconfined radicalism and fierce, relentless and bigoted fanaticism."[76]

Francis Bowen, the editor of the *North American Review*, the bastion of intellectually conservative Whiggery, argued that the so-called Hungarian Revolution was not a movement in favor of national independence and republicanism but actually was a "war of races," in which the "arrogant, cruel, and tyrannical" Magyars sought their own state in order to dominate

---

[75] Spencer, *Louis Kossuth and Young America*, pp. 45 (battlefield), 114 (Jackson Association), 117-8 (transfer); Komlos, *Louis Kossuth in America 1851-1852*, p. 91.

[76] Spencer, *Louis Kossuth and Young America*, pp. 103, 106 (juggernautic).

ethnic minorities, particularly the Slavs, which had enjoyed the protection of the Austrian Empire. Orestes Bronson and the Catholic hierarchy in the United States warned that Kossuth represented radicalism and aggressive Protestantism. Irish immigrants opposed Kossuth's appeal for an Anglo-American alliance. Interventionism, one New York writer claimed, was the "great question" of the day, because it had proved remarkably adaptable to annexationist schemes:

> The annexation of Texas and the Lopez expedition in Cuba – both peculiarly southern measures – were only parts of the same platform of universal, everlasting intervention which is now becoming the reigning idea of Northern and Western States, as expounded by Webster, Kossuth, Cass, Kinkel, and all the rest. . . . We are in the midst . . . of a radical, total, unextinquishable revolution . . . which will be productive of the most momentous contingencies that this country has ever seen.[77]

The Whig administration of Millard Fillmore was placed in a difficult position by these countervailing forces of public opinion. Webster, who recently had fanned the flames of American nationalism with his reply to Hülsemann, now leaned hard in the other direction. He was especially concerned that "Kossuth mania" might spill over into greater political support for aggressive expansionism and filibustering in the Western hemisphere, which would in turn generate a political backlash that would destroy the Union. "You cannot fail to see how very probable it is that a more warlike administration than that which now exists is likely to come into power fifteen months hence," Webster wrote to his friend Abbot Lawrence. "There is not only existing among us a spirit favorable to further territorial acquisition, but a zeal also for intervention in the affairs of other states, of a fearful character and already of considerable extent. This spirit has gained great strength and vivacity from Kossuth's visit and speeches. At one time the whole – or nearly the whole – city of New York seemed quite crazy." Webster hoped that sober minds from North and South would abate the Kossuth fever, but he feared that a large section of the Democratic party intended to take advantage of his presence "to bring the country, if they can, to the doctrine and the practice of intervention." "I am at a great loss

---

[77] Francis Bowen, North American Review 70 (January 1850): 121; 72 (January 1851): 238-40; Spencer, Louis Kossuth and Young America, p. 43; Riepma, "Young America," p. 160 (unextinguishable).

what to do, and what to say. I hope I may be able to steer clear of trouble, on both sides." [78]

The President's Annual Message in December 1851, delivered just before Kossuth's arrival in New York, had already reflected these countervailing pressures. Fillmore cited Washington's maxim of friendly relations with all, but entangling alliances with none, and reiterated the line of argument from the previous Message that had drawn praise from Hülsemann. "Our true mission is not to propagate our opinions or impose upon other countries our form of government by artifice or force, but to teach by example and show by our success, moderation, and justice the blessings of self-government and the advantages of free institutions. Let every people choose for itself and make and alter its political institutions to suit its own condition and convenience." However, Fillmore was not willing simply to ignore America's interest in favorable conditions for liberal regime change:

> while we avow and maintain this neutral policy ourselves, we are anxious to see the same forbearance on the part of other nations whose forms of government are different from our own. The deep interest which we feel in the spread of liberal principles and the establishment of free governments and the sympathy with which we witness every struggle against oppression forbid that we should be indifferent to a case in which the strong arm of a foreign power is invoked to stifle public sentiment and repress the spirit of freedom in any country.

Fillmore left it to Congress to determine the manner in which "Governor Kossuth and his companions" should be received and treated. [79]

In his correspondence with Lawrence, Webster took credit for the Message, which "will have shown you the ground on which I stand, with the entire *concurrence* and *support* of the President, and the other heads of department. You perceive how difficult it is to prevent these lawless invasions of other countries, but we shall do all we can." Webster was especially fearful that if the "miserable government" of Mexico collapsed, it would invite "aggression and ... cupidity in all quarters." He favored a policy, if it could be sustained, "to uphold Mexico and save her government from disunion, for the reason

---

[78] Webster to Abbot Lawrence, 29 December 1851, *The Writings and Speeches of Daniel Webster: National Edition*, 4: 633-5; Spencer, *Louis Kossuth and Young America*, p. 46; Komlos, *Louis Kossuth in America 1851-1852*, p. 98; Webster to Paige, 25 December 1851, *The Writings and Speeches of Daniel Webster: National Edition*, 18: 499.

[79] Fillmore, Annual Message to Congress, 2 December 1851, at http://www.presidency.ucsb.edu/ws/index.php?pid=29492.

that it is better for us that Mexico should be able to maintain an independent government, than that she should break to pieces and fall into other hands, even though those hands were our own." [80]

To Welcome or Not to Welcome Kossuth: The Senate Debates

With these domestic and international variables in mind, Webster decided that he could not go too far in the direction of caution and cede the high moral ground on the matter of Kossuth. He persuaded Senator Foote to introduce a resolution of welcome to Kossuth, offering the Senate's "profound respect" for the Hungarian cause. Foote made no secret of the fact that he had been put up to it by the Secretary of State.[81] Foote chastised those Whigs who were reluctant to offer such a courtesy. "I discover in certain quarters that hints have already been given, that it would be a dangerous thing for Kossuth to be allowed to come to this country and deliver such bold and soul-stirring harangues in favor of the great principles of which he is the champion, from the fear that his eloquence might have the effect of unduly liberalizing the minds of the people of America, and might impart a still more republican cast to the minds of thinking millions in this country."

> ... there is a great struggle going on at this moment in all parts of the civilized world between the principles of freedom and the principles of slavery. The tyrants of the earth have combined for the overthrow of liberty. In some instances open attempts are made to break down political and religious freedom. In others, the means employed by the enemies of freedom are more disguised and insidious, but not all less dangerous. At such a moment does it behove [sic] the American people to join the side of despotism, or to stand by the cause of freedom? We must do one or the other. We cannot avoid the solemn alternative presented. Those who are not for us are against us. Those who are not for freedom are for slavery.[82]

Foote's observation – "those who are not for freedom are for slavery" – triggered the predictable rejoinder of the staunch anti-slavery Senator from New Hampshire, John P. Hale: "Exactly." Hale offered an amendment to Foote's resolution that expressed sympathy not only for Kossuth but for

---

[80] Webster to Abbot Lawrence, 29 December 1851, *The Writings and Speeches of Daniel Webster: National Edition*, 4: 633-5.

[81] Riepma, "Young America," p. 128. Foote also introduced a resolution calling for the relief of the Irish who had been exiled after their abortive revolution of 1848.

[82] *Congressional Globe*, 32:1, pp. 22-3.

the "victims of oppression everywhere," such as the Irish and, implicitly, American slaves, an implication which the southern members of both parties immediately resented.[83]

Lewis Cass expressed dismay that once again, the weight of America's moral authority was being squandered by such divisions. "I had hoped that this resolution would have met with no opposition, for we cannot conceal from ourselves the fact that it will lose a great part of its value, both at home and abroad, unless it meets with the unanimous consent of the two Houses of Congress." Cass argued that Kossuth represented a cause even greater than that of national (Hungarian) independence, as important as that was – "he comes here as the representative of a sacred cause – of a great and glorious cause, involving the human rights in every nation of the globe." Cass opposed Hale's formulation of the problem, meant clearly "to bring up the old question of slavery. . . . I am, therefore, opposed to this abstract declaration as to the rights of man, though I believe in my soul I am just as good a friend to them as the gentlemen from New Hampshire. . . . When a proposition comes up of any practical description, in which the rights of man are concerned, I will go as far as any gentleman."[84]

Senate opposition to Foote's resolution of welcome grew as reports of Kossuth's more strident rhetoric in New York reached Washington. Senator Underwood agreed with Cass's premise about the need to avoid abstract and unconditional statements about human rights, but he drew the opposite conclusion. "But every Senator must perceive that if we commence the system of complimenting foreigners for distinguished services in their own country in behalf of human liberty, there is no end; there is no limit to the exercise of this power, from this time forever." They would be legitimizing "that intervention in the affairs of other nations which has been hostile to the genius of our government and to the practice of every administration from Washington down to this day." Underwood and Senator Jeremiah Clemens of Alabama also challenged Kossuth's credentials as a republican: they noted that he had asserted while in England that a monarchy as well as a republic could serve the cause of freedom; and they cited Hungarian revolutionaries who had opposed the formation of a republican government in 1848-9. Clemens characterized Kossuth as a dictator and the leader of a war to establish the supremacy of the Magyar race. Senator William Dawson warned that if a resolution of welcome passed, Kossuth would proceed to Washington on the mistaken assumption

---

[83] *Congressional Globe*, 32:1, p. 23.

[84] *Congressional Globe*, 32:1, pp. 23-5.

that the U.S. government endorsed his policy agenda and the policy of intervention for non-intervention. "Is it not, then, due to candor – do not honor and magnanimity require us to announce to Kossuth that this Government has no such design?" Dawson asked. If a resolution of any sort was passed, he favored an amendment that would "announce to him that he is mistaken; that he is not to come to the seat of Government of this great nation under the expectation that this Government gives any pledge, or any assurance, that they will sustain him at any time." [85]

Seward and the Progressive Whig Case for Kossuth

To prevent defeat or the narrow passage of the Foote Resolution, progressive Whig William Seward offered a substitute which merely expressed a "cordial welcome" to Kossuth and his associates. Seward believed that Foote, a supporter of Webster's presidential aspirations, had been persuaded by the Secretary of State to introduce his original resolution in order to take political advantage of Kossuth's visit – and to preempt Seward's role as the leading exponent of Kossuth's cause and the progressive Whig case for promoting liberty abroad. [86] Over the next few months, Seward attempted to reclaim that role and to set out his understanding of a proper forward policy for the United States. In coming years Seward would appeal to a "higher law" than the Constitution to condemn slavery; here he appealed to a "higher and greater tribunal" than the U.S. Congress:

> It is a tribunal whose existence and jurisdiction and authority we have acknowledged, and to whose judgment-seat we have already called the Turk, the Austrian, and the Russian, to account for their action in regard to Hungary and to Kossuth. It is the tribunal of the public opinion of the world – the public opinion of mankind. Sir, that tribunal is unerring in its judgments. It is constituted of the great, the wise, and the good of all nations – not only of the great, and wise, and good who are now living, but of the great, the wise, and the good of all ages. Before that tribunal, states, great and small, are equal. Ay, before that tribunal the proudest empire is equaled by its humblest citizen or subject. Yes, the

---

[85] *Congressional Globe*, 32:1, pp. 21-2, 25-6, 52, 71-2; Komlos, *Louis Kossuth in America 1851-1852*, p. 76.

[86] Spencer, *Louis Kossuth and Young America*, pp. 74-5; Komlos, *Louis Kossuth in America 1851-1852*, p. 81.

Indian and the serf are equal there to the American Republic and to the Russian Empire.[87]

When America was called before the tribunal of the public opinion of the world to justify its response to Kossuth, it would be more than entitled – it would be required – to explain that it had done everything that was not positively forbidden by the law of nations to promote human rights and liberalized regime change. "I believe that no man will deny the principle, that a nation may do for the cause of liberty in other nations whatever the laws of nations do not forbid. I plant myself upon that principle. What the laws of nations do not forbid, any nation may do for the cause of liberty in any other nation, in any other country.

> Now, the laws of nations do not forbid hospitality. The laws of nations do not forbid us to sympathize with the exile – to sympathize with the overthrown champion of freedom. The laws of nature demand that hospitality, and from the very inmost sources of our nature springs up that sympathy. . . . Sir, the laws of nature require – the laws of nations command hospitality to those who fly from oppression and despair. And this is all that we have done, and all that we propose to do. . . .
>
> I shall be told, that we may not intervene in this, which is a domestic affair of a foreign government. It is true that we may not intervene in the affair of any government for unjust purposes, nor can we intervene by force for even just purposes. But this is the only restraint imposed on us by the law of nations. That law, while it declares that every government has the absolute right to deal with its own citizens, according to its own laws, independently of any other, affords a large verge and scope for the exercise of offices of courtesy, kindness, benevolence, and charity. It is Montesquieu who says that "the law of nations is founded upon the principle, that every nation is bound in time of peace to do to every other nation all the good it possibly can, and in time of war, the least evil it possibly can consistently with its own real interests."

The failure to offer Kossuth the common courtesy of a "warm, generous, a cordial welcome" would not only demoralize the American public and "discourage the hopes and expectations of the friends of freedom throughout the

---

[87] Seward text taken primarily from *Congressional Globe*, 32:1, pp. 88-9; see also pp. 41-2, 66-7, 72-3; and Appendix, pp. 243-7.

world"; it would "encourage the advocates of oppression throughout Europe in their efforts to prevent the transition of the nations of that continent from under the system of force to the voluntary system of government which we have established and commended to their adoption." Seward pointed out that England had already shown its willingness to honor Kossuth and offer him exile. "Are you prepared to give the world evidence that *you* cannot receive the representative of liberty and republicanism, whom England can honor, shelter and protect?" America would effectively cede its pride of place as a defender of human liberty to England, the nation which most New Democrats professed to hate most of all (although Seward did not make that point explicitly).

Seward was willing to grant that prudential considerations must enter into calculations about precisely how far the United States should push the boundaries of activities permitted under the law of nations. He did not believe, for instance, that "intervention in the affairs of Europe," particularly military intervention, was required:

> Mr. President, I am a lover of peace. I shall never freely give my consent to any measure which I shall think will tend to involve this nation in the calamities of foreign war. I believe that our mission is a mission of republicanism. But I believe that we shall best execute it by maintaining peace at home and with all mankind; and if I saw in this measure a step in advance toward the bloody field of contention in the affairs of Europe, I, too, would hesitate long before adopting it. But I see no advance toward any such danger in doing a simple act of national justice and magnanimity.

Seward was not prepared to accept the slippery-slope argument made by critics of an activist foreign policy – that because the nation could not easily distinguish among legitimate and illegitimate means to support regime change abroad, it must categorically and preemptively reject all such means.

> Again, Mr. President, it will be said that if we adopt this resolution, it will, however harmless it be in itself, furnish a precedent for mischievous intervention, either by ourselves in the affairs of other states, or by other states in our affairs hereafter. To admit this argument is to admit distrust of ourselves. We certainly do not distrust our own sense of justice. We do not distrust our own wisdom. So long as we remain here, then, we shall be able to guard against any such abuse of this precedent. Let us also be generous instead of egotistical, and let us believe that neither wisdom nor justice will die with those who occupy these places now, but that

our successors will be as just and as wise as we are. So far as the objection anticipates an abuse of this precedent by foreign states, I have only to say, that if a foreign state shall ask of us just what we now propose, and no more, we shall have no difficulty and no ground of complaint.

Seward also addressed the critics of Kossuth, who challenged his bona fides as a champion of liberalism and republicanism. Unlike many of the New Democrats, Seward was willing to accept constitutional monarchy, as well as wholly popular government, as a legitimate regime for those seeking to overthrow the despotisms of Europe. He was willing to place such monarchies on the side of liberty. Seward also embraced civic nationalism, rather than ethnic nationalism, as the *logos* for liberalized regime change.

Kossuth's first public action in early youth, was an effort, through the Hungarian Diet, to extend equal privileges of representation, of suffrage, and of taxation, to all the people of Hungary, without distinction of rank, or caste, or race. For his fidelity to the great cause of human equality and freedom, he was imprisoned three long years in a dungeon in the castle of Buda by the hand of the Austrian despot. When he came out from that captivity, he commenced that career of agitation for the restoration of the constitution of his country, which ended with success in the year 1848. When he had wrung that charter from the Emperor of Austria, his constitutional king, the first exercise of Hungarian authority by the legislature which he directed, was an act which abolished all the feudal tenures, that brought land within the reach of all, and put the Croat, the Wallachian, the Elyrian, the Jew, and the Magyar, upon the same platform of equality before the law, equality before the government, equality in representation, equality in suffrage, and equality in enduring the burdens of government. It was for this that he was hunted from his native land and came an exile to your shores. Who pursued him there with reproaches of falsehood to freedom? Not the Jew, the Croat, or the Slav, but the tyrant of Austria, who has reduced all the people of Hungary, of whatever rank or race or caste, to the level of slaves.

According to Seward, despotisms naturally combined whenever efforts were made to overthrow the government of one of their kind. Those who advocated the cause of constitutional liberty, whether of a monarchical or republican form, must also recognize their common cause.

Now whatever people leads the way at any time in any crisis in this contest for civil liberty, becomes the representative of the nations of the earth. We once occupied that proud and interesting position, and we engaged the sympathies of civilized men throughout the world. No one can deny, that recently Hungary assumed that same position; and the records of our own legislature show that we, in common with the friends of civil liberty in Europe, held Hungary to be the representative of the nations of the earth in this great cause. We had a messenger [Mann] on the verge of the battlefield ready to acknowledge her independence.

By the same token, "whenever a nation thus assumes to open this controversy for liberty, in behalf of the nations of the earth, some one man more than another becomes identified with the struggle by his virtues, by his valor, by his wisdom, or by his sufferings, until he eclipses others who may be associated with him, and comes to be regarded by the country itself, in whose behalf he labors and struggles, and by mankind, as the representative of that nation, and of that cause." Such was the case of William Tell and Switzerland, William Wallace and Scotland, and of course Washington and America. Although Seward made a point of praising the "towering fame" of Hungary and Kossuth, he implied that even if any particular country or any particular leader fell short of perfection in its pursuit of liberty, the benefit to that cause from such "leading" nations and men outweighed those failings and ought not be overly dwelled upon if they were on the right side of the great struggle.

Seward had no doubt that this struggle was soon coming to a great climax, one of fundamental importance to the United States. "We cannot extinguish sympathy for freedom elsewhere, without extinguishing the spirit of freedom which is the life of our own republic." For those who wanted a more material and practical justification for supporting the Hungarian and similar causes, Seward added:

Again, sir, you may reject Kossuth; you may, if you please, propitiate despotic favor by trampling the exiles of all Europe under your feet. But what will you have gained? This republic is, and forever must be, a living offence to Russia and to Austria, and to despotic powers everywhere. You will never, by whatever humiliations, gain one friend or secure one ally in Europe or America that wears a crown. It is clear that the days of despotism are numbered. We do not know whether its end is to come this year, or next year, or the year after; in this quarter of a century, or in this half of a century. But there is to come, sooner or later, a struggle between the representative and the arbitrary systems of government. Europe is the field on which that struggle must take place. While the representative principle is gaining strength among the people, the power of Russia is seen to culminate. That struggle will be between Russia, whose power extends across the whole northern part of the Eastern Hemisphere, and all the people of Southern and Western Europe. If the Russian autocrat prevail in that contest, we shall be left without friends or allies in the Eastern World. Is it wise to deny ourselves the benefits of alliances with states kindred in political interests and constitutions? Far otherwise; true wisdom dictates that we lend to European nations, struggling for civil liberty, all possible moral aid to sustain them until they can mature and perfect their strength for that great conflict, through which they are doomed to pass. The nations that we thus lawfully aid to raise up, will constitute a lasting and impregnable bulwark for ourselves.

Douglas and the New Democrat Case for Kossuth

Senator Stephen A. Douglas, for his part, sought to push forward the distinctive New Democrat argument, which differed in important respects from that of Seward and the progressive Whigs. "We should not close our eyes to the fact, that a great movement is in progress, which threatens the existence of every absolute government in Europe. It will be a struggle between liberal and absolute principles – between Republicanism and Despotism. Are we to remain cold and indifferent spectators when the time of action will arrive, and the exciting scene shall be presented to our view? Will it not become our duty to do whatever the interests, honor and glory of the country may require, in pursuance of the law of nations, to give encouragement to that great nation?"

Douglas cited several common instruments of that policy of encouraging liberalization and regime change: "to recognize every republican government as soon as it was established; to open regular diplomatic intercourse and negotiate treaties of commerce; and to extend the hand of friendship and every possible courtesy." Kossuth's policy axiom – non-intervention in the affairs of others – was an axiom of the law of nations, one which every nation ought to respect. Douglas supported an explicit endorsement of that axiom by the Senate, one that would authorize the interposition of any state that had sufficient interest in the matter at hand to vindicate the law of nations. In the case of Russian intervention, Douglas judged that either the United States or

Britain would have been justified to intervene on behalf of Hungary, if either had chosen to do so.

That was water under the bridge, however. Douglas raised the question of how the United States ought to respond if another alliance of despots formed to destroy the remaining vestiges of liberty in Europe. He would not commit the United States to a blanket policy of non-intervention, "as most Senators have." To say that the United States would not intervene gave the green light to despotic intervention – precisely as the American hands-off policy had encouraged Spain to execute Lopez and American citizens caught in the recently failed filibustering attempt against Cuba. On the other hand, Douglas would not commit the United States in advance to intervene. That might be looked upon as bluster, an empty threat. The United States instead should retain control over its own actions by deciding each case as it arose.

Douglas's line of argument suggested an intriguing possibility. If England and America both had been entitled as a matter of duty and interest to intervene on behalf of Hungary (even if neither had), would it not make sense, as Kossuth and some Progressive Whigs had argued, to join with England in future joint action on behalf of the cause of freedom? Douglas, however, would not back down from his long-standing view that Britain was the enemy of liberty as well as of the manifest destiny of the United States. Here was a central point of difference with the progressive Whigs.

> Sir, something has been said about an alliance with England, to restrain the march of Russia over the European Continent. I am free to say that I desire no alliance with England, or with other crowned heads. I am not willing to acknowledge that America needs England to maintain the principles of our Government. Nor am I willing to go to the rescue of England to save her from the power of the Autocrat, until she assimilates her institutions to ours. Hers is a half-way house between despotism and republicanism. She is responsible, as much as any power in Europe, for the failure of the revolutionary movements which have occurred within the last four years. English diplomacy, English intrigue and English perfidy put down the revolution in Sicily and in Italy, and was the greatest barrier to its success even in Hungary. So long as England shall by her diplomacy, attempt to defeat the liberal movements in Europe, I am utterly averse to an alliance with her to sustain her monarch, her nobles, and her privileged classes.

Revolution and Regime Change

For Douglas, Britain would have to undertake fundamental reforms, in fact alter its regime, before any Anglo-American cooperation was conceivable. The immediate litmus test for London was to "do justice to Ireland, and the Irish patriots in exile, and to the masses of her own people, by relieving them from the oppressive taxation imposed to sustain the privileged classes, and by adopting republican institutions. . . . Republicanism has nothing to hope, therefore, from England so long as she maintains her existing government and preserves her present policy."

> I wish no alliance with monarchs. No republican movement will ever succeed so long as the people put their trust in princes. The fatal error committed in Italy, in Germany, in France, wherever the experiment was tried, consisted in placing a prince at the head of the popular movement. The princes all sympathized with the dynasties from which they were descended, and seized the first opportunity to produce a reaction, and to betray people into the hands of their oppressors. There is reason to believe that much of this was accomplished through British diplomacy and intrigue. What [is] more natural? The power of the British Government is in the hands of the princes and the nobility. Their sympathies are all with the privileged classes of other countries, in every movement which does not affect the immediate interests of their own kingdom.

"The peculiar position of our country requires that we should have an *American policy* in our foreign relations, based upon the principles of our own Government, and adapted to the spirit of the age," Douglas argued. He rejected the argument that a resolution of welcome for Kossuth should be opposed on the grounds that he asked more of the United States than it was prepared to give. Douglas said that he would not provide any satisfaction or encouragement to despots by muting the nation's support for revolutionaries like Kossuth – but neither would he mislead Kossuth by inciting hopes that might not be realized.[88]

Senators continued to try to shape the debate through various alternative formulations. Illinois Senator James Shields, a New Democrat supporter of Stephen Douglas, along with Free Soiler Hale and progressive Whig Charles Sumner offered various substitute resolutions calling for the creation of a committee of introduction for Kossuth. Senator John Berrien, a Georgia Whig, offered an amendment that would reaffirm the

---

[88] *Congressional Globe*, 32:1, pp. 70-1.

established policy of the United States of refraining from all interference with the domestic concerns of other nations. That amendment was defeated by a vote of 27-16.[89] Senator Isaac P. Walker, a Wisconsin New Democrat, introduced a resolution (never voted on) that pushed the forward policy into outright interventionism:

> Whereas, the signs of the times are portentous of an approaching struggle in Europe, between the republican masses for constitutional government on one side, and the advocates of monarchy for absolute governments on the other; and whereas, it pressingly behooves the representatives of the American people, and of the united sovereign States of America to seriously consider, and betimes to inquire into the relations of the Government and country in this struggle, and their duty in view of it to themselves, to foreign nations, and the international law; therefore,
>
> *Be it resolved,* That the Committee on Foreign Relations be instructed to inquire into, and report upon the expediency of an open declaration by Congress, to foreign nations and the world, that the United States hold strictly to the policy and principle that each individual nation, state, or power possesses, for itself, the exclusive right and sole power to take care and dispose of its own internal concerns, without and exempt from the intervention and interference of any foreign government, state, confederacy, alliance, or power whatsoever; and that any such Intervention or interference by, or on the part of any foreign government, state, confederacy, alliance or power, constitutes an infraction of the law of nations, authorising and justifying the interposition of any or all other governments, confederacies, or powers, at their discretion, to prevent such intervention, and to repair such infraction of the law of nations.
>
> *Resolved further.* That the same committee be instructed to inquire, also, into the expediency of requesting the President of the United States to cause negotiations to be opened with all other constitutional governments, with a view, and to the end of obtaining their co-operation with the United States in the declaration aforesaid, and the policy and principle thereof, and in the

---

[89] *Congressional Globe,* 32: 1, pp. 83, 86, 185; Riepma, "Young America," pp. 134-7; May, *Contemporary American Opinion of the Mid-Century Revolutions,* p. 83.

observance, defense, and maintenance of the law of nations in this respect.[90]

In the end, Seward's substitute was adopted by a large majority but a subsequent resolution to print Kossuth's letter of thanks passed by only one vote. A spirited debate also took place in the House. Seward's proposed language was originally defeated in that body, but the House acquiesced 181-16 once the Senate passed the measure. The Senate then passed a resolution to receive Kossuth in the Senate chambers. William Hunter, Clerk of the Department of State, carried the official invitation to Kossuth in New York.[91]

Kossuth in Washington

While the Congressional debate was in progress, President Fillmore had sent his son and private secretary to New York, to inquire unofficially about Kossuth's plans. Kossuth apparently interpreted this as an urgent invitation to Washington. He told young Fillmore that he was confused and upset by the reported dispute in the Senate and was not inclined to travel to the capital under those circumstances. When Hunter made the invitation official, however, Kossuth made plans to travel to the capital, with festivities and fundraising activities planned at stops in between.[92]

Daniel Webster continued to try to maintain his self-understood role as the balancer among what he regarded as foreign policy extremists and as the defender of the American national interest. He warned Abbott Lawrence that "a large section of the Democratic party intend taking advantage of his presence to bring the country, if they can, to the doctrine and practice of intervention." Webster informed another friend: "I shall treat him [Kossuth] with all personal and individual respect, but if he should speak to me of the policy of 'intervention,' I shall 'have ears more deaf than adders.'" On the other hand, Webster and Baron Hülsemann were no longer on speaking terms over the administration's allegedly improper conduct vis-à-vis Kossuth, including the cannon salute (which Webster insisted was a matter for the Navy Department, not the State Department), and the invitation to Kossuth to visit Washington. Webster insisted that their communications take place only in writing. Hülsemann, meanwhile, informed the President that he could no longer remain

---

[90] *Congressional Globe*, 32:1, p. 111.

[91] Spencer, *Louis Kossuth and Young America*, p. 144; May, *Contemporary American Opinion of the Mid-Century Revolutions*, p. 84; Komlos, *Louis Kossuth in America 1851-1852*, p. 84.

[92] Komlos, *Louis Kossuth in America 1851-1852*, p. 81.

at the capital while Webster remained in office. He also indicated that the Russian minister might also withdraw in support of his Austrian colleague.[93]

When Kossuth reached Washington, Webster arranged for an audience with the President and his Cabinet. The Hungarian revolutionary was escorted by Whig Senator Seward and Illinois Democrat James Shields. What was supposed to be a courtesy visit went poorly. Webster, on the basis of a previous discussion with Kossuth, had assured Fillmore that Kossuth would not "make a speech," in the sense of not pressing for American intervention. Kossuth, apparently under the impression that Webster meant that he was not supposed to speak at length, kept his remarks brief. He spoke, moreover, as if the United States had already committed itself to the Hungarian cause by obtaining his freedom, inviting him to Washington, and treating him as a head of state. Kossuth added that "the star-spangled banner was seen cast in protection around me, announcing to the world that there is a nation, alike powerful as free, ready to protect the laws of nations, even in distant parts of the world and in the person of a poor exile." He quoted from the part of the President's Message that spoke of America's support for the cause of freedom, but without noting any of the President's prior insistence on non-interference. Kossuth was possibly so forward because somehow he had gained the impression from Webster or others that the United States was prepared to recognize Hungary as soon as another uprising occurred, and that the American naval squadron in the Mediterranean was now prepared to cooperate with England (and Turkey) on behalf of the liberal cause in Europe.[94]

Fillmore, apparently caught off guard, replied somewhat frostily:

> I am happy, Governor Kossuth, to welcome you to this land of freedom – and it gives me pleasure to congratulate you upon your release from a long confinement in Turkey, and your safe arrival here. As an individual, I sympathized deeply with you in your brave struggle for the independence and freedom of your native land. The American people can never be indifferent to such a contest; but our policy as a nation in this respect has been uniform, from the commencement of our government; and my own views, as the chief executive magistrate of this nation, are fully and freely expressed in my recent message to Congress, to which you have been pleased

---

[93] Webster to Abbot Lawrence, 29 December 1851, *The Writings and Speeches of Daniel Webster: National Edition,* loc. cit.; Komlos, *Louis Kossuth in America 1851-1852,* p. 92; Webster to Blatchford, 30 December 1851, *The Papers of Daniel Webster,* Diplomatic Papers, 2: 96; Curti, *Austria and the United States, 1848-1852,* pp. 181-3, 187.

[94] Komlos, *Louis Kossuth in America 1851-1852,* pp. 101-2 (star-spangled).

to allude. They are the same, whether speaking to Congress here, or to the nations of Europe. Should your country be restored to independence and freedom, I should then wish you, as the greatest blessing you could enjoy, a restoration to your native land; but, should that never happen, I can only repeat my welcome to you and your companions here, and pray that God's blessing may rest upon you wherever your lot may be cast.

Fillmore saw that this exchange was printed in the New York *Herald*, and reprinted in other Whig newspapers and pamphlets.[95]

"The President received him with great propriety, and his address was all right; sympathy, personal respect and kindness, but no departure from our established policy," Webster recorded hopefully. Senator Shields, a New Democrat, had a somewhat different view: "The administration has treated him shabbily. You ought to have seen Fillmore when he was received, as rigid as a midshipman on a quarter-deck. He got himself into position and tried to look dignified, but the dignity of intellect and refinement was not there. You have read his (Fillmore's) reply, it was worse spoken than it read."[96]

Webster continued to seek to define the middle ground. To offset Fillmore's cold reception to Kossuth, Webster decided to attend a Congressional dinner honoring the Hungarian. He insisted to Fillmore, and later to Hülsemann, that he was doing so in a private capacity, not as Secretary of State. "I have come to the conclusion that it is well for some of us to go to the dinner this evening," he informed Fillmore.

The President of the Senate is to preside, and the Speaker of the House is to act as Vice-President. It has been said that assurances have been given that nothing shall be said that shall justly be offensive to these gentlemen as anti-intervention men. But what chiefly influences me, is, that I learned yesterday that preparations were making for a good deal of an attack upon us, if no member of the administration should pay Kossuth the respect of attending the dinner given to him by members of Congress, of all parties, as the nation's guest. I wish the Heads of Department could see their way clear to go, as I think I shall go myself. In the present state of the

---

[95] See, for instance, *American Whig Review* 15 (February 1852): 188.

[96] Webster to Blatchford, 31 December 1851, *The Writings and Speeches of Daniel Webster: National Edition*, 2: 502; Spencer, *Louis Kossuth and Young America*, pp. 87-9; Thomas J. McCormick, ed., *Memoirs of Gustav Koerner, 1809-1896*, 2 vols. (Cedar Rapids, Iowa: Torch Press, 1909), 1: 579 (Shields quote).

country, especially in the interior, where Kossuth is going, I should not like unnecessarily to provoke popular attack.[97]

In his prepared remarks at the Congressional banquet, Webster reiterated his views about the importance of the role of the United States in marshalling world public opinion on behalf of the law of nations and the rule of comprehensive non-intervention; he affirmed the right of a distinct and self-sufficient people to determine their own form of government free of foreign interference. "There is nothing that satisfies the human mind in an enlightened age, unless man is governed by his own country and the institutions of this own government. No matter how easy be the yoke of a foreign power, no matter how lightly it sits upon the shoulders, if it is not imposed by the voice of his own nation and of his own country, he will not, he cannot, he *means* not to be happy under its burden." This was the great truth and objective of the American Revolution and it ought not be denied to other nations, to the extent that they met certain criteria for true national self-determination. "Wherever this is, in the Christian and civilized world, a nationality of character – wherever there exists a nation of sufficient knowledge and wealth and population to constitute a government, then a national government is a necessary and proper result of nationality of character."

Webster argued that Hungarian independence, rightly understood, would benefit Austria itself. "The imposition of a foreign yoke upon a people capable of self-government, while it oppresses and depresses that people, adds nothing to the strength of those that impose that yoke. In my opinion, Austria would be a better and stronger government tomorrow if she confined the limits of her power to the hereditary and German domains, especially if she saw in Hungary a strong, sensible, independent neighboring nation; because I think that the cost of keeping Hungary quiet is not repaid by any benefit derived from Hungarian levies or tributes." As to the proper form of government for Hungary, Webster acknowledged that "we would be glad to see her, when she becomes independent, embrace that system of government which is most acceptable to ourselves. We shall rejoice to see our American model upon the Lower Danube and on the Mountains of Hungary." But that was not the first or necessary step:

> The first prayer shall be that Hungary may become independent of all foreign power – that her destinies may be entrusted to her own hands, and to her own discretion. I do not profess to understand the

---

[97] Webster to Fillmore, 7 January 1852, *The Papers of Daniel Webster,* Diplomatic Papers, 2: 96-7.

social relations and connection of races, and of twenty other things that may affect the public institutions of Hungary. All I say is, that Hungary can regulate these matters for herself infinitely better than they can be regulated for her by Austria; and, therefore, I limit my aspirations for Hungary, for the present, to that single and simple point, – Hungarian independence, Hungarian self-government, Hungarian control of Hungarian destinies.

Webster concluded his remarks by offering a toast to "Hungarian Independence, Hungarian control of her own destinies – Hungary a distinct nationality among the nations of Europe." [98]

After the Congressional banquet, Hülsemann angrily addressed a private note of complaint to Fillmore. The President responded that he had not yet had time to read Webster's speech; if, however, Webster's remarks reflected views other than those that the President had expressed in his Annual Message and in his response to Kossuth at the President's Mansion, they were not to be understood as reflecting the policies of the U.S. government. Fillmore refused Hülsemann's suggestion that he disavow Webster's speech through an anonymous editorial in the semi-official Whig newspaper, the *Republic*. The President, however, went so far as to prepare a written statement to the Russian Minister, Alexander Bodisco, which affirmed that Webster had not expressed the views of the U.S. government. [99] Webster himself instructed the American *charge* in Vienna, Charles McCurdy, to assure that government that the United States did not countenance intervention or "involving this Government in European wars from causes affecting only the nations of Europe." Webster's guidance included the following:

> You may say, in as explicit terms as you may judge proper, that neither the President nor his Cabinet countenance any such thing as "intervention," or involving the Government in European wars, from causes affecting only the nations of Europe. Public men in this Country, as well as private men, are accustomed to speak their opinions freely. This belongs to our system, and although in this respect individuals may sometimes be indiscreet, yet there is no where any power of control; and there are some public men, as well as private individuals, who are ready to take a part in the troubles, and in the wars of other States. It is believed however, that the sober sense of the country will settle down on

---

[98] Speech at the Kossuth Banquet, *The Papers of Daniel Webster*, Diplomatic Papers, 2: 101-5.

[99] Curti, *Austria and the United States, 1848-1852*, p. 192.

more prudent and pacific ideas. While there is no probability that the Government will lend aid or countenance to Kossuth, there is no reason to suppose that the amount of private contributions made for him will be large. On the whole, the enthusiasm felt for him is not increasing; and having visited most of the large Northern Cities, where there has existed the greatest readiness to subscribe, his success elsewhere is not likely to be distinguished. And I venture to say, that the "Intervention" feeling will doubtless subside gradually and rapidly, if nothing should take place, calculated to kindle it into a new flame. [100]

On the other hand, Webster refused to patch up the strained relationship with Austria by offering his own unofficial disclaimer through party newspapers, a step which Fillmore may have wanted his Secretary of State to take. But Webster did agree to publish a modified, toned-down version of his speech. After reports from the U.S. diplomatic representatives indicated considerable disquiet on the part of European governments about the reception of Kossuth, and a general expectation that a major shift in American foreign policy was in the offing, Webster agreed to publish an interview in the *Republic* that reaffirmed the doctrine of non-intervention. [101]

Domestic critics of an activist policy toward Hungary and Europe also came forward. When Kossuth paid a courtesy visit to Henry Clay, who was on his sickbed (he would die within a few months), the one-time Whig advocate of global human rights expressed his "liveliest sympathies" with the Hungarians. Clay argued, however, that the practical effects of providing "material aid" to Kossuth by the United States would probably be war with one or more European powers. Clay pointed out that the United States lacked the means to carry out military operations on the European continent, and that a maritime war would "result in mutual annoyance to commerce, but little else." Once the United States engaged (ineffectually) in such a war, it would have (effectually) abandoned its "ancient policy of amity and non-intervention in the affairs of other nations." The European powers would feel justified "in abandoning the terms of forbearance and non-intervention," which they had so far preserved toward the American Republic. "After the downfall, perhaps, of the friends of liberal institutions in Europe, her despots,

---

[100] Webster to McCurdy, 15 January 1852, *The Papers of Daniel Webster,* Diplomatic Papers, 2: 109-11.

[101] Curti, *Austria and the United States, 1848-1852,* loc. cit.; Komlos, *Louis Kossuth in America 1851-1852,* pp. 110-2.

imitating and provoked by our fatal example," might turn upon the United States in its hour of weakness and exhaustion.

"Sir," Clay concluded, "the recent subversion of the republican government of France [by Louis Napoleon's coup of December 2, 1851] and that enlightened nation voluntarily placing its neck under the yoke of despotism, teach us to despair of any present success for liberal institutions in Europe."

> But if we should involve ourselves in the tangled web of European politics, in a war in which we could effect nothing, *and in that struggle Hungary should go down, and we should go down with her*, where then would be the last hope of the friends of freedom throughout the world? Far better is it for ourselves, for Hungary, and for the cause of liberty, that . . . we should keep the lamp burning brightly on this Western shore as a light to all nations, than to hazard its ultimate extinction, amid the ruins of fallen or falling republics in Europe.[102]

Clay and his Whig Party supporters made certain that his admonitory remarks to Kossuth were widely published. Georgia Whig Congressman Alexander Stephens organized a Congressional dinner to counter the earlier pro-Kossuth affair, on the occasion of Washington's Birthday. "The dinner is an anti-Kossuth affair, or at least it is intended as a demonstration in favor of the neutral policy of Washington," Stephens informed Senator Crittenden, who he asked to provide the keynote for the evening.[103] Crittenden had been a cautious supporter of Senate efforts to hail the French revolutionaries of 1848, but the turn of events there and elsewhere in Europe left him very much of Clay's mind when it came to Kossuth. The recent execution of Crittenden's son by Spanish authorities in Cuba, in the wake of a disastrous filibustering expedition by Narciso Lopez, could not have been far from Crittenden's mind.

In his dinner address, Crittenden stressed two related themes from Washington's Farewell Address – the necessity of Union; and the imperative "to be jealous of all foreign influence, and enter into entangling alliances with none." Crittenden acknowledged that the use of force was a legitimate means to defend the rights and liberties of a people who had already exercised those rights, whose "heart" was "prepared for liberty," and who understood "what it is, and how to value it." If such a people

---

[102] Remarks to Kossuth, 9 January 1852, *The Papers of Henry Clay,* 10: 944-6; Spencer, *Louis Kossuth and Young America*, p. 94. Emphasis in the original.

[103] Coleman, ed., *The Life of John J. Crittenden,* 2: 27, 34.

obtained arms, "I'll warrant you they will obtain and sustain their freedom. We have given the world an example of that success. But three millions, scattered over a vast territory, opposed to the most powerful enemy on earth, we went triumphantly through our Revolution and established our liberties." The implication, of course, was that if the Hungarians possessed such an understanding of liberty, and the sort of leadership capabilities possessed by men like Washington, they would have been able to overcome foreign intervention quite on their own.

Setting the internal situation of Hungary aside, Crittenden asked if the United States would ever be justified in intervening to tip the balance on behalf of a nation fighting for its liberties? Crittenden agreed that the United States possessed such a right, but "it is always a question of expediency."

> There are cases so connected with our own interests, and with the cause of humanity, that interference would be proper. But still, it is a question for the sound discretion of this people, – a question always of expediency, – whether you will or will not interfere; and it is just because it is a question of that character, and because our passions and sympathies may often tempt us to err upon it, that Washington has made it the subject of this emphatic admonition. It is not because we have not the right to interfere, but it is because we have the right, and because we are surrounded by temptations – by the temptations of generous hearts and noble principles – to transcend the limits of prudence and of policy, and to interfere in the affairs of our neighbors, that he has admonished us. Washington, with that forecast and that prophetic spirit which constituted a part of his character, saw through all this. He knew the warm and generous natures of his countrymen. He knew their susceptibility, and he knew where the danger of error was; and it is there that his wisdom has erected, as far as his advice can do it, a bulwark for our protection. He tells you, "Stand upon your own ground." That is the ground to stand upon.

Crittenden argued that there is comparatively little that "the bayonet and the sword can do. The plowshare does a thousand times more than either. The time was when arms were powerful instruments of oppression; but they cannot do much now, unless they are aided by the mercenary and degenerate spirit of the people over whom they are brandished."

> Our mission, so far as it concerns our distant brethren, is not a mission of arms. We are here to do what Washington advised

us to do, – take care of our Union, have a proper respect for the Constitution and laws of our country, cultivate peace and commerce with all nations, do equal justice to all nations, and thereby set an example to them, and show forth in ourselves the blessings of self-government to all the world. Thus you will best convince mankind. Seeing you prosper, they will follow your example, and do likewise. It is by that power of opinion, by that power of reformation, that you can render the mightiest and greatest service that is in your power towards the spread of liberty all over the world. Adopt the policy of interference, and what is its consequence? War, endless war. If one interferes, another will interfere, and another, and another, and so this doctrine for the protection of republican liberty and human rights results in a perpetual, widespread, and wider-spreading war, until all mankind, overcome by slaughter and ruin, shall fall down bleeding and exhausted. [104]

In other words, national and personal liberty must be established first by and among a people striving to obtain the separate and equal station to which the Laws of Nature and of Nature's God entitle them. Foreign attempts to support the cause of republican liberty and human rights would actually generate a wider war that would harm the particular cause of a people like the Hungarians, as well as that of humanity at large.

Even some New Democrats had begun to put some distance between themselves and Kossuth. Douglas, a leading candidate for the party's presidential nomination in 1852, resisted efforts by Young American George Sanders to identify him with a highly aggressive U.S. policy toward European revolutions. Massachusetts Democrat Caleb Cushing warned Douglas of the peril of having his name associated with the cause of the European "Reds," thus affronting the Catholic vote, making the party appear to be the tool of "professional agitators," and threatening the unity among northern and southern Democrats. For Douglas, Manifest Destiny and international republicanism were not precisely identical; he was prepared to be sympathetic with, but not wedded to, the latter cause. Douglas was mainly interested in expanding American territory in the Western Hemisphere, which put him strongly at odds with Great Britain (and, *inter alia*, made him a strong supporter of the Irish cause). At the Congressional banquet honoring Kossuth, and at a Jackson Day dinner, Douglas stressed these expansionist and anti-British themes rather than the cause of Hungarian or European revolution. He used

---

[104] Coleman, ed., *The Life of John J. Crittenden*, loc. cit.

those occasions to attack the Fillmore administration for interfering with filibustering expeditions against Cuba and to support a policy of intervention for annexation. [105]

In mid-January 1852, Kossuth, disappointed at his reception in Washington, departed the capital to tour the country in support of his cause. Meanwhile, Rhode Island Senator John H. Clarke, a Whig, introduced a resolution designed to take the political initiative away from the supporters of an activist American foreign policy. [106] (A similar resolution was placed before the House by Congressman Albert Brown of Mississippi.) Clarke asked the Senate to endorse formally the advice given in Washington's Farewell Address ("why quit our own to stand on foreign ground?"), and in Jefferson's First Inaugural ("peace, commerce, and honest friendship with all nations, entangling alliances with none.") America, Clark insisted, was doing "far more . . . for the liberation of man by our quiet and peaceful example" than by "resorting to war and putting at hazard the rich inheritance of freedom." [107]

New Democrat and progressive Whigs responded with their own legislative language. "I have seen Cass and we mean to amend it [Clarke's resolution] in a way as to indicate a determination to throw our weight with the great Liberal party of the world . . . ," Senator James Shields told Gustav Koerner. Cass's substitute resolution would have the Senate warn that the United States would not watch "without deep concern" another violation of Hungary's nationality. [108] Seward proposed a more general statement:

> The United States, in defense of their own interests and the common interests of mankind, do solemnly protest against the conduct of Russia . . . as a wanton and tyrannical infraction of the laws of nations. And the United States do further declare, that they will not hereafter be indifferent to similar acts

---

[105] Spencer, *Louis Kossuth and Young America*, pp. 107, 116; Riepma, "Young America," pp. 158, 164-7, 181 (Reds). In addition, Sanders, by his personal attacks on the other contenders for the nomination on behalf of Douglas, also alienated much of the party establishment and irritated Douglas.

[106] For a more detailed account of this second major Congressional debate on Kossuth and Hungary, see Garrity, *American Views on Regime Change and the European Revolutions of 1848*, pp. 93-111.

[107] Riepma, "Young America," pp. 197-8; *Congressional Globe*, 32:1, p. 298; *Congressional Globe*, 32:1, Appendix, p. 144.

[108] McCormick, ed., *Memoirs of Gustav Koerner*, loc. cit.; Komlos, *Louis Kossuth in America 1851-1852*, p. 104.

of national injustice, oppression, and usurpation, whenever or wherever they may occur.[109]

The ensuing debate provided the advocates of an activist policy with their final opportunity to define an approach that would offer a plausible middle ground between war on the one hand, and feckless and offensive rhetoric on the other.

In the end, none of these resolutions or amendments ever came to a vote. The conservative Whigs, aligned with the Fillmore administration, and a strong majority of Southerners of both parties, constituted a substantial opposition to the New Democrats and progressive Whigs on this issue. By the time Kossuth returned to Washington in mid-April, Kossuth mania had largely passed. Only a few Senators, Seward among them, bothered to pay him courtesy calls before he departed for New England and eventually for Europe. Kossuth, meanwhile, had further muddied the waters by becoming involved in a proposed expedition to protect the white-ruled San Domingo against incorporation by the new self-proclaimed Emperor of Haiti, Faustin I. "If the Spaniards are beaten off the island by the negroes, we are in favor of encouraging an immediate descent of Americans and their setting up a republic for themselves . . . and the introduction there of all the political institutions of this country, including domestic slavery," George Sanders declared in the *Democratic Review*. The proposed expedition would establish a colony within the Dominican portion of the island, consisting of 1500 American and foreign fighting men under the leadership of Colonel John T. Pickett of Kentucky, then proceed to subjugate Haiti. The expeditionary force would then have been available to Kossuth for use in Europe. Kossuth claimed to oppose the Haitian Emperor because he was a despot under the sway of the Czar of Russia, but reports of this scheme scarcely endeared him to the American anti-slavery movement.[110]

Conclusion

The Presidential election of 1852 did not turn on the question of American attitudes towards Kossuth and future European revolutions. New Hampshire Democrat Franklin Pierce, the "dark horse" nominee who was regarded as reliable by the southern interests in the party, easily defeated the candidate of a weakened Whig Party, Winfield Scott, as well as Free Soiler John Hale, whom

---

[109] *Congressional Globe*, 32:1, p. 310.

[110] Spencer, *Louis Kossuth and Young America*, p. 155; Komlos, *Louis Kossuth in America*, pp. 122-6 *(Democratic Review)*.

both sides had regarded as something of a gadfly over the slavery question during the Senate debates discussed above.

The Democratic Party platform, formulated with the South in mind, ignored the issue of intervention entirely and cast the matter as one of defending American constitutional liberty, rightly understood:

> Resolved, That, in view of the condition of popular institutions in the Old World, a high and sacred duty is devolved, with increased responsibility upon the democratic party of this country, as the party of the people, to uphold and maintain the rights of every State, and thereby the Union of the States, and to sustain and advance among us constitutional liberty, by continuing to resist all monopolies and exclusive legislation for the benefit of the few at the expense of the many, and by a vigilant and constant adherence to those principles and compromises of the constitution, which are broad enough and strong enough to embrace and uphold the Union as it was, the Union as it is, and the Union as it shall be, in the full expansion of the energies and capacity of this great and progressive people. [111]

The Whig Party platform articulated the default position of American foreign policy, that of strict non-intervention in the affairs of others and the exemplary role of the Republic:

> That while struggling freedom everywhere enlists the warmest sympathy of the Whig party, we still adhere to the doctrines of the Father of his Country, as announced in his Farewell Address, of keeping ourselves free from all entangling alliances with foreign countries, and of never quitting our own to stand upon foreign ground; that our mission as a republic is not to propagate our opinions, or impose on other countries our form of government by artifice or force; but to teach, by example, and show by our success, moderation and justice, the blessings of self-government, and the advantages of free institutions. [112]

The Free Soil Party alone explicitly advocated American activism:

---

[111] 1852 Democratic Party Platform, 1 June 1852, at http://www.presidency.ucsb.edu/ws/index.php?pid=29575.

[112] 1852 Whig Party Platform, 17 June 1852, at http://www.presidency.ucsb.edu/ws/index.php?pid=25856.

> That every nation has a clear right to alter or change its own government and to administer its own concerns in such manner as may best secure the rights and promote the happiness of the people; and foreign interference with that right is a dangerous violation of the law of nations, against which all independent governments should protest, and endeavor by all proper means to prevent; and especially is it the duty of the American government, representing the chief republic of the world, to protest against, and by all proper means to prevent, the intervention of kings and emperors against nations seeking to establish for themselves republican or constitutional governments. . . .
>
> That the independence of Haiti ought to be recognized by our government, and our commercial relations with it placed on the footing of the most favored nations.[113]

The precise attitude of Pierce himself toward European affairs was unknown when he took office. Party conservatives thought him safe against the wilder interventionist notions of the New Democrats (by now generally known as "Young America"), while some observers believed that he secretly harbored Young America-type ambitions. His Inaugural Address was taken as a repudiation of Fillmore's cautious approach, certainly with respect to official American assertiveness in the Western Hemisphere – although not to illegal filibustering. Pierce was less precise toward Europe:

> With an experience thus suggestive and cheering, the policy of my Administration will not be controlled by any timid forebodings of evil from expansion. Indeed, it is not to be disguised that our attitude as a nation and our position on the globe render the acquisition of certain possessions not within our jurisdiction eminently important for our protection, if not in the future essential for the preservation of the rights of commerce and the peace of the world. Should they be obtained, it will be through no grasping spirit, but with a view to obvious national interest and security, and in a manner entirely consistent with the strictest observance of national faith. We have nothing in our history or position to

---

[113] 1852 Free Soil Platform, 11 August 1852, in Thomas Hudson McKee, ed., *The National Conventions and Platforms of All Political Parties, 1789 to 1904*, 5th ed. (Baltimore: The Friedenwald Company, 1904), p. 83.

invite aggression; we have everything to beckon us to the cultivation of relations of peace and amity with all nations.

Purposes, therefore, at once just and pacific will be significantly marked in the conduct of our foreign affairs. I intend that my Administration shall leave no blot upon our fair record, and trust I may safely give the assurance that no act within the legitimate scope of my constitutional control will be tolerated on the part of any portion of our citizens which can not challenge a ready justification before the tribunal of the civilized world. . . . Of the complicated European systems of national polity we have heretofore been independent. From their wars, their tumults, and anxieties we have been, happily, almost entirely exempt. Whilst these are confined to the nations which gave them existence, and within their legitimate jurisdiction, they can not affect us except as they appeal to our sympathies in the cause of human freedom and universal advancement. But the vast interests of commerce are common to all mankind, and the advantages of trade and international intercourse must always present a noble field for the moral influence of a great people.[114]

Kossuth, for his part, had decided to abandon any pretensions of political neutrality and effectively endorsed Pierce before leaving the United States. Kossuth sent one of his associates to attend Pierce's inauguration and ascertain his views on supporting actively a new Hungarian Revolution. If the new President was found willing, the envoy was to propose that the United State support Turkey diplomatically against Russia, strengthen the U.S. Navy in the Mediterranean, and establish a steamship line directly between New York and Constantinople. The United States would also provide military supplies and financial contributions and agree that, in the case of an insurrection, it would transport volunteers from America at the U.S. government's expense. Kossuth also sent private requests to Colonel John Pickett, encouraging him to organize volunteers and make his men available for an expedition to Italy, Hungary or Turkey.[115]

Kossuth's emissary received no response or encouragement from Pierce or his high-level appointees. The new Secretary of State, William Marcy of New York, had largely ignored Kossuth during his visit to America.

---

[114] Franklin Pierce, Inaugural Address, 4 March 1852, at http://millercenter.org/scripps/archive/speeches/detail/3553.

[115] Riepma, "Young America," pp. 232-5; Komlos, *Louis Kossuth in America*, pp. 130-2, 171.

Secretary of War Jefferson Davis, while a Senator from Mississippi, had been critical of Kossuth during the Senate debates. One of the key New Democrats remaining in Congress, Stephen Douglas (who had unsuccessfully sought the presidential nomination) emphasized the hemispheric rather than the transatlantic dimensions of an assertive foreign policy: one built around assisting revolutionary movements in Cuba, opposing British influence in Central America, and excluding other European powers entirely from the New World. When a European war broke out over the Crimea, Pierce ignored an inquiry from Kossuth as to whether the United States was prepared to recognize the independence of Hungary, Poland and Italy if they established *de facto* governments, and to accord them the benefits of commercial and neutral rights. [116]

There were still prospects of combining a hemispheric and transatlantic New Democrat agenda, however. Several of the Pierce administration's diplomatic appointments – which were made to accommodate factional interests within the Democratic Party – believed that by encouraging revolutions in Europe, the United States would enable the completion of its territorial and political ambitions in the New World. These appointees included Pierre Soulé as Minister to Spain, John L. O'Sullivan as Minister to Portugal, James Buchanan as Minister to Great Britain, Daniel Sickles as the secretary of the American legation in London, and George Sanders as the U.S. consul there. Sanders organized what became a famous, or notorious, dinner for the exiled European revolutionary leaders then in England, including Kossuth, Garibaldi, Mazzini, Herzen and Ledru-Roland. Buchanan's appearance at the dinner gave it the appearance of a U.S.-sanctioned meeting in support of revolution. Soulé was the most active of the group. He conspired with Spanish rebels to overthrow the monarchy in hopes that a republican government there would cede Cuba to the United States, and of trying to bring about a war between Britain and Spain over Cuba, during which the resulting interruption of American cotton and corn supplies would destabilize the European social order and lead to the overthrow of its monarchies. Finally, he was also accused of collaborating with potential assassins of Napoleon III. [117]

Any such free-lancing by U.S. diplomats was effectively curtailed after the fiasco of the Ostend Manifesto, which publicized to domestic and international audiences the extent of American willingness to pressure Spain over Cuba. Pierce, and later President Buchanan, continued to enforce American

---

[116] Riepma, "Young America," loc. cit.; Komlos, *Louis Kossuth in America*, pp. 169-71.

[117] Eyal, *The Young America Movement*, pp. 93, 110-5; Blumenthal, *A Reappraisal of Franco-American Relations*, pp. 28-9.

neutrality laws against filibustering expeditions despite their private sympathies toward their aims. Such political circumstances in the United States created the possibility of filibustering that would result in the creation of independent (or client) regimes, rather than additions to American territory. The adventurer William Walker landed in Nicaragua in June 1855 and eventually established a puppet government under his control. Walker subsequently won the presidency through rigged elections, reinstituted chattel slavery, and established English as a second language. He envisioned the creation of a white-ruled Central American Union based on slavery and closely tied to the southern states. Walker's regime was recognized by the U.S. government and defended by New Americans such as Stephen Douglas. [118]

In time, Walker overextended himself and was executed; his legacy, however, and that of the other filibusters, deeply affected American politics as well as U.S. relations with Latin America. In 1861, President-elect Abraham Lincoln, who had once identified himself with the progressive Whigs, rejected a series of compromises proposed by Senator Crittenden aimed at heading off the Civil War. "Filibustering for all South of us, and making slave states would follow . . . to put us again on the high road to a slave empire," Lincoln wrote. "A year will not pass, till we shall have to take Cuba as a condition upon which they will stay in the Union." [119] As the nation slid deeper into domestic crisis over slavery during the 1850s, the prospect for a new political coalition based on an assertive foreign policy and an aggressive approach to foreign regime change disappeared.

---

[118] Herring, *From Colony to Superpower*, p. 220; Walter McDougall, *Throes of Democracy: The American Civil War Era, 1829-1877* (New York: HarperCollins, 2008), p. 346.

[119] James McPherson, *Abraham Lincoln and the Second American Revolution* (New York: Oxford University Press, 1991), pp. 118-9 (filibustering).

CHAPTER FIVE

The American Regime Change Debates of the 1890s:
A Matter of Principle and Interest

The late 19th century was a time of great hope and anxiety for the United States. Several decades of extraordinary growth had transformed the United States into the world's leading industrial power, yet a financial panic in 1893 plunged the nation into a major economic depression. The American people were a generation removed from the divisions created by the Civil War (setting apart the continuing mistreatment of African-Americans), but potentially serious and violent fault lines had emerged between country and city, East and West, and labor and capital. Americans watched with concern as the major European powers scrambled for new colonies and influence in Africa, the Middle East and Asia. These revitalized European empires threatened to exclude American business from vital overseas markets and to expand into the Western Hemisphere, thereby challenging American security. New technologies, especially steam power, the telegraph, and railroads, pointed to major changes in the conduct of warfare and arguably lessened the traditional security provided to the United States by its distance from Europe. Yet there was considerable hope that science, commerce and civilization had reached the point where great power conflict might be prevented, or at least limited, by international cooperation.

Many Americans felt that their bourgeoning economic power and the moral authority of their democratic society entitled – indeed, compelled – them to exert greater influence over this brave yet frightening new world. They disagreed considerably over the means and ends of doing so, however – especially when the exertion of American power, or the claims of American example, required the United States to consider actively intervening in the affairs of other peoples and nations. This chapter examines two of the major controversies of this sort that emerged during the 1890s.[1]

- The 1896-1898 debate over possible American intervention in the Cuban civil war (or insurrection or revolution, depending on one's viewpoint), which focused on the desirability and feasibility of removing the Spanish imperial regime in favor of Cuban independence, or some other form of political governance over the island.

- The "imperial debate" of 1898-1900, in which Americans argued whether their national interest and moral authority required them to go beyond the removal of a European power in the Philippines and replace it with a regime, temporarily or permanently, under American political control.

These debates were driven, in a conceptual sense at least, by those who considered themselves "large Americans," heirs to the expansionist tradition of the pre-Civil War republic, a tradition they believed must be revived and adapted properly to the conditions of the time. The unification of the nation in the years following the Civil War, and the increased threat represented by European colonialism, both allowed and required the United States to become more "outward-looking." Events in East Asia, as well as in Latin America, directly affected the economic strength and security of the United States. To retain its freedom of action, America would have to increase substantially its naval forces, and enhance its ability to operate away from its shores by acquiring strategically located bases.

There seemed to be no good reason why America's Manifest Destiny should halt at the eastern edge of the Pacific Ocean. War was an essential, even beneficial element of national policy; the maintenance of armed forces and the most modern weapons were the best guarantees of peace and security. The United States did not necessarily have to expand territorially, save in a few strategically critical locations (e.g., Hawaii), but it did have to widen its methods of political control outside of the continental United States. These methods included protectorates and neo-colonial arrangements (by and large, "large Americans" insisted that they did not

---

[1] A third major debate occurred over the Hawaiian Islands in 1893, when the Cleveland administration considered restoring the native Hawaiian monarchy following a republican "revolution" fostered by American planters, who then sought annexation by the United States. This is discussed in an extended version of this chapter, *The American Regime Change Debates of the 1890s* (Ashland, Ohio: Ashbrook Center for Public Affairs, January 2010), pp. 5-30. Accessible at http://strategyanddiplomacy.typepad.com/strategyanddiplomacy/afprc/afprc4.pdf. The islands were annexed to the United States in 1898, during the Spanish-American War.

favor establishing European-style empires). To the extent that foreigners, whether colonial powers or natives, resisted American political intervention, they would be subject to more forceful action and a change of regime. Alfred Thayer Mahan, Theodore Roosevelt, and Henry Cabot Lodge were among those promoting the "large" view, but it was supported by substantial figures from the old-line Republican Party, such as Benjamin Harrison.

The opposing intellectual camp went under various names, including "little Americanism," "anti-expansionism," and "anti-imperialism." As a rule, those in this camp did not regard the activities of the European powers as representing a significant threat to the security of the United States. The economic well-being of the nation was best secured through free trade, a small, non-offensive navy, and no overseas bases. Any further territorial expansion (with the possible exception of Canada) was unnecessary, and would only involve the United States in foreign entanglements. Armaments were the cause of war and hence ought to be limited or abolished, through international agreement or unilateral actions. The anti-imperialists emphasized morality rather than self-interest as the core of their argument: the principles of the American regime compelled policymakers to concern themselves first with the welfare of citizens of the United States, and to avoid interference with or intervention in the affairs of other nations, especially when it came to the constitution of their regimes. The health of the American regime would be undermined if it attempted to emulate the Europeans and establish a full-blown empire in which it would rule other peoples without their consent, or deny other peoples their right to national and political self-determination. The leading anti-imperialists included individuals from various backgrounds and from both major political parties, including Carl Schurz, David Starr Jordan, and William Jennings Bryan. This outlook was particularly identified with the Democratic Party.

In the practical political arena, as this chapter will demonstrate, the division between these two foreign policy schools was not quite that clear-cut. Many of those who considered themselves to be anti-imperialists, such as Bryan, came to support what they regarded as humanitarian intervention in Cuba, which meant the overthrow of the Spanish colonial regime. Bryan, for tactical political reasons, also supported ratification of the Treaty of Paris and with it the acquisition of the Philippines. Some of those who might have counted themselves in the large American camp, such as Harrison, opposed the acquisition of those islands because they were "a bridge too far." Overshadowing the debates was the enigmatic William McKinley. The new President was closely associated with the business interests of the Republican Party, and leading businessmen by and large opposed war over Cuba. McKinley himself promised "no jingo nonsense," yet he led the nation into conflicts in which regime change was actively promoted. The debates were often driven by Republican and Democratic partisans, notably Roosevelt and Bryan, who believed that they might be able to use foreign policy issues to bring about an enduring and decisive domestic political realignment.

This chapter offers a modest and selective reprise of these debates, designed to educe the major arguments of both camps and to demonstrate their complexity when applied to the policy world. The chapter will also elucidate the broader elements – e.g., strategic, constitutional and moral – that framed the debates. These arguments still resonate strongly in current policy discourse and offer much upon which to reflect in our present circumstances. We cannot offer a detailed account of the 1890s or all the associated regime change issues, which would be necessary for a full evaluation of the success or failure of various American approaches to foreign regime change. The reader will be referred in the footnotes to major secondary sources for more information on the historical context.

The Decision to Intervene in Cuba, 1896-1898

Cuba, along with Puerto Rico, remained colonies of Spain after most of Madrid's great empire in the Western Hemisphere had achieved independence in the early 19th century. Americans had long been interested in Cuba. The island's strategic location was such that it commanded critical maritime lines of communication into the Gulf of Mexico. Thomas Jefferson and John Quincy Adams both thought that the island's geographic position made it naturally part of a North American confederation. Before and during the Civil War, leading southerners anticipated Cuba's acquisition as a future slave state. Throughout the 19th century American businessmen held substantial investments on the island or otherwise had an interest in the orientation of the Cuban economy. Americans sympathized generally with efforts by native Cubans to improve their domestic situation and favored their desire for autonomy or independence from Spain. During a major popular insurrection against Spanish rule (the Ten Years War, 1868-78), however, Presidents Grant and Hayes chose to avoid direct American intervention.

The standard of popular rebellion was raised again in 1895 as living conditions in Cuba worsened. The island suffered from an economic crisis inadvertently created in part by a new American tariff on Cuban sugar, as well as by the general hemispheric aftereffects of the economic Panic of 1893.

The *insurrectos*, as the anti-Spanish forces were known, waged guerrilla war aimed at destroying the economic basis of Spanish rule, especially the sugar plantations and cattle ranches. Cubans in the United States and their American sympathizers – including some with substantial business interests on the island – raised money for their cause and attempted to smuggle supplies and men onto the island. (Many Cuban leaders, such as the famous writer José Martí, who died in a skirmish in 1895, admired much about the United States but wanted to avoid a close connection. They feared that the United States might choose to annex the island rather than support independence.) A new Spanish commander, General Valeriano Weyler, waged a counterinsurgency campaign that brought the civilian population into concentration camps. Those outside the camps were treated as rebels. Due to poor sanitation and lack of food and medicine, tens of thousands of civilian *reconcentrados* died of disease and starvation. The precise casualty toll is unknown but perhaps 200,000 lives were lost on both sides during the three-year conflict, most of them non-combatants, out of a total population of 1.8 million. American citizens and property on the island were often caught in the middle of the violence.

The humanitarian disaster in Cuba caught the attention of the popular press in the United States. These "yellow journalists" sensationalized the atrocities of "Butcher" Weyler and encouraged popular enthusiasm for American intervention to stop the bloodshed. William Randolph Hearst's *New York Journal* and Joseph Pulitzer's *New York World* competed to scoop each other with stories of Spain's brutality and the heroism of the *insurrectos*.

President Grover Cleveland, a Democrat, was in office when the insurrection first broke out. He was decidedly in the anti-interventionist camp. Cleveland sought to protect American citizens and property while encouraging a peaceful settlement of the conflict. He represented an enduring element of American culture that distrusted war as an instrument of policy, except in self-defense. Americans had not forgotten the devastation of the Civil War. As noted in more detail below, white southerners in general feared that a supposedly "humanitarian" intervention in Cuba would be fought in the interests of the industrial north, resulting in a stronger federal government, weakened states' rights, and perhaps new efforts to challenge Jim Crow. Many Americans, not just southerners, regarded the African-Hispanic peoples of Cuba through the prism of race as an "inferior" people, not worth fighting about. Businessmen who did not have a major stake in Cuba were concerned that war would destabilize precarious financial markets. In the view of this broad anti-war coalition, American intervention in Cuba would likely trigger, rather than deter, counter-intervention by European powers on behalf of Spain.

Security and honor for the United States, they concluded, meant staying out of the quarrels of others rather than rushing to join the imperial scramble for bases and colonies. As to the humanitarian question, those opposed to war pointed to serious human rights abuses by the *insurrectos*.

Interventionists, by contrast, argued that a great nation like the United States could not honorably stand by while Cuba was devastated and depopulated. They insisted that the demonstration of American weakness on its own doorstep would embolden European powers to challenge U.S. hemispheric interests and global aspirations. They warned that Spain might cede the island to a more potent and dangerous nation like Germany. These "war hawks," following the geopolitical arguments made popular by Captain Alfred Thayer Mahan, also stressed the importance of Cuba in the context of broader American security concerns. To deal with an increasingly dangerous world, militant pro-interventionists insisted that the United States obtain naval bases and secure critical naval lines of communication and commerce in the Western Hemisphere and in the Pacific. The United States, as Mahan put it, must "look outward." A war with Spain over Cuba would provide the political-military impetus for America to acquire or control critical assets such as Hawaii and the site of a future Isthmian Canal.

The Election of 1896

The election of 1896, coming so shortly after the renewed insurrection in Cuba, might have been a referendum on U.S. intervention. It was not. The Democratic Party platform merely noted: "The Monroe doctrine, as originally declared, and as interpreted by succeeding Presidents, is a permanent part of the foreign policy of the United States, and must at all times be maintained. We extend our sympathy to the people of Cuba in their heroic struggle for liberty and independence." The Republican platform reasserted:

> the Monroe Doctrine in its full extent, and we reaffirm the rights of the United States to give the Doctrine effect by responding to the appeal of any American State for friendly intervention in case of European encroachment. . . . We watch with deep and abiding interest the heroic battles of the Cuban patriots against cruelty and oppression, and best hopes go out for the full success of their determined contest for liberty. The government of Spain, having lost control of Cuba, and being unable to protect the property or lives of resident American citizens, or to comply with its Treaty obligations, we believe that the government of the United States

should actively use its influence and good offices to restore peace and give independence to the Island.[2]

The major issue of 1896 was not foreign or defense policy; it was the currency question – crudely put, gold versus silver. More fundamentally, it concerned the organization of American society and government – a concern that had been fanned by the financial conditions set off by the Panic of 1893. The issue cut across party lines. New York Senator T.C. Platt wrote on the eve of the vote: "There has been no more important election in this country since the [Civil] war; in fact, the issues involved in the campaign which are now drawing to a close are of more vital concern than any that have ever been raised since the foundation of the Republic."[3] Most politicians and commentators at the time concurred with Platt's assessment. American politics were very much in a state of flux as the nation approached the 20th century. The political alignment first created by the election of 1860 and confirmed by the Civil War seemed to be breaking down. Despite Republican domination of presidential elections since Lincoln's first term (28 of the 36 years), the Democratic Party had been very competitive at the Congressional and local levels. Now the old-line foundation of the Republican Party was being challenged by forces that were at once radical and reactionary. Whether or not those forces succeeded in 1896, or proved a temporary aberration, conservatives in both parties were afraid of losing their grip on affairs – and not just on the currency matter.

The Republican nominee, William McKinley of Ohio, was considered an old-line Republican, albeit not a reactionary. He built his reputation as an expert on the tariff. His party was the national party, the party of the Union, which believed in economic funding, spending and regulation. He was publicly associated with big business interests, most notably through his friend, Mark Hanna. As a Congressman, however, McKinley had favored such measures as civil service reform and federal protection of voting rights to the point where some considered him a liberal Republican. "I always felt that McKinley represented the newer view," no less an authority than Robert La Follette would recall. "Of course, McKinley was a high protectionist, but on the great new issues as they arose he was generally on the side of the public

---

[2] Platforms accessed at http://www.presidency.ucsb.edu/platforms.php. According to the People's Party platform: "We tender to the patriotic people of the country our deepest sympathies in their heroic struggle for political freedom and independence, and we believe the time has come when the United States, the great Republic of the world, should recognize that Cuba is and of right ought to be a free and independent State." Accessed at http://projects.vassar.edu/1896/peoplesplatform.html.

[3] T.C. Platt, "The Effect of Republican Victory," *North American Review* 163 (November 1896): 513.

and against private interests."[4] Concerning the issue at hand, McKinley was solidly in the camp of the hard-money gold bugs. He warned that free silver would prove inflationary and thereby threaten the value of income and savings. Prosperity meant a Republican tariff and an expanding export trade; it also meant a national rather than a narrow class-based party.

> My countrymen, the most un-American of all appeals observable in this campaign is the one which seeks to array labor against capital, employer against unemployed. It is most unpatriotic and is fraught with the greatest peril to all concerned. We are all political equals here – equal in privilege and opportunity, dependent upon each other, and the prosperity of the one is the prosperity of the other.[5]

While business-oriented Republicans chafed over the silver heresy, Theodore Roosevelt, then New York City Police Commissioner and a rising star in the party, longed to bring another issue to the front. "Though I feel very strongly indeed on such questions as municipal reform and civil service reform, I feel even more strongly on the question of our attitude towards the outside world, with all that implies, from seacoast defense and a first class navy, to a properly vigorous foreign policy," he announced in April 1896. "I think we ought to interfere in Cuba . . ."[6] Had Cleveland or one of his sound-money associates been the Democratic nominee, Roosevelt might well have pushed to make American policy toward Spain the campaign's principal issue. As it was, he had to place the money question first.

> It is earnestly to be hoped that the Republican Party will also make an aggressive fight on the question of America's foreign policy. A policy of buncombe and spread-eagleism in foreign affairs would be sincerely to be deprecated; but a policy of tame submission to insult is even worse. In its foreign policy the present Democratic administration has offered a most unpleasant contrast to the preceding Republican administration. The very Democrats who have stood stoutest in warring against the great majority of their own party for sound finance have also been unpleasantly conspicuous in forcing their party to adopt a thoroughly improper and un-American tone in

---

[4] Cited by Margaret Leech, *In the Days of McKinley* (New York: Harper & Brothers, 1959), p. 485.

[5] H. Wayne Morgan, *From Hayes to McKinley: National Party Politics, 1877-1896* (Syracuse, NY: Syracuse University Press, 1969), p. 518.

[6] Roosevelt to Cowles, April 5, 1896, in Elting Morison, et al., eds. *The Letters of Theodore Roosevelt*, 8 vols. (Cambridge: Harvard University Press, 1951-1954), 1: 524. Hereafter referred to as *Roosevelt Letters*.

foreign affairs. Unfortunately, very many decent men in the country, and especially in the Northeast, are too timid, or too unpatriotic, to wish the United States to play the part it should among the nations of the earth. America must never play the part of a bully; but even less must she play the part of a coward; and it is this last most unpleasant part which, during the last two years of Democratic administration, she has once or twice come near playing.[7]

The Democratic Party of President Grover Cleveland was in a sorry state as Roosevelt penned those words in late 1895. The elections of 1894 had proven disastrous for the party, reversing the promising results of 1890 and 1892. In the 54th Congress, the Democratic majority in the House was wiped out; only 104 Democrats would face 245 Republicans. Nebraska Congressman William Jennings Bryan, beset by an intra-party rivalry, was one of those Democrats who failed at re-election. Cleveland, in the meantime, had lost control of his own party, which was split between silver and gold, populist and Bourbon factions.[8]

On the face of events, the Democratic nominee in 1896 should have been a sacrificial lamb. The currency question, however, cut across sections and parties; as Platt noted, "party lines, for the time being, have been practically obliterated."[9] Might not a Democrat who disregarded the party's conservatism on monetary and social matters be able to command a new majority, and bring about another Revolution of 1800? The key would be a West-South agrarian alliance within the party, replacing the old East-South Bourbon alliance. This was the foundation of the proposed "popocrat" coalition. With 224 electoral votes necessary to elect the President, the 83 electoral votes in the section west of the Mississippi and the 159 electoral votes in the South (including Delaware) would be sufficient for victory. A win in competitive states in the Midwest would even offset possible defections in the West and South. In short, a silver Democratic candidate with Populist support could be elected President without winning a single Northern state east of the Mississippi.[10] As Kansas' David Overmeyer proclaimed, it did

---

[7] Theodore Roosevelt, "The Issues of 1896: A Republican View," *Century Illustrated Monthly* (November 1895): 71.

[8] Morgan, *From Hayes to McKinley,* pp. 477-8; Allan Nevins, *Grover Cleveland: A Study in Courage* (New York: Dodd, Mead, 1932), pp. 679, 681.

[9] Platt, "Republican Victory," p. 514.

[10] Louis W. Koenig, *Bryan: A Political Biography of William Jennings Bryan* (New York: Putnam, 1971), p. 143.

seem as if "the seat of empire" had been transferred from "the Atlantic to the great Mississippi Valley," if not even farther west. [11]

The heir to that transformation was unclear as the Democrats met in Chicago. The Cleveland forces were bloodied but unbowed, and they warned that no Democrat could win without carrying some of the East. Still, the candidate would likely be a silverite, perhaps Richard "Silver Dick" Bland of Missouri. Few gave much thought to a former Nebraska Congressman named Bryan who was just old enough to qualify for the office, and who had attended the Republican convention as a reporter. Fortune, nevertheless, placed Bryan on the rostrum at the right moment, and he delivered the speech that he was confident would gain him the nomination. He had given almost the identical Cross of Gold speech earlier in Congress, but the convention was the perfect platform for his style and message. Sunlight filtered onto Bryan during the address and, as he finished, Bryan raised his arms in a crucifixion stance. The Democrats had found a candidate, and for the first time a Presidential nominee resided west of the Missouri River. [12]

Republicans were clearly worried about the effect that the "Boy Orator of the Platte" could have on the campaign. (The Platte, Lodge could not help remarking, "is a stream 1250 miles long, with an average depth of six inches and a wide mouth." [13]) Bryan was an excellent speaker with a radical message; while McKinley conducted the traditional and dignified front porch campaign, Bryan was constantly on the road. He began the campaign with a swing into the enemy's camp, the Northeast, where he accepted formal notification of the Democratic nomination at Madison Square Garden in New York. Bryan's announced foreign policy views were tied up with his views on the currency question. He vigorously denied that he was a sectional candidate, claiming instead that "national character is being weakened and national independence threatened by servile submission to foreign dictation." This dictation was being fostered by an international conspiracy in favor of gold, led by Britain, in alliance with the moneyed interests of the East. It was against those interests that Bryan led his crusade.

> Today the Democratic Party stands between two great forces, each inviting its support. On the one side stand the corporate interests of the nation, its moneyed institutions, its aggregations

---

[11] Cited by Koenig, *Bryan*, p. 192.

[12] Ibid., p. 212; Morgan, *From Hayes to McKinley*, p. 504. For a sympathetic modern biography of Bryan, see Michael Kazin, *A Godly Hero: The Life of William Jennings Bryan* (New York: Anchor Books, 2006).

[13] Cited by John A. Garraty, *Henry Cabot Lodge: A Biography* (New York: Knopf, 1953), p. 174.

of wealth and capital, imperious, arrogant, compassionless. They demand special legislation, favors, privileges, and immunities. They can subscribe magnificently to campaign funds; they can strike down opposition with their all-pervading influence, and to those who fawn and flatter, bring ease and plenty. They demand that the Democratic Party shall become their agent to execute their merciless decrees. On the other side stands that unnumbered throng which gave a name to the Democratic Party and for which it has assumed to speak. Work-worn and dust-begrimed, they make their sad appeal. They hear of average wealth increased on every side and feel the inequality of its distribution. They see an overproduction of everything desired because of the under-production of the ability to buy. They cannot pay for loyalty except with their suffrages, and can only punish betrayal with their condemnation. Although the ones, who most deserve the fostering care of government, their cries for help too often beat in vain against the outer wall, while others less deserving find ready access to legislative halls. [14]

Bryan traced the lineage of his Democratic party through Andrew Jackson to Thomas Jefferson, the political progenitor of agrarian populism.

Let us, then, with the courage of Andrew Jackson, apply to the present conditions the principles taught by Thomas Jefferson – Thomas Jefferson, the greatest constructive statesman whom the world has ever known; the grandest warrior who ever battled for human liberty. He gave apt expression to the hopes that had nestled in the heart of man for ages and he set forth the principles upon whose strength all popular government must rest. In the Declaration of American Independence he proclaimed the principle with which there is, without which there cannot be, "a government of the people, by the people, and for the people." He declared that "all men are created equal; that they are endowed by their Creator with certain inalienable rights; that among these are life, liberty, and the pursuit of happiness, and that to secure these rights, governments are instituted among men, deriving their just powers from the consent of the governed."

---

[14] Genevieve Forbes Herrick and John Origen Herrick, *The Life of William Jennings Bryan* (Chicago: Buxton Publishing House, 1925), p. 95. This speech was given on August 16, 1893. See also J.C. Long, *Bryan: The Great Commoner* (New York: D. Appleton & Company, 1928), p. 94.

> He comprehended all that lies between the Alpha and Omega of democracy.

> Alexander "wept for other worlds to conquer" after he had carried his victorious banner throughout the then known world. Napoleon "rearranged the map of Europe with his sword" amid the lamentations of those by whose blood he was exalted; but when these and other military heroes are forgotten and their achievements disappear in the cycle's sweep of years, children will still lisp the name of Jefferson, and free men will ascribe due praise to him who filled the kneeling subject's heart with hope and bade him stand erect – a sovereign among his peers.[15]

Bryan also anticipated the rhetoric of a man whose Secretary of State he would become, Woodrow Wilson.

> The money question is not too deep to be understood by the American people. The great questions of state, are, after all, simple in their last analysis. Every great political question is first a great economic question, and every great economic question is in reality a great moral question. Questions are not settled until the right and wrong of the questions are determined. Questions are not settled by a discussion of the details; they are not settled until the people grasp the fundamental principles, and when these principles are fully comprehended, then the people settle the question and they settle it for a generation.[16]

Although the silver question was foremost during the campaign of 1896, Bryan's election would clearly mean a new direction for American politics. As Boston Mayor Josiah Quincy pointed out in August, there were a large number of voters "who were thoroughly tired of the old political parties and the leadership which has controlled them," and who might therefore welcome the prospect of creating political disruption through the election of Bryan. In a normal election, the Republican candidate would stand to benefit from the disaffection with the Cleveland administration, but the Democrats had cut themselves "loose so entirely from the present administration and from existing political conditions, that (they offer) to the country a much more pronounced change than the Republican Party." The Republicans had

---

[15] Herrick and Herrick, *William Jennings Bryan*, pp. 97-8. This speech was given on March 19, 1895.

[16] Cited in ibid., p. 148.

become the defenders of the present order, while Bryan offered a program of radical and far-reaching change. [17]

McKinley was elected as Chief Executive in November 1896, despite the fact that Bryan received more votes than any other Democratic candidate in history. McKinley's 271-176 margin in the Electoral College included the doubtful states of Delaware, Maryland, West Virginia, Kentucky, Iowa, Minnesota, North Dakota, California and Oregon. [18] The geographical pattern of votes was nonetheless striking, with the traditionally Democratic South aligned with most of the plain and Rocky Mountain states. The Republican electoral coalition was shaky at best. Was this only a temporary division over the currency question, or was there a deeper polarization? The growing foreign policy crisis over Cuba – and the debate over whether the United States should intervene to terminate the Spanish colonial regime over that island – might decisively affect the political direction of the American regime, one way or another.

The Cuban Rebellion: McKinley's Cautious Conservatism

McKinley's initial position on the Cuban situation seemed ambiguous and satisfactory both to the interventionist and anti-interventionist isolationist camps. In his Inaugural Address, he did not even specifically refer to Cuba, but instead articulated the conservative's foreign policy creed.

> We have cherished the policy of non-interference with the affairs of foreign governments, wisely inaugurated by Washington, keeping ourselves free from entanglements either as allies or foes, content to leave undisturbed with them the settlement of their own domestic concerns. It will be our aim to pursue a firm and dignified foreign policy which shall be just and impartial, ever-watchful of our national honor and always insisting upon the enforcement of the lawful rights of American citizens. We want no wars of conquest. We must avoid the temptation of territorial aggression. War should never be entered upon until every agency of peace has failed; peace is preferable to war in almost

---

[17] Josiah Quincy, "Issues and Prospects of the Campaign," *North American Review* 163 (August 1896): 194.

[18] The Electoral College results can be accessed at http://www.usconstitution.net/ev_1896.html. For an analysis see Harold U. Faulkner, *Politics: Reform and Expansion, 1890-1900* (New York: Harper & Brothers, 1959).

every contingency. Arbitration is the true method of settlement of international as well as local or individual differences. [19]

McKinley told Carl Schurz that "there will be no jingo nonsense under my administration"; and added that he had submitted a treaty to annex Hawaii to the Senate in 1897 only to test public opinion on that topic. [20] His object was the traditional one of peace and prosperity. "Cuba . . . is very much on his mind and I found that he had given it a great deal of thought," Lodge wrote Roosevelt before the inauguration. "He very naturally does not want to be obliged to go to war as soon as he comes in, for of course his great ambition is to restore business and bring back good times and he dislikes the idea of such interruption." [21] There were possible complications with Europe that might attend any American intervention. And then there was the experience of ex-Union Major McKinley in such matters: "I have been through one war. I have seen the dead piled up, and I do not want to see another." [22]

On the surface, McKinley's policy toward Spain was not all that much different than that of the previous administration. Both refused to recognize the belligerent status of the Cuban rebels, or to recognize Cuban independence, as many interventionists had demanded. McKinley, like Cleveland, preferred a negotiated settlement. Moreover, the Republican President was much more direct in his diplomatic criticism of Spanish atrocities, and demanded that Spain's pacification campaign be conducted "according to the military codes of civilization." He protested "against the cruel employment of fire and famine to accomplish by uncertain indirection what the military arm seems powerless to directly accomplish." Unlike the Cleveland administration, which was prepared to disregard the wishes of the rebels in order to achieve a satisfactory settlement, McKinley refused to impose a solution unacceptable to the Cubans, even if Madrid accepted his offer of mediation. If the Cuban people were determined to achieve independence, there would be no basis for negotiation if, as it soon became

---

[19] McKinley's Inaugural Address, 4 March 1897, accessed at http://millercenter.org/scripps/archive/speeches/detail/3562.

[20] Sylvester K. Stevens, *American Expansion in Hawaii, 1842-1898* (Harrisburg: Archives Publishing Company of Pennsylvania, 1945), p. 290.

[21] Ernest R. May, *Imperial Democracy: The Emergence of America as a Great Power* (New York: Harper & Row, 1973), p. 117.

[22] Edmund Morris, *The Rise of Theodore Roosevelt* (New York: Coward, McCann & Geoghegan, 1979), p. 600.

apparent, Spain was equally determined not to leave the island. McKinley's course, therefore, seemed to lead either to stalemate or to war.[23]

Radical interventionists bitterly protested against the President's reluctance to push matters with Spain to a head, but the more strategic minded initially accepted his caution. McKinley "has done so much that I don't feel like being discontented," Roosevelt admitted in 1897.[24] The anti-interventionists could likewise grudgingly accept McKinley's stance against the demands for war. "McKinley has behaved extremely well, and has done everything that a man in his position could do, for peace, partly because he sincerely dislikes war, and partly because the effect of war on his fortunes would be very uncertain," E.L. Godkin wrote James Bryce in early 1898. Godkin speculated that the President intended to prolong the negotiations until after the November congressional elections, and perhaps even until he was re-nominated and reelected. "We keep edging towards war fast enough to keep the jingoes quiet, and yet not fast enough to frighten or alarm the good people." (Still, Godkin could not help adding: "The newspapers are filled with promises, although everyone acknowledges in private that he is an intriguing ass . . ."[25]) Critics accused McKinley of being a scheming politician out to satisfy everyone at once, or merely an unprincipled weakling with the backbone of a chocolate éclair. The *Baltimore News* reflected:

> One merit should be unanimously conceded to the president's eagerly awaited message. It is that which was assigned to one of our best-known northern universities by a Japanese student, some years ago. Being asked how he was pleased with the institution, the Japanese replied: "It is admirable. The teaching is so bad that we are compelled to do all our own thinking." If the president's object was to say just enough to set congress and the people to thinking very hard, and not enough to show them either what they ought to think or what he thinks himself, he has succeeded to a nicety.[26]

McKinley's supporters contended that his course was statesmanlike and conservative, rejecting both radical extremes of indifference and war until events resolved the situation one way or another. "The weak man in his

---

[23] J.A.S. Grenville and George B. Young, *Politics, Strategy and American Diplomacy: Studies in Foreign Policy, 1873-1917* (New Haven: Yale University Press, 1966), p. 249.

[24] May, *Imperial Democracy*, p. 123.

[25] Godkin to James Bryce, March 22 and April 1, 1898, in William M. Armstrong, ed. *The Gilded Age Letters of E.L. Godkin* (Albany. State University of New York, 1974), pp. 502 3.

[26] Cited in *Public Opinion* 24 (April 21, 1898): 487.

place would have long ago rushed into war under the awful pressure exerted," Charles Dawes, a McKinley aide, recorded in his journal. "The ultra papers are heaping abuse upon the President, but the conservative press of the country sustains him." [27]

William Claflin, a former governor of Massachusetts, wrote to Secretary of the Navy John Davis Long, "The country believes in him, will follow him in all his efforts for peace. All the jingoes will be left high and dry, by and by, and will have about the same name as the Hartford Conventionists, in the great hereafter." [28] But many of those jingoes were also Republicans, good Republicans like Roosevelt and Lodge. The members of the Hartford Convention had been Federalists, after all, and that party's opposition to the War of 1812 and its suspected disloyalty served as its death knell. The struggle over Cuban policy was thus very much a struggle over the soul of McKinley, and the future direction of his party.

Many leading Republican businessmen opposed intervention. "First, I do not believe the American people want war," Maine Republican Senator Hale asserted on February 9, 1898. "It is too intolerable that to-day, with our industries reviving, with the demand for peace reviving, the American people want war." [29] Commercial classes were not the only groups opposing intervention; conservatives in both parties concurred with McKinley's remark, "I had rather that my administration were an ignominious failure than that it should become responsible for an unjust war." The *Philadelphia Record* chastised those who would refuse a monetary indemnity from Spain if that power was found culpable for the fatal explosion aboard the battleship *Maine*. "If there could be no indemnity for the offense there could be no end of the war save in the ruin of one of the combatants. Nations have found in arbitration and indemnity far better methods of settling their differences than by the arbitrament of arms."

> A war would not prove Spain to be in the wrong, while it would betray to the world not only a want of foresight but of public morality in the American people should they rush into an assault upon a weak power without adequate cause. The weakness and decrepitude of Spain afford no reason why a brave and magnanimous nation should make war upon her. On the contrary, the feebleness

---

[27] Bascom N. Timmons, ed., *A Journal of the McKinley Years by Charles G. Dawes* (Chicago: The Lakeside Press, 1950), pp. 150-1. Hereafter referred to as *Dawes Journal*.

[28] Claflin to Long, April 3, 1898, Gardner Weld Allen, ed., *Papers of John Davis Long, 1897-1904* (Norwood: Massachusetts Historical Society, 1939), p. 83.

[29] *Congressional Record* 32, 55: 2, part 2, February 9, 1898, p. 1577.

> of Spain and her utter incapacity to cope with a country of the inexhaustible resources of the United States should be with a great nation strong reason for forbearance. To inflict a war upon Spain merely to gratify the military spirit or for no better cause would be like the act of Tom Hood's bully, who gave a man two black eyes for being blind.[30]

Any war with Spain would place the United States in the wrong in world public opinion, Godkin cautioned. "The Franco-Prussian war of 1870 demonstrated that the world's sympathy is a great factor in wars at the present day. Even when not accompanied by active help, it encourages one side and depresses the other."[31] And at home, Godkin asked: Are there no gentlemen left in American public life? "We have had six or eight years of constant Jingo excitement to make our national temper irritable and suspicious. We have had dark plots and designs of foreign nations held up before us as bogies. National good faith, the sincerity of a desire for peace, the sanctity of treaties, the strength of diplomatic methods and moral forces – all have been scouted as delusions of lethargic and luxury-loving citizens."

> It must not be forgotten that we are to-day making precedents and concocting doctrines for what is practically a new people. No one denies that the national character, partly as a result of the [Civil] war and partly as a result of the influence of greatly increased facility in making money, has undergone serious modifications. The old expectation of peaceful development and the self-reliance which were the chief characteristics of American society before the war, have well-nigh disappeared. A large portion of the population is filled with a desire to employ force to gratify our own desires and ambitions, to become a great military and naval power, and to use this power to have our own way, in disregard of law and precedent. The cheap press preaches these things incessantly, and the cheap press now has an influence on the government of the nation which no one dreamed of fifty years ago.[32]

The anti-interventionists' bane was indeed the so-called "yellow press," with its lurid reporting of alleged atrocities by the Spanish military. "There are probably more able bodied liars to the square inch in Cuba than

---

[30] Cited in *Literary Digest* 16 (March 12, 1898): 302-3.

[31] *Nation* (April 14, 1898), p. 279.

[32] *Nation* (February 24, 1898), p. 142, and (April 21, 1898), pp. 296-7.

in any other section of the globe," the *Los Angeles Times* had admonished in 1896.[33] Godkin was even more explicit. He publicly doubted whether the Cuban rebels had either the sympathy or support of a majority on the island. He reported that prominent citizens in Havana had signed a statement to the effect that eighty percent of the island's property owners opposed the rebellion and autonomy from Spain. Godkin predicted that the withdrawal of Spanish troops from Cuba would result not in peace but in a new revolution. Further, he applauded Senator Hale's statement that the rebels had committed greater atrocities than had the Spaniards: "This fact has been leaking out for some time . . . the answer of the jingo politicians and newspapers is that this mode of warfare is excusable in those struggling for 'liberty' but not for their oppressors – an answer which does not go far to help families whose fields have been devastated, their houses and sugar mills burned, and themselves, if not slaughtered, turned into the highway to perish."[34]

Then there were the political arguments against intervention. Speaker of the House Thomas B. Reed, a Maine Republican, defended himself against charges that he was pro-Spanish to his one-time supporter, Senator Lodge. Unless there was a clear advantage to the United States, Reed explained, he preferred not to spill any American blood. "As I have said to you before, let us assimilate Pettigrew and Teller [Silver Republican Senators from South Dakota and Colorado] before we try something harder." "As for gratitude of nations, that is not worth counting. If we help another people to liberty we either do it for our own interests or it will seem so when their interests become diverse. In fact until the federation of the world let each nation look out for itself."[35]

Could McKinley rely upon the support of all sections and interests should he choose intervention? An editorial in the *Chattanooga Times* in mid-March 1898 asked the South to be slow in crying "war," since the brunt of any war with Spain over Cuba would fall upon the South. The lightly defended Southern coast would be attacked, and if Spain allied itself with France, that coast might well be threatened with an invasion. A free Cuba would mean nothing to the South. In fact, the island would probably become the scene of

---

[33] Cited by Omer A. Weston, "The Attitude of California Toward Intervention in Cuba and American Imperialism, 1895-1900," M.A. Thesis, Claremont Graduate School, 1952, p. 23.

[34] *Nation* (March 10 and 17, 1898), pp. 178, 199; *New York Evening Post*, January 29 and March 10, 1898, cited by Joseph E. Wisan, *The Cuban Crisis as Reflected in the New York Press, 1895-1898* (New York: Columbia University Press, 1934), p. 96.

[35] William A. Robinson, *Thomas B. Reed, Parliamentarian* (New York: Dodd, Mead and Company, 1930), pp. 358-9.

an internecine war of extermination, to the point that American intervention would be necessary to restore order and revive industry. What, then, would happen to the South's sugar industry? What compensation could Cuba offer for the sacrifice of thousands of warm-blooded young men?[36]

The Interventionists: A Definition of Nationalism

It is unnecessary here to recount in detail the diplomatic moves and political debates that led the United States into war with Spain.[37] The relatively liberal Spanish government in Madrid had to account for serious domestic pressures against surrendering the last vestiges of the once-great empire; it offered only limited reforms and the recall of General Weyler. The Cuban *insurrectos*, who wanted complete independence, also rejected compromise. The American press published an inflammatory private letter from the Spanish Minister to the United States, Enrique Dupuy de Lôme, which disparaged McKinley personally and made clear that Spain's promise of reforms was not seriously intended. On February 15, 1898, the battleship *Maine* exploded while on a "goodwill visit" to Havana harbor. The official U.S. investigation concluded that the ship had been destroyed by a submarine mine of unknown origin, but the obvious conclusion was that Spain had planted the device. Public opinion moved sharply in the direction of intervention after the explosion of the *Maine*.[38] The President now insisted on Spanish acceptance of U.S. mediation. He declined the offers of European powers, led by Germany and France, to mediate the dispute, and rejected a Spanish offer to suspend hostilities. On April 11, 1898, McKinley sent Congress a message that asked for the authority to use the army and navy to end hostilities in Cuba.[39]

How did the debate evolve during 1895-1898, to reach the point where the United States found itself on the verge of military intervention in Cuba with widespread popular support, despite the previous deep-seated resistance to

---

[36] Cited in *Public Opinion* 24 (March 17, 1898): 325.

[37] This is usefully presented by John L. Offner, *An Unwanted War: The Diplomacy of the United States and Spain over Cuba, 1895-1898* (Chapel Hill: University of North Carolina Press, 1992); and Lewis L. Gould, *The Spanish-American War and President McKinley* (Lawrence: University Press of Kansas, 1982).

[38] Secretary of the Navy Long noted: "There is intense difference of opinion as to the cause of the blowing up of the *Maine*. In this, as in everything else, the opinion of the individual is determined by his original bias. If he is a conservative, he is sure it was an accident; if he is a jingo, he is equally sure that it was by design." Lawrence Shaw Mayo, ed., *America of Yesterday, as Reflected in the Journal of John Davis Long* (Boston: The Atlantic Press, 1923), pp. 163-4. Hereafter cited as the *Long Journal*.

[39] Accessed at http://www.mtholyoke.edu/acad/intrel/mkinly2.htm.

American involvement and McKinley's apparent reluctance to go to war? The "jingo alliance" that eventually coalesced behind intervention in Cuba was a curious one, uniting many Western and Southern silverites of both parties and the hard-money expansionists of the Republican Party. Their common foe was the conservative anti-interventionist business interests of the Northeast. Massachusetts Republican Senator George F. Hoar drew the fire of the *New York World* as being "indifferent to the slaughter of the insurgents because the commercial sentiment of New England states deprecates any interference by Spain with their coast-wide trade.... [His] change of front was dictated by the chilly pulse of Boston." [40] Senator Lodge explained in his later history of the Spanish-American War:

> Against the sentiment springing from the popular instinct which at the great crisis of American history has always been true and right, an opposition strong in purpose although in large measure concealed, was arrayed. The naturally timid and conservative elements of the community shrank from war, and the powerful financial interests of the Eastern cities, too short-sighted to see that their selfish advantage was in the certainty of action and not in suspense, exerted their great force to stop every forward step along the inevitable path. [41]

The *Denver Times* warned that the "'commercial instinct' has triumphed and the higher impulses have been subordinated at the command of mercenary interests." [42] This theme was particularly popular in the West. "Mr. President," cried Utah's Frank J. Cannon, a Silver Republican, before the Senate,

> I charge now that the purpose of the Administration in delaying action is in consonance with, if not in direct co-partnership with, the will of the Spanish bondholders, who are determined that before Cuba shall be allowed her freedom in the world, and before there shall be recognition of her independence by Spain, there shall be security upon that blood-stained island for the major part of the debt which has been incurred by Spain. [43]

And Senator William V. Allen, a Nebraska Populist:

---

[40] *New York World,* March 12, 1897, cited by Wisan, *The Cuban Crisis,* p. 120.

[41] Henry Cabot Lodge, *The War with Spain* (New York: Arno Press & the New York Times, 1970), p. 32.

[42] Cited in *Public Opinion* 24 (April 21, 1898): 486.

[43] *Congressional Record* 31, 55: 2, part 2, February 9, 1898, p. 1574.

> But, unfortunately for the advancement and elevation of the human race and for the glory of our country, we have entered an era of cold and merciless commercialism that freezes the blood of patriotism in its veins and that is willing to sacrifice human rights, the honor of women, and the lives of children, if need be, that the course of business may not be checked or that the channels of trade be not obstructed. [44]

The interventionists also contended that a resolution on the bloodshed in Cuba would actually be a boon to business. The *Philadelphia Record* spoke of America's "expensive neutrality," i.e., the loss of millions of dollars in trade with a peaceful Cuba. [45] The *Cincinnati Enquirer*, a Silver Democrat newspaper, portrayed Cuba as a nation capable of "becoming a tremendous factor in the commerce of the world. Spain has restrained its development, and has thus interfered with the business and progress of other countries on this side of the Atlantic. She has been a drawback to civilization and advancement for a century. Now is the time to strike off the shackles." [46]

Senator William E. Mason, an Illinois Republican, recalled Secretary of State William Seward's protest in 1863 against French interference in Mexico. He reminded the Senate that this protest was based on American interests – "a statement of the Monroe doctrine in another way."

> In other words, it was not the Monroe doctrine, but it was "American interests." In Cuba, what was our interest? Buying from her millions of dollars of her products and selling to her millions of dollars of our products. That commerce has been interfered with. Commerce is absolutely dead between the two; and now the gentlemen say that we have no more right to interfere and stop that which destroys our commerce, which threatens the health of the American people than Spain had a right to interfere in the Chicago riots. [47]

The commercial motive of the interventionists, however, was decidedly secondary to that of principle. President McKinley seemed to many to be unable to articulate the outrage of the nation over Cuba. In the opinion of the Denver Times, McKinley's supposed war message "is not in harmony with the

---

[44] Ibid., part 1, December 8, 1897, p. 40.

[45] *Philadelphia Record*, cited in Public Opinion 24 (March 17, 1898): 325.

[46] Loc. cit.

[47] *Congressional Record* 31, 55: 2, part 2, February 9, 1898, p. 1579.

principles enunciated in the declaration of independence, nor does it satisfy the demands of liberty and justice upon which the foundations of our government are laid. It will carry no inspiration to humanity." [48] At the time, most estimates (including those of the Spaniards) calculated that 400,000 Cubans had died during the revolt – more than one quarter of the island's population. [49] If McKinley could not express America's horror at this massacre, and its demand that the killing cease, the interventionists had no lack of those who could. "It is the duty of the United States, as guardians of the Western hemisphere, to see that Cuba is not turned into an Armenia, and massacre made a substitute for war," the New York Mail and Express proclaimed in 1896. [50] Or, as Lodge reflected after the war: "Diplomats might plan, and twist, and devise, and exchange notes, and deal in all the forms so futile at a great crisis, but the American people had made up their minds that the only real and possible solution was the end of Spanish rule in Cuba." [51]

The American people had help in making up their minds. In a century when politicians and statesmen took pride in their rhetorical prowess, the orators of 1898 took second place to no one. There was Senator Mason:

> Mr. President, one moment we are charged with being for war and the next with being soft-hearted sentimentalists, because we seek our party to keep its promise, because we stand in line with civilization for peace and the growth of the people of the continent, because we insist upon a strictly broad and, if necessary, a new construction of the Monroe doctrine. The world moves. We can make history and we can make precedent. The precedent that is made along the line of liberty and civilization will live when we are gone. A precedent that we establish that is against the line of civilization and good conduct will die when our betters shall take our places.
>
> I like precedents just as well as any one when they are on my side of the case. "Sentimentalists," they say, "you want us to go and interfere in other people's business." All right, I am a sentimentalist. I do not deny it. The world without it would not be much. The Boston Tea Party was a sentimental party, not a social function,

---

[48] Cited in *Public Opinion* 24 (April 21, 1898): 486.

[49] May, *Imperial Democracy*, p. 127, reports that postwar estimates placed the number of dead at "only" 100,000. Other scholarly estimates are in the 200,000 range.

[50] Cited by Wisan, *The Cuban Crisis*, p. 91.

[51] Lodge, *The War with Spain*, p. 33.

as I remember it. This Government was established on sentiment, and it was a sentiment that sent you here and sent me here, to represent a principle. Sentiment laid the foundation of this building. Sentiment writes the laws! but when we get away from the moorings of sentiment, when we take the bucket shop and worship it in the joss house, when before we vote we listen to the ticker to know the state of the market, when the vicious people of the nation write the songs and the trusts and the bucket shops write the laws, the dawn of our day of decay is upon us and the night is not far off.

Mr. President, I am a sentimentalist. You people on the Democratic side have not forgotten the sentiments of your party, nor we ours. One of the proud and happy considerations of life is to read the history of my party, which is a part of my faith in life. The first platform of our party was an inspiration for liberty. The Republican Party has never written a platform with a view to capturing votes. God help us if at this late day we will go to the American people who put us in power in the White House and in the House of Congress and say to them, "Truly, we have broken faith, but the resolution was for buncombe, to get your votes in 1896." Did we mean anything by our platform when we wrote it? Go on with your plan of cowardice. Teach your children to say, "Peace at any price." Let them forget the fathers and the struggle for independence. Let the friendly (?) nations of Europe own slaves on your continent, and sell them and butcher them at will, while you lie still, and dip the Stars and Stripes to salute murderers, and but a few generations will come until the stern and warlike nations of the world will perch themselves in your harbor, waiting to divide the spoils of war. I have the same respect for a boy who will not fight for his rights that I have for a nation that will not fight for its rights. The boy grows usually but halfway, the nation the same.[52]

And perhaps the most representative of them all, Mason's Populist colleague from Nebraska, Senator William A. Harris on April 5, 1898:

Sir, I have seen war. If to die were to reach the summit of human calamity, if to weep and mourn for the loved and lost were to make up the sum of human woe, then nothing would be worse than war. But, sir, there is a crucifixion of the soul when honor dies, there is a

---

[52] *Congressional Record* 31, 55: 2, part 2, February 9, 1898, pp. 1581-2.

death of a nation "when the jingle of the guinea heals the hurt that honor feels;" there is an existence, when patriotic pride is dead, "that doth murder sleep" and life becomes a horrid nightmare, and men shun their fellows, and the laugh of little children becomes a taunt and a mockery. True, there have been men who could exist and thrive and fatten without national honor or pride or patriotism, like worms in a muck heap, but that nation has been the scorned of all time and has quickly died. God forbid that any such should ever be called Americans.

Sir, I shall never consent that our dead shall lie in Spanish soil and under the Spanish flag. Brave American sailors can know no rest there. When it becomes consecrated by freedom, when that flag has trailed in the dust, when the Cuban Republic is raised as a monument to the men who went down in the *Maine*, then, and then only, will they sleep.

Do you say this is revenge, and that revenge is unworthy of a great nation? No, Mr. President, a righteous wrath and just resentment, the swift punishment of the assassin and the wrongdoer, are wholly different from revenge and are the safeguards and protection of a nation among nations, and enable us to look the whole world in the face. What sight more glorious than a nation roused in such a cause as this! God hates a coward, and a nation timid, halting, and hesitating in its foreign policy is a sight despised of God and man. A just war promotes and preserves all that is highest and best in national life.[53]

As to the nature of the regime change, both Roosevelt and Lodge had their doubts whether the Cubans would have much success with their attempts at self-government, but concluded that anything would be better than Spanish misrule. "This is a world of comparative progress, and freedom from Spain would be to Cuba a long step in advance on the highroad of advancing civilization," Lodge wrote in May 1896. "The interests of humanity are the controlling reasons which demand the beneficent interposition of the United States to bring an end to this savage war and give to the island peace and independence."[54]

---

[53] Ibid., part 4, April 5, 1898, p. 3547.

[54] Lodge, "Our Duty to Cuba," *Forum* 21 (May 1898): 287. See also Roosevelt to Anna Cowles Roosevelt, January 2, 1897, *Roosevelt Letters*, 1: 573-4.

It did not seem to Roosevelt that Cuba ought to be annexed to the United States. "I don't want it to seem that we are engaged merely in a land-grabbing war," he wrote to Robert Bacon, a friend and businessman. "Let us fight on the broad grounds of securing the independence of a people who, whether they amount to much or not, have been treated with hideous brutality by their oppressors." Intervention in Cuba would have the added utility of "putting a medieval power once for all out of the western world."[55] Roosevelt had expressed his concern with the fate of the island as part of a much broader policy:

> My feeling about these matters is just this: I wish we had a perfectly consistent foreign policy, and that this policy was that ultimately every European power should be driven out of America, and every foot of American soil, including the nearest islands in both the Pacific and the Atlantic, should be in the hands of independent American states, and so far as possible in the possession of the United States or under its protection. With this end in view I should take every opportunity to oust each European power in turn from this continent, and to acquire for ourselves every military coign of vantage; and I would treat as cause for war any effort by a European power to get so much as a fresh foothold of any kind on American soil.[56]

If the United States were to act, it would first have to overcome its inhibitions against intervention in the affairs of other nations. Senator Harris argued that the doctrine of non-intervention was formulated by the bloody-handed Cain, who insolently answered his God, "Am I my brother's keeper?" His followers had neither advanced nor improved the doctrine, Harris concluded.[57] Senator Mason, in the meantime, responded to the accusation that he wished the United States to become the world's policeman:

> But we are told that this may involve ourselves; that if we demand peace in Cuba we may get into trouble. That is the answer the

---

[55] Roosevelt to Robert Bacon, April 8, 1898, ibid., 2: 814.

[56] Roosevelt to Chandler, December 23, 1897, ibid., 1: 746. When Roosevelt wrote his letter, he admitted that, at present, "owing mainly to the change in Spanish policy, it is not possible at the moment to do anything about Cuba." It was, however, possible to acquire Hawaii – indeed, necessary – because "otherwise it will pass into the hands of some strong nation." Cuba was in the hands of a weak and decadent nation, which made its position much less pressing; nevertheless, "I earnestly hope that events will so shape themselves that we must interfere sometime in the not distant future." Events developed even more rapidly than Roosevelt imagined.

[57] *Congressional Record* 31, 55: 2, part 4, April 5, 1898, p. 3546.

coward always gives when he permits a bully to destroy a crippled child. But, my friend says, "Is Uncle Sam a policeman?" Yes, yes. This is not couched in the language of international law; but it is international law. Uncle Sam is a policeman. Monroe put the policeman's star upon his breast and gave him charge concerning a continent, and all history shows that every time Uncle Sam has said to the people who attempted to interfere in Hawaii, in Mexico, in Cuba, or anywhere else on this continent, he exercised his power as a police officer, and the people of this country have stood behind him with the Army and the Navy and the Treasury of the Government. Less than two years ago, when England sought to gather but a few miles of territory in Venezuela, Grover Cleveland gave notice to them to stop and pointed to this doctrine of Monroe (which I am pleased to call the police powers of the continent), and when the President of the United States, Mr. Cleveland, served that notice upon England and told her that she must keep hands off Venezuela, he simply acted as a police officer. All Christendom said "amen," and England consented to the truth of our position and contention when she arbitrated as to Venezuela.[58]

Mason also endeavored to explain why he sought intervention when President Grant, the great Republican war hero, had declined to interfere or even recognize the Cuban insurgents in the 1870s. The European situation then was such that the United States might have become involved, Mason explained; that danger no longer existed because the European nations were busily watching each other, and did not care to become embroiled in a quarrel with the United States. Also, America had then not yet recovered from its own Civil War. The United States was now strong, but an even more important change had come "in the evolution of the sentiment of the American people. More liberty is demanded by Americans for Americans than was the case twenty years ago, when we stood near the shadow of our own slave pens."[59]

Americans were also becoming aware of the strategic aspects of any war and the presumed threat that Spain posed to the American regime. The *New York Journal* printed brief extracts from an 1876 book by Spanish Minister de Lôme, which predicted the ultimate partition of the United States into three nations: East, North, and South.[60] The *Journal* also cited a Havana reporter's

---

[58] Ibid., part 2, February 9, 1898, p. 1581.

[59] Ibid., p. 1580.

[60] Cited in Wisan, *The Cuban Crisis*, p. 381.

prediction that, in the event of war, the American southwest would rebel and form a new republic under the protection of Spain, Mexico and France.[61] The *New York Sun* had warned in 1895 that Spain was using its military power to keep the key to the Gulf of Mexico under European control.[62]

Captain Alfred Thayer Mahan provided the most influential account of the strategic importance of Cuba in an October 1897 article in *Harper's New Monthly Magazine*. Mahan noted the similarities between the Caribbean/ Gulf of Mexico and the Mediterranean Sea. In the Mediterranean, however, the Land Powers (Germany, Austria, Russia) were superior to the Sea Powers (Britain, France, Italy), while the Caribbean was pre-eminently the domain of sea power. The Gulf had one major position of commercial importance (the mouth of the Mississippi River), as did the Caribbean (the Isthmus). The lines of communication to and from these centers were vulnerable to interdiction by a superior naval power operating from Cuba or, secondarily, Jamaica.

> Cuba presents a condition wholly unique among the islands of the Caribbean and of the Gulf of Mexico; of both which it, and it alone of all the archipelago, belongs. It is unique in its size, which should render it largely self-supporting, either by its own production or by the accumulation of foreign necessaries which naturally obtains in a large and prosperous maritime community; and it is unique in that such supplies can be conveyed from one point to the other, according to the needs of a fleet, by interlines, not exposed to the risks of maritime capture. The extent of the coast line, its numerous harbors, and the many directions from which approach can be made, minimize the dangers of total blockade to which all islands are subject. Such conditions are in themselves advantageous, but they are especially so to a navy inferior to its adversary, for they convey the power – subject, of course, to conditions of skill – of shifting operations from side to side, and finding refuge and supplies in either direction.[63]

American interventionists understandably were concerned that Spain, or some other hostile European power, would one day use Cuba against the United States. They could point to an April 1897 article in the *North American Review* by Captain Jose Gutierrez Sobral, the naval attaché at the Spanish lega-

---

[61] Cited in ibid., p. 273.

[62] Cited in ibid., pp. 85-6.

[63] Mahan, "The Strategic Features of the Gulf of Mexico and the Caribbean Sea," *Harper's New Monthly Magazine* 95 (October 1897): 680-91.

tion in Washington, for proof of their concern. Captain Sobral explained that Spain, as the owner of Cuba, must at all times exercise a powerful influence in the Gulf of Mexico, and that it was capable of becoming the commanding influence there. If the United States persisted in its plan to construct an isthmian canal, Sobral insisted, Spain would in turn fortify its West Indian possessions, and maintain such a fleet in those waters as to neutralize American control of the canal, at least to some extent. [64]

McKinley: Dilemma or Opportunity?

The President was clearly under increasing pressure by leading elements of both parties to "do something" about Cuba after the *Maine* catastrophe and the leak of the de Lôme letter. "But the time has at last arrived when patience ceases to be a virtue and magnanimity becomes folly," the *New York Mail and Express* warned in February 1898. [65] The *Denver Times*, a Republican newspaper that characterized its President as "a man who failed to rise to a great occasion – a man of good intentions, but not of great attainments." [66] This was a relatively mild criticism compared to that of the *Minneapolis Times*:

> What ails the man? Has he gone daft, or does he really believe that this is a nation of fools and cowards? In all the history of the nation there was never a more humiliating exhibition of cowardice in the White House as this indecisive, evasive, and thoroughly insincere message. It is impossible to discuss the situation with any degree of equanimity. The unpatriotic, almost imbecile message of the president places the American people in a most humiliating and painful attitude, which can only be relieved by the prompt and patriotic action of congress. [67]

The Democratic *New York Journal* leveled probably the unkindest charge of all against a Republican administration:

> The President has sounded the retreat. It is not that it would be the shame of Americans to follow him. Instead taking a step, firm and irretraceable, for the expulsion of the Spaniards from Cuba, the president begs shamefacedly for power to compel a compromise

---

[64] J.G. Sobral, "A Spanish View of the Nicaraguan Canal," *North American Review* 164 (April 1897): 462-71.

[65] Cited in *Public Opinion* 24 (February 17, 1898): 198.

[66] Cited in ibid., (April 21, 1898): 486.

[67] Cited in ibid., (April 7, 1898): 420.

between the Spaniards and Cubans. Compromise! The very word implies the yielding to Spain of some rights still of sovereignty in the islands it has desolated. No considerations of loyalty to the national government can compel acquiescence in a policy which seeks to betray Cuban freedom into the clutches of Spanish monarchy. Aggressive Americanism was promised for the president by his spokesmen. Prompt vengeance for the foul destruction of the Maine it was said he would promise. What did we find instead? Wordy palavering, laborious citations of the words of men like Jackson, who in this crisis would have indicated in deeds, not words, his solvent for the problem. The assassination of the Maine set aside as a matter to be determined in the interminable loquacities of diplomacy. An aggressive Americanism? Not a manifestation of it appears in the president's marshaling of studied phrases. Not one ounce of the spirit that burned at Bunker Hill, in Independence Hall on July 4, 1776, or in the hearts of the brave men who stood by Jackson in the Louisiana swamps in 1814 gleams from the muckish mass of sordid words and pitiable timidity which McKinley sent to Congress in lieu of a call to arms. [68]

Henry Cabot Lodge had admonished President Cleveland in 1896, "If one Administration declines to meet our national responsibilities as they should be met, there should be put in power another Administration which will neither neglect nor shun its plain duty to the United States and to the cause of freedom and humanity." [69] Many Republican leaders feared that Lodge's prophesy would be proven only too true for Cleveland's successor. They dreaded the Democratic slogan in the elections of 1900: "Free Cuba" and "Free Silver." Certain silverites had been in the vanguard of the interventionist movement from its inception. Nebraska Populist Allen hammered on Republican vulnerabilities:

> I do not belong to that circle that is rusting and rotting out for want of action, miscalling itself conservative. I have not said one word about it – the *Maine*. Every man in the United States who has quit thinking is conservative. Every man who wants to let things run along and drift as they will is a conservative man. Every man who leaves his plow in the field to rust and lets the weeds grow is a conservative man. I have no earthly respect for that kind of

---

[68] Cited in ibid., (April 21, 1898): 484.

[69] Lodge, "Our Duty to Cuba," p. 287.

conservatism or those conservatives, and I rejoice in the title such men give me. . . .

Sir, this is my country as much as it is yours or any other man's. While I would hesitate long before taking any step resulting in a breach between this country and Spain or any other nation, I would rather muster every ship that floats on the sea and every man capable of bearing arms and hurl them against Spain than to see the barbarities, the inhumanity, go on longer in Cuba. And if this is radicalism, if this is not conservatism, then those who condemn me may condemn to their heart's content. I shall not feel particularly chagrined by it. [70]

At the end of March 1898, Bryan called in newspaper reporters and announced, "the time for intervention has arrived. Humanity demands that we shall act. Cuba lies almost within sight of our shores, and the sufferings of her people cannot be ignored unless we, as a nation, have become so engrossed in money-making as to be indifferent to distress." [71] The partisan gauntlet had been thrown down. Moreover, McKinley did not appear to have much additional time. He had already been heavily criticized for his procrastination by interventionists such as Republican Senator John M. Thurston of Nebraska in a February 23, 1898 speech to the Senate:

I have never ceased to regret that we did not act then [in passing resolutions calling for the recognition of belligerent status for the Cuban revolutionaries], for I believe that if we had acted then the Cuban revolutionaries would have been given such standing on land and sea, under a recognized flag, and in the money markets of the world that they would, ere this, without further trouble to the United States, and without involving us in the danger of a terrible war, have achieved their own independence, and have been in possession of the Island of Cuba under the Cuban flag. [72]

Lodge concurred with Thurston's judgment.

If two years ago we had recognized the belligerency of the Cuban insurgents they would have been able to raise money . . . and open a port; they would have won their independence . . . and we never should have been involved. . . . if we had today, as we ought to have,

---

[70] *Congressional Record* 31, 55: 2, part 3, February 23, 1898, pp. 2079-80.

[71] Cited by May, *Imperial Democracy,* pp. 145-6.

[72] *Congressional Record* 31, 55: 2, part 3, February 23, 1898, p. 2078.

twenty battle ships and a hundred torpedo boats; there never would have been a Cuban question; . . . the contest would have been so hopeless that it never would have been entered upon. . . . If we had clung to the old faiths, if we had kept our Navy and our defenses as Washington advised, if we had looked a little further ahead into what the Monroe Doctrine meant, we should not be standing on the verge of war today.[73]

In his history of the war, Lodge would later acknowledge that even recognition would probably have been insufficient to allow the insurgents to drive out the Spaniards – but that recognition represented the only chance for the United States to avoid intervention and war.[74] Despite these protestations, the anti-interventionists were convinced that arguments in favor of recognition were only a subterfuge for war, because of the likelihood that the Spanish would regard such a declaration as *casus belli*.

As Assistant Secretary of the Navy, Roosevelt in particular was concerned at McKinley's delays – but for reasons other than political necessity. Roosevelt warned his superior, Secretary Long, on January 22, 1898:

I would also respectfully call your attention to the steady way in which the Spanish force grows relatively to our own. If we had had war with Spain a year ago they would have had but three ironclads to put against us. Now they can probably put seven. Six or eight months hence they will probably be able to put nine or ten. During all this time our own force has remained and will remain at seven battleships and armored cruisers. Even when they get all these ironclads our force will be superior, thanks to the quality of our men, but instead of the superiority being overwhelming, as it was a year ago, it will be small, so far as the Atlantic Ocean is concerned. The naval situation has steadily turned a little to our disadvantage, and is continuing so to turn.[75]

But was McKinley's caution that of a scheming politician, or that of a statesman determined to exhaust all reasonable chances for success, and to ensure strong public support if drastic remedies were necessary? Even Roosevelt seemed concerned that a repetition of the War of 1812 might be the result of too firm a policy. "I sometimes grow to fear that the [New York] *Sun*

---

[73] Ibid., part 4, April 13, 1898, pp. 3782-3.

[74] Lodge, *War with Spain*, p. 19.

[75] Roosevelt to Long, January 22, 1898, *Long Journal*, pp. 41-2.

and a few Senators are the only representatives of true American sentiment, in naval and foreign affairs which we have in the Northeast," Roosevelt wrote Charles Dana in June 1897.[76]

The early verdict of McKinley's political strategy of waiting until public opinion had come around to the side of intervention was most apparent in the South, where the President, well aware of the circumstances, appointed two former Confederate cavalry officers (Fitzhugh Lee and Joseph Wheeler) as major generals in the volunteer army. "The whole South stands behind you," Stuyvesant Fish told the President after he had refused to remove the United States consul-general of Cuba despite the insistence of the Spanish government, "as it has never stood behind any of your predecessors, Republican or Democrat."[77] Or as the *Richmond Times* editorialized:

> That our relations with Spain have become severely strained goes without saying. That we must necessarily have war by no means follows. Nevertheless, whenever the president takes his stand, if it involves us in war, then the people of the whole country, must back him as one man. It will be a case of "the country, whether right or wrong, the country." And the nation may turn its eyes with perfect confidence to the south. Upon any battlefield of the war the confederate veterans and their sons will be seen upholding the national honor and guarding the country's safety with all the steadiness and resolution that characterized them in the early sixties.[78]

Major General Joseph ("Fighting Joe") Wheeler was especially anxious to be the first to encounter "the Yankees – damn it, I mean the Spaniards."[79] In some decisive ways, the Spanish-American War marked the end of the American Civil War, just as the War of 1812 marked the end of the War of Independence. The 1815 military stalemate (at best) with Britain ushered in the Era of Good Feelings in American politics. The smashing triumph of 1898, however, threatened to result in a much less happy outcome.

---

[76] Roosevelt to Charles Anderson Dana, June 7, 1897, *Roosevelt Letters*, 1: 621.

[77] Howard B. Schonberger, *Transportation to the Seaboard* (Westport, Conn.: Greenwood Publishing Corporation, 1971), p. 203.

[78] Cited in *Public Opinion* 24 (March 17, 1898): 326.

[79] Morris, *Rise of Roosevelt*, p. 639.

The Imperial Debate, 1898-1900

On April 11, 1898, McKinley sent Congress a message requesting authority to use the army and navy to end hostilities in Cuba. He and his Congressional supporters carefully orchestrated a joint resolution that supported Cuban independence and authorized the use of force. The resolution passed on April 19 by a vote of 311 to 6 in the House and 42 to 35 in the Senate. To promote cooperation with the Cuban *insurrectos* and reassure European powers of U.S. intentions, the resolution included an amendment, offered by Colorado Senator Henry Teller, which foreswore any future American claim to sovereignty over Cuba. There would be regime change in Cuba in the direction of independence rather than absorption by the United States.

The U.S. Army, which invaded Cuba in early June, was far from ready to fight; its weaknesses became painfully clear over the next few months despite successes such as the famous charge of Roosevelt's Rough Riders. McKinley and his advisers, therefore, decided that the war would be won primarily at sea. The newly-modernized U.S. Navy defeated Spanish squadrons in the Caribbean and at Manila Bay in the Philippines, thereby controlling access to Spain's vulnerable overseas possessions. U.S. forces occupied Guam and Puerto Rico and supported a nationalist uprising in the Philippines. During the war, Congress also passed a joint resolution that annexed the hitherto independent Republic of Hawaii. Within three months, the Spanish government sued for peace. Hostilities were halted on August 12, 1898. The two sides signed a peace treaty in Paris on December 10, which included Madrid's recognition of Cuban independence and cession of most of its other overseas territories to the United States, including the Philippines. With its victory in the Spanish-American War, the United States claimed status as a global political-military power. Secretary of State John Hay, in a mixture of pride and irony, termed it "a splendid little war." Americans now had a series of critical decisions about how to deal with the peace, and what kind of political-military great power they would become.

At the time of the Spanish-American conflict, the United States had not been at war for over thirty years. It had not been at war with a foreign nation for fifty years. And it had not been at war with a European power for more than three-quarters of a century. The war, as events turned out, was short and militarily successful, when some had feared catastrophe. Its outcome, however, would divide public opinion in the most fundamental manner for some time to come – and continues to divide scholars and strategists today. The War with Spain cannot be separated from the world of 1898, or at least the world as Americans saw it. Neither interventionists nor their opponents believed that Spain posed a serious threat to the security of the United States, however brutal that decrepit empire might have been in Cuba. It was, rather, the complications that might arise from the final disintegration of the Spanish Empire, or from a dozen other noteworthy events, which were the gravest matter of strategic concern. The perceived threat posed by the expansive nationalism of Germany and Japan, and the risk of having to fight a two-front (ocean) war, was very much on the minds of the "large Americans," as much or perhaps more than the need to preserve economic access to the markets of China and East Asia. This threat perception shaped fundamentally their views on the peace treaty with Spain and the possible acquisition of the Philippine Islands and other Spanish possessions.[80]

The Case Against Acquisition: Isolationist Morality

Although the nation was substantially united on the issue of war with Spain, that consensus quickly broke down over the terms of peace and, more precisely, over the disposition of the Philippine Islands. At one level, this question revealed the disjunction between the "large Americans" and the anti-imperialists in an entirely new light. Many of the expansionists of the 1890s were taken aback by proposals to acquire the Philippines. Some, like former President Harrison, elected to drop into opposition. The anti-imperialists were themselves divided as to policy and, in the end were unsuccessful in imposing either legal or electoral restrictions on the McKinley administration. The debate over American foreign policy in the aftermath of the momentous events of 1898, moreover, reveals many elements of the classic divisions of the 20th century. There is one partial exception – the precise relationship between the United States and the continent of Europe. That relationship would become fully contentious during Roosevelt's mediation efforts in the Moroccan crisis of 1905, which itself was a preview of the debate over intervention in the great European war a decade later.

Many anti-imperialists, however, believed that the reasoning that had brought the McKinley administration to its decision about the Philippines would inexorably lead the United States into interference with strictly European concerns. "To acquire these islands," warned Democratic Senator George Gray of Delaware, a member of the Peace Commission, "would be to reverse the accepted continental policy of the country, declared and acted upon throughout our history. Propinquity governs the case of Cuba and

---

[80] For a discussion of these strategic concerns, see Garrity, *The American Regime Change Debates of the 1890s*, pp. 53-70.

Puerto Rico. Policy proposed introduces us into European politics and entangling alliances, against which Washington and all American statesmen have protested." [81] (Gray's opinion, needless to say, was not the controlling one of the Commission.) In this regard, Democratic Senator Donelson Caffery (Louisiana) recalled the warnings of Jefferson and Lincoln, and asked:

> Were they "little Americans," Mr. President? When Washington besought his countrymen to avoid all foreign complications and entanglements was he a little American? Who had greater opportunity to advance the sword above the plowshare and to wrench from Britain and Spain their contiguous territory? Sir, he counseled that sobriety and considerateness of conduct and bearing toward the world which Solomon taught us to practice in our prosperity. And when the marvelous valor of our countrymen has thrown into our lap possessions which have been a thorn in the side of our defeated foe, let us carefully and patriotically weigh ourselves in the scale of our Constitution, of our principles of government, of our honor, our race, our interest, and our duty. [82]

The meaning of Washington's Farewell Address was explained by Stanford University President and peace activist David Starr Jordan:

> that America should grow strong within herself, should keep out of all fights and friendships not her own, should secure no territory in which a free man cannot live, and should own no possessions that may not in time be numbered among the United States. . . . In other words, America should not be a power among the nations, but a nation among the powers. This view of the function our country rests on is no mere accident of revolution or isolation. It has its base in sound political common-sense, and in the rush of new claims and new possibilities we should not forget this old wisdom. [83]

The tradition parallel to the Farewell Address, the Monroe Doctrine, likewise served as the foundation for the anti-imperialists' objection to the acquisition of the Philippines. "The Monroe Doctrine is gone," lamented Senator George Hoar. "Every European nation, every European alliance, has the right to acquire dominion in this hemisphere when we acquire it in the

---

[81] Gray to Hay, October 25, 1898, *Papers Relating to the Foreign Relations of the United States (FRUS)*, 1898 (Washington, D.C.: U.S. Government Printing Office, 1898), p. 934.

[82] *Congressional Record* 32, 55:3, part 1, January 9, 1899, p. 501.

[83] David Starr Jordan, *Imperial Democracy* (New York: Garland Press, 1972), p. 42.

other." [84] The anti-imperialists regarded the Monroe Doctrine as much more than a strategic statement of the separation between Europe and America. As Jordan explained: "The purpose of the Monroe Doctrine is not to keep the European flag from America. Its function is to prevent the extension here of European colonial methods, the domination of weak races by strong, of one race for the good of another, of the principle of inequality of right which underlies slavery." [85] For William Jennings Bryan, the Doctrine was a positive statement of the need to promote liberty in the Western Hemisphere – to "hold up the torches of freedom before the nations of the world and prove that the governments derive their just powers from the consent of the governed and not from the rights of hereditary powers." [86]

Bryan perceived a fundamental distinction between the traditional American regime and that which the expansionists wished to graft onto public opinion. He rejected "the splendors of a heterogeneous empire encircling the globe" in favor of "bringing enduring happiness to a homogeneous people."

> The forcible annexation of the Philippine Islands is not necessary to make the United States a world power. For over ten decades our nation has been a world power. During its brief-existence it has exerted that influence without the use of sword or Gatling gun. Mexico and the republics of Central and South America testify to the benign influence of our institutions, while Europe and Asia give evidence of the working of the leaven of self-government. In the growth of democracy we observe the triumphant march of an idea – an idea that would be weighted down rather than aided by the armor and weapons proffered by imperialism. [87]

The annexations demanded security through physical control, when there were better and more moral means of self defense. Charles Francis Adams Jr. recalled "the war of spoliation" against Mexico in the 1840s, a war that his grandfather, John Quincy Adams, had opposed:

> Under the theory now gaining in vogue, it would then have been our plain duty to make of Mexico an extra-territorial dependency, and protect it against itself. We wisely took a different course. Like other Spanish communities in America, Mexico then passed

---

[84] *Congressional Record* 32, 55: 3, part 1, January 9, 1899, p. 501.

[85] Jordan, *Imperial Democracy*, p. 108.

[86] *New York Times*, 17 December 1897, cited by Koenig, *Bryan*, p. 261.

[87] William Jennings Bryan, *Bryan on Imperialism* (Chicago: The Independence Company, 1900), pp. 4, 23.

through a succession of revolutions, from which it became apparent the people were not in a fit condition for self-government. Nevertheless, sternly insisting on noninterference by outside powers, we ourselves wisely left that country to work out its own salvation in its own way. In 1862, when the United States was involved in the War of the Rebellion, the Europeans took advantage of the situation to invade Mexico, and to establish there a "stable government." They undertook to protect that people against themselves, and to erect for them a species of protectorate, such as we now propose for the Philippines. As soon as our war was over, we insisted upon the withdrawal of Europe from Mexico. What followed is a matter of recent history. It is unnecessary to recall it. We did not reduce Mexico into a condition of "tutelage" or establish over it a "protectorate" of our own. We, on the contrary, insisted that it should stand on its own legs; and, by so doing, learn to stand firmly on them, just as a child learns to walk, by being compelled to try to walk, not by being kept everlastingly in "leading strings." This was the American, as contradistinguished from the European policy; and Mexico today walks firmly.[88]

The degeneration of American purpose would be immediately matched by a decline in American behavior. An active foreign policy, a nation constantly on the verge of war, required a strong government, but not necessarily self-government. "Democracy yields before diplomacy . . . ," Jordan cautioned. "We cannot try civic experiments with a foe at our gates." An editorial in the *San Francisco Argonaut* speculated on what such a condition meant in the present circumstances: "We shall have to adopt the same methods pursued by European colonial powers, if we continue in our imperialistic groove."

For example, in the Philippines we may have to adopt Spanish methods in many ways. We may find it necessary to stir up one tribe of natives against another. Thus we could arm the Visayans, drill them, and ship them to Luzon. The Visayans hate the Tagalos [Tagalogs], and we could set the two tribes to fighting together, and with the Visayans we might exterminate the Tagalos. Then, after the Tagalos were exterminated or subjected, we could stir up the fierce Moros of Mindanao against the Visayans. By judiciously fomenting strife we could exterminate the Visayans. There would

---

[88] William Jennings Bryan, et al., *Republic or Empire? The Philippine Question* (Chicago: The Independence Company, 1899), pp. 217-8.

then remain only the Moros, and probably we could get away with them ourselves. Here is another suggestion. The Spaniards have always found it necessary to use treachery, torture and bribery in the Philippines. We shall probably have to do the same. The Anglo-Saxon methods of warfare do not appeal to the Malay. In pursuance of our imperialistic plans, it would be well to hire some of the insurgent lieutenants to betray [Philippine revolutionary leader Emilio] Aguinaldo and other chieftains into our clutches. A little bribery, a little treachery, and a little ambuscading, and we could trap Aguinaldo and his chieftains. Then, instead of putting them to death in the ordinary way, it might be well to torture them. The Spaniards have left behind them some means to that end in the dungeons in Manila. The rack, the thumbscrew, the trial by fire, the trial by molten lead, boiling insurgents alive, crushing their bones in ingenious mechanisms of torture – these are some of the methods that would impress the Malay mind. It would show them that we are in earnest. Ordinary, decent, Christian, and civilized methods, such as the United States have always pursued in warfare, will only lead them to believe that we are weaklings and cowards, and that we are therefore to be steadily and sturdily combated. [89]

And to what end? To accept the responsibilities of empire would mean an endless preoccupation with the balance of power. Who could doubt, Democratic Senator Augustus Bacon of Georgia asked his colleagues in January 1899, "that if we reach out and take these islands we have put ourselves in a position where we are in danger at any time of being involved in a world war?" And do not think that such a war would be confined to the Orient, Bacon admonished. "If that war comes it will involve every leading nation of the world. If that war comes, not only will our young men lay their bones upon the distant soil of Asia, but our own country still will have to stand its defense." What good would the Philippines be in such a global conflagration?

If we become involved in a war with a foreign power – the Philippine Islands would be our weak spot. It was the weak spot of Spain – and we struck it first because it was the weak spot, and if we succeeded to her dominion it would be our weak spot, and any foreign government with which we engaged in war would strike that first. Mr. President, if we were to maintain our authority, if we

---

[89] Cited in Jordan, *Imperial Democracy*, pp. 35, 149.

were to meet that stroke, at least 100,000 men must be transported across the Pacific Ocean 7,000 miles. [90]

The anti-imperialists also challenged the vision of commercial plenty that would be promoted by the acquisition of the Philippines. Andrew Carnegie reasoned that colonial expansion was actually inimical to commercial expansion; the Philippines would "place the whole republic within the zone of wars and rumors of wars, and the rumor of war, it must be remembered, is in itself destructive to commerce." [91] H.D. Money, in an essay in *The Arena* of April 1900, pointed out that the United States had become the world's greatest exporting nation without the benefit of a single colony. Great Britain, the world's most impressive empire, had lost five percent of its trade in the past seven years, during which time the United States gained eighteen percent in its export trade. Only seven percent of Great Britain's trade was with India, the empire's greatest possession. Money contended that London's success as a world trader did not stem from the colonies, but from England's commercial efficiency. [92]

Senator Caffery hammered upon this theme during the debates over ratification of the treaty of peace with Spain in early 1899. Less than one-tenth of American trade was with Asia, Africa and South America combined; nine-tenths of exports from the United States went to Western Europe. Caffery explained that men in the tropics would never consume significant quantities of manufactured goods, and that the American surplus could only be sent to Europe. [93] "I know what I'd do if I was Mac (McKinley)," reflected the immortal Mr. Hennessy. "I'd hist a flag over th' Ph'lipeens, an' I'd take in th' whole lot iv thim." "An' yet," retorted Mr. Dooley, "'tis not more than two months since ye learned whether they were islands or canned goods." [94]

With education, the anti-imperialists hoped to convince the public that the Philippines in no way represented canned goods but a distinct polity, with a large population, and no government. If the United States did not acquire the Philippines, and if American public opinion would not permit

---

[90] *Congressional Record* 32, 55: 3, part 1, January 15, 1899, p. 737.

[91] Andrew Carnegie, "Commercial Expansion vs. Colonial Expansion: An Open Letter," Anti-Imperialist Leaflet No. 11 (Washington, n.d., but undoubtedly December 1898), cited in Robert L. Beisner, *Twelve Against Empire: The Anti-Imperialists, 1898-1900* (New York: McGraw-Hill, 1968), p. 178.

[92] H.D. Money, "Conquest and the Constitution," *Arena* 23 (April 1900): 339-40.

[93] *Congressional Record* 32, 55:3, part 1, January 6, 1899, p. 438.

[94] Finley Peter Dunne, "Mr. Dooley on the Philippines," in Anti-Imperialist Broadside No. 2 (December 1898), cited by Beisner, *Twelve Against Empire*, p. 181.

them to be returned to the tender mercies of Spain, then what did the anti-imperialists propose to do with the spoils of war? Some advocated the simple expedient of declaring them independent and sailing away. The more common proposal was that of Bryan: independence as soon as practical, with the United States to declare a protectorate over the islands, while retaining a coaling station at Manila.

> A European protectorate often results in the plundering of the ward by the guardian. An American protectorate gives to the nation protected the advantage of our strength, without making it the victim of our greed. For three-quarters of a century the Monroe Doctrine has been a shield to neighboring republics and yet it has imposed no pecuniary burden upon us. After the Filipinos had aided us in the war against Spain, we could not honorably turn them over to their former masters; we could not leave them to be the victims of the ambitious designs of European nations, and since we do not desire to make them a part of us or to hold them as subjects, we propose the only alternative, namely, to give them independence and guard them against molestation from without.[95]

Another possibility, suggested by Edward Atkinson, a founder of the Anti-Imperialist League, and Senator Hoar, was to neutralize the islands by international agreement. As Atkinson analyzed the problem:

> The alternative is an agreement among the great powers to neutralize these islands. We have precedents in the neutralization of Belgium by agreement; in the neutralization of Switzerland by agreement. . . . We have a precedent in the neutralization of the Suez Canal. Why should we not continue on these lines? England does not wish and will not risk her soldiers in taking possession of the Philippine Islands, even if the opportunity were offered. Germany will not take them; Japan might not take them; no other nation desires to take them; each nation desires that the other shall not; each nation desires a coaling station; the open door to commerce, the development of the wants of the Filipinos through commerce to the end that their demand for manufactures may increase; [and] the development of their own products correspondingly. The necessities of war, of military occupation, of defense against aggression, increase the burden and diminish the

---

[95] Bryan, *Bryan on Imperialism*, p. 90.

> commerce; and whereas if by agreement it were ordained that all fortifications should be destroyed, that no naval warfare should be permitted within the waters of the Philippine Islands, that all nations might buy coaling stations, land commodities and enjoy commerce under the same system of collecting the revenue, called the open door . . . [96]

The anti-imperialist position assumed that the United States had the power either to establish a protectorate or to ensure a neutral Philippines. Jordan waved aside any suggestion of great power interference.

> But this German bugaboo is set up merely as an excuse. No nation on earth would dare set the heel of oppression on any land our flag has made free. The idea that every little nation must be subject to some great one is one of the most contemptible products of military commercialism. No nation, little or big, is "derelict" that minds its own business, maintains law and order, and respects the development of its own people. If we behave honorably towards the people we have freed, we shall set a fashion which the powers never dare to disregard. [97]

Aside from the reasons of national self-interest, the anti-imperialists raised serious constitutional objections to the acquisition of the Philippines. These objections were summarized most notably in the Vest Resolution, which Missouri Senator George Vest (Democrat) introduced in the Senate on December 1, 1898:

> . . . That under the Constitution of the United States no power is given to the Federal Government to acquire territory to be held and governed permanently as colonies. The colonial system of European nations cannot be established under our present Constitution but all territory acquired by the Government, except such small amount as may be necessary for coaling stations, connection of boundaries, and similar governmental purposes, must be acquired and governed with the purpose of ultimately organizing such territory into States suitable for admission into the Union. [98]

---

[96] Beisner, *Twelve Against Empire*, pp. 95-6. See also Hoar letter to the editor of the *Boston Herald*, January 2, 1900, cited by Richard E. Welch, Jr., "Senator George Frisbie Hoar and the Defeat of Anti-Imperialism, 1898-1900," *Historian* 26 (May 1964): 369.

[97] Jordan, *Imperial Democracy*, pp. 72-3.

[98] See, for example, *Congressional Record* 32, 55: 3, part 1, December 12, 1898, p. 93.

The anti-imperialists denied that they were anti-expansionists. They defined "expansion" as "the taking in of territory which can be created into states," while imperialism involved "the conversion of a republic into an empire, wherein part of the people govern themselves and also govern the colonies." [99] Legally, if the Philippines were acquired from Spain, they must be governed by the Constitution (which mandated preparation for statehood). They could not legally be governed outside the Constitution, for that would be despotism. The anti-imperialists argued that there was no sentiment toward granting the Philippines statehood, now or ever. Carl Schurz predicted catastrophe if any tropical territory was permanently incorporated into the Union.

> Have you thought of it, what this means? . . . fancy ten or twelve tropical States added to the Southern States we already possess; fancy the Senators and Representatives of ten or twelve millions of tropical people, people of the Latin race mixed with Indian and African blood; . . . fancy them sitting in the Halls of Congress, throwing the weight of their intelligence, their morality, their political notions and habits, their prejudices and passions, into the scale of the destinies of this Republic; and, what is more, fancy the Government of this Republic making itself responsible for order and security and republican institutions in such States, inhabited by such people; fancy this, and then tell me, does not your imagination recoil from the picture? [100]

The main authority for this anti-imperialist interpretation of the Constitution, interestingly enough, was the decision of the Supreme Court in the 1857 case of *Dred Scott v. Sanford*. Vest admitted that the decision of the court in regard to slavery had been overturned "by shot and shell and saber stroke for all time to come." [101] Still, according to Vest, there was a portion of that opinion that was accepted by all nine judges, including dissenting Justices McLean and Curtis, and that was still binding. The relevant portion of Taney's decision read:

> There is certainly no power given by the Constitution to the Federal Government to establish or maintain colonies bordering on the United States or at a distance to be ruled and governed at its own pleasure, nor to enlarge its territorial limits in any way except by

---

[99] Paul W. Glad, *The Trumpet Soundeth* (Lincoln: University of Nebraska Press, 1960), p. 75.

[100] Beisner, *Twelve Against Empire*, pp. 23-4.

[101] *Congressional Record* 32, 55: 3, part 2, February 2, 1899, p. 1380.

the admission of new States. That power is plainly given; and if a new State is admitted it needs no further legislation by Congress because the Constitution itself defines the relative rights and powers and duties of the State and the citizens of the State and the Federal Government. But no power is given to acquire a territory to be held and governed permanently in that character. [102]

Needless to say, the pro-annexationists derived a great deal of amusement and political capital from this tainted source of their opponents' argument. Anti-imperialists, however, argued that this position was inherent in the Constitution and that it existed quite apart from the slavery question. Senator Bacon recalled the position of Massachusetts Federalist Congressman Josiah Quincy in 1811 – that the government of the United States had no constitutional authority to acquire any foreign territory, and that such a course would be sufficient reason for New England to withdraw from the Union. (Bacon doubted seriously whether Quincy had any interest in the maintenance of slavery as a motivation for his argument. [103]) Jordan contended that even a continental Union became possible only as the result of the development of transportation (i.e., railroads and the telegraph). Without these improvements, even the Louisiana Purchase would have had a dubious constitutional status. On these grounds, Jordan challenged the legal validity of the purchase of Alaska. [104]

The heart of the anti-imperialist position, however, rested in the belief that incorporation of the Philippines was immoral as well as illegal. "The question is this," Senator Hoar declared. "Have we the right, as doubtless we have the physical power, to enter upon the government of ten or twelve million subject people without constitutional restraint?" [105] The analogy that the opponents of the McKinley policy raised over and over again was that of the great slavery controversy. Just as Lincoln denied that the Union would remain half slave and half free, so the anti-imperialists claimed it could not remain half republic, half empire. "Mr. President, Abraham Lincoln said, 'No man was ever created good enough to own another man,'" Hoar reminded the Senate, adding, "No nation was ever created good enough to own another." To say that the United States would govern the Philippines for its own good was no different than the slaveholder's claim that he owned men for their own good. [106]

---

[102] Ibid., part 1, December 12, 1898, p. 83.

[103] Ibid., part 2, February 2, 1898, p. 1378.

[104] Jordan, *Imperial Democracy*, pp. 21, 93.

[105] *Congressional Record* 32, 55: 3, part 1, January 9, 1899, p. 494.

[106] Ibid., pp. 496, 501.

Jordan recalled Steven A. Douglas' statement: "I am for the black man, as against the alligator, but between black man and white man, I am for the white man every time." This inequality before the law, Jordan explained, was the essence of slavery, and the essence of imperialism, which itself was nothing more than the master-slave relationship as applied to nations. [107]

For nearly a hundred years, Senator Mason argued, the United States "piled up the wealth of unrequited toil of the slaves. We said, 'This is the land of the free and the home of the brave,' and sold women and children to the highest and best bidder for cash. No picture could be painted of the genius of our country in which the slave pen and whipping post did not rear their heads." The country had forgotten the law of compensation and wrongly believed that there was no vicarious atonement for a nation's crime. In the end, the slave pen and the auction block were torn down, but even they did not provide enough material to make headboards for the graves. America, Mason warned, was on the verge of forgetting the law of compensation again in the Philippines.

> You cannot govern the Philippine Islands . . . without taxing them. You have not their consent to tax them. You propose again to tax without representation! Look out for tea parties. Those semi-social functions are liable to occur, for Yankee Doodle and Dixie and the Star Spangled Banner have been heard in the Archipelago.

And what of the contention that the Filipinos were incapable of governing themselves?

> But, Mr. President, we are told that they cannot govern themselves. Where is the student of evolution who talks like this? Where is the man who has read who does not know that all government is made to fit the people and does not rise either above or below the people themselves? Who does not know the difference between "canned liberty," as the distinguished Speaker of the House calls it, and the genuine liberty which we enjoy? No, no; they cannot govern themselves. I was told so the other day by one of my beloved constituents, who never governs himself fifteen minutes at a time; but he was willing to take an assignment under the present Administration to govern all the Philippines at a fair salary. (Laughter) [108]

---

[107] Jordan, *Imperial Democracy*, p. 100.

[108] *Congressional Record* 32, 55: 3, part 1, January 10, 1899, p. 529.

The great statement of American morality – indeed, universal morality – for the anti-imperialists was the Declaration of Independence. "To give up the idea of 'equality of all men before the law' would be to abandon our sole excuse for being as a nation," Jordan maintained. "We would then become a mere geographical expression or police arrangement, and logically might as well join Canada as a dependency of Great Britain." [109] Congressman Reed, the Republican Speaker of the House and an opponent of annexation, reflected that "our fathers did not make their Declaration of Independence as a piece of rhetoric but as a guide of national life." [110] That great document did more than declare the independence of America – it proclaimed the dignity of human nature itself. [111]

The Democratic Party taunted the expansionist Republicans for accepting Douglas' interpretation of the Declaration. As Minnesota Democratic Senator Charles A. Towne pointed out in the November 1900 issue of the *Forum*, Douglas had held that the Declaration referred only to the fact that British subjects in North America were equal to British subjects born and residing in Great Britain. The *New York Sun*, a Democratic newspaper that had consistently supported McKinley, was cited by Towne as stating:

> The Declaration of Independence was made to suit a particular existing condition of things. The Declaration meant simply that the colonies had become tired of British domination, deeming it oppressive, and intended to set up a government of their own by the right of revolution.

And also the *New York Tribune*: "The Declaration of Independence was a formal notice that the inhabitants of the colonies consented no longer to British rule."

To which Towne was pleased to give the reply of Lincoln to Douglas in a speech at Springfield, Illinois on June 26, 1857:

> The assertion 'that all men are created equal' was of no practical use in effecting our separation from Great Britain; and it was placed in the Declaration, not for that, but for future use. Its authors meant it to be – as, thank God, it is now proving itself – a stumbling block to all those who in after times might seek to turn a free people

---

[109] Jordan, *Imperial Democracy*, p. 76.

[110] Robinson, *Thomas B. Reed*, pp. 378-9.

[111] *Congressional Record* 32, 55: 3, part 1, January 9, 1899, p. 500.

back into the hateful paths of despotism. They knew the proneness of prosperity to breed tyrants, and they meant, when such should reappear in this fair land and commence their vocation, they should find left for them at least one hard nut to crack.[112]

Senator Hoar, a Civil War-era Republican like Reed, warned against reading the Declaration of Independence out of the Constitution. "The Declaration of Independence is coequal with the Constitution, the one being a grant of power and the other a sovereign rule of interpretation." "The Constitution must be interpreted in the light of the Declaration of Independence, and, therefore . . . we have no right under the Constitution to acquire territory for the purpose of governing a people without their consent."

> Expositio contemporanea maxime valet. The great contemporaneous exposition of the Constitution is to be found in the Declaration of Independence. Over every clause, syllable, and letter of the Constitution the Declaration of Independence pours its blazing torchlight. The same men framed it. The same States confirmed it. The same people pledged their lives, their fortunes, and their sacred honor to support it. The great characters in the Constitutional Convention were the great characters of the Continental Congress. There are undoubtedly, among its burning and shining truths, one or two which the convention that adopted it were not prepared themselves at once to put into practice. But they placed them before their countrymen as an ideal moral law to which the liberty of the people was to aspire and to ascend as soon as the nature of existing conditions would admit. Doubtless slavery was inconsistent with it, as Jefferson, its great author, has in more than one place left on record. But at last in the strife of a great civil war the truth of the Declaration prevailed and the falsehood of slavery went down, and at last the Constitution of the United States conformed to the Declaration and it has become the law of the land, and its great doctrines of liberty are written upon the American flag wherever the American flag floats. Who shall haul them down?[113]

---

[112] Charles A. Towne, "Reasons for Democratic Success," *Forum* 30 (November 1900): 276-7, which cites the above newspaper editorials.

[113] *Congressional Record* 32, 55: 3, part 1, January 9, 1899, pp. 494, 499; January 10, 1899, p. 528.

Connecticut Senator Orville H. Platt raised the ire of both Hoar and Mason when he observed, as a matter of fact, that the just powers of government were derived from the consent of *some* of the governed. Mason rushed to the defense of what he regarded as the original meaning of the Declaration.

> This sentence, Mr. President, has been a pillar of fire by night and a cloud by day to the downtrodden and oppressed all over the world. In the light of this sentence crowns have fallen to the dust and men have stood anew in their own manhood. In the light of this sentence Simon Bolivar, the liberator of South America, laid in blood and carnage the foundation stones of the South American Republics. In the light of this sentence Kosciusko led his Spartan hand against the hosts of Russian and Austrian oppressors of his native Poland. This burning sentence attracted the attention of Lafayette, across the water, and his ships set sail for our relief. In the light of this sentence Garibaldi struck down Bourbon tyranny and carved his name not only in the hearts of lovers of liberty in Italy, but all over the world. No, Mr. President, we will not amend that sentence now. We will not insert the word "some" just yet. It has passed beyond the power of this country to amend the Declaration of Independence, and when the distinguished Senator from Connecticut and I and all the rest of us are moldering in forgotten dust, that sentence will continue to live and to burn, a menace to tyrants and a beacon light to the downtrodden and the oppressed.[114]

The anti-imperialists feared that, if the nation was allowed to drift into empire without careful consideration, because of the siren call of "destiny" or "necessity," the moral character of the people would be forever corrupted. Hoar insisted that he did not distrust the American public. "But the strongest frame may get mortal sickness from one exposure; the most vigorous health or life may be destroyed by a single drop of poison, and what poison is to the human frame the abandonment of our great doctrine of liberty will be to the Republic."

> After all, I am old-fashioned enough to think that our fathers, who won the Revolution and who framed the Constitution, were the wisest builders of states the world has yet seen. I think that they knew where to seek for the best lessons of experience and they knew

---

[114] Ibid., January 10, 1899, p. 530.

how to lay down the rules which should be the best guides for their descendants. They did not disdain to study ancient history. They knew what caused the downfall of the mighty Roman Republic. They read, as Chatham said he did, the history of the freedom, of the decay, and the enslavement of Greece. They knew to what she owed her glory and to what she owed her ruin. They learned from her the doctrine that while there is little else that a democracy can not accomplish it cannot rule over vassal states or subject peoples without bringing in the elements of death into its own constitution. The Americans have been aptly called the Greeks of modern times. The versatile, enterprising, adventurous Yankee has been likened to the people of Athens, who were of the Ionian race, and the brave, constant, inflexible men of the South to the brave, constant, and inflexible Sparta, whose people were Dorians.

There are two lessons our fathers learned from the history of Greece which they hoped their children would remember: the danger of disunion and domestic strife and an indulgence in the greed and lust of empire. The Greeks stood together against the power of Persia as the American states stood together against the tyranny of England. For us the danger of disunion has happily passed by. Our Athenians and our Spartans are bound and welded together again, each lending to the other the strength of their steel and the sharpness of their tempered blade in an indissoluble Union. Our danger to-day is from the lust of empire. It is a little remarkable that the temptation that besets us now lured and brought to ruin the Athenian people in ancient times. I hope that we may be able to resist and avert that danger as we resisted and averted the peril of disunion. [115]

"I heard much calculated to excite the imagination of the youth seeking wealth, of the youth charmed by the dream of empire," Hoar responded to a speech by Indiana's exuberant Senator, Albert Beveridge, in January 1900. "But the words Right, Justice, Duty, Freedom were absent." [116] Beveridge and the so-called progressives promised reform at home; how could they consistently permit such fundamental abuses abroad? "Is there some place in the Pacific Ocean where we change the code of ethics and good morals as we change the calendar and the ship's clocks in crossing?" Senator Mason

---

[115] Ibid., January 9, 1899, p. 494.

[116] Ibid., 33, 56: 1, January 9, 1900, p. 712.

wondered. "God Almighty help the party that seeks to give civilization and Christian liberty hypodermically with 13-inch guns." [117]

The patriotism of many of the anti-imperialists inevitably came into question. Bryan, who had supported the war and who had helped form a volunteer regiment from Nebraska, warned McKinley in September that his men had joined "to attempt to break the yoke of Spain in Cuba, and for nothing else. They did not volunteer to attempt to subjugate other peoples, or establish United States sovereignty elsewhere." [118] Bryan subsequently resigned his commission under politically controversial circumstances.

The most controversial position, however, was that of Harvard Professor Charles Eliot Norton. In a speech that was condemned even by such anti-imperialists as Hoar, Norton advised students not to enlist.

> The country is in no peril. There is always in a vast population like ours an immense, a sufficient supply of material of a fighting order, often of a heroic courage, ready and eager for the excitement of battle, filled with the old notion that patriotism is best expressed in readiness to fight for your country, be she right or wrong. Better the paying of bounties to such men to fill the ranks than that they should be filled by those whose higher duty is to fit themselves for the service of their country in the patriotic labors of peace. We mourn the deaths of our noble youth fallen in the cause of their country when she stands for the right; but we may mourn with a deeper sadness for those who have fallen in a cause which their generous hearts mistook for one worthy of the last sacrifice. [119]

None of the amendments and resolutions in Congress intended to limit the McKinley administration in the Philippines were adopted during the 55th or 56th Congress. The anti-imperialists were nonetheless optimistic that the elections of 1898 and, most importantly, 1900, would turn the tide. They were hopeful that, by defeating the reelection bid of President McKinley, they could achieve an electoral revolution equivalent to that of Lincoln and the Republicans in 1860. In fact, the early impetus to the organization of the anti-imperialist movement came from many of the old anti-slavery and abolitionist voices, such as Schurz, who had supported Lincoln. The

---

[117] Ibid., 32, 55: 3, part 1, January 10, 1899, pp. 530-1.

[118] Paolo E. Coletta, *William Jennings Bryan: Political Evangelist, 1860-1908* (Lincoln: University of Nebraska Press, 1964), p. 229.

[119] Sara Norton and M.A. Dewolfe Howe, eds., *Letters of Charles Eliot Norton*, 2 vols. (Boston and New York: Houghton Mifflin Company, 1913), 2: 268; Beisner, *Twelve Against Empire*, p. 80, 486.

anti-imperialists recalled that the anti-slavery stance of the Republican Party, which took practical form in opposition to the repeal of the Missouri Compromise, had attracted a variety of otherwise disparate elements into a successful political coalition. Thus, the following resolution of the New York Anti-Imperialist League on May 24, 1900:

> Resolved that the question of imperialism overshadows in importance all other public questions; that the approval or disapproval of the imperialistic policy pursued by the present Administration should be the supreme issue in the coming election; and that all American citizens having the good name and best interests of our free institutions at heart should unite in an earnest effort to secure the condemnation of that policy and the sternest possible rebuke to its authors by a decisive popular vote. [120]

With the right candidate, the Philippine issue might re-unite the Gold and Silver wings of the Democratic Party, as well as attract disaffected Republicans and various independents, who had separated from the Republican Party in the 1872 "Liberal Republican" revolt or the 1884 "Mugwump" movement. Politics has made stranger bedfellows than the old-line Northern Republican abolitionists and the old-line Southern Democratic racists. By January 1899, even Hoar, the impeccable Republican who once called the Mugwumps the "vilest set of political assassins that ever disgraced this or any other country," was corresponding with charter Mugwumps Schurz and Moorfield Storey. [121]

After toying with the possibility of launching a third party for the 1900 elections, most anti-imperialist leaders decided to support the Democratic Party's nominee. The party's choice again was Bryan, even though his credentials as an anti-imperialist were suspect because of his support, for tactical reasons, of the Peace Treaty's ratification. Neither the Great Commoner's support for free silver nor his image as a radical was particularly helpful. Many of Bryan's supporters urged him to concentrate on the imperialism issue as the one common rallying point for the Democrats. William A. Croffut, secretary and founder of the Washington Anti-Imperialist League, wrote to Bryan in September 1899 that "imperialism is certainly to be the great issue next summer."

---

[120] E. Berkeley Tompkins, "Scylla and Charybdis: The Anti-Imperialist Dilemma in the Election of 1900," *Pacific Historical Review* 36 (May 1967): 152.

[121] Cited in Fred H. Harrington, "The Anti-Imperialist Movement in the United States, 1898-1900," *Mississippi Valley Historical Review* 36 (May 1967): 152.

> If there were no other issue than that I believe you would be elected, and I beg you to think profoundly before encumbering the platform with anything else. If you will leave in abeyance the definite demand for free silver, I don't believe anything can beat you. If that demand is explicitly reiterated, you cannot carry Massachusetts, Connecticut or New York. You will be fifty electoral votes short and our country will be cursed with a continuation of this monstrous and wicked policy. Let us be politic this time . . .[122]

In another echo of Lincoln's policy in the campaigns of 1858 and 1860, George Boutwell, an old-line Republican and president of the New England Anti-Imperialist League, argued that the imperial question was the only decisive issue in American politics.

> In the month of November, 1900, the future of the nation will be decided, Republic or Empire? That is the question, the only question of any importance before the country. If any false financial or industrial policies are entered upon by a new administration, adequate corrections may be applied in four or eight years, but a policy by which Puerto Rico and the Philippines are incorporated in the Union, or attached to it as vassal dependencies, can never be reversed until this republic is numbered among the states that have fallen through an unjust and criminal greed for empire and power.[123]

Or, as Jordan conceived of the situation, "The greatest political problems the world has ever known are ours today and still unsolved – the problems of free men in freedom." Jordan did not accept the imperial urge as an indication of a vigorous national character but rather as a manifestation of weakness and cowardice toward essential domestic problems. "Because these are hard and trying [the labor problem, the corporation problem, the race problem, the problem of coinage] we would shirk them in order to meddle with the affairs of our weak-minded neighbors."[124]

As the Democratic Party's candidate for the presidency in 1900, Bryan disregarded the advice to concentrate on the issue of imperialism. On the one hand, he regarded it neither principled nor expedient to abandon free silver, a stance that had allowed him to become a national figure. In addition, Bryan

---

[122] Croffut to Bryan, September 9, 1899, Croffut Papers, Library of Congress, cited in Tompkins, "The Election of 1900," p. 144.

[123] Cited in ibid., p. 146.

[124] Jordan, *Imperial Democracy*, pp. 58-9.

professed to see a link between McKinley's foreign and domestic policies; he believed that these policies were best attacked as a whole. "The issue presented in the campaign of 1900 is the issue between plutocracy and democracy," he began an article in the June 1900 *North American Review*. "All the questions under discussion will, in their last analysis, disclose the conflict between the dollar and the man – a conflict as old as the human race, and one which will continue as long as the human race endures." In the circumstances of 1900, Bryan concluded, this great general conflict had three particular manifestations: the money question, the trust question, and imperialism. [125] "In the future, as in the past, the desire to be free will be stronger than the desire to enjoy a mere physical existence," Bryan told a Cincinnati audience in January 1899. "The conflict between right and might will continue here and everywhere until a day is reached when the love of money will no longer sear the national conscience and hypocrisy no longer hide the hideous features of avarice behind the mask of philanthropy." [126]

The various aspects of the money question were clearly paramount in the Nebraska Democrat's mind; according to historian Paolo E. Coletta, Bryan spoke more against the trusts than any other subject during the 1900 campaign. [127] In this context, Bryan argued that acquisition of the Philippines would offer no benefit to the common man, only to the privileged few.

> Imperialism would be profitable to the army contractors; it would be profitable to the ship owners, who would carry live soldiers to the Philippines and bring dead soldiers back; it would be profitable to those who would seize upon the franchises, and it would be profitable to the officials whose salaries would be fixt (sic) here and paid over there; but to the farmer, to the laboring man and to the vast majority of those engaged in other occupations it would bring expenditure without return and risk without reward. [128]

Bryan attempted to capture the essence of his teaching during a well-publicized speech in Madison Square Garden: "When I tell you that the first and most important object of government is not money-making or the extension of commerce or even the care of property, but rather the protection of human rights, I am not asserting an original proposition, I

---

[125] Bryan, "The Issue in the Presidential Campaign," *North American Review* 170 (June 1900): 753, 758.

[126] Bryan, *Bryan on Imperialism*, p. 12.

[127] Coletta, *William Jennings Bryan*, p. 277.

[128] David Healy, *U.S. Expansionism* (Madison: University of Wisconsin Press, 1970), p. 243.

am not promulgating a western theory; I am simply giving expression to a fundamental truth." [129]

The Case for Acquisition: Expansive Necessity

Historians have long struggled to explain America's sudden foray into what Samuel Flagg Bemis termed the "Great Aberration." There was unquestionably an element of haste and indecision about the acquisition of the Philippines. "The march of events rules and overrules human action," McKinley noted in his directions to the American Peace Commission in September 1898. [130] When William Howard Taft supposedly told McKinley that he did not approve of the administration's policy and that he did not want the Philippines, the President answered, "Neither do I, but that isn't the question. We've got them." [131] John Hay admitted to Andrew Carnegie in a letter dated August 22, 1898, "I have read with keenest interest your article in the *North American Review*. I am not allowed to say in my present fix, how much I agree with you. The only question in my mind is how far it is now *possible* for us to withdraw from the Philippines." [132]

Even those arch-large Americans, Roosevelt, Mahan and Lodge, were caught off guard for the moment. "I myself, though rather an expansionist, have not fully adjusted myself to the idea of taking them, from our own standpoint of advantage," Mahan admitted at one point to Lodge. The Massachusetts Senator himself toyed with the idea of exchanging all or part of the Philippines with Great Britain in return for certain British possessions in the Caribbean. [133] The intellectual bent of the large Americans and their decision to retain most of Spain's Asian empire was entirely predictable, even if it was driven by the pressure of events. McKinley's famous account of his conversion to a pro-annexationist stance parallels that of many American leaders.

> The truth is I didn't want the Philippines and when they came to us as a gift from the gods, I did not know what to do with them. . . . I sought counsel from all sides – Democrats as well as Republicans – but got little help. I thought first we would

---

[129] *The Commoner*, 12 February 1904, cited by Coletta, *William Jennings Bryan*, p. 295.

[130] Cited by May, *Imperial Democracy*, p. 251.

[131] Foster Rhea Dulles, *America in the Pacific* (Boston and New York: Houghton Mifflin Co., 1932), p. 259.

[132] Hay to Carnegie, August 22, 1898, John Hay, *Letters of John Hay and Extracts from his Diary*, 3 vols. (New York: Gordian Press, 1969), 3: 129.

[133] Healy, *U.S. Expansionism*, p. 60.

take only Manila; then Luzon; then other islands, perhaps, also. I walked the floor of the White House night after night until midnight; and I am not ashamed to tell you, gentlemen, that I went down on my knees and prayed Almighty God for light and guidance more than one night. And one night late it came to me this way – I don't know how it was, but it came: (1) that we could not give them back to Spain – that would be cowardly and dishonorable; (2) that we could not turn them over to France or Germany – our commercial rivals in the Orient – that would be bad business and discreditable; (3) that we could not leave them to themselves – they were unfit for self-government – and they would soon have anarchy and misrule over there worse than Spain's was; and (4) that there was nothing left for us to do but to take them all, and to educate the Filipinos, and uplift and civilize and Christianize them, and by God's grace do the very best we could by them as our fellow-men for whom Christ also died. And then I went to bed, and went to sleep and slept soundly. [134]

The significance of McKinley's analysis consists not in his appeal to the divine, but in the fact that he took this step without the influence of leading figures of the large America movement. "Unless I am utterly and profoundly mistaken," Lodge wrote to Roosevelt on May 24, 1898, "the Administration is now fully committed to the large policy that we both desire." [135] That new "large policy," however, was not immediately that of the jingoes of the 1890s, regardless of how much they might have prepared the way. Lodge was hardly an intimate of McKinley, who was actually much closer to Lodge's anti-imperialist colleague from Massachusetts, Senator George F. Hoar. Roosevelt, the *enfant terrible* of the Navy Department, had resigned his post to help train an obscure lot of would-be cavalrymen. Mahan was an adviser to Navy Secretary Long, but he hardly constituted a decisive vote. The Spanish-American War was fought, won and settled under the direction of the mainstream of the Republican Party. That direction was not infirm. Tradition has it that McKinley, upon hearing of Dewey's victory at Manila Bay on May 1, turned to a globe to discover where the Philippines actually

---

[134] Cited by James Ford Rhodes, *The McKinley and Roosevelt Administrations* (New York: The MacMillan Company, 1923), p. 107. Lewis Gould examines the accuracy of this quote, which was recalled four years later, in *The Presidency of William McKinley* (Lawrence: University Press of Kansas, 1980), pp. 140-2.

[135] Lodge to Roosevelt, May 24, 1898, *Selections from the Correspondence of Theodore Roosevelt and Henry Cabot Lodge, 1884-1918*, 2 vols. (New York: Charles Scribner's Sons, 1925): 1: 300.

were located. But Charles Dawes, a close confidant of the President, recorded in his diary on May 3 that McKinley "is much pleased at the outcome of this movement at Manila as he issued the orders a week ago for the fleet to proceed to Manila and destroy the Spanish ships." [136]

Why did the administration prefer, in the end, to acquire all of the Philippines, instead of taking a less controversial course? Most of the intelligence that McKinley received indicated that the islands could neither be divided nor made independent. McKinley's private secretary gave him a copy of the July 1898 issue of the *Contemporary Review*, in which John Foreman, an Englishman who was regarded as the foremost authority on the islands, painted a pessimistic picture. The Tagalog insurrection was hardly of a nationalist character, Foreman explained; the Filipinos were sharply divided by tribal and racial differences. "The Philippine Islands . . . would not remain one year peaceful under an independent native government. It is an impossibility." McKinley was also advised officially by the Japanese Foreign Minister that the Filipinos were incapable of self-government. [137]

On September 30, the President received a report from Brigadier General Francis V. Greene, who had commanded a brigade in the islands during the Battle of Manila. Greene informed McKinley that a restoration of Spanish rule was impossible. He also argued that the rebel leader Aguinaldo's scheme of government would be a pure despotism, a dictatorship of the South American type. The inhabitants of the central islands, the Visayans, would probably oppose the Tagalog insurrection of Aguinaldo. Greene claimed that the educated and propertied Filipinos in Manila had little faith in Aguinaldo, and that this group would support a Philippine Republic under American protection. [138]

In the meantime, Commander R.B. Bradford, the U.S. Navy's adviser to the Peace Commission, had been asked to make a strategic evaluation of the islands. Bradford concluded that it would be less difficult to defend the entire group than a single island. If Manila Bay or Luzon were taken alone, they would be vulnerable to attack from almost any direction. Bradford favored acquiring all of the Landrones as well as Guam, plus the Carolines. When pressed to suggest a lesser division, Bradford drew a line around Luzon that veered back to include Mindoro and Palawan, and other islands to the southwest. If the United States allowed Spain to retain some of the islands, Bradford warned, Spain would shortly sell them to Germany. An attempted partition of

---

[136] *Dawes Journal*, p. 158.

[137] May, *Imperial Democracy*, p. 254; Leech, *In the Days of McKinley*, p. 325.

[138] Leech, *In the Days of McKinley*, pp. 334-5.

the islands between the United States and certain European powers, or joint administration of the Philippines, would almost certainly end in great controversy. [139] If the United States permitted the islands to fall into the hands of a continental power, for example, it seemed unlikely that Britain would stand idly by and see its Far Eastern lines of communication so threatened. French possession of the Philippines, along with France's colonies Annam and Cambodia, would serve to close the South China Sea. The British might have acquiesced in Japanese occupation, but this would alarm Tokyo's and London's great Asian rival, Russia. The most likely course for the United States seemed to be to cede the islands to Britain, in return for concessions in the Western Hemisphere. Lodge had favored this course at one time, and Roosevelt agreed to that idea in July 1899, "if she [Britain] would leave this continent. The relations between Canada and England always tend to bring on friction between us and both of them." [140] British possession of the Philippines, however, was also open to serious objections. Its enemies would regard her possession of the islands as a drive for Far Eastern hegemony –placing Britain on the flanks of France's colonies in Indochina, for instance.

The balance of European and Asian power seemed to McKinley to require American annexation of the Philippines. "By holding the Philippines we ... postpone at least a general European war," Charles Denby, the former U.S. Minister to China, contended. [141] "Our duty to mankind enjoins us not to precipitate a general war, and the surest mode of discharging that duty is to take the Philippines ourselves," writer Mayo W. Hazeltine concurred. [142] Britain urged Washington to keep the islands; so too did Japan. Senator Albert Beveridge was told by Marquis Ito, Japan's Premier, "First you must keep the islands ... because if you do not, another Power will immediately take them involving the world in war in all probability, for which you will be responsible." [143]

Why not establish a protectorate over the Philippines, as many of the anti-imperialists desired? As Roosevelt answered, citing William Howard

---

[139] Ibid., pp. 326-7, 339-40. To pull out of the islands altogether, in the opinion of the expansionists, meant that "almost all Europe [would be] on their backs the next morning before breakfast." See Senator Foraker in *Congressional Record* 32, 55: 3, part l, January 11, 1899, p. 571.

[140] Roosevelt to Wilson, July 12, 1899, *Roosevelt Letters*, 2: 1032.

[141] Charles Denby, "Shall We Keep the Philippines?" *Forum* 26 (November 1898): 280-1.

[142] Mayo W. Hazeltine, "What Shall Be Done About the Philippines?" North American Review 167 (October 1898): 388.

[143] Claude G. Bowers, *Beveridge and the Progressive Era* (Boston: Houghlin Mifflin, 1932), p. 110.

Taft, "to abandon the Islands and yet establish a protectorate over them, simply meant to pledge ourselves to perpetual war . . ."[144] The United States would be committed to the defense of the Philippines without exercising any control over the actions of a future native government in Manila. To extend the Monroe Doctrine to the Philippines – for that was the practical effect of the anti-imperialist's proposal – seemed even more radical than acquiring the islands. Charles Dicks made this point in the November 1900 issue of the *Forum*:

> The Monroe Doctrine is not globe encircling, and in a senseless attempt to extend it to the Eastern hemisphere we should destroy it. To maintain a protectorate over the islands would be a greater task than to govern them. We must not set up a government which is to be managed by others, but at the same time requires our land and naval forces to uphold it. We must be masters of the situation or abandon it. There is no middle ground. It is too late to debate the question of retaining these islands.[145]

American possession of the Philippines held out the prospect that the United States could exercise strong – and perhaps decisive – influence over events in China. Denby later admitted that "I advocated the acquisition of these islands chiefly on the ground that their possession would enable us to prevent the partition of China. Holding enormous territories in the Far East, we would have the right to intervene in any matter which points to the destruction of our interests."[146] The annexation of the Philippines would provide the United States with the needed leverage in the Far East, Hazeltine stated, because:

> Such is their strategic relation to China that our possession of them would give us an influence at Peking second only to that of Russia and Great Britain, an influence that we could use to thwart such of the European powers as contemplate a thoroughgoing partition of the Middle Kingdom, and to cooperate effectively with those that are resolved to uphold what is left of China's territorial integrity and to keep at all events an open door to that most populous and resourceful section of the Celestial Empire which is watered by the Yang-tse-Kiang. It is, in a word, freedom of access for American

---

[144] Roosevelt to Van Nest, September 1, 1900, *Roosevelt Letters*, 2: 1396.

[145] Charles Dicks, "Why the Republicans Should Be Endorsed," *Forum* 30 (November 1900): 267 8.

[146] Healy, *U.S. Expansionism*, p. 192.

manufacturers to the best part of China which would be powerfully furthered by our retention of the Philippines.[147]

Or as Lodge commented to Elihu B. Hayes, a Massachusetts friend, in May 1898, "All Europe is seizing on China and if we do not establish ourselves in the Far East, from which we must draw our future prosperity, and that great region in which alone we can hope to find the new markets so essential to us, will be practically closed to us forever."[148] The only alternative, Denby warned, was for the United States to seize territory in China itself.[149]

Most large Americans adjusted quickly to the need to acquire the Philippines because of their belief that the Pacific Basin represented the center of future world power. The *Journal of Commerce* asserted: "The one all-controlling reason is that we have an imperative need for an impregnable defensive position in the Pacific, and that we have no other way of getting it than by keeping these Islands, and cannot calculate upon another opportunity if this be neglected."[150] Linked with other American possessions in the Pacific, Alabama Senator John T. Morgan, a Democrat, noted that the Philippines were a valuable strategic asset.

> The necessary care of our commercial affairs, and the defense of our coasts, will require the annexation of Hawaii, and the establishment of a naval station in Pango Pango Bay, in Samoa, where we have this right, by treaty. A military post in the Philippines, connecting with these other islands and with Asia, would form a strategic situation of immense value in time of war, and would place us on an equal footing with all other powers in the control of the commerce of the Southern Pacific Ocean.

Morgan insisted, however, that such power would never be intended to support a policy of conquest or colonization but only to protect the rights of American citizens, and the liberty of commerce. Besides, "the Philippines are not within the sphere of American political influence, but are Asiatic, and should remain Asiatic." The United States had no justifiable motive in acquiring the islands (Morgan wrote in the June 1898 *North American Review*), "unless that is the only feasible way of saving those

---

[147] Hazeltine, "What Shall Be Done About the Philippines?" pp. 389-90.

[148] Lodge to Hayes, May 18, 1898, Lodge Papers, cited by Garraty, *Henry Cabot Lodge*, p. 204.

[149] Denby, "Shall We Keep the Philippines?" p. 280.

[150] Dulles, *America in the Pacific*, p. 234.

people from destruction; or unless those islands become indispensable to our national safety." [151]

The issue of whether America was to become a world power (at least by European standards) was squarely joined in the settlement of the Spanish-American war. Lodge believed there to be no acceptable substitute for greatness.

> Now is the accepted time. I do not want this generation to fail in the task which has been imposed upon it: I do not want our children and our children's children reaping a bitter harvest which has grown from our mistakes or our cowardice. . . . I want them to be able to say of us that we saw that the United States could not be turned into a gigantic Switzerland or Holland, that it could not be a hermit nation hiding a defenseless, feeble body within a huge shell; that it could not be shut up and kept from its share of the world's commerce until it was smothered by a power hostile to it in every conception . . . when it might have prevented such a fate. [152]

While the opponents of the acquisition of the Philippines preferred to call themselves anti-imperialists, most of the advocates of annexation insisted that they were not imperialists. During the debate over the Philippines they generally styled themselves as expansionists, in the great tradition of American expansion. "I do not think that there is any such thing as imperialism,'" Lodge declared, "but I am clearly of the opinion that there is such a thing as 'expansion' and that the United States must control some distant dependencies." [153] Roosevelt asserted in his letter of acceptance of the Republican Vice Presidential nomination: "The simple truth is, there is nothing even remotely resembling 'imperialism' . . . involved in the present development of that policy of expansion which has become part of the history of America from the day she became a nation. The words mean absolutely nothing as applied to our present policy in the Philippines." [154]

The expansionists recognized that the weight of such traditional pronouncements as the Monroe Doctrine and Washington's Farewell Address

---

[131] John T. Morgan, "What Shall We Do with the Conquered Islands?" *North American Review* 166 (June 1898): 645-9.

[152] *Boston Herald*, 1 November 1899, cited by William C. Widenor, *Henry Cabot Lodge and the Search for an American Foreign Policy* (Berkeley: University of California Press, 1980), pp. 114, 158.

[153] Howard K. Beale, *Theodore Roosevelt and the Rise of America to World Power* (New York: Oxford University Press, 1956), pp. 68-9.

[154] *Roosevelt Letters*, September 15, 1900, 2: 1403.

seemed to be against them. In some cases, this called for an argument that these traditions were not truly being challenged; in other instances, the expansionists frankly argued that the traditions were outmoded. The former approach appeared in a letter from a friend to Secretary Long:

> The foreign policy of the United States, as formulated in the "Farewell Address," the Monroe message and subsequent applications of the same is limited exclusively to our intervention in European politics and European intervention in American politics. It was based upon our determination not to be drawn into the questions raised by the balance of power in Europe, nor to allow Europe to introduce questions of European balance of power into America. Its prime object of attack was the Holy Alliance, which has been succeeded by the doctrines of the primacy of the great powers and the concert of Europe. Therefore, whether the dominant factor of European politics be the balance of power or the succeeding schemes for European dynastic control, it is as utterly apart from the interest and policy of the United States, as are the structure and conditions of life on the planet Mars. Hence our foreign policy outside of America and Europe – whether in the Pacific, eastern Asia or southern Africa has no connection with, nor can it in any way affect our Monroe Doctrine for good or evil. [155]

Outsiders, such as British sociologist Benjamin Kidd, envisioned a different set of principles governing American action.

> The meaning of Washington's Farewell Address, delivered when the United States contained only about 6,000,000 people, surrounded on every side by hostile powers and hostile natural conditions, appears to be lost when they will be 200,000,000. The people whom Henry Adams described as living at the beginning of the nineteenth century "in an isolation like that of the Jutes and Angles of the fifth century" have tamed a continent, have covered it with a vast network of the most magnificent railroads in the world, have grown to be the largest and most heterogeneous nation on the face of the earth, with a great world-movement behind it, and certain a great world-part in the future before it. It is because the man in the Western states to-day, in a dim and instinctive way, realizes these things, because he has himself been in the

---

[155] Horace N. Fisher to Long, July 21, 1898, *Long Journal*, p. 158.

midst of this development, and has even been a factor in it, that he seems to be willing to take the risks which more theoretical minds hesitate at. [156]

"The fetish of isolation must be cut down," Whitelaw Reid's *New York Tribune* proclaimed near the end of the War. Reid would become one of McKinley's selections for the U.S. Peace Commission that would negotiation with Spain. [157]

The most familiar justification for the acquisition of the Philippines was that of trade. "The administration seems to be hesitating about the Philippines," Lodge informed Roosevelt in August 1898, "but I hope they will at least keep Manila, which is the great prize, and the thing which will give us the Eastern trade." [158] Overproduction was the great economic fear of the 1890s, and the vast markets of Asia seemed to be the solution, as Beveridge told an audience in Boston two days after the declaration of war against Spain.

> American factories are making more than the American people can use; American soil is producing more than they can consume. Fate has written our policy for us; the trade of the world must and shall be ours. And we will get it as our mother [England] has told us how. We will establish trading-posts throughout the world as distributing-points for American products. We will cover the ocean with our merchant marine. We will build a navy to the measure of our greatness. Great colonies governing themselves, flying our flag and trading with us, will grow about our posts of trade. Our institutions will follow our flag on the wings of our commerce. And American law, American order, American civilization, and the American flag will plant themselves on shores hitherto bloody and benighted, but by those agencies of God hence to be made beautiful and bright. [159]

Beveridge finished the thought in a controversial speech before the Senate on January 9, 1900:

> But to hold it [the Philippines] will be no mistake. Our largest trade henceforth must be with Asia. The Pacific is our ocean.

---

[156] Benjamin Kidd, "The United States and the Control of the Tropics," *Atlantic Monthly* 82 (December 1898): 724.

[157] Bingham Duncan, *Whitelaw Reid: Journalist, Politician, Diplomat* (Athens: University of Georgia Press, 1975), pp. 182-3.

[158] Lodge to Roosevelt, August 15, 1898, *Roosevelt-Lodge Correspondence*, 1: 337.

[159] Bowers, *Beveridge and the Progressive Era*, p. 69.

More and more Europe will manufacture the most it needs, and secure from its colonies the most it consumes. Where shall we turn for consumers of our surplus? Geography answers the question. China is our natural customer. She is nearer to us than to England, Germany, or Russia, the commercial powers of the present and the future. They have moved nearer to China by securing permanent bases on her borders. The Philippines give us a base at the door of all the East. Lines of navigation from our ports to the Orient, and Australia from the Isthmian Canal to Asia; from all Oriental ports to Australia, converge at and separate from the Philippines. They are a self-supporting, dividend-paying fleet, permanently anchored at a spot selected by the strategy of Providence, commanding the Pacific. And the Pacific is the ocean of the commerce of the future. Most future wars will be conflicts for commerce. The power that rules the Pacific, therefore, is the power that rules the world. And, with the Philippines, that power is and will forever be the American Republic. [160]

McKinley had informed his Peace Commission in September 1898 that the protection of American trade was indeed official policy, although he did not consider it to be of the first rank, at least for the record. "Incidental to our tenure of the Philippines is the commercial opportunity to which American statesmanship cannot be indifferent," his instructions read. "It is just to use every legitimate means for the enlargement of American trade; but we seek no advantages in the Orient which are not common to all. Asking only the open door for ourselves, we are ready to accord the open door to others." [161]

The expansionists had to defend themselves from the charge that they were solely motivated by the sordid greed common to imperialists. Lodge told the Senate on March 7, 1900:

> When these arguments are offered in behalf of our Philippine policy the opponents of that policy stigmatize them as sordid. I have never been able to see why they were any more sordid than arguments of exactly the same character urged against the retention of the islands, but we may let that inconsistency pass as one of the familiar incidents of political discussion. I do not myself consider

---

[160] *Congressional Record* 33, 56: 1, part 1, January 9, 1900, p. 704.

[161] Senate Documents, (Ser. 4039), 56: 2, no. 148, February 27, 1901, pp. 6-7, cited by Outten Jones Clinard, *Japan's Influence on American Naval Power, 1897-1917* (Berkeley: University of California Press, 1947), p. 28.

them sordid, for anything which involves the material interests and the general welfare of the people of the United States seems to me of the highest merit and the greatest importance. Whatever duty to others might seem to demand, I should pause long before supporting any policy if there were the slightest suspicion that is was not for the benefit of the people of the United States.

I conceive my first duty to be always to the American people, and I have ever considered it the cardinal principle of American statesmanship to advocate policies which would operate for the benefit of the people of the United States, and most particularly for the advantage of our farmers and our workmen, upon whose well-being, and upon whose full employment at the highest wages, our entire fabric of society and government rests. In a policy which gives us a foothold in the East, which will open a new market in the Philippines, and enable us to increase our commerce with China, I see great advantages to all our people and more especially to our farmers and our workingmen. [162]

"Nations are selfish," Republican Senator John C. Spooner of Wisconsin had argued in the debates over ratification of the Peace Treaty a year earlier. "They must be selfish or they cannot live. I do not mean grasping and overweening of necessity, but they must look to their own interests and the interests of their own people." When Spooner attempted to compare the acquisition of Puerto Rico – to which there was little opposition – with that of the Philippines, he provoked the following exchange with Senator Bacon:

> Mr. BACON. I think, Mr. President that the attitude of the United States in that particular is entirely justified upon the ground that the continued possession by Spain of any West India island is recognized as inimical to the interests and to the peace of this country, and, for that reason, on the ground of the safety of this country and the future peace of this country, not only has the Government of the United States made that demand as to Porto *sic* Rico, but as to all the other West India possessions of Spain.

> Mr. SPOONER. Mr. President, I thank the Senator from Georgia. He has in a single sentence made a more powerful argument in support of my contention than I could ever hope to make. He says

---

[162] *Congressional Record* 33, 56: 1, part 3, March 7, 1900, p. 2627.

that the Declaration of Independence is suspended in the West Indies. Why? Because it is for the interest of the United States.

Mr. BACON. No.

Mr. SPOONER. Yes.

Mr. BACON. I beg the Senator's pardon; not the interest.

Mr. SPOONER. Yes.

Mr. BACON. To the public safety, which goes beyond interest.

Mr. SPOONER. Oh, the United States, Mr. President, is interested in its public safety. (Laughter)

Mr. BACON. There are a great many things, however, that are to the interest of the country which are not essential to its safety.

Mr. SPOONER. But this is the particular thing that we are talking about, Mr. President; not a great many other things. The Senator justifies the taking of Porto Rico, as he must, without asking the consent of the inhabitants. Otherwise we could not probably take it at all. He bases his justification upon the fact, for it is a fact, that we require it in our business; in other words, that we regard it –

Mr. BACON. The Senator must take my words, and not use other words. I say necessary, not for our interest, not for our business, but essential to our safety. Now, if the Senator will use that word, I will stand by it; and I will say further that I go fully with him to the extent –

Mr. SPOONER. Spain occupied it for one hundred and twenty years and we were safe.

Mr. BACON. To the extent that the acquisition of territory necessary to our safety is perfectly justifiable under the Declaration of Independence and our Constitution.

Mr. SPOONER. The Senator has surrendered.

Mr. BACON. Safety, not interest.

Mr. SPOONER. I accept his surrender.

Mr. BACON. No.

Mr. SPOONER. Mr. President, there is no escape from it. That is the principle upon which nations transact business.

Mr. BACON. If the Senator can show that the Philippines are essential to our safety, I am with him.

Mr. SPOONER. Wait a moment. It is the same sort of selfishness which leads a man to prefer the interest of his own children to the interest of the public. It is the same sort of selfishness that leads a man to safeguard his own home. It is the foundation of all society. It is the one thing that we ought never to lose sight of. We ought to legislate and we ought to deal, where we can, with reference primarily to the interests of our people, not to the interest of any other people, not to please any other Government. [163]

John Barrett, a journalist and adviser to Admiral Dewey, in his August 1899 *North American Review* article entitled "The Paramount Power of the Pacific," argued that the markets of the Far East would unite the nation on the basis of self-interest. If the annexation of the Philippines and the search for trade in China had been merely sectional issues, Barrett agreed that "there might be a grave question as to the advisability of taking a strong position as to the future of the empire." But America's Western states were in a position to provide China and other Asiatic nations with flour and timber. In time, Asian-Pacific demand for cotton might take up the South's surplus supply of this staple. The North and East, in turn, could provide the manufactured cotton, iron, steel and miscellaneous products to the teeming millions of the Far East. "The farmers of the West and South can unite with the laboring man of the North and East in supporting the shippers, manufacturers and exporters in developing a strong Asiatic policy." [164]

As to the objection of the anti-imperialists that the United States had not the Constitutional authority to acquire the Philippines without the intention of preparing the islands for statehood, the expansionists were delighted to take the Hamiltonian high ground. After all, were not the anti-imperialists taking their authority from that vehicle of states' rights, the Dred Scott decision? Charles Dawes' speech at a Lincoln Day banquet in 1900 stressed that "the Republican party stands now as in the days of Lincoln, behind the nation's sovereignty." [165] The "little Americans" advocated a constitutional doctrine that denied the government of the United States legitimate powers possessed by every other sovereign entity. They refused to accept the verdict of the Civil

---

[163] Ibid., 32, 55: 3, part 2, February 2, 1899, pp. 1383-4.

[164] John Barrett, "The Paramount Power of the Pacific," *North American Review* 169 (August 1899): 169-70.

[165] *Dawes Journal*, p. 215.

War, which found the United States to be one nation, in favor of the verdict of Dred Scott. Senator Teller elaborated on this theme in December 1898:

> Mr. President, that question was settled, and settled for all time. It was settled when Lee handed his sword to Grant at Appomattox. Whatever might have been the difference of opinion amongst the American people up to that hour, in the minds and in the hearts of the American people we took our place as a nation, as a nation endowed with all the powers and all the dignity of any nation in the world. Why should it not be, Mr. President? Why should it not be in the case of a great nation containing within itself forty-five other nations, all yielding obedience to it, all recognizing in national affairs that the nation was supreme, they themselves nations in some sense of the term, as Chief Justice Marshall said in 1821, sovereigns and yet subordinates, sovereign in their local affairs, subordinate when it came to international affairs, their international sovereignty having been merged into the sovereignty of this great nation of ours? Mr. President, it is strange to me, and I think it will be strange to the American people, that we should be now discussing the question in the American Senate whether this is a nation with all the prerogatives and all the powers and all the dignity of any nation in the world. The American people, North and South, East and West, believe it is a nation. Everywhere there is a national sentiment which denies to this Government no power that any other nation in the world claims.[166]

Of course, debate over the meaning of the Constitution preceded the Civil War by many years, going back even to the ratification of the basic document itself. The heart of the debate was over the validity of Hamilton's formulation of implied powers which, in the eyes of the large Americans/expansionists, was intended to protect both the nation and the Constitution:

> Now a constitution, however marvelous its intrinsic excellences a hundred years ago, and however wonderfully adapted to the wants of a growing nation, could not, in the nature of things, make definite and specific provisions for such new conditions. Moreover, the demands made by the new conditions cannot be set aside: on the contrary, they are often imperative and irresistible. No intelligent people will ever be permanently bound by an obstructing

---

[166] *Congressional Record* 32, 55: 3, part 1, December 20, 1898, p. 325.

law, or even an obstructing constitution, that cannot be changed. If, therefore, the Constitution, in case it unmistakably and persistently resists the demands of public opinion, cannot be modified, it will either bend or break. In the development of the country thus far it has, with all needed flexibility, yielded to new necessities. The inference as to what is likely to occur in the future is unmistakably plain; and the question, as to the propriety and desirability of the permanent occupation of insular territory, so far from being one of constitutional law, is simply one to be determined by considerations of national policy. [167]

And then there were those, New York Senator T. C. Platt contended, whose appeal to tradition was meant to obscure their rejection of this healthy constitutional doctrine.

There has never been absent from the floor of the Senate that class of intellect which has found, in the Constitution its warrant for opposing new things. It has always been a superior class of intellect, without doubt earnest and sincere, but not always to be appreciated by ordinary minds that believe in finding a practical solution for practical questions as they arise one after another in the course of national experience, and that starts out in its consideration of all public questions with the assumption that the founders of our Government did not intend it to be anything less than a competent government. Nor is it new things only which are so resolutely opposed in the name of the fathers. It is old things, with new faces, as well. Here we have been for a whole century annexing territory – annexing with a club or with a caress, just as the necessities demanded and yet Senators are discovering to one another the most acute distress over what they boldly describe as a "departure from time honored traditions." [168]

The national history of the United States had been one of almost continuous expansion. Even that arch-enemy of Hamilton, Thomas Jefferson, swallowed his constitutional scruples and permitted the purchase of Louisiana. Beveridge could not understand why the latter-day Jeffersonians railed against further expansion in the name of that same Constitution.

---

[167] Charles Kendall Adams, "Colonies and Other Dependencies," *Forum* 27 (March 1899): 42

[168] *Congressional Record* 32, 55: 3, part 2, January 27, 1899, p. 1155.

The power to govern all territory the nation may acquire would have been in Congress if the language affirming that power had not been written in the Constitution. For not all powers of the National Government are expressed. Its principal powers are implied. The written Constitution is but the index of the living Constitution. Had this not been true, the Constitution would have failed. For the people in any event would have developed and progressed. And if the Constitution had not had the capacity for growth corresponding with the growth of the nation, the Constitution would and should have been abandoned as the Articles of Confederation were abandoned. For the Constitution is not immortal in itself, is not useful even in itself. The Constitution is immortal and even useful only as it serves the orderly development of the nation. The nation alone is immortal. The nation alone is sacred. The Army is its servant. The Navy is its servant. The President is its servant. This Senate is its servant. Our laws are its methods. Our Constitution is its instrument. This is the golden rule of constitutional interpretation: The Constitution was made for the people, not the people for the Constitution.

Beveridge and some (but not all) of the annexationists believed that even if the people of the United States were not the final cause of expansion, they were the efficient cause.

Mr. President, this question is deeper than any question of party politics; deeper than any question of the isolated policy of our country even; deeper even than any question of constitutional power. It is elemental. It is racial. God has not been preparing the English-speaking and Teutonic peoples for a thousand years for nothing but vain and idle self-contemplation and self-admiration. No. He has made us the master organizers of the world to establish system where chaos reigns. He has given us the spirit of progress to overwhelm the forces of reaction throughout the earth. He has made us adept in government that we may administer government among savage and senile peoples. Were it not for such a force as this the world would relapse into barbarism and night. And of all our race He has marked the American people as His chosen nation to finally lead in the regeneration of the world. This is the divine mission of America, and it holds for us all the profit, all the glory, all the happiness, possible to man. We are trustees of the world's progress, guardians of its righteous peace. The judgment of the

Master is upon us: "Ye have been faithful over a few things; I will make you ruler over many things." [169]

Nor was it sufficient for Beveridge that all previous territorial acquisitions (with the exception of Alaska and Hawaii) had been contiguous to the United States. "Is there a geographical interpretation to the Constitution? Do degrees of longitude fix constitutional limitations?" The ocean separating the Philippines was not a barrier, but a highway. "Land may separate men from their desire, the ocean never." [170] Technology – steam power and electricity – had brought the globe together in the same way that the North American continent had been united by the railroad and the telegraph.

Senator Platt (Connecticut) objected on similar grounds to Vest's position that the United States was constitutionally unable to acquire territory without intending to incorporate that territory as states. After all, the anti-imperialists admitted exceptions to that rule, for example, the establishment of coaling stations in the Philippines.

> The Senator from Missouri himself does not accept it without qualification. He says that we cannot acquire territory except to make new States of it and to establish coaling stations and to correct boundaries. The Senator himself is not willing to go to the full length of the dictum of Judge Taney. Where is a specific clause to be found in the Constitution declaring that we may acquire territory for coaling stations? How large may a station be? To what limits must it be circumscribed? If we can acquire property for a coaling station, why not for a naval station, which the Senator does not incorporate in his resolution or admit by it? And how much territory may we acquire for a naval station? And if acquired, what sort of government may we establish in connection with our naval station? The doctrine of the resolution seems frivolous. [171]

But what of the moral argument: even if the United States had the power, did it also have the right to annex the Philippines? The expansionists were required to address the challenge of their opponents, that the "conquest" of these islands violated the very core of the American regime, as embodied in the principles of the Declaration of Independence. Some chose to admit the anti-imperialists' point, while arguing (as did Amos K. Fiske, a long-time

---

[169] Ibid., 33, 56: 1, part 1, January 9, 1900, p. 711.

[170] Ibid., p. 710.

[171] Ibid., 32, 55: 3, part 1, December 19, 1898, p. 292.

editorial writer of the *New York Times* and *The Journal of Commerce*) that the Declaration "consecrated to perpetuity some of the most obvious fallacies that were ever promulgated to mislead men." The Declaration was proclaimed as part of the emergency represented by the revolt of the thirteen colonies, and was not intended "for the future government of this or any other people." The Founders "prefaced their Declaration with that sweeping and glowing utterance, which had a Broad application as to the truth of their case, but which becomes a delusive bundle of fallacies when promiscuously applied to the universal state of man." Fiske believed, however, that in no sense was "the Revolution based upon any self-evident truth of the equality of men, or upon the theory that governments derive their just powers from the consent of the governed."

> They proclaimed it to be a self-evident truth "that all men are created equal; that they are endowed by their Creator with certain inalienable rights; that among these are life, liberty and the pursuit of happiness." Whatever interpretation and exegesis may do for this declaration, in the sense in which it is commonly accepted and used in the place of argument, it is neither self-evident nor truth. There is nothing more evident to human observation and human reason than the inequalities with which men come into the world and pass through it and out of it. Not only are different races unequal in capacities of various kinds, but the members of the same race present every diversity of inequality. Nor can any power at the command of mankind make them equal in this world or in the processes of time whatever may be their destiny in eternity.
>
> It is useless to argue around this immutable fact, or try to interpret into the Declaration a meaning which it does not contain. All men are simply not created equal in any possible sense of the word. The negroes held in slavery by some of the signers of the Declaration of Independence were not created the equals of their masters nor of the average members of the race to which their masters belonged. The mass of the white people of the colonies were not all created equal, nor were the people of Mexico and South America at that time created equal to the people inhabiting the Republic then in the throes of birth. [172]

---

[172] Amos K. Fiske, "Some Consecrated Fallacies," *North American Review* 169 (December 1899): 221-8.

Harvard Professor A. Lawrence Lowell also sought to grapple with the Declaration's statement that "all men are created equal." In a February 1899 article in the *Atlantic Monthly*, Lowell divided the doctrine of human equality into civil and political rights, of which there was no necessary connection. Civil equality was an essential principle of common law, the unshakable creed of all civilized nations, extending back to such traditions as the Magna Charta. Political equality was quite another matter. It was obviously not true in the strict sense that a worthless street loafer and Abraham Lincoln were equally fit to be entrusted with the direction of public affairs. If such inequalities were not too severe, then the doctrine of political equality might be close enough to the truth to act upon. The Northern states, for example, where the population was tolerably homogenous and political education tolerably diffuse, qualified as such an area. In the larger cities, however, "where the inequalities of social condition are enormous, and where there is a huge mass of foreigners untrained in self-government, the Utopia foretold by the prophets of democracy has not been quite fulfilled. Tammany does not altogether realize the dreams of Jefferson." [173]

Lodge and many of the other expansionists implied that the principles of self-government were limited in their application, perhaps decisively, by conditions of race, geography and climate.

> The capacity of a people, moreover, for free and representative government is not in the least a matter of guesswork. The forms of government to which nations or races naturally tend may easily be discovered from history. You can follow the story of political freedom and representative government among the English-speaking people back across the centuries until you reach the Teutonic tribes emerging from the forests of Germany and bringing with them forms of local self-government which are repeated to-day in the pure democracies of the New England town meeting. The tendencies and instincts of the Teutonic race which, reaching from the Arctic Circle to the Alps, swept down upon the Roman Empire, were clear at the outset. Yet the individual freedom and the highly developed forms of free government in which these tendencies and instincts have culminated in certain countries and under the most favorable conditions have been the slow growth of nearly fifteen hundred years.

---

[173] A. Lawrence Lowell, "The Colonial Expansion of the United States," *Atlantic Monthly* 83 (February 1899): 149-50. Jefferson probably would have agreed.

There never has been, on the other hand, the slightest indication of any desire for what we call freedom or representative government east of Constantinople. The battle of Marathon was but the struggle between a race which had the instinct and desire for freedom and the opposite principle. The form of government natural to the Asiatic has always been a despotism. You may search the history of Asia and of the East for the slightest trace, not merely of any understanding, but of any desire for political liberty, as we understand the word.

One could not alter the tendencies of race in a moment, Lodge cautioned; those peculiarities were capable of being modified only by very slow processes. "Buckle's theory, that you could make a Hottentot into a European if you only took possession of him in infancy, and gave him a European education among suitable surroundings, has been abandoned alike by science and history as grotesquely false." [174]

Anti-imperialists were reading too much into the Declaration, in the opinion of Ohio Republican Senator Joseph B. Foraker:

You will not find there any complaint against the colonial system of government. You find there only a recitation of wrongs and grievances and outrages and tyrannies, as they are characterized, which the people of the colonies had suffered at the hands of the British ministry, and their sole purpose, as they claimed over and over again, both before the war and for nearly a year after the war commenced, was, not to secure independence, but simply to redress the wrongs and grievances to which they had been subjected by the mother country. There was no complaint about the colonial system proper. [175]

As a consequence of such misinterpretations, Americans had been taught to overlook the maintenance of civil and economic rights as secured by the Constitution, in favor of certain less important political dogmas. "Our public orators have created a fictitious, theoretical Constitution, into which fragments of the real Constitution and scraps of the Declaration of Independence, have been worked as in a mosaic," an unsigned commentary in the February 1899 issue of the *Yale Review* explained:

---

[174] *Congressional Record* 33, 56 :1, part 3, March 7, 1900, p. 2621.

[175] Ibid., 32, 55: 3, part 1, January 11, 1899, p. 565.

> Historically, the Declaration of Independence cannot for a moment be put upon the same plane as the Constitution. The former was a political manifesto, issued by a revolutionary body, and like most such manifestoes, was a rhetorical appeal for support. The latter is the fundamental law of the country, which can be quoted in court, and according to which the rights of the individual may be gauged. Leaving aside rhetoric and an appeal to the feelings, it lays down carefully and exactly the really essential maxims of good government. It very wisely leaves the subject of political rights almost untouched, allowing the States to decide for themselves who shall vote, and how the votes shall be counted; but it does lay great emphasis upon the maintenance of civil rights. It protects the citizen against unjust searches and seizures; it secures him against the loss of life, liberty, and property, without due process of law; it guarantees him the right of trial by jury in criminal suits. Practically these civil rights have done much more to make our country prosperous and great than the possession of political rights. People flock to our shores, not because they can vote, for the inhabitants of most European countries from which we receive immigrants already enjoy that right at home; but they come here because they are free to earn their own living in their own way, secure in their persons and property, and exempt from the burden of a standing army and of a military aristocracy. The right of suffrage is worth little without the ability to earn a comfortable living, as we may see in the case of the Negroes, and the lack of the right of suffrage does not seriously impair the attractiveness of the country as long as there is a chance to earn good wages, as is seen in the case of the Chinese.[176]

The expansionists were placed on the rhetorical defensive by Senator Orville Platt's statement, made in response to a question by Hoar, that he regarded government to derive its just powers from the consent of *some* of the governed. Lodge supported Platt's interpretation of the Declaration, noting that Jefferson's language did not include either the word "some," or "all."

> In order to interpret Jefferson's language aright let us see what kind of a government he was himself engaged in setting up, for there alone can we get light as to his meaning. The Declaration

---

[176] *Yale Review* 7 (February 1899): 358-9.

of Independence was the announcement of the existence of a new revolutionary government upon American soil. Upon whose consent did it rest? Was it upon that of all the people of the colonies duly expressed? Most assuredly not. In the first place we must throw out all negroes and persons of African descent, who formed about one quarter of the population, and who were not consulted at all as to the proposed change of government. So we must immediately insert the word "white" in Jefferson's sentence. Let us go a step further. Were women included in the word "governed?" They certainly were not permitted by voice or vote to express an opinion on this momentous question. They must, therefore, be excluded, and we must add the word "white" to the word "male" as a further limitation upon the governed to whom Jefferson had in mind.

Did the revolutionary government rest on the consent of all the white males in the colonies? Most assuredly not. There was the usual age limitation which shut out all male persons under twenty-one, and manhood suffrage, as we understand it, did not exist in a single colony. Everywhere the suffrage was limited, generally by property qualifications, sometimes by other restrictions. So another amendment becomes necessary to Jefferson's phrase if we are going to make it fit the government which he was actually engaged in setting up. Conforming to the facts the sentence then would read something like this: "deriving their just powers from the consent of the white male governed who have the right to vote according to the laws of the various colonies."

Nor was that all. The nation was further divided into those who supported the Revolution, and those who opposed it. The revolutionaries imposed their new government on the Loyalists at the point of the bayonet, forcing them to choose between accepting that government or exile. Lodge attributed the sentiments in the Declaration to the influence of Rousseau and the doctrines of the social compact. "What Jefferson really did – with Rousseau and the theory of the social compact in mind – was to put in the form of a large generalization the principle for which the colonies engaged in the Revolution, which was that they were not to be taxed without representation and without their consent." Jefferson did not therein intend to establish a constitution providing for all contingencies and creating all sorts of limitations. "To pull a sentence out of a revolutionary manifesto and deal with it as if it was one of the labored and chiseled clauses of the Constitution shows a sad confusion of thought." The phrase "consent of the governed," Lodge insisted, represented a great and just principle, but whose application in practice would be determined by actual facts and conditions.[177]

Among those conditions, Senator Teller explained, was the fact that not everyone was permitted to participate in the affairs of government: aliens were excluded, as were the vicious and ignorant, women and infants. And yet all of the above were liable to pay taxes.[178] The problem arose from trying to apply an abstract doctrine, even if philosophically true, to the world of concrete circumstances. Senator Spooner, who made this point in February 1899, believed that the "consent" doctrine, along with one or two others conjoined with it, were intended to form the theoretical basis for the right of revolution. Spooner argued that abstractions often had to give way to practical affairs, and would remain that way "until the millennium comes. It never can be while government is entrusted to men and holds sway over men. It never can be until perfection comes into life, and until the weaknesses, the passions, the violence, the faults, and the foibles of our common humanity are eliminated."[179] For Republicans, there was also the political truth of the recent past.

> There cannot be much doubt that if our brethren of the South had been accorded the privilege "of the consent of the governed," there would be here now four republics, or monarchies, instead of one great and indestructible Union, which honorably and rightly and justly in spite of all this sentimentalism was pinned together by bayonets.[180]

Even if it was true, as Lodge said, that the United States had the power and right to "govern the Philippines without making them economically or politically part of our system," the annexationists did not intend to govern the islands tyrannically. How could the United States deprive the residents of the Philippines of their liberty when they had possessed none prior to the arrival of the flag and armed forces of the United States?[181] This seemed to imply that there was a higher political good than governing according to the consent of the governed. "The consent of the governed doctrine must not in my opinion be pushed to an extent that would restore savagery," Roosevelt wrote after his election as Vice President in November 1900. ". . . it is not true that the

---

[177] *Congressional Record* 33, 56:1, part 3, March 7, 1900, p. 2618.

[178] Ibid., 32, 55: 3, part 1, December 20, 1898, p. 326.

[179] Ibid., part 2, February 2, 1899, p. 1382.

[180] Charles Denby, "Do We Owe Independence to the Philippines?" *Forum* 29 (June 1900): 405.

[181] *Congressional Record* 33, 56:1, part 3, March 7, 1900, p. 2618.

democratic system of government is fit for all men." If a government were to be established "on strict limitations of savagery, we would violate the theory of the Declaration of Independence if pushed to its extreme form, just as much as we violated it upon insisting that we may govern the Philippines now." [182]

Roosevelt told cartoonist Finley Peter Dunne that his criticism that the expansionists wished to "take up the white man's burden and put it on the coon," hit the weak spot in his position. [183] And yet it seemed to Elihu Root, the new Secretary of War, that there was a sharp distinction between those peoples who were capable of self-government, and those who were not. The essential point was not, therefore, consent of the governed, but that each society should have an adequate government. Even if a society was incapable of providing for itself, it was still necessary "that the weak shall be protected, that cruelty and lust shall be restrained, whether there be consent or not." Was it a violation of Jeffersonian principles "for the external forces of civilization to replace brutal and oppressive government, with which . . . people in ignorance are content, by ordered liberty and individual freedom"? [184]

Root and others, from this line of analysis, concluded that the Philippines need not be made independent immediately. Nor did it mean, in the opinion of Teller, that the islands would ever be admitted as states, or that their citizens would be given elective franchise. "But it does mean that you shall give them that moral aid, that moral encouragement, which will enable them to take care of themselves." [185] Even more concretely, Senator Orville Platt believed that the United States operated under moral obligations and constraints in its relations with the Philippines.

> We must legislate on the great principles which underlie our institutions, with liberty, justice, and the protection of individual rights in view. We must legislate in the spirit of republicanism, not in the monarchical or despotic spirit. We must legislate with the idea of the right of self-government, when people shall become fitted for self-government, always in view. We must legislate for the security of every personal right which the individual is fitted to appreciate and enjoy. In other words, we must provide for the people of any territory that we may acquire the most liberal, just, and beneficent government which they may be

---

[182] Roosevelt to Love, November 24, 1900, *Roosevelt Letters*, 2: 1441-2.

[183] Roosevelt to Dunne, January 16, 1900, ibid., 2: 1134.

[184] Healy, *U.S. Expansionism*, p. 148.

[185] *Congressional Record* 32, 55: 3, part 1, December 20, 1898, p. 330.

capable of enjoying, always with reference to their development and welfare and in the hope that they may be finally fitted for independent self-government.[186]

Neither Platt nor Lodge believed that any Congressional resolution intending to bind the government to any course of action, constitutional or otherwise, was at all advisable.

> When that treaty is ratified, we have full power and are absolutely free to do with those islands as we please; and the opposition to its ratification may be summed up in a single sentence, that the American people and the American Congress are not to be trusted with that power and with that freedom of action in regard to the inhabitants of those distant islands. Every one of the resolutions thus far offered on this subject is an expression of distrust in the character, ability, honesty, and wisdom of the American people and an attempt to make us promise to be good and wise and honest in the future and in our dealings with other people. It is a well-meant effort to make us give bonds to fate by means of a Congressional resolution.[187]

In fact, many of the expansionists claimed that they were much more radically democratic than their opponents. An editorial in the October 1898 issue of the *Outlook* asserted that,

> the radical difference between the expansionist and the continentalist – that is, between the one who believes that American ideas and institutions are good for the whole world, and the one who thinks they are adapted only to the continent of North America – is not that the former is an imperialist and the latter a democrat, but that the former is a more radical, a more enthusiastic, and a more optimistic democrat than the latter.[188]

Lodge made the following comparison: Bryan and the Democrats "think we should abandon the Philippines because they are not fit for self-government. I believe that for the same reason we should retain them."[189] Those who shrank from such a task were cowardly rather than principled;

---

[186] Ibid., December 19, 1898, p. 295.

[187] Ibid., January 24, 1899, p. 959.

[188] Healy, *U.S. Expansionism*, p. 62.

[189] Garraty, *Henry Cabot Lodge*, p. 206.

Roosevelt accused them of using moral arguments to rationalize abdication of responsibility. [190]

To what degree did morality require the United States to undertake a global civilizing mission? Even though Mahan believed that interest and altruism ran together by bringing backward peoples forward, thus alleviating the barbarian threat – duty must be in the forefront. "If the ideas get inverted, and the nation sees in its new responsibilities, first of all, markets and profits, with incidental resultant benefits to the natives, it will go wrong," Mahan wrote in 1899. [191] Or as Roosevelt argued in February 1900 about Puerto Rico: "Our only justification for keeping the islands is that we intend to benefit them. If we do not intend to so benefit them, then for Heaven's sake let them go and strike out for themselves!" [192]

For some of the expansionists, the nation's task for spreading civilization was a primary function of "large Americanism." Senator Orville Platt spoke of the government's "mission to relieve the oppressed, to right every wrong, and to extend the institutions of free government." [193] Beveridge reasoned that the Declaration of Independence could not forbid the American nation to do its part in the regeneration of the world. "If it did, the Declaration would be wrong – just as the Articles of Confederation, drafted by the very same men who signed the Declaration, was found to be wrong." [194]

In principle, the expansionists acknowledged that the Philippines could one day become independent or (much less likely) be admitted as a state of the Union. Their present status as a territory of the United States was a condition of circumstance, a circumstance that admittedly was likely to continue for some time. Roosevelt expressed the expansionists' official creed in a letter to Charles William Eliot on November 14, 1900:

> By every consideration of honor and humanity we are bound to stay in the Philippines to put down the insurrection, establish order and then give a constantly increasing measure of liberty and self-government, while ruling with wisdom and justice. Whenever the islands can stand alone I should be only too glad to withdraw. At present to withdraw would be on a small scale to work the infinite

---

[190] Healy, *U.S. Expansionism*, p. 124.

[191] Ibid., p. 129.

[192] Roosevelt to Root, February 13, 1900, *Roosevelt Letters*, 2: 1183.

[193] *Congressional Record* 32, 55: 3, part 1, December 19, 1898, p. 297.

[194] Ibid., 33, 56: 1, part 1, January 9, 1900, p. 710.

damage that would be worked in India by following out the views of the "Perish India" school of English politicians.[195]

But the expansionists, unlike the anti-imperialists, refused to make any legally binding commitment to the permanent status of the Philippines. The anti-imperialists alleged that the annexationists' hesitation stemmed from political expediency – in fact, the Administration had no intention of ever freeing the islands. The expansionists responded by pointing to the delicate situation in the Far East, with an insurrection smoldering in the Philippines and a potential war in sight over the partition of China. Any binding Congressional action would destroy the freedom of action essential to the policy-making discretion of the executive. Lodge characterized this anti-annexationist tactic as "both diaphanous and elusive."

> Another proposition is that we should treat the Philippines as we treat Cuba. That is precisely what we are doing. But what is really meant by this demand is not that we should treat the Philippines as we treat Cuba, but that we should make to them a promise as to the future. And that is what every proposition made by those opposed to the Republican Party comes down to, a promise as to the future. We are to put down insurrection and disorder and hold the islands temporarily without the consent of the governed, but simultaneously we are to make large promises as to the future, which will look well in print and keep insurrection and disorder alive.

Negotiations, concessions, promises and hesitations were only proofs of weakness to the Asiatic mind, Lodge emphasized:

> The resolutions offered by Senators on the other side and the tenor of their speeches are all of this description. They present no policy, but invite us to make promises. Promises are neither action nor policy, and, in the form of legislation, are a grave mistake. Those which involve us in pledges of independence have the additional disadvantage of being the one sure means of keeping alive war and disorder in the islands. Those who offer them or urge them proceed on the assumption that you can deal with an Asiatic in the same manner and expect from him the same results as from a European or an American. This shows, it seems to me, a fatal misconception. The Asiatic mind and habit of thought are utterly different from

---

[195] Roosevelt to Norton, November 14, 1900, *Roosevelt Letters*, 2: 1415.

ours. Words or acts which to us would show generosity and kindness and would bring peace and order, to an Asiatic mean simply weakness and timidity and are to him an incentive to riot, resistance, and bloodshed. Promises of this kind, therefore, are neither effective action nor intelligent policy, but the sure breeders of war. If we must abandon the Philippines, let us abandon them frankly. If we mean to turn them over to domestic anarchy or foreign control, let us do it squarely. If we are to retain them, let us deal manfully with the problems as they arise. [196]

Senator Orville Platt opposed a resolution introduced by Senator Bacon, which would have declared the right of the Philippine people to independence. The resolution would do more than place the United States on record as being committed to eventual independence for the Philippines – it would have direct and disastrous consequences, precisely as the anti-imperialists intended.

> Mr. Aguinaldo would come with the joint resolution in his hand and say, "You passed a solemn resolution in order to ratify the treaty, saying we were entitled to independence, and that it was not the purpose of the Government 'to secure and maintain permanent dominion over the same . . . or to incorporate the inhabitants thereof as citizens of the United States.' You disclaimed any disposition or intent to exercise permanent sovereignty." He would also point to this clause, "announced in the great Declaration that governments derive 'their just powers from the consent of the governed;' that 'the Government of the United States recognizes that the people of the Philippine Islands of right ought to be free and independent.'" And would he not have a right to say so? Would not every nation in Europe say that Aguinaldo, with that joint resolution passed in the Senate, had a right to insist on the immediate independence of the Philippine Islands, because governments could only derive their just powers from the consent of the governed, and he did not consent to the United States in those islands at all, and his government did not, because the joint resolution declared that the Filipinos of right ought to be free and Independent. [197]

---

[196] *Congressional Record* 33, 56: 1, part 3, March 7, 1900, pp. 2617-8.

[197] Ibid. 32, 55: 3, part 2, January 31, 1899, p. 1302.

Even talk about a firm commitment to Philippine independence would only fan the fires of insurrection – and whet the appetite of certain European powers – thus jeopardizing the lives of American soldiers. Roosevelt denounced "the peace-at-any-price Senators and publicists," on whose shoulders rested a heavy responsibility for the outbreak of hostilities between American forces and those of Aguinaldo in early 1899.[198] "The bullets that slay our men in Luzon are inspired by the denouncers of America here," Roosevelt fumed. The Filipino will stop killing our soldiers very soon after he becomes convinced that he will receive no aid in the effort from the party of which Mr. Bryan is chief.[199] Beveridge joined the attack during his well-publicized Senate speech of January 9, 1900:

> Mr. President, reluctantly and only from a sense of duty am I forced to say that American opposition to the war has been the chief factor in prolonging it. Had Aguinaldo not understood that in America, even in the American Congress, even here in the Senate, he and his cause were supported; had he not known that it was proclaimed on the stump and in the press of a faction in the United States that every shot his misguided followers fired into the breasts of American soldiers was like the volleys fired by Washington's men against the soldiers of King George his insurrection would have dissolved before it entirely crystallized. . . . It is believed and stated in Luzon, Panay, and Cuba that the Filipinos have only to fight, harass, retreat, break up into small parties, if necessary, as they are doing now, but by any means hold out until the next Presidential election, and our forces will be withdrawn.
>
> All this has aided the enemy more than climate, arms, and battle. Senators, I have heard these reports myself; I have talked with the people; I have seen our mangled boys in the hospital, and field; I have stood on the firing line and beheld our dead soldiers, their faces turned to the pitiless southern sky, and in sorrow rather than anger I say to those whose voices in America have cheered those misguided natives on to shoot our soldiers down, that the blood of those dead and wounded boys of ours is on their hands, and the flood of all the years can never wash that stain away. In sorrow

---

[198] Roosevelt to Root, February 6, 1899, *Roosevelt Letters*, 2. 933.

[199] Beale, *Theodore Roosevelt*, p. 70.

rather than anger I say these words, for I earnestly believe that our brothers knew not what they did.[200]

The expansionists argued that such anti-American behavior by the anti-imperialists belied the latter's contention that the "large Americans" were bent on destroying the character of the American regime. (How could Bryan demand the "consent of the governed" in the Philippines, Roosevelt wondered, when he and the Democrats "profited by the denial of this same so-called right in North Carolina and Alabama.")[201] Roosevelt branded the anti-imperialists as "the political heirs and assigns" of the copperheads of the Civil War, and reminded Americans that the Democrats had accused Lincoln of wanting to become emperor. In Detroit during the campaign of 1900, he asked the men in uniform in the audience to stand up, and then told the cheering crowd, "Behold your tyrants."[202]

The political battle between the annexationists and anti-imperialists, in its essence, involved a struggle to articulate the commanding definition of American expansionism. Just as the new expansionists sought to claim the Federalist-Whig-Republican nationalist heritage in domestic matters, so too did they wish to capture the expansionist tradition which had largely been a Democratic province during the 19th century. The "small American" doctrine, in this case, a too-literal reading of the Declaration of Independence, "would have turned back the Mayflower from Plymouth Rock," in the words of Connecticut's Platt.[203] Senator Foraker wondered further: if the territory of Florida, or the territory commanding the mouth of the Mississippi, had been inhabited by people who were incapable of self-government, "would that have precluded this Government from acquiring that territory . . . to promote the interests of the people and advancing them?" The United States, obviously, had not been so precluded and it did in fact acquire these strategic possessions without consulting the wishes of the local inhabitants.[204]

The great American expansionist tradition had always been opposed by an anti-expansionist opposition, Lodge emphasized, and he noted that the "small Americans" of past times had made arguments similar to those of the contemporary anti-imperialists:

---

[200] *Congressional Record* 33, 56: 1, part 1, January 9, 1900, p. 708.

[201] Roosevelt to Johnson, August 18, 1900, *Roosevelt Letters*, 2: 1385.

[202] Beale, *Theodore Roosevelt*, p. 68.

[203] *Congressional Record* 32, 55: 3, part 1, January 9, 1899, p. 502.

[204] Ibid., January 11, 1899, p. 569.

Prophets of evil are not lacking to declare ruin inevitable if we persist in our career of expansion and in setting no fixed bounds to the progress of the country. Like the raven of Macbeth they croak themselves hoarse in predicting the downfall of the Republic. These dire forebodings are not new. Look back to the debates of 1803 and the succeeding years, and you will find there all that is being said now in almost the same language, and with the same certainty of swift-coming disaster. In view of the results of the Louisiana Purchase the gloomy prophecies of these old Cassandras look very queer and make us smile. But they are no queerer than the black predictions of their successors of to-day will appear to the next generation. The downfall of the Republic has been constantly and confidently foretold many times since the foundation of the Government, generally on trivial grounds, and always when a great expansion of territory took place. Never has it come true. Only once was the great peril real and near, and that was not when men were trying to widen the bounds of the Republic, but when they sought to divide it and make it small.

If the annexation of the Philippines was morally wrong in the light of the Declaration of Independence, Lodge reflected, "then our whole past record of expansion is a crime, and Thomas Jefferson, and John Quincy Adams, and James Monroe, and all the rest of our Presidents and statesmen who have added to our national domain are traitors to the cause of liberty and to the Declaration of Independence." That record, far from violating the great Declaration, succeeded in spreading its principles over vast regions where they were previously unknown. [205]

Conclusion: The United States on the Eve of the 20th Century

To sum up: As the 19th century came to a close, Americans were increasingly concerned about the strategic and economic threats posed by the expansion of conflicting European empires – and, in the case of Spain, by an empire in terminal decline. The rapid American success in the war against Spain – a conflict justified in large part because of human rights concerns – left the United States in possession of a number of former Spanish territories, including the Philippines. Americans confronted the fundamental question: Should the United States itself become a formal, European-style empire, with colonies and a permanent division between the center and the periphery?

---

[205] *Congressional Record* 33, 56: 1, part 3, March 7, 1900, p. 2620.

A significant group of Senators – and their public advocates, such as Theodore Roosevelt – favored an overtly imperial solution to the matter of the Philippines (or at least they refused to preclude that option). They saw the acquisition of those islands, as well as the annexation of Hawaii, as the first steps in the emergence of a formal American empire (or at least they refused to preclude that option). In any case, they insisted that a "large America" would be qualitatively different from the European empires. Another significant group of Senators – and another vigorous, outside group, including Mark Twain – saw these actions as contrary to the principles of the Declaration of Independence and fatal to the republican character of the American regime. (Some in this group, especially from the South, also rejected the acquisition squarely on grounds of racism and economic self-interest.) The anti-imperialist solution was to renounce American sovereignty and grant the Filipinos full independence as soon as possible.

A middle group emerged that eventually carried the day, at least in practical terms. The Philippines, for reasons of necessity and circumstance, would become U.S. territory, but the theory of American federalism remained unchanged. That is, when the Filipino peoples became capable of self-government – and it was the United States' obligation to govern the islands so as to bring them to that point – the islands would either be admitted to the Union as a full member or members (a highly unlikely outcome), or be granted their independence. The acquisition and governance of the Philippines, as a colony, would not become the future norm for United States foreign policy. The debate shifted to one of not if, but when, the Filipinos would gain their independence; and particularly, whether the United States should make a formal commitment to that end, with a specific termination date of its sovereignty. The Republican and Democratic presidential administrations also differed over the means by which the Filipinos would be prepared for independence and self-government.[206]

The fierce resistance to American rule in the islands only strengthened the growing national opinion that by and large favored strategic and economic expansion but opposed formal political imperialism. When hostilities with Spain ceased in August 1898, the United States was already deeply involved in the domestic affairs of the islands. Commodore (later Admiral) Dewey had supported the Filipino revolutionary group led by Aguinaldo,

---

[206] For a detailed assessment of the different American approaches to the development of the Philippines, beginning with McKinley's policy of "Benevolent Assimilation," see Priscilla Tacujan, "An Evaluation of the Philosophical Foundations of Philippine Liberal-Democracy," Ph.D. Dissertation, Claremont Graduate School, 1996.

who returned from exile in Hong Kong aboard an American warship. The native forces captured most of Spanish-occupied territory except Manila, which the Spaniards surrendered to the Americans. In June 1898, Aguinaldo declared the independence of the Philippines. Class, ethnic, language and religious differences divided the Filipinos from each other as well as from the Americans. Some natives, especially the wealthy elites, welcomed American rule. Many were undecided or apathetic. Nevertheless, tensions with the occupying American forces grew steadily. Fighting broke out in February 1899 between Aguinaldo's troops and the U.S. Army. In the short run, news of the conflict may have tipped the balance in the U.S. Senate in favor of ratification of the peace treaty, as undecided members decided to support American troops under fire. Even so, the treaty was barely ratified by the required two-thirds majority, 57-27.

Any lingering prospect that the Philippines might be the immediate jumping off point for a new American Empire or Large America, however, was put to rest by stiff Filipino resistance in the jungles, swamps and mountains of the islands. The U.S. military, after a period of trial and error, waged an effective counterinsurgency campaign that was aided by sympathetic natives. The United States eventually deployed over 120,000 men in the Philippines and suffered more than 4,000 deaths, with roughly a fourth killed in action. The capture of Aguinaldo in March 1901 deprived the resistance of its most visible leader. However, the American military's techniques, especially its resort to concentration camps, resulted unintentionally in considerable civilian deaths due to disease (200,000 or more, by some estimates). Stories of outright military atrocities by U.S. troops also troubled Americans.[207] The Philippine peoples, for the most part, collectively came to terms with American rule although some resistance continued after 1902. Nonetheless, the logic of American politics, and facts on the grounds, pointed toward eventual independence.

The fierce U.S. debate over the Philippines indicated the limits of popular support for expansionism, even if Americans remained proud of what they regarded as an honorable military triumph over Spain. President McKinley's victory against Bryan in the election of 1900 did not turn on issues of imperialism but rather on the increasingly prosperous American economy and the resultant ebb of Bryan's agrarian/economic populism. The economic and strategic interests that led to the acquisition of the Philippines did not disappear, however. The United States explored other – less intrusive, but still controversial – means to achieve its objectives, such as the Open Door.

---

[207] Brian McAllister Linn provides a careful and balanced account of the campaign in *The Philippine War, 1899-1902* (Lawrence: University of Kansas Press, 2000).

The McKinley administration's policy, and that of the political middle ground, did not point toward the establishment of a formal U.S. empire. Public opinion was deeply influenced by a strong anti-imperialist movement, even if the anti-imperialists did not always win out on particular policy matters. Interest, ideals and experience pointed toward solutions other than territorial expansion and a foreign policy that actively promoted regime change. Americans retained a deep attachment to the principle that peoples could be governed only with their own consent. The United States arguably could obtain access to overseas markets and military bases without establishing colonies. Perhaps domestic economic and political change was the answer to industrial overproduction.

Racist assumptions cut both ways. Many supporters of an interventionist American foreign policy, as well as their opponents, did not want the country "tainted" by acquiring non-white peoples. And, if foreign cultures were indeed highly resistant to change, perhaps the costs and risks of "civilizing" others was simply too great. The coming 20th century would witness Americans trying to operate in a difficult, contentious middle ground between empire and non-intervention.

About the Author

Dr. Patrick J. Garrity is a Research Faculty Associate with the Miller Center of Public Affairs at the University of Virginia, where he is a member of the Center's Presidential Recordings Program. He holds the Ph.D. in Government from Claremont Graduate University. He has been a Senior Policy Analyst (Technical Staff Member) at the Los Alamos National Laboratory, where he specialized in arms control and deterrence policy, and is now a Guest Scientist. Dr. Garrity was a Research Fellow at the Center for Strategic and International Studies (CSIS), and a Visiting Fellow at the Johns Hopkins University School of Advanced International Studies (SAIS). He taught at the Catholic University of America and the Naval Postgraduate School, and has served as a consultant for the National Institute for Public Policy (NIPP). Additionally, he has published on American national security policy and historical topics in such journals as *Survival, Washington Quarterly, The National Interest, Parameters, Comparative Strategy* and *Journal of Strategic Studies*. Dr. Garrity is co-author of *A Sacred Union of Citizens: George Washington's Farewell Address and the American Character* (Lanham, MD: Rowman and Littlefield, 1996); he is co-editor of *Nuclear Weapons in the Changing World: Perspectives From Europe, Asia, and North America* (New York: Plenum, 1992).

Index

Aan het Folk van Nederland (van der Capellen tot den Pol), 60–61
Abbé Correa. *See* Serra, José Correia da
Adams, Charles Francis, 139
Adams, Charles Francis, Jr., 374–375
Adams, John
  for Anglo-American Union, xii, 3
  on balance of power, 31, 40–41, 51
  Barbary regencies and, 82–83
  for Barbary regency tribute, 82
  against Barbary War, 82–83
  on Britain, 44–50
  for British Constitution, 10–11
  for Dutch Republic, xii, 2–3, 52–67
  on Europe, xii, 30, 74
  failures of, 67–68
  for finances, 43, 53, 55–56
  France and, xi–xii, 2, 34, 36–39
  Franklin and, 41–44, 72
  on Joseph II, 70–71
  JQA Address and, 171n46
  Livingston against, 67–72
  for Massachusetts Constitution, 47–48
  Memorial by, 57–61, 63, 66, 70–72
  militia diplomacy of, xi–xii
  on monarchy, 64
  on new international system, 50–52
  Russia and, 59
  self-defense of, 69–72
  Vergennes and, 38–39, 43–45, 60
Adams, John Quincy. *See also* JQA Address; South America
  against American Colonization Society, 202, 203n98
  against Barbary regencies, 93–94
  against Bradley, 139–141
  Cabinet of, 239–240
  Clay and, xv, 158, 194, 211–212, 212n113, 239, 251
  criticism of, 212
  Europe and, 151–152, 222, 222n131
  against Europe's colonialism, xiv
  to Everett, 179 180
  fallacy of, xv–xvi, 251–252
  First Annual Message of, 243
  for Florida, 152–154
  for France, 34–35
  isolationism of, xiii–xiv, 149
  on Karamanli, H., 138–141
  on Karamanli, H., family, 140–141
  Lexington Doctrine and, 181, 184
  Louisiana Purchase and, 200–203
  Manifest Destiny and, 201–202, 202n97
  on monarchy, 228–229
  against Monroe, 191
  neutrality for, 186–188, 186n65
  optimism of, 212
  for Panama Congress, 239–243, 247–250
  on prisoners, 140
  realist-idealist success of, xvi, 252
  on recognition, 186–188
  on regime change policy, 257–258
  republicanism for, 216
  slavery and, 184, 199
  Southern states' secession and, 151
  Spain and, 152
  Spanish colonies and, 153–155
  Walsh and, 165–166
  on war, 182–184, 182n57, 184n62, 186–187, 210
  warnings of, xiii–xiv
Adams, Samuel, 66
Adams-Onís Treaty (Transcontinental Treaty), 153–154, 198–199
Aguinaldo, Emilio
  against America, 419, 423
  capture of, 423
  despotism of, 393
  for Philippines independence, 376, 393, 418–419, 422–423
  support for, 419
Alexander of Russia (emperor), 151
  Holy Alliance and, 206–207
  perspective of, 233–234, 233n148
  South America and, 221
Algiers, 82
  in Barbary War Treaty, 133–134, 143
  Britain's truce with, 85

Dey of, 81, 85–89, 89n29, 101–102
Eaton against, 92–93, 101
Humphreys against, 93
Jones for, 84–85
JQA Address on, 183–184, 184n62
navy against, 85
O'Brien and, 89, 102
tribute for, 86–89, 87n23, 99–101
Tripoli and, 90, 90n31, 95, 95n42

Allen, William V.
against commercialism, 358–359
for Cuba intervention, 358–359, 367–368

America. *See also* Southern states
Aguinaldo against, 419, 423
balance of power and, 206–207, 207n106, 208n108
boundaries of, 198–200, 199nn92–93
Britain's affinity with, 165–166
criticism about, 178
for defense *versus* offense, 227–228
Dutch Patriot movement and, 56–57
Dutch Republic compared to, 57–58
Edinburgh Doctrine against, 165–166
Europe compared with, 204–205, 213–214, 227, 374–375
Europe's reform and, 166–167
expansionism of, 198–199, 199nn92–93
Greece compared to, 386
Holy Alliance to, 228–231
Hungary compared to, 318, 329–330
internationalization of, 37–40
among nations, 177, 330–331, 397
reputation of, 93–94
South America compared with, 194–195
South America related to, 159–161
sovereignty of, 403–404
Spain compared with, 30, 375–376
Spanish colonies' independence and, 152–154
uniqueness of, 39
as world power, 397

American colonies
as asylum, 22, 22n43, 29
beliefs of, 3–9
for British Constitution, 4–5
commerce for, xi, 10
emigration to, 22, 22n43, 29
for Enlightenment, 5–6

generalizability of, 10–12, 17
against imperialist conspiracy, 9–12
liberty of, 4–5
moderates in, 15
morality of, 11–12, 21–22
for reform, 10–11
rights of, 172–175
role of, 8–9
slavery and, 202–203, 203n98

American Colonization Society, 202, 203n98

American consuls. *See also* Barbary regencies' treaties; *specific consuls*
George Washington and, 88–89, 92, 97

American Hemisphere, 160–161

American regime change, 31–35
case against, 12–16
case for, 16–18
as model, 20–21, 27, 73, 204–205, 257, 293, 298
for republic, 21, 29

American Revolution, 1n1. *See also specific founders*
agenda for, 176
basis of, 174–175
Britain's impact from, 44–47
colonial background of, 3–9
effects of, 72
Europe related to, 14, 31–32, 40, 42–43, 61–62, 70–71, 298
foreign policy debate from, 35–37
French Revolution and, 194
internationalization of, 31–32, 257
legitimacy of, 31–34
regime change and, 31–35
strategy and diplomacy of, 27–37
support for, 296–297

American revolutionaries
for balance of power, 24–25
commerce for, 22–23, 40
Declaration of Independence for, 18–21
documents from, 18
in Europe, 27–31
Europe related to, 166, 205
Europe's allies for, 16–18, 20–21, 23–24
France's alliance with, xi, 2–3, 34–39
goals of, 2, 11–12, 21–22, 24

Model Treaty from, 25, 51
  for non-interference, 24
American System, 220
  Bolivar for, 198–199
  Clay for, 160, 169
  against Holy Alliance, 169
  Panama Congress and, 245
  for South America, 197–198
Americans, Asians compared to, 417–418
Ames, Fisher, 131–132
anarchy
  Declaration of Independence without, 175–176
  Enlightenment or, 12
Anglo-American Union, xiv. *See also* Edinburgh Doctrine
  Adams, J., for, xii, 3
anti-expansionism, 388, 407
  of Bryan, 341–342, 374, 387
  of Cleveland, 343
  expansionism compared to, 341
  expansionism with, xix–xx
  intervention with, 341–342
  Lodge against, 420–421
  morality of, xix
  in regime change of 1890s, xix–xx
anti-imperialism. *See* anti-expansionism
anti-interventionism. *See* anti-expansionism
Armitage, David, 20
Armstrong, John, 117–118
Articles of Confederation, 176, 213
Asians, Americans compared to, 417–418
Atkinson, Edward, 378–379
Atlantic Monthly, 409
Austria, 271. *See also* Hülsemann, Baron; Hungarian Revolution; Webster, Daniel
  de-recognition of, 284–288
  despotism from, 155–156
  Hungarian Revolution for, 326
  Joseph II of, 70–71
  Schwartzenberg for, 277

Bacon, Augustus, 381
  Spooner against, 401–402
  against war, 376–377
Bailyn, Bernard, 4–6
Bainbridge, William, 89
  in Barbary War, 115
  on Barbary War Treaty, 124–125
  intelligence from, 120–121
  on price of peace, 124–125
balance
  from Britain, 12–14
  for Declaration of Independence, 18–19
  of Webster, 253–254
balance of power
  Adams, J., on, 31, 40–41, 51
  America and, 206–207, 207n106, 208n108
  American revolutionaries for, 24–25
  for Europe, 206–207
  Philippines acquisition and, 393–394, 394n139
Baltimore News, 353
Barbary regencies. *See also* Karamanli, Yusuf
  accommodation of, 75
  Adams, J., and, 82–83
  Adams, J. Q., against, 93–94
  authority in, 76–77, 77nn3–4
  Barbary War Treaty and, 143–145
  behavior change for, 75–76
  blockade of, 83–84
  Britain and, 78, 80
  commerce with, 80
  Denmark and, 102
  Europe and, 77–79
  France and, 78, 80–81, 89n29
  Jefferson and, xii–xiii, 83–84, 98–99
  limited liability policy for, xii–xiii, 75–76
  Panama Congress and, 248–249
  piracy of, 75, 77–81, 85–86
  privateering of, 77–78
  relations between, 79
  statehood of, 76–77, 77n3
  support among, 102
  tribute for, 82–84, 86–88, 88n27, 102, 122

Tripoli blockade and, 108–109
Barbary regencies' treaties. *See also*
    Algiers; Morocco; Tunis
  American consuls against, 92–97, 92n35,
    95nn42–43
  America's reputation related to, 93–94
  Cathcart against, 91–92, 92n33, 92n35
  collapse of, 88–92, 88n27, 90nn30–31,
    91n33
  Eaton for, 87, 87n23, 89
  Jones for, 84–85
  religion and, 87–88
  resources for, 81–82, 81n11
  Sultan and, 94–96, 95n43
  Tripoli in, 94

Barbary War, 183. *See also* Eaton, William;
    Karamanli, Hamet; Karamanli,
    Yusuf; Preble, Edward
  Adams, J., against, 82–83
  Bainbridge in, 115
  Beaussier in, 119–120
  cost of, 133, 142
  Europe and, 117, 144
  failures in, 102, 102n56
  first phase of, 97–100
  Gallatin against, 110
  Jefferson and, 97–100, 111–112, 116–117,
    121–122, 133–136, 142, 144
  law and, 99
  Lear on, 118, 120
  naval deployment to, 100–101
  naval deterrence in, 101–104, 142
  naval squadron blockade in, 98–100, 103
  offensive against, 103, 113–118, 142
  peace price in, 124–125
  Philadelphia in, 115–117, 116n85,
    117n87
  Preble's campaign against, 112–121,
    112n77, 113n79, 117n87
  reevaluation about, 110–113
  second deployment of, 104–106
  settlement debate over, 131–141
  Smith, R., for, 111
  strategic options for, 101–104
  successes in, 101, 119
  Tangier in, 114–115, 115n82
  Tripoli's upper hand in, 106–110
  Turkey and, 123
  victory in, 100

Barbary War Treaty
  Algiers in, 133–134, 143
  Ames against, 131–132
  Bainbridge on, 124–125
  Barbary regencies and, 143–145
  Barron for, 124–126, 126n105
  Bradley on, 141
  concessions in, 133–134
  conclusions about, 141–145
  debate over, 131–141
  Dghies on, 124
  Eaton against, 132–133, 133n115
  Jefferson and, 133, 136
  with Karamanli, Y., 124–125, 127–129,
    128nn109–110, 131–145
  Lear and, 127–128, 128n110, 131–134,
    136, 138, 140–141
  Nissen for, 124, 127, 127n108
  prisoners in, 127–128, 128n109, 132–
    133, 133n115
  ratification of, 135–136, 141
  regime change and, 132, 134–135
  resolutions for, 135–136, 141

Barclay, Thomas, 81
Barlow, Joel, 86–87
Barrett, John, 403
Barron, James, 120
  for Barbary War Treaty, 124–126,
    126n105
  blockade by, 123
  force for, 121–122
  limitations of, 139
  orders for, 121–122
Beaumarchais, Pierre, 17–18
Beaussier, 117
  in Barbary War, 119–120
Bemis, Samuel Flagg, 391
Berrien, John, 321–322
Beveridge, Albert, 386, 394
  on Constitution's implied powers, 406
  on contiguity, 407
  morality of, 416
  for Orient commerce, 399–400
  on Philippines independence, 419–420
Bodisco, Alexander, 327

Bolivar, Simon, 239
  for American System, 198–199
Boutwell, George, 389
Boutwell, James, 307
Bowen, Francis, 309–310
Bradford, R. B., 393–394
Bradley, Stephen R.
  Adams, J. Q., against, 139–141
  on Barbary War Treaty, 141
  for Karamanli, H., 136–138, 141
  against Lear, 138
  on Tripoli regime change, 137–138
Brazil
  Calhoun and, 215
  Clay and, 216n122
  monarchy for, 215
  recognition of, 215–216
  republicanism in, 216
Britain
  absolutism or, 13–14
  Adams, J., on, 44–50
  Algiers' truce with, 85
  alliance with, xii, xiv, 3, 207–210, 320–321
  American Revolution impact on, 44–47
  America's affinity with, 165–166
  balance from, 12–14
  Barbary regencies and, 78, 80
  British Constitution for, 208
  colonial islands of, 46
  commerce and, 26–27, 44, 209–210
  conspiracy of, xi, 1, 9
  corruption of, 10–11
  criticism from, 178
  Cuba and, 224
  decline of, 209–210
  disrespect from, 147–148
  against Dutch Republic, 53, 65–66
  France compared to, 4, 38
  Gordon Riots in, 50
  Holy Alliance and, 232
  hostility of, 49–50, 208–209
  invasion of, 33
  Ireland and, 46–47, 259, 321
  Jefferson on, 223
  In JQA Address, 171–172, 178
  liberty in, 167
  Madison for, 223–224
  Manifest Destiny and, 262
  maritime tyranny of, 9–10, 26–27, 31–32, 44–45
  Massachusetts Constitution and, 47–48
  nature of, 225
  Navigation Acts from, 9–10
  for non-interference, 155
  peace for, 46
  people of, 32–33, 49–50
  Philippines acquisition related to, 394
  pride of, 49–50
  privateering and, 77–78, 80
  reform for, 48, 50, 155, 167–168, 207–210, 230
  republicanism in, 46–47
  revolution for, 45–46, 48–49
  rights in, 171–172
  South America and, 188, 222–225
  Spanish colonies and, 188–190
  Whigs and, 268–269
British Constitution
  Adams, J., for, 10–11
  American colonies for, 4–5
  for Britain, 208
  corruption of, 9–10
  in Enlightenment, 6–7
  as model, 6–7
Brougham, Henry, 165
Brown, Albert, 332
Bryan, William Jennings, xix
  anti-expansionism of, 341–342, 374, 387
  campaign of, 348–351
  Croffut to, 388–389
  for Cuba intervention, 368
  in imperial debate of 1898-1900, 388–391
  for Jefferson, 349–350
  loss of, 347, 351
  on Monroe Doctrine, 374
  nomination of, 348
  Wilson with, 350
Buchanan, John, 337
  for Stiles, 278–279
Buenos Aires, 158, 189–190, 211
Burke, Edmund, 6, 11, 174

Caffery, Donelson, 373, 377
Calhoun, John C., 151
  Brazil and, 215
  for caution, 254
  for Germany, 273–274
  on Holy Alliance, 231–232
Calkoen, Hendrik, 57
Canada
  Canning, S., and, 199n93
  filibustering against, 261, 264
  incorporation of, 33, 199, 199n93, 341
  invasion of, 33
Canning, George, 221–222, 224
Canning, Stratford
  Canada and, 199n93
  JQA Address and, 148–149
Cannon, Frank J., 358
Caribbean, 365. *See also* Cuba; Haiti
Carnegie, Andrew, 377
Cass, Lewis, 254–255, 259–260
  for de-recognition, 284–286
  for Germany, 289–290
  for Kossuth, 313
  Taylor and, 289–290
Castlereagh, Lord, 163, 189
Cathcart, James Leander
  advice of, 94–96, 95n42
  against Barbary regencies' treaties, 91–92, 92n33, 92n35
  Karamanli, Y., and, 91–92, 92n33, 95–96
  O'Brien against, 92n35
  Tripoli negotiations with, 105
Chattanooga Times, 356
China
  commerce with, 400
  Philippines acquisition and, 395–396
Choate, Rufus, 253–254
Christian civilization, 182–183
Cincinnati Enquirer, 359
civil equality, 409

civil liberty
  Hungary for, 318
  principle of, 217–218
  religion and, 217–218, 218n125, 241–242
  for South America, 217–218, 218n125
civil rights, 411
Civil War, 291
  America's sovereignty from, 403–404
  consent doctrine related to, 413, 420
Claflin, William, 354
Clarke, John H., 332
Clay, Henry, 152
  Adams, J. Q., and, xv, 158, 194, 211–212, 212n113, 239, 251
  ambitions of, 157, 211–212, 212n113
  for American System, 160, 169
  Brazil and, 216l22
  against de-recognition, 287–289
  for Greece, 164–165, 235, 270
  against impartial neutrality, 158, 161
  for independent regimes, 269
  Kossuth and, 328–329
  for Lexington Doctrine, xiv, 156–165
  against Madison, 157
  for opportunities, 251
  on progress, 288
  for South America, xiv–xv, 157–164, 270
  for Texas independence, 269
  for unification, 165, 165n34
  war and, 186–187, 187n67
Clayton, John M.
  to Donelson, 276
  Germany and, 275–276
  Hülsemann and, 283–284
  Hungary and, 281–284
Clemens, Jeremiah, 313
Cleveland, Grover
  anti-expansionism of, 343
  Lodge against, 367
  losses for, 347
  for Venezuela, 364
coercive diplomacy
  with Mexico, 265–266
  for New Democrats, 265
Coletta, Paolo E., 390

— 432 —

Colombia
  Cuba and, 219
  government form of, 218–219
  republicanism of, 218–219
  Salazar for, 238

colonialism. *See also* Europe's colonialism
  in JQA Address elaboration, 180–181

colonies, 30, 410. *See also specific countries*
  Britain's islands as, 46
  for Enlightenment, 5–8
  non-colonization, 246–247

commerce. *See also* Treaty of Amity and Commerce
  for American colonies, xi, 10
  for American revolutionaries, 22–23, 40
  with Barbary regencies, 80
  Britain and, 26–27, 44, 209–210
  with China, 400
  criticism of, 400–401
  Cuba intervention related to, 358–359
  from Declaration of Independence, 176–177
  despite geographic isolation, 294
  in Enlightenment, 8
  for Europe, 40
  expansionism for, 399–400
  Hamilton on, 25
  beyond isolationism, 256–257, 294
  for liberalism, 25–26, 26n54
  liberty and, 25
  Lodge for, 400–401
  Mason, W. E., on, 359
  McKinley for, 400
  with Orient, 399–400
  at Panama Congress, 245–246
  from Philippines acquisition, 399–401, 403
  regime change of 1890s and, xvii–xviii
  South America and, 160, 216–217, 217n124
  with Turkey, 237n155

commercialism, 358–359

Common Sense (Paine), 18, 20, 23–24

Compromise of 1850, 289
  Webster and, 292

consent doctrine

adequate government or, 414
Civil War related to, 413, 420
in Declaration of Independence, 385, 411–412
Foraker on, 420
Platt, O. H., on, 385, 411
Roosevelt on, 413–414, 420
Spooner on, 413
Teller on, 413

conservativism, 286

Constitution. *See also* British Constitution
  Declaration of Independence compared to, 411
  Declaration of Independence with, 384
  implied powers of, 404–406
  misinterpretation of, 404–406
  nation compared to, 406
  Philippines acquisition despite, 384, 403–404
  Platt, T. C., on, 405
  public opinion related to, 405
  tradition of, 405

Constitution of the Commonwealth of Massachusetts, 47–48

constitutional liberalism, 155

constitutional monarchies, 236, 286, 317

continentalism, 415

Cool Thoughts (Galloway), 45, 45n103

Correa, Abbé. *See* Serra, José Correia da

Crittenden, John J., xvii, 256
  Hungarian Revolution and, 280–281, 329–330
  on war, 329–331
  Washington and, 329–331

Croffut, William A., 388–389

Cuba, xviii–xix, 338, 340
  Britain and, 224
  Colombia and, 219
  guerrilla war in, 343–344
  investments in, 342–343
  Lopez for, 264
  regime change issues about, 362–363
  Soulé for, 337
  strategic importance of, 365–366
  Teller for, 371

Cuba intervention
    Allen for, 358–359, 367–368
    background on, 342
    Bryan for, 368
    Cannon on, 358
    case against, 343–344
    case for, 344
    commerce related to, 358–359
    decision for, 342–366
    election of 1896 and, 344–351
    Godkin against, 355–356
    Harris, W. A., for, 361–362
    Lodge on, 358, 368–369
    Mason, W. E., for, 360–361, 363–364
    Philippines acquisition compared to, 417
    public opinion for, 364, 366–370
    Republicans against, 354–355
    Roosevelt for, 363, 363n56
    Southern states and, 343, 356–357, 370
    Spanish-American War as, 369–372
    transition to, 357–360
    Wheeler for, 370
    yellow press and, 355–356
Cuban Rebellion, 351
    deaths in, 343–344, 360, 360n49
    Weyler against, 343
Cuba's recognition
    Lodge for, 368–369
    People's Party for, 345n2
    Thurston for, 368
Cushing, Caleb, 331

Dale, Richard, 100, 104
    advice from, 103
    authority of, 98, 101–102, 102n56
    limitation of, 99, 101–102, 102n56
    purpose of, 98
Dallas, George M., 280
Dana, Francis, 42–43
Davis, George
    for Karamanli, H., family, 128n110
    on Tripoli attack, 116, 118
    Tunis and, 129–130
Davis, Jefferson, 300, 337
Dawes, Charles

    for McKinley, 353–354, 393
    on Republican Party, 403
Dawson, William, 313–314
Deane, Silas, 28
Decatur, Stephen, 183–184
Declaration of Independence
    for American revolutionaries, 18–21
    without anarchy, 175–176
    balance for, 18–19
    civil rights in, 411
    clarification of, 385
    colonial system in, 410
    commerce from, 176–177
    consent doctrine in, 385, 411–412
    Constitution compared to, 411
    Constitution with, 384
    context of, 20
    Europe and, 28, 272
    fallacies in, 407–408
    Fiske on, 407–408
    Foraker on, 410
    France and, 28
    gender and, 412
    generalizability of, 20–21
    Hancock on, 28
    Hoar on, 384
    in imperial debate of 1898-1900, 383–385
    Jordan on, 383
    in JQA Address, 173–176, 173n47, 181–182
    Lodge on, 411–412
    Lowell on, 409
    Mason, G., on, 385
    misinterpretations of, 408–412
    morality of, 416
    new international system from, 22–27
    for non-interference, 20
    Philippines acquisition related to, 407–413
    property and, 412
    Reed on, 383
    role of, 173–176, 173n47
    slavery and, 384, 412
    specificities of, 20
    spirit of, 178
    Town on, 383–384
    Treaty of Amity and Commerce and,

216–217
defense, 295
Democratic Party, xix. *See also* New Democrats; *specific Democrats*
　alliances within, 347–348
　factions within, 340n14, 348–349
　foreign policy of, 346–347
　platform of, 334
　radicalism of, 350–351

Democratic Review, 266

Denby, Charles, 394, 396

Denmark, 106. *See also* Nissen, Nicholas
　Barbary regencies and, 102

Denver Times, 358–360, 366

de-recognition
　of Austria, 284–288
　Cass for, 284–286
　Clay against, 287–289
　frequency of, 286
　Hale and, 287
　as intervention, 287–289
　from public opinion, 285–286
　of Russia, 287
　substitutes for, 289–290

despotism, 293
　of Aguinaldo, 393
　from Austria, 155–156
　enlightened, 7
　in Europe, 164

Detroit *Free Press*, 308

Dey of Algiers
　demands of, 81, 85–89
　with Tripoli, 101–102
　war from, 89, 89n29

Dghies, Sidi Mohammad, 124

Dickinson, John, 10

Dicks, Charles, 395

Dom Joao (John) VI, 215

Dom Pedro I, 215

Donelson, Andrew
　Clayton to, 276
　for Germany, 271–272, 274–276
　instructions for, 274–276

perspective of, 275

Douglas, Stephen A., xvii, 254–255
　against filibustering, 265, 331–332
　for Hungary, 319–321
　against monarchies, 321
　perspectives of, 331–332
　against Sanders, 331, 332n105
　for Walker, W., 338

Dred Scott v. Sanford, 380–381, 403

Dumas, C. W. F., 17

Dutch Patriot movement
　America and, 56–57
　aristocracy in, 56
　loans from, 55–56
　rebellion and, 60–61
　William V and, 56–57, 56n131

Dutch Republic, 17
　Adams, J., for, xii, 2–3, 52–67
　alliance with, xii, 57–67
　America compared to, 57–58
　Britain against, 53, 65–66
　France and, 52, 57–61
　loans from, 53, 55–56, 66
　moderation in, 65
　patience related to, 58–59
　political structure in, 54–55
　public opinion in, 62–63
　rebellion for, 60–61, 63
　recognition from, 66–67
　reform for, 59, 63
　republicanism in, 56–65
　sovereignty of, 56, 56n131
　Treaty of Amity and Commerce with, 66
　understanding about, 62–63

Eaton, William, 89–90, 100
　against Algiers, 92–93, 101
　for Barbary regencies' treaties, 87, 87n23, 89
　against Barbary War Treaty, 132–133, 133n115
　ground forces of, 124, 124n102, 126, 129
　plausible deniability and, 135, 135n118
　against Tripoli, 103, 108
　for Tripoli's regime change, 104, 123–126, 126n105, 132

Edinburgh Doctrine, xiv, 149

against America, 165–166
deconstruction of, 203–210
JQA Address and, 165–170, 181
in JQA Address elaboration, 203–210
Naples and, 169–170
source of, 165

Edinburgh Review, 165–169, 207–209

1890s, 339

election of 1896. *See also* Bryan, William Jennings
Cuba intervention and, 344–351
currencies in, 345–346
economics in, 345
Monroe Doctrine and, 344–345
Platt, T. C., on, 345
results of, 351

election of 1900, 387–389

emigration, 22, 22n43, 29

England. *See* Britain

enlightened despotism, 7

Enlightenment
American colonies for, 5–6
anarchy or, 12
British Constitution in, 6–7
commerce in, 8
internationalism in, 7–8
leaders of, 6
power in, 6–7
for reform process, 7

Enterprise, 100

equality
civil, 409
gender and, 412–413
political, 409
race and, 408, 412

Europe. *See also* revolutions of 1848; specific countries
Adams, J., on, xii, 30, 74
Adams, J. Q., and, 151–152, 222, 222n131
America compared with, 204–205, 213–214, 227, 374–375
American Revolution related to, 14, 31–32, 40, 42–43, 61–62, 70–71, 298
American revolutionaries' allies from, 16–18, 20–21, 23–24
American revolutionaries in, 27–31
American revolutionaries related to, 166, 205
balance of power for, 206–207
Barbary regencies and, 77–79
Barbary War and, 117, 144
commerce for, 40
constitutional liberalism in, 155
Declaration of Independence and, 28, 272
despotism in, 164
evolution of, xii, 235–236, 318–319
fears of, 29–30
Holy Alliance for, 151, 153, 156, 228–231
hostility of, 205–206
Manifest Destiny for, 261–262
in Mexico, 374–375
non-intervention in, 203–210, 226, 234–236, 249–250
Pierce on, 336
recognition in, 162
repression in, 258–259
Russia and, 225–226, 226n137, 229–230
against South America, 162–163, 186–188
South America with, 163–164
Treaties of Amity and Commerce from, 52
war with, 328–329

Europe's colonialism, xiv, xviii–xix. *See also specific countries*
France and, 181
JQA Address against, 173–174, 180–181

Europe's reform, 169
America and, 166–167

Everett, Edward, 199, 297
Adams, J. Q., to, 179–180

evolution
of Europe, xii, 235–236, 318–319
of republicanism, 250–251
of South America, 185–186

expansionism, xiv, xviii. *See also* anti-expansionism
Adams, C. F., Jr., against, 374–375
of America, 198–199, 199nn92–93

for commerce, 399–400
contiguity in, 407
continentalism compared to, 415
imperialism compared to, 380, 397
morality related to, 341
Pierce for, 335
Platt, O. H., against, 407
political control as, 340–341
in protectorates, xix
racism in, 406–407
reality of, 404–405
in regime change of 1890s, xviii–xix
Washington's Farewell Address and, 397–398

Famin, Joseph, 86, 87n23

Ferdinand VII (Spain), 154, 181, 189, 221

filibustering
against Canada, 261, 264
Douglas against, 265, 331–332
Lincoln against, 338
neutrality against, 337–338
for republicanism, 264–265
slavery and, 338
Walker, W., for, 338

Fillmore, Millard
Kossuth with, 324–325
for neutrality, 311
Webster and, 325, 327

Fish, Stuyvesant, 370

Fiske, Amos K., 407–408

Florida
Adams, J. Q., for, 152–154
South America and, 163

Foote, Henry S., 289
for Kossuth, 302–303, 312

Foraker, Joseph B.
on consent doctrine, 420
on Declaration of Independence, 410

foreign policy
of Democratic Party, 346–347
indirectness for, xv, 73–74
"monsters to destroy" in, 148–149, 177–178, 200, 250, 257–258
patience for, xiv–xv, 250–251

of Roosevelt, T., 346–347
foreign policy debates. *See also* imperial debate of 1898-1900
from American Revolution, 35–37
modernity of, xvii
public opinion of, xx
racism in, xx, 424

Foreman, John, 393

Fourth of July, 173n47

France, 259, 284. *See also* French Revolution
Adams, J., and, xi–xii, 2, 34, 36–39
Adams, J. Q., for, 34–35
American revolutionaries' alliance with, xi, 2–3, 34–39
Barbary regencies and, 78, 80–81, 89n29
Britain compared to, 4, 38
character of, 42
Declaration of Independence and, 28
Dutch Republic and, 52, 57–61
Europe's colonialism and, 181
Franklin and, xii, 2–3, 41–42
French and Indian War, 4–5
Gerard for, 35–36
gratitude towards, 42
language with, 233
limitations by, 38–39
Louis 18th of, 181
Morocco and, 81
navy of, 32–33
privateering of, 77–78
Spain's invasion by, 234–235
treaties with, 33–34
Treaty of Amity and Commerce with, 216–217, 217n124
Tripoli and, 106

Franklin, Benjamin
Adams, J., and, 41–44, 72
against alliances, 41
autonomy and, 5
France and, xii, 2–3, 41–42
on French Revolution, 72–73
against good war, 31
on liberty, x–xi, 1, 28–29
as Mason, 72
for patience, 14–15, 15n27, 43
predictions of, 9

reassurance of, 28
Free Soil Party
   Hale for, 287, 333–334
   perspective of, 270–271
   platform of, 334–335
freedom. *See* liberty
French and Indian War, 4–5
French Revolution, 162, 271
   American Revolution and, 194
   Franklin on, 72–73
   recognition from, 254

Gallatin, Albert, 233n148
   against Barbary War, 110
   for Greece, 234
Galloway, Joseph, 13–14, 36
   against sedition, 33, 45, 45n103
Garrison, William Lloyd, 309
Gavino, John, 100
gender
   Declaration of Independence and, 412
   equality and, 412–413
George Washington, 88–89, 92, 97
Gerard, Conrad Alexander, 35–36
Germany, 255
   Calhoun for, 273–274
   Cass for, 289–290
   Clayton and, 275–276
   Donelson for, 271–272, 274–276
   monarchy in, 275
   navy for, 272–273, 273n31
   Polk for, 272–273
   recognition for, 272–273
   unification of, 273–276
Gerolt, Friedrich von, 273
Gerry, Elbridge, 47
Giddings, Joshua, 270
Gleig, George Robert, 147–148, 148n2
Godkin, E. L.
   against Cuba intervention, 355–356
   for McKinley, 353
government forms

   of Colombia, 218–219
   independence and, 229, 229n142
   Lodge on, 409–410
   race and, 409–410
   republicanism related to, 228–229
   Seward and, 317
   for South America, 213–216, 242–243
   treaties and, 24
   Webster on, 268–269
Gray, George, 372–373
Greece
   America compared to, 386
   Clay for, 164–165, 235, 270
   Gallatin for, 234
   support for, 234–237, 235n152, 237n155
   Turkey and, 237
Greeley, Horace, 270–271
   for Kossuth, 306–307
Greene, Francis V., 393
Guizot, François, 263–264
Gulf of Mexico, 365

Haiti, 243–244
   Kossuth and, 333
   slavery and, 333
Hale, John P., 312–313
   de-recognition and, 287
   for Free Soil Party, 287, 333–334
   Pierce over, 333–334
Hamilton, Alexander
   on commerce, 25
   implied powers of, 404–405
Hampton, Moses, 307–308
Hancock, John, 10
   on Declaration of Independence, 28
Harper's New Monthly Magazine, 365
Harris, Levitt, 117
Harris, William A.
   for Cuba intervention, 361–362
   on morality, 363
Harrison, Benjamin, xix–xx
Hawaii

annexation of, 371
independence for, 269–270
monarchy in, 340n1
regime change in, 269–270, 340n1
for Whigs, 269–270

Hay, John, 371
against imperialism, 391

Hazeltine, Mayo W., 394
for Philippines acquisition, 395–396

Hendrickson, David, 258, 300

Hoar, George F., 358, 381
on Declaration of Independence, 384
on founders, 385–386
against imperialism, 373–374

Holy Alliance
Alexander of Russia and, 206–207
to America, 228–231
American System against, 169
Britain and, 232
Calhoun on, 231–232
for Europe, 151, 153, 156, 228–231
military force against, 232–233, 233n146
Poletica for, 206
to South America, 228–232
Spanish colonies and, 153

House of Representatives, U.S., 211. *See also* JQA Address
presidency and, 239

Howe, Daniel Walker, 260–261, 270

Hülsemann, Baron, 255. *See also* Webster-Hülsemann debate
Clayton and, 283–284
Mann and, 290–291, 297–298, 301
observations of, 283
warnings from, 291–292

human rights
democratization and, ix–x
monarchies or, 293
Whigs for, 270–271

Humboldt, Alexander von, xv, 158–159

Hume, David, 8

Humphreys, David, 86
against Algiers, 93
against piracies, 96–97

Hungarian Revolution, 255–256. *See also* Kossuth, Lajos
for Austria, 326
Crittenden and, 280–281, 329–330
implications of, 279, 326–327
Lincoln for, 280
Mann and, 281–284, 284n46, 297–298
rationale for, 299–300
refugees from, 302–303
support for, 280
Taylor on, 283–284, 284n46

Hungary, xvi, 255. *See also* Stiles, William H.; Webster, Daniel
America compared to, 318, 329–330
for civil liberty, 318
Clayton and, 281–284
Douglas for, 319–321
New Democrats and, xvii, 319–323
recognition of, 280–284, 284n46, 287–288, 297
Russia against, 282–284, 295–296, 304–305
Russia and, 279
self-government for, 326–327

Hunter, William, 323

Huntington, Samuel, 30–31

Hutchinson, Thomas, 12–13

imperial debate of 1898-1900, xviii–xx, 371
Boutwell, G., in, 389
Bryan in, 388–391
case against in, 372–391
case for in, 391–421
commercialism in, 377
Declaration of Independence in, 383–385
Dred Scott v. Sanford related to, 380–381
election of 1900 and, 387–389
independence in, 378
Jordan in, 389
methods of control in, 375–376
morality in, 381–383
neutralization in, 378–379
Norton in, 387
party politics in, 388
protectorate in, 378

racism in, 380
self-government in, 382
slavery related to, 380–382
taxation in, 382
Vest Resolution in, 379
world war in, 376–377

imperialism
  Caffery against, 373
  expansionism compared to, 380, 397
  Gray against, 372–373
  Hay against, 391
  Hoar against, 373–374
  Jordan against, 379
  Mason, G., against, 386–387
  profitability of, 390

imperialist conspiracy, 9–12

independence. *See also* Declaration of Independence; Philippines independence; Spanish colonies' independence
  Catholic religion and, 196
  government form and, 229, 229n142
  for Hawaii, 269–270
  in imperial debate of 1898-1900, 378
  of India, 199
  political, 192
  for Texas, 269

India, 199

indirect approach, x–xii, 73–74

internationalism
  in Enlightenment, 7–8
  of Manifest Destiny, 261–262

internationalization
  of America, 37–40
  of American Revolution, 31–32, 257
  of recognition, 188–191

intervention. *See also* Cuba intervention
  anti-expansionism with, 341–342
  de-recognition as, 287–289
  Monroe on, 169–170
  nationalism of, 357–366
  for non-intervention, 304–305
  sympathy or, 294
  temptations for, 203–204
  Walker for, 322–323

Ireland

  Britain and, 46–47, 259, 321
  O'Connell for, 259
  republicanism in, 46–47, 321

isolation, geographic, 294

isolationism
  of Adams, J. Q., xiii–xiv, 149
  commerce beyond, 256–257, 294
  inaccuracy of term, xiv, 256–257

Jackson, Andrew, 153

Jay, John, 12–13, 36

Jefferson, Thomas. *See also* Declaration of Independence
  Barbary regencies and, xii–xiii, 83–84, 98–99
  for Barbary regency blockade, 83–84
  against Barbary regency tribute, 83–84
  Barbary War and, 97–100, 108–109, 111–112, 116–117, 121–122, 133–136, 142, 144
  Barbary War Treaty and, 133, 136
  on Britain, 223
  British with, 10
  Bryan for, 349–350
  limited liability policy of, xiii, 139
  on social compact, 412

Jones, John Paul, 33, 48, 84–85

Jordan, David Starr, xix
  on Declaration of Independence, 383
  in imperial debate of 1898-1900, 389
  against imperialism, 379
  on Monroe Doctrine, 374
  on Washington's Farewell Address, 373

Joseph II (emperor), 70–71

Journal of Commerce, 396

JQA Address
  Adams, J., and, 171n46
  on Algiers, 183–184, 184n62
  American colonies' rights in, 172–175
  Britain in, 171–172, 178
  Canning, S., and, 148–149
  cautions about, 147, 147n1
  Christian civilization for, 182–183
  context of, 150–155
  Declaration of Independence role in,

173–176, 173n47, 181–182
  as demonstration, 180
  Edinburgh Doctrine and, 165–170, 181
  against Europe's colonialism, 173–174, 180–181
  formal argument of, 170–178, 171n46, 173n47, 174n48
  Gleig and, 147–148, 148n2
  hypocrisy and, 148
  intentions of, 179–180
  invitation for, 147
  justice in, 173
  Lexington doctrine and, 156–165
  liberty in, 170
  main points of, 180
  "monsters to destroy" in, 148–150, 177–178, 200, 250, 257–258
  regrets after, 179
  religion and, 171, 171n46
  slavery and, 182, 182nn57–58, 184
  South America in, 158–163, 180, 184–185
  status and, 148
  sympathy in, 173–174, 174n48
  on war, 182, 182n57
  on Washington's Farewell Address, 257–258

JQA Address elaboration, 182–184
  colonialism in, 180–181
  Edinburgh Doctrine deconstruction in, 203–210
  Lexington Doctrine deconstruction in, 194–203
  reaction to, 178–179
  recognition and regime change criteria, 191–193
  South America in, 185–191

Karamanli, Hamet
  Adams, J. Q., on, 138–141
  Bradley for, 136–138, 141
  family of, 107, 128, 128n110, 135–136, 140–141
  Preble and, 113–114
  promises of, 123–124, 124n101
  support limitations for, 125–126, 126n105, 139–140
  as Tripoli regime change, 104–106, 122–128, 124n101, 142–143

Karamanli, Yusuf, 90
  Barbary War Treaty with, 124–125, 127–129, 128nn109–110, 131–145
  Cathcart and, 91–92, 92n33, 95–96
  coercion of, 142–143
  demands of, 91–92, 96, 100–101, 119–120
  pride of, 143
  Sultan and, 95–96
  threat from, 125
  for Tripoli, 87, 90–91, 90n31, 91n33
  Tripoli regime change against, 103–106, 123–128, 124n101, 142–143

Kidd, Benjamin, 398–399

King, Rufus, 86

Kossuth, Lajos (Louis), xvi–xvii
  activities of, 317
  arrival of, 304
  asylum for, 302–303
  Cass for, 313
  Clay and, 328–329
  Clemens against, 313
  Dawson against, 313–314
  debate over, 312–314
  demands of, 305
  endorsements for, 306–309
  Fillmore with, 324–325
  Foote for, 302–303, 312
  funding for, 328
  Garrison against, 309
  Greeley for, 306–307
  Haiti and, 333
  injustices against, 317
  Monroe Doctrine related to, 304–305
  New Democrat case for, 319–323
  opposition to, 309–312
  for Pickett, 333, 336
  Pierce and, 336–337
  Progressive Whig case for, 314–319
  Sanders for, 308
  Seward for, 314–319, 323
  Shields with, 324–325
  slavery and, 306, 309, 333
  to Stiles, 278
  support for, 255
  Underwood against, 313
  for war, 305–306
  in Washington, D.C., 323–333

Webster against, 310–311

La Follette, Robert, 345
Lafayette, Marquis de, 64
Lang, Daniel George, 8
Laurens, Henry, 53
law of nations, 154, 187, 192, 287
   defense of, 295–296
   neutrality for, 295
   for non-interference, 7
   principles of, 315
   sympathies under, 298–299
Lawrence, Abbot, 310–313
League of Armed Neutrality, 51, 53, 59
Lear, Tobias, 114–115
   advice from, 116
   authority of, 122–123
   on Barbary War, 118, 120
   Barbary War Treaty and, 127–128, 128n110, 131–134, 136, 138, 140–141
   Bradley against, 138
   successes of, 133
   against Tripoli regime change, 127
Lee, Arthur, 31, 36
Lee, William, 28, 33, 53
Leonard, Daniel, 13
Lerner, Ralph, 6
Lexington Doctrine, 149
   Adams, J. Q., and, 181, 184
   Clay for, xiv, 156–165
   deconstruction of, 194–203
   JQA Address and, 156–165
liberty, 170, 200, 251. *See also* civil liberty
   of American colonies, 4–5
   in Britain, 167
   commerce and, 25
   Franklin on, x–xi, 1, 28–29
   geographic isolation for, 294
   maritime, 51–52
   representative of, 317–319

Life of Washington (Marshall), 166, 166n37

limited liability policy
   Barbary regencies and, xii–xiii, 75–76
   criticism of, xiii, 76
   of Jefferson, xiii, 139

Lincoln, Abraham, 280, 338
Lisle, Peter. *See* Reis, Murad
Livingston, Robert R., 26, 117
   against Adams, J., 67–72
   to Madison, 95n43
   against political intrigue, 67–69
Lodge, Henry Cabot, xix
   against anti-expansionism, 420–421
   on Asians, 417–418
   against Cleveland, 367
   for commerce, 400–401
   on Cuba intervention, 358, 368–369
   for Cuba's recognition, 368–369
   on Declaration of Independence, 411–412
   on government forms, 409–410
   for Philippines acquisition, 396, 399–401, 413
   against promises, 417–418
   on social compact, 412
Lôme, Enrique Dupuy de, 357
Long, John Davis, 357n38
Lopez, Narciso, 264
Los Angeles Times, 355–356
Louis 18th (France), 181
Louisiana Purchase, 200–203
Louis-Philippe, 254, 271
Lovell, James, 70
Lowell, A. Lawrence, 409

Macon, Nathaniel, 243
Madison, James, 26, 85, 85n21
   to Armstrong, 117–118
   for Britain, 223–224
   Clay against, 157
   Livingston to, 95n43
   for Tripoli regime change, 105–106
   on Tripoli tribute, 111–112
Mahan, Alfred Thayer, xix, 391
   on Cuba's strategic importance, 365

geopolitics of, 344
Maier, Pauline, 18
Maine, 354, 357, 357n38
Manent, Pierre, 26n54
Manifest Destiny, 263–264
  Adams, J. Q., and, 201–202, 202n97
  Britain and, 262
  for Europe, 261–262
  internationalism of, 261–262
  New Democrats for, 260
  Texas and, 260–261, 261n10
Mann, A. Dudley
  approval for, 283–284, 284n46
  Hülsemann and, 290–291, 297–298, 301
  Hungarian Revolution and, 281–284, 284n46, 297–298
  success of, 281–282
  Webster-Hülsemann debate related to, 297–298, 301
Mansfield, Harvey, 6–7
Marcy, William, 336
Marsh, George P., 302–303
Marshall, John, 166, 166n37
Mason, George, 17
  on Declaration of Independence, 385
  against imperialism, 386–387
  against slavery, 382
Mason, William E., 359–361, 363–364
Masonic Lodge of the Grand Sisters, 72
Massachusetts Constitution. *See* Constitution of the Commonwealth of Massachusetts
May, Ernest R., 212n113
McCurdy, Charles, 327–328
McKenzie, William Lyon, 264
McKinley, William, xx
  annexation conversion of, 391–392
  for commerce, 400
  criticism of, 353–354, 366–369
  Dawes for, 353–354, 393
  Godkin for, 353
  on non-intervention, 351–352

politics of, 345–346
for regime changes, 341–342
Roosevelt, T., for, 353
Spain and, 352–353
support for, 353–356, 370
against war, 352–354
for war, 357

Mediterranean Sea, 365. *See also specific countries*

Memorial To their High Mightinesses, the States General of the United Provinces of the Low Countries (*Memorial*) (Adams, J.), 57–58
  Joseph II and, 70–71
  results from, 59–61, 63, 66, 70–72

Mexico
  coercive diplomacy with, 265–266
  Europe in, 374–375
  recognition of, 212–213
  slavery and, 266n20
  war with, 266–267
  Webster on, 311–312

Middleton, Henry, 206–207

Minneapolis Times, 366

Missouri, 150–151

Model Treaty (Plan of 1776), 18, 25, 51

monarchies, 7. *See also specific monarchs*
  Adams, J., on, 64
  Adams, J. Q., on, 228–229
  for Brazil, 215
  constitutional, 236, 286, 317
  Douglas against, 321
  in Germany, 275
  in Hawaii, 340n1
  human rights or, 293
  republicanism or, 321
  for South America, 214–215

Money, H. D., 377

Monroe, James
  Adams, J. Q., against, 191
  consultations of, 222–223, 223n132
  criticism of, 237–238
  on intervention, 169–170
  Spanish colonies' independence and, 152

Monroe Doctrine, xv–xvi. *See also* Russia
   Bryan on, 374
   development toward, 221–237
   election of 1896 and, 344–345
   Jordan on, 374
   Kossuth related to, 304–305
   Polk Corollary to, 265
   reference to, 150n7

Montesquieu, Charles Louis de Secondat, 6, 8, 315

Moore, John Bassett, 281–282

morality, x, xix
   of American colonies, 11–12, 21–22
   of Beveridge, 416
   of Declaration of Independence, 416
   expansionism related to, 341
   Harris, W. A., on, 363
   in imperial debate of 1898-1900, 381–383
   of Philippines acquisition, 407–408, 414–417, 421
   of Platt, O. H., 414–416
   of Puerto Rico acquisition, 416
   of Roosevelt, 416–417
   South America and, 161

Morgan, John T., 396–397

Morocco, 77, 77n3
   France and, 81
   treaty with, 80
   tribute for, 87n23
   Tripoli blockade and, 108–109

Morris, Richard
   attack by, 107
   limitations of, 108–109
   Murray with, 109–110
   negotiations of, 107
   orders for, 104–106
   plan of, 113, 113n79
   presumptions of, 107

Murray, Alexander, 109–110

Naples, 169–170

Napoleon, 117, 194

nation, 406
   most favored, 192

nationalism. *See also specific countries*
   civic or ethnic, 317
   of intervention, 357–366

Native Americans, 199

Navigation Acts, 9–10

navy, 85. *See also* Dale, Richard; Morris, Richard; *specific countries*
   Enterprise, 100
   George Washington, 88–89, 92, 97
   Maine, 354, 357, 357n38
   Philadelphia, 115–117, 116n85, 117n87

Nelson, Admiral, 116

Nesselrode, Count, 225–226

Netherlands. *See* Dutch Republic

Neufville, Jean de, 53

neutrality, 51, 53, 59, 158, 161
   for Adams, J. Q., 186–188, 186n65
   against filibustering, 337–338
   Fillmore for, 311
   for law of nations, 295
   at Panama Congress, 240, 248–249
   recognition and, 192–193

neutralization, 378–379

New Democrats. *See also* Polk, James K.
   coercive diplomacy for, 265
   factionalism within, 267
   goals of, 260
   Hungary and, xvii, 319–323
   for Manifest Destiny, 260
   membership of, 259–260
   resistance to, 262–263
   role of, 254
   for Texas, 263
   use of term, 259n7
   Webster and, 297n59
   Whigs against, xvi–xvii, 256, 267–268, 271

new international system
   Adams, J., on, 50–52
   from Declaration of Independence, 22–27
   maritime liberty in, 51–52
   popular sentiment in, 50–51

New York Anti-Imperialist League, 388

New York Herald, 324–325

New York Journal, 364–365, 366–367

New York Mail and Express, 366

New York Sun, 365, 383

New York Tribune, 271, 383, 399

New York World, 358

Nicaragua, 338

Nissen, Nicholas, 101, 108, 117, 120
   for Barbary War Treaty, 124, 127, 127n108
   warnings from, 106, 125

non-interference, 351. *See also* Washington's Farewell Address
   Britain for, 155
   Declaration of Independence for, 20
   law of nations for, 7
   Vattel for, 23–24

non-intervention
   in Europe, 203–210, 226, 234–236, 249–250
   in Hungary, xvii
   intervention for, 304–305
   McKinley on, 351–352

North America. *See also* Canada
   expansionism of, 198–199, 199nn92–93
   South America's unification with, 220

North American Review, 365–366, 390, 403

Norton, Charles Eliot, 387

O'Brien, Richard, 86–87
   Algiers and, 89, 102
   against Cathcart, 92n35
   George Washington and, 97

O'Connell, Daniel, 259

Onís, Luis de, 153–154, 161, 198–199

Onuf, Nicholas, 8, 23

Onuf, Peter, 8, 22, 23

Ostend Manifesto, 337

O'Sullivan, John L., 259–260, 337

Outlook, 415

Overmeyer, David, 347–348

Paine, Thomas, 18, 20, 23–24

Palmer, Robert R., 73

Panama Congress
   Adams, J. Q., for, 239–243, 247–250
   American System and, 245
   background on, 237–238
   Barbary regencies and, 248–249
   commerce at, 245–246
   for friendship, 247–248
   instructions for, 240–241
   invitation to, 239
   neutrality at, 240, 248–249
   non-colonization related to, 246–247
   opposition to, 243–247, 243n166
   for peace, 248
   religion and, 247, 249
   republicanism related to, 241–242
   slave trade and, 246
   against Spain, 245
   Washington's Farewell Address related to, 244

peace, 26
   for Britain, 46
   as natural state, 23–24
   Panama Congress for, 248
   price of, 124–125

Peace Reduction Act (1801), 98n48

People's Party, 345n2

Philadelphia, 115–117, 116n85, 117n87

Philadelphia Record, 354, 359

Philippines acquisition, xviii. *See also* imperial debate of 1898-1900
   balance of power and, 393–394, 394n139
   Barrett for, 403
   Britain related to, 394
   China and, 395–396
   commerce from, 399–401, 403
   Cuba intervention compared to, 417
   Declaration of Independence related to, 407–413
   Hazeltine for, 395–396
   indivisibility of, 393–394
   Lodge for, 396, 399–401, 413

morality of, 407–408, 414–417, 421
Morgan for, 396–397
permanent status of, 417–419
as protectorate, 394–395
Puerto Rico acquisition compared to, 401–402
resolutions on, 415
sectionalism in, 403
self-government and, 393, 415–416
statehood in, 407
as strategic asset, 396–397
strategic evaluation for, 393–394

Philippines independence, 407
Aguinaldo for, 376, 393, 418–419, 422–423
Beveridge on, 419–420
debate for, 417–420, 422
Platt, O. H., on, 418
war and, 419–420, 422–423

Pickering, Secretary of State, 96

Pickett, John T., 333, 336

Pierce, Franklin
on Europe, 336
for expansionism, 335
Kossuth and, 336–337
over Hale, 333–334

Platt, Orville H.
on consent doctrine, 385, 411
against expansionism, 407
morality of, 414–416
on Philippines independence, 418

Platt, T. C.
on Constitution, 405
on election of 1896, 345

plausible deniability, 135, 135n118

Poletica, Pierre de, 148
for Holy Alliance, 206

political equality, 409

political rights, 411

Polk, James K., 266
for Germany, 265, 272–273

Polk Corollary, 265

Porte, 76–77, 77n4, 90

Portugal, 155

Pownall, Thomas, 45, 45n103

Preble, Edward
attacks by, 118–121
complaints of, 115
Karamanli, H., and, 113–114
negotiations by, 116–117, 117n87, 119–120
orders for, 112–113
plans of, 113–114, 113n79
ships for, 112, 112n77, 118
Tunis and, 118

press. *See also specific newspapers*
yellow, 355–356

privateering, 77–78, 80

protectorates, xix
in imperial debate of 1898-1900, 378
Philippines acquisition as, 394–395
Roosevelt against, 394–395
Taft against, 394–395

public opinion, xx
Constitution related to, 405
for Cuba intervention, 364, 366–370
de-recognition from, 285–286
in Dutch Republic, 62–63
revolution related to, 286
Seward on, 314–315
war and, 294–295, 355

Puerto Rico acquisition
morality of, 416
Philippines acquisition compared to, 401–402
Roosevelt on, 416

Quincy, Josiah, 350, 381

race, 409–410

racism
in expansionism, 406–407
in foreign policy debates, xx, 380, 424

Randolph, John, 238

Rebello, Silvestre, 215–216

recognition, 299

Adams, J. Q., on, 186–187
of Brazil, 215–216
of Buenos Aires, 158, 189–190, 211
criteria for, 191–193
for Cuba, 345n2, 368–369
from Dutch Republic, 66–67
in Europe, 162
from French Revolution, 254
for Germany, 272–273
of Hungary, 280–284, 284n46, 287–288, 297
internationalization of, 188–191
law of nations for, 192
of Mexico, 212–213
most favored nation status and, 192
neutrality and, 192–193
physical control for, 192
political independence for, 192
from Rush, 254
of South America, 185–191, 211
of Spanish colonies, 161–163, 186–191, 210–211, 224
of Texas, 261, 261n10
war over, 193, 193n80

Reed, Thomas B.
on Declaration of Independence, 383
against war, 356

reform
American colonies for, 10–11
for Britain, 48, 50, 155, 167–168, 207–210, 230
for Dutch Republic, 59, 63
Enlightenment for, 7
in Europe, 166–167, 169

regime change. *See also* American regime change; Tripoli regime change
American Revolution and, 31–35
Barbary War Treaty and, 132, 134–135
criteria for, 191–193
Cuba's issues about, 362–363
debates over, ix–x
democratization and, ix–x
description of, ix
forcible interference in, 293
in Hawaii, 269–270, 340n1
indirect approach to, x–xii, 73–74
McKinley for, 341–342
new standard for, 19–22, 47–48

policy on, 257–258
for Spanish colonies, 152–154

regime change of 1890s. *See also specific countries*
anti-expansionism in, xix–xx
commerce and, xvii–xviii
expansionism in, xviii–xix

Reid, Whitelaw, 399

Reis, Murad (Lisle, Peter), 100

religion, 128–129, 196
Barbary regencies' treaties and, 87–88
Christian civilization and, 182–183
civil liberty and, 217–218, 218n125, 241–242
civil rights and, 217–218
JQA Address and, 171, 171n46
Panama Congress and, 247, 249
in South America, 159–160
state's separation from, 241–242

Republican Party, xix. *See also specific Republicans*
Dawes on, 403
platform of, 344–345

republicanism
for Adams, J. Q., 216
in Brazil, 216
in Britain, 46–47
of Colombia, 218–219
in Dutch Republic, 56–65
evolution of, 250–251
filibustering for, 264–265
generic, 6
government form related to, 228–229
in Ireland, 47–48, 321
monarchies or, 321
Panama Congress related to, 241–242
principles of, 228–229
without propagandism, 231, 242

revolutions. *See also specific countries*
for Britain, 45–46, 48–49
criteria for, 19
public opinion related to, 286
in Texas, 260–261

revolutions of 1848, xvi–xvii. *See also specific countries*
argument limitations about, 256

perspective of, 253–254
scope of, 271

Richmond Times, 370

Riepma, Siert, 261–262

Roberts, Timothy, 270

Rodgers, John, 111
authority of, 130–131
Tunis treaty from, 129–131

Roosevelt, Theodore, xix
on consent doctrine, 413–414, 420
for Cuba intervention, 363, 363n56
foreign policy of, 346–347
for McKinley, 353
morality of, 416–417
against protectorate, 394–395
on Puerto Rico acquisition, 416
on Spain's navy, 369

Root, Elihu, 414

Rush, Richard, 189
recognition from, 254
replacement of, 276n35
South America and, 224, 224n135

Russia. *See also* Alexander of Russia
Adams, J., and, 59
claims of, 221
de-recognition of, 287
Europe and, 225–226, 226n137, 229–230
against Hungary, 282–284, 295–296, 304–305
Hungary and, 279
Salazar related to, 238
Seward against, 332–333
Seward on, 319
threat of, 304–305

Salazar, Jose Maria, 238

San Francisco Argonaut, 375–376

Sanders, George, 337
Douglas against, 331, 332n105
for Kossuth, 308

SCFR. *See* Senate Committee on Foreign Relations

Schurz, Carl, xix, 380

Schwartzenberg, Prince, 277

Scott, Winfield, 333–334

sectionalism, 403. *See also* Southern states

self-government
for Hungary, 326–327
in imperial debate of 1898-1900, 382
Philippines acquisition and, 393, 415–416
race related to, 409–410

Senate Committee on Foreign Relations (SCFR), 243–247

Serra, José Correia da (Correa, Abbé), 197–198, 198n89

Seward, William, xvii, 255–256
on globalization, 267–268
government forms and, 317
for Kossuth, 314–319, 323
on law of nations, 315
on precedence, 316–317
on public opinion, 314–315
on representative of liberty, 317–319
against Russia, 332–333
on Russia, 319
on war, 316

Sheffield, Lord, 80

Shields, James, 321, 332
Kossuth with, 324–325

Sickles, Daniel, 337

Simpson, James, 109

slavery, 246
Adams, J. Q., and, 184, 199
American colonies and, 202–203, 203n98
Declaration of Independence and, 384, 412
filibustering and, 338
Garrison and, 309
Haiti and, 333
imperial debate of 1898-1900 related to, 380–382
impressment compared to, 182n57
JQA Address and, 182, 182nn57–58, 184
Kossuth and, 306, 309, 333
Mason, G., against, 382
Mexico and, 266n20

– 448 –

Smith, Adam, 25
Smith, Robert
  for Barbary War, 111
  Preble's orders from, 112–113
Sobral, Jose Gutierrez, 365–366
Soulé, Pierre, 260, 302
  for Cuba, 337
South America. *See also* Panama Congress; Spanish colonies
  Alexander of Russia and, 221
  America compared with, 194–196
  America related to, 159–161
  American Hemisphere and, 160–161
  American System for, 197–198
  appropriations for, 157–158
  Britain and, 188, 222–225
  Canning, G., and, 221–222, 224
  civil liberty for, 217–218, 218n125
  Clay for, xiv–xv, 157–164, 270
  commerce and, 160, 216–217, 217n124
  confederation of, 220–221
  dissatisfaction from, 197
  Europe against, 162–163, 186–188
  Europe with, 163–164
  evolution of, 185–186
  Florida and, 163
  government form for, 213–216, 242–243
  Holy Alliance to, 228–232
  in JQA Address, 158–163, 180, 184–185
  JQA Address elaboration on, 185–191
  monarchies for, 214–215
  morality and, 161
  North America's unification with, 220
  opportunities in, xv
  recognition of, 185–191, 211
  religion in, 159–160
  Rush and, 224, 224n135
  Serra for, 197–198, 198n89
  Spain compared with, 195–196
  traits in, 158–159
  unification of, 219–220
  war over, 162–163
Southern states
  Cuba intervention and, 343, 356–357, 370
  secession of, 151
Spain

Adams, J. Q., and, 152
America compared with, 30, 375–376
brutality of, 185, 185n63
Ferdinand VII for, 181, 221
France's invasion of, 234–235
honor for, 31
McKinley and, 352–353
navy of, 369
Panama Congress against, 245
rebellions in, 154, 163–164
South America compared with, 195–196
war with, 186–188, 352–356, 369–372

Spanish colonies, xiii–xvi. *See also* Cuba
  Adams, J. Q., and, 153–155
  Adams-Onís agreement on, 153–154, 198–199
  Britain and, 188–190
  Holy Alliance and, 153
  recognition of, 161–163, 186–191, 210–213, 224
  regime change for, 152–154
  Vives and, 153–154
Spanish colonies' independence
  America and, 152–154
  inevitability of, 185–186, 185n64
  Monroe and, 152
  origins of, 195

Spencer, Donald, 297, 297n59

Spooner, John C.
  against Bacon, 401–402
  on consent doctrine, 413

Staloff, Darren, 25

state, religion's separation from, 241–242

statehood
  of Barbary regencies, 76–77, 77n3
  in Philippines acquisition, 407

Stephens, Alexander, 329

Stiles, William H.
  Buchanan for, 278–279
  caution of, 277–279
  Kossuth to, 278
  on larger implications, 279
  refusal from, 276–277
  Schwartzenberg with, 277
  Windischgrätz to, 278

Stockton, Robert, 266
Strickland, Walter, 61
Sumner, Charles, 321
Sumner, George, 282
Sweden, 96, 106

Taft, William Howard, 391
   against protectorate, 394–395
Tangier, 114–115, 115n82
taxation, 382
Taylor, Zachary
   Cass and, 289–290
   on Hungarian Revolution, 283–284, 284n46
Teller, Henry, 414
   on consent doctrine, 413
   for Cuba, 371
Texas, 201–202, 202n97
   independence for, 269
   Manifest Destiny and, 260–261, 261n10
   New Democrats for, 263
   recognition of, 261, 261n10
   revolution in, 260–261
Thurston, John M., 368
Torres, Manuel, 211
Town, Charles A., 383–384
Tracy, Uriah, 135–136
Transcontinental Treaty (Adams-Onís Treaty), 153–154, 198–199
treaties. *See also* Barbary War Treaty
   with France, 33–34
   government form and, 24
   Model, 18, 25, 51
   with Morocco, 80
   Transcontinental, 153–154, 198–199
   Tripoli regime change and, 132, 134–135
   with Tunis, 129–131
Treaty of Amity and Commerce, 52
   Declaration of Independence and, 216–217
   with Dutch Republic, 66
   with France, 216–217, 217n124

tribute
   for Algiers, 86–89, 87n23, 99–101
   for Barbary regencies, 82–84, 86–88, 88n27, 102, 122
   for Morocco, 87n23
   for Tripoli, 90–91, 111–112
   for Tunis, 112, 112n76
Tripoli, 76–77. *See also* Barbary War
   agreement with, 87–88
   Algiers and, 90, 90n31, 95, 95n42
   attack on, 116, 118
   in Barbary regencies' treaties, 94
   blockade of, 108–109
   Cathcart negotiations with, 105
   consul advice about, 94–96, 95nn42–43
   Dey of Algiers with, 101–102
   Eaton against, 103, 108
   France and, 106
   Karamanli, Y., for, 87, 90–91, 90n31, 91n33
   Sweden with, 96, 106
   tribute for, 90–91, 111–112
   upper hand of, 106–110
Tripoli regime change
   Bradley on, 137–138
   coercion and, 142–143
   deterrence in absence of, 129–131
   Eaton for, 104, 123–126, 126n105, 132
   Karamanli, H., as, 104–106, 122–128, 124n101, 142–143
   against Karamanli, Y., 103–106, 123–128, 124n101, 142–143
   Lear against, 127
   Madison for, 105–106
   treaty and, 132, 134–135
Tunis, 86–87
   Davis, G., and, 129–130
   demands from, 115–116
   Preble and, 118
   treaty with, 129–131
   tribute for, 112, 112n76
Turkey
   Barbary War and, 123
   commerce with, 237n155
   Greece and, 237
Tuyll, Baron de, 221, 230

Underwood, Joseph R., 289
  against Kossuth, 313

Van Buren, Martin, 243

van der Capellen tot den Pol, Joan Derk, 60–61, 63

Van der Kemp, François Adriaan, 61

Van Doren, Carl, 72

Vattel, Emmerich de, 7–8
  for non-interference, 23–24

Vauguyon, Duke De La, 57, 60

Venezuela, 364

Vergennes, comte de, 80, 82
  Adams, J., and, 38–39, 43–45, 60
  France's navy and, 33

Vest, George, 379

Vest Resolution, 379

Vives, Francisco, 153–154

Walker, Isaac P., 322–323

Walker, Robert J., 304

Walker, William, 338

Walsh, Robert, 165–166

war, 31, 343–344. *See also specific countries; specific wars*
  Adams, J. Q., on, 182–184, 182n57, 184n62, 186–187, 210
  Bacon against, 376–377
  Clay and, 186–187, 187n67
  Crittenden on, 329–331
  from Dey of Algiers, 89, 89n29
  with Europe, 328–329
  JQA Address on, 182, 182n57
  Kossuth for, 305–306
  McKinley against, 352–354
  with Mexico, 266–267
  over recognition, 193, 193n80
  over South America, 162–163
  Philippines independence and, 419–420, 422–423
  public opinion and, 294–295, 355
  Reed against, 356
  Seward on, 316
  with Spain, 186–188, 352–356, 369–372

War of 1812, 150

Warren, Joseph, 10

Washington, D.C., 323–333

Washington, George, 32–33
  biography of, 166, 166n37
  Crittenden and, 329–331

Washington's Farewell Address (Washington Doctrine), 229n142, 329
  expansionism and, 397–398
  irrelevance of, 398–399
  Jordan on, 373
  JQA Address on, 257–258
  Kidd on, 398–399
  Panama Congress related to, 244
  resolutions for, 332–333
  Whigs against, 333

Webster, Daniel, xvii, 235
  balance of, 253–254
  Compromise of 1850 and, 292
  Fillmore and, 325, 327
  on government forms, 268–269
  against Kossuth, 310–311
  for law of nations defense, 295–296
  to McCurdy, 327–328
  on Mexico, 311–312
  middle policy of, 292–298, 323–326
  New Democrats and, 297n59
  on principle, 169

Webster-Hülsemann debate, 291–292, 296, 297n59
  aftermath of, 323–324, 327
  Mann related to, 297–298, 301
  national self-determination in, 299–300
  publication of, 300–301

West, Samuel, 19, 239

Weyler, Valeriano, 343

Wheeler, Joseph, 370

Whigs, xvi, 333. *See also* Edinburgh Doctrine; Fillmore, Millard; Taylor, Zachary
  Britain and, 268–269
  Hawaii for, 269–270
  for human rights, 270–271

against New Democrats, xvi–xvii, 256, 267–268, 271
platform of, 334
Progressive, 314–319
role of, 254

Wilentz, Sean, 258–259

William V (king), 54–55
Dutch Patriot movement and, 56–57, 56n131

Willis, William, 95

Wilson, Woodrow, 350

Windischgrätz, Field Marshall, 278

Wirt, William, 215, 230

Wood, Gordon, 4

Woodbury, Levi, 261

world war, 376–377

XYZ controversy, 77–78

Yale Review, 410–411

Yorke, Joseph, 65

Ypsilantis, Alexander, 155

www.ingramcontent.com/pod-product-compliance
Lightning Source LLC
Chambersburg PA
CBHW071958150426
43194CB00008B/922